The Baseball Record Companion

Other Books by Joseph L. Reichler

The Baseball Encyclopedia (*editor*)

The World Series

The Game and the Glory

The Great Game

Baseball's Greatest Moments

The Mickey Walker Story

It's Good to Be Alive

The History of Baseball

Baseball's Unforgettable Games

The Baseball Record Companion

Joseph L. Reichler

COLLIER BOOKS
MACMILLAN PUBLISHING COMPANY
NEW YORK
COLLIER MACMILLAN PUBLISHERS
LONDON

Macmillan Publishing Company
866 Third Avenue, New York, N.Y. 10022
Collier Macmillan Canada, Inc.

Library of Congress Cataloging-in-Publication Data

Reichler, Joseph L., 1915–
The baseball record companion.
1. Baseball—United States—Records. I. Title.
GV877.R37 1987 796.357'0973021 86-12980
ISBN 0-02-028030-0

Macmillan books are available at special discounts for bulk purchases for sales promotions, premiums, fund-raising, or educational use. For details, contact:

Special Sales Director
Macmillan Publishing Company
866 Third Avenue
New York, N.Y. 10022

10 9 8 7 6 5 4 3 2 1

Printed in the United States of America

All photographs not otherwise credited are reprinted courtesy of Major League Baseball Promotions Corporation.

Editorial and Production Staff

Jackie Dickens
Robert Keefe
Casey Kwang-Chong Lee
Jeffrey Neuman
Fred C. Richardson
Jonathan Simon

Contents

ROOKIES

TEAM RECORDS

Acknowledgments

I would like to gratefully acknowledge the efforts of the Society for American Baseball Research. SABR's efforts in delving, digging, and divining new areas of research, and filling the gaps in the ones that already exist, are a credit to all who take the game seriously. Special thanks go to Pete Palmer, Ron Liebman, Bob McConnell, Bob Davids, Frank Williams, John Husman, Ted DiTullio, Jim Smith, John Schwartz, and Paul Doherty. Thanks also to Jon Simon for his tireless efforts in preparing this book for publication.

Individual Batting Records

Two Grand Slams in One Game

Player	Team	Date
Tony Lazzeri	NY A	May 24, 1936
Jim Tabor	BOS A	Jul 4, 1939
Rudy York	BOS A	Jul 27, 1946
Jim Gentile	BAL A	May 9, 1961
Tony Cloninger	ATL N	Jul 3, 1966
Jim Northrup	DET A	Jun 24, 1968
Frank Robinson	BAL A	Jun 26, 1970

Most Grand Slams, Career

Player	Total
Lou Gehrig	23
Willie McCovey	18
Jimmie Foxx	17
Ted Williams	17
Hank Aaron	16
Dave Kingman	16
Babe Ruth	16
Gil Hodges	14
Eddie Murray	14
Joe DiMaggio	13
George Foster	13
Ralph Kiner	13
Ernie Banks	12
Rogers Hornsby	12
Joe Rudi	12
Rudy York	12
Johnny Bench	11
Hank Greenberg	11
Reggie Jackson	11
Harmon Killebrew	11
Lee May	11
Willie Stargell	11
Joe Adcock	10
Don Baylor	10
Jeff Burroughs	10
Gary Carter	10
John Milner	10
Roy Sievers	10
Al Simmons	10
Vern Stephens	10
Vic Wertz	10

"The Iron Horse," Lou Gehrig, led the Yankees to six World Championships while playing in a record 2130 consecutive games. Over his career Gehrig batted .340 and slugged .632, while amassing 1990 RBIs.

Grand Slam In Two Consecutive Games, AL

Player	Team	Date
Babe Ruth	NY	Sep 27, 1927
	NY	Sep 29, 1927
	NY	Aug 6, 1929
	NY	Aug 7, 1929
Bill Dickey	NY	Aug 3, 1937
	NY	Aug 4, 1937
Jimmie Foxx	BOS	May 20, 1940
	BOS	May 21, 1940
Jim Busby	CLE	Jul 5, 1956
	CLE	Jul 6, 1956
Brooks Robinson	BAL	May 6, 1962
	BAL	May 9, 1962
Willie Aikens	CAL	Jun 13, 1979
	CAL	Jun 14, 1979

Grand Slam In Two Consecutive Games, NL

Player	Team	Date
Jimmy Bannon	BOS	Aug 6, 1894
	BOS	Aug 7, 1894
Jimmy Sheckard	BKN	Sep 23, 1901
	BKN	Sep 24, 1901
Phil Garner	PIT	Sep 14, 1978
	PIT	Sep 15, 1978

Grand Slam in First Major League Game

Player	Team	Date
Bill Duggleby	PHI N	Apr 21, 1898
Bobby Bonds	SF N	Jun 25, 1968

Most Grand Slams, Season, AL

Player	Team	Year	Total
Jim Gentile	BAL	1961	5
Babe Ruth	BOS	1919	4
Lou Gehrig	NY	1934	4
Rudy York	DET	1938	4
Tommy Henrich	NY	1948	4
Al Rosen	CLE	1951	4
Ray Boone	CLE	1953	
	DET	1953	4
Jim Northrup	DET	1968	4
Tris Speaker	CLE	1923	3
Lou Gehrig	NY	1927	3
Babe Ruth	NY	1929	3
Lou Gehrig	NY	1931	3
Jimmie Foxx	PHI	1932	3
	PHI	1934	3
Joe DiMaggio	NY	1937	3
Jimmie Foxx	BOS	1938	3
Bob Johnson	PHI	1938	3
Jimmie Foxx	BOS	1940	3
Don Lenhardt	BOS	1952	
	DET	1952	3
Gus Zernial	PHI	1952	3
Ted Williams	BOS	1955	3
Vic Wertz	BOS	1960	3
Bob Allison	MIN	1961	3
Dick Stuart	BOS	1964	3
Pete Ward	CHI	1964	3
Willie Horton	DET	1969	3
Carl Yastrzemski	BOS	1969	3
Rico Petrocelli	BOS	1972	3
Jeff Burroughs	TEX	1973	3
Gene Tenace	OAK	1974	3
Rod Carew	MIN	1976	3
Reggie Jackson	BAL	1976	3
Joe Rudi	CAL	1978	3
	CAL	1979	3
Andre Thornton	CLE	1979	3
Larry Parrish	TEX	1982	3
Dave Kingman	OAK	1984	3
Kent Hrbek	MIN	1985	3
Eddie Murray	BAL	1985	3

Most Grand Slams, Season, NL

Player	Team	Year	Total
Ernie Banks	CHI	1955	5
Wildfire Schulte	CHI	1911	4
Vince DiMaggio	PHI	1945	4
Ralph Kiner	PIT	1949	4
Sid Gordon	BOS	1950	4
George Kelly	NY	1921	3
Jim Bottomley	STL	1925	3
Cy Williams	PHI	1926	3
Chuck Klein	PHI	1932	3
Sid Gordon	NY	1948	3
Ralph Kiner	PIT	1951	3
Wes Westrum	NY	1951	3
Del Crandall	MIL	1955	3
Gene Freese	PHI	1959	3
Hank Aaron	MIL	1962	3
Willie McCovey	SF	1967	3
Lee May	CIN	1970	3
John Milner	NY	1976	3
Keith Hernandez	STL	1977	3
Ray Knight	CIN	1980	3

Pinch-Hit Home Runs

Most Pinch-Hit Home Runs, Career

Player	Total
Cliff Johnson	20
Jerry Lynch	18
Gates Brown	16
Smoky Burgess	16
Willie McCovey	16
George Crowe	14
Joe Adcock	12
Bob Cerv	12
Fred Whitfield	11
Cy Williams	11
Don Mincher	10
Wally Post	10
Champ Summers	10
Gus Zernial	10

Pinch-Hit Home Runs by Same Player in Most Consecutive At-Bats

Player	Team	Date
Lee Lacy	LA N	May 2, 1978
	LA N	May 6, 1978
	LA N	May 17, 1978
Del Unser	PHI N	Jun 30, 1979
	PHI N	Jul 5, 1979
	PHI N	Jul 10, 1979

Rudy York (*left*) holds the record for most home runs in a month: 18 in July 1937. *Above*: Two of the game's greatest sluggers, Ernie Banks and Hank Aaron, played in a combined 38 All-Star Games.

Most Pinch-Hit Grand Slams, Career

Player	Team	Date	Total	Opp.	Opp. Pitcher
Ron Northey	STL N	Sep 3, 1947		CHI	Doyle Lade
	STL N	May 30, 1948		PIT	Elmer Singleton
	CHI N	Sep 18, 1950	3	BKN	Dan Bankhead
Willie McCovey	SF N	Jun 12, 1960		MIL	Carl Willey
	SF N	Sep 10, 1965		CHI	Ted Abernathy
	SD N	May 30, 1975	3	NY	Bob Apodaca
Rich Reese	MIN A	Aug 3, 1969		BAL	Dave McNally
	MIN A	Jun 7, 1970		WAS	Dick Bosman
	MIN A	Jul 9, 1972	3	NY	Lindy McDaniel
Yogi Berra	NY A	Jun 7, 1953		STL	Satchel Paige
	NY A	Jun 23, 1962	2	DET	Phil Regan
Bill Skowron	NY A	Aug 17, 1954		PHI	Al Sima
	NY A	Jul 14, 1957	2	CHI	Jim Wilson
Gene Freese	PHI N	Apr 18, 1959		CIN	Mike Cuellar
	PHI N	Jul 2, 1959	2	CIN	Jim Brosnan
Vic Wertz	BOS A	Aug 14, 1959		NY	Ryne Duren
	BOS A	Aug 25, 1960	2	CLE	Don Newcombe
Ed Bailey	SF N	Jun 26, 1962		CIN	Joey Jay
	SF N	Apr 10, 1963	2	HOU	Don McMahon
Reggie Jackson	OAK A	Sep 5, 1970		KC	Tom Burgmeier
	BAL A	Aug 22, 1976	2	CHI	Terry Forster
Dave Parker	PIT N	Sep 8, 1974		MON	Tom Walker
	CIN N	Jul 13, 1986	2	MON	Bob McClure
Ted Simmons	STL N	Jun 23, 1975		NY	Jon Matlack
	ATL N	Jun 3, 1986	2	PIT	Cecilio Guante
Champ Summers	CHI N	Aug 23, 1975		HOU	Jim York
	SD N	Apr 10, 1984	2	STL	Bob Forsch
Terry Crowley	BAL A	Sep 9, 1977		CLE	Larry Andersen
	BAL A	Aug 8, 1982	2	KC	Mike Armstrong
Davey Johnson	PHI N	Apr 30, 1978		SD	Bob Shirley
	PHI N	Jun 3, 1978	2	LA	Terry Forster
Mike Ivie	SF N	May 28, 1978		LA	Don Sutton
	SF N	Jun 30, 1978	2	ATL	Dave Campbell
John Milner	PIT N	Aug 5, 1979		PHI	Tug McGraw
	PIT N	Aug 15, 1982	2	STL	Steve Mura

Pinch-Hit Home Run in First At-Bat in Majors, AL

Player	Team	Date	Inn.
Ace Parker	PHI	Apr 30, 1937	9
John Kennedy	WAS	Sep 5, 1962	6
Gates Brown	DET	Jun 19, 1963	5
Bill Roman	DET	Sep 30, 1964	7
Brant Alyea	WAS	Sep 12, 1965	6
Joe Keough	OAK	Aug 7, 1968	8
Al Woods	TOR	Apr 7, 1977	5

Pinch-Hit Home Run in First At-Bat in Majors, NL

Player	Team	Date	Inn.
Eddie Morgan	STL	Apr 14, 1936	7
Les Layton	NY	May 21, 1948	9
Ted Tappe	CIN	Sep 14, 1950	8
Chuck Tanner	MIL	Apr 12, 1955	8

Most Home Runs, Season, AL

Player	Team	Year	HR	Player	Team	Year	HR
Roger Maris	NY	1961	61	Jimmie Foxx	PHI	1934	44
Babe Ruth	NY	1927	60	Hank Greenberg	DET	1946	44
	NY	1921	59	Harmon Killebrew	MIN	1967	44
Jimmie Foxx	PHI	1932	58	Carl Yastrzemski	BOS	1967	44
Hank Greenberg	DET	1938	58	Frank Howard	WAS	1968	44
Babe Ruth	NY	1920	54		WAS	1970	44
	NY	1928	54	Ted Williams	BOS	1949	43
Mickey Mantle	NY	1961	54	Al Rosen	CLE	1953	43
	NY	1956	52	Tony Armas	BOS	1984	43
Jimmie Foxx	BOS	1938	50	Hal Trosky	CLE	1936	42
Babe Ruth	NY	1930	49	Gus Zernial	PHI	1953	42
Lou Gehrig	NY	1934	49	Roy Sievers	WAS	1957	42
	NY	1936	49	Mickey Mantle	NY	1958	42
Harmon Killebrew	MIN	1964	49	Rocky Colavito	CLE	1959	42
Frank Robinson	BAL	1966	49	Harmon Killebrew	WAS	1959	42
Harmon Killebrew	MIN	1969	49	Dick Stuart	BOS	1963	42
Jimmie Foxx	PHI	1933	48	Babe Ruth	NY	1923	41
Harmon Killebrew	MIN	1962	48	Lou Gehrig	NY	1930	41
Frank Howard	WAS	1969	48	Babe Ruth	NY	1932	41
Babe Ruth	NY	1926	47	Jimmie Foxx	BOS	1936	41
Lou Gehrig	NY	1927	47	Hank Greenberg	DET	1940	41
Reggie Jackson	OAK	1969	47	Rocky Colavito	CLE	1958	41
Babe Ruth	NY	1924	46	Norm Cash	DET	1961	41
	NY	1929	46	Harmon Killebrew	MIN	1970	41
Lou Gehrig	NY	1931	46	Reggie Jackson	NY	1980	41
Babe Ruth	NY	1931	46	Ben Oglivie	MIL	1980	41
Joe DiMaggio	NY	1937	46	Hank Greenberg	DET	1937	40
Jim Gentile	BAL	1961	46	Mickey Mantle	NY	1960	40
Harmon Killebrew	MIN	1961	46	Rico Petrocelli	BOS	1969	40
Jim Rice	BOS	1978	46	Carl Yastrzemski	BOS	1969	40
Rocky Colavito	DET	1961	45		BOS	1970	40
Harmon Killebrew	MIN	1963	45	Darrell Evans	DET	1985	40
Gorman Thomas	MIL	1979	45	Jesse Barfield	TOR	1986	40

Most Home Runs, Season, NL

Player	Team	Year	HR	Player	Team	Year	HR
Hack Wilson	CHI	1930	56	Eddie Mathews	MIL	1953	47
Ralph Kiner	PIT	1949	54	Ted Kluszewski	CIN	1955	47
Willie Mays	SF	1965	52	Ernie Banks	CHI	1958	47
George Foster	CIN	1977	52	Willie Mays	SF	1964	47
Ralph Kiner	PIT	1947	51	Hank Aaron	ATL	1971	47
Johnny Mize	NY	1947	51	Eddie Mathews	MIL	1959	46
Willie Mays	NY	1955	51	Orlando Cepeda	SF	1961	46
Ted Kluszewski	CIN	1954	49	Ernie Banks	CHI	1959	45
Willie Mays	SF	1962	49	Hank Aaron	MIL	1962	45
Willie Stargell	PIT	1971	48	Willie McCovey	SF	1969	45
Dave Kingman	CHI	1979	48	Johnny Bench	CIN	1970	45
Mike Schmidt	PHI	1980	48	Mike Schmidt	PHI	1979	45
Ralph Kiner	PIT	1950	47	Ernie Banks	CHI	1955	44

Most Home Runs, Season, NL *(cont'd)*

Player	Team	Year	HR
Hank Aaron	MIL	1957	44
	MIL	1963	44
Willie McCovey	SF	1963	44
Hank Aaron	ATL	1966	44
	ATL	1969	44
Willie Stargell	PIT	1973	44
Chuck Klein	PHI	1929	43
Johnny Mize	STL	1940	43
Duke Snider	BKN	1956	43
Ernie Banks	CHI	1957	43
Davey Johnson	ATL	1973	43
Rogers Hornsby	STL	1922	42
Mel Ott	NY	1929	42
Ralph Kiner	PIT	1951	42
Duke Snider	BKN	1953	42
Gil Hodges	BKN	1954	42
Duke Snider	BKN	1955	42
Billy Williams	CHI	1970	42
Cy Williams	PHI	1923	41
Roy Campanella	BKN	1953	41
Willie Mays	NY	1954	41
Hank Sauer	CHI	1954	41
Eddie Mathews	MIL	1955	41
Ernie Banks	CHI	1960	41
Darrell Evans	ATL	1973	41
Jeff Burroughs	ATL	1977	41
Chuck Klein	PHI	1930	40
Ralph Kiner	PIT	1948	40
Johnny Mize	NY	1948	40
Gil Hodges	BKN	1951	40
Ted Kluszewski	CIN	1953	40
Eddie Mathews	MIL	1954	40
Duke Snider	BKN	1954	40
Wally Post	CIN	1955	40
Duke Snider	BKN	1957	40
Hank Aaron	MIL	1960	40
Willie Mays	SF	1961	40
Dick Allen	PHI	1966	40
Tony Perez	CIN	1970	40
Johnny Bench	CIN	1972	40
Hank Aaron	ATL	1973	40
George Foster	CIN	1978	40
Mike Schmidt	PHI	1983	40

Yankee slugger Roger Maris (*left*) chased a legend with his 61 home runs in 1961. Only Babe Ruth hit homers more often than Ralph Kiner (*right*), who led the National League in 4-baggers for seven straight seasons (1946–52).

Most Home Runs, Career

Player	HR	Player	HR
Hank Aaron	755	Eddie Mathews	512
Babe Ruth	714	Mel Ott	511
Willie Mays	660	Mike Schmidt	495
Frank Robinson	586	Lou Gehrig	493
Harmon Killebrew	573	Stan Musial	475
Reggie Jackson	548	Willie Stargell	475
Mickey Mantle	536	Carl Yastrzemski	452
Jimmie Foxx	534	Dave Kingman	442
Ted Williams	521	Billy Williams	426
Willie McCovey	521	Duke Snider	407
Ernie Banks	512		

The swing that beat the Babe: On April 8, 1974, Hank Aaron (*left*) sent his 715th home run into the Atlanta night. Still swinging at age 41, Reggie Jackson (*right*) leads active players in homers (548), and all players in strikeouts (2500).

Best Home Run Ratio, Career

Player	HR	AB	Ratio
Babe Ruth	714	8399	11.76
Ralph Kiner	369	5205	14.11
Harmon Killebrew	573	8147	14.22
Eddie Mathews	512	8537	14.67
Mike Schmidt	495	7292	14.73
Ted Williams	521	7706	14.79
Dave Kingman	442	6677	15.11
Mickey Mantle	536	8102	15.12
Jimmie Foxx	534	8134	15.23
Hank Greenberg	331	5193	15.69
Willie McCovey	521	8197	15.73
Lou Gehrig	493	8001	16.23
Hank Aaron	755	12364	16.38
Willie Mays	660	10881	16.49
Bob Horner	215	3571	16.61
Hank Sauer	288	4796	16.65
Eddie Mathews	512	8537	16.67
Willie Stargell	475	7927	16.69
Frank Howard	382	6488	16.98
Frank Robinson	583	10006	17.16
Roy Campanella	242	4205	17.38
Rocky Colavito	374	6503	17.39
Reggie Jackson	548	9528	17.39
Gus Zernial	237	4131	17.43
Gorman Thomas	268	4677	17.45
Dick Stuart	228	3997	17.53
Duke Snider	407	7161	17.59
Norm Cash	377	6705	17.79
Johnny Mize	359	6443	17.95
Dick Allen	351	6332	18.04
Ernie Banks	512	9421	18.40
Mel Ott	511	9456	18.50
Roger Maris	275	5101	18.55
Dale Murphy	266	5017	18.86
Joe DiMaggio	361	6821	18.89
Gil Hodges	370	7030	19.00
Wally Post	210	4007	19.08
Al Rosen	192	3725	19.40
Hack Wilson	244	4760	19.51
Joe Adcock	336	6606	19.66
Bob Allison	256	5032	19.66
Johnny Bench	389	7658	19.69
Boog Powell	339	6681	19.71

Most Home Runs by Position, Career, AL

Player	Pos.	HR
Lou Gehrig	1B	493
Jimmie Foxx	1B	473
Norm Cash	1B	375
Joe Gordon	2B	246
Bobby Doerr	2B	223
Charlie Gehringer	2B	183
Graig Nettles	3B	319
Brooks Robinson	3B	267
Sal Bando	3B	232
Vern Stephens	SS	213
Joe Cronin	SS	151
Rico Petrocelli	SS	129
Babe Ruth	OF	686
Ted Williams	OF	521
Mickey Mantle	OF	496
Yogi Berra	C	313
Carlton Fisk	C	255
Bill Dickey	C	202
Wes Ferrell	P	36
Red Ruffing	P	35
Earl Wilson	P	35

Most Home Runs by Position, Career, NL

Player	Pos.	HR
Willie McCovey	1B	439
Gil Hodges	1B	355
Orlando Cepeda	1B	334
Rogers Hornsby	2B	263
Joe Morgan	2B	260
Bill Mazeroski	2B	138
Eddie Mathews	3B	482
Mike Schmidt	3B	478
Ron Santo	3B	334
Ernie Banks	SS	293
Pee Wee Reese	SS	124
Leo Cardenas	SS	117
Hank Aaron	OF	661
Willie Mays	OF	643
Mel Ott	OF	475
Johnny Bench	C	325
Roy Campanella	C	242
Gabby Hartnett	C	233
Warren Spahn	P	35
Don Drysdale	P	29
Bob Gibson	P	24

Most Home Runs by Position, Season, AL

Player	Team	Year	Pos.	HR
Hank Greenberg	DET	1938	1B	58
Joe Gordon	CLE	1948	2B	32
Al Rosen	CLE	1953	3B	43
Rico Petrocelli	BOS	1969	SS	40
Roger Maris	NY	1961	OF	61
Carlton Fisk	CHI	1985	C	33
Wes Ferrell	CLE	1931	P	9

Most Home Runs by Position, Season, NL

Player	Team	Year	Pos.	HR
Johnny Mize	NY	1947	1B	51
Rogers Hornsby	STL	1922	2B	42
Davey Johnson	ATL	1973	2B	42
Mike Schmidt	PHI	1980	3B	48
Ernie Banks	CHI	1958	SS	47
Hack Wilson	CHI	1930	OF	56
Roy Campanella	BKN	1953	C	40
Don Newcombe	BKN	1955	P	7
Don Drysdale	LA	1958	P	7
	LA	1965	P	7

Home Run in First Appearance in Majors, AL

Player	Team	Date
Earl Averill	CLE	Apr 16, 1929
Ace Parker	PHI	Apr 30, 1937
Bill LeFebvre	BOS	Jun 10, 1938
Hack Miller	DET	Apr 23, 1944
Eddie Pellagrini	BOS	Apr 22, 1946
George Vico	DET	Apr 20, 1948
Bob Nieman	STL	Sep 14, 1951
John Kennedy	WAS	Sep 5, 1962
Buster Narum	BAL	May 3, 1963
Gates Brown	DET	Jun 19, 1963
Bert Campaneris	KC	Jul 23, 1964
Bill Roman	DET	Sep 30, 1964
Brant Alyea	WAS	Sep 12, 1965
John Miller	NY	Sep 11, 1966
Rick Renick	MIN	Jul 11, 1968
Joe Keough	OAK	Aug 7, 1968
Gene Lamont	DET	Sep 2, 1970
Don Rose	CAL	May 24, 1972
Reggie Sanders	DET	Sep 1, 1974
Dave McKay	MIN	Aug 22, 1975
Al Woods	TOR	Apr 7, 1977
Dave Machemer	CAL	Jun 21, 1978
Gary Gaetti	MIN	Sep 20, 1981
Andre David	MIN	Jun 29, 1984
Will Clark	SF	Apr 8, 1986
Terry Steinbach	OAK	Sep 12, 1986
Jay Bell	CLE	Sep 29, 1986

Home Run in First Appearance in Majors, NL

Player	Team	Date
Bill Duggleby	PHI	Apr 21, 1898
Johnny Bates	BOS	Apr 12, 1906
Clise Dudley	BKN	Apr 27, 1929
Gordon Slade	BKN	May 24, 1930
Eddie Morgan	STL	Apr 14, 1936
Ernie Koy	BKN	Apr 19, 1938
Emmett Mueller	PHI	Apr 19, 1938
Clyde Vollmer	CIN	May 31, 1942
Buddy Kerr	NY	Sep 8, 1943
Whitey Lockman	NY	Jul 5, 1945
Dan Bankhead	BKN	Aug 26, 1947
Les Layton	NY	May 21, 1948
Ed Sanicki	PHI	Sep 14, 1949
Ted Tappe	CIN	Sep 14, 1950
Hoyt Wilhelm	NY	Apr 23, 1952
Wally Moon	STL	Apr 13, 1954
Chuck Tanner	MIL	Apr 12, 1955
Bill White	NY	May 7, 1956
Frank Ernaga	CHI	May 24, 1957
Don Leppert	PIT	Jun 18, 1961
Cuno Barragan	CHI	Sep 1, 1961
Benny Ayala	NY	Aug 27, 1974
Jose Sosa	HOU	Jul 30, 1975
Johnnie LeMaster	SF	Sep 2, 1975
Mike Fitzgerald	NY	Sep 13, 1983

Home Run on First Pitch in Majors, AL

Player	Team	Date
George Vico	DET	Apr 20, 1948
Bert Campaneris	KC	Jul 23, 1964
Brant Alyea	WAS	Sep 12, 1965
Don Rose	CAL	May 24, 1972

Home Run on First Pitch in Majors, NL

Player	Team	Date
Clise Dudley	BKN	Apr 27, 1929
Eddie Morgan	STL	Apr 14, 1936
Clyde Vollmer	CIN	May 31, 1942
Chuck Tanner	MIL	Apr 12, 1955

Two Home Runs in One Inning, AL

Player	Team	Date	Inn.
Ken Williams	STL	Aug 7, 1922	6
Bill Regan	BOS	Jun 16, 1928	4
Joe DiMaggio	NY	Jun 24, 1936	5
Al Kaline	DET	Apr 17, 1955	6
Jim Lemon	WAS	Sep 5, 1959	3
Joe Pepitone	NY	May 23, 1962	8
Rick Reichardt	CAL	Apr 30, 1966	8
Cliff Johnson	NY	Jun 30, 1977	8

Two Home Runs in One Inning, NL

Player	Team	Date	Inn.
Charley Jones	BOS	Jun 10, 1880	8
Bobby Lowe	BOS	May 30, 1894	3
Jake Stenzel	PIT	Jun 6, 1894	3
Hack Wilson	NY	Jul 1, 1925	3
Hank Leiber	NY	Aug 24, 1935	2
Andy Seminick	PHI	Jun 2, 1949	8
Sid Gordon	NY	Jul 31, 1949	2
Willie McCovey	SF	Apr 12, 1973	4
John Boccabella	MON	Jul 6, 1973	6
Lee May	HOU	Apr 29, 1974	6
Willie McCovey	SF	Jun 27, 1977	6
Andre Dawson	MON	Jul 30, 1978	3
Ray Knight	CIN	May 13, 1980	5
Von Hayes	PHI	Jun 11, 1985	1
Andre Dawson	MON	Sep 24, 1985	5

A mainstay of the Expos' lineup from 1976 to 1986, Andre Dawson possesses the rare combination of speed (253 career SB) and power (225 HR).

Two Home Runs in One Game Most Often

Player	G
Babe Ruth	72
Willie Mays	63
Hank Aaron	62
Jimmie Foxx	55
Frank Robinson	54
Eddie Mathews	49
Mel Ott	49
Harmon Killebrew	46
Mickey Mantle	46
Willie McCovey	44
Lou Gehrig	43
Dave Kingman	43
Ernie Banks	42
Reggie Jackson	42
Mike Schmidt	41
Ralph Kiner	40
Stan Musial	37
Ted Williams	37
Willie Stargell	36
Joe DiMaggio	35
Hank Greenberg	35
Lee May	35
Jim Rice	34
Duke Snider	34
Dick Allen	32
Rocky Colavito	32
Gus Zernial	32
Hank Sauer	31
Billy Williams	31
Gil Hodges	30
Willie Horton	30
Johnny Mize	30

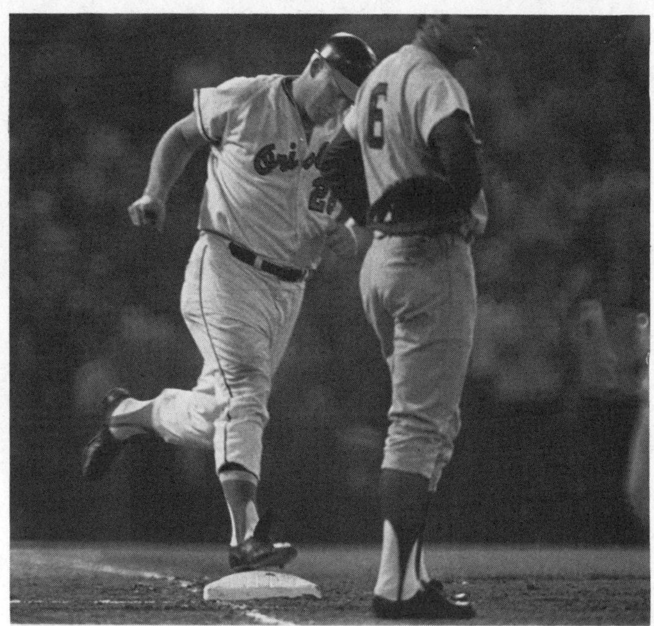

Goose Goslin (*left*) led the Washington Senators to their first championship with an 11-hit, 3-homer World Series performance against the Giants in 1924. Boog Powell (*above*) gave the Orioles the power at first they needed to win it all in 1966 and 1970.

Three Home Runs in One Game, AL

Player	Team	Date	H/A	Cons.
Ken Williams	STL	Apr 22, 1922	Home	No
Joe Hauser	PHI	Aug 2, 1924	Away	No
Ty Cobb	DET	May 5, 1925	Away	No
Mickey Cochrane	PHI	May 21, 1925	Away	No
Goose Goslin	WAS	Jun 19, 1925	Away	No
Tony Lazzeri	NY	Jun 8, 1927	Home	No
Lou Gehrig	NY	Jun 23, 1927	Away	No
	NY	May 4, 1929	Away	No
Babe Ruth	NY	May 21, 1930	Away	No
Lou Gehrig	NY	May 22, 1930	Away	No
Carl Reynolds	CHI	Jul 2, 1930	Away	Yes
Goose Goslin	STL	Aug 19, 1930	Away	Yes
Earl Averill	CLE	Sep 17, 1930	Home	Yes
Goose Goslin	STL	Jun 23, 1932	Home	Yes
Ben Chapman	NY	Jul 9, 1932	Home	Yes
Jimmie Foxx	PHI	Jul 10, 1932	Away	Yes
Al Simmons	PHI	Jul 15, 1932	Home	Yes
Jimmie Foxx	PHI	Jun 8, 1933	Home	Yes
Hal Trosky	CLE	May 30, 1934	Home	Yes
Ed Coleman	PHI	Aug 17, 1934	Home	Yes
Pinky Higgins	PHI	Jun 27, 1935	Home	Yes
Moose Solters	STL	Jul 7, 1935	Away	Yes
Tony Lazzeri	NY	May 24, 1936	Away	No
Joe DiMaggio	NY	Jun 13, 1937	Away	Yes
Hal Trosky	CLE	Jul 5, 1937	Away	No
Merv Connors	CHI	Sep 17, 1938	Home	Yes

Three Home Runs in One Game, AL *(cont'd)*

Player	Team	Date	H/A	Cons.
Ken Keltner	CLE	May 25, 1939	Away	Yes
Jim Tabor	BOS	Jul 4, 1939	Away	No
Bill Dickey	NY	Jul 26, 1939	Home	Yes
Pinky Higgins	DET	May 20, 1940	Home	Yes
Charlie Keller	NY	Jul 28, 1940	Away	No
Rudy York	DET	Sep 1, 1941	Home	No
Pat Seerey	CLE	Jul 13, 1945	Away	No
Ted Williams	BOS	Jul 14, 1946	Home	No
Sam Chapman	PHI	Aug 15, 1946	Away	No
Joe DiMaggio	NY	May 23, 1948	Away	Yes
Pat Mullin	DET	Jun 26, 1949	Away	No
Bobby Doerr	BOS	Jun 8, 1950	Home	No
Larry Doby	CLE	Aug 2, 1950	Home	Yes
Joe DiMaggio	NY	Sep 10, 1950	Away	No
Johnny Mize	NY	Sep 15, 1950	Away	Yes
Gus Zernial	CHI	Oct 1, 1950	Home	No
Bobby Avila	CLE	Jun 20, 1951	Away	No
Clyde Vollmer	BOS	Jul 26, 1951	Home	No
Al Rosen	CLE	Apr 29, 1952	Away	No
Bill Glynn	CLE	Jul 5, 1954	Away	Yes
Al Kaline	DET	Apr 17, 1955	Home	No
Mickey Mantle	NY	May 13, 1955	Home	No
Norm Zauchin	BOS	May 27, 1955	Home	No
Jim Lemon	WAS	Aug 31, 1956	Home	Yes
Ted Williams	BOS	May 8, 1957	Away	No
	BOS	Jun 13, 1957	Away	No
Hector Lopez	KC	Jun 26, 1958	Home	No
Preston Ward	KC	Sep 9, 1958	Home	Yes
Charlie Maxwell	DET	May 3, 1959	Home	Yes
Bob Cerv	KC	Aug 20, 1959	Home	No
Willie Kirkland	CLE	Jul 9, 1961	Home	Yes
Rocky Colavito	DET	Aug 27, 1961	Away	No
Lee Thomas	LA	Sep 5, 1961	Away	No
Rocky Colavito	DET	Jul 5, 1962	Away	Yes
Steve Boros	DET	Aug 6, 1962	Away	No
Don Leppert	WAS	Apr 11, 1963	Home	Yes
Bob Allison	MIN	May 17, 1963	Away	Yes
Boog Powell	BAL	Aug 10, 1963	Away	Yes
Harmon Killebrew	MIN	Sep 21, 1963	Away	No
Jim King	WAS	Jun 8, 1964	Home	No
Boog Powell	BAL	Jun 27, 1964	Away	No
Manny Jimenez	KC	Jul 4, 1964	Away	Yes
Tom Tresh	NY	Jun 6, 1965	Home	Yes
Boog Powell	BAL	Aug 15, 1966	Away	No
Tom McCraw	CHI	May 24, 1967	Away	No
Curt Blefary	BAL	Jun 6, 1967	Away	No
Ken Harrelson	BOS	Jun 14, 1968	Away	Yes
Mike Epstein	WAS	May 16, 1969	Away	No
Joe Lahoud	BOS	Jun 11, 1969	Away	No
Bill Melton	CHI	Jun 24, 1969	Away	Yes
Reggie Jackson	OAK	Jul 2, 1969	Home	No

Three Home Runs in One Game, AL ***(cont'd)***

Player	Team	Date	H/A	Cons.
Paul Blair	BAL	Apr 29, 1970	Away	No
Tony Horton	CLE	May 24, 1970	Home	No
Willie Horton	DET	Jun 9, 1970	Home	No
Bobby Murcer	NY	Jun 24, 1970	Home	Yes
Bill Freehan	DET	Aug 9, 1971	Away	No
George Hendrick	CLE	Jun 19, 1973	Home	Yes
Tony Oliva	MIN	Jul 3, 1973	Away	No
Leroy Stanton	CAL	Jul 10, 1973	Away	No
Bobby Murcer	NY	Jul 13, 1973	Home	No
Bobby Grich	BAL	Jun 18, 1974	Home	Yes
Fred Lynn	BOS	Jun 18, 1975	Away	No
John Mayberry	KC	Jul 1, 1975	Away	No
Don Baylor	BAL	Jul 2, 1975	Away	Yes
Tony Solaita	KC	Sep 7, 1975	Away	Yes
Carl Yastrzemski	BOS	May 19, 1976	Away	No
Willie Horton	TEX	May 15, 1977	Away	No
John Mayberry	KC	Jun 1, 1977	Away	Yes
Cliff Johnson	NY	Jun 30, 1977	Away	Yes
Jim Rice	BOS	Aug 29, 1977	Home	Yes
Al Oliver	TEX	May 23, 1979	Home	No
Ben Oglivie	MIL	Jul 8, 1979	Home	No
Claudell Washington	CHI	Jul 14, 1979	Home	No
George Brett	KC	Jul 22, 1979	Away	No
Cecil Cooper	MIL	Jul 27, 1979	Home	No
Eddie Murray	BAL	Aug 29, 1979	Away	Yes
Carney Lansford	CAL	Sep 1, 1979	Away	Yes
Otto Velez	TOR	May 4, 1980	Home	No
Freddie Patek	CAL	Jun 20, 1980	Away	No
Al Oliver	TEX	Aug 17, 1980	Away	No
Eddie Murray	BAL	Sep 14, 1980	Away	No
Jeff Burroughs	SEA	Aug 14, 1981	Away	No
Paul Molitor	MIL	May 12, 1982	Away	No
Larry Herndon	DET	May 18, 1982	Home	Yes
Ben Oglivie	MIL	Jun 20, 1982	Away	No
Harold Baines	CHI	Jul 7, 1982	Home	No
Doug DeCinces	CAL	Aug 3, 1982	Home	No
	CAL	Aug 8, 1982	Away	No
George Brett	KC	Apr 20, 1983	Away	No
Ben Oglivie	MIL	May 14, 1983	Home	No
Dan Ford	BAL	Jul 20, 1983	Away	No
Jim Rice	BOS	Aug 29, 1983	Away	No
Dave Kingman	OAK	Apr 16, 1984	Away	Yes
Harold Baines	CHI	Sep 17, 1984	Away	No
Gorman Thomas	SEA	Apr 11, 1985	Home	No
Larry Parrish	TEX	Apr 19, 1985	Home	Yes
Eddie Murray	BAL	Aug 26, 1985	Away	No
Lee Lacy	BAL	Jun 8, 1986	Away	No
Juan Beniquez	BAL	Jun 12, 1986	Home	Yes
Joe Carter	CLE	Aug 29, 1986	Away	No
Jim Presley	SEA	Sep 1, 1986	Home	No
Reggie Jackson	CAL	Sep 18, 1986	Home	No

Wille McCovey (*left*) blasts his 500th homer in Atlanta on June 30, 1978. *Below left:* Johnny Bench anchored the Big Red Machine, belting 389 home runs in 17 years. *Below*: Darryl Strawberry's sleek frame and powerful looping swing have produced 108 homers and 100 steals in four years with the Mets.

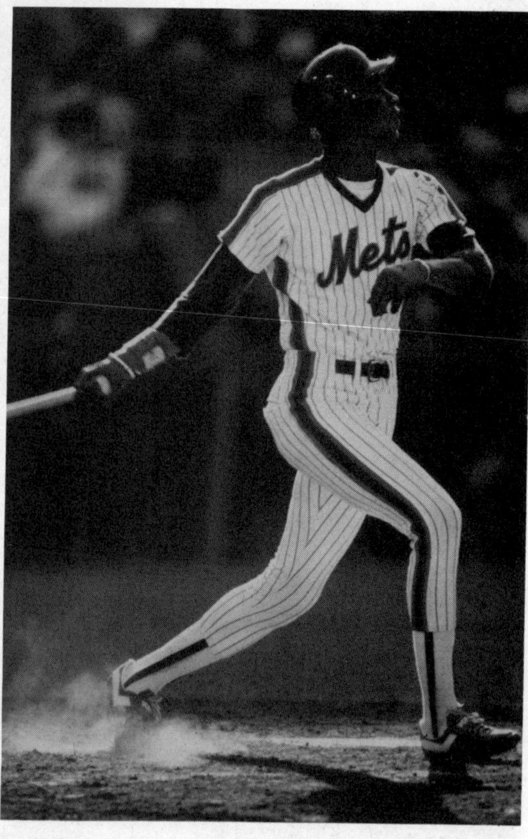

Three Home Runs in One Game, NL

Player	Team	Date	H/A	Cons.
Ned Williamson	CHI	May 30, 1884	Home	No
Cap Anson	CHI	Aug 6, 1884	Home	Yes
Jack Manning	PHI	Oct 9, 1884	Away	Yes
Dan Brouthers	DET	Sep 10, 1886	Away	No
Roger Connor	NY	May 9, 1888	Away	No
Frank Shugart	STL	May 10, 1894	Away	No
Bill Joyce	WAS	Aug 20, 1894	Home	Yes
Tom McCreery	LOU	Jul 12, 1897	Away	No
Jake Beckley	CIN	Sep 26, 1897	Away	No
Butch Henline	PHI	Sep 15, 1922	Home	No
Cy Williams	PHI	May 11, 1923	Home	No
George Kelly	NY	Sep 17, 1923	Away	Yes
	NY	Jun 14, 1924	Home	No
Jack Fournier	BKN	Jul 13, 1926	Away	No
Les Bell	BOS	Jun 2, 1928	Home	No
George Harper	STL	Sep 20, 1928	Away	Yes
Hack Wilson	CHI	Jul 26, 1930	Away	No
Mel Ott	NY	Aug 31, 1930	Home	Yes
Rogers Hornsby	CHI	Apr 24, 1931	Away	Yes
George Watkins	STL	Jun 24, 1931	Away	Yes
Bill Terry	NY	Aug 13, 1932	Home	No
Babe Herman	CHI	Jul 20, 1933	Home	No
Hal Lee	BOS	Jul 6, 1934	Away	No
Babe Ruth	BOS	May 25, 1935	Away	No
Johnny Moore	PHI	Jul 22, 1936	Home	Yes
Alex Kampouris	CIN	May 9, 1937	Away	No
Johnny Mize	STL	Jul 13, 1938	Home	Yes
	STL	Jul 20, 1938	Home	No
Hank Leiber	CHI	Jul 4, 1939	Home	Yes
Johnny Mize	STL	May 13, 1940	Away	No
	STL	Sep 8, 1940	Home	Yes
Jim Tobin	BOS	May 13, 1942	Home	Yes
Clyde McCullough	CHI	Jul 26, 1942	Away	Yes
Bill Nicholson	CHI	Jul 23, 1944	Away	Yes
Johnny Mize	NY	Apr 24, 1947	Away	Yes
Willard Marshall	NY	Jul 18, 1947	Home	Yes
Ralph Kiner	PIT	Aug 16, 1947	Home	Yes
	PIT	Sep 11, 1947	Home	Yes
	PIT	Jul 5, 1948	Home	No
Gene Hermanski	BKN	Aug 5, 1948	Home	Yes
Andy Seminick	PHI	Jun 2, 1949	Home	No
Walker Cooper	CIN	Jul 6, 1949	Home	No
Bob Elliott	BOS	Sep 24, 1949	Away	Yes
Duke Snider	BKN	May 30, 1950	Home	Yes
Wes Westrum	NY	Jun 24, 1950	Home	No
Andy Pafko	CHI	Aug 2, 1950	Away	Yes
Roy Campanella	BKN	Aug 26, 1950	Away	Yes
Hank Sauer	CHI	Aug 28, 1950	Home	Yes
Tommy Brown	BKN	Sep 18, 1950	Home	Yes
Ralph Kiner	PIT	Jul 18, 1951	Away	No
Del Wilber	PHI	Aug 27, 1951	Home	Yes

Three Home Runs in One Game, NL ***(cont'd)***

Player	Team	Date	H/A	Cons.
Don Mueller	NY	Sep 1, 1951	Home	No
Hank Sauer	CHI	Jun 11, 1952	Home	No
Eddie Mathews	BOS	Sep 27, 1952	Away	Yes
Dusty Rhodes	NY	Aug 26, 1953	Home	Yes
Jim Pendleton	MIL	Aug 30, 1953	Away	No
Stan Musial	STL	May 2, 1954	Home	No
Hank Thompson	NY	Jun 3, 1954	Away	Yes
Dusty Rhodes	NY	Jul 28, 1954	Home	Yes
Duke Snider	BKN	Jun 1, 1955	Home	No
Gus Bell	CIN	Jul 21, 1955	Away	Yes
Del Ennis	PHI	Jul 23, 1955	Home	No
Smoky Burgess	CIN	Jul 29, 1955	Home	No
Ernie Banks	CHI	Aug 4, 1955	Home	No
Gus Bell	CIN	May 29, 1956	Away	Yes
Ed Bailey	CIN	Jun 24, 1956	Away	No
Ted Kluszewski	CIN	Jul 1, 1956	Away	No
Bob Thurman	CIN	Aug 18, 1956	Home	Yes
Ernie Banks	CHI	Sep 14, 1957	Home	Yes
Roman Mejias	PIT	May 4, 1958	Away	No
Walt Moryn	CHI	May 30, 1958	Home	No
Frank Thomas	PIT	Aug 16, 1958	Away	Yes
Lee Walls	CHI	Aug 24, 1958	Away	No
Don Demeter	LA	Apr 21, 1959	Home	No
Hank Aaron	MIL	Jun 21, 1959	Away	No
Frank Robinson	CIN	Aug 22, 1959	Home	Yes
Dick Stuart	PIT	Jun 30, 1960	Home	No
Willie Mays	SF	Jun 29, 1961	Away	No
Bill White	STL	Jul 5, 1961	Away	Yes
Don Demeter	PHI	Sep 12, 1961	Away	No
Ernie Banks	CHI	May 29, 1962	Home	Yes
Stan Musial	STL	Jul 8, 1962	Away	Yes
Willie Mays	SF	Jun 2, 1963	Away	No
Ernie Banks	CHI	Jun 9, 1963	Home	No
Willie McCovey	SF	Sep 22, 1963	Home	Yes
	SF	Apr 22, 1964	Away	Yes
Johnny Callison	PHI	Sep 27, 1964	Home	Yes
	PHI	Jun 6, 1965	Away	No
Willie Stargell	PIT	Jun 24, 1965	Away	No
Jim Hickman	NY	Sep 3, 1965	Away	Yes
Gene Oliver	ATL	Jul 30, 1966	Home	No
Art Shamsky	CIN	Aug 12, 1966	Home	Yes
Willie McCovey	SF	Sep 17, 1966	Home	No
Roberto Clemente	PIT	May 15, 1967	Away	No
Adolfo Phillips	CHI	Jun 11, 1967	Home	Yes
Jimmy Wynn	HOU	Jun 15, 1967	Home	Yes
Willie Stargell	PIT	May 22, 1968	Away	No
Billy Williams	CHI	Sep 10, 1968	Home	No
Dick Allen	PHI	Sep 29, 1968	Away	Yes
Bob Tillman	ATL	Jul 30, 1969	Away	No
Roberto Clemente	PIT	Aug 13, 1969	Away	Yes
Rico Carty	ATL	May 31, 1970	Home	No

Three Home Runs in One Game, NL *(cont'd)*

Player	Team	Date	H/A	Cons.
Mike Lum	ATL	Jul 3, 1970	Home	No
Johnny Bench	CIN	Jul 26, 1970	Home	Yes
Orlando Cepeda	ATL	Jul 26, 1970	Away	Yes
Willie Stargell	PIT	Apr 10, 1971	Away	No
	PIT	Apr 21, 1971	Home	Yes
Deron Johnson	PHI	Jul 11, 1971	Home	Yes
Rick Monday	CHI	May 16, 1972	Away	Yes
Nate Colbert	SD	Aug 1, 1972	Away	No
Johnny Bench	CIN	May 9, 1973	Away	No
Lee May	HOU	Jun 21, 1973	Away	No
George Mitterwald	CHI	Apr 17, 1974	Home	No
Jimmy Wynn	LA	May 11, 1974	Away	No
Davey Lopes	LA	Aug 20, 1974	Away	No
Reggie Smith	STL	May 22, 1976	Away	No
Dave Kingman	NY	Jun 4, 1976	Away	No
Bill Robinson	PIT	Jun 5, 1976	Home	No
Gary Matthews	SF	Sep 25, 1976	Home	No
Gary Carter	MON	Apr 20, 1977	Home	Yes
Larry Parrish	MON	May 29, 1977	Away	Yes
George Foster	CIN	Jul 14, 1977	Home	Yes
Pete Rose	CIN	Apr 29, 1978	Away	No
Dave Kingman	CHI	May 14, 1978	Away	No
Larry Parrish	MON	Jul 30, 1978	Away	Yes
Dave Kingman	CHI	May 17, 1979	Home	No
Dale Murphy	ATL	May 18, 1979	Home	No
Mike Schmidt	PHI	Jul 7, 1979	Home	Yes
Dave Kingman	CHI	Jul 28, 1979	Away	Yes
Larry Parrish	MON	Apr 25, 1980	Away	No
Johnny Bench	CIN	May 29, 1980	Home	No
Claudell Washington	NY	Jun 22, 1980	Away	Yes
Darrell Evans	SF	Jun 15, 1983	Home	No
Darryl Strawberry	NY	Aug 26, 1985	Away	No
Gary Carter	NY	Sep 3, 1985	Away	Yes
Andre Dawson	MON	Sep 24, 1985	Away	No
Ken Griffey	ATL	Jul 22, 1986	Away	No
Eric Davis	CIN	Sep 10, 1986	Away	No

Four Home Runs in One Game, AL

Player	Team	Date	H/A	Cons.	Inns.
Lou Gehrig	NY	Jun 3, 1932	Away	No	9
Pat Seerey	CHI	Jul 18, 1948	Away	No	11
Rocky Colavito	CLE	Jun 10, 1959	Away	No	9

Four Home Runs in One Game, NL

Player	Team	Date	H/A	Cons.	Inns.
Bobby Lowe	BOS	May 30, 1894	Home	No	9
Ed Delahanty	PHI	Jul 13, 1896	Away	Yes	9
Chuck Klein	PHI	Jul 10, 1936	Away	No	10
Gil Hodges	BKN	Aug 31, 1950	Home	No	9
Joe Adcock	MIL	Jul 31, 1954	Away	Yes	9
Willie Mays	SF	Apr 30, 1961	Away	No	9
Mike Schmidt	PHI	Jul 17, 1976	Away	No	10
Bob Horner	ATL	Jul 6, 1986	Home	No	9

Most Home Runs in a Doubleheader, AL

Player	Team	Date	HR
Earl Averill	CLE	Sep 17, 1930	4
Jimmie Foxx	PHI	Jul 2, 1933	4
Jim Tabor	BOS	Jul 4, 1939	4
Gus Zernial	CHI	Oct 1, 1950	4
Charlie Maxwell	DET	May 3, 1959	4
Roger Maris	NY	Jul 25, 1961	4
Rocky Colavito	DET	Aug 27, 1961	4
Harmon Killebrew	MIN	Sep 21, 1963	4
Bobby Murcer	NY	Jun 24, 1970	4
Graig Nettles	NY	Apr 14, 1974	4
Otto Velez	TOR	May 4, 1980	4
Al Oliver	TEX	Aug 17, 1980	4

Most Home Runs in a Doubleheader, NL

Player	Team	Date	HR
Stan Musial	STL	May 2, 1954	5
Nate Colbert	SD	Aug 1, 1972	5
Bill Nicholson	CHI	Jul 23, 1944	4
Ralph Kiner	PIT	Sep 11, 1947	4
Wally Post	CIN	Apr 29, 1956	4
Bobby Thomson	MIL	May 30, 1956	4
Leo Cardenas	CIN	Jun 5, 1966	4
Adolfo Phillips	CHI	Jun 11, 1967	4
Lee May	CIN	Jul 15, 1969	4
Rusty Staub	MON	Aug 1, 1970	4
Jason Thompson	PIT	Jun 26, 1984	4

Bob Horner (*above*) and teammate Dale Murphy have combined for 479 home runs for Atlanta since 1978, reminding Braves' fans of a pair named Aaron and Matthews.

Leadoff Home Runs in Two Consecutive Games, AL

Player	Team	Date	Opp.
Harry Hooper	BOS	May 30, 1913	WAS
	BOS	May 30, 1913	WAS
Sherry Robertson	WAS	Sep 17, 1946	CLE
	WAS	Sep 18, 1946	CLE
Hank Bauer	NY	Aug 6, 1957	WAS
	NY	Aug 7, 1957	WAS
Tony Kubek	NY	Sep 6, 1964	KC
	NY	Sep 7, 1964	MIN
Dick McAuliffe	DET	Apr 28, 1969	WAS
	DET	Apr 29, 1969	WAS
Al Bumbry	BAL	Aug 4, 1982	BOS
	BAL	Aug 5, 1982	KC
Lou Whitaker	DET	May 6, 1983	CAL
	DET	May 7, 1983	CAL
Damaso Garcia	TOR	Jun 1, 1983	DET
	TOR	Jun 2, 1983	DET
Oddibe McDowell	TEX	Jul 27, 1985	NY
	TEX	Jul 28, 1985	NY
Kirby Puckett	MIN	May 2, 1986	DET
	MIN	May 3, 1986	DET

Leadoff Home Runs in Two Consecutive Games, NL

Player	Team	Date	Opp.
John Crooks	STL	May 10, 1892	PHI
	STL	May 11, 1892	BAL
Sam Mertes	CHI	Jun 8, 1900	BOS
	CHI	Jun 9, 1900	BOS
Jesse Burkett	STL	May 22, 1901	BKN
	STL	May 23, 1901	PHI
Carl Furillo	BKN	Jul 12, 1951	CHI
	BKN	Jul 13, 1951	CHI
Whitey Lockman	NY	Jul 18, 1953	CHI
	NY	Jul 19, 1953	MIL
Denis Menke	MIL	Jul 26, 1964	CIN
	MIL	Jul 27, 1964	CIN
Felipe Alou	MIL	Jul 26, 1965	HOU
	MIL	Jul 27, 1965	HOU
	ATL	Aug 9, 1966	LA
	ATL	Aug 10, 1966	LA
Bobby Bonds	SF	Jun 5, 1973	PIT
	SF	Jun 6, 1973	PIT
Pete Rose	CIN	Jul 25, 1976	ATL
	CIN	Jul 26, 1976	SF
Gary Redus	CIN	Jul 1, 1983	ATL
	CIN	Jul 2, 1983	ATL
Eddie Milner	CIN	Jun 24, 1984	SD
	CIN	Jun 25, 1984	SF
Dan Gladden	SF	Oct 1, 1985	CIN
	SF	Oct 2, 1985	HOU

Al Bumbry (*top*) holds the Orioles' record with 252 career stolen bases. Felipe Alou (*above*) was the most prolific of the Alou brothers, collecting 2101 hits in 17 seasons.

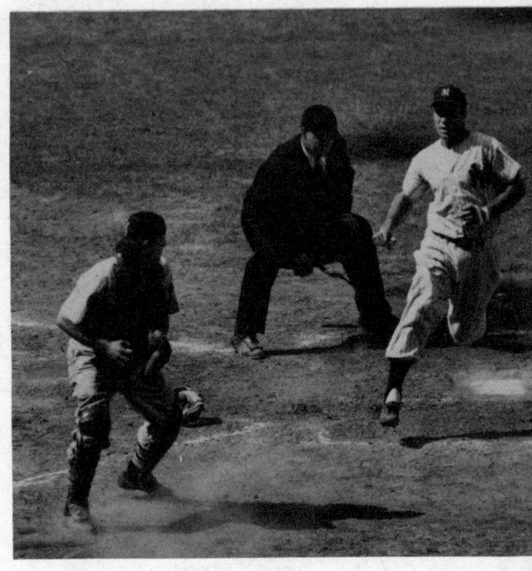

Bobby Bonds (*above*) became the most powerful leadoff man in history, hitting 30 home runs and stealing 30 bases in five separate seasons. *Right*: Hank Bauer's steady hitting helped the Yankees dominate the 1950s.

Most Leadoff Home Runs, Career

Player	Total
Bobby Bonds	35
Rickey Henderson	28
Eddie Yost	28
Davey Lopes	26
Lou Brock	22
Jimmy Ryan	22
Felipe Alou	20
Eddie Joost	19
Dick McAuliffe	19
Hank Bauer	18
Lou Whitaker	18
Pete Rose	17
Tommy Harper	16
Rick Monday	16
Don Buford	15
Bert Campaneris	14

Player	Total
Frankie Crosetti	14
Paul Molitor	14
Terry Puhl	13
Bill Bruton	12
Al Bumbry	12
Joe Morgan	12
Al Smith	12
Tom Brown	11
Ralph Garr	11
Mickey Rivers	11
Earle Combs	10
Brian Downing	10
Johnny Frederick	10
Harry Hooper	10
Don Money	10
Wally Moses	10

Home Runs

Switch-Hit Home Runs in One Game, AL

Player	Team	Date
Johnny Lucadello	STL	Sep 16, 1940
Mickey Mantle	NY	May 13, 1955
	NY	Aug 15, 1955
	NY	May 18, 1956
	NY	Jul 1, 1956
	NY	Jun 12, 1957
	NY	Jul 28, 1958
	NY	Sep 15, 1959
	NY	Apr 26, 1961
	NY	May 6, 1962
Tom Tresh	NY	Sep 1, 1963
	NY	Jul 13, 1964
Mickey Mantle	NY	Aug 12, 1964
Tom Tresh	NY	Jun 6, 1965
Reggie Smith	BOS	Aug 20, 1967
	BOS	Aug 11, 1968
Don Buford	BAL	Apr 9, 1970
Roy White	NY	May 7, 1970
Reggie Smith	BOS	Jul 2, 1972
	BOS	Apr 16, 1973
Roy White	NY	Aug 13, 1973
Roy White	NY	Apr 23, 1975
Ken Henderson	CHI	Aug 29, 1975
Eddie Murray	BAL	Aug 3, 1977
Roy White	NY	Jun 13, 1978
Larry Milbourne	SEA	Jul 15, 1978
Willie Wilson	KC	Jun 15, 1979
Eddie Murray	BAL	Aug 29, 1979
U. L. Washington	KC	Sep 21, 1979
Eddie Murray	BAL	Aug 16, 1981
	BAL	Apr 24, 1982
Ted Simmons	MIL	May 2, 1982
Eddie Murray	BAL	Aug 26, 1982
Roy Smalley	NY	Sep 5, 1982
Donnie Scott	SEA	Apr 29, 1985
Mike Young	BAL	Aug 13, 1985
Eddie Murray	BAL	Aug 26, 1985
Nelson Simmons	DET	Sep 16, 1985
Roy Smalley	MIN	May 30, 1986
Tony Bernazard	CLE	Jul 1, 1986
Ruben Sierra	TEX	Sep 13, 1986

Switch-Hit Home Runs in One Game, NL

Player	Team	Date
Augie Galan	CHI	Jun 25, 1937
Jim Russell	BOS	Jun 7, 1948
	BKN	Jul 26, 1950
Red Schoendienst	STL	Jul 8, 1951
Maury Wills	LA	May 30, 1962
Ellis Burton	CHI	Aug 1, 1963
	CHI	Sep 7, 1964
Jim Lefebyre	LA	May 7, 1966
Wes Parker	LA	Jun 5, 1966
Pete Rose	CIN	Aug 30, 1966
Pete Rose	CIN	Aug 2, 1967
Ted Simmons	STL	Apr 17, 1975
Reggie Smith	STL	May 4, 1975
	STL	May 22, 1976
Lee Mazzilli	NY	Sep 3, 1978
Ted Simmons	STL	Jun 11, 1979
Alan Ashby	HOU	Sep 27, 1982
Chili Davis	SF	Jun 5, 1983
Mark Bailey	HOU	Sep 16, 1984

Most Extra-Inning Home Runs, Career

Player	Total
Willie Mays	22
Babe Ruth	16
Frank Robinson	15
Jimmie Foxx	14
Mickey Mantle	14
Hank Aaron	13
Ted Williams	13
Harmon Killebrew	11
Stan Musial	11
Willie Stargell	11

Twenty Home Runs with 50 Stolen Bases, Season

Player	Team	Year	G	SB	HR
Lou Brock	STL N	1967	159	52	21
Cesar Cedeno	HOU N	1972	139	55	22
	HOU N	1973	139	56	25
Joe Morgan	CIN N	1973	157	67	26
Cesar Cedeno	HOU N	1974	160	57	26
Joe Morgan	CIN N	1974	149	58	22
	CIN N	1976	141	60	27
Rickey Henderson	NY A	1985	143	80	24
Ryne Sandberg	CHI N	1985	153	54	26
Eric Davis	CIN N	1986	132	80	27
Rickey Henderson	NY A	1986	153	87	28

Thirty Home Runs with 30 Stolen Bases, Season, AL

Player	Team	Year	G	SB	HR
Ken Williams	STL	1922	153	37	39
Tommy Harper	MIL	1970	154	38	31
Bobby Bonds	NY	1975	145	30	32
	CAL	1977	158	41	37
	CHI	1978			
	TEX	1978	156	43	31

Thirty Home Runs with 30 Stolen Bases, Season, NL

Player	Team	Year	G	SB	HR
Willie Mays	NY	1956	152	40	36
	NY	1957	152	38	35
Hank Aaron	MIL	1963	161	31	44
Bobby Bonds	SF	1969	158	45	32
	SF	1973	160	43	39
Dale Murphy	ATL	1983	162	30	36

Most Home Runs in Final Season

Player	Team	Year	G	AB	HR
Ted Williams	BOS A	1960	113	310	29
Hank Greenberg	PIT N	1947	125	405	25
Roy Cullenbine	DET A	1947	142	464	24
Joe Gordon	CLE A	1950	119	368	19
Ralph Kiner	CLE A	1955	113	321	18
Joe Adcock	CAL A	1966	83	231	18
Mickey Mantle	NY A	1968	144	435	18
Tony Horton	CLE A	1970	115	413	17
Al Rosen	CLE A	1956	121	416	15
Ted Kluszewski	LA A	1961	107	263	15

Brothers with Most Home Runs, Career

Player	HR
Hank Aaron	755
Tommie Aaron	13
Total	768
Joe DiMaggio	361
Vince DiMaggio	125
Dom DiMaggio	87
Total	573
Ken Boyer	282
Clete Boyer	162
Total	444
Lee May	354
Carlos May	90
Total	444
Graig Nettles	384
Jim Nettles	16
Total	400
Dick Allen	351
Hank Allen	6
Ron Allen	1
Total	358
Bob Johnson	288

Player	HR
Roy Johnson	58
Total	346
Hank Sauer	288
Ed Sauer	5
Total	293
Eddie Murray	275
Rich Murray	4
Total	279
Felipe Alou	206
Jesus Alou	32
Matty Alou	31
Total	269
Joe Torre	252
Frank Torre	13
Total	265
Bob Meusel	156
Irish Meusel	106
Total	262
Sal Bando	242
Chris Bando	19
Total	261

Playing in the shadows: Tommie Aaron (*above*) toiled on his brother's team for seven years, hitting just 742 fewer homers than Hank. Dom DiMaggio's professorial appearance (*left*) belied his hitting ability: 1046 runs and a .298 average in 11 seasons.

Home Runs by Brothers in One Game

Player	Team	Date	Inn.	Opp.	Opp. Pitcher
Lloyd Waner	PIT N	Sep 4, 1927	5	CIN	Dolf Luque
Paul Waner	PIT N	Sep 4, 1927	5	CIN	Dolf Luque
	PIT N	Jun 9, 1929	5	BKN	Doug McWeeny
Lloyd Waner	PIT N	Jun 29, 1929	7	BKN	Doug McWeeny
Rick Ferrell	BOS A	Jul 19, 1933	4	CLE	Wes Ferrell
Wes Ferrell	CLE A	Jul 19, 1933	4	BOS	Hank Johnson
Tony Cuccinello	BKN N	Jul 5, 1935	8	NY	Leon Chagnon
Al Cuccinello	NY N	Jul 5, 1935	9	BKN	Johnny Babich
Lloyd Waner	PIT N	Sep 15, 1938	5	NY	Cliff Melton
Paul Waner	PIT N	Sep 15, 1938	5	NY	Cliff Melton
Dom DiMaggio	BOS A	Jun 30, 1950	6	NY	Joe Ostrowski
Joe DiMaggio	NY A	Jun 30, 1950	8	BOS	Walt Masterson
Felipe Alou	SF N	May 15, 1961	1	CHI	Dick Ellsworth
Matty Alou	SF N	May 15, 1961	8	CHI	Joe Schaffernoth
Hank Aaron	MIL N	Jun 12, 1962	2	LA	Phil Ortega
Tommie Aaron	MIL N	Jun 12, 1962	8	LA	Ed Roebuck
	MIL N	Jul 12, 1962	9	STL	Larry Jackson
Hank Aaron	MIL N	Jul 12, 1962	9	STL	Lindy McDaniel
Tommie Aaron	MIL N	Aug 14, 1962	6	CIN	Johnny Klippstein
Hank Aaron	MIL N	Aug 14, 1962	7	CIN	Ted Wills
Jesus Alou	SF N	Aug 12, 1965	6	PIT	Bob Friend
Matty Alou	SF N	Aug 12, 1965	8	PIT	Don Schwall
Billy Conigliaro	BOS A	Jul 4, 1970	4	CLE	Steve Dunning
Tony Conigliaro	BOS A	Jul 4, 1970	7	CLE	Fred Lasher
Billy Conigliaro	BOS A	Sep 19, 1970	4	WAS	Jim Hannan
Tony Conigliaro	BOS A	Sep 19, 1970	7	WAS	Joe Grzenda
Graig Nettles	NY A	Sep 14, 1974	1	DET	Mickey Lolich
Jim Nettles	DET A	Sep 14, 1974	2	NY	Pat Dobson

Most Extra-Base Hits, Game, AL

Player	Team	Date	2B	3B	HR	Total
Lou Boudreau	CLE	Jul 14, 1946	4	0	1	5

Most Extra-Base Hits, Game, NL

Player	Team	Date	2B	3B	HR	Total
George Gore	CHI	Jul 9, 1885	2	3	0	5
Larry Twitchell	CLE	Aug 15, 1889	1	3	1	5
Joe Adcock	MIL	Jul 13, 1954	1	0	4	5
Willie Stargell	PIT	Aug 1, 1970	3	0	2	5
Steve Garvey	LA	Aug 28, 1977	3	0	2	5

Most Extra-Base Hits, Game, Other Leagues

Player	Team	Date	2B	3B	HR	Total
George Strief	PHI AA	Jun 25, 1885	1	4	0	5

Most Extra-Base Hits in a Doubleheader, AL

Player	Team	Date	2B	3B	HR	Total	Inns.
John Stone	DET	May 30, 1933	4	0	2	6	
Jimmie Foxx	PHI	Jul 2, 1933	1	1	4	6	19
Hank Majeski	PHI	Aug 27, 1948	6	0	0	6	
Hal McRae	KC	Aug 27, 1974	5	0	1	6	
Al Oliver	TEX	Aug 17, 1980	1	1	4	6	

Most Extra-Base Hits in a Doubleheader, NL

Player	Team	Date	2B	3B	HR	Total	Inns.
Chick Hafey	STL	Jul 28, 1928	4	0	2	6	21
Mel Ott	NY	Jun 19, 1929	4	0	2	6	20
Joe Medwick	STL	May 30, 1935	5	1	0	6	
Red Schoendienst	STL	Jun 6, 1948	5	0	1	6	
Dusty Rhodes	NY	Aug 29, 1954	2	2	2	6	20

Most Consecutive Games with Extra-Base Hit

Player	Team	Date	G	2B	3B	HR
Paul Waner	PIT N	Jun 3, 1927				
	PIT N	Jun 19, 1927	14	12	4	1
Babe Ruth	NY A	Aug 28, 1921				
	NY A	Sep 8, 1921	11	7	1	3

Most Doubles, Game, AL

Player	Team	Date	2B
Pop Dillon	DET	Apr 25, 1901	4
Bill Werber	BOS	Jul 17, 1935	4
Frankie Hayes	PHI	Jul 25, 1936	4
Mike Kreevich	CHI	Sep 4, 1937	4
Marv Owen	CHI	Apr 23, 1939	4
Johnny Lindell	NY	Aug 17, 1944	4
Lou Boudreau	CLE	Jul 14, 1946	4
Al Zarilla	BOS	Jun 8, 1950	4
Vic Wertz	CLE	Sep 26, 1956	4
Charlie Lau	BAL	Jul 13, 1962	4
Bill Bruton	DET	May 19, 1963	4
Orlando Cepeda	BOS	Aug 8, 1973	4
Jim Mason	NY	Jul 8, 1974	4
Dave Duncan	BAL	Jun 30, 1975	4
Rick Miller	BOS	May 11, 1981	4
Damaso Garcia	TOR	Jun 27, 1986	4

Most Doubles, Game, NL

Player	Team	Date	2B
John O'Rourke	BOS	Sep 15, 1880	4
Abner Dalrymple	CHI	Jul 3, 1883	4
Cap Anson	CHI	Jul 3, 1883	4
Tommy Tucker	BOS	Jul 22, 1893	4
Frank Bonner	BAL	Aug 4, 1894	4
Joe Kelley	BAL	Sep 3, 1894	4
Ed Delahanty	PHI	May 13, 1899	4
Gavvy Cravath	PHI	Aug 8, 1915	4
Denny Sothern	PHI	Jun 6, 1930	4
Paul Waner	PIT	May 20, 1932	4
Dick Bartell	PHI	Apr 25, 1933	4
Ernie Lombardi	CIN	May 8, 1935	4
Joe Medwick	STL	Aug 4, 1937	4
Bill Werber	CIN	May 13, 1940	4
Willie Jones	PHI	Apr 20, 1949	4
Jim Greengrass	CIN	Apr 13, 1954	4
Billy Williams	CHI	Apr 9, 1969	4

Most Doubles, Game, Other Leagues

Player	Team	Date	2B
Henry Larkin	PHI AA	Jul 29, 1885	4
Jocko Milligan	PHI AA	May 2, 1886	4

Most Triples, Game, AL

Player	Team	Date	3B	Inns.
Elmer Flick	CLE	Jul 6, 1902	3	
Bill Bradley	CLE	Jul 28, 1903	3	
Patsy Dougherty	BOS	Sep 5, 1903	3	
Billy Lush	DET	Sep 26, 1903	3	
Nap Lajoie	CLE	Jul 13, 1904	3	
Hal Chase	NY	Aug 30, 1906	3	10
Joe Jackson	CLE	Jun 30, 1912	3	
Gus Williams	STL	Apr 24, 1913	3	
Joe Judge	WAS	Aug 9, 1921	3	19
Baby Doll Jacobson	STL	Sep 9, 1922	3	
Jackie Tavener	DET	Sep 12, 1925	3	13
Earle Combs	NY	Sep 22, 1927	3	
Charlie Gehringer	DET	Aug 5, 1929	3	
Joe Kuhel	WAS	May 13, 1937	3	
Joe DiMaggio	NY	Aug 27, 1938	3	
Ben Chapman	CLE	Jul 3, 1939	3	
Bert Campaneris	KC	Aug 29, 1967	3	10
Al Bumbry	BAL	Sep 22, 1973	3	
Ken Landreaux	MIN	Jul 3, 1980	3	

Most Triples, Game, NL

Player	Team	Date	3B
Bill Joyce	NY	May 18, 1897	4
George Hall	PHI	Jun 14, 1876	3
Ezra Sutton	PHI	Jun 14, 1876	3
Buck Ewing	NY	Jun 9, 1883	3
King Kelly	CHI	Sep 29, 1885	3
Hardy Richardson	DET	Sep 9, 1886	3
Sam Thompson	DET	May 13, 1887	3
Marty Sullivan	CHI	May 17, 1887	3
Larry Twitchell	CLE	Aug 15, 1889	3
Long John Reilly	CIN	Jun 14, 1890	3
Bid McPhee	CIN	Jun 28, 1890	3
George Davis	CLE	Apr 25, 1891	3
Billy Hamilton	PHI	Jul 14, 1891	3
Harry Stovey	BAL	Jul 21, 1892	3
Jouett Meekin	NY	Jul 4, 1894	3
George Davis	NY	Jul 14, 1894	3
Bill Hassamaer	WAS	Jul 25, 1894	3
Hugh Duffy	BOS	Sep 18, 1894	3
Frank Shugart	LOU	Jul 30, 1895	3
Bill Dahlen	CHI	May 3, 1896	3
Jake Beckley	CIN	May 19, 1898	3
Bill Dahlen	CHI	Jun 6, 1898	3
Elmer Flick	PHI	Jun 20, 1898	3
Ginger Beaumont	PIT	Aug 9, 1899	3
Harry Wolverton	PHI	Jul 13, 1900	3
Jimmy Sheckard	BKN	Apr 18, 1901	3
Mike Donlin	CIN	Sep 22, 1903	3

Most Triples, Game, NL ***(cont'd)***

Player	Team	Date	3B	Inns.
Miller Huggins	CIN	Oct 8, 1904	3	
Dave Brain	STL	May 29, 1905	3	
	STL	Aug 8, 1905	3	10
Pat Moran	BOS	Aug 10, 1905	3	
Owen Wilson	PIT	Jul 24, 1911	3	
Ross Youngs	NY	May 11, 1920	3	
Ray Powell	BOS	Sep 27, 1921	3	
Charlie Hollocher	CHI	Aug 13, 1922	3	
Jim Bottomley	STL	May 15, 1923	3	
Les Bell	STL	Sep 22, 1926	3	
Jim Bottomley	STL	Jun 21, 1927	3	
Lance Richbourg	BOS	Jul 31, 1929	3	
Carlos Bernier	PIT	May 2, 1953	3	
Danny O'Connell	MIL	Jun 13, 1956	3	
Roberto Clemente	PIT	Sep 8, 1958	3	
Willie Mays	SF	Sep 15, 1960	3	11
Ernie Banks	CHI	Jun 11, 1966	3	
Doug Flynn	NY	Aug 5, 1980	3	
Craig Reynolds	HOU	May 16, 1981	3	

Most Triples, Game, Other Leagues

Player	Team	Date	3B
George Strief	PHI AA	Jun 25, 1885	4
Dave Rowe	STL U	Jun 24, 1884	3
Charley Jones	CIN AA	Jul 20, 1884	3
Harry Stovey	PHI AA	Aug 18, 1884	3
Sadie Houck	PHI AA	Aug 27, 1884	3
Oyster Burns	BAL AA	Jun 13, 1887	3
Billy Hamilton	KC AA	Jun 28, 1889	3
Sid Farrar	PHI P	Aug 28, 1890	3
Tom Brown	BOS AA	May 7, 1891	3
Jack Lewis	PIT F	May 7, 1914	3
Fred Smith	BUF F	Apr 27, 1915	3
Al Shaw	KC F	Jul 4, 1915	3

Twenty Doubles, 20 Triples, and 20 Home Runs, Season, AL

Player	Team	Year	G	2B	3B	HR	BA
Jeff Heath	CLE	1941	151	32	20	24	.340
George Brett	KC	1979	154	42	20	23	.329

Twenty Doubles, 20 Triples, and 20 Home Runs, Season, NL

Player	Team	Year	G	2B	3B	HR	BA
Buck Freeman	WAS	1899	155	20	26	25	.318
Wildfire Schulte	CHI	1911	154	30	21	21	.300
Jim Bottomley	STL	1928	149	42	20	31	.325
Willie Mays	NY	1957	152	26	20	35	.333

Most Total Bases, Game, AL

Player	Team	Date	1B	2B	3B	HR	TB	Inns.
Ty Cobb	DET	May 5, 1925	2	1	0	3	16	
Lou Gehrig	NY	Jun 3, 1932	0	0	0	4	16	
Jimmie Foxx	PHI	Jul 10, 1932	2	1	0	3	16	18
Pat Seerey	CHI	Jul 18, 1948	0	0	0	4	16	11
Rocky Colavito	CLE	Jun 10, 1959	0	0	0	4	16	
Fred Lynn	BOS	Jun 18, 1975	1	0	1	3	16	
Tony Lazzeri	NY	May 24, 1936	0	0	1	3	15	
Pat Seerey	CLE	Jul 13, 1945	0	0	1	3	15	
Bobby Avila	CLE	Jun 20, 1951	1	1	0	3	15	

Most Total Bases, Game, NL

Player	Team	Date	1B	2B	3B	HR	TB	Inns.
Joe Adcock	MIL	Jul 31, 1954	0	1	0	4	18	
Bobby Lowe	BOS	May 30, 1894	1	0	0	4	17	
Ed Delahanty	PHI	Jul 13, 1896	1	0	0	4	17	
Gil Hodges	BKN	Aug 31, 1950	1	0	0	4	17	
Mike Schmidt	PHI	Apr 17, 1976	1	0	0	4	17	10
Larry Twitchell	CLE	Aug 15, 1889	1	1	3	1	16	
Chuck Klein	PHI	Jul 10, 1936	0	0	0	4	16	10
Willie Mays	SF	Apr 30, 1961	0	0	0	4	16	
Dan Brouthers	DET	Sep 10, 1886	1	1	0	3	15	
George Kelly	NY	Sep 17, 1923	1	1	0	3	15	
Les Bell	BOS	Jun 2, 1928	0	0	1	3	15	
Walker Cooper	CIN	Jul 6, 1949	3	0	0	3	15	
Wes Westrum	NY	Jun 24, 1950	0	0	1	3	15	
Willie Mays	SF	May 13, 1958	1	0	2	2	15	
Willie Stargell	PIT	May 22, 1968	1	1	0	3	15	
Davey Lopes	LA	Aug 20, 1974	1	1	0	3	15	

Most Total Bases, Season, AL

Player	Team	Year	TB
Babe Ruth	NY	1921	457
Lou Gehrig	NY	1927	447
Jimmie Foxx	PHI	1932	438
Lou Gehrig	NY	1930	419
Joe DiMaggio	NY	1937	418
Babe Ruth	NY	1927	417
Lou Gehrig	NY	1931	410
	NY	1934	409
Jim Rice	BOS	1978	406
Hal Trosky	CLE	1936	405
Jimmie Foxx	PHI	1933	403
Lou Gehrig	NY	1936	403

Most Total Bases, Season, NL

Player	Team	Year	TB
Rogers Hornsby	STL	1922	450
Chuck Klein	PHI	1930	445
Stan Musial	STL	1948	429
Hack Wilson	CHI	1930	423
Chuck Klein	PHI	1932	420
Babe Herman	BKN	1930	416
Rogers Hornsby	CHI	1929	409
Joe Medwick	STL	1937	406
Chuck Klein	PHI	1929	405
Hank Aaron	MIL	1959	400

One of the most feared hitters of today: George Brett (*above left*) has batted .319, slugged .539, and hit 135 home runs in the 1980s. Walker Cooper (*above*) caught for two World Champions with the Cards before being traded seven times in the next 11 years. Willie Mays (*left*) was one of the greatest outfielders ever to play the game: 660 home runs, .302 average, 338 SB, and 11 consecutive Gold Glove awards.

Most Times Walked, Game, AL

Player	Team	Date	BB
Jimmie Foxx	BOS	Jun 16, 1938	6
Andre Thornton	CLE	May 2, 1984	6
Sammy Strang	CHI	Apr 27, 1902	5
Kid Elberfeld	DET	Aug 1, 1902	5
Charlie Hemphill	NY	Aug 3, 1911	5
Tris Speaker	BOS	Oct 1, 1912	5
Roger Peckinpaugh	NY	Jun 2, 1919	5
Whitey Witt	NY	Jul 2, 1924	5
Ira Flagstead	BOS	May 8, 1925	5
Max Bishop	PHI	Apr 29, 1929	5
	PHI	May 21, 1930	5
Earl Averill	CLE	Aug 29, 1932	5
Jo-Jo White	DET	Apr 18, 1935	5
Lou Gehrig	NY	Aug 27, 1935	5
Ben Chapman	NY	May 24, 1936	5

Most Times Walked, Game, AL *(cont'd)*

Player	Team	Date	BB	Inns.
Billy Rogell	DET	Aug 8, 1938	5	
Charlie Keller	NY	Aug 17, 1939	5	10
Herschel Martin	NY	Sep 1, 1944	5	
Russ Derry	NY	Sep 6, 1945	5	
Ted Williams	BOS	May 23, 1951	5	
Larry Doby	CLE	Sep 19, 1951	5	
	CLE	Jul 1, 1952	5	19
Danny Walton	MIL	May 22, 1970	5	
Carl Yastrzemski	BOS	May 25, 1971	5	11
Tony Muser	CHI	Jul 3, 1973	5	
Billy North	OAK	Sep 17, 1973	5	13
Sal Bando	MIL	May 29, 1977	5	11
Jim Norris	CLE	Jul 8, 1977	5	
Roy Smalley	MIN	May 7, 1978	5	
Rickey Henderson	OAK	Apr 8, 1982	5	16

Most Times Walked, Game, NL

Player	Team	Date	BB	Player	Team	Date	BB
Walt Wilmot	CHI	Aug 22, 1891	6	Mel Ott	NY	Apr 30, 1944	5
Fred Carroll	PIT	Jul 4, 1889	5	Max West	PIT	Apr 25, 1948	5
	PIT	Jul 27, 1889	5	Gene Hermanski	BKN	Sep 22, 1949	5
Pop Smith	BOS	Apr 17, 1890	5	Solly Hemus	STL	Sep 15, 1951	5
Jimmy Ryan	CHI	May 28, 1892	5	Andy Seminick	PHI	Sep 30, 1951	5
Piggy Ward	CIN	Jun 18, 1893	5	Richie Ashburn	PHI	Jul 16, 1954	5
Elmer Flick	PHI	Oct 15, 1898	5	Hank Aaron	MIL	Sep 3, 1960	5
Kip Selbach	CIN	Jun 11, 1899	5	Joe Morgan	HOU	Jun 2, 1966	5
Sam Mertes	NY	Aug 12, 1903	5	Dick Allen	PHI	Aug 16, 1968	5
Fred Tenney	BOS	Aug 16, 1907	5	Hank Aaron	ATL	Jul 11, 1972	5
Heinie Groh	NY	May 26, 1922	5	Ellie Hendricks	CHI	Sep 16, 1972	5
Hughie Critz	CIN	May 28, 1926	5	Tim Foli	MON	Sep 7, 1973	5
Mel Ott	NY	Oct 5, 1929	5	Ted Sizemore	STL	Aug 12, 1974	5
Gus Suhr	PIT	Apr 29, 1930	5	Joe Ferguson	HOU	Jun 24, 1978	5
Paul Waner	PIT	Sep 22, 1931	5	Johnny Bench	CIN	Jul 22, 1979	5
Mel Ott	NY	Sep 1, 1933	5	Rodney Scott	MON	Apr 12, 1980	5
	NY	Jun 7, 1943	5	Dale Murphy	ATL	Apr 22, 1983	5

Struck Out Twice in One Inning, AL

Player	Team	Date	Inn.	Player	Team	Date	Inn.
Billy Purtell	CHI	May 10, 1910	6	Babe Ruth	NY	Jul 31, 1934	1
Del Gainor	DET	Aug 15, 1913	9	Gee Walker	DET	Jul 16, 1937	6
Bob Groom	STL	Aug 29, 1916	7	Mickey Mantle	NY	May 24, 1951	6
Joe Judge	WAS	Jul 27, 1920	2	Rudy May	CAL	Jun 12, 1965	6
Elmer Miller	BOS	Sep 7, 1922	7	Boog Powell	BAL	Jul 19, 1966	5
Lefty Gomez	NY	Jul 24, 1932	7	Chuck Manuel	MIN	Jun 30, 1969	9
Frankie Crosetti	NY	Sep 9, 1932	7	Deron Johnson	OAK	Sep 23, 1973	5

Struck Out Twice in One Inning, NL

Player	Team	Date	Inn.	Player	Team	Date	Inn.
Walt Wilmot	CHI	Aug 12, 1891	6	Chris Krug	CHI	Aug 8, 1965	9
Edd Roush	CIN	Jul 22, 1916	6	Curt Flood	STL	Apr 17, 1966	7
Joe Oeschger	PHI	Aug 26, 1917	3	Billy O'Dell	PIT	Jun 9, 1967	5
Lynn Brenton	CIN	Oct 2, 1920	7	Duffy Dyer	NY	May 9, 1969	5
Tony Kaufmann	CHI	Aug 25, 1922	2	Amos Otis	NY	May 14, 1969	8
Van Mungo	BKN	May 16, 1932	4	Jose Arcia	SD	Aug 16, 1970	1
Pep Young	PIT	Jul 3, 1937	7	John Bateman	MON	Aug 29, 1971	2
Jackie Robinson	BKN	Aug 30, 1953	3	Bob Gibson	STL	Aug 2, 1972	4
Duke Snider	BKN	Aug 14, 1954	6	Larry McWilliams	ATL	Apr 22, 1979	4
Ed Roebuck	BKN	Sep 4, 1957	8				

Most Times Struck Out, Game, AL

Player	Team	Date	SO	Inns.
Carl Weilman	STL	Jul 25, 1913	6	15
Rick Reichardt	CAL	May 31, 1966	6	17
Billy Cowan	CAL	Jul 9, 1971	6	20
Cecil Cooper	BOS	Jun 14, 1974	6	15
Donie Bush	DET	May 1, 1910	5	10
Cy Morgan	PHI	Sep 18, 1911	5	12
Lefty Williams	CHI	May 15, 1918	5	18
Scott Perry	PHI	Apr 25, 1919	5	11
Ossie Bluege	WAS	Jun 17, 1923	5	11
Lefty Grove	PHI	Jun 10, 1933	5	
Johnny Broaca	NY	Jun 25, 1934	5	
Chet Laabs	DET	Oct 2, 1938	5	
Larry Doby	CLE	Apr 25, 1948	5	
Jim Landis	CHI	Jul 28, 1957	5	
Bill Skowron	NY	Jun 7, 1964	5	15
Bob Allison	MIN	Sep 2, 1965	5	
George Scott	BOS	Apr 15, 1966	5	12
Sandy Valdespino	MIN	Aug 9, 1967	5	20
Reggie Jackson	OAK	Sep 27, 1968	5	
Ray Jarvis	BOS	Apr 20, 1969	5	
Rick Monday	OAK	Apr 29, 1970	5	
Frank Howard	WAS	Sep 19, 1970	5	
Tony Conigliaro	CAL	Jul 9, 1971	5	20
Don Buford	BAL	Aug 26, 1971	5	
Bobby Darwin	MIN	May 12, 1972	5	22
Roy Smalley	MIN	Aug 28, 1976	5	17
Rick Manning	CLE	May 15, 1977	5	
Gorman Thomas	MIL	Jul 13, 1979	5	17
Kevin Bell	CHI	Apr 26, 1980	5	12
Dave Stegman	CHI	May 4, 1984	5	25

Most Times Struck Out, Game, NL

Player	Team	Date	SO	Inns.
Don Hoak	CHI	May 2, 1956	6	17
Oscar Walker	BUF	Jun 20, 1879	5	
Harry Stovey	BOS	Jun 30, 1891	5	10
Pete Dowling	LOU	Aug 15, 1899	5	
Benny Kauff	NY	May 23, 1918	5	14
Les Bell	STL	May 12, 1927	5	11
Pep Young	PIT	Sep 29, 1935	5	
Steve Bilko	STL	May 28, 1953	5	10
Ron Kline	PIT	Sep 22, 1958	5	14
Bob Sadowski	MIL	Apr 20, 1964	5	
Dick Allen	PHI	Jun 28, 1964	5	
Deron Johnson	CIN	Aug 29, 1964	5	11
	CIN	Sep 30, 1964	5	16
Adolfo Phillips	CHI	Aug 10, 1966	5	10
Ron Swoboda	NY	Jun 22, 1969	5	
Steve Whitaker	SF	Apr 14, 1970	5	
Dick Allen	STL	May 24, 1970	5	10
Larry Hisle	PHI	May 28, 1970	5	11
Bill Russell	LA	Jun 9, 1971	5	
Pepe Mangual	MON	Aug 11, 1975	5	
Frank Taveras	NY	May 1, 1979	5	
Dave Kingman	NY	May 28, 1982	5	

Amos Otis's speed (341 SB) and steady fielding (3 Gold Gloves) helped Kansas City dominate the A.L.'s Western Division in the late 1970s.

Most Hits, Game, AL

Player	Team	Date	H	AB	2B	3B	HR	Inns.
Johnny Burnett	CLE	Jul 10, 1932	9	11	2	0	0	18
Rocky Colavito	DET	Jun 24, 1962	7	10	0	1	0	22
Cesar Gutierrez	DET	Jun 21, 1970	7	7	1	0	0	12
Mike Donlin	BAL	Jun 24, 1901	6	6	2	2	0	
Doc Nance	DET	Jul 13, 1901	6	6	1	0	0	
Ervin Harvey	CLE	Apr 25, 1902	6	6	0	0	0	
Danny Murphy	PHI	Jul 8, 1902	6	6	0	0	1	
Jimmy Williams	BAL	Aug 25, 1902	6	6	1	1	0	
Bobby Veach	DET	Sep 17, 1920	6	6	1	1	1	12
George Sisler	STL	Aug 9, 1921	6	9	0	1	0	19
Frank Brower	CLE	Aug 7, 1923	6	6	1	0	0	
George Burns	CLE	Jun 19, 1924	6	6	3	1	0	
Ty Cobb	DET	May 5, 1925	6	6	1	0	3	
Jimmie Foxx	PHI	May 30, 1930	6	7	2	1	0	
Doc Cramer	PHI	Jun 20, 1932	6	6	0	0	0	
Jimmie Foxx	PHI	Jul 10, 1932	6	9	1	0	3	18
Sammy West	STL	Apr 13, 1933	6	6	1	0	0	11
Myril Hoag	NY	Jun 6, 1934	6	6	0	0	0	
Bob Johnson	PHI	Jun 16, 1934	6	6	1	0	2	11
Doc Cramer	PHI	Jul 13, 1935	6	6	1	0	0	
Bruce Campbell	CLE	Jul 2, 1936	6	6	1	0	0	
Rip Radcliff	CHI	Jul 18, 1936	6	7	2	0	0	
Hank Steinbacher	CHI	Jun 22, 1938	6	6	1	0	0	
George Myatt	WAS	May 1, 1944	6	6	1	0	0	
Stan Spence	WAS	Jun 1, 1944	6	6	0	0	1	
George Kell	DET	Sep 20, 1946	6	7	1	0	0	
Jim Fridley	CLE	Apr 29, 1952	6	6	0	0	0	
Jimmy Piersall	BOS	Jun 10, 1953	6	6	1	0	0	
Joe DeMaestri	KC	Jul 8, 1955	6	6	0	0	0	11
Pete Runnels	BOS	Aug 30, 1960	6	7	1	0	0	15
Floyd Robinson	CHI	Jul 22, 1962	6	6	0	0	0	
Bob Oliver	KC	May 4, 1969	6	6	1	0	1	
Jim Northrup	DET	Aug 28, 1969	6	6	0	0	2	13
John Briggs	MIL	Aug 4, 1973	6	6	2	0	0	
Jorge Orta	CLE	Jun 15, 1980	6	6	1	0	0	
Jerry Remy	BOS	Sep 3, 1981	6	10	0	0	0	20

Most Hits, Game, NL

Player	Team	Date	H	AB	2B	3B	HR	Inns.
Wilbert Robinson	BAL	Jun 10, 1892	7	7	1	0	0	
Rennie Stennett	PIT	Sep 16, 1975	7	7	2	1	0	
Davy Force	PHI	Jun 27, 1876	6	6	1	0	0	
Cal McVey	CHI	Jul 22, 1876	6	7	1	0	0	
	CHI	Jul 25, 1876	6	7	1	0	0	
Ross Barnes	CHI	Jul 27, 1876	6	6	1	1	0	
Paul Hines	PRO	Aug 26, 1879	6	6	0	0	0	10
George Gore	CHI	May 7, 1880	6	6	0	0	0	
Buttercup Dickerson	WOR	Jun 16, 1881	6	6	0	1	0	
Sam Wise	BOS	Jun 20, 1883	6	7	1	1	0	

Most Hits, Game, NL *(cont'd)*

Player	Team	Date	H	AB	2B	3B	HR	Inns.
Dan Brouthers	BUF	Jul 19, 1883	6	6	2	0	0	
Danny Richardson	NY	Jun 11, 1887	6	7	0	0	0	
King Kelly	BOS	Aug 27, 1887	6	7	1	0	1	
Jerry Denny	IND	May 4, 1889	6	6	1	0	1	
Larry Twitchell	CLE	Aug 15, 1889	6	6	1	3	1	
Jack Glasscock	NY	Sep 27, 1890	6	6	0	0	0	
Bobby Lowe	BOS	Jun 11, 1891	6	6	1	0	1	
Henry Larkin	WAS	Jun 7, 1892	6	7	0	1	0	
Jack Boyle	PHI	Jul 6, 1893	6	6	1	0	0	11
Duff Cooley	STL	Sep 30, 1893	6	6	1	0	0	
Ed Delahanty	PHI	Jun 16, 1894	6	6	1	0	0	
Steve Brodie	BAL	Jul 9, 1894	6	6	2	1	0	
Chief Zimmer	CLE	Jul 11, 1894	6	6	2	0	0	10
Sam Thompson	PHI	Aug 17, 1894	6	7	1	1	1	
Roger Connor	STL	Jun 1, 1895	6	6	2	1	0	
George Davis	NY	Aug 15, 1895	6	6	2	1	0	
Jake Stenzel	PIT	May 14, 1896	6	6	0	0	0	
Fred Tenney	BOS	May 31, 1897	6	8	1	0	0	
Dick Harley	STL	Jun 24, 1897	6	6	1	0	0	12
Barry McCormick	CHI	Jun 29, 1897	6	8	0	1	1	
Tommy Tucker	WAS	Jul 15, 1897	6	6	1	0	0	
Willie Keeler	BAL	Sep 3, 1897	6	6	0	1	0	
Jack Doyle	BAL	Sep 3, 1897	6	6	2	0	0	
Chick Stahl	BOS	May 31, 1899	6	6	0	0	0	
Ginger Beaumont	PIT	Jul 22, 1899	6	6	0	0	0	
Kip Selbach	NY	Jun 9, 1901	6	7	2	0	0	
George Cutshaw	BKN	Aug 9, 1915	6	6	0	0	0	
Carson Bigbee	PIT	Aug 22, 1917	6	11	0	0	0	22
Dave Bancroft	NY	Jun 28, 1920	6	6	0	0	0	
Johnny Gooch	PIT	Jul 7, 1922	6	8	1	0	0	18
Max Carey	PIT	Jul 7, 1922	6	6	1	0	0	18
Jack Fournier	BKN	Jun 29, 1923	6	6	2	0	1	
Kiki Cuyler	PIT	Aug 9, 1924	6	6	3	1	0	
Frankie Frisch	NY	Sep 10, 1924	6	7	0	0	1	
Jim Bottomley	STL	Sep 16, 1924	6	6	1	0	2	
Paul Waner	PIT	Aug 26, 1926	6	6	2	1	0	
Lloyd Waner	PIT	Jun 15, 1929	6	8	1	1	0	14
Hank DeBerry	BKN	Jun 23, 1929	6	7	0	0	0	14
Wally Gilbert	BKN	May 30, 1931	6	7	1	0	0	
Jim Bottomley	STL	Aug 5, 1931	6	6	1	0	0	
Tony Cuccinello	CIN	Aug 13, 1931	6	6	2	1	0	
Terry Moore	STL	Sep 5, 1935	6	6	1	0	0	
Ernie Lombardi	CIN	May 9, 1937	6	6	1	0	0	
Frank Demaree	CHI	Jul 5, 1937	6	7	3	0	0	14
Cookie Lavagetto	BKN	Sep 23, 1939	6	6	1	1	0	
Walker Cooper	CIN	Jul 6, 1949	6	7	0	0	3	
Johnny Hopp	PIT	May 14, 1950	6	6	0	0	2	
Connie Ryan	PHI	Apr 16, 1953	6	6	2	0	0	
Dick Groat	PIT	May 13, 1960	6	6	3	0	0	
Jesus Alou	SF	Jul 10, 1964	6	6	0	0	1	
Joe Morgan	HOU	Jul 8, 1965	6	6	0	1	2	12

Most Hits, Game, NL *(cont'd)*

Player	Team	Date	H	AB	2B	3B	HR	Inns.
Felix Millan	ATL	Jul 6, 1970	6	6	1	1	0	
Don Kessinger	CHI	Jul 17, 1971	6	6	1	0	0	10
Willie Davis	LA	May 24, 1973	6	9	0	0	0	19
Bill Madlock	CHI	Jul 26, 1975	6	6	0	1	0	10
Jose Cardenal	CHI	May 2, 1976	6	7	1	0	1	14
Gene Richards	SD	Jul 26, 1977	6	7	1	0	0	15
Joe Lefebvre	SD	Sep 13, 1982	6	8	1	0	1	16

Most Hits, Game, Other Leagues

Player	Team	Date	H	AB	2B	3B	HR
Denny Mack	LOU AA	May 26, 1882	6	6	0	0	0
Hick Carpenter	CIN AA	Sep 12, 1883	6	7	0	0	0
Long John Reilly	CIN AA	Sep 12, 1883	6	7	1	1	1
Oscar Walker	BKN AA	May 31, 1884	6	6	1	1	0
Lon Knight	PHI AA	Jul 30, 1884	6	6	0	1	0
Dave Orr	NY AA	Jun 12, 1885	6	6	2	1	1
Henry Larkin	PHI AA	Jun 16, 1885	6	6	2	1	1
George Pinckney	BKN AA	Jun 25, 1885	6	6	0	0	0
Arlie Latham	STL AA	Apr 24, 1886	6	6	0	1	0
Guy Hecker	LOU AA	Aug 15, 1886	6	7	0	0	3
Denny Lyons	PHI AA	Apr 26, 1887	6	6	2	1	0
Pete Hotaling	CLE AA	Jun 6, 1888	6	7	0	1	0
Jim McTamany	KC AA	Jun 15, 1888	6	6	0	0	1
Darby O'Brien	BKN AA	Aug 8, 1889	6	6	3	0	0
Farmer Weaver	LOU AA	Aug 12, 1890	6	6	1	2	1
Frank Scheibeck	TOL AA	Sep 27, 1890	6	6	1	1	0
Ed Delahanty	CLE P	Jun 2, 1890	6	6	1	1	0
Bill Shindle	PHI P	Aug 26, 1890	6	6	2	1	0

Most Games with Five or More Hits, Career

Player	G
Ty Cobb	14
Ed Delahanty	11
Cap Anson	10
Pete Rose	10
Max Carey	9
Fred Clarke	9
Willie Keeler	9
Roberto Clemente	8
Stan Musial	8
Lefty O'Doul	8

Two Hits in One Inning Twice in One Game

Player	Team	Date	Inn.	Inn.
Max Carey	PIT N	Jun 22, 1925	1	8
Johnny Hodapp	CLE A	Jul 29, 1928	2	6
Sherm Lollar	CHI A	Apr 23, 1955	2	6
Rennie Stennett	PIT N	Sep 16, 1975	1	5

Babe Ruth (*above left*), baseball's most enduring legend, hit 714 homers despite being walked over 2000 times, and compiled a 94–46, 2.28 ERA pitching record. Roberto Clemente (*above*) led the N.L. in batting four times, and won 12 straight Gold Gloves for the Pirates. *Left:* Mickey Rivers's flashy style helped the Yankees to World Series victories in 1977 and '78.

.300 Batting Average in Final Season (Min. 100 G)

Player	Team	Year	G	AB	H	BA
Joe Jackson	CHI A	1920	146	470	218	.382
Dave Orr	BKN P	1890	107	464	173	.373
Happy Felsch	CHI A	1920	142	556	188	.338
Henry Moore	WAS U	1884	111	461	155	.336
Buck Weaver	CHI A	1920	151	630	210	.333
Bill Lange	CHI N	1899	107	416	135	.325
Chicken Hawks	PHI N	1925	105	320	103	.322
Sam Dungan	WAS A	1901	138	559	179	.320
Bill Keister	PHI N	1903	100	400	128	.320
Ted Williams	BOS A	1960	113	310	98	.316
Tex Vache	BOS A	1925	110	252	79	.313
Buzz Arlett	PHI N	1931	121	418	131	.313
Joe Knight	CIN N	1890	127	481	150	.312
Johnny Hodapp	BOS A	1933	115	413	129	.312
Roberto Clemente	PIT N	1972	102	378	118	.312
Sam Wise	WAS N	1893	122	521	162	.311
Irv Waldron	MIL A	1901				
	WAS A	1901	141	598	186	.311
Vin Campbell	NWK F	1915	127	525	163	.310
Jack Tobin	BOS A	1927	111	374	116	.310
George Sisler	BOS N	1930	116	431	133	.309
Steve Evans	BKN F	1915				
	BAL F	1915	151	556	171	.308
Tony Cuccinello	CHI A	1945	118	402	124	.308
Curt Walker	CIN N	1930	134	472	145	.307
Richie Ashburn	NY N	1962	135	389	119	.306
Lou Brock	STL N	1979	120	405	123	.304
Ray Chapman	CLE A	1920	111	435	132	.303
Del Pratt	DET A	1924	121	429	130	.303
Perry Werden	LOU N	1897	131	506	153	.302
Cap Anson	CHI N	1897	114	424	128	.302
Johnny Dickshot	CHI A	1945	130	486	147	.302
Rene Monteagudo	PHI N	1945	114	193	58	.301
Mickey Rivers	TEX A	1984	102	313	94	.300

Most Combined Hits and Walks, Season, AL

Player	Team	Year	H	BB	Total
Babe Ruth	NY	1923	205	170	375
Ted Williams	BOS	1949	194	162	356
Babe Ruth	NY	1921	204	144	348
Ted Williams	BOS	1947	181	162	343
Babe Ruth	NY	1924	200	142	342
Wade Boggs	BOS	1985	240	96	336
Lou Gehrig	NY	1936	205	130	335
Ted Williams	BOS	1946	176	156	332
	BOS	1942	186	145	331
Babe Ruth	NY	1927	192	138	330
Ted Williams	BOS	1941	185	145	330
Jimmie Foxx	PHI	1932	213	116	329

Most Combined Hits and Walks, Season, AL ***(cont'd)***

Player	Team	Year	H	BB	Total
Babe Ruth	NY	1926	184	144	328
Lou Gehrig	NY	1931	211	117	328
	NY	1927	218	109	327
Babe Ruth	NY	1931	199	128	327
Lou Gehrig	NY	1937	200	127	327
Ty Cobb	DET	1915	208	118	326
Babe Ruth	NY	1930	186	136	322
Lou Gehrig	NY	1930	220	101	321
Babe Ruth	NY	1920	172	148	320
Lou Gehrig	NY	1934	210	109	319
Mickey Mantle	NY	1957	173	146	319
Norm Cash	DET	1961	193	124	317
Lou Gehrig	NY	1932	208	108	316
Jimmie Foxx	BOS	1938	197	119	316
Ted Williams	BOS	1948	186	126	314
Carl Yastrzemski	BOS	1970	186	128	314
Charlie Gehringer	DET	1934	214	99	313
Ted Williams	BOS	1951	169	144	313
Wade Boggs	BOS	1986	207	105	312
Tris Speaker	CLE	1920	214	97	311
	CLE	1923	218	93	311
Buddy Myer	WAS	1935	215	96	311
Charlie Gehringer	DET	1936	227	83	310
Eddie Yost	WAS	1950	169	141	310
Babe Ruth	NY	1928	173	135	308
Lou Gehrig	NY	1935	176	132	308
Rod Carew	MIN	1977	239	69	308
Lu Blue	CHI	1931	179	127	306
Lou Gehrig	NY	1928	210	95	305
Tris Speaker	BOS	1912	222	82	304
George Sisler	STL	1920	257	46	303
Jimmie Foxx	BOS	1936	198	105	303
Charlie Jamieson	CLE	1923	222	80	302
Hank Greenberg	DET	1937	200	102	302
Wade Boggs	BOS	1983	210	92	302
Jimmie Foxx	PHI	1933	204	96	300
Mickey Mantle	NY	1956	188	112	300

Most Combined Hits and Walks, Season, NL

Player	Team	Year	H	BB	Total
Billy Hamilton	PHI	1894	223	126	346
Lefty O'Doul	PHI	1929	254	76	330
Rogers Hornsby	STL	1924	227	89	316
	CHI	1929	229	87	316
	STL	1922	250	65	315
Woody English	CHI	1930	214	100	314
Stan Musial	STL	1949	207	107	314
Hack Wilson	CHI	1930	208	105	313
Richie Ashburn	PHI	1958	215	97	312

Most Combined Hits and Walks, Season, NL ***(cont'd)***

Player	Team	Year	H	BB	Total
Bill Terry	NY	1930	254	57	311
Jesse Burkett	CLE	1895	235	74	309
Stan Musial	STL	1948	230	79	309
Arky Vaughan	PIT	1936	190	118	308
Babe Herman	BKN	1930	241	66	307
Joe Kelley	BAL	1894	199	107	306
Pete Rose	CIN	1969	218	88	306
Stan Musial	STL	1953	200	105	305
Chuck Klein	PHI	1930	250	54	304
Stan Musial	STL	1951	205	98	303
Pete Rose	PHI	1979	208	95	303
Hugh Duffy	BOS	1894	236	66	302
Eddie Stanky	NY	1950	158	144	302
Billy Hamilton	BOS	1896	191	110	301
Stan Musial	STL	1946	228	73	301
Ralph Kiner	PIT	1951	164	137	301
Pete Rose	CIN	1976	215	86	301
Paul Waner	PIT	1928	223	77	300
Kiki Cuyler	CHI	1930	228	72	300
Richie Ashburn	PHI	1954	175	125	300

Easiest to Double Up, Career (Min. 1000 G)

Player	LH/RH	AB	DP	Ratio
Ernie Lombardi	RH	5260	261	20.1
Walt Dropo	RH	4124	166	24.8
Jim Rice	RH	7127	271	26.3
George Scott	RH	7433	287	26.8
Jerry Adair	RH	4019	149	27.0
Sammy White	RH	3502	129	27.1
Rico Carty	RH	5606	206	27.2
Hal Lanier	RH	3703	135	27.4
Joe Torre	RH	7874	284	27.7
Danny Cater	RH	4451	160	27.8
Ray Knight	RH	3967	141	28.1
Lou Piniella	RH	5867	209	28.1
Earl Battey	RH	3586	127	28.2
Jackie Jensen	RH	5236	185	28.3
Bill Jurges	RH	5564	195	28.5
Sid Gordon	RH	4992	174	28.7
Bill Skowron	RH	5547	192	28.9
Ken Singleton	LH/RH	7189	248	29.0
Sherm Lollar	RH	5351	184	29.1
Walker Cooper	RH	4702	160	29.4
Roy Campanella	RH	4205	143	29.4
Joe Adcock	RH	6606	223	29.6
Frank Howard	RH	6488	219	29.6
Bill Tuttle	RH	4268	143	29.8
Rich Dauer	RH	3829	128	29.9
Mickey Owen	RH	3649	122	29.9

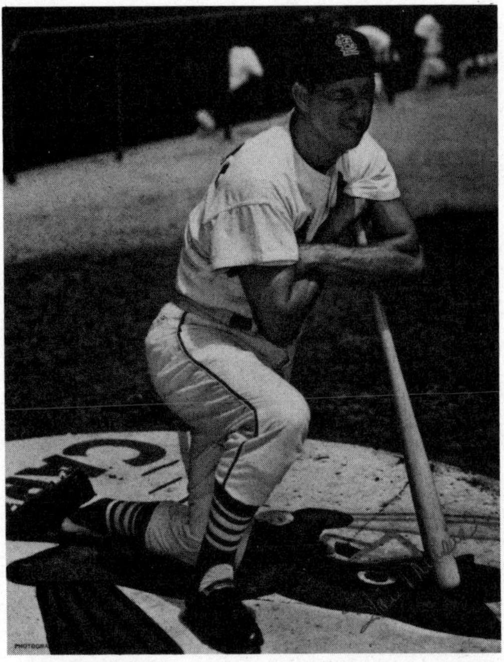

In 22 years with St. Louis, Stan "The Man" Musial won three MVP awards, led the league in batting seven times, and played in a record 24 All-Star Games.

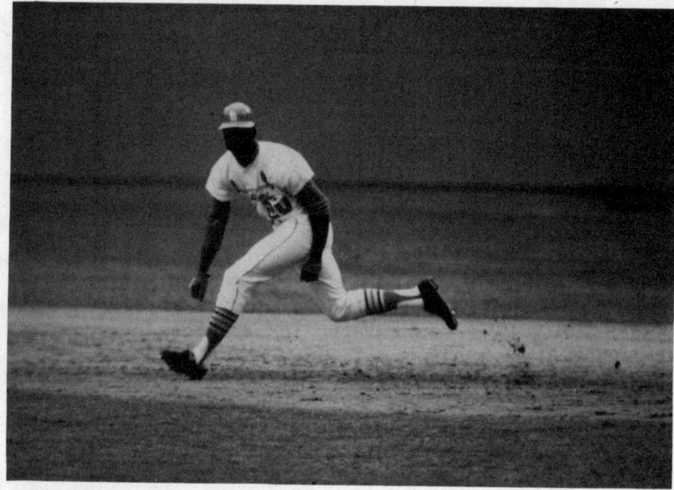

Left: Speedster Willie Wilson's 705 at bats in 1980 are a major-league record. *Above*: Lou Brock terrorized enemy basepaths for 19 years, amassing 938 SB and 141 triples.

Hardest to Double Up, Career (Min. 1,000 G)

Player	AB	DP	Ratio
Don Buford	4553	33	138.0
Mickey Rivers	5621	44	127.9
Don Blasingame	5296	43	123.2
Willie Wilson	4908	40	122.7
Omar Moreno	4992	45	110.9
Joe Moore	5053	48	105.3
Richie Ashburn	8365	83	100.8
Cesar Tovar	5569	58	96.0
George Case	4494	48	93.6
Vic Davalillo	4017	43	93.4
Stan Hack	7100	78	91.0
Bill Nicholson	5534	61	90.7
Lou Brock	10332	114	90.6
Bud Harrelson	4744	53	89.5
Wally Moses	5188	58	89.4
Craig Reynolds	3742	42	89.1

Player	AB	DP	Ratio
Joe Morgan	9277	105	88.4
Arky Vaughan	6125	70	87.5
Whitey Lockman	5940	68	87.4
Rick Monday	6136	71	86.4
Terry Puhl	4086	48	85.1
Alfredo Griffin	4408	52	84.8
Del Unser	5215	62	84.1
Bill Bruton	6066	73	83.1
Dave Collins	4484	54	83.0
Maury Wills	7588	92	82.5
Augie Galan	5937	72	82.5
Sandy Alomar	4760	58	82.1
Bert Campaneris	8684	106	81.9
Mel Ott	6669	82	81.3
Don Gutteridge	4202	52	80.8
Dick McAuliffe	6185	77	80.3

Grounded into Most Double Plays, Game, AL

Player	Team	Date	DP	Opp.
Goose Goslin	DET	Apr 28, 1934	4	CLE
Mike Kreevich	CHI	Aug 4, 1939	4	WAS
Riggs Stephenson	CLE	Sep 30, 1924	3	CHI
Sammy Hale	PHI	May 12, 1927	3	DET
Zeke Bonura	CHI	May 11, 1934	3	WAS
Earl Averill	CLE	Jul 8, 1939	3	STL
Eddie Robinson	NY	May 30, 1955	3	NY
Jerry Terrell	MIN	Apr 11, 1977	3	SEA
Jose Morales	MIN	May 17, 1980	3	MIL
Jim Presley	SEA	Apr 27, 1985	3	CAL
Rich Gedman	BOS	Apr 23, 1986	3	DET

Grounded into Most Double Plays, Game, NL

Player	Team	Date	DP	Opp.
Joe Torre	NY	Jul 21, 1975	4	CIN
Hal Irelan	PHI	Sep 5, 1914	3	BOS
Walt Cruise	BOS	Sep 18, 1921	3	CIN
Burleigh Grimes	BKN	Sep 22, 1925	3	CIN
Adam Comorosky	CIN	Jul 22, 1934	3	NY
Babe Herman	CIN	Jun 26, 1936	3	PHI
Bill Brubaker	PIT	Sep 19, 1936	3	CIN
Johnny Hudson	BKN	Aug 25, 1938	3	CHI
Zeke Bonura	NY	Jul 8, 1939	3	BKN
Roy Hughes	PHI	Sep 5, 1939	3	NY
Billy Herman	CHI	Aug 17, 1940	3	PIT
Ralph Kiner	PIT	Sep 4, 1946	3	CIN
Monte Irvin	NY	Jul 30, 1953	3	MIL
Randy Jackson	CHI	Aug 15, 1953	3	MIL
Joe Adcock	MIL	Jul 20, 1955	3	PIT
Richie Ashburn	PHI	Jun 28, 1959	3	SF
Jesus Alou	SF	Jul 17, 1966	3	PIT
Tommie Agee	NY	May 29, 1970	3	HOU
Roberto Clemente	PIT	May 23, 1972	3	STL

Batting Champion with Two Different Clubs

Player	Team	Year	BA
Ed Delahanty	PHI N	1899	.408
	WAS A	1902	.376
Nap Lajoie	PHI A	1901	.422
	CLE A	1903	.355
	CLE A	1904	.381
Rogers Hornsby	STL N	1920	.370
	STL N	1921	.397
	STL N	1922	.401
	STL N	1923	.384
	STL N	1924	.424

Player	Team	Year	BA
Rogers Hornsby	STL N	1925	.403
	BOS N	1928	.387
Lefty O'Doul	PHI N	1929	.398
	BKN N	1932	.368
Ernie Lombardi	CIN N	1938	.342
	BOS N	1942	.330
Bill Madlock	CHI N	1975	.354
	CHI N	1976	.339
	PIT N	1981	.341
	PIT N	1983	.323

Hardest to Strike Out, Career (Min. 1,000 G)

Player	Yrs.	AB	SO	Ratio	Player	Yrs.	AB	SO	Ratio
Joe Sewell	14	7132	114	62.6	Stuffy McInnis	15	6667	189	35.3
Lloyd Waner	18	7772	173	44.9	Andy High	13	4400	130	33.8
Nellie Fox	19	9232	216	42.7	Sam Rice	20	9269	215	33.7
Tommy Holmes	11	4992	122	40.9	Frankie Frisch	19	9112	272	33.5
Tris Speaker	16	7899	220	35.9	Johnny Cooney	20	3372	107	31.5

Easiest to Strike Out, Career (Min. 1,000 G)

Player	Yrs.	AB	SO	Ratio	Player	Yrs.	AB	SO	Ratio
Gorman Thomas	13	4677	1339	3.49	Larry Hisle	14	4205	941	4.47
Dave Kingman	16	6677	1816	3.68	Deron Johnson	16	5940	1318	4.51
Reggie Jackson	20	9528	2500	3.81	Dale Murphy	11	5017	1094	4.59
Bobby Bonds	14	7043	1757	4.01	Vince DiMaggio	10	3849	837	4.60
Dick Allen	15	6332	1556	4.06	Jimmy Wynn	15	6653	1427	4.66
Rick Monday	19	6136	1513	4.06	Dwayne Murphy	9	3828	822	4.66
Donn Clendenon	12	4648	1140	4.08	Mickey Mantle	18	8102	1710	4.74
Willie Stargell	21	7927	1936	4.09	Jim Hickman	13	3974	832	4.78
Mike Schmidt	15	7292	1744	4.18	Harmon Killebrew	22	8147	1699	4.80
Dick Stuart	10	3997	957	4.18	Lee May	18	7609	1570	4.85
Tommie Agee	12	3912	918	4.26	Bob Allison	13	5032	1033	4.87
Woodie Held	14	4019	944	4.26	Jeff Burroughs	16	5536	1135	4.88
Tony Armas	11	4513	1055	4.28	Doug Rader	11	5186	1057	4.90
Bobby Knoop	9	3622	833	4.35	Steve Yeager	14	3454	703	4.91
Greg Luzinski	15	6505	1495	4.35	Wally Post	15	4007	813	4.93
Gene Tenace	15	4390	998	4.40	Steve Yeager	15	3584	726	4.94
Frank Howard	16	6488	1460	4.44	George Foster	18	7023	1419	4.95

Far left: Joe Sewell never struck out more than 20 times in a season, en route to a lifetime .312 mark. *Left*: Gorman Thomas's powerful swing has brought him an average of 31 homers and 136 strikeouts over his last eight full seasons.

Triple Crown Winners, AL

Player	Team	Year	HR	RBI	BA
Nap Lajoie	PHI	1901	14	125	.422
Ty Cobb	DET	1909	9	115	.377
Jimmie Foxx	PHI	1933	48	163	.356
Lou Gehrig	NY	1934	49	165	.363
Ted Williams	BOS	1942	36	137	.356
	BOS	1947	32	114	.343
Mickey Mantle	NY	1956	52	130	.353
Frank Robinson	BAL	1966	49	122	.316
Carl Yastrzemski	BOS	1967	44	121	.326

Triple Crown Winners, NL

Player	Team	Year	HR	RBI	BA
Paul Hines	PRO	1878	4	50	.358
Hugh Duffy	BOS	1894	18	145	.438
Heinie Zimmerman	CHI	1912	14	103	.372
Rogers Hornsby	STL	1922	42	152	.401
	STL	1925	39	143	.403
Chuck Klein	PHI	1933	28	120	.368
Joe Medwick	STL	1937	31	154	.374

Players Who Just Missed Triple Crowns, AL

Player	Team	Year	HR	RBI	BA	2nd
Ty Cobb	DET	1907	5	119	.350	HR
	DET	1911	8	127	.420	HR
Babe Ruth	NY	1923	41	130	.393	BA
	NY	1924	46	121	.378	RBI
	NY	1926	47	145	.372	BA
Jimmie Foxx	PHI	1932	58	169	.364	BA
	BOS	1938	50	175	.349	HR
Ted Williams	BOS	1949	43	159	.343	BA
Al Rosen	CLE	1953	43	145	.336	BA

Players Who Just Missed Triple Crowns, NL

Player	Team	Year	HR	RBI	BA	2nd
Honus Wagner	PIT	1908	10	109	.354	HR
Gavvy Cravath	PHI	1913	19	128	.341	BA
Rogers Hornsby	STL	1921	21	126	.397	HR
Stan Musial	STL	1948	39	131	.376	HR

Two Legs of Triple Crown, AL

Player	Team	Year	HR	RBI	BA
Buck Freeman	BOS	1903	13	104	
Nap Lajoie	CLE	1904		102	.381
Harry Davis	PHI	1905	8	83	
	PHI	1906	12	96	
Ty Cobb	DET	1907		119	.350
	DET	1908		108	.324
	DET	1911		127	.420
Frank Baker	PHI	1912	10	130	
	PHI	1913	12	117	
Sam Crawford	DET	1914	8	104	
Babe Ruth	BOS	1919	29	112	
	NY	1920	54	137	
	NY	1921	59	171	
Ken Williams	STL	1922	39	155	
Babe Ruth	NY	1923	41	131	
	NY	1924	46		.378
Bob Meusel	NY	1925	33	138	
Babe Ruth	NY	1926	47	145	
	NY	1928	54	142	
Lou Gehrig	NY	1931	46	184	
Jimmie Foxx	PHI	1932	58	169	
Hank Greenberg	DET	1935	36	170	
Jimmie Foxx	BOS	1938		175	.349
Hank Greenberg	DET	1940	41	150	
Ted Williams	BOS	1941	37		.406
Rudy York	DET	1943	34	118	
Hank Greenberg	DET	1946	44	127	
Joe DiMaggio	NY	1948	39	155	
Ted Williams	BOS	1949	43	159	
Gus Zernial	CHI	1951			
	PHI	1951	33	129	
Al Rosen	CLE	1953	43	145	
Larry Doby	CLE	1954	32	126	
Roy Sievers	WAS	1957	42	114	
Roger Maris	NY	1961	61	142	
Harmon Killebrew	MIN	1962	48	126	
	MIN	1969	49	140	
Frank Howard	WAS	1970	44	126	
Dick Allen	CHI	1972	37	113	
Reggie Jackson	OAK	1973	32	117	
George Scott	MIL	1975	36	109	
Jim Rice	BOS	1978	46	139	
Eddie Murray	BAL	1981	22	78	
Jim Rice	BOS	1983	39	126	
Tony Armas	BOS	1984	43	123	

Right: Jim Rice's right-handed power (351 HR in 13 years) and fielding reflexes are perfectly suited to Fenway Park. Honus Wagner (*far right*) led the N.L. in batting eight times, in slugging six times, and in stolen bases five times.

Two Legs of Triple Crown, NL

Player	Team	Year	HR	RBI	BA
Deacon White	BOS	1877		49	.387
Cap Anson	CHI	1881		82	.399
Sam Thompson	DET	1887		166	.372
Cap Anson	CHI	1888		84	.344
Dan Brouthers	BKN	1892		124	.335
Ed Delahanty	PHI	1893	19	146	
Sam Thompson	PHI	1895	18	165	
Ed Delahanty	PHI	1899		137	.408
Cy Seymour	CIN	1905		121	.377
Honus Wagner	PIT	1908		109	.354
	PIT	1909		100	.339
Sherry Magee	PHI	1910		123	.331
Wildfire Schulte	CHI	1911	21	107	
Gavvy Cravath	PHI	1913	19	128	
	PHI	1915	24	115	
Rogers Hornsby	STL	1920		94	.370
	STL	1921		126	.397
Paul Waner	PIT	1927		131	.380
Jim Bottomley	STL	1928	31	136	
Hack Wilson	CHI	1930	56	190	
Chuck Klein	PHI	1931	31	121	
Mel Ott	NY	1934	35	135	
Wally Berger	BOS	1935	34	130	
Johnny Mize	STL	1939	28		.349
	STL	1940	43	137	
Dolf Camilli	BKN	1941	34	120	

Two Legs of Triple Crown, NL *(cont'd)*

Player	Team	Year	HR	RBI	BA
Bill Nicholson	CHI	1943	29	128	
	CHI	1944	33	122	
Johnny Mize	NY	1947	51	138	
Stan Musial	STL	1948		131	.376
Ralph Kiner	PIT	1949	54	127	
Hank Sauer	CHI	1952	37	121	
Ted Kluszewski	CIN	1954	49	141	
Hank Aaron	MIL	1957	44	132	
Ernie Banks	CHI	1958	47	129	
Orlando Cepeda	SF	1961	46	142	
Tommy Davis	LA	1962		153	.346
Hank Aaron	MIL	1963	44	130	
	ATL	1966	44	127	
Willie McCovey	SF	1968	36	105	
	SF	1969	45	126	
Johnny Bench	CIN	1970	45	148	
Joe Torre	STL	1971		137	.363
Johnny Bench	CIN	1972	40	125	
Willie Stargell	PIT	1973	44	119	
George Foster	CIN	1977	52	149	
	CIN	1978	40	120	
Mike Schmidt	PHI	1980	48	121	
	PHI	1981	31	91	
Al Oliver	MON	1982		109	.331
Mike Schmidt	PHI	1983	36	106	
	PHI	1986	37	119	

In 1986 Philadelphia's Mike Schmidt (*far left*) led the N.L. in homers for the eighth time, while winning his record-tying third MVP award. From 1876-97 Adrian "Cap" Anson (*left*) racked up 3041 hits and a .334 average for Chicago.

Cycle Hitters, AL

Player	Team	Date
Earl Averill	CLE	Aug 17, 1933
Frank Baker	PHI	Jul 3, 1911
Lyman Bostock	MIN	Jul 24, 1976
Bill Bradley	CLE	Sep 24, 1903
George Brett	KC	May 28, 1979
Jack Brohamer	CHI	Sep 24, 1977
Rod Carew	MIN	May 20, 1970
Roy Carlyle	BOS	Jul 21, 1925
Sam Chapman	PHI	May 5, 1939
Lu Clinton	BOS	Jul 13, 1962
Otis Clymer	WAS	Oct 2, 1908
Mickey Cochrane	PHI	Jul 22, 1932
	PHI	Aug 2, 1933
Doc Cramer	PHI	Jun 10, 1934
Joe Cronin	WAS	Sep 2, 1929
	BOS	Aug 2, 1940
Mike Cubbage	MIN	Jul 27, 1978
Leon Culberson	BOS	Jul 3, 1943
Bert Daniels	NY	Jul 25, 1910
Harry Davis	PHI	Jul 10, 1901
Joe DiMaggio	NY	Jul 9, 1937
	NY	May 20, 1948
Larry Doby	CLE	May 4, 1952
Bobby Doerr	BOS	May 17, 1944
	BOS	May 13, 1947
Patsy Dougherty	BOS	Jul 29, 1903
Dwight Evans	BOS	Jun 28, 1984
Hoot Evers	DET	Sep 7, 1950
Carlton Fisk	CHI	May 16, 1984
Dan Ford	CAL	Aug 10, 1979
Bob Fothergill	DET	Sep 26, 1926
Jimmie Foxx	PHI	Aug 14, 1933
Buck Freeman	BOS	Jun 21, 1903
Jim Fregosi	LA	Jul 28, 1964
	CAL	May 20, 1968
Rich Gedman	BOS	Sep 18, 1985
Lou Gehrig	NY	Jun 25, 1934
	NY	Aug 1, 1937
Charlie Gehringer	DET	May 27, 1939
Joe Gordon	NY	Sep 8, 1940
Goose Goslin	WAS	Aug 28, 1924
Odell Hale	CLE	Jul 12, 1938
Mike Hegan	MIL	Sep 3, 1976
Pinky Higgins	PHI	Aug 6, 1933

Player	Team	Date
Larry Hisle	MIN	Jun 4, 1976
Tony Horton	CLE	Jul 2, 1970
Baby Doll Jacobson	STL	Apr 17, 1924
Bob Johnson	BOS	Jul 6, 1944
George Kell	DET	Jun 2, 1950
Jim King	WAS	May 26, 1964
Nap Lajoie	PHI	Jul 30, 1901
Tony Lazzeri	NY	Jun 3, 1932
Fred Lynn	BOS	May 13, 1980
Mickey Mantle	NY	Jul 23, 1957
John Mayberry	KC	Aug 5, 1977
Oddibe McDowell	TEX	Jul 23, 1985
George McQuinn	STL	Jul 19, 1941
Oscar Melillo	STL	May 23, 1929
Bob Meusel	NY	May 7, 1921
	NY	Jul 3, 1922
	NY	Jul 26, 1928
Charlie Moore	MIL	Oct 1, 1980
Bobby Murcer	NY	Aug 29, 1972
Danny Murphy	PHI	Aug 25, 1910
Freddie Patek	KC	Jul 9, 1971
Tony Phillips	OAK	May 16, 1986
Kirby Puckett	MIN	Aug 1, 1986
Cal Ripken	BAL	May 6, 1984
Brooks Robinson	BAL	Jul 15, 1960
Buddy Rosar	NY	Jul 19, 1940
Ray Schalk	CHI	Jun 27, 1922
George Sisler	STL	Aug 8, 1920
	STL	Aug 13, 1921
Moose Solters	BOS	Aug 19, 1934
Tris Speaker	BOS	Jun 9, 1912
Andre Thornton	CLE	Apr 22, 1978
Cesar Tovar	MIN	Sep 19, 1972
Elmer Valo	PHI	Aug 2, 1950
Bobby Veach	DET	Sep 17, 1920
Mickey Vernon	WAS	May 19, 1946
Gee Walker	DET	Apr 20, 1937
Gary Ward	MIN	Sep 18, 1980
Bob Watson	BOS	Sep 15, 1979
Vic Wertz	DET	Sep 14, 1947
Frank White	KC	Sep 26, 1979
	KC	Aug 3, 1982
Ted Williams	BOS	Jul 21, 1946
Carl Yastrzemski	BOS	May 14, 1965

Above: Jackie Robinson's speed and versatility helped him to a .311 average, and Brooklyn to six World Series. Napoleon Lajoie (*right*) batted above .350 10 times, including a .422 performance in 1901.

Cycle Hitters, NL

Player	Team	Date
Tommie Agee	NY	Jul 6, 1970
Dave Bancroft	NY	Jun 1, 1921
Johnny Bates	BOS	Apr 26, 1907
Gus Bell	PIT	Jun 4, 1951
Jim Bottomley	STL	Jul 15, 1927
Ken Boyer	STL	Sep 14, 1961
	STL	Jun 16, 1964
Lou Brock	STL	May 27, 1975
George Burns	NY	Sep 17, 1920
Oyster Burns	BKN	Aug 1, 1890
Johnny Callison	PHI	Jun 27, 1963
Max Carey	PIT	Jun 20, 1925
Fred Carroll	PIT	May 2, 1887
Ed Cartwright	WAS	Sep 30, 1895
Cesar Cedeno	HOU	Aug 2, 1972
Cesar Cedeno	HOU	Aug 9, 1976
Fred Clarke	PIT	Jul 23, 1901
	PIT	May 7, 1903
Bill Collins	BOS	Oct 6, 1910
Duff Cooley	BOS	Jun 20, 1904
Harry Craft	CIN	Jun 8, 1940
Lave Cross	PHI	Apr 24, 1894
Kiki Cuyler	PIT	Jun 4, 1925
Harry Danning	NY	Jun 15, 1940
Ivan DeJesus	CHI	Apr 22, 1980
Tommy Dowd	STL	Aug 16, 1895
Fred Dunlap	STL	May 24, 1886
Mike Easler	PIT	Jun 12, 1980
Bob Elliott	PIT	Jul 15, 1945
Curry Foley	BUF	May 25, 1882

Cycle Hitters, NL *(cont'd)*

Player	Team	Date
Tim Foli	MON	Apr 22, 1976
Jack Glasscock	IND	Aug 8, 1889
Heinie Groh	CIN	Jul 5, 1915
Chick Hafey	STL	Aug 21, 1930
Jim Ray Hart	SF	Jul 8, 1970
Bill Hassamaer	WAS	Jun 13, 1894
Cliff Heathcote	STL	Jun 13, 1918
Babe Herman	BKN	May 18, 1931
	BKN	Jul 24, 1931
	CHI	Sep 30, 1933
Keith Hernandez	NY	Jul 4, 1985
Jim Hickman	NY	Aug 7, 1963
Gil Hodges	BKN	Jun 25, 1949
Randy Hundley	CHI	Aug 11, 1966
Jimmy Johnston	BKN	May 25, 1922
Bill Joyce	WAS	May 30, 1896
Ralph Kiner	PIT	Jun 25, 1950
Dave Kingman	SF	Apr 16, 1972
Chuck Klein	PHI	Jul 1, 1931
	PHI	May 26, 1933
Jeffrey Leonard	SF	Jun 27, 1985
Sam Leslie	NY	May 24, 1936
Freddie Lindstrom	NY	May 8, 1930
Herman Long	BOS	May 9, 1896
Pepper Martin	STL	May 5, 1933
Willie McGee	STL	Jun 23, 1984
Mox McQuery	DET	Sep 28, 1885
Joe Medwick	STL	Jun 29, 1935
Sam Mertes	NY	Oct 4, 1904
Chief Meyers	NY	Jun 10, 1912
Mike Mitchell	CIN	Aug 11, 1911
Johnny Mize	STL	Jul 13, 1940
Don Mueller	NY	Jul 11, 1954
Stan Musial	STL	Jul 24, 1949
Jim O'Rourke	BUF	Jun 16, 1884
Mel Ott	NY	May 16, 1929

Player	Team	Date
Wes Parker	LA	May 7, 1970
Tom Parrott	CIN	Sep 28, 1894
Mike Phillips	NY	Jun 25, 1976
Long John Reilly	CIN	Aug 6, 1890
Dave Robertson	PIT	Aug 30, 1921
Frank Robinson	CIN	May 2, 1959
Jackie Robinson	BKN	Aug 29, 1948
Jack Rowe	DET	Aug 21, 1886
Jimmy Ryan	CHI	Jul 28, 1888
	CHI	Jul 1, 1891
Bill Salkeld	PIT	Aug 4, 1945
Roy Smalley	CHI	Jun 28, 1950
Chris Speier	MON	Jul 20, 1978
Willie Stargell	PIT	Jul 22, 1964
Bill Terry	NY	May 29, 1928
Sam Thompson	PHI	Aug 17, 1894
Mike Tiernan	NY	Aug 25, 1888
Joe Torre	STL	Jun 27, 1973
Pie Traynor	PIT	Jul 7, 1923
Larry Twitchell	CLE	Aug 15, 1889
Arky Vaughan	PIT	Jun 24, 1933
	PIT	Jul 19, 1939
Honus Wagner	PIT	Aug 22, 1912
Dixie Walker	BKN	Sep 2, 1944
Lee Walls	CHI	Jul 2, 1957
Bob Watson	HOU	Jun 24, 1977
Wally Westlake	PIT	Jul 30, 1948
	PIT	Jun 14, 1949
Bill White	STL	Aug 14, 1960
Billy Williams	CHI	Jul 17, 1966
Cy Williams	PHI	Aug 5, 1927
Hack Wilson	CHI	Jun 23, 1930
Owen Wilson	PIT	Jul 3, 1910
George Wood	DET	Jun 13, 1885
Ross Youngs	NY	Apr 29, 1922
Richie Zisk	PIT	Jun 9, 1974

Cycle Hitters, Other Leagues

Player	Team	Date
Sam Barkley	KC AA	Jun 13, 1888
Pete Browning	LOU AA	Aug 8, 1886
	LOU AA	Jun 7, 1889
Roger Connor	NY P	Jul 21, 1890
Abner Dalrymple	C-M AA	Sep 12, 1891
Jumbo Davis	B-B AA	Jul 18, 1890
Lon Knight	PHI AA	Jul 30, 1883
Henry Larkin	PHI AA	Jun 16, 1885
Ed Lennox	PIT F	May 6, 1914
Chippy McGarr	PHI AA	Sep 23, 1886

Player	Team	Date
Bid McPhee	CIN AA	Aug 26, 1887
Tip O'Neill	STL AA	Apr 30, 1887
	STL AA	May 7, 1887
Dave Orr	NY AA	Jun 12, 1885
	NY AA	Aug 10, 1887
Long John Reilly	CIN AA	Sep 12, 1883
	CIN AA	Sep 19, 1883
Harry Stovey	PHI AA	May 15, 1888
Bill Van Dyke	TOL AA	Jul 5, 1890
Farmer Weaver	LOU AA	Aug 12, 1890

The Worst Hitters (Min. 2,500 AB)

Player	G	AB	H	BA	Player	G	AB	H	BA
Bill Bergen	947	3028	516	.170	Jim Hegan	1666	4772	1087	.228
Billy Sullivan	1146	3657	777	.212	Hal Lanier	1196	3703	843	.228
Dave Duncan	929	2885	617	.214	Steve Yeager	1269	3584	816	.228
Bobby Wine	1164	3172	682	.215	Rabbit Warstler	1206	4088	935	.229
Dal Maxvill	1423	3443	748	.217	John Bateman	1017	3330	765	.230
George McBride	1658	5526	1203	.218	Mickey Doolan	1727	5976	1376	.230
Malachi Kittredge	1215	4030	882	.219	Roger Metzger	1219	4201	972	.231
Lee Tannehill	1089	3778	833	.220	Bob Swift	1001	2750	635	.231
Lou Criger	1012	3202	709	.221	Eddie Ainsmith	1068	3048	707	.232
Johnnie LeMaster	1019	3167	707	.223	Larry Brown	1129	3449	803	.233
Ed Brinkman	1818	5970	1337	.224	Clay Dalrymple	1079	3042	710	.233
George Strickland	971	2824	633	.224	Wayne Gross	1103	3123	727	.233
Buck Martinez	1049	2743	618	.225	Monte Cross	1681	5817	1364	.234
Gorman Thomas	1435	4677	1051	.225	Ron Hansen	1384	4311	1007	.234
Charley O'Leary	954	3230	731	.226	Oscar Stanage	1094	3503	819	.234
Dick Schofield	1321	3083	699	.227	Andy Etchebarren	948	2618	615	.235
Mark Belanger	2016	5784	1316	.228	Don Zimmer	1095	3283	773	.235

The .400 Hitters, AL

Player	Team	Year	G	AB	H	2B	3B	HR	R	RBI	BA
Nap Lajoie	PHI	1901	131	543	229	48	14	14	146	125	.422
Ty Cobb	DET	1911	146	591	248	47	24	8	147	144	.420
George Sisler	STL	1922	142	586	246	52	18	8	134	105	.420
Ty Cobb	DET	1912	140	553	227	30	23	7	119	90	.410
Joe Jackson	CLE	1911	147	571	233	43	19	7	126	83	.408
George Sisler	STL	1920	154	631	257	49	18	19	136	122	.407
Ted Williams	BOS	1941	143	456	185	33	3	37	135	120	.406
Harry Heilmann	DET	1923	144	524	211	44	11	18	121	115	.403
Ty Cobb	DET	1922	137	526	211	42	16	4	99	99	.401

The .400 Hitters, NL

Player	Team	Year	G	AB	H	2B	3B	HR	R	RBI	BA
Hugh Duffy	BOS	1894	124	539	236	50	13	18	160	145	.438
Willie Keeler	BAL	1897	128	562	243	27	19	1	147	74	.432
Rogers Hornsby	STL	1924	143	536	227	43	14	25	121	94	.424
Jesse Burkett	CLE	1895	132	555	235	21	15	5	149	83	.423
	CLE	1896	133	585	240	26	16	6	159	72	.410
Ed Delahanty	PHI	1899	145	573	234	56	9	9	123	137	.408
Fred Clarke	LOU	1897	129	525	213	28	15	6	122	67	.406
Sam Thompson	PHI	1894	102	458	185	29	27	13	115	141	.404
Rogers Hornsby	STL	1925	138	504	203	41	10	39	123	143	.403
Jesse Burkett	STL	1899	138	567	228	17	10	7	115	71	.402
Rogers Hornsby	STL	1922	154	623	250	46	14	42	141	152	.401
Bill Terry	NY	1930	154	633	254	39	15	23	139	129	.401
Ed Delahanty	PHI	1894	114	497	199	36	16	4	149	131	.400

Ty Cobb ranks in the top five in career hits, doubles, triples, runs, RBIs, and stolen bases. His .367 career batting average is one of baseball's unmatchable accomplishments.

The .400 Hitters, Other Leagues

Player	Team	Year	G	AB	H	2B	3B	HR	R	BA
Tip O'Neill	STL AA	1887	124	517	225	52	19	14	167	.435
Fred Dunlap	STL U	1884	101	449	185	39	8	13	160	.412
Pete Browning	LOU AA	1887	134	547	220	36	18	4	137	.402
Harry Stovey	PHI AA	1884	104	448	179	25	25	11	126	.400

Highest Batting Average, Career

Player	BA
Ty Cobb	.367
Rogers Hornsby	.358
Joe Jackson	.356
Ed Delahanty	.345
Willie Keeler	.345
Billy Hamilton	.344
Tris Speaker	.344
Ted Williams	.344
Dan Brouthers	.343
Pete Browning	.343
Harry Heilmann	.342

Player	BA
Babe Ruth	.342
Jesse Burkett	.341
Bill Terry	.341
George Sisler	.340
Lou Gehrig	.340
Nap Lajoie	.339
Riggs Stephenson	.336
Cap Anson	.334
Al Simmons	.334
Eddie Collins	.333
Paul Waner	.333

The 3,000-Hit Club

Player	Yrs.	G	AB	H	BA
Pete Rose	23	3490	13816	4204	.304
Ty Cobb	24	3033	11429	4191	.367
Hank Aaron	23	3298	12364	3771	.305
Stan Musial	22	3026	10972	3630	.331
Tris Speaker	22	2790	10196	3515	.345
Honus Wagner	21	2785	10427	3430	.329
Carl Yastrzemski	23	3308	11988	3419	.285
Eddie Collins	25	2826	9949	3311	.333
Babe Martin	22	2992	10881	3283	.302
Nap Lajoie	21	2475	9589	3251	.339
Paul Waner	20	2549	9459	3152	.333
Rod Carew	19	2469	9315	3053	.328
Cap Anson	22	2276	9120	3041	.333
Lou Brock	19	2616	10332	3023	.292
Al Kaline	22	2834	10116	3007	.297
Roberto Clemente	18	2433	9454	3000	.317

The 3,000th Hit

Player	Team	Date	Age	Yrs.	H	Opp.	Opp. Pitcher
Cap Anson	CHI N	Jul 18, 1897	45	22	1B	BAL	
Honus Wagner	PIT N	Jun 9, 1914	40	18	2B	PHI	
Nap Lajoie	CLE A	Sep 27, 1914	39	20	2B	STL	
Ty Cobb	DET A	Aug 19, 1921	34	17	1B	BOS	Elmer Myers
Tris Speaker	CLE A	May 17, 1925	37	18	1B	WAS	Tom Zachary
Eddie Collins	CHI A	Jun 3, 1925	38	18	1B	DET	Rip Collins
Paul Waner	BOS N	Jun 19, 1942	39	17	1B	PIT	Rip Sewell
Stan Musial	STL N	May 13, 1958	37	16	2B	CHI	Moe Drabowsky
Hank Aaron	ATL N	May 17, 1970	36	17	1B	CIN	Wayne Simpson
Willie Mays	SF N	Jul 18, 1970	39	19	1B	MON	Mike Wegener
Roberto Clemente	PIT N	Sep 30, 1972	38	18	2B	NY	Jon Matlack
Al Kaline	DET A	Sep 24, 1974	39	21	2B	BAL	Dave McNally
Pete Rose	CIN N	May 5, 1978	37	16	1B	MON	Steve Rogers
Lou Brock	STL N	Aug 13, 1979	37	18	1B	CHI	Dennis Lamp
Carl Yastrzemski	BOS A	Sep 12, 1979	40	19	1B	NY	Jim Beattie
Rod Carew	CAL A	Aug 4, 1985	39	19	1B	MIN	Frank Viola

Most Seasons with 200 Hits

Player	Total	Best
Pete Rose	10	230
Ty Cobb	9	248
Lou Gehrig	8	220
Willie Keeler	8	239
Paul Waner	8	237
Charlie Gehringer	7	227
Rogers Hornsby	7	250
Jesse Burkett	6	240
Steve Garvey	6	210
Stan Musial	6	230
Sam Rice	6	227
Al Simmons	6	253
George Sisler	6	257
Bill Terry	6	254
Chuck Klein	5	250
Nap Lajoie	5	229

Pete Rose, seen here slashing his 4192d hit, has played more games, had more at bats, and collected more hits than any player in history. His .321 average in 62 postseason games has led his teams to three World Championships.

More Walks than Hits, Season, AL

Player	Team	Year	BB	H	BA
Max Bishop	PHI	1926	116	106	.265
	PHI	1927	105	103	.277
	PHI	1929	128	110	.232
	PHI	1930	128	111	.252
	PHI	1932	110	104	.254
Roy Cullenbine	DET	1947	137	104	.224
Eddie Joost	PHI	1947	114	111	.206
	PHI	1949	149	138	.263
Ted Williams	BOS	1954	136	133	.345
Eddie Yost	WAS	1956	151	119	.231
Mickey Mantle	NY	1962	122	121	.321
	NY	1968	106	103	.237
Gene Tenace	OAK	1974	110	102	.211

More Walks than Hits, Season, NL

Player	Team	Year	BB	H	BA
Eddie Stanky	BKN	1945	148	143	.258
	BKN	1946	137	132	.273
Hank Greenberg	PIT	1947	104	100	.249
Eddie Stanky	NY	1951	127	127	.247
Jimmy Wynn	HOU	1969	148	133	.269
	LA	1975	110	102	.248
Gene Tenace	SD	1977	125	102	.233

Batting Champion by Widest Margin, AL

Player	Team	Year	BA	Diff.
Nap Lajoie	PHI	1901	.422	
Mike Donlin	BAL	1901	.340	.082
Rod Carew	MIN	1977	.388	
Lyman Bostock	MIN	1977	.336	.052
Rod Carew	MIN	1974	.364	
Jorge Orta	CHI	1974	.316	.048
Ted Williams	BOS	1941	.406	
Cecil Travis	WAS	1941	.359	.047
Rod Carew	MIN	1973	.350	
George Scott	MIL	1973	.306	.044

Batting Champion by Widest Margin, NL

Player	Team	Year	BA	Diff.
Rogers Hornsby	STL	1924	.424	
Zack Wheat	BKN	1924	.375	.049
Rogers Hornsby	STL	1922	.401	
Ray Grimes	CHI	1922	.354	.047
Harry Walker	PHI	1947		
	STL	1947	.363	
Bob Elliott	BOS	1947	.317	.046
Rogers Hornsby	STL	1921	.397	
Edd Roush	CIN	1921	.352	.045
Stan Musial	STL	1948	.376	
Richie Ashburn	PHI	1948	.333	.043
Rico Carty	ATL	1970	.366	
Joe Torre	STL	1970	.325	.041

No-Hit Spoilers - The Only Hit Most Often

Player	Team	Date	H	Opp.	Opp. Pitcher
Cesar Tovar	MIN A	Apr 30, 1967	1	WAS	Barry Moore
	MIN A	May 15, 1969	1	BAL	Dave McNally
	MIN A	Aug 10, 1969	1	BAL	Mike Cuellar
	MIN A	Aug 13, 1970	1	WAS	Dick Bosman
	TEX A	May 31, 1975	1	NY	Catfish Hunter
Eddie Milner	CIN N	Apr 28, 1982	1	CHI	Dickie Noles
	CIN N	Jun 11, 1982	1	LA	Jerry Reuss
	CIN N	Aug 24, 1983	1	CHI	Chuck Rainey
	CIN N	Jun 14, 1984	1	ATL	Len Barker
				ATL	Donnie Moore
	CIN N	Aug 2, 1986	1	LA	Alejandro Pena
				LA	Tom Niedenfuer
Don Blasingame	CIN N	Jul 13, 1962	1	CHI	Cal Koonce
	WAS A	Aug 6, 1963	1	NY	Stan Williams
	WAS A	Aug 20, 1963	1	KC	Moe Drabowsky
	WAS A	Sep 25, 1965	1	MIN	Mudcat Grant
Patsy Dougherty	BOS A	May 2, 1904	1	PHI	Rube Waddell
	CHI A	Sep 24, 1904	1	NY	Joe Lake
	CHI A	Aug 28, 1909	1	WAS	Dolly Gray

No-Hit Spoilers - The Only Hit Most Often *(cont'd)*

Player	Team	Date	H	Opp.	Opp. Pitcher
Patsy Dougherty	CHI A	Jul 29, 1910	1	DET	Ed Summers
Sherry Magee	PHI N	Sep 8, 1906	1	BOS	Irv Young
	PHI N	Jun 13, 1908	2	CHI	Three Finger Brown
	PHI N	May 6, 1910	1	CHI	Orval Overall
	BOS N	Sep 29, 1915	1	PHI	Grover Alexander
Ed Konetchy	STL N	Jun 22, 1913	1	CHI	George Pearce
	BOS N	Sep 28, 1916	1	NY	Ferdie Schupp
	BOS N	Sep 30, 1916	1	NY	Rube Benton
	BOS N	Aug 21, 1917	1	STL	Marv Goodwin
Billy Williams	CHI N	Sep 24, 1961	2	MIL	Warren Spahn
	CHI N	Jul 5, 1966	3	PIT	Woodie Fryman
	CHI N	Sep 5, 1969	4	PIT	Steve Blass
	CHI N	Jul 25, 1970	2	ATL	Phil Niekro
Zoilo Versalles	MIN A	Sep 10, 1962	1	LA	Dean Chance
	MIN A	Sep 2, 1964	1	BAL	Milt Pappas
	MIN A	Sep 6, 1964	1	BOS	Bill Monbouquette
	LA N	May 28, 1968	1	CIN	Jim Maloney
Al Bumbry	BAL A	Jun 10, 1975	1	OAK	Jim Perry
	BAL A	May 24, 1976	1	CLE	Dennis Eckersley
				CLE	Stan Thomas
	BAL A	Aug 16, 1983	1	TEX	John Butcher
	BAL A	Sep 15, 1984	2	MIL	Bob Gibson
Jake Stahl	WAS A	Jul 8, 1904	1	PHI	Eddie Plank
	WAS A	May 21, 1905	1	CHI	Frank Smith
	WAS A	Aug 31, 1905	1	CHI	Frank Smith
Honus Wagner	PIT N	Sep 12, 1905	2	STL	Jack Taylor
	PIT N	May 27, 1911	1	CIN	Art Fromme
	PIT N	Oct 2, 1914	1	CIN	Phil Douglas
Buck Weaver	CHI A	Jul 6, 1912	1	DET	Jean Dubuc
	CHI A	Jul 6, 1913	1	CLE	Willie Mitchell
	CHI A	May 5, 1917	1	STL	Ernie Koob
Harry Hooper	BOS A	Jul 14, 1913	1	CHI	Reb Russell
	BOS A	Apr 4, 1915	1	PHI	Herb Pennock
	BOS A	Sep 9, 1915	1	WAS	Walter Johnson
Terry Turner	CLE A	Jun 20, 1909	1	CHI	Ed Walsh
	CLE A	Jun 2, 1914	1	STL	Wiley Taylor
	CLE A	Jul 27, 1915	1	WAS	Bert Gallia
Fred Pfeffer	CHI N	May 11, 1886	1	BOS	Bill Stemmyer
	CHI N	Aug 6, 1887	1	PHI	Charlie Buffinton
	CHI N	Aug 9, 1887	1	PHI	Charlie Buffinton
Freddy Parent	BOS A	Sep 11, 1905	1	WAS	Cy Falkenberg
	BOS A	May 1, 1906	1	NY	Bill Hogg
	BOS A	Aug 7, 1908	2	CLE	Addie Joss
Possum Whitted	PHI N	Sep 9, 1915	1	STL	Red Ames
	PIT N	Aug 28, 1919	1	STL	Ferdie Schupp
	PIT N	Jun 30, 1920	1	CHI	Hippo Vaughn
Billy Southworth	PIT N	Jul 25, 1918	1	BKN	Burleigh Grimes
	PIT N	Sep 16, 1920	1	NY	Art Nehf
	STL N	Jun 27, 1926	1	CHI	Sheriff Blake
Fred Snodgrass	NY N	Apr 21, 1911	1	PHI	Earl Moore
	NY N	Sep 1, 1915	1	CIN	Fred Toney

No-Hit Spoilers - The Only Hit Most Often *(cont'd)*

Player	Team	Date	H	Opp.	Opp. Pitcher
Fred Snodgrass	BOS N	Jul 7, 1916	1	CHI	Gene Packard
Harlond Clift	STL A	Jun 12, 1938	1	PHI	Bud Thomas
	STL A	May 29, 1941	1	CHI	Bill Dietrich
	STL A	Sep 2, 1942	1	NY	Hank Borowy
Bob Johnson	PHI A	Jun 8, 1937	1	DET	Eldon Auker
	PHI A	Jun 30, 1937	1	NY	Lefty Gomez
	BOS A	Aug 30, 1945	1	NY	Bill Bevens
Bob Elliott	PIT N	Aug 8, 1941	1	CHI	Paul Erickson
	PIT N	Sep 12, 1943	1	CIN	Elmer Riddle
	BOS N	May 15, 1951	1	CIN	Ewell Blackwell
Del Ennis	PHI N	Jun 8, 1946	1	STL	Red Barrett
	PHI N	Apr 22, 1947	1	BKN	Hal Gregg
	PHI N	Apr 29, 1956	1	NY	Ray Monzant
Jim Northrup	DET A	Apr 24, 1968	1	CLE	Steve Hargan
	DET A	May 6, 1968	1	BAL	Dave Leonhard
	DET A	Apr 12, 1969	1	NY	Mel Stottlemyre
Tony Perez	CIN N	Sep 5, 1969	1	ATL	Phil Niekro
	CIN N	Sep 17, 1971	1	HOU	Don Wilson
	CIN N	Sep 4, 1974	1	HOU	Don Wilson
				HOU	Mike Cosgrove
Phil Cavarretta	CHI N	Sep 6, 1937	1	CIN	Lee Grissom
	CHI N	Sep 19, 1949	1	BKN	Rex Barney
	CHI N	Sep 2, 1950	1	CIN	Ewell Blackwell
Enos Slaughter	STL N	Sep 25, 1940	2	CIN	Junior Thompson
	STL N	Jul 18, 1947	1	BKN	Ralph Branca
	NY A	Sep 9, 1954	1	BAL	Joe Coleman
Denis Menke	MIL N	Apr 19, 1965	1	CIN	Jim Maloney
	ATL N	May 4, 1966	2	PHI	Chris Short
	HOU N	Jul 6, 1969	1	SD	Dick Kelley
Tommy Holmes	BOS N	Jun 13, 1942	1	CHI	Bill Fleming
	BOS N	Aug 25, 1942	3	PIT	Rip Sewell
	BOS N	Aug 28, 1943	2	NY	Van Mungo
Lou Brock	STL N	May 24, 1967	1	ATL	Denny Lemaster
	STL N	Apr 27, 1973	2	SF	Jim Barr
	STL N	May 18, 1975	2	SF	Jim Barr
John Stearns	NY N	May 3, 1975	1	MON	Woodie Fryman
	NY N	Jun 10, 1977	2	HOU	Joaquin Andujar
	NY N	Aug 12, 1978	1	STL	John Denny
				STL	Roy Thomas
Ralph Kiner	PIT N	Jun 24, 1949	2	BKN	Rex Barney
	PIT N	Jun 23, 1951	1	BKN	Don Newcombe
	PIT N	Aug 5, 1951	1	PHI	Bubba Church
Jimmy Wynn	HOU N	May 18, 1964	1	PHI	Jim Bunning
	HOU N	Jun 19, 1971	1	LA	Don Sutton
	LA N	Jun 13, 1975	2	PHI	Jim Lonborg
Duane Kuiper	CLE A	Jul 2, 1977	1	KC	Andy Hassler
	CLE A	May 5, 1978	1	CAL	Nolan Ryan
	CLE A	Sep 24, 1978	2	NY	Ron Guidry
John Mayberry	TOR A	Jul 7, 1979	1	TEX	Doc Medich
				TEX	Jim Kern
	TOR A	Jun 6, 1980	1	MIN	Geoff Zahn

No-Hit Spoilers - The Only Hit Most Often *(cont'd)*

Player	Team	Date	H	Opp.	Opp. Pitcher
John Mayberry	TOR A	Sep 26, 1980	1	BOS	Dennis Eckersley
Ken Griffey	CIN N	May 12, 1977	1	STL	John D'Acquisto
				STL	Buddy Schultz
				STL	Al Hrabosky
	CIN N	Aug 27, 1981	1	MON	Ray Burris
				MON	Jeff Reardon
	NY A	Oct 2, 1983	1	BAL	Mike Boddicker
				BAL	Sammy Stewart

Batted .300 after Age 40

Player	Team	Birth Date	Age	Year	G	AB	H	2B	3B	HR	BA
Ty Cobb	PHI A	Dec 16, 1886	40	1927	134	490	175	32	7	5	.357
Sam Rice	WAS A	Feb 20, 1890	40	1930	147	593	207	35	13	1	.349
Stan Musial	STL N	Nov 21, 1920	41	1962	135	433	143	18	1	19	.330
Pete Rose	PHI N	Apr 14, 1941	40	1981	107	431	140	18	5	0	.325
Ty Cobb	PHI A	Dec 16, 1886	41	1928	95	353	114	27	4	1	.323
Sam Rice	WAS A	Feb 20, 1890	42	1932	106	288	93	16	7	1	.323
Johnny Cooney	BOS N	Mar 18, 1901	40	1941	123	442	141	25	2	0	.319
Ted Williams	BOS A	Aug 30, 1918	41	1960	113	310	98	15	0	29	.316
Luke Appling	CHI A	Apr 2, 1907	41	1948	139	497	156	16	2	0	.314
Sam Rice	WAS A	Feb 20, 1890	41	1931	120	413	128	21	8	0	.310
Luke Appling	CHI A	Apr 2, 1907	40	1947	139	503	154	29	0	8	.306
Lou Brock	STL N	Jun 18, 1939	40	1979	120	405	123	15	4	5	.304
Luke Appling	CHI A	Apr 2, 1907	42	1949	142	492	148	21	5	5	.301

Most Runs, Season, AL

Player	Team	Year	R
Babe Ruth	NY	1921	177
Lou Gehrig	NY	1936	167
Babe Ruth	NY	1928	163
Lou Gehrig	NY	1931	163
Babe Ruth	NY	1920	158
Babe Ruth	NY	1927	158
	NY	1923	151
Jimmie Foxx	PHI	1932	151
Joe DiMaggio	NY	1937	151

Most Runs, Season, NL

Player	Team	Year	R
Billy Hamilton	PHI	1894	196
Joe Kelley	BAL	1894	167
Billy Hamilton	PHI	1895	166
Willie Keeler	BAL	1894	165
	BAL	1895	162
Hugh Duffy	BOS	1894	160
Jesse Burkett	CLE	1896	160
Hughie Jennings	BAL	1895	159
Bobby Lowe	BOS	1894	158
Chuck Klein	PHI	1930	158

Most Runs, Career

Player	R
Ty Cobb	2245
Hank Aaron	2174
Babe Ruth	2174
Pete Rose	2150
Willie Mays	2062
Stan Musial	1949
Lou Gehrig	1888
Tris Speaker	1881
Mel Ott	1859
Frank Robinson	1829
Eddie Collins	1818
Carl Yastrzemski	1816
Ted Williams	1798
Charlie Gehringer	1774
Jimmie Foxx	1751
Honus Wagner	1740
Willie Keeler	1722
Cap Anson	1719
Jesse Burkett	1713
Billy Hamilton	1692

Mel Ott's unique batting stance put him a leg up on pitchers—to the tune of 511 home runs.

Most Runs, Game, AL

Player	Team	Date	R
Johnny Pesky	BOS	May 8, 1946	6
Spike Owen	BOS	Aug 21, 1986	6

Most Runs, Game, NL

Player	Team	Date	R
Jim Whitney	BOS	Jun 9, 1883	6
Cap Anson	CHI	Aug 24, 1886	6
Mike Tiernan	NY	Jun 15, 1887	6
King Kelly	BOS	Aug 27, 1887	6
Ezra Sutton	BOS	Aug 27, 1887	6
Jimmy Ryan	CHI	Jul 25, 1894	6
Bobby Lowe	BOS	May 3, 1895	6
Ginger Beaumont	PIT	Jul 22, 1899	6
Mel Ott	NY	Aug 4, 1934	6
	NY	Apr 30, 1944	6
Frank Torre	MIL	Sep 2, 1957	6

Most Runs, Game, Other Leagues

Player	Team	Date	R
Guy Hecker	LOU AA	Aug 15, 1886	7
Long John Reilly	CIN AA	Sep 12, 1883	6
Monk Cline	KC AA	Sep 30, 1888	6

Most RBIs, Season, AL

Player	Team	Year	RBI
Lou Gehrig	NY	1931	184
Hank Greenberg	DET	1937	183
Lou Gehrig	NY	1927	175
Jimmie Foxx	BOS	1938	175
Lou Gehrig	NY	1930	174
Babe Ruth	NY	1921	171
Hank Greenberg	DET	1935	170
Jimmie Foxx	PHI	1932	169
Joe DiMaggio	NY	1937	167
Al Simmons	PHI	1930	165
Lou Gehrig	NY	1934	165

Most RBIs, Season, NL

Player	Team	Year	RBI
Hack Wilson	CHI	1930	190
Chuck Klein	PHI	1930	170
Sam Thompson	DET	1887	166
	PHI	1895	165
Hack Wilson	CHI	1929	159
Joe Medwick	STL	1937	154
Tommy Davis	LA	1962	153
Rogers Hornsby	STL	1922	152
Mel Ott	NY	1929	151
Rogers Hornsby	CHI	1929	149
George Foster	CIN	1977	149

A volatile member of St. Louis' Gashouse Gang, left fielder Joe Medwick's scuffle with Tigers third baseman Marv Owen in Game Seven of the 1934 Series prompted fans to pelt Medwick with garbage and led to his removal from the game.

Most RBIs, Career

Player	RBI
Hank Aaron	2297
Babe Ruth	2211
Lou Gehrig	1990
Ty Cobb	1961
Stan Musial	1951
Jimmie Foxx	1921
Willie Mays	1903
Mel Ott	1860
Carl Yastrzemski	1844
Ted Williams	1839
Al Simmons	1827
Frank Robinson	1812
Honus Wagner	1732
Cap Anson	1715
Ernie Banks	1636
Tony Perez	1623
Goose Goslin	1609
Nap Lajoie	1599
Rogers Hornsby	1584
Harmon Killebrew	1584
Al Kaline	1583

Most Runs Produced, Season, AL

Player	Team	Year	R	RBI	HR	RP
Lou Gehrig	NY	1931	163	184	46	301
Babe Ruth	NY	1921	177	171	59	289
Ty Cobb	DET	1911	147	144	8	283
Al Simmons	PHI	1930	152	165	36	281
Hank Greenberg	DET	1937	137	183	40	280
Lou Gehrig	NY	1927	149	175	47	277
	NY	1930	143	174	41	276
Joe DiMaggio	NY	1937	151	167	46	272
Lou Gehrig	NY	1936	167	152	49	270
Babe Ruth	NY	1931	149	163	46	266
Ted Williams	BOS	1949	150	159	43	266
Jimmie Foxx	BOS	1938	139	175	50	264
Babe Ruth	NY	1927	158	164	60	262
Jimmie Foxx	PHI	1932	151	169	58	262
Al Simmons	PHI	1932	144	151	35	260
Lou Gehrig	NY	1937	138	159	37	260
Nap Lajoie	PHI	1901	145	125	14	256
Lou Gehrig	NY	1932	138	151	34	255
Hank Greenberg	DET	1935	121	170	36	255
Lou Gehrig	NY	1928	139	142	27	254
Babe Ruth	NY	1930	150	153	49	254
	NY	1928	163	142	54	251
Earl Averill	CLE	1931	140	143	32	251
Charlie Gehringer	DET	1934	134	127	11	250

Most Runs Produced, Season, NL

Player	Team	Year	R	RBI	HR	RP
Chuck Klein	PHI	1930	158	170	40	288
Hugh Duffy	BOS	1894	160	145	18	287
Hughie Jennings	BAL	1895	159	125	4	280
Hack Wilson	CHI	1930	146	190	56	280
Billy Hamilton	PHI	1894	196	87	4	279
Sam Thompson	PHI	1895	131	165	18	278
Ed Delahanty	PHI	1894	149	131	4	276
Kiki Cuyler	CHI	1930	155	134	13	276
Sam Thompson	DET	1887	118	166	11	273
Ed Delahanty	PHI	1893	145	146	19	272
Joe Kelley	BAL	1894	167	111	6	272
	BAL	1895	148	134	10	272
Rogers Hornsby	CHI	1929	156	149	40	265
Ed Delahanty	PHI	1899	133	137	9	261
Hugh Duffy	BOS	1893	147	118	6	259
Dan Brouthers	BAL	1894	137	128	9	256
Bobby Lowe	BOS	1894	158	115	17	256
Hack Wilson	CHI	1929	135	159	39	255
Cap Anson	CHI	1886	117	147	10	254
Willie Keeler	BAL	1894	165	94	5	254
Rogers Hornsby	STL	1922	141	152	42	251
Chuck Klein	PHI	1932	152	137	38	251

Most Runs Produced, Career

Player	R	RBI	HR	RP
Ty Cobb	2244	1959	118	4085
Hank Aaron	2174	2297	755	3716
Babe Ruth	2174	2204	714	3664
Stan Musial	1949	1951	475	3425
Lou Gehrig	1888	1990	493	3385
Honus Wagner	1740	1732	101	3371
Cap Anson	1719	1715	96	3338
Tris Speaker	1881	1562	117	3326
Pete Rose	2165	1314	160	3319
Willie Mays	2062	1903	660	3305
Mel Ott	1859	1860	511	3208
Carl Yastrzemski	1816	1844	452	3208
Jimmie Foxx	1751	1921	534	3138
Ted Williams	1798	1839	521	3116
Jake Beckley	1600	1575	88	3087
Eddie Collins	1818	1299	47	3070
Frank Robinson	1829	1812	586	3055
Al Simmons	1507	1827	307	3027
Nap Lajoie	1503	1599	83	3019
Charlie Gehringer	1774	1427	184	3017
Ed Delahanty	1599	1464	100	2963
George Davis	1544	1435	73	2906

Player	R	RBI	HR	RP
Rogers Hornsby	1584	1579	301	2862
Goose Goslin	1483	1609	248	2844
Paul Waner	1626	1309	112	2823
Sam Crawford	1393	1525	97	2821
Al Kaline	1622	1583	399	2806
Bill Dahlen	1611	1233	84	2760
Hugh Duffy	1553	1299	103	2749
Frankie Frisch	1532	1244	105	2671
Harry Heilmann	1291	1551	183	2659
Mickey Mantle	1677	1509	536	2650
Lave Cross	1332	1345	47	2630
Reggie Jackson	1509	1659	548	2620
Jimmy Ryan	1643	1093	118	2618
Jesse Burkett	1713	952	75	2590
George Van Haltren	1639	1014	69	2584
Fred Clarke	1626	1015	67	2574
Joe DiMaggio	1390	1537	361	2566
Roger Connor	1621	1078	136	2563
Sam Rice	1515	1078	34	2559
Joe Kelley	1426	1193	65	2553
Tony Perez	1272	1652	379	2545
Joe Morgan	1651	1134	268	2517

Most RBIs in One Inning, AL

Player	Team	Date	RBI	Inn.
Bob Johnson	PHI	Aug 29, 1937	6	1
Tom McBride	BOS	Aug 4, 1945	6	4
Joe Astroth	PHI	Sep 23, 1950	6	6
Gil McDougald	NY	May 3, 1951	6	9
Sam Mele	CHI	Jun 10, 1952	6	4
Jim Lemon	WAS	Sep 5, 1959	6	3
Ty Cobb	DET	Aug 27, 1909	5	4
Ray Bates	PHI	May 14, 1917	5	7
Chick Gandil	CHI	Jul 3, 1919	5	4
Al Simmons	PHI	May 22, 1929	5	5
Joe DiMaggio	NY	Jun 24, 1936	5	5
Mike Cubbage	MIN	Aug 7, 1977	5	4

Most RBIs in One Inning, NL

Player	Team	Date	RBI	Inn.
Fred Merkle	NY	May 13, 1911	6	1
Jim Ray Hart	SF	Jul 8, 1970	6	5
Andre Dawson	MON	Sep 24, 1985	6	5
Chick Hafey	STL	May 7, 1930	5	5
Billy Williams	CHI	May 1, 1964	5	1
Felix Millan	ATL	Sep 20, 1972	5	2
John Boccabella	MON	Jul 6, 1973	5	6
Dusty Baker	LA	Sep 13, 1977	5	2
Ray Knight	CIN	May 13, 1980	5	5
Von Hayes	PHI	Jun 11, 1985	5	1

Left: Hack Wilson's 1930 season included 56 home runs, a .723 slugging percentage, and an incredible 190 RBIs. Hammerin' Hank Greenberg (*above*) pounded out a lifetime .605 slugging average.

Most RBIs in One Inning, Other Leagues

Player	Team	Date	RBI	Inn.
Ed Cartwright	STL AA	Sep 23, 1890	7	3

Most RBIs, Game, AL

Player	Team	Date	RBI
Tony Lazzeri	NY	May 24, 1936	11
Rudy York	BOS	Jul 27, 1946	10
Norm Zauchin	BOS	May 27, 1955	10
Reggie Jackson	OAK	Jun 14, 1969	10
Fred Lynn	BOS	Jun 18, 1975	10
Jimmie Foxx	PHI	Aug 14, 1933	9
Jim Tabor	BOS	Jul 4, 1939	9
Jackie Jensen	BOS	Aug 2, 1956	9
Jim Gentile	BAL	May 9, 1961	9
Roy Howell	TOR	Sep 10, 1977	9
Eddie Murray	BAL	Aug 26, 1985	9

Most RBIs, Game, NL

Player	Team	Date	RBI
Jim Bottomley	STL	Sep 16, 1924	12
Wilbert Robinson	BAL	Jun 10, 1892	11
Phil Weintraub	NY	Apr 30, 1944	11
Walker Cooper	CIN	Jul 6, 1949	10
Harry Staley	BOS	Jun 1, 1893	9
Heinie Zimmerman	CHI	Jun 11, 1911	9
Johnny Rizzo	PIT	May 30, 1939	9
Gil Hodges	BKN	Aug 31, 1950	9
Smoky Burgess	CIN	Jul 29, 1955	9
Tony Cloninger	ATL	Jul 3, 1966	9

More RBIs than Games Played, Season, AL

Player	Team	Year	RBI	G	Diff.
Lou Gehrig	NY	1931	184	155	29
Hank Greenberg	DET	1937	183	154	29
Al Simmons	PHI	1930	165	138	27
Jimmie Foxx	BOS	1938	175	149	26
Lou Gehrig	NY	1927	175	155	20
	NY	1930	174	154	20
Babe Ruth	NY	1921	171	152	19
	NY	1929	154	135	19
	NY	1931	153	145	18
Hank Greenberg	DET	1935	170	152	18
Joe DiMaggio	NY	1937	167	151	16
Jimmie Foxx	PHI	1932	169	154	15
Al Simmons	PHI	1929	157	143	14
Jimmie Foxx	PHI	1933	163	149	14
Babe Ruth	NY	1927	164	151	13
Lou Gehrig	NY	1934	165	154	11
Hal Trosky	CLE	1936	162	151	11
Babe Ruth	NY	1930	153	145	8
Walt Dropo	BOS	1950	144	136	8
Joe DiMaggio	NY	1939	126	120	6
Babe Ruth	NY	1932	137	133	4
Vern Stephens	BOS	1949	159	155	4
Ted Williams	BOS	1949	159	155	4
Ken Williams	STL	1925	105	102	3
Jimmie Foxx	PHI	1930	156	153	3

More RBIs than Games Played, Season, AL *(cont'd)*

Player	Team	Year	RBI	G	Diff.
Ken Williams	STL	1922	155	153	2
Al Simmons	PHI	1927	108	106	2
Lou Gehrig	NY	1937	159	157	2
Hank Greenberg	DET	1940	150	148	2
Joe DiMaggio	NY	1948	155	153	2
	NY	1940	133	132	1
George Brett	KC	1980	118	117	1

More RBIs than Games Played, Season, NL

Player	Team	Year	RBI	G	Diff.
Hack Wilson	CHI	1930	190	155	35
Chuck Klein	PHI	1930	170	156	14
Hack Wilson	CHI	1929	159	150	9
Rogers Hornsby	STL	1925	143	138	5
Mel Ott	NY	1929	151	150	1

Most Stolen Bases, Season, AL

Player	Team	Year	SB
Rickey Henderson	OAK	1982	130
	OAK	1983	108
	OAK	1980	100
Ty Cobb	DET	1915	96
Clyde Milan	WAS	1912	88
Rickey Henderson	NY	1986	87
Ty Cobb	DET	1911	83
Willie Wilson	KC	1979	83
Eddie Collins	PHI	1910	81
Rickey Henderson	NY	1985	80

Player	Team	Year	SB
Willie Wilson	KC	1980	79
Ron LeFlore	DET	1979	78
Rudy Law	CHI	1983	77
Ty Cobb	DET	1909	76
Clyde Milan	WAS	1913	75
Billy North	OAK	1976	75
Fritz Maisel	NY	1914	74
Tommy Harper	SEA	1969	73
Mickey Rivers	CAL	1975	70

Most Stolen Bases, Season, NL

Player	Team	Year	SB
Lou Brock	STL	1974	118
Vince Coleman	STL	1985	110
	STL	1986	107
Maury Wills	LA	1962	104
Ron LeFlore	MON	1980	97
Omar Moreno	PIT	1980	96
Maury Wills	LA	1965	94
Tim Raines	MON	1983	90
Bob Bescher	CIN	1911	81
Eric Davis	CIN	1986	80
Dave Collins	CIN	1980	79
Tim Raines	MON	1982	78
Jimmy Sheckard	BAL	1899	77
Davey Lopes	LA	1975	77

Player	Team	Year	SB
Omar Moreno	PIT	1979	77
Tim Raines	MON	1984	75
Lou Brock	STL	1966	74
John McGraw	BAL	1899	73
Juan Samuel	PHI	1984	72
Omar Moreno	PIT	1978	71
Tim Raines	MON	1981	71
Bob Bescher	CIN	1910	70
Lou Brock	STL	1973	70
Frank Taveras	PIT	1977	70
Alan Wiggins	SD	1984	70
Tim Raines	MON	1985	70
	MON	1986	70

Most Stolen Bases, Career

Player	SB
Lou Brock	938
Ty Cobb	892
Eddie Collins	743
Max Carey	738
Honus Wagner	703
Joe Morgan	689
Bert Campaneris	649
Maury Wills	586
Rickey Henderson	573
Cesar Cedeno	549
Davey Lopes	530
Luis Aparicio	506
Clyde Milan	495
Omar Moreno	470
Bobby Bonds	461
Jimmy Sheckard	460
Ron LeFlore	455
Sherry Magee	441
Willie Wilson	436
Tris Speaker	433
Bob Bescher	428
Frankie Frisch	419
Tommy Harper	408
Frank Chance	405
Donie Bush	403

Most Stolen Bases, Game, AL

Player	Team	Date	SB
Eddie Collins	PHI	Sep 11, 1912	6
	PHI	Sep 22, 1912	6
Clyde Milan	WAS	Jun 14, 1912	5
Johnny Neun	DET	Jul 9, 1927	5
Amos Otis	KC	Sep 7, 1971	5
Bert Campaneris	OAK	Apr 24, 1976	5

Most Stolen Bases, Game, NL

Player	Team	Date	SB
Dan McGann	NY	May 27, 1904	5
Davey Lopes	LA	Aug 24, 1974	5
Lonnie Smith	STL	Sep 4, 1982	5
Alan Wiggins	SD	May 17, 1984	5
Tony Gwynn	SD	Sep 20, 1986	5

Stole 2nd, 3rd, and Home in One Game, AL

Player	Team	Date
Dave Fultz	PHI	Sep 4, 1902
Wild Bill Donovan	DET	May 7, 1906
Bill Coughlin	DET	Jun 6, 1906
Ty Cobb	DET	Sep 2, 1907
	DET	Jul 23, 1909
	DET	Jul 12, 1911
	DET	Jul 4, 1912
Joe Jackson	CLE	Aug 11, 1912
Eddie Collins	PHI	Sep 22, 1912
Eddie Ainsmith	WAS	Jun 26, 1913
Fritz Maisel	NY	Apr 17, 1915
Red Faber	CHI	Jul 14, 1915
Danny Moeller	WAS	Jul 19, 1915
Ty Cobb	DET	Jun 18, 1917
Buck Weaver	CHI	Sep 6, 1919
Braggo Roth	WAS	May 31, 1920
Ty Cobb	DET	Aug 10, 1924
Bob Meusel	NY	May 16, 1927
Jackie Tavener	DET	Jul 10, 1927
	DET	Jul 25, 1928
Don Kolloway	CHI	Jun 28, 1941
Rod Carew	MIN	May 18, 1969
Dave Nelson	TEX	Aug 30, 1974

Stole 2nd, 3rd, and Home in One Game, NL

Player	Team	Date
Honus Wagner	PIT	Jun 15, 1902
	PIT	Sep 25, 1907
Buck Herzog	NY	Sep 9, 1908
Hans Lobert	CIN	Sep 27, 1908
Honus Wagner	PIT	May 2, 1909
Bill O'Hara	NY	Aug 8, 1909
Dode Paskert	CIN	May 23, 1910
Wilbur Good	CHI	Aug 18, 1915
Jimmy Johnston	BKN	Sep 22, 1916
Greasy Neale	CIN	Aug 15, 1919
Max Carey	PIT	Aug 18, 1923
	PIT	Aug 26, 1925
Harvey Hendrick	BKN	Jun 12, 1928
Jackie Robinson	BKN	Apr 23, 1954
Pete Rose	PHI	May 11, 1980
Dusty Baker	SF	Jun 27, 1984

Shortstop Bert Campaneris (*above*) led off for Oakland in three straight victorious World Series. Eddie Collins (*right*) holds the record for most stolen bases in World Series play: 14.

Most Steals of Home, Career

Player	Total
Ty Cobb	50
George Burns	27
Sherry Magee	23
Wildfire Schulte	22
Johnny Evers	21
Frankie Frisch	19
Jackie Robinson	19
George Sisler	19
Jimmy Sheckard	18
Rod Carew	17
Eddie Collins	17
Larry Doyle	17
Joe Tinker	17
Lou Gehrig	15
Tris Speaker	15
Max Carey	14

Player	Total
Ben Chapman	14
Fritz Maisel	14
Vic Saier	14
Honus Wagner	14
Heinie Zimmerman	13
Harry Hooper	11
Fred Merkle	11
George Moriarty	11
Braggo Roth	11
Shano Collins	10
Buck Herzog	10
Jimmy Johnston	10
Sam Rice	10
Babe Ruth	10
Bill Werber	10
Ross Youngs	10

Most Times Caught Stealing, Game, AL

Player	Team	Date	Total	Opp.
Tris Speaker	BOS	Jul 22, 1912	3	NY
Larry Chappell	CHI	Aug 20, 1913	3	BOS
Eddie Murphy	PHI	Jun 20, 1914	3	STL
Fritz Maisel	NY	Apr 26, 1916	3	PHI
Larry Gardner	BOS	Jun 27, 1916	3	PHI
Lee Magee	NY	Jun 29, 1916	3	PHI
Rickey Henderson	OAK	Jul 27, 1982	3	CAL

Most Times Caught Stealing, Game, NL

Player	Team	Date	Total	Inns.	Opp.
Robby Thompson	SF	Jun 27, 1986	4	12	CIN
Rabbit Maranville	BOS	Jun 6, 1913	3		CHI
Miller Huggins	STL	Jul 14, 1914	3		BOS
Bill McKechnie	NY	May 30, 1916	3		PHI
Jack Smith	STL	Jun 1, 1916	3		CIN
Tommy Long	STL	Apr 14, 1917	3		CIN
Fred Toney	CIN	Jun 24, 1917	3		STL
Hy Myers	BKN	Aug 25, 1917	3		STL
Rodney Scott	MON	Apr 15, 1979	3		CHI

Most Pinch Hits, Season, AL

Player	Team	Year	Total
Dave Philley	BAL	1961	24
Smoky Burgess	CHI	1966	21
Ed Coleman	STL	1936	20
Smoky Burgess	CHI	1965	20
Bob Fothergill	DET	1929	19
Johnny Mize	NY	1953	19
Bob Hale	CLE	1960	19
Joe Cronin	BOS	1943	18
Julio Becquer	WAS	1957	18
Gates Brown	DET	1968	18
Jerry Hairston	CHI	1984	18
Sammy Hale	DET	1920	17

Player	Team	Year	Total
Bob Boyd	BAL	1960	17
Vic Wertz	DET	1962	17
Pete Ward	CHI	1969	17
Jerry Hairston	CHI	1983	17
Bill Rumler	STL	1917	16
Enos Slaughter	NY	1955	
	KC	1955	16
Dick Williams	BOS	1963	16
Gomer Hodge	CLE	1971	16
Winston Llenas	CAL	1973	16
Gates Brown	DET	1974	16
Rick Miller	BOS	1983	16

Most Pinch Hits, Season, NL

Player	Team	Year	Total
Jose Morales	MON	1976	25
Vic Davalillo	STL	1970	24
Rusty Staub	NY	1983	24
Sam Leslie	NY	1932	22
Peanuts Lowrey	STL	1953	22
Red Schoendienst	STL	1962	22
Merv Rettenmund	SD	1977	21
Doc Miller	PHI	1913	20
Frenchy Bordagaray	STL	1938	20

Player	Team	Year	Total
Joe Frazier	STL	1954	20
Ken Boswell	HOU	1976	20
Jerry Turner	SD	1978	20
Thad Bosley	CHI	1985	20
Chris Chambliss	ATL	1986	20
Jerry Lynch	CIN	1960	19
	CIN	1961	19
Jose Pagan	PIT	1969	19
Greg Gross	PHI	1982	19

Most Pinch Hits, Season, NL *(cont'd)*

Player	Team	Year	Total
Rene Monteagudo	PHI	1945	18
Dave Philley	PHI	1958	18
Rusty Staub	NY	1982	18
Jim Bolger	CHI	1957	17
George Crowe	STL	1959	17
Bob Will	CHI	1962	17
Merritt Ranew	CHI	1963	17
Carl Taylor	PIT	1969	17
Ramon Webster	SD	1970	17
Ed Kranepool	NY	1974	17
Tony Taylor	PHI	1974	17
Mike Lum	ATL	1979	17
Kurt Bevacqua	SD	1980	
	PIT	1980	17
Jesus Figueroa	CHI	1980	17
Steve Braun	STL	1984	17
Candy Maldonado	SF	1986	17
Sid Gautreaux	BKN	1936	16
Mike Rogodzinski	PHI	1973	16
Jesus Alou	HOU	1978	16
Charlie Spikes	ATL	1979	16
Duane Walker	CIN	1983	16
Lee Mazzilli	PIT	1985	16

Most Pinch Hits, Career

Player	Total
Manny Mota	149
Smoky Burgess	145
Jose Morales	123
Jerry Lynch	116
Red Lucas	114
Steve Braun	113
Terry Crowley	108
Greg Gross	108
Gates Brown	107
Mike Lum	103
Rusty Staub	100
Larry Biittner	95
Vic Davalillo	95
Dave Philley	93
Jay Johnstone	92
Ed Kranepool	90
Elmer Valo	90
Jerry Hairston	85
Jesus Alou	82
Kurt Bevacqua	82
Tim McCarver	82
Tito Francona	81
Dalton Jones	81
Tom Hutton	79
Enos Slaughter	77
George Crowe	76
Bob Fothergill	76

Pinch-hitter extraordinaire Jose Morales led the league in pinch hits four times, including his record of 25 for the Expos in 1976.

Most Consecutive Pinch Hits

Player	Team	Year	Total	Player	Team	Year	Total
Dave Philley	PHI	1958		Rogers Hornsby	STL	1933	5
	PHI	1959	9	Max Macon	BKN	1942	5
Rusty Staub	NY	1983	8	Johnny Mize	NY	1953	5
Peanuts Lowrey	STL	1952	7	Bob Hale	CLE	1960	5
Bill Stein	TEX	1981	7	Vic Wertz	DET	1962	5
Bobby Adams	CHI	1958	6	Andre Rodgers	PIT	1965	5
Bob Johnson	BAL	1964	6	Charley Smith	NY	1968	5
Mike Vail	CHI	1978	6	Richie Scheinblum	KC	1972	5
Joe Schultz	STL	1922	5	Rowland Office	ATL	1975	5

Longest Hitting Streaks, AL

Player	Team	Year	G	Player	Team	Year	G
Joe DiMaggio	NY	1941	56	Sam Rice	WAS	1930	28
George Sisler	STL	1922	41	Hal Trosky	CLE	1936	28
Ty Cobb	DET	1911	40	Wade Boggs	BOS	1985	28
	DET	1917	35	Socks Seybold	PHI	1901	27
George Sisler	STL	1925	34	Hal Chase	NY	1907	27
John Stone	DET	1930	34	Heinie Manush	STL	1930	
George McQuinn	STL	1938	34		WAS	1930	27
Dom DiMaggio	BOS	1949	34	Al Simmons	PHI	1931	27
Heinie Manush	WAS	1933	33	Luke Appling	CHI	1936	27
Sam Rice	WAS	1924	31	Gee Walker	DET	1937	27
Ken Landreaux	MIN	1980	31	Bruce Campbell	CLE	1938	27
Tris Speaker	BOS	1912	30	Bob Dillinger	STL	1948	27
Goose Goslin	DET	1934	30	Dom DiMaggio	BOS	1951	27
Ron LeFlore	DET	1976	30	Ron LeFlore	DET	1978	27
George Brett	KC	1980	30	Harry Bay	CLE	1902	26
Bill Bradley	CLE	1902	29	Buck Freeman	BOS	1902	26
Roger Peckinpaugh	NY	1919	29	Hobe Ferris	STL	1908	26
Sam Rice	WAS	1920	29	Babe Ruth	NY	1921	26
Bill Lamar	PHI	1925	29	Heinie Manush	WAS	1933	26
Dale Alexander	DET	1930	29	Bob Johnson	PHI	1938	26
Earle Combs	NY	1931	29	Guy Curtright	CHI	1943	26
Pete Fox	DET	1935	29	Johnny Pesky	BOS	1947	26
Mel Almada	STL	1938	29	Kid Gleason	DET	1901	25
Joe Gordon	NY	1942	29	Ty Cobb	DET	1906	25
Nap Lajoie	PHI	1901	28	George Sisler	STL	1920	25
Joe Jackson	CLE	1911	28	Goose Goslin	WAS	1928	25
Ken Williams	STL	1922	28	Catfish Metkovich	BOS	1944	25
Bing Miller	PHI	1929	28	Rod Carew	CAL	1982	25

Longest Hitting Streaks, NL

Player	Team	Year	G
Willie Keeler	BAL	1897	44
Pete Rose	CIN	1978	44
Bill Dahlen	CHI	1894	42
Tommy Holmes	BOS	1945	37
Billy Hamilton	PHI	1894	36
Fred Clarke	LOU	1895	35
George Davis	NY	1893	33
Rogers Hornsby	STL	1922	32
Ed Delahanty	PHI	1899	31
Willie Davis	LA	1969	31
Rico Carty	ATL	1970	31
Elmer Smith	CIN	1898	30
Stan Musial	STL	1950	30
Zack Wheat	BKN	1916	29
Harry Walker	STL	1943	29
Ken Boyer	STL	1959	29
Rowland Office	ATL	1976	29
Bill Dahlen	CHI	1894	28
Joe Medwick	STL	1935	28
Red Schoendienst	STL	1954	28
Ron Santo	CHI	1966	28
Jimmy Williams	PIT	1899	27
Piano Legs Hickman	NY	1900	27
Edd Roush	CIN	1920	27
	CIN	1924	27
Hack Wilson	CHI	1929	27
Joe Medwick	BKN	1942	27
Duke Snider	BKN	1953	27
Vada Pinson	CIN	1965	27
Glenn Beckert	CHI	1968	27
Hugh Duffy	BOS	1894	26
George Decker	CHI	1896	26
Willie Keeler	BAL	1896	26
Jimmy Williams	PIT	1899	26
Willie Keeler	BKN	1902	26
Bill Sweeney	BOS	1911	26
Zack Wheat	BKN	1918	26
Chuck Klein	PHI	1930	26
	PHI	1930	26
Gabby Hartnett	CHI	1937	26
Danny O'Connell	PIT	1953	26
Lou Brock	STL	1971	26
Glenn Beckert	CHI	1973	26
Jack Clark	SF	1978	26
Charlie Grimm	PIT	1923	25
Clyde Barnhart	PIT	1925	25
Hack Wilson	CHI	1926	25
Rube Bressler	CIN	1927	25
Harvey Hendrick	BKN	1929	25
Freddie Lindstrom	PIT	1933	25
Buzz Boyle	BKN	1934	25
Hank Aaron	MIL	1956	25
	MIL	1962	25
Pete Rose	CIN	1967	25
Willie Davis	LA	1971	25
Tony Gwynn	SD	1983	25
Steve Sax	LA	1986	25

Most Consecutive Games Played

Player	G
Lou Gehrig	2130
Everett Scott	1307
Steve Garvey	1207
Billy Williams	1117
Joe Sewell	1103
Stan Musial	895
Eddie Yost	829
Gus Suhr	822
Nellie Fox	798
Cal Ripken	765
Pete Rose	745
Dale Murphy	740
Richie Ashburn	730
Ernie Banks	717
Pete Rose	678
Earl Averill	673
Frank McCormick	652
Sandy Alomar	648
Eddie Brown	618
Roy McMillan	598
George Pinckney	577
Steve Brodie	574
Aaron Ward	565
Candy LaChance	540
Buck Freeman	535
Fred Luderus	533
Clyde Milan	512
Charlie Gehringer	511
Vada Pinson	508
Tony Cuccinello	504
Charlie Gehringer	504
Omar Moreno	503

Fewest Games Missed (10-Year Period)

Player	First	Last	G	G Mis	Pct.
Lou Gehrig	1929	1938	1543	0	100.0
Pete Rose	1973	1982	1562	4	99.7
Billy Williams	1962	1971	1614	10	99.4
Cap Anson	1883	1892	1258	11	99.1
Nellie Fox	1952	1961	1544	15	99.0
Stan Musial	1946	1955	1533	17	98.9
John Morrill	1878	1887	957	13	98.7
Ron Santo	1961	1970	1595	23	98.6
Richie Ashburn	1949	1958	1524	22	98.6
Roger Connor	1880	1889	1083	17	98.5
George Van Haltren	1891	1900	1389	22	98.4
George Burns	1914	1923	1487	25	98.3
Willie Mays	1954	1963	1536	26	98.3
Jim O'Rourke	1876	1885	819	14	98.3
Jimmie Foxx	1929	1938	1495	30	98.0
Brooks Robinson	1960	1969	1578	33	98.0
Sam Crawford	1906	1915	1507	33	97.9
Hugh Duffy	1889	1898	1350	30	97.8
Paul Hines	1877	1886	896	21	97.7
Hank Aaron	1955	1964	1534	37	97.6
Mel Ott	1929	1938	1498	38	97.5

RBI in Most Consecutive Games, AL

Player	Team	Last Date	G	RBI
Taffy Wright	CHI	May 20, 1941	13	22
Joe Cronin	BOS	Jul 9, 1939	12	19
Ted Williams	BOS	Sep 13, 1942	12	18
Al Simmons	PHI	May 12, 1931	11	20
Babe Ruth	NY	Jul 2, 1931	11	18
Ted Williams	BOS	Jun 10, 1950	11	21
Frank White	KC	Jun 22, 1983	11	13

RBI in Most Consecutive Games, NL

Player	Team	Last Date	G	RBI
Ray Grimes	CHI	Jul 23, 1922	17	27
Paul Waner	PIT	Jun 16, 1939	12	20
Mel Ott	NY	Jun 20, 1929	11	27

Most Consecutive Hits, AL

Player	Team	Year	H
Pinky Higgins	BOS	1938	12
Walt Dropo	DET	1952	12
Tris Speaker	CLE	1920	11
Johnny Pesky	BOS	1946	11
George Sisler	STL	1921	10
Harry Heilmann	DET	1922	10
Harry McCurdy	CHI	1926	10
Ken Singleton	BAL	1981	10
Doc Johnston	CLE	1919	9
Ty Cobb	DET	1925	9
Sam Rice	WAS	1925	9
Hal Trosky	CLE	1936	9
Ted Williams	BOS	1939	9
Tony Oliva	MIN	1967	9
Nap Lajoie	CLE	1910	8
George Sisler	STL	1922	8
	STL	1927	8
Buddy Myer	WAS	1929	8
Oscar Melillo	STL	1931	8
Sammy West	STL	1933	8
Hank Bauer	NY	1952	8
Johnny Groth	DET	1950	8
Don Baylor	CAL	1978	8
Dan Ford	CAL	1979	8
Jorge Orta	CLE	1980	8

Five-foot four-and-a-half-inch Wee Willie Keeler (*above left*) hit over .370 six times, including his .432 for Baltimore in 1897. Harry Heilmann (*above*) led the A.L. in batting four times on his way to a .342 career mark. Joe Cronin (*left*) led the Senators and Red Sox on the field and in the dugout, assuming managerial duties at age 26.

Most Consecutive Hits, NL

Player	Team	Year	H	Player	Team	Year	H
Ed Delahanty	PHI	1897	10	Ron Cey	LA	1977	9
Jake Gettman	WAS	1897	10	Roger Connor	STL	1895	8
Ed Konetchy	BKN	1919	10	Sammy Strang	CHI	1900	8
Kiki Cuyler	PIT	1925	10	Jack Fournier	BKN	1923	8
Chick Hafey	STL	1929	10	Jimmy Johnston	BKN	1923	8
Joe Medwick	STL	1936	10	Glenn Wright	PIT	1924	8
Buddy Hassett	BOS	1940	10	Chick Hafey	STL	1928	8
Woody Williams	CIN	1943	10	Lefty O'Doul	NY	1933	8
Joe Kelley	BAL	1894	9	Kiki Cuyler	CIN	1936	8
Rogers Hornsby	STL	1924	9	Augie Galan	BKN	1944	8
Taylor Douthit	STL	1926	9	Wayne Terwilliger	CHI	1949	8
Babe Herman	BKN	1926	9	Dick Sisler	PHI	1950	8
Bill Jurges	NY	1941	9	Eddie Waitkus	PHI	1950	8
Terry Moore	STL	1947	9	Sid Gordon	BOS	1952	8
Dave Philley	PHI	1958		Lee Walls	CHI	1958	8
	PHI	1959	9	Curt Flood	STL	1964	8
Felipe Alou	SF	1962	9	Jerry Grote	NY	1970	8
Willie Stargell	PIT	1966	9	Billy Williams	CHI	1972	8
Rennie Stennett	PIT	1975	9	Dave Winfield	SD	1979	8

Most Consecutive Times Struck Out, AL

Player	Team	Year	SO
Dean Chance	CAL	1965	11
Joe Grzenda	WAS	1970	10
Dick Drago	KC	1970	9
Ray Culp	BOS	1971	8
Dave Lemonds	CHI	1972	8
Jim Fuller	BAL	1973	8
Gorman Thomas	MIL	1975	8
Rusty Staub	NY	1983	8
Steve Nicosia	SF	1984	8

Most Consecutive Times Struck Out, NL

Player	Team	Year	SO
Sandy Koufax	BKN	1955	12
Tommie Sisk	PIT	1965	10
Adolfo Phillips	PHI	1966	9
Gary Gentry	NY	1969	9
Wayne Twitchell	PHI	1973	9
Jerry Koosman	NY	1969	8
Richie Hebner	PIT	1971	8

Dave Philley took his lifetime .270 batting average to 10 teams in 12 years, from 1951–62.

"The Beast," Jimmie Foxx (*above*), feasted on pitchers for 534 home runs. *Above right*: Speedy Kiki Cuyler led the N.L. in stolen bases four times and smacked 26 triples for Pittsburgh in 1925. *Right*: Dave Winfield's 104 RBIs in 1986 made him the first player since Willie Mays to drive in 100 runs in five straight seasons.

Home Runs in Most Consecutive At-Bats, AL

Player	Team	Date	HR	Total
Lou Gehrig	NY	Jun 3, 1932	4	4
Jimmie Foxx	PHI	Jun 7, 1933	1	
	PHI	Jun 8, 1933	3	4
Hank Greenberg	DET	Jul 26, 1938	2	
	DET	Jul 27, 1938	2	4
Ted Williams	BOS	Sep 17, 1957	1	
	BOS	Sep 20, 1957	1	
	BOS	Sep 21, 1957	1	
	BOS	Sep 22, 1957	1	4
Charlie Maxwell	DET	May 3, 1959	1	
	DET	May 3, 1959	3	4
Rocky Colavito	CLE	Jun 10, 1959	4	4
Willie Kirkland	CLE	Jul 9, 1961	3	
	CLE	Jul 13, 1961	1	4
Johnny Blanchard	NY	Jul 21, 1961	1	
	NY	Jul 22, 1961	1	
	NY	Jul 26, 1961	2	4
Mickey Mantle	NY	Jul 4, 1962	2	
	NY	Jul 6, 1962	2	4
Bobby Murcer	NY	Jun 24, 1970	1	
	NY	Jun 24, 1970	3	4
Mike Epstein	OAK	Jun 15, 1971	2	
	OAK	Jun 16, 1971	2	4
Don Baylor	BAL	Jul 1, 1975	1	
	BAL	Jul 2, 1975	3	4
Larry Herndon	DET	May 16, 1982	1	
	DET	May 18, 1982	3	4

Home Runs in Most Consecutive At-Bats, NL

Player	Team	Date	HR	Total
Bobby Lowe	BOS	May 30, 1894	4	4
Bill Nicholson	CHI	Jul 22, 1944	1	
	CHI	Jul 23, 1944	3	4
Ralph Kiner	PIT	Aug 15, 1947	1	
	PIT	Aug 16, 1947	3	4
	PIT	Sep 11, 1949	2	
	PIT	Sep 13, 1949	2	4
Stan Musial	STL	Jul 7, 1962	1	
	STL	Jul 8, 1962	3	4
Art Shamsky	CIN	Aug 12, 1966	3	
	CIN	Aug 14, 1966	1	4
Deron Johnson	PHI	Jul 10, 1971	1	
	PHI	Jul 11, 1971	3	4
Mike Schmidt	PHI	Apr 17, 1976	4	4
	PHI	Jul 6, 1979	1	
	PHI	Jul 7, 1979	3	4

Individual Pitching Records

"The Big Train," Walter Johnson (*left*), won 60 percent of his games over 21 years. *Above*: Giants' ace Christy Mathewson posted the following performance in the 1905 World Series: 3–0, 27 IP, 0.00 ERA, 18 Ks.

Most Shutouts, Career

Player	ShO
Walter Johnson	110
Grover Alexander	90
Christy Mathewson	80
Cy Young	76
Eddie Plank	69
Warren Spahn	63
Tom Seaver	61
Don Sutton	58
Three Finger Brown	57
Pud Galvin	57
Ed Walsh	57
Bob Gibson	56
Steve Carlton	55
Bert Blyleven	54
Nolan Ryan	54
Jim Palmer	53
Gaylord Perry	53
Juan Marichal	52
Rube Waddell	50
Vic Willis	50

Player	ShO
Don Drysdale	49
Ferguson Jenkins	49
Luis Tiant	49
Early Wynn	49
Kid Nichols	48
Red Ruffing	48
Babe Adams	47
Jack Powell	47
Bob Feller	46
Addie Joss	46
Doc White	46
Whitey Ford	45
Tommy John	45
Phil Niekro	45
Robin Roberts	45
Milt Pappas	43
Catfish Hunter	42
Bucky Walters	42
Chief Bender	41
Mickey Lolich	41

Most Shutouts, Career *(cont'd)*

Player	ShO
Hippo Vaughn	41
Jim Bunning	40
Larry French	40
Tim Keefe	40
Sandy Koufax	40
Claude Osteen	40
Ed Reulbach	40
Mel Stottlemyre	40
Mickey Welch	40
Sam Leever	39
Eppa Rixey	39
Stan Coveleski	38
Billy Pierce	38
Nap Rucker	38
Vida Blue	37
John Clarkson	37
Larry Jackson	37
Steve Rogers	37
Tommy Bond	36
Eddie Cicotte	36
Wilbur Cooper	36
Mike Cuellar	36
Bill Doak	36
Bob Friend	36
Carl Hubbell	36
Sad Sam Jones	36
Camilo Pascual	36
Jerry Reuss	36
Allie Reynolds	36
Curt Simmons	36
Will White	36
Joe Bush	35
Jack Chesbro	35
Jack Coombs	35
Wild Bill Donovan	35
Burleigh Grimes	35
Lefty Grove	35
George Mullin	35
Herb Pennock	35
Old Hoss Radbourn	35
Virgil Trucks	35

Most Shutout Losses, Career

Player	ShO L
Walter Johnson	65
Cy Young	48
Phil Niekro	47
Claude Osteen	47
Bob Friend	45
Ferguson Jenkins	45
Early Wynn	45
Robin Roberts	44
Jim McCormick	43
Pud Galvin	42
Gaylord Perry	42
Jack Powell	42
Jim Bunning	41
Mickey Lolich	41
Nolan Ryan	39
Grover Alexander	38
Red Ames	38
Fritz Peterson	38
Stan Bahnsen	37
Steve Carlton	37
Bobo Newsom	37
Hippo Vaughn	37
Vic Willis	37
Paul Derringer	36
Don Drysdale	36
Burleigh Grimes	36
Rudy May	36
Nap Rucker	36
Tom Seaver	36
Jim Kaat	35

Most Shutouts, Season, AL

Player	Team	Year	ShO
Jack Coombs	PHI	1910	13
Ed Walsh	CHI	1908	12
Walter Johnson	WAS	1913	12
Dean Chance	LA	1964	11
Cy Young	BOS	1904	10
Ed Walsh	CHI	1906	10
Joe Wood	BOS	1912	10
Walter Johnson	WAS	1914	10
Bob Feller	CLE	1946	10
Bob Lemon	CLE	1948	10
Jim Palmer	BAL	1975	10

Most Shutouts, Season, NL

Player	Team	Year	ShO
George Bradley	STL	1876	16
Grover Alexander	PHI	1916	16
Bob Gibson	STL	1968	13
Tommy Bond	BOS	1879	12
Pud Galvin	BUF	1884	12
Christy Mathewson	NY	1908	12
Grover Alexander	PHI	1915	12
Old Hoss Radbourn	PRO	1884	11
Sandy Koufax	LA	1963	11
John Clarkson	CHI	1885	10
Three Finger Brown	CHI	1906	10
Carl Hubbell	NY	1933	10
Mort Cooper	STL	1942	10
Juan Marichal	SF	1965	10
John Tudor	STL	1985	10

Most Shutout Losses, Season, AL

Player	Team	Year	ShO L	W	L
Walter Johnson	WAS	1909	10	13	25
Casey Patten	WAS	1904	9	15	23
Patsy Flaherty	CHI	1903	8	11	25
Harry Howell	STL	1905	8	15	22
Joe Harris	BOS	1906	8	3	21
Fred Glade	STL	1906	8	16	15
Ed Walsh	CHI	1907	8	24	18
Tom Murphy	CAL	1971	8	6	17
Nolan Ryan	CAL	1976	8	17	18

Most Shutout Losses, Season, NL

Player	Team	Year	ShO L	W	L
Jim Devlin	LOU	1876	14	30	35
Dupee Shaw	PRO	1885	11	23	26
Bugs Raymond	STL	1908	11	14	25
Jim McCormick	CLE	1880	10	45	28
	CLE	1879	9	20	40
Irv Young	BOS	1906	9	16	25
Roger Craig	NY	1963	9	5	22
Ferguson Jenkins	CHI	1968	9	20	15
Tommy Bond	BOS	1880	8	26	29
Will White	CIN	1880	8	18	42
Jim McCormick	CLE	1882	8	35	29
Vive Lindaman	BOS	1906	8	12	23
Jim Pastorius	BKN	1908	8	4	20
George McQuillan	PHI	1908	8	23	17
Erv Kantlehner	PIT	1915	8	6	12
Bob Bruce	HOU	1965	8	9	18
Ray Sadecki	SF	1968	8	12	18

Left: Fernando Valenzuela's screwball has averaged him 16 wins and 210 strikeouts in his first six full seasons. Grover Cleveland Alexander (*below left*) had an ERA under 2.00 six seasons in a row, starting with a 31–10, 1.22 mark in 1915. Dave McNally (*below*) had four consecutive 20-win seasons from 1968–71.

Shutout in First Start in Majors, AL

Player	Team	Date	Score	Inns.	Opp.
Bill Cristall	CLE	Sep 2, 1901	4-0		BOS
Addie Joss	CLE	Apr 26, 1902	3-0		STL
Jack Coombs	PHI	Jul 5, 1906	3-0		WAS
Slow Joe Doyle	NY	Aug 25, 1906	2-0		CLE
Rube Kroh	BOS	Sep 30, 1906	2-0		STL
Tex Neuer	NY	Aug 28, 1907	1-0		BOS
Pete Wilson	NY	Sep 15, 1908	1-0		BOS
King Brady	BOS	Oct 5, 1908	4-0		NY
Jim Scott	CHI	Apr 25, 1909	1-0		STL
Larry Pape	BOS	Jul 6, 1909	2-0		WAS
Sailor Stroud	DET	Apr 29, 1910	5-0		STL
Fred Blanding	CLE	Sep 15, 1910	3-0		WAS
Lefty Russell	PHI	Oct 1, 1910	3-0		BOS
Buck O'Brien	BOS	Sep 9, 1911	2-0		PHI
Elmer Brown	STL	Sep 16, 1911	6-0		WAS
Stan Coveleski	PHI	Sep 12, 1912	3-0		DET
Jack Bentley	WAS	Oct 1, 1913	1-0	8	PHI
Adam Johnson	BOS	Apr 13, 1914	5-0		WAS
George Dumont	WAS	Sep 14, 1915	3-0		CLE
Elmer Myers	PHI	Oct 6, 1915	4-0		WAS
Claude Thomas	WAS	Sep 18, 1916	1-0		PHI
Bob Clark	CLE	Aug 15, 1920	5-0		DET
Ray Benge	CLE	Sep 26, 1925	6-0		PHI
Bob Weiland	CHI	Sep 30, 1928	1-0		PHI
Schoolboy Rowe	DET	Apr 15, 1933	3-0		CHI
Russ Van Atta	NY	Apr 25, 1933	16-0		WAS
Johnny Marcum	PHI	Sep 7, 1933	6-0		CLE
George Hockette	BOS	Sep 17, 1934	3-0		STL
Vito Tamulis	NY	Sep 25, 1934	5-0		PHI
Henry Coppola	WAS	Jun 6, 1935	3-0		PHI
George Gill	DET	May 13, 1937	4-0		BOS
Boo Ferriss	BOS	Apr 29, 1945	2-0		PHI
Bill McCahan	PHI	Sep 15, 1946	2-0	7	CLE
Fred Sanford	STL	Sep 15, 1946	1-0		NY
Sandy Consuegra	WAS	Jun 10, 1950	6-0	5	CHI
Mike Fornieles	WAS	Sep 2, 1952	5-0		PHI
Raul Sanchez	WAS	Sep 5, 1952	2-0		BOS
Bobo Holloman	STL	May 6, 1953	6-0		PHI
Ben Flowers	BOS	Aug 5, 1953	5-0		STL
Wally Burnette	KC	Jul 15, 1956	8-0		WAS
Charlie Beamon	BAL	Sep 26, 1956	1-0		NY
Lew Krausse	KC	Jun 16, 1961	4-0		LA
Dave McNally	BAL	Sep 26, 1962	3-0		KC
Dave Morehead	BOS	Apr 13, 1963	3-0		WAS
Luis Tiant	CLE	Jul 19, 1964	3-0		NY
Don Loun	WAS	Sep 23, 1964	1-0		BOS
Tom Phoebus	BAL	Sep 15, 1966	2-0		CAL
Billy Rohr	BOS	Apr 14, 1967	3-0		NY
Mike Norris	OAK	Apr 10, 1975	9-0		CHI

Shutout in First Start in Majors, NL

Player	Team	Date	Score	Inns.	Opp.
Al Spalding	CHI	Apr 25, 1876	4-0		LOU
Monte Ward	PRO	Jul 20, 1878	3-0		IND
John Hibbard	CHI	Jul 31, 1884	4-0		DET
John Henry	CLE	Aug 13, 1884	1-0		DET
Bill Stemmyer	BOS	Oct 3, 1885	18-0	6	BUF
Frank Dwyer	CHI	Sep 20, 1888	11-0		WAS
John Scheible	CLE	Sep 8, 1893	7-0		WAS
Roger Bresnahan	WAS	Aug 27, 1897	3-0		STL
Jim Hughes	BAL	Apr 18, 1898	9-0		WAS
Bill Phyle	CHI	Sep 17, 1898	9-0		WAS
Alex Hardy	CHI	Sep 4, 1902	1-0		BKN
Red Ames	NY	Sep 14, 1903	5-0	5	STL
Lefty Leifield	PIT	Sep 3, 1905	1-0	6	CHI
Vive Lindaman	BOS	Apr 14, 1906	1-0		BKN
Nick Maddox	PIT	Sep 13, 1907	4-0		STL
Bob Spade	CIN	Sep 22, 1907	1-0		NY
Tom Tuckey	BOS	Aug 11, 1908	2-0		STL
Cliff Curtis	BOS	Sep 2, 1909	1-0		PIT
King Cole	CHI	Oct 6, 1909	8-0		STL
Eddie Stack	PHI	Jun 7, 1910	1-0		CHI
Wilbur Cooper	PIT	Sep 6, 1912	8-0		STL
Al Demaree	NY	Sep 26, 1912	4-0		BOS
Erv Kantlehner	PIT	Apr 17, 1914	2-0		STL
Pete Schneider	CIN	Jun 28, 1914	1-0		PIT
Carmen Hill	PIT	Sep 17, 1915	5-0		NY
Harry Shriver	BKN	May 1, 1922	2-0		PHI
Earl Caldwell	PHI	Sep 8, 1928	4-0		BOS
Van Mungo	BKN	Sep 7, 1931	2-0		BOS
Ray Starr	STL	Sep 15, 1932	3-0		BKN
Hal Smith	PIT	Sep 22, 1932	7-0		CHI
Bill Lee	CHI	May 7, 1934	2-0		PHI
Hal Kelleher	PHI	Sep 17, 1935	1-0		CIN
Tot Pressnell	BKN	Apr 21, 1938	9-0		PHI
Don Newcombe	BKN	May 22, 1949	3-0		CIN
Bill Macdonald	PIT	May 23, 1950	6-0		PHI
Paul LaPalme	PIT	Jun 5, 1951	8-0		BOS
Niles Jordan	PHI	Aug 26, 1951	2-0		CIN
Jackie Collum	STL	Sep 21, 1951	6-0		CHI
Stu Miller	STL	Aug 12, 1952	1-0		CHI
Al Worthington	NY	Jul 6, 1953	6-0		PIT
Karl Spooner	BKN	Sep 22, 1954	3-0		NY
Von McDaniel	STL	Jun 21, 1957	2-0		BKN
Carl Willey	MIL	Jun 23, 1958	7-0		SF
Juan Marichal	SF	Jul 19, 1960	2-0		PHI
Nick Willhite	LA	Jun 16, 1963	2-0		CHI
Grover Powell	NY	Aug 20, 1963	4-0		PHI
Dick Rusteck	NY	Jun 10, 1966	5-0		CIN
Jim Cosman	STL	Oct 2, 1966	2-0		CHI
Wayne Simpson	CIN	Apr 9, 1970	3-0		LA
Ed Acosta	SD	Aug 24, 1971	2-0		PHI
Dave Downs	PHI	Sep 2, 1972	3-0		ATL

Shutout in First Start in Majors, NL *(cont'd)*

Player	Team	Date	Score	Inns.	Opp.
Eric Rasmussen	STL	Jul 21, 1975	4-0		SD
Charlie Leibrandt	CIN	Apr 13, 1980	5-0		ATL
Marty Bystrom	PHI	Sep 10, 1980	5-0		NY
Fernando Valenzuela	LA	Apr 9, 1981	2-0		HOU
Jimmy Jones	SD	Sep 21, 1986	5-0		HOU

Shutout in First Two Major League Games, AL

Player	Team	Date	Score	Opp.
Slow Joe Doyle	NY	Aug 25, 1906	2-0	CLE
	NY	Aug 30, 1906	5-0	WAS
Johnny Marcum	PHI	Sep 7, 1933	6-0	CLE
	PHI	Sep 11, 1933	8-0	CHI
Boo Ferriss	BOS	Apr 29, 1945	2-0	PHI
	BOS	May 6, 1945	5-0	NY
Tom Phoebus	BAL	Sep 15, 1966	2-0	CAL
	BAL	Sep 20, 1966	4-0	KC

Shutout in First Two Major League Games, NL

Player	Team	Date	Score	Opp.
Al Spalding	CHI	Apr 25, 1876	4-0	LOU
	CHI	Apr 27, 1876	10-0	LOU
Monte Ward	PRO	Jul 18, 1878	3-0	IND
	PRO	Jul 20, 1878	4-0	IND
Jim Hughes	BAL	Apr 18, 1898	9-0	WAS
	BAL	Apr 22, 1898	8-0	BOS
Al Worthington	NY	Jul 6, 1953	6-0	PIT
	NY	Jul 11, 1953	6-0	BKN
Karl Spooner	BKN	Sep 22, 1954	3-0	NY
	BKN	Sep 26, 1954	1-0	PIT

Shutout with Most Hits Allowed, AL

Player	Team	Date	Score	H	Inns.	Opp.
Walter Johnson	WAS	Jul 3, 1913	1-0	15	15	BOS
Milt Gaston	WAS	Jul 10, 1928	9-0	14		CLE
Mudcat Grant	MIN	Jul 15, 1964	6-0	13		WAS
Bob Shawkey	NY	Jul 13, 1920	14-0	12		CLE
Duster Mails	CLE	Jul 10, 1921	10-0	12		PHI
Stan Bahnsen	CHI	Jun 21, 1973	2-0	12		OAK
Harry Howell	STL	Jun 23, 1906	9-0	11		CLE
Jack Chesbro	NY	Aug 19, 1908	8-0	11		DET
Reb Russell	CHI	May 24, 1917	1-0	11	12	WAS
Jim Bagby	CLE	Aug 6, 1918	1-0	11	10	WAS
Waite Hoyt	NY	Jul 1, 1924	7-0	11		PHI
Earl Whitehill	DET	Jul 5, 1924	3-0	11		STL
Herb Pennock	NY	Jun 6, 1933	4-0	11		BOS
Ed Lopat	NY	Jul 17, 1948	4-0	11		STL
Bob Kuzava	NY	Aug 17, 1953	9-0	11		PHI
Robin Roberts	BAL	Jul 17, 1964	5-0	11		DET
Jim Kaat	MIN	Apr 11, 1971	6-0	11		CHI
Marty Pattin	MIL	Jun 26, 1971	5-0	11		MIN
Gaylord Perry	TEX	Jul 28, 1977	3-0	11		TOR
Rick Lysander	MIN	Aug 1, 1983	7-0	11		OAK

Shutout with Most Hits Allowed, NL

Player	Team	Date	Score	H	Opp.
Larry Cheney	CHI	Sep 14, 1913	7-0	14	NY
Scott Stratton	LOU	Sep 19, 1893	3-0	13	NY
Ned Garvin	CHI	Sep 22, 1899	3-0	13	BOS
Bill Lee	CHI	Sep 17, 1938	4-0	13	NY
Nixey Callahan	CHI	Apr 30, 1899	4-0	12	STL
Pol Perritt	NY	Sep 14, 1917	5-0	12	BOS
Rube Benton	NY	Aug 28, 1920	4-0	12	CIN
Leon Cadore	BKN	Sep 4, 1920	10-0	12	BOS
George Smith	PHI	Aug 12, 1921	4-0	12	BOS
Hal Schumacher	NY	Jul 19, 1934	4-0	12	CIN
Fritz Ostermueller	PIT	May 17, 1947	4-0	12	BKN
Bob Friend	PIT	Sep 24, 1959	6-0	12	STL
Jouett Meekin	NY	Jun 17, 1897	5-0	11	CLE
Bill Damman	CIN	May 6, 1899	11-0	11	STL
Charlie Case	PIT	Aug 1, 1904	4-0	11	CHI
Babe Adams	PIT	Aug 9, 1910	10-0	11	BOS
Three Finger Brown	CHI	Aug 15, 1910	14-0	11	BKN
Christy Mathewson	NY	Aug 11, 1911	6-0	11	PHI
Dan Griner	STL	Jun 24, 1913	1-0	11	CHI
Fred Baczewski	CIN	Jun 10, 1954	6-0	11	PIT
Bob Purkey	CIN	Aug 15, 1960	4-0	11	MIL
Billy O'Dell	SF	Jul 30, 1963	5-0	11	PHI

No-Hitters, AL (9 innings or more)

Player	Team	Date	Score	BB	SO	E	Opp.	Opp. Pitcher
Earl Moore	CLE	May 9, 1901	2-4	4	4	1	CHI	John Katoll
Nixey Callahan	CHI	Sep 20, 1902	3-0	2	2	1	DET	Wish Egan
Cy Young	BOS	May 5, 1904	3-0	0	8	0	PHI	Rube Waddell
Jesse Tannehill	BOS	Aug 17, 1904	6-0	1	4	0	CHI	Ed Walsh
Weldon Henley	PHI	Jul 22, 1905	6-0	3	5	1	STL	Barney Pelty
Frank Smith	CHI	Sep 6, 1905	15-0	3	8	0	DET	Jimmy Wiggs
Bill Dinneen	BOS	Sep 27, 1905	2-0	2	6	0	CHI	Frank Owen
Cy Young	BOS	Jun 30, 1908	8-0	1	2	0	NY	Rube Manning
Bob Rhoads	CLE	Sep 18, 1908	2-1	2	2	2	BOS	Frank Arellanes
Frank Smith	CHI	Sep 20, 1908	1-0	1	2	1	PHI	Eddie Plank
Addie Joss	CLE	Oct 2, 1908	1-0	0	3	0	CHI	Ed Walsh
	CLE	Apr 20, 1910	1-0	2	2	1	CHI	Doc White
Chief Bender	PHI	May 12, 1910	4-0	1	4	0	CLE	Fred Link
Tom Hughes	NY	Aug 30, 1910	0-5	0	4	1	CLE	George Kahler
Joe Wood	BOS	Jul 29, 1911	5-0	2	12	1	STL	Joe Lake
Ed Walsh	CHI	Aug 27, 1911	5-0	1	8	0	BOS	Ray Collins
George Mullin	DET	Jul 4, 1912	7-0	5	5	1	STL	Willie Adams
Earl Hamilton	STL	Aug 30, 1912	5-1	2	3	2	DET	Jean Dubuc
Jim Scott	CHI	May 14, 1914	0-1	3	2	3	WAS	Doc Ayers
Joe Benz	CHI	May 31, 1914	6-1	2	6	3	CLE	Abe Bowman
Rube Foster	BOS	Jun 21, 1916	2-0	3	3	0	NY	Bob Shawkey
Joe Bush	PHI	Aug 26, 1916	5-0	1	7	0	CLE	Stan Coveleski
Dutch Leonard	BOS	Aug 30, 1916	4-0	2	5	0	STL	Carl Weilman
Eddie Cicotte	CHI	Apr 14, 1917	11-0	3	5	1	STL	Earl Hamilton
George Mogridge	NY	Apr 24, 1917	2-1	3	3	3	BOS	Dutch Leonard
Ernie Koob	STL	May 5, 1917	1-0	5	2	2	CHI	Eddie Cicotte
Bob Groom	STL	May 6, 1917	3-0	3	4	0	CHI	Joe Benz
Ernie Shore	BOS	Jun 23, 1917	4-0	0	2	0	WAS	Doc Ayers
Dutch Leonard	BOS	Jun 3, 1918	5-0	1	4	0	DET	Hooks Dauss
Ray Caldwell	CLE	Sep 10, 1919	3-0	1	5	1	NY	Carl Mays
Walter Johnson	WAS	Jul 1, 1920	1-0	0	10	1	BOS	Harry Harper
Charlie Robertson	CHI	Apr 30, 1922	2-0	0	6	0	DET	Herman Pillette
Sad Sam Jones	NY	Sep 4, 1923	2-0	1	0	1	PHI	Bob Hasty
Howard Ehmke	BOS	Sep 7, 1923	4-0	1	1	1	PHI	Slim Harriss
Ted Lyons	CHI	Aug 21, 1926	6-0	1	2	1	BOS	Slim Harriss
Wes Ferrell	CLE	Apr 29, 1931	9-0	3	8	3	STL	Sam Gray
Bobby Burke	WAS	Aug 8, 1931	5-0	5	8	0	BOS	Wilcy Moore
Bobo Newsom	STL	Sep 18, 1934	1-2	7	9	3	BOS	Wes Ferrell
Vern Kennedy	CHI	Aug 31, 1935	5-0	4	5	0	CLE	Willis Hudlin
Bill Dietrich	CHI	Jun 1, 1937	8-0	2	5	1	STL	Chief Hogsett
Monte Pearson	NY	Aug 27, 1938	13-0	2	7	0	CLE	John Humphries
Bob Feller	CLE	Apr 16, 1940	1-0	5	8	1	CHI	Eddie Smith
Dick Fowler	PHI	Sep 9, 1945	1-0	4	6	0	STL	Ox Miller
Bob Feller	CLE	Apr 30, 1946	1-0	5	11	2	NY	Bill Bevens
Don Black	CLE	Jul 10, 1947	3-0	6	5	0	PHI	Bill McCahan
Bill McCahan	PHI	Sep 3, 1947	3-0	0	2	1	WAS	Ray Scarborough
Bob Lemon	CLE	Jun 30, 1948	2-0	3	4	0	DET	Art Houtteman
Bob Feller	CLE	Jul 1, 1951	2-1	3	5	2	DET	Bob Cain
Allie Reynolds	NY	Jul 12, 1951	1-0	3	4	1	CLE	Bob Feller
	NY	Sep 28, 1951	8-0	4	9	1	BOS	Mel Parnell
Virgil Trucks	DET	May 15, 1952	1-0	1	7	3	WAS	Bob Porterfield

No-Hitters, AL (9 innings or more) *(cont'd)*

Player	Team	Date	Score	BB	SO	E	Opp.	Opp. Pitcher
Virgil Trucks	DET	Aug 25, 1952	1-0	1	8	2	NY	Bill Miller
Bobo Holloman	STL	May 6, 1953	6-0	5	3	1	PHI	Morrie Martin
Mel Parnell	BOS	Jul 14, 1956	4-0	2	4	0	CHI	Jim McDonald
Don Larsen	NY	Oct 8, 1956	2-0	0	7	0	BKN	Sal Maglie
Bob Keegan	CHI	Aug 20, 1957	6-0	2	1	0	WAS	Chuck Stobbs
Jim Bunning	DET	Jul 20, 1958	3-0	2	12	0	BOS	Frank Sullivan
Hoyt Wilhelm	BAL	Sep 20, 1958	1-0	2	8	0	NY	Don Larsen
Bo Belinsky	LA	May 1, 1962	2-0	5	9	1	BAL	Steve Barber
Earl Wilson	BOS	Jun 26, 1962	2-0	4	5	0	LA	Bo Belinsky
Bill Monbouquette	BOS	Aug 1, 1962	1-0	1	7	0	CHI	Early Wynn
Jack Kralick	MIN	Aug 26, 1962	1-0	1	3	0	KC	Bill Fischer
Dave Morehead	BOS	Sep 16, 1965	2-0	1	8	0	CLE	Luis Tiant
Sonny Siebert	CLE	Jun 10, 1966	2-0	1	7	1	WAS	Phil Ortega
Dean Chance	MIN	Aug 25, 1967	2-1	5	9	1	CLE	Sonny Siebert
Joe Horlen	CHI	Sep 10, 1967	6-0	0	4	1	DET	Joe Sparma
Tom Phoebus	BAL	Apr 27, 1968	6-0	3	9	0	BOS	Gary Waslewski
Catfish Hunter	OAK	May 8, 1968	4-0	0	11	0	MIN	Dave Boswell
Jim Palmer	BAL	Aug 13, 1969	8-0	6	8	2	OAK	Chuck Dobson
Clyde Wright	CAL	Jul 3, 1970	4-0	3	1	0	OAK	Chuck Dobson
Vida Blue	OAK	Sep 21, 1970	6-0	1	9	0	MIN	Jim Perry
Steve Busby	KC	Apr 27, 1973	3-0	6	4	0	DET	Jim Perry
Nolan Ryan	CAL	May 15, 1973	3-0	3	12	0	KC	Bruce Dal Canton
	CAL	Jul 15, 1973	6-0	4	17	0	DET	Jim Perry
Jim Bibby	TEX	Jul 30, 1973	8-0	6	13	0	OAK	Vida Blue
Steve Busby	KC	Jun 19, 1974	2-0	1	3	0	MIL	Clyde Wright
Dick Bosman	CLE	Jul 19, 1974	4-0	0	4	1	OAK	Dave Hamilton
Nolan Ryan	CAL	Sep 28, 1974	4-0	8	15	0	MIN	Joe Decker
	CAL	Jun 1, 1975	1-0	4	9	1	BAL	Ross Grimsley
Jim Colborn	KC	May 14, 1977	6-0	1	6	0	TEX	Tommy Boggs
Dennis Eckersley	CLE	May 30, 1977	1-0	1	12	0	CAL	Frank Tanana
Bert Blyleven	TEX	Sep 22, 1977	6-0	1	7	0	CAL	Paul Hartzell
Len Barker	CLE	May 15, 1981	3-0	0	11	0	TOR	Luis Leal
Dave Righetti	NY	Jul 4, 1983	4-0	4	9	0	BOS	John Tudor
Mike Warren	OAK	Sep 29, 1983	3-0	3	5	0	CHI	Britt Burns
Jack Morris	DET	Apr 7, 1984	4-0	6	8	0	CHI	Floyd Bannister
Mike Witt	CAL	Sep 30, 1984	1-0	0	10	0	TEX	Charlie Hough
Joe Cowley	CHI	Sep 19, 1986	7-1	7	8	0	CAL	Kirk McCaskill

No-Hitters, NL (9 innings or more)

Player	Team	Date	Score	BB	SO	E	Opp.	Opp. Pitcher
George Bradley	STL	Jul 15, 1876	2-0	1	3	3	HAR	Tommy Bond
Lee Richmond	WOR	Jun 12, 1880	1-0	0	5	0	CLE	Jim McCormick
Monte Ward	PRO	Jun 17, 1880	5-0	0	7	0	BUF	Pud Galvin
Larry Corcoran	CHI	Aug 19, 1880	6-0	2	4	2	BOS	Tommy Bond
Pud Galvin	BUF	Aug 20, 1880	1-0	0	2	6	WOR	Fred Corey
Larry Corcoran	CHI	Sep 20, 1882	5-0	1	3	4	WOR	Frank Mountain
Old Hoss Radbourn	PRO	Jul 25, 1883	8-0	0	6	1	CLE	One Arm Daily
One Arm Daily	CLE	Sep 13, 1883	1-0	3	2	2	PHI	John Coleman
Larry Corcoran	CHI	Jun 27, 1884	6-0	1	6	6	PRO	Charlie Sweeney
Pud Galvin	BUF	Aug 4, 1884	18-0	0	7	2	DET	Frank Meinke

No-Hitters, NL (9 innings or more) *(cont'd)*

Player	Team	Date	Score	BB	SO	E	Opp.	Opp. Pitcher
John Clarkson	CHI	Jul 27, 1885	4-0	0	4	5	PRO	Old Hoss Radbourn
Charlie Ferguson	PHI	Aug 29, 1885	1-0	2	8	6	PRO	Dupee Shaw
Tom Lovett	BKN	Jun 22, 1891	4-0	3	4	0	NY	Amos Rusie
Amos Rusie	NY	Jul 31, 1891	6-0	8	4	2	BKN	Adonis Terry
Jack Stivetts	BOS	Aug 6, 1892	11-0	5	6	3	BKN	Ed Stein
Ben Sanders	LOU	Aug 22, 1892	6-2	3	0	4	BAL	Sadie McMahon
Bumpus Jones	CIN	Oct 15, 1892	7-1	3	1	0	PIT	Mark Baldwin
Bill Hawke	BAL	Aug 16, 1893	5-0	2	6	0	WAS	George Stephens
Cy Young	CLE	Sep 18, 1897	6-0	1	3	3	CIN	Billy Rhines
Ted Breitenstein	CIN	Apr 22, 1898	11-0	1	2	1	PIT	Charlie Hastings
Jim Hughes	BAL	Apr 22, 1898	8-0	2	3	0	BOS	Ted Lewis
Red Donahue	PHI	Jul 8, 1898	5-0	2	1	0	BOS	Vic Willis
Walter Thornton	CHI	Aug 21, 1898	2-0	3	3	0	BKN	Brickyard Kennedy
Deacon Phillippe	LOU	May 25, 1899	7-0	2	1	0	NY	Ed Doheny
Vic Willis	BOS	Aug 7, 1899	7-1	4	5	3	WAS	Bill Dinneen
Noodles Hahn	CIN	Jul 12, 1900	4-0	2	8	1	PHI	Bill Bernhard
Christy Mathewson	NY	Jul 15, 1901	5-0	4	4	1	STL	Willie Sudhoff
Chick Fraser	PHI	Sep 18, 1903	10-0	5	4	4	CHI	Peaches Graham
Bob Wicker	CHI	Jun 11, 1904	1-0	1	10	1	NY	Joe McGinnity
Christy Mathewson	NY	Jun 13, 1905	1-0	0	2	2	CHI	Three Finger Brown
Johnny Lush	PHI	May 1, 1906	1-0	3	11	1	BKN	Mal Eason
Mal Eason	BKN	Jul 20, 1906	2-0	3	5	1	STL	Gus Thompson
Harry McIntyre	BKN	Aug 1, 1906	0-1	1	8	1	PIT	Lefty Leifield
Big Jeff Pfeffer	BOS	May 8, 1907	6-0	1	3	1	CIN	Del Mason
Nick Maddox	PIT	Sep 20, 1907	2-1	3	5	2	BKN	Elmer Stricklett
Hooks Wiltse	NY	Jul 4, 1908	1-0	0	6	0	PHI	George McQuillan
Nap Rucker	BKN	Sep 5, 1908	6-0	0	14	3	BOS	Patsy Flaherty
Red Ames	NY	Apr 15, 1909	0-3	2	9	0	BKN	Kaiser Wilhelm
Jeff Tesreau	NY	Sep 6, 1912	3-0	2	2	2	PHI	Eppa Rixey
George Davis	BOS	Sep 9, 1914	7-0	5	4	2	PHI	Ben Tincup
Rube Marquard	NY	Apr 15, 1915	2-0	2	2	1	BKN	Nap Rucker
Jimmy Lavender	CHI	Aug 31, 1915	2-0	1	8	1	NY	Rube Schauer
Tom Hughes	BOS	Jun 16, 1916	2-0	2	3	0	PIT	Erv Kantlehner
Fred Toney	CIN	May 2, 1917	1-0	2	3	0	CHI	Hippo Vaughn
Hippo Vaughn	CHI	May 2, 1917	0-1	2	10	2	CIN	Fred Toney
Hod Eller	CIN	May 11, 1919	6-0	3	8	0	STL	Jakie May
Jesse Barnes	NY	May 7, 1922	6-0	1	5	0	PHI	Lee Meadows
Jesse Haines	STL	Jul 17, 1924	5-0	3	5	2	BOS	Tim McNamara
Dazzy Vance	BKN	Sep 13, 1925	10-1	1	9	3	PHI	Clarence Mitchell
Carl Hubbell	NY	May 8, 1929	11-0	1	4	3	PIT	Jesse Petty
Paul Dean	STL	Sep 21, 1934	3-0	1	6	0	BKN	Ray Benge
Johnny Vander Meer	CIN	Jun 11, 1938	3-0	3	4	0	BOS	Danny MacFayden
	CIN	Jun 15, 1938	6-0	8	7	0	BKN	Max Butcher
Tex Carleton	BKN	May 30, 1940	3-0	2	4	3	CIN	Jim Turner
Lon Warneke	STL	Aug 30, 1941	2-0	1	2	2	CIN	Elmer Riddle
Jim Tobin	BOS	Apr 27, 1944	2-0	2	6	0	BKN	Fritz Ostermueller
Clyde Shoun	CIN	May 15, 1944	1-0	1	1	0	BOS	Jim Tobin
Ed Head	BKN	Apr 23, 1946	5-0	3	2	1	BOS	Mort Cooper
Ewell Blackwell	CIN	Jun 18, 1947	6-0	4	3	0	BOS	Ed Wright
Rex Barney	BKN	Sep 9, 1948	2-0	3	4	2	NY	Monte Kennedy
Vern Bickford	BOS	Aug 11, 1950	7-0	4	3	0	BKN	Carl Erskine

No-Hitters, NL (9 innings or more) ***(cont'd)***

Player	Team	Date	Score	BB	SO	E	Opp.	Opp. Pitcher
Cliff Chambers	PIT	May 6, 1951	3-0	8	4	0	BOS	George Estock
Carl Erskine	BKN	Jun 19, 1952	5-0	1	1	0	CHI	Warren Hacker
Jim Wilson	MIL	Jun 12, 1954	2-0	2	6	0	PHI	Robin Roberts
Sam Jones	CHI	May 12, 1955	4-0	7	6	0	PIT	Nellie King
Carl Erskine	BKN	May 12, 1956	3-0	2	3	0	NY	Al Worthington
Sal Maglie	BKN	Sep 25, 1956	5-0	2	3	0	PHI	Jack Meyer
Harvey Haddix	PIT	May 26, 1959	0-1	1	8	0	MIL	Lew Burdette
Don Cardwell	CHI	May 15, 1960	4-0	1	7	0	STL	Lindy McDaniel
Lew Burdette	MIL	Aug 18, 1960	1-0	0	3	0	PHI	Gene Conley
Warren Spahn	MIL	Sep 16, 1960	4-0	2	15	0	PHI	John Buzhardt
	MIL	Apr 28, 1961	1-0	2	9	0	SF	Sam Jones
Sandy Koufax	LA	Jun 30, 1962	5-0	5	13	0	NY	Bob Miller
	LA	May 11, 1963	8-0	2	4	0	SF	Juan Marichal
Don Nottebart	HOU	May 17, 1963	4-1	3	8	1	PHI	Jack Hamilton
Juan Marichal	SF	Jun 15, 1963	1-0	2	5	0	HOU	Dick Drott
Ken Johnson	HOU	Apr 23, 1964	0-1	2	9	2	CIN	Joe Nuxhall
Sandy Koufax	LA	Jun 4, 1964	3-0	1	10	0	PHI	Chris Short
Jim Bunning	PHI	Jun 21, 1964	6-0	0	10	0	NY	Tracy Stallard
Jim Maloney	CIN	Jun 14, 1965	0-1	1	18	0	NY	Larry Bearnarth
	CIN	Aug 19, 1965	1-0	10	12	1	CHI	Larry Jackson
Sandy Koufax	LA	Sep 9, 1965	1-0	0	14	0	CHI	Bob Hendley
Don Wilson	HOU	Jun 18, 1967	2-0	3	15	0	ATL	Phil Niekro
George Culver	CIN	Jul 29, 1968	6-1	5	4	3	PHI	Chris Short
Gaylord Perry	SF	Sep 17, 1968	1-0	2	9	1	STL	Bob Gibson
Ray Washburn	STL	Sep 18, 1968	2-0	5	8	0	SF	Bobby Bolin
Bill Stoneman	MON	Apr 17, 1969	7-0	5	8	0	PHI	Jerry Johnson
Jim Maloney	CIN	Apr 30, 1969	10-0	5	13	0	HOU	Wade Blasingame
Don Wilson	HOU	May 1, 1969	4-0	6	15	1	CIN	Jim Merritt
Ken Holtzman	CHI	Aug 19, 1969	3-0	3	0	0	ATL	Phil Niekro
Bob Moose	PIT	Sep 20, 1969	4-0	3	6	0	NY	Gary Gentry
Dock Ellis	PIT	Jun 12, 1970	2-0	8	6	0	SD	Dave Roberts
Bill Singer	LA	Jul 20, 1970	5-0	0	10	2	PHI	Woodie Fryman
Ken Holtzman	CHI	Jun 3, 1971	1-0	4	6	0	CIN	Gary Nolan
Rick Wise	PHI	Jun 23, 1971	4-0	1	3	0	CIN	Ross Grimsley
Bob Gibson	STL	Aug 14, 1971	11-0	3	10	0	PIT	Bob Johnson
Burt Hooton	CHI	Apr 16, 1972	4-0	7	7	0	PHI	Dick Selma
Milt Pappas	CHI	Sep 2, 1972	8-0	1	6	0	SD	Mike Caldwell
Bill Stoneman	MON	Oct 2, 1972	7-0	7	9	1	NY	Jim McAndrew
Phil Niekro	ATL	Aug 5, 1973	9-0	3	4	2	SD	Steve Arlin
Ed Halicki	SF	Aug 24, 1975	6-0	2	10	1	NY	Craig Swan
Larry Dierker	HOU	Jul 9, 1976	6-0	4	8	0	MON	Don Stanhouse
John Candelaria	PIT	Aug 9, 1976	2-0	1	7	2	LA	Doug Rau
John Montefusco	SF	Sep 29, 1976	9-0	1	4	0	ATL	Jamie Easterly
Bob Forsch	STL	Apr 16, 1978	5-0	2	3	1	PHI	Randy Lerch
Tom Seaver	CIN	Jun 16, 1978	4-0	3	3	1	STL	John Denny
Ken Forsch	HOU	Apr 7, 1979	6-0	2	5	0	ATL	Larry McWilliams
Jerry Reuss	LA	Jun 27, 1980	8-0	0	2	1	SF	Vida Blue
Charlie Lea	MON	May 10, 1981	4-0	4	8	0	SF	Ed Whitson
Nolan Ryan	HOU	Sep 26, 1981	5-0	3	11	0	LA	Ted Power
Bob Forsch	STL	Sep 26, 1983	3-0	0	6	1	MON	Steve Rogers
Mike Scott	HOU	Sep 25, 1986	2-0	2	13	0	SF	Juan Berenguer

No-Hitters, Other Leagues

Player	Team	Date	Score	Opp.
Tony Mullane	LOU AA	Sep 11, 1882	2-0	CIN
Guy Hecker	LOU AA	Sep 19, 1882	3-1	PIT
Al Atkinson	PHI AA	May 24, 1884	10-1	PIT
Ed Morris	COL AA	May 29, 1884	5-0	PIT
Frank Mountain	COL AA	Jun 5, 1884	12-0	WAS
Sam Kimber	BKN AA	Oct 4, 1884	0-0	TOL
Al Atkinson	PHI AA	May 1, 1886	3-2	NY
Adonis Terry	BKN AA	Jul 24, 1886	1-0	STL
Matt Kilroy	BAL AA	Oct 6, 1886	6-0	PIT
Adonis Terry	BKN AA	May 27, 1888	4-0	LOU
Henry Porter	KC AA	Jun 6, 1888	4-0	BAL
Ed Seward	PHI AA	Jul 26, 1888	12-2	CIN
Gus Weyhing	PHI AA	Jul 31, 1888	4-0	KC
Cannonball Titcomb	ROC AA	Sep 15, 1890	7-0	SYR
Ted Breitenstein	STL AA	Oct 4, 1891	8-0	LOU
Dick Burns	CIN U	Aug 26, 1884	3-1	KC
Ed Cushman	MIL U	Sep 28, 1884	5-0	WAS
Ed Lafitte	BKN F	Sep 19, 1914	6-2	KC
Frank Allen	PIT F	Apr 24, 1915	2-0	STL
Claude Hendrix	CHI F	May 15, 1915	10-0	PIT
Alex Main	KC F	Aug 16, 1915	3-0	BUF
Dave Davenport	STL F	Sep 7, 1915	3-0	CHI

Johnny Vander Meer (*left*) accomplished one of baseball's most amazing feats, hurling consecutive no-hitters against the Braves and the Dodgers in 1938. California's lanky ace Mike Witt (*above*) is the last pitcher to throw a perfect game.

Left: Nolan Ryan's 100-mph fastballs have struck out and walked more batters than anyone in history. Five straight 20-win seasons and an uncanny knack for pitching in the World Series earned Catfish Hunter (*below left*) a 1987 election to the Hall of Fame. *Below*: Sandy Koufax led the N.L. in ERA in each of his last six seasons, retiring after a 27–9, 1.73, 317 K performance.

Most No-Hitters, Career

Player	Team	Date	Score	Opp.
Nolan Ryan	CAL A	May 15, 1973	3-0	KC
	CAL A	Jul 15, 1973	6-0	DET
	CAL A	Sep 28, 1974	4-0	DET
	CAL A	Jun 1, 1975	1-0	BAL
	HOU N	Sep 26, 1981	5-0	LA
Sandy Koufax	LA N	Jun 30, 1962	5-0	NY
	LA N	May 11, 1963	8-0	SF
	LA N	Jun 4, 1964	3-0	PHI
	LA N	Sep 9, 1965	1-0	CHI
Larry Corcoran	CHI N	Aug 19, 1880	6-0	BOS
	CHI N	Sep 20, 1882	5-0	WOR
	CHI N	Jun 27, 1884	6-0	PRO
Cy Young	CLE N	Sep 18, 1897	6-0	CIN
	BOS A	May 5, 1904	3-0	PHI
	BOS A	Jun 30, 1908	8-0	NY
Bob Feller	CLE A	Apr 16, 1940	1-0	CHI
	CLE A	Apr 30, 1946	1-0	NY
	CLE A	Jul 1, 1951	2-1	DET
Jim Maloney	CIN N	Jun 14, 1965	0-1	NY
	CIN N	Aug 19, 1965	1-0	CHI
	CIN N	Apr 30, 1969	10-0	HOU
Christy Mathewson	NY N	Jul 15, 1901	5-0	STL
	NY N	Jun 13, 1905	1-0	CHI
Addie Joss	CLE A	Oct 2, 1908	1-0	CHI
	CLE A	Apr 20, 1910	1-0	CHI
Johnny Vander Meer	CIN N	Jun 11, 1938	3-0	BOS
	CIN N	Jun 15, 1938	6-0	BKN
Allie Reynolds	NY A	Jul 12, 1951	1-0	CLE
	NY A	Sep 28, 1951	8-0	BOS
Virgil Trucks	DET A	May 15, 1952	1-0	WAS
	DET A	Aug 25, 1952	1-0	NY
Jim Bunning	DET A	Jul 20, 1958	3-0	BOS
	PHI N	Jun 21, 1964	6-0	NY
Warren Spahn	MIL N	Sep 16, 1960	4-0	PHI
	MIL N	Apr 28, 1961	1-0	SF
Ken Holtzman	CHI N	Aug 19, 1969	3-0	ATL
	CHI N	Jun 3, 1971	1-0	CIN
Bill Stoneman	MON N	Apr 17, 1969	7-0	PHI
	MON N	Oct 2, 1972	7-0	NY
Steve Busby	KC A	Apr 27, 1973	3-0	DET
	KC A	Jun 19, 1974	2-0	MIL
Frank Smith	CHI A	Sep 6, 1905	15-0	DET
	CHI A	Sep 20, 1908	1-0	PHI
Tom Hughes	NY A	Aug 30, 1910	0-5	CLE
	BOS N	Jun 16, 1916	2-0	PIT
Dutch Leonard	BOS A	Aug 30, 1916	4-0	STL
	BOS A	Jun 3, 1918	5-0	DET
Carl Erskine	BKN N	Jun 19, 1952	5-0	CHI
	BKN N	May 12, 1956	3-0	NY
Don Wilson	HOU N	Jun 18, 1967	2-0	ATL
	HOU N	May 1, 1969	4-0	CIN

Most No-Hitters, Career *(cont'd)*

Player	Team	Date	Score	Opp.
Al Atkinson	PHI AA	May 24, 1884	10-1	PIT
	PHI AA	May 1, 1886	3-2	NY
Adonis Terry	BKN AA	Jul 24, 1886	1-0	STL
	BKN AA	May 27, 1888	4-0	LOU
Pud Galvin	BUF N	Aug 20, 1880	1-0	WOR
	BUF N	Aug 4, 1884	18-0	DET
Bob Forsch	STL N	Apr 16, 1978	5-0	PHI
	STL N	Sep 26, 1983	3-0	MON

Perfect Games (9 innings or more)

Player	Team	Date	Score	SO	Opp.	Opp. Pitcher
Lee Richmond	WOR N	Jun 12, 1880	1-0	5	CLE	Jim McCormick
Monte Ward	PRO N	Jun 17, 1880	5-0	7	BUF	Pud Galvin
Cy Young	BOS A	May 5, 1904	3-0	8	PHI	Rube Waddell
Addie Joss	CLE A	Oct 2, 1908	1-0	3	CHI	Ed Walsh
Ernie Shore	BOS A	Jun 23, 1917	4-0	2	WAS	Doc Ayers
Charlie Robertson	CHI A	Apr 30, 1922	2-0	6	DET	Herman Pillette
Don Larsen	NY A	Oct 8, 1956	2-0	7	BKN	Sal Maglie
Harvey Haddix	PIT N	May 26, 1959	0-1	8	MIL	Lew Burdette
Jim Bunning	PHI N	Jun 21, 1964	6-0	10	NY	Tracy Stallard
Sandy Koufax	LA N	Sep 9, 1965	1-0	14	CHI	Bob Hendley
Catfish Hunter	OAK A	May 8, 1968	4-0	11	MIN	Dave Boswell
Len Barker	CLE A	May 15, 1981	3-0	11	TOR	Luis Leal
Mike Witt	CAL A	Sep 30, 1984	1-0	10	TEX	Charlie Hough

Most Complete 1-0 Wins, Career

Player	Total
Walter Johnson	38
Grover Alexander	17
Eddie Plank	15
Bert Blyleven	14
Christy Mathewson	14
Three Finger Brown	13
Dean Chance	13
Ed Walsh	13
Doc White	13
Cy Young	13
Steve Carlton	12
Stan Coveleski	12
Gaylord Perry	12

Player	Total
Ferguson Jenkins	11
Kid Nichols	11
Nap Rucker	11
Joe Bush	10
Paul Derringer	10
Bill Doak	10
Addie Joss	10
Sandy Koufax	10
Dick Rudolph	10
Nolan Ryan	10
Warren Spahn	10
Lefty Tyler	10
Hippo Vaughn	10

Jim Bunning had eight seasons of 15 wins or more, and he is one of only four pitchers to throw no-hitters in both the American and National Leagues.

Most 1-0 Losses, Career

Player	Total
Walter Johnson	26
Jim Bunning	15
Ferguson Jenkins	13
Lee Meadows	13
Jack Powell	13
Eddie Cicotte	12
Eddie Plank	12
Wilbur Cooper	11
Christy Mathewson	11
Doc White	11
Three Finger Brown	10
Bob Gibson	10
Larry Jackson	10
Ken Raffensberger	10
Nap Rucker	10

Worst Won-Lost Record, Season (12 or more losses)

Player	Team	Year	W	L	Pct.	ERA
Terry Felton	MIN A	1982	0	13	.000	4.99
Steve Gerkin	PHI A	1945	0	12	.000	3.62
Russ Miller	PHI N	1928	0	12	.000	5.42
Jack Nabors	PHI A	1916	1	19	.050	3.47
Frank Bates	STL N	1899				
	CLE N	1899	1	18	.053	6.90
Art Hagan	PHI N	1883				
	BUF N	1883	1	16	.059	5.27
Tom Sheehan	PHI A	1916	1	16	.059	3.69
Mike Parrott	SEA A	1980	1	16	.059	7.28
Howie Judson	CHI A	1949	1	14	.067	4.54
Fred Corey	WOR N	1882	1	13	.071	3.56
Jim McElroy	PHI N	1884				
	WIL U	1884	1	13	.071	5.12
Tony Madigan	WAS N	1886	1	13	.071	5.06
Guy Morton	CLE A	1914	1	13	.071	3.02
Roy Moore	PHI A	1920	1	13	.071	4.68
Pascual Perez	ATL N	1985	1	13	.071	6.14
Steve Hargan	CLE A	1971	1	13	.071	6.21
Troy Herriage	KC A	1956	1	13	.071	6.64
George Gill	DET A	1939				
	STL A	1939	1	13	.071	7.21
Walt Leverenz	STL A	1914	1	12	.077	3.80
Carl Scheib	PHI A	1951	1	12	.077	4.47
Bob Miller	NY N	1962	1	12	.077	4.89
Tricky Nichols	BAL AA	1882	1	12	.077	5.02
Wally Hebert	STL A	1932	1	12	.077	6.48
Jim Walkup	STL A	1938	1	12	.077	6.80

Lefty Grove (*above*) had a season winning percentage of .750 or better seven times for the A's and the Red Sox. *Right*: Ron Guidry has averaged 16 wins per season over his 10 years in the Yankees' regular rotation.

Best Won-Lost Record, Season, AL (20 or more wins)

Player	Team	Year	W	L	Pct.
Ron Guidry	NY	1978	25	3	.893
Lefty Grove	PHI	1931	31	4	.886
Joe Wood	BOS	1912	34	5	.872
Wild Bill Donovan	DET	1907	25	4	.862
Whitey Ford	NY	1961	25	4	.862
Roger Clemens	BOS	1986	24	4	.857
Lefty Grove	PHI	1930	28	5	.848
Lefty Gomez	NY	1934	26	5	.839
Denny McLain	DET	1968	31	6	.838
Walter Johnson	WAS	1913	36	7	.837
Spud Chandler	NY	1943	20	4	.833
Chief Bender	PHI	1910	23	5	.821
Russ Ford	NY	1910	26	6	.813
Eddie Plank	PHI	1912	26	6	.813
General Crowder	STL	1928	21	5	.808
Bobo Newsom	DET	1940	21	5	.808
Ernie Bonham	NY	1942	21	5	.808
Dave McNally	BAL	1971	21	5	.808
Catfish Hunter	OAK	1973	21	5	.808
Eddie Cicotte	CHI	1919	29	7	.806
Boo Ferriss	BOS	1946	25	6	.806
Stan Coveleski	WAS	1925	20	5	.800

Left: Carl Hubbell's screwball baffled Giants' opponents for 16 years, earning Hubbell the nickname "King Carl." Preacher Roe (*above*) racked up a .715 winning percentage in seven years with Brooklyn.

Best Won-Lost Record, Season, NL (20 or more wins)

Player	Team	Year	W	L	Pct.
Preacher Roe	BKN	1951	22	3	.880
Fred Goldsmith	CHI	1880	21	3	.875
Dwight Gooden	NY	1985	24	4	.857
Old Hoss Radbourn	PRO	1884	60	12	.833
King Cole	CHI	1910	20	4	.833
Sandy Koufax	LA	1963	25	5	.833
Jim Hughes	BKN	1899	28	6	.824
Jack Chesbro	PIT	1902	28	6	.824
Dazzy Vance	BKN	1924	28	6	.824
Bob Purkey	CIN	1962	23	5	.821
Joe McGinnity	NY	1904	35	8	.814
Three Finger Brown	CHI	1906	26	6	.813
Carl Hubbell	NY	1936	26	6	.813
Bill Hoffer	BAL	1895	30	7	.811
Dizzy Dean	STL	1934	30	7	.811
Larry Jansen	NY	1947	21	5	.808
Howie Camnitz	PIT	1909	25	6	.806
Christy Mathewson	NY	1909	25	6	.806
Juan Marichal	SF	1966	25	6	.806
Jocko Flynn	CHI	1886	24	6	.800
Sam Leever	PIT	1905	20	5	.800
Robin Roberts	PHI	1952	28	7	.800
Don Newcombe	BKN	1955	20	5	.800
John Candelaria	PIT	1977	20	5	.800

Armed with the most dangerous slider in the major leagues, Steve Carlton struck out over 4000 batters and ranks second only to Warren Spahn in wins by a lefthander with 323.

Twenty Wins One Year, 20 Losses the Next, AL

Player	Team	Year	W	L
George Mullin	DET	1906	21	18
	DET	1907	20	20
Al Orth	NY	1906	27	17
	NY	1907	14	21
Russ Ford	NY	1911	22	11
	NY	1912	13	21
Walter Johnson	WAS	1915	27	13
	WAS	1916	25	20
Hooks Dauss	DET	1919	21	9
	DET	1920	13	21
Alex Kellner	PHI	1949	20	12
	PHI	1950	8	20
Mel Stottlemyre	NY	1965	20	9
	NY	1966	12	20
Luis Tiant	CLE	1968	21	9
	CLE	1969	9	20
Stan Bahnsen	CHI	1972	21	16
	CHI	1973	18	21
Wilbur Wood	CHI	1972	24	17
	CHI	1973	24	20
	CHI	1974	20	19
	CHI	1975	16	20

Twenty Wins One Year, 20 Losses the Next, NL since 1900

Player	Team	Year	W	L
Togie Pittinger	BOS	1902	27	14
	BOS	1903	19	23
Jack Taylor	STL	1904	20	19
	STL	1905	15	21
Irv Young	BOS	1905	20	21
	BOS	1906	16	25
Nap Rucker	BKN	1911	22	18
	BKN	1912	18	21
Rube Marquard	NY	1913	23	10
	NY	1914	12	22
Eppa Rixey	PHI	1916	22	10
	PHI	1917	16	21
Joe Oeschger	BOS	1921	20	14
	BOS	1922	6	21
Murry Dickson	PIT	1951	20	16
	PIT	1952	14	21
Larry Jackson	CHI	1964	24	11
	CHI	1965	14	21
Steve Carlton	PHI	1972	27	10
	PHI	1973	13	20
Jerry Koosman	NY	1976	21	10
	NY	1977	8	20

Twenty Wins with Last-Place Team, AL

Player	Team	Year	W	L	Team W	Team L
Scott Perry	PHI	1918	21	19	52	76
Howard Ehmke	BOS	1923	20	17	61	91
Sloppy Thurston	CHI	1924	20	14	66	87
Ned Garver	STL	1951	20	12	52	102
Nolan Ryan	CAL	1974	22	16	68	94

Twenty Wins with Last-Place Team, NL

Player	Team	Year	W	L	Team W	Team L
Lee Richmond	WOR	1881	25	26	32	50
Mark Baldwin	PIT	1891	22	28	55	80
Sadie McMahon	BAL	1892	20	25	46	101
Noodles Hahn	CIN	1901	22	19	52	87
Steve Carlton	PHI	1972	27	10	59	97

Highest Percentage of Team's Wins, AL

Player	Team	Year	W	L	Team W	Team L	Pct.
Ed Walsh	CHI	1908	40	15	88	64	45.5
Jack Chesbro	NY	1904	41	12	92	59	44.6
Cy Young	BOS	1901	33	10	79	57	41.8
Joe Bush	PHI	1916	15	22	36	117	41.7
Cy Young	BOS	1902	32	11	77	60	41.6
Eddie Rommel	PHI	1922	27	13	65	89	41.5
Scott Perry	PHI	1918	21	19	52	76	40.4
Red Faber	CHI	1921	25	15	62	92	40.3
Walter Johnson	WAS	1913	36	7	90	64	40.0

Highest Percentage of Team's Wins, NL since 1900

Player	Team	Year	W	L	Team W	Team L	Pct.
Steve Carlton	PHI	1972	27	10	59	97	45.8
Noodles Hahn	CIN	1901	22	19	52	87	42.3

Twenty Wins and 20 Losses in Same Year, AL

Player	Team	Year	W	L
Joe McGinnity	BAL	1901	26	21
Bill Dinneen	BOS	1902	21	21
George Mullin	DET	1905	21	20
	DET	1907	20	20
Jim Scott	CHI	1913	20	20
Walter Johnson	WAS	1916	25	20
Wilbur Wood	CHI	1973	24	20

Twenty Wins and 20 Losses, Season, NL since 1900

Player	Team	Year	W	L
Joe McGinnity	NY	1903	31	20
Irv Young	BOS	1906	20	21
Phil Niekro	ATL	1979	21	20

Thirty-Game Winners, AL

Player	Team	Year	W	L	Pct.	ERA	IP	BB	SO	ShO
Jack Chesbro	NY	1904	41	12	.774	1.82	455	88	239	6
Ed Walsh	CHI	1908	40	15	.727	1.42	464	56	269	12
Walter Johnson	WAS	1913	36	7	.837	1.09	346	38	243	12
Joe Wood	BOS	1912	34	5	.872	1.91	344	82	258	10
Cy Young	BOS	1901	33	10	.767	1.62	371	36	119	4
	BOS	1902	32	10	.762	2.15	385	33	166	3
Walter Johnson	WAS	1912	32	12	.727	1.39	368	76	303	8
Lefty Grove	PHI	1931	31	4	.886	2.06	289	62	175	3
Denny McLain	DET	1968	31	6	.838	1.96	336	63	280	6
Jack Coombs	PHI	1910	31	9	.769	1.30	353	115	224	13
Jim Bagby	CLE	1920	31	12	.721	2.89	340	79	73	3

Jack Chesbro's 41 wins for the Yankees in 1904 is tops in the twentieth century. Chesbro finished his career with a more modest 198–132, 2.68 ERA record, and a plaque in Cooperstown.

Thirty-Game Winners, NL since 1900

Player	Team	Year	W	L	Pct.	ERA	IP	BB	SO	ShO
Christy Mathewson	NY	1908	37	11	.771	1.43	391	42	259	12
Joe McGinnity	NY	1904	35	8	.814	1.61	408	86	144	9
Christy Mathewson	NY	1904	33	12	.733	2.03	368	78	212	4
Grover Alexander	PHI	1916	33	12	.733	1.55	389	50	167	16
Christy Mathewson	NY	1905	31	8	.795	1.27	339	64	206	9
Grover Alexander	PHI	1915	31	10	.756	1.22	376	64	241	12
Joe McGinnity	NY	1903	31	20	.608	2.43	434	109	171	3
Dizzy Dean	STL	1934	30	7	.811	2.66	312	75	195	7
Grover Alexander	PHI	1917	30	13	.698	1.86	388	58	201	8
Christy Mathewson	NY	1903	30	13	.698	2.26	366	100	267	3

Most 20-Win Seasons

Player	Total
Cy Young	16
Christy Mathewson	13
Warren Spahn	13
Walter Johnson	12
Kid Nichols	11
Pud Galvin	10
Grover Alexander	9
Old Hoss Radbourn	9
Mickey Welch	9
John Clarkson	8
Lefty Grove	8
Jim McCormick	8

Player	Total
Joe McGinnity	8
Tony Mullane	8
Jim Palmer	8
Eddie Plank	8
Amos Rusie	8
Charlie Buffinton	7
Clark Griffith	7
Ferguson Jenkins	7
Tim Keefe	7
Bob Lemon	7
Gus Weyhing	7
Vic Willis	7

Undefeated Seasons (5 or more wins)

Player	Team	Year	W
Tom Zachary	NY A	1929	12
Dennis Lamp	TOR A	1985	11
Howie Krist	STL N	1941	10
Joe Pate	PHI A	1926	9
Ken Holtzman	CHI N	1967	9
Ted Wilks	STL N	1946	8
Grant Jackson	BAL A	1973	8
Piano Legs Hickman	BOS N	1899	7
Duster Mails	CLE A	1920	7
Wes Stock	BAL A	1963	7
Mike Wallace	PHI N	1974	
	NY A	1974	7
Ed Rodriguez	MIL A	1975	7
Tom Burgmeier	BOS A	1982	7
Tom Filer	TOR A	1985	7
Roy Thomas	SEA A	1985	7
Earl Hamilton	PIT N	1918	6
Allyn Stout	STL N	1931	6

Player	Team	Year	W
Max Lanier	STL N	1946	6
Freddie Martin	STL N	1949	6
Luis Aloma	CHI A	1951	6
Sandy Consuegra	WAS A	1952	6
Moe Drabowsky	BAL A	1966	6
Bob Veale	PIT N	1971	6
Fred Beene	NY A	1973	6
Rob Murphy	CIN N	1986	6
Jack Taylor	CHI N	1898	5
Archie McKain	DET A	1940	5
Bill Connelly	NY N	1952	5
Wes Stock	BAL A	1961	5
Joe Nuxhall	CIN N	1962	
	LA A	1962	5
Bill Stafford	NY A	1964	5
Fred Gladding	DET A	1966	5
Ramon Hernandez	PIT N	1972	5
Marty Bystrom	PHI N	1980	5

Individual Pitching Records

Most Wins, Career

Player	W	L
Cy Young	511	313
Walter Johnson	416	279
Christy Mathewson	373	188
Grover Alexander	373	208
Warren Spahn	363	245
Pud Galvin	361	309
Kid Nichols	360	202
Tim Keefe	344	225
Eddie Plank	327	192
John Clarkson	326	177
Steve Carlton	323	229
Gaylord Perry	314	265
Tom Seaver	311	205
Mickey Welch	311	207
Phil Niekro	311	261
Don Sutton	310	239
Old Hoss Radbourn	308	191
Lefty Grove	300	141
Early Wynn	300	244
Robin Roberts	286	245
Tony Mullane	285	215
Ferguson Jenkins	284	226
Jim Kaat	283	237
Red Ruffing	273	225
Burleigh Grimes	270	212
Jim Palmer	268	152
Bob Feller	266	162
Eppa Rixey	266	251
Tommy John	264	210
Jim McCormick	264	214
Gus Weyhing	264	224
Ted Lyons	260	230
Red Faber	254	212
Carl Hubbell	253	154
Nolan Ryan	253	226
Bob Gibson	251	174
Vic Willis	248	208
Jack Powell	248	254
Joe McGinnity	247	145
Jack Quinn	247	216
Juan Marichal	243	142
Amos Rusie	243	160

Player	W	L
Herb Pennock	241	162
Three Finger Brown	239	130
Waite Hoyt	237	182
Whitey Ford	236	106
Charlie Buffinton	231	151
Will White	229	166
Luis Tiant	229	172
George Mullin	229	195
Bert Blyleven	229	197
Sad Sam Jones	229	217
Catfish Hunter	224	166
Jim Bunning	224	184
Mel Harder	223	186
Paul Derringer	223	212
Jerry Koosman	222	209
Hooks Dauss	221	183
Bob Caruthers	218	99
Earl Whitehill	218	185
Freddie Fitzsimmons	217	146
Mickey Lolich	217	191
Wilbur Cooper	216	178
Jim Perry	215	174
Stan Coveleski	214	141
Joe Niekro	213	190
Billy Pierce	211	169
Bobo Newsom	211	222
Chief Bender	210	128
Eddie Cicotte	210	148
Jesse Haines	210	158
Vida Blue	209	161
Milt Pappas	209	164
Don Drysdale	209	166
Carl Mays	208	126
Bob Lemon	207	128
Jack Stivetts	207	131
Hal Newhouser	207	150
Silver King	206	152
Lew Burdette	203	144
Charlie Root	201	160
Rube Marquard	201	177
George Uhle	200	166

The 300-Win Club

Player	W	L	ERA	ShO	SO
Cy Young	511	313	2.63	77	2799
Walter Johnson	416	279	2.17	110	3508
Christy Mathewson	373	188	2.13	83	2511
Grover Alexander	373	208	2.56	91	2199
Warren Spahn	363	245	3.09	63	2583
Pud Galvin	361	309	2.87	57	1799
Kid Nichols	360	202	2.94	48	1885
Tim Keefe	344	225	2.62	40	2533
Eddie Plank	327	192	2.34	70	2261
John Clarkson	326	177	2.81	37	2015
Steve Carlton	323	229	3.11	55	4040
Gaylord Perry	314	265	3.10	53	3534
Tom Seaver	311	205	2.86	61	3640
Mickey Welch	311	207	2.71	40	1850
Phil Niekro	311	261	3.27	45	3278
Don Sutton	310	239	3.19	58	3431
Old Hoss Radbourn	308	191	2.67	35	1830
Lefty Grove	300	141	3.06	35	2266
Early Wynn	300	244	3.54	49	2334

Most Wins by Age, Season, AL

Player	Team	Year	Age	W
Bob Feller	CLE	1936	17	5
	CLE	1937	18	9
Wally Bunker	BAL	1964	19	19
Bob Feller	CLE	1939	20	24
	CLE	1940	21	27
Joe Wood	BOS	1912	22	34
Hal Newhouser	DET	1944	23	29
Walter Johnson	WAS	1912	24	32
	WAS	1913	25	36
Ed Walsh	CHI	1908	26	40
Walter Johnson	WAS	1915	27	27
George Uhle	CLE	1926	27	27
George Mullin	DET	1909	28	29
Walter Johnson	WAS	1916	29	25
Jack Chesbro	NY	1904	30	41
Lefty Grove	PHI	1931	31	31
Jim Bagby	CLE	1920	32	31
Eddie Cicotte	CHI	1917	33	28
Cy Young	BOS	1901	34	33
	BOS	1902	35	32
	BOS	1903	36	28
	BOS	1904	37	27
	BOS	1905	38	18
Early Wynn	CHI	1959	39	22
Cy Young	BOS	1907	40	22
	BOS	1908	41	21
	CLE	1909	42	19

Cleveland sensation Bob "Rapid Robert" Feller had 55 wins before his 21st birthday, and a fastball that led the A.L. in Ks seven times.

Most Wins by Age, Season, AL *(cont'd)*

Player	Team	Year	Age	W
Jack Quinn	PHI	1927	43	15
	PHI	1928	44	18
Phil Niekro	NY	1984	45	16
	NY	1985	46	16
	CLE	1986	47	11

Most Wins by Age, Season, NL since 1900

Player	Team	Year	Age	W
Mike McCormick	NY	1957	18	3
Dwight Gooden	NY	1984	19	17
	NY	1985	20	24
Rube Marquard	NY	1911	21	24
Christy Mathewson	NY	1903	22	30
	NY	1904	23	33
	NY	1905	24	31
Robin Roberts	PHI	1952	25	28
Vic Willis	BOS	1902	26	27
Dick Rudolph	BOS	1914	26	27
Christy Mathewson	NY	1908	27	37
Grover Alexander	PHI	1915	28	31
	PHI	1916	29	33
	PHI	1917	30	30
Three Finger Brown	CHI	1908	31	29
Joe McGinnity	NY	1903	32	31
	NY	1904	33	35
Burleigh Grimes	PIT	1928	34	25
Joe McGinnity	NY	1906	35	27
Grover Alexander	CHI	1923	36	22
Steve Carlton	PHI	1982	37	23
Warren Spahn	MIL	1959	38	21
	MIL	1960	39	21
Grover Alexander	STL	1927	40	21
Warren Spahn	MIL	1961	40	21
Phil Niekro	ATL	1979	40	21
Warren Spahn	MIL	1962	41	18
	MIL	1963	42	23
Phil Niekro	ATL	1982	43	17
	ATL	1983	44	11
Hoyt Wilhelm	ATL	1969	45	2
	ATL	1970		
	CHI	1970	46	6
Jack Quinn	BKN	1931	47	5
	BKN	1932	48	3

Using a knuckleball that baffles hitters and preserves his arm, Phil Niekro (*top*) has won 114 games since his 40th birthday. At age 22, Dwight Gooden (*above*) has a 58–19 record, 2.28 ERA, and 744 strikeouts in three years with the Mets.

Strikeouts and Walks

Most Strikeouts, Season, AL

Player	Team	Year	SO
Nolan Ryan	CAL	1973	383
	CAL	1974	367
Rube Waddell	PHI	1904	349
Bob Feller	CLE	1946	348
Nolan Ryan	CAL	1977	341
	CAL	1972	329
	CAL	1976	327
Sam McDowell	CLE	1965	325
Walter Johnson	WAS	1910	313
Mickey Lolich	DET	1971	308
Sam McDowell	CLE	1970	304
Walter Johnson	WAS	1912	303
Rube Waddell	PHI	1903	302
Vida Blue	OAK	1971	301
Rube Waddell	PHI	1905	287
Sam McDowell	CLE	1968	283
Denny McLain	DET	1968	280
Sam McDowell	CLE	1969	279
Hal Newhouser	DET	1946	275
Mickey Lolich	DET	1969	271
Ed Walsh	CHI	1908	269
Frank Tanana	CAL	1975	269
Luis Tiant	CLE	1968	264
Herb Score	CLE	1956	263
Bob Feller	CLE	1940	261
Frank Tanana	CAL	1976	261
Bob Feller	CLE	1941	260
Nolan Ryan	CAL	1978	260
Ed Walsh	CHI	1910	258
Joe Wood	BOS	1912	258
Bert Blyleven	MIN	1973	258
Ed Walsh	CHI	1911	255
	CHI	1912	254
Mickey Lolich	DET	1972	250
Bert Blyleven	MIN	1974	249
Ron Guidry	NY	1978	248
Bob Feller	CLE	1939	246
Jim Lonborg	BOS	1967	246
Herb Score	CLE	1955	245
Mark Langston	SEA	1986	245
Dennis Leonard	KC	1977	244
Walter Johnson	WAS	1913	243
Bill Singer	CAL	1973	241
Bob Feller	CLE	1938	240
Jack Chesbro	NY	1904	239
Gaylord Perry	CLE	1973	238
Roger Clemens	BOS	1986	238
Sam McDowell	CLE	1967	236
Joe Coleman	DET	1971	236
Dean Chance	MIN	1968	234
Gaylord Perry	CLE	1972	234
Bert Blyleven	MIN	1975	233
Gaylord Perry	TEX	1975	233
Rube Waddell	PHI	1907	232
	STL	1908	232
Jack Morris	DET	1983	232
Joe Wood	BOS	1911	231
Mickey Lolich	DET	1970	230
Walter Johnson	WAS	1916	228
Bert Blyleven	MIN	1972	228
Bobo Newsom	STL	1938	226
Mickey Lolich	DET	1965	226
Walter Johnson	WAS	1914	225
Sam McDowell	CLE	1966	225
Ferguson Jenkins	TEX	1974	225
Jack Coombs	PHI	1910	224
Bert Blyleven	MIN	1971	224
Nolan Ryan	CAL	1979	223
Jack Morris	DET	1986	223
Joe Coleman	DET	1972	222
Camilo Pascual	MIN	1961	221
Dean Chance	MIN	1967	220
Luis Tiant	CLE	1967	219
Bert Blyleven	TEX	1976	219
Al Downing	NY	1964	217
Gaylord Perry	CLE	1974	216
Gary Peters	CHI	1967	215
Bert Blyleven	MIN	1986	215
Mickey Lolich	DET	1973	214
Camilo Pascual	MIN	1964	213
Hal Newhouser	DET	1945	212
Jim Kaat	MIN	1967	211
Andy Messersmith	CAL	1969	211
Rube Waddell	PHI	1902	210
Eddie Plank	PHI	1905	210
Bob Turley	NY	1955	210
Wilbur Wood	CHI	1971	210
Russ Ford	NY	1910	209
Lefty Grove	PHI	1930	209
Whitey Ford	NY	1961	209
Tom Bradley	CHI	1972	209
Floyd Bannister	SEA	1982	209
Cy Young	BOS	1905	208
Mike Witt	CAL	1986	208
Walter Johnson	WAS	1911	207
Dean Chance	LA	1964	207
Ted Higuera	MIL	1986	207
Ed Walsh	CHI	1907	206
Camilo Pascual	MIN	1962	206
Bob Johnson	KC	1970	206
Tom Bradley	CHI	1971	206
Luis Tiant	BOS	1973	206

Most Strikeouts, Season, AL *(cont'd)*

Player	Team	Year	SO	Player	Team	Year	SO
Bert Blyleven	CLE	1985		Joe Coleman	DET	1973	202
	MIN	1985	206	Mickey Lolich	DET	1974	202
Gary Peters	CHI	1964	205	Mark Langston	SEA	1984	202
Jim Kaat	MIN	1966	205	Kirk McCaskill	CAL	1986	202
Frank Tanana	CAL	1977	205	Eddie Plank	PHI	1904	201
Dave Boswell	MIN	1967	204	Jim Bunning	DET	1959	201
Cy Young	BOS	1904	203		DET	1960	201
Walter Johnson	WAS	1915	203	Ron Guidry	NY	1979	201
Jack Powell	NY	1904	202	Earl Wilson	BOS	1966	
Camilo Pascual	MIN	1963	202		DET	1966	200
Dave McNally	BAL	1968	202	Dennis Eckersley	CLE	1976	200

Most Strikeouts, Season, NL since 1900

Player	Team	Year	SO	Player	Team	Year	SO
Sandy Koufax	LA	1965	382	Tom Seaver	NY	1973	251
	LA	1966	317	Bob Veale	PIT	1964	250
J. R. Richard	HOU	1979	313	Tom Seaver	NY	1972	249
Steve Carlton	PHI	1972	310	Juan Marichal	SF	1963	248
Sandy Koufax	LA	1963	306	Phil Niekro	ATL	1978	248
Mike Scott	HOU	1986	306	Bill Singer	LA	1969	247
J. R. Richard	HOU	1978	303	Don Drysdale	LA	1960	246
Tom Seaver	NY	1971	289	Bob Gibson	STL	1964	245
Steve Carlton	PHI	1980	286	Nolan Ryan	HOU	1982	245
	PHI	1982	286	Jim Maloney	CIN	1965	244
Tom Seaver	NY	1970	283	Tom Seaver	NY	1975	243
Bob Veale	PIT	1965	276	Don Drysdale	LA	1959	242
Dwight Gooden	NY	1984	276	Mario Soto	CIN	1983	242
Steve Carlton	PHI	1983	275	Fernando Valenzuela	LA	1986	242
Bob Gibson	STL	1970	274	Grover Alexander	PHI	1912	241
Ferguson Jenkins	CHI	1970	274	Juan Marichal	SF	1965	240
Mario Soto	CIN	1982	274	Steve Carlton	PHI	1974	240
Ferguson Jenkins	CHI	1969	273	Fernando Valenzuela	LA	1984	240
Bob Gibson	STL	1965	270	Noodles Hahn	CIN	1901	239
Sandy Koufax	LA	1961	269	Van Mungo	BKN	1936	238
Bob Gibson	STL	1969	269	Rube Marquard	NY	1911	237
Jim Bunning	PHI	1965	268	Don Drysdale	LA	1964	237
Bob Gibson	STL	1968	268	Chris Short	PHI	1965	237
Dwight Gooden	NY	1985	268	Ferguson Jenkins	CHI	1967	236
Christy Mathewson	NY	1903	267	Don Wilson	HOU	1969	235
Jim Maloney	CIN	1963	265	Tom Seaver	NY	1976	235
Ferguson Jenkins	CHI	1971	263	Gaylord Perry	SF	1969	233
Dazzy Vance	BKN	1924	262	Don Drysdale	LA	1962	232
Phil Niekro	ATL	1977	262	Larry Dierker	HOU	1969	232
Ferguson Jenkins	CHI	1968	260	Clay Kirby	SD	1971	231
Christy Mathewson	NY	1908	259	Gaylord Perry	SF	1967	230
Jim Bunning	PHI	1967	253	Bob Veale	PIT	1966	229
	PHI	1966	252	Grover Alexander	PHI	1911	227
Don Drysdale	LA	1963	251	Bill Singer	LA	1968	227
Bill Stoneman	MON	1971	251	Wild Bill Donovan	BKN	1901	226

Most Strikeouts, Season, NL since 1900 *(cont'd)*

Player	Team	Year	SO
Tom Seaver	CIN	1978	226
Long Tom Hughes	CHI	1901	225
Vic Willis	BOS	1902	225
Sam Jones	STL	1958	225
Bob Gibson	STL	1966	225
Sandy Koufax	LA	1964	223
Steve Carlton	PHI	1973	223
Juan Marichal	SF	1966	222
Christy Mathewson	NY	1901	221
Dazzy Vance	BKN	1925	221
Andy Messersmith	LA	1974	221
Jim Bunning	PHI	1964	219
Juan Marichal	SF	1967	218
Don Sutton	LA	1969	217
Sandy Koufax	LA	1962	216
Jim Maloney	CIN	1966	216
John Montefusco	SF	1975	215
Grover Alexander	PHI	1914	214
Jim Maloney	CIN	1964	214
Gaylord Perry	SF	1970	214
J. R. Richard	HOU	1976	214
	HOU	1977	214
Mario Soto	CIN	1985	214
Bob Veale	PIT	1969	213
Andy Messersmith	LA	1975	213
Steve Carlton	PHI	1979	213
Christy Mathewson	NY	1904	212
Tony Cloninger	MIL	1965	211
Don Drysdale	LA	1965	210
Steve Carlton	STL	1969	210
Sam Jones	SF	1959	209
Don Sutton	LA	1966	209
Nolan Ryan	HOU	1985	209
Bob Gibson	STL	1962	208
Tom Seaver	NY	1969	208
Bob Gibson	STL	1972	208
Phil Niekro	ATL	1979	208
Fernando Valenzuela	LA	1985	208
Don Sutton	LA	1972	207
Christy Mathewson	NY	1905	206
Juan Marichal	SF	1964	206
Gary Nolan	CIN	1967	206
Ray Sadecki	SF	1968	206
Steve Rogers	MON	1977	206
Orval Overall	CHI	1909	205
Stan Williams	LA	1961	205
Tom Seaver	NY	1968	205
Juan Marichal	SF	1969	205
Jon Matlack	NY	1973	205
Bob Gibson	STL	1963	204
Dick Farrell	HOU	1962	203
Mike Cuellar	HOU	1967	203
Johnny Vander Meer	CIN	1941	202
Chris Short	PHI	1968	202
Ken Holtzman	CHI	1970	202
Floyd Youmans	MON	1986	202
Nap Rucker	BKN	1909	201
Grover Alexander	PHI	1917	201
Gaylord Perry	SF	1966	201
Don Sutton	LA	1970	201
Tom Seaver	NY	1974	201
Dazzy Vance	BKN	1928	200
Tom Griffin	HOU	1969	200
Don Sutton	LA	1973	200
Jerry Koosman	NY	1976	200
Nolan Ryan	HOU	1980	200
Sid Fernandez	NY	1986	200
Dwight Gooden	NY	1986	200

Most Strikeouts, Season before 1900

Player	Team	Year	SO
Matt Kilroy	BAL AA	1886	513
Toad Ramsey	LOU AA	1886	499
One Arm Daily	C-P U	1884	
	WAS U	1884	483
Dupee Shaw	DET N	1884	
	BOS U	1884	451
Old Hoss Radbourn	PRO N	1884	441
Charlie Buffinton	BOS N	1884	417
Guy Hecker	LOU AA	1884	385
Bill Sweeney	BAL U	1884	374
Pud Galvin	BUF N	1884	369
Mark Baldwin	COL AA	1889	368
Tim Keefe	NY AA	1883	361
Toad Ramsey	LOU AA	1887	355
Hardie Henderson	BAL AA	1884	346
Jim Whitney	BOS N	1883	345
Mickey Welch	NY N	1884	345
Amos Rusie	NY N	1890	345
Jim McCormick	CLE N	1884	
	CIN U	1884	343
John Clarkson	CHI N	1886	340
Charlie Sweeney	PRO N	1884	
	STL U	1884	337
Amos Rusie	NY N	1891	337

Most Strikeouts, Season before 1900 ***(cont'd)***

Player	Team	Year	SO	Player	Team	Year	SO
Tony Mullane	TOL AA	1884	334	Bill Hutchison	CHI N	1892	316
Tim Keefe	NY N	1888	333	Old Hoss Radbourn	PRO N	1883	315
Ed Morris	PIT AA	1886	326	Larry McKeon	IND AA	1884	308
Tim Keefe	NY AA	1884	323	Amos Rusie	NY N	1892	303
Lady Baldwin	DET N	1886	323	Ed Morris	COL AA	1884	302
John Clarkson	CHI N	1885	318				

Most Strikeouts, Career

Player	SO	Player	SO
Nolan Ryan	4277	Bert Blyleven	3090
Steve Carlton	4040	Jim Bunning	2855
Tom Seaver	3640	Mickey Lolich	2832
Gaylord Perry	3534	Cy Young	2799
Walter Johnson	3508	Warren Spahn	2583
Don Sutton	3431	Bob Feller	2581
Phil Niekro	3278	Jerry Koosman	2556
Ferguson Jenkins	3192	Tim Keefe	2533
Bob Gibson	3117	Christy Mathewson	2502

Four Strikeouts in One Inning, AL

Player	Team	Date	Inn.	Opp.	Opp. Batters
Walter Johnson	WAS	Apr 15, 1911	5	BOS	Ray Collins
	WAS			BOS	Larry Gardner
	WAS			BOS	Harry Hooper
	WAS			BOS	Duffy Lewis
Guy Morton	CLE	Jun 11, 1916	6	PHI	Whitey Witt
	CLE			PHI	Charlie Pick
	CLE			PHI	Nap Lajoie
	CLE			PHI	Stuffy McInnis
Ryne Duren	LA	May 18, 1961	7	CHI	Minnie Minoso
	LA			CHI	Roy Sievers
	LA			CHI	J. C. Martin
	LA			CHI	Sammy Esposito
Lee Stange	CLE	Sep 2, 1964	7	WAS	Don Lock
	CLE			WAS	Willie Kirkland
	CLE			WAS	Mike Brumley
	CLE			WAS	Don Zimmer
Mike Cuellar	BAL	May 29, 1970	4	CAL	Alex Johnson
	BAL			CAL	Ken McMullen
	BAL			CAL	Tommie Reynolds
	BAL			CAL	Jim Spencer
Mike Paxton	CLE	Jul 21, 1978	5	SEA	Bruce Bochte
	CLE			SEA	Tom Paciorek
	CLE			SEA	Dan Meyer
	CLE			SEA	Bill Stein

Four Strikeouts in One Inning, NL

Player	Team	Date	Inn.	Opp.	Opp. Batters
Cannonball Crane	NY	Oct 4, 1888	5	CHI	Fred Pfeffer
	NY			CHI	Ned Williamson
	NY			CHI	Tom Burns
	NY			CHI	John Tener
Hooks Wiltse	NY	May 15, 1906	5	CIN	Jim Delahanty
	NY			CIN	Tommy Corcoran
	NY			CIN	Admiral Schlei
	NY			CIN	Chick Fraser
Jim Davis	CHI	May 27, 1956	6	STL	Hal Smith
	CHI			STL	Jackie Brandt
	CHI			STL	Lindy McDaniel
	CHI			STL	Don Blasingame
Joe Nuxhall	CIN	Aug 11, 1959	6	MIL	Eddie Mathews
	CIN			MIL	Joe Adcock
	CIN			MIL	Del Crandall
	CIN			MIL	Johnny Logan
Pete Richert	LA	Apr 12, 1962	3	CIN	Frank Robinson
	LA			CIN	Gordy Coleman
	LA			CIN	Wally Post
	LA			CIN	Johnny Edwards
Don Drysdale	LA	Apr 17, 1965	2	PHI	Wes Covington
	LA			PHI	Tony Gonzalez
	LA			PHI	Dick Stuart
	LA			PHI	Clay Dalrymple
Bob Gibson	STL	Jun 7, 1966	4	PIT	Jerry Lynch
	STL			PIT	Jim Pagliaroni
	STL			PIT	Bill Mazeroski
	STL			PIT	Don Cardwell
Bill Bonham	CHI	Jul 31, 1974	2	MON	Mike Torrez
	CHI			MON	Ron Hunt
	CHI			MON	Tim Foli
	CHI			MON	Willie Davis
Phil Niekro	ATL	Jul 29, 1977	6	PIT	Dave Parker
	ATL			PIT	Bill Robinson
	ATL			PIT	Rennie Stennett
	ATL			PIT	Omar Moreno
Mario Soto	CIN	May 17, 1984	3	CHI	Tom Veryzer
	CIN			CHI	Dick Ruthven
	CIN			CHI	Bob Dernier
	CIN			CHI	Ryne Sandberg
Mike Scott	HOU	Sep 3, 1986	5	CHI	Chris Speier
	HOU			CHI	Chico Walker
	HOU			CHI	Dave Martinez
	HOU			CHI	Ryne Sandberg

Four Strikeouts in One Inning, Other Leagues

Player	Team	Date	Inn.	Opp.	Opp. Batters
Bobby Mathews	PHI AA	Sep 30, 1885	7	PIT	Charlie Eden
	PHI AA			PIT	Art Whitney
	PHI AA			PIT	Fred Mann
	PHI AA			PIT	Frank Ringo

Perfect Innings, AL (3 strikeouts on 9 pitches)

Player	Team	Date	Inn.	Opp.
Rube Waddell	PHI	Jul 1, 1902	3	BAL
Sloppy Thurston	CHI	Aug 22, 1923	12	PHI
Lefty Grove	PHI	Aug 23, 1928	2	CLE
	PHI	Sep 27, 1928	7	CHI
Jim Bunning	DET	Aug 2, 1959	9	BOS
Al Downing	NY	Aug 11, 1967	2	CLE
Nolan Ryan	CAL	Jul 9, 1972	2	BOS
Ron Guidry	NY	Aug 7, 1984	9	CHI

Perfect Innings, NL (3 strikeouts on 9 pitches)

Player	Team	Date	Inn.	Opp.
Pat Ragan	BKN	Oct 5, 1914	8	BOS
Hod Eller	CIN	Aug 21, 1917	9	NY
Joe Oeschger	BOS	Sep 8, 1921	4	PHI
Dazzy Vance	BKN	Sep 14, 1924	3	CHI
Sandy Koufax	LA	Jun 30, 1962	1	PHI
	LA	Apr 18, 1964	3	CIN
Bob Bruce	HOU	Apr 19, 1964	8	STL
Nolan Ryan	NY	Apr 19, 1968	3	PIT
Bob Gibson	STL	May 12, 1969	7	LA
Lynn McGlothen	STL	Aug 19, 1975	2	CIN
Bruce Sutter	CHI	Sep 8, 1977	9	STL

Most Strikeouts in Nine-Inning Game, AL

Player	Team	Date	SO	Opp.
Roger Clemens	BOS	Apr 29, 1986	20	SEA
Nolan Ryan	CAL	Aug 12, 1974	19	BOS
Bob Feller	CLE	Oct 2, 1938	18	DET
Nolan Ryan	CAL	Sep 10, 1976	18	CHI
Ron Guidry	NY	Jun 17, 1978	18	CAL
Bob Feller	CLE	Sep 13, 1936	17	PHI
Bill Monbouquette	BOS	May 12, 1961	17	WAS
Nolan Ryan	CAL	Sep 30, 1972	17	MIN
	CAL	Jul 15, 1973	17	DET
Frank Tanana	CAL	Jun 21, 1975	17	TEX
Rube Waddell	STL	Jul 29, 1908	16	PHI
Bob Feller	CLE	Aug 25, 1937	16	BOS
Jack Harshman	CHI	Jul 25, 1954	16	BOS
Herb Score	CLE	May 1, 1955	16	BOS

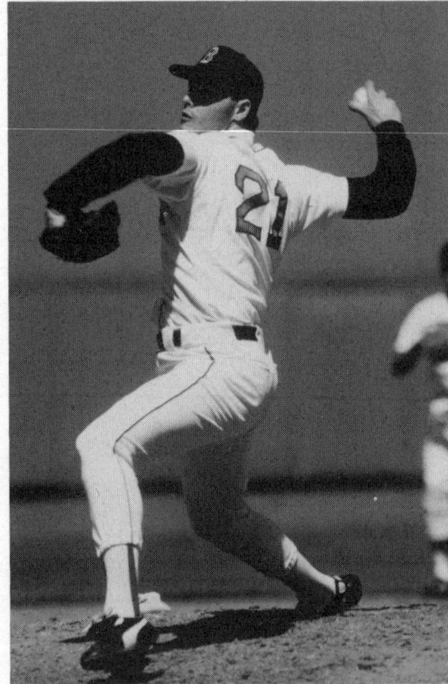

Rube Waddell (*top*) ranks sixth on the all-time list with a 2.16 career ERA. *Above*: Roger Clemens emerged in 1986 as one of the premier pitchers in baseball, becoming the first starter to win the MVP since Vida Blue in 1971.

Most Strikeouts in Nine-Inning Game, AL *(cont'd)*

Player	Team	Date	SO	Opp.
Luis Tiant	CLE	Aug 22, 1967	16	CAL
Sam McDowell	CLE	May 1, 1968	16	OAK
Luis Tiant	CLE	Sep 9, 1968	16	MIN
Mickey Lolich	DET	May 23, 1969	16	CAL
	DET	Jun 9, 1969	16	SEA
Nolan Ryan	CAL	Jul 1, 1972	16	OAK
	CAL	Jul 9, 1972	16	BOS
Rudy May	CAL	Aug 10, 1972	16	MIN
Nolan Ryan	CAL	Jun 9, 1979	16	DET
Mike Witt	CAL	Jul 23, 1984	16	SEA
Jose Rijo	OAK	Apr 19, 1986	16	SEA

Most Strikeouts in Nine-Inning Game, NL

Player	Team	Date	SO	Opp.
Charlie Sweeney	PRO	Jun 7, 1884	19	BOS
Steve Carlton	STL	Sep 15, 1969	19	NY
Tom Seaver	NY	Apr 22, 1970	19	SD
Sandy Koufax	LA	Aug 31, 1959	18	SF
	LA	Apr 24, 1962	18	CHI
Don Wilson	HOU	Jul 14, 1968	18	CIN
Bill Gullickson	MON	Sep 10, 1980	18	NY
Charlie Buffinton	BOS	Sep 2, 1884	17	CLE
Dizzy Dean	STL	Jul 30, 1933	17	CHI
Art Mahaffey	PHI	Apr 23, 1961	17	CHI
Jim Whitney	BOS	Jun 14, 1883	16	CHI
Charlie Buffinton	BOS	Jul 30, 1885	16	DET
John Clarkson	CHI	Aug 18, 1886	16	KC
Frank Gilmore	WAS	Sep 28, 1886	16	STL
Noodles Hahn	CIN	May 22, 1901	16	BOS
Christy Mathewson	NY	Oct 3, 1904	16	STL
Nap Rucker	BKN	Jul 24, 1909	16	PIT
Sandy Koufax	LA	Jun 22, 1959	16	PHI
	LA	May 26, 1962	16	PHI
Jim Maloney	CIN	May 21, 1963	16	MIL
Bob Veale	PIT	Jun 1, 1965	16	PHI
Steve Carlton	STL	Sep 20, 1967	16	PHI
Don Wilson	HOU	Sep 10, 1968	16	CIN
Steve Carlton	STL	May 21, 1970	16	PHI
Bob Gibson	STL	May 23, 1970	16	PHI
Nolan Ryan	NY	May 29, 1971	16	SD
Tom Seaver	NY	May 29, 1973	16	SF
Steve Carlton	PHI	Jun 9, 1982	16	CHI
Dwight Gooden	NY	Sep 12, 1984	16	PIT
	NY	Sep 17, 1984	16	PHI
	NY	Aug 20, 1985	16	SF

Called "Tom Terrific" by fans and opponents alike, Tom Seaver (*top*) struck out at least 200 batters a record nine seasons in a row. Dizzy Dean (*above*) rang up a 135–75 record in just six full seasons with the Cardinals.

Most Strikeouts in Nine-Inning Game, Other Leagues

Player	Team	Date	SO	Opp.
One Arm Daily	C-P U	Jul 7, 1884	19	BOS
Dupee Shaw	BOS U	Jul 19, 1884	18	STL
Henry Porter	MIL U	Oct 3, 1884	18	BOS
Guy Hecker	LOU AA	Aug 26, 1884	17	COL
Toad Ramsey	LOU AA	Aug 7, 1886	17	NY
	LOU AA	Jun 21, 1887	17	CLE
Jack Lynch	NY AA	Aug 12, 1884	16	RIC
Larry McKeon	IND AA	Oct 1, 1884	16	RIC
Ed Cushman	MIL U	Oct 4, 1884	16	BOS
Bobby Mathews	PHI AA	Oct 13, 1884	16	CLE
Toad Ramsey	LOU AA	Jul 29, 1886	16	BAL
Matt Kilroy	BAL AA	Aug 24, 1886	16	PHI
Toad Ramsey	LOU AA	Jun 30, 1887	16	STL

Most Strikeouts in Extra-Inning Game, AL

Player	Team	Date	SO	Inns.	Opp.
Tom Cheney	WAS	Sep 12, 1962	21	16	BOS
Luis Tiant	CLE	Jul 3, 1968	19	10	MIN
Nolan Ryan	CAL	Jun 14, 1974	19	12	BOS
	CAL	Aug 20, 1974	19	11	DET
	CAL	Jun 8, 1977	19	10	TOR
Jack Coombs	PHI	Sep 1, 1906	18	24	BOS
Rube Waddell	PHI	Sep 5, 1905	17	13	BOS
	STL	Sep 20, 1908	17	10	WAS
Vida Blue	OAK	Jul 9, 1971	17	11	CAL
Nolan Ryan	CAL	Aug 18, 1975	17	17	DET
Rube Waddell	PHI	Jul 9, 1902	16	17	BOS
	PHI	Apr 21, 1904	16	12	NY
	PHI	Oct 18, 1905	16	12	STL
Walter Johnson	WAS	Jul 25, 1913	16	11	STL
Nolan Ryan	CAL	Sep 27, 1973	16	11	MIN

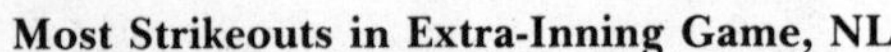

Most Strikeouts in Extra-Inning Game, NL

Player	Team	Date	SO	Inns.	Opp.
Jim Whitney	BOS	Jun 14, 1884	18	15	PRO
Warren Spahn	BOS	Jun 14, 1952	18	15	CHI
Jim Maloney	CIN	Jun 14, 1965	18	11	NY
Chris Short	PHI	Oct 2, 1965	18	15	NY
Jack Pfiester	CHI	May 30, 1906	17	15	STL
Dazzy Vance	BKN	Jul 20, 1925	17	10	STL
Bob Veale	PIT	Sep 30, 1964	16	12	CIN
Sandy Koufax	LA	Jul 27, 1966	16	11	PHI
Tom Seaver	NY	May 1, 1974	16	12	LA

Top: Tom Cheney never put together a winning season despite averaging 6.7 Ks per nine innings over eight seasons. Warren Spahn (*above*) won 20 games 13 times, despite never striking out 200 batters in a season.

Most Walks in One Game, AL

Player	Team	Date	BB	Inns.	Opp.
Bruno Haas	PHI	Jun 23, 1915	16		NY
Tommy Byrne	NY	Aug 22, 1951	16	13	WAS
Boardwalk Brown	NY	Jul 12, 1915	15		DET
Skipper Friday	WAS	Jun 17, 1923	14		CHI
George Turbeville	PHI	Aug 24, 1935	13	15	CLE
Tommy Byrne	NY	Jun 8, 1949	13	11	DET
Dick Weik	WAS	Sep 1, 1949	13		CHI
Jack Townsend	WAS	Aug 1, 1902	12		DET
John Wyckoff	PHI	Sep 24, 1913	12		BOS
Cap Crowell	PHI	Sep 8, 1915	12		BOS
Bud Davis	PHI	Sep 20, 1915	12		CLE
Carl Ray	PHI	May 9, 1916	12		DET
Sam Gibson	DET	Jul 13, 1927	12		WAS
Tommy Bridges	DET	Aug 25, 1930	12		STL
Bobby Burke	WAS	May 3, 1932	12		NY
Fritz Ostermueller	BOS	Jul 30, 1935	12		WAS
Bobo Newsom	WAS	Aug 27, 1935	12		STL
Vallie Eaves	CHI	Apr 22, 1940	12		DET
Bill Kennedy	STL	Jun 21, 1948	12		PHI
Sid Hudson	WAS	Aug 7, 1948	12		DET
Bob Turley	bal	Jul 25, 1954	12		PHI
Jack Fisher	BAL	Aug 30, 1961	12		LA

Most Walks in One Game, NL

Player	Team	Date	BB	Inns.	Opp.
Bill George	NY	May 30, 1887	16		CHI
George Van Haltren	CHI	Jun 27, 1887	16		BOS
Cannonball Crane	WAS	Sep 1, 1886	14		CHI
Piano Legs Hickman	BOS	Aug 16, 1899	14		LOU
Henry Mathewson	NY	Oct 5, 1906	14		BOS
Bill George	NY	May 17, 1887	13		IND
John Kirby	IND	Jun 9, 1887	13		DET
Bill George	NY	Jun 15, 1887	13		IND
Jesse Burkett	NY	Sep 23, 1890	13		PIT
Cy Seymour	NY	May 24, 1899	13	10	CIN
Mal Eason	BOS	Sep 3, 1902	13		PIT
Pete Schneider	CIN	Jul 6, 1918	13		PHI
Bud Podbielan	CIN	May 18, 1953	13	11	BKN
Henry Gruber	CLE	Sep 9, 1889	12		NY
Crazy Schmit	PIT	Jun 12, 1890	12		CHI
George Nicol	PIT	Jun 13, 1894	12		PHI
Wiley Piatt	BOS	Jun 10, 1903	12		CHI
	BOS	Aug 14, 1903	12		CHI
Fred Mitchell	PHI	Aug 27, 1903	12		BKN
Red Causey	BOS	Sep 8, 1919	12		PIT
Bob Smith	BOS	Sep 28, 1928	12	15	STL
Johnny Vander Meer	CIN	Apr 21, 1948	12		STL
Curt Simmons	PHI	Sep 6, 1948	12	7	NY

Most Games with 10 or More Strikeouts, Career

Player	G	Player	G
Nolan Ryan	162	Dazzy Vance	33
Sandy Koufax	98	Jim Maloney	32
Steve Carlton	83	Luis Tiant	32
Sam McDowell	74	Dwight Gooden	31
Bob Gibson	72	Don Sutton	30
Tom Seaver	70	Christy Mathewson	29
Rube Waddell	70	Vida Blue	28
Bob Feller	54	Toad Ramsey	28
Walter Johnson	53	Frank Tanana	28
Mickey Lolich	50	Don Drysdale	27
Jim Bunning	49	Mario Soto	27
Bert Blyleven	48	Lefty Grove	26
Ferguson Jenkins	46	Bill Singer	26
Gaylord Perry	41	Jerry Koosman	25
Camilo Pascual	39	Juan Marichal	25
J. R. Richard	39		

Most Strikeouts per Nine Innings, Career (Min. 1,500 IP)

Player	W	L	IP	SO	Ratio
Nolan Ryan	253	226	4115	4277	9.35
Sandy Koufax	165	87	2324	2396	9.28
Sam McDowell	141	134	2492	2453	8.86
J. R. Richard	107	71	1606	1493	8.37
Bob Veale	120	95	1926	1703	7.96
Mario Soto	95	83	1612	1404	7.84
Jim Maloney	134	84	1849	1605	7.81
Sam Jones	102	101	1643	1376	7.54
Fernando Valenzuela	99	68	1554	1274	7.38
Bob Gibson	251	174	3885	3117	7.22
Steve Carlton	323	229	5055	4040	7.19
Rube Waddell	191	141	2842	2250	7.04
Mickey Lolich	217	191	3640	2832	7.00
Bert Blyleven	229	197	3987	3090	6.98
Floyd Bannister	101	117	1832	1405	6.90
Rollie Fingers	114	118	1701	1299	6.87
Tom Seaver	311	205	4782	3640	6.85
Jim Bunning	224	184	3760	2855	6.83
Juan Pizarro	131	105	2034	1522	6.73
Bobby Bolin	88	75	1576	1175	6.71
Ray Culp	122	101	1897	1411	6.69
Ron Guidry	163	80	2219	1650	6.69
Camilo Pascual	174	170	2930	2167	6.66
Stan Williams	109	94	1764	1305	6.66
Bob Turley	101	85	1713	1265	6.65
Don Wilson	104	92	1748	1283	6.60
Tug McGraw	96	92	1516	1109	6.58
Denny Lemaster	90	105	1788	1305	6.57
Andy Messersmith	130	99	2230	1625	6.56
Don Drysdale	209	166	3432	2486	6.52
Al Downing	123	107	2268	1639	6.50

Most Consecutive Wins, AL

Player	Team	Year	W	Player	Team	Year	W
Walter Johnson	WAS	1912	16	Whitey Ford	NY	1961	14
Joe Wood	BOS	1912	16	Steve Stone	BAL	1980	14
Lefty Grove	PHI	1931	16	Roger Clemens	BOS	1986	14
Schoolboy Rowe	DET	1934	16	Walter Johnson	WAS	1924	13
General Crowder	WAS	1932	15	Stan Coveleski	WAS	1925	13
Johnny Allen	CLE	1937	15	Wes Ferrell	CLE	1930	13
Dave McNally	BAL	1969	15	Bobo Newsom	DET	1940	13
Gaylord Perry	CLE	1974	15	Ellis Kinder	BOS	1949	13
Jack Chesbro	NY	1904	14	Dave McNally	BAL	1971	13
Walter Johnson	WAS	1913	14	Catfish Hunter	OAK	1973	13
Chief Bender	PHI	1914	14	Ron Guidry	NY	1978	13
Lefty Grove	PHI	1928	14	LaMarr Hoyt	CHI	1983	13

Most Consecutive Wins, NL

Player	Team	Year	W	Player	Team	Year	W
Tim Keefe	NY	1888	19	Joe McGinnity	NY	1904	14
Rube Marquard	NY	1912	19	Ed Reulbach	CHI	1909	14
Old Hoss Radbourn	PRO	1884	18	Rick Sutcliffe	CHI	1984	14
Mickey Welch	NY	1885	17	Dwight Gooden	NY	1985	14
Pat Luby	CHI	1890	17	Larry Corcoran	CHI	1880	13
Roy Face	PIT	1959	17	Charlie Buffinton	BOS	1884	13
Jim McCormick	CHI	1886	16	Cy Young	CLE	1892	13
Carl Hubbell	NY	1936	16	Frank Dwyer	CIN	1896	13
Ewell Blackwell	CIN	1947	16	Christy Mathewson	NY	1909	13
Jack Sanford	SF	1962	16	Deacon Phillippe	PIT	1910	13
Dazzy Vance	BKN	1924	15	Burleigh Grimes	NY	1927	13
Bob Gibson	STL	1968	15	Brooks Lawrence	CIN	1956	13
Steve Carlton	PHI	1972	15	Phil Regan	LA	1966	13
Jim McCormick	CHI	1885	14	Dock Ellis	PIT	1971	13
Jocko Flynn	CHI	1886	14				

Most Consecutive Losses, AL

Player	Team	Year	L	Player	Team	Year	L
Bob Groom	WAS	1909	19	Dutch Henry	CHI	1930	13
Jack Nabors	PHI	1916	19	Lum Harris	PHI	1943	13
Mike Parrott	SEA	1980	16	Terry Felton	MIN	1982	13
Joe Harris	BOS	1906	14	Red Ruffing	BOS	1929	12
Paul Calvert	WAS	1949	14	Milt Gaston	BOS	1931	12
Howie Judson	CHI	1949	14	Walt Masterson	WAS	1940	12
Matt Keough	OAK	1979	14	Steve Gerkin	PHI	1945	12
Guy Morton	CLE	1914	13	Bobo Newsom	PHI	1945	12
Roy Moore	PHI	1920	13	Charlie Bishop	PHI	1953	12

Most Consecutive Losses, NL

Player	Team	Year	L	Player	Team	Year	L
Cliff Curtis	BOS	1910	18	Dutch McCall	CHI	1948	13
Roger Craig	NY	1963	18	Blondie Purcell	CIN	1880	12
Dory Dean	CIN	1876	16	John Coleman	PHI	1883	12
Sam Weaver	MIL	1878	16	Henry Thielman	CIN	1902	12
Jim Hughey	CLE	1899	16	Mal Eason	BKN	1905	12
Craig Anderson	NY	1962	16	Rube Marquard	NY	1914	12
Frank Gilmore	WAS	1887	14	Pete Schneider	CIN	1914	12
Frank Bates	CLE	1899	14	Russ Miller	PHI	1928	12
Jim Pastorius	BKN	1908	14	Si Johnson	CIN	1933	12
Buster Brown	BOS	1911	14	Max Butcher	PHI		
Sam Moffett	CLE	1884	13		PIT	1939	12
Burleigh Grimes	PIT	1917	13	Hugh Mulcahy	PHI	1940	12
Joe Oeschger	BOS	1922	13	Bob Miller	NY	1962	12
Ben Cantwell	BOS	1935	13	Ken Reynolds	PHI	1972	12

Most Consecutive Strikeouts, AL

Player	Team	Date	SO	Opp.
Nolan Ryan	CAL	Jul 9, 1972	8	BOS
	CAL	Jul 15, 1973	8	DET
Ron Davis	NY	May 4, 1981	8	OAK
Roger Clemens	BOS	Apr 29, 1986	8	SEA
Ryne Duren	LA	Jun 9, 1961	7	BOS
Denny McLain	DET	Jun 15, 1965	7	BOS
Pete Richert	WAS	Apr 24, 1966	7	DET
Phil Ortega	WAS	May 29, 1966	7	BOS
Jim Merritt	MIN	Jul 21, 1966	7	WAS
John Hiller	DET	Oct 1, 1970	7	CLE
Sammy Stewart	BAL	Sep 1, 1978	7	CLE
Mark Langston	SEA	Jun 15, 1984	7	BOS
Joe Cowley	CHI	May 28, 1986	7	TEX

Most Consecutive Strikeouts, NL

Player	Team	Date	SO	Opp.
Tom Seaver	NY	Apr 22, 1970	10	SD
Mickey Welch	NY	Aug 28, 1884	9	PIT
Charlie Buffinton	BOS	Sep 2, 1884	8	CLE
Max Surkont	MIL	May 25, 1953	8	CIN
Johnny Podres	LA	Jul 2, 1962	8	PHI
Jim Maloney	CIN	May 21, 1963	8	MIL
Don Wilson	HOU	Jul 14, 1968	8	CIN
Jim Deshaies	HOU	Sep 23, 1986	8	LA
John Clarkson	CHI	Sep 30, 1884	7	NY
Hooks Wiltse	NY	May 15, 1906	7	CIN
Dazzy Vance	BKN	Aug 1, 1924	7	CHI
Van Mungo	BKN	Jun 25, 1936	7	CIN
Juan Marichal	SF	Sep 6, 1964	7	PHI
Steve Renko	MON	Oct 3, 1972	7	NY
Al Downing	LA	Jul 14, 1973	7	CHI

Gaylord Perry (*left*) defined longevity in pitching, collecting 314 wins in 22 seasons for eight different teams. Tug McGraw (*above*) made believers out of hitters, appearing in 824 games and helping his teams into three World Series.

Most Consecutive Strikeouts, Other Leagues

Player	Team	Date	SO	Opp.
Ed Cushman	NY AA	Sep 16, 1885	8	PIT
Jack Stivetts	STL AA	May 3, 1890	7	LOU

Most Relief Wins, Career

Player	W
Hoyt Wilhelm	123
Lindy McDaniel	119
Rollie Fingers	107
Sparky Lyle	99
Roy Face	96
Mike Marshall	92
Don McMahon	90
Tug McGraw	89
Clay Carroll	88
Goose Gossage	87

Player	W
Tom Burgmeier	79
Stu Miller	79
Ron Perranoski	79
Gary Lavelle	78
Bill Campbell	77
Kent Tekulve	74
Johnny Murphy	73
John Hiller	72
Dick Hall	71

Most Relief Wins, Season, AL

Player	Team	Year	W
John Hiller	DET	1974	17
Bill Campbell	MIN	1976	17
Dick Radatz	BOS	1964	16
Tom Johnson	MIN	1977	16
Luis Arroyo	NY	1961	15
Dick Radatz	BOS	1963	15
Eddie Fisher	CHI	1965	15
Stu Miller	BAL	1965	14
Ron Davis	NY	1979	14
Mark Clear	BOS	1982	14
Mark Eichhorn	TOR	1986	14
Gerry Staley	CHI	1960	13
Rollie Fingers	OAK	1976	13
Sparky Lyle	NY	1977	13
Jim Kern	TEX	1979	13
Aurelio Lopez	DET	1980	13
Goose Gossage	NY	1983	13
Johnny Murphy	NY	1937	12
	NY	1943	12
Hoyt Wilhelm	CHI	1964	12
Wilbur Wood	CHI	1968	12
Lindy McDaniel	NY	1973	12
Sid Monge	CLE	1979	12
Dan Quisenberry	KC	1980	12
Clint Brown	CHI	1939	11
Joe Heving	BOS	1939	11
Rollie Fingers	OAK	1972	11
John Hiller	DET	1976	11
Mark Clear	CAL	1979	11
	CAL	1980	11

Hoyt Wilhelm (*left*) pitched in a record 1070 games and had a career ERA of 2.52. Sparky Lyle (*above*) protected the Yankees' championships in the late 1970s, going 3–0 with a 1.89 ERA in 10 postseason games.

The year after Roy Face posted an amazing 18–1 record, he helped secure Pittsburgh's World Series victory over the Yankees by recording saves in Games One, Four, and Five.

Most Relief Wins, Season, NL

Player	Team	Year	W
Roy Face	PIT	1959	18
Jim Konstanty	PHI	1950	16
Ron Perranoski	LA	1963	16
Mace Brown	PIT	1938	15
Hoyt Wilhelm	NY	1952	15
Mike Marshall	LA	1974	15
Dale Murray	MON	1975	15
Stu Miller	SF	1961	14
Phil Regan	LA	1966	14
Frank Linzy	SF	1969	14
Mike Marshall	MON	1972	14
	MON	1973	14
Roger McDowell	NY	1986	14
Clyde Shoun	CIN	1943	13
Lindy McDaniel	STL	1959	13
Larry Sherry	LA	1960	13
Lindy McDaniel	CHI	1963	13
Al Hrabosky	STL	1975	13
Jesse Orosco	NY	1983	13
Hoyt Wilhelm	NY	1954	12
Lindy McDaniel	STL	1960	12
Jack Baldschun	PHI	1962	12
Ron Kline	PIT	1968	12
Phil Regan	LA	1968	
	CHI	1968	12
	CHI	1969	12
Jerry Johnson	SF	1971	12
Charlie Hough	LA	1976	12
Hugh Casey	BKN	1946	11
Roy Face	PIT	1956	11
Jack Baldschun	PHI	1963	11
Hal Woodeshick	HOU	1963	11
Al McBean	PIT	1963	11
Clay Carroll	CIN	1969	11
Tug McGraw	NY	1971	11
Pedro Borbon	CIN	1973	11
Goose Gossage	PIT	1977	11
Doug Bair	CIN	1979	11
Dick Tidrow	CHI	1979	11
Rollie Fingers	SD	1980	11

Most Relief Losses, Career

Player	L
Rollie Fingers	102
Hoyt Wilhelm	102
Mike Marshall	98
Gene Garber	89
Lindy McDaniel	87
Roy Face	82
Sparky Lyle	76
Ron Perranoski	74
Gary Lavelle	71
Kent Tekulve	71
Darold Knowles	69
Clay Carroll	68
Tug McGraw	67
Stu Miller	67
Bruce Sutter	67
Don McMahon	66
Goose Gossage	60
Bill Campbell	58
John Hiller	57
Frank Linzy	57
Tom Burgmeier	53
Jim Kern	52
Dave LaRoche	52
Randy Moffitt	52
Dick Farrell	51
Claude Raymond	51
Dale Murray	50
Al Worthington	50

Most Relief Losses, Season, AL

Player	Team	Year	L
Darold Knowles	WAS	1970	14
John Hiller	DET	1974	14
Mike Marshall	MIN	1979	14
Wilbur Wood	CHI	1970	13
Ken Sanders	MIL	1971	12
Jim Willoughby	BOS	1976	12
Mike Marshall	MIN	1978	12
Frank Funk	CLE	1961	11
Dick Radatz	BOS	1965	11
Wilbur Wood	CHI	1968	11
	CHI	1969	11
Rollie Fingers	OAK	1976	11
Goose Gossage	NY	1978	11
Dave Heaverlo	OAK	1979	11
Dave LaRoche	CAL	1979	11
Mark Clear	CAL	1980	11
Jim Kern	TEX	1980	11
Ron Davis	MIN	1984	11

Most Relief Losses, Season, NL

Player	Team	Year	L
Gene Garber	ATL	1979	16
Mike Marshall	LA	1975	14
Rollie Fingers	SD	1978	13
Skip Lockwood	NY	1978	13
Roy Face	PIT	1956	12
	PIT	1961	12
Mike Marshall	LA	1974	12
Gene Garber	PHI	1975	12
Charlie Hough	LA	1977	12
Kent Tekulve	PIT	1980	12
Ken Howell	LA	1986	12
Nels Potter	BOS	1949	11
Frank Linzy	SF	1966	11
Mike Marshall	MON	1973	11
Greg Minton	SF	1983	11
Mark Davis	SF	1985	11

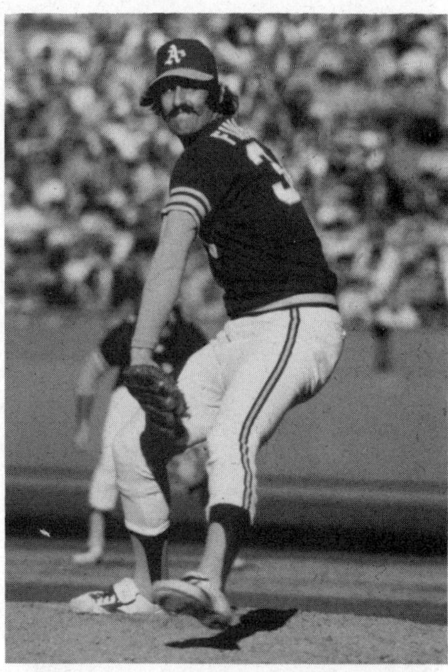

Rollie Fingers (*top*) saved a record six World Series games for Oakland during the 1972–74 championship seasons. Bruce Sutter (*above*) put together nine consecutive seasons (1977-85) of 20 or more saves.

Most Saves, Career

Player	SV
Rollie Fingers	341
Bruce Sutter	286
Goose Gossage	278
Sparky Lyle	238
Dan Quisenberry	229
Hoyt Wilhelm	227
Gene Garber	194
Roy Face	193
Mike Marshall	188
Tug McGraw	180
Ron Perranoski	179
Kent Tekulve	176
Lindy McDaniel	172
Jeff Reardon	162
Stu Miller	154
Don McMahon	153
Ted Abernathy	148
Dave Giusti	145
Lee Smith	144
Clay Carroll	143
Darold Knowles	143
Gary Lavelle	135
Jim Brewer	132
Ron Davis	130
Terry Forster	127
Bill Campbell	126
Dave LaRoche	126
John Hiller	125
Greg Minton	124
Jack Aker	123
Bob Stanley	123
Dick Radatz	122
Tippy Martinez	115
Willie Hernandez	114
Frank Linzy	111
Al Worthington	110
Fred Gladding	109
Wayne Granger	108
Ron Kline	108
Johnny Murphy	107
Dave Righetti	107
Bill Caudill	105
Ron Reed	103
John Wyatt	103
Tom Burgmeier	102
Ellis Kinder	102
Firpo Marberry	101
Dave Smith	100

Most Saves, Season, AL

Player	Team	Year	SV	Player	Team	Year	SV
Dave Righetti	NY	1986	46	Jack Aker	KC	1966	32
Dan Quisenberry	KC	1983	45	Mike Marshall	MIN	1979	32
	KC	1984	44	Willie Hernandez	DET	1984	32
John Hiller	DET	1973	38	Bob James	CHI	1985	32
Dan Quisenberry	KC	1985	37	Ron Perranoski	MIN	1969	31
Bill Caudill	OAK	1984	36	Ken Sanders	MIL	1971	31
Sparky Lyle	NY	1972	35	Bill Campbell	BOS	1977	31
Dan Quisenberry	KC	1982	35	Dave Righetti	NY	1984	31
Ron Perranoski	MIN	1970	34	Willie Hernandez	DET	1985	31
Don Aase	BAL	1986	34	Donnie Moore	CAL	1985	31
Goose Gossage	NY	1980	33	Ed Farmer	CHI	1980	30
Dan Quisenberry	KC	1980	33	Goose Gossage	NY	1982	30
Bob Stanley	BOS	1983	33	Ron Davis	MIN	1983	30

Most Saves, Season, NL

Player	Team	Year	SV	Player	Team	Year	SV
Bruce Sutter	STL	1984	45	Dave Smith	HOU	1986	33
Jeff Reardon	MON	1985	41	Ted Abernathy	CHI	1965	31
Clay Carroll	CIN	1972	37	Mike Marshall	MON	1973	31
Rollie Fingers	SD	1978	37	Bruce Sutter	CHI	1977	31
Bruce Sutter	CHI	1979	37	Kent Tekulve	PIT	1978	31
	STL	1982	36		PIT	1979	31
Todd Worrell	STL	1986	36	Jesse Orosco	NY	1984	31
Wayne Granger	CIN	1970	35	Lee Smith	CHI	1986	31
Rollie Fingers	SD	1977	35	Dave Giusti	PIT	1971	30
Jeff Reardon	MON	1986	35	Gene Garber	ATL	1982	30
Lee Smith	CHI	1984	33	Greg Minton	SF	1982	30
	CHI	1985	33				

Most Wins Plus Saves, Season

Player	Team	Year	G	IP	SO	W	L	SV	W & S	ERA
Dave Righetti	NY A	1986	74	107	83	8	8	46	54	2.45
Bruce Sutter	STL N	1984	71	123	77	5	7	45	50	1.54
Dan Quisenberry	KC A	1983	69	139	48	5	3	45	50	1.94
	KC A	1984	72	129	41	6	3	44	50	2.64
John Hiller	DET A	1973	65	125	124	10	5	38	48	1.44
Todd Worrell	STL N	1986	74	104	73	9	10	36	45	2.08
Dick Radatz	BOS A	1964	79	157	181	16	9	29	45	2.29
Dan Quisenberry	KC A	1985	84	129	54	8	9	37	45	2.37
Mike Marshall	MON N	1973	92	179	124	14	11	31	45	2.66
Bill Caudill	OAK A	1984	68	96	89	9	7	36	45	2.71
Bruce Sutter	STL N	1982	70	102	61	9	8	36	45	2.90
Dan Quisenberry	KC A	1980	75	128	37	12	7	33	45	3.11
Sparky Lyle	NY A	1972	59	108	75	9	5	35	44	1.92
Luis Arroyo	NY A	1961	65	119	87	15	5	29	44	2.19
Dan Quisenberry	KC A	1982	72	137	46	9	7	35	44	2.57
Bill Campbell	BOS A	1977	69	140	114	13	9	31	44	2.96
Bruce Sutter	CHI N	1979	62	101	110	6	6	37	43	2.23

Most Wins Plus Saves, Season ***(cont'd)***

Player	Team	Year	G	IP	SO	W	L	SV	W & S	ERA
Clay Carroll	CIN N	1972	65	96	51	6	4	37	43	2.25
Rollie Fingers	SD N	1978	67	107	72	6	13	37	43	2.52
	SD N	1977	78	132	113	8	9	35	43	3.00
Jeff Reardon	MON N	1985	63	88	67	2	8	41	43	3.18
Jim Kern	TEX A	1979	71	143	136	13	5	29	42	1.57
Mike Marshall	MIN A	1979	90	143	81	10	15	32	42	2.64
Lee Smith	CHI N	1984	69	101	86	9	7	33	42	3.65
Jeff Reardon	MON N	1986	62	89	67	7	9	35	42	3.94
Willie Hernandez	DET A	1984	80	140	112	9	3	32	41	1.92
Ron Perranoski	MIN A	1970	67	111	55	7	8	34	41	2.43
Jesse Orosco	NY N	1984	60	87	85	10	6	31	41	2.59
Wayne Granger	CIN N	1970	67	85	38	6	5	35	41	2.65
Kent Tekulve	PIT N	1979	74	134	75	10	8	31	41	2.75
Dave Righetti	NY A	1985	74	107	92	12	7	29	41	2.78
Bob Stanley	BOS A	1983	64	145	65	8	10	33	41	2.85
Greg Minton	SF N	1982	78	123	58	10	4	30	40	1.83
Dick Radatz	BOS A	1963	66	125	162	15	6	25	40	1.97
Jack Aker	KC A	1966	66	113	68	8	4	32	40	1.99
Ron Perranoski	MIN A	1969	75	120	62	9	10	31	40	2.11
Bob James	CHI A	1985	69	110	88	8	7	32	40	2.13
Don Aase	BAL A	1986	66	82	67	6	7	34	40	2.98
Lee Smith	CHI N	1985	65	98	112	7	4	33	40	3.04
	CHI N	1986	66	90	93	9	9	31	40	3.09

Master of the submarine pitch, the Royals' Dan Quisenberry (*above*) has averaged 32 saves per year since 1980. *Right*: Just three years after hurling a no-hitter against Boston, Dave Righetti saved a record 46 games in 1986.

Two Complete Game Wins in One Day, AL

Player	Team	Date	Score	H	SO	BB	Opp.
Frank Owen	CHI	Jul 1, 1905	3-2	4	2	3	STL
	CHI	Jul 1, 1905	3-0	3	0	0	STL
George Mullin	DET	Sep 22, 1906	5-3	11	4	1	WAS
	DET	Sep 22, 1906	4-3	9	5	2	WAS
Ed Summers	DET	Sep 25, 1908	7-2	6	1	3	PHI
	DET	Sep 25, 1908	1-0	2	6	0	PHI
Ed Walsh	CHI	Sep 29, 1908	5-1	3	10	0	BOS
	CHI	Sep 29, 1908	2-0	4	5	1	BOS
Ray Collins	BOS	Sep 22, 1914	5-3	12	3	1	DET
	BOS	Sep 22, 1914	5-0	4	0	1	DET
Dave Davenport	STL	Jul 29, 1916	3-1	4	4	3	NY
	STL	Jul 29, 1916	3-2	7	7	3	NY
Carl Mays	BOS	Aug 30, 1918	12-0	9	2	0	PHI
	BOS	Aug 30, 1918	4-1	4	3	2	PHI
Urban Shocker	STL	Sep 6, 1924	6-2	9	1	1	CHI
	STL	Sep 6, 1924	6-2	5	0	4	CHI
Dutch Levsen	CLE	Aug 28, 1926	6-1	4	0	1	BOS
	CLE	Aug 28, 1926	5-1	4	0	2	BOS

Two Complete Game Wins in One Day, NL since 1900

Player	Team	Date	Score	H	SO	BB	Opp.
Joe McGinnity	NY	Aug 1, 1903	4-1	6	5	1	BOS
	NY	Aug 1, 1903	5-2	6	3	1	BOS
	NY	Aug 8, 1903	6-1	8	2	0	BKN
	NY	Aug 8, 1903	4-3	5	5	4	BKN
	NY	Aug 31, 1903	4-1	5	4	3	PHI
	NY	Aug 31, 1903	9-2	6	9	1	PHI
Doc Scanlan	BKN	Oct 3, 1905	4-0	3	8	2	STL
	BKN	Oct 3, 1905	3-2	9	5	0	STL
Ed Reulbach	CHI	Sep 26, 1908	5-0	5	6	1	BKN
	CHI	Sep 26, 1908	3-0	3	4	4	BKN
Pol Perritt	NY	Sep 9, 1916	3-1	4	3	2	PHI
	NY	Sep 9, 1916	3-0	4	0	3	PHI
Al Demaree	PHI	Sep 20, 1916	7-0	9	4	2	PIT
	PHI	Sep 20, 1916	3-2	12	3	0	PIT
Grover Alexander	PHI	Sep 23, 1916	7-3	12	3	0	CIN
	PHI	Sep 23, 1916	4-0	8	4	1	CIN
Fred Toney	CIN	Jul 1, 1917	4-1	3	3	1	PIT
	CIN	Jul 1, 1917	5-1	3	1	1	PIT
Grover Alexander	PHI	Sep 3, 1917	5-0	4	5	1	BKN
	PHI	Sep 3, 1917	9-3	9	2	0	BKN
Bill Doak	STL	Sep 18, 1917	2-0	2	1	1	BKN
	STL	Sep 18, 1917	12-4	12	4	2	BKN
Mule Watson	BOS	Aug 13, 1921	4-3	9	2	2	PHI
	BOS	Aug 13, 1921	8-0	2	5	0	PHI
Johnny Stuart	STL	Jul 10, 1923	11-1	3	0	2	BOS
	STL	Jul 10, 1923	6-3	10	0	2	BOS
Hi Bell	STL	Jul 19, 1924	6-1	4	2	1	BOS
	STL	Jul 19, 1924	2-1	9	1	1	BOS

Two Complete Game Wins in One Day, NL before 1900

Player	Team	Date	Score	Inns.	Opp.
Candy Cummings	HAR	Sep 9, 1876	14-4		CIN
	HAR	Sep 9, 1876	8-4		CIN
Monte Ward	PRO	Aug 9, 1878	12-6		IND
	PRO	Aug 9, 1878	8-5		IND
Pud Galvin	BUF	Jul 12, 1879	4-3		TRO
	BUF	Jul 12, 1879	5-4	12	TRO
Mickey Welch	TRO	Jul 4, 1881	8-0		BUF
	TRO	Jul 4, 1881	12-3		BUF
Pud Galvin	BUF	Jul 4, 1882	9-5		WOR
	BUF	Jul 4, 1882	18-8		WOR
Old Hoss Radbourn	PRO	May 30, 1884	12-9		CHI
	PRO	May 30, 1884	9-2		CHI
Dupee Shaw	PRO	Oct 7, 1885	4-0	5	BUF
	PRO	Oct 7, 1885	6-1	5	BUF
	PRO	Oct 10, 1885	3-0	6	BUF
	PRO	Oct 10, 1885	7-3	5	BUF
Charlie Ferguson	PHI	Oct 9, 1886	5-1		DET
	PHI	Oct 9, 1886	6-1	6	DET
Jim Whitney	WAS	Aug 20, 1887	3-1		BOS
	WAS	Aug 20, 1887	4-3		BOS
John Clarkson	BOS	Sep 12, 1889	3-2		CLE
	BOS	Sep 12, 1889	5-0		CLE
Bill Hutchison	CHI	May 30, 1890	6-4		BKN
	CHI	May 30, 1890	11-7		BKN
Cy Young	CLE	Oct 4, 1890	5-1		PHI
	CLE	Oct 4, 1890	7-3		PHI
Mark Baldwin	PIT	Sep 12, 1891	13-3		BKN
	PIT	Sep 12, 1891	8-4		BKN
Amos Rusie	NY	Sep 26, 1891	10-4		BOS
	NY	Sep 26, 1891	13-5	6	BOS
Mark Baldwin	PIT	May 30, 1892	11-1		BAL
	PIT	May 30, 1892	4-3		BAL
Amos Rusie	NY	Oct 4, 1892	6-4		WAS
	NY	Oct 4, 1892	9-5		WAS
Cy Seymour	NY	Jun 3, 1897	6-1		LOU
	NY	Jun 3, 1897	10-6	7	LOU

Two Complete Game Wins in One Day, Other Leagues

Player	Team	Date	Score	Inns.	Opp.
Tim Keefe	NY AA	Jul 4, 1883	9-1		COL
	NY AA	Jul 4, 1883	3-0		COL
Guy Hecker	LOU AA	Jul 4, 1884	5-4		BKN
	LOU AA	Jul 4, 1884	8-2		BKN
Matt Kilroy	BAL AA	Jul 26, 1887	8-0	7	COL
	BAL AA	Jul 26, 1887	9-1		COL
	BAL AA	Oct 1, 1887	5-2		PHI
	BAL AA	Oct 1, 1887	8-1	7	PHI
Tony Mullane	CIN AA	Sep 20, 1888	1-0		PHI
	CIN AA	Sep 20, 1888	2-1		PHI

Two Complete Game Wins in One Day, Other Leagues *(cont'd)*

Player	Team	Date	Score	Inns.	Opp.
Henry Gruber	CLE P	Jul 26, 1890	6-1		NY
	CLE P	Jul 26, 1890	8-7		NY
Bert Cunningham	BUF P	Aug 20, 1890	6-2		CHI
	BUF P	Aug 20, 1890	7-0		CHI
Cannonball Crane	NY P	Sep 27, 1890	9-8		BUF
	NY P	Sep 27, 1890	8-3		BUF

Best Control Pitchers, Career

Player	IP	BB	Ratio	Player	IP	BB	Ratio
Deacon Phillippe	2607	363	1.25	Carl Hubbell	3589	724	1.82
Babe Adams	2995	430	1.29	Juan Marichal	3509	709	1.82
Addie Joss	2336	370	1.43	Slim Sallee	2819	572	1.83
Cy Young	7356	1217	1.49	Lew Burdette	3068	628	1.84
Jesse Tannehill	2770	478	1.55	Curt Davis	2325	479	1.85
Christy Mathewson	4782	846	1.59	Ed Walsh	2964	617	1.87
Red Lucas	2542	455	1.61	Paul Derringer	3646	761	1.88
Nick Altrock	1515	272	1.62	Ken Raffensberger	2152	449	1.88
Grover Alexander	5189	953	1.65	Three Finger Brown	3172	673	1.91
Ernie Bonham	1551	287	1.67	Sherry Smith	2053	440	1.93
Noodles Hahn	2012	379	1.70	Bill Swift	1638	351	1.93
Fritz Peterson	2218	426	1.73	Jack Quinn	3935	859	1.96
Robin Roberts	4689	902	1.73	Watty Clark	1747	383	1.97
Al Orth	3355	661	1.77	Doc White	3059	670	1.97
Dick Rudolph	2049	402	1.77	Ferguson Jenkins	4500	997	1.99
Jesse Barnes	2570	515	1.80	Sam Leever	2661	587	1.99
Pete Donohue	2112	422	1.80				

Babe Adams (*left*) led the Pirates to World Series victory over Detroit in 1909, recording complete-game wins in Games One, Five, and Seven. Cub ace Ferguson Jenkins (*above*) won 20 or more games every year from 1967–72.

Lowest ERA, Season, AL

Player	Team	Year	ERA
Dutch Leonard	BOS	1914	1.01
Walter Johnson	WAS	1913	1.09
Addie Joss	CLE	1908	1.16
Cy Young	BOS	1908	1.26
Ed Walsh	CHI	1910	1.27
Walter Johnson	WAS	1918	1.27
Jack Coombs	PHI	1910	1.30
Walter Johnson	WAS	1910	1.35
Harry Krause	PHI	1909	1.39
Walter Johnson	WAS	1912	1.39
Ed Walsh	CHI	1909	1.41
	CHI	1908	1.42
Rube Waddell	PHI	1905	1.48
Joe Wood	BOS	1915	1.49
Walter Johnson	WAS	1919	1.49

Lowest ERA, Season, NL

Player	Team	Year	ERA
Three Finger Brown	CHI	1906	1.04
Bob Gibson	STL	1968	1.12
Christy Mathewson	NY	1909	1.14
Jack Pfiester	CHI	1907	1.15
Carl Lundgren	CHI	1907	1.17
Grover Alexander	PHI	1915	1.22
Christy Mathewson	NY	1905	1.27
Three Finger Brown	CHI	1909	1.31
Jack Taylor	CHI	1902	1.33
Three Finger Brown	CHI	1907	1.39
Ed Reulbach	CHI	1905	1.42
Orval Overall	CHI	1909	1.42
Christy Mathewson	NY	1908	1.43
Three Finger Brown	CHI	1908	1.47

Bob Gibson was overpowering in October as well. His World Series record: 7–2, 1.89 ERA, 92 Ks, and two shutouts.

Most Innings Pitched, Game, AL

Player	Team	Date	IP	H	R	SO	BB	Score	Opp.
Jack Coombs	PHI	Sep 1, 1906	24	15	1	18	6	4-1	BOS
Joe Harris	BOS	Sep 1, 1906	24	16	4	14	2	1-4	PHI
Ted Lyons	CHI	May 24, 1929	21	24	6	4	2	5-6	DET
Rube Waddell	PHI	Jul 4, 1905	20	15	2	11	4	4-2	BOS
Cy Young	BOS	Jul 4, 1905	20	13	4	9	0	2-4	PHI
George Uhle	DET	May 24, 1929	20	17	5	4	3	6-5	CHI
Les Mueller	DET	Jul 21, 1945	19.2	13	1	6	5	1-1	PHI
Eddie Plank	PHI	Sep 27, 1912	19	12	5	10	6	4-5	WAS
Stan Coveleski	CLE	May 24, 1918	19	12	2	4	6	3-2	NY
Dixie Davis	STL	Aug 9, 1921	19	13	6	8	5	8-6	WAS
Ed Summers	DET	Jul 16, 1909	18	7	0	10	1	0-0	WAS
Walter Johnson	WAS	May 15, 1918	18	10	0	9	1	1-0	CHI
Lefty Williams	CHI	May 15, 1918	18	8	1	3	2	0-1	WAS

Most Innings Pitched, Game, NL

Player	Team	Date	IP	H	R	SO	BB	Score	Opp.
Leon Cadore	BKN	May 1, 1920	26	15	1	7	5	1-1	BOS
Joe Oeschger	BOS	May 1, 1920	26	9	1	7	4	1-1	BKN
Bob Smith	BOS	May 17, 1927	22	20	4	5	9	3-4	CHI
Rube Marquard	NY	May 17, 1914	21	15	1	2	2	3-1	PIT
Babe Adams	PIT	May 17, 1914	21	12	3	6	0	1-3	NY
Lefty Tyler	CHI	Jul 17, 1918	21	13	1	8	1	2-1	PHI
Art Nehf	BOS	Aug 1, 1918	21	12	2	8	5	0-2	PIT
Ad Gumbert	CHI	Jun 30, 1892	20	12	7	2	3	7-7	CIN
Tony Mullane	CIN	Jun 30, 1892	20	14	7	5	3	7-7	CHI
Ed Reulbach	CHI	Aug 24, 1905	20	13	1	7	4	2-1	PHI
Tully Sparks	PHI	Aug 24, 1905	20	19	2	6	1	1-2	CHI
Milt Watson	PHI	Jul 17, 1918	20	19	2	5	4	1-2	CHI
Joe Oeschger	PHI	Apr 30, 1919	20	22	9	2	5	9-9	BKN
Burleigh Grimes	BKN	Apr 30, 1919	20	15	9	7	7	9-9	PHI
Jack Taylor	CHI	Jun 22, 1902	19	14	2	6	1	3-2	PIT
Otto Hess	BOS	Jul 31, 1912	19	14	7	3	8	6-7	PIT
Dana Fillingim	BOS	May 3, 1920	19	12	1	4	4	2-1	BKN
Deacon Phillippe	PIT	Jun 22, 1902	18.2	14	3	6	3	2-3	CHI
Zip Zabel	CHI	Jun 17, 1915	18.1	15	2	6	1	4-3	BKN
Jeff Pfeffer	BKN	Jun 17, 1915	18.1	15	4	6	8	3-4	CHI
Sherry Smith	BKN	May 3, 1920	18.1	13	2	3	5	1-2	BOS
Monte Ward	PRO	Aug 17, 1882	18	9	0	4	1	1-0	DET
Wild Bill Donovan	BKN	Aug 17, 1902	18	14	7	13	7	7-7	STL
Ed Reulbach	CHI	Jun 24, 1905	18	14	1	6	6	2-1	STL
Jack Taylor	STL	Jun 24, 1905	18	11	2	7	4	1-2	CHI
Jeff Pfeffer	BKN	Jun 1, 1919	18	23	10	6	3	9-10	PHI
Guy Bush	CHI	May 14, 1927	18	11	2	5	8	7-2	BOS
Carl Hubbell	NY	Jul 2, 1933	18	6	0	12	0	1-0	STL
Vern Law	PIT	Jul 19, 1955	18	9	2	12	3	4-3	MIL

Triple-Crown Pitchers, AL (most wins, lowest ERA, most strikeouts)

Player	Team	Year	W	L	SO	ERA
Cy Young	BOS	1901	33	10	158	1.62
Rube Waddell	PHI	1905	26	11	287	1.48
Walter Johnson	WAS	1913	36	7	303	1.09
	WAS	1918	23	13	162	1.27
	WAS	1924	23	7	158	2.72
Lefty Grove	PHI	1930	28	5	209	2.54
	PHI	1931	31	4	175	2.06
Lefty Gomez	NY	1934	26	5	158	2.33
	NY	1937	21	11	194	2.33
Hal Newhouser	DET	1945	25	9	212	1.81

Triple-Crown Pitchers, NL (most wins, lowest ERA, most strikeouts)

Player	Team	Year	W	L	SO	ERA
Tommy Bond	BOS	1877	40	17	170	2.11
Old Hoss Radbourn	PRO	1884	60	12	441	1.38
Tim Keefe	NY	1888	35	12	333	1.74
John Clarkson	BOS	1889	49	19	284	2.73
Amos Rusie	NY	1894	36	13	195	2.78
Christy Mathewson	NY	1905	31	8	206	1.27
	NY	1908	37	11	259	1.43
Grover Alexander	PHI	1915	31	10	241	1.22
	PHI	1916	33	12	167	1.55
	PHI	1917	30	13	201	1.86
Hippo Vaughn	CHI	1918	22	10	148	1.74
Grover Alexander	CHI	1920	27	14	173	1.91
Dazzy Vance	BKN	1924	28	6	262	2.16
Bucky Walters	CIN	1939	27	11	137	2.29
Sandy Koufax	LA	1963	25	5	306	1.88
	LA	1965	26	8	382	2.04
	LA	1966	27	9	317	1.73
Steve Carlton	PHI	1972	27	10	310	1.97
Dwight Gooden	NY	1985	24	4	268	1.53

Fewest Base Runners per Nine Innings, Career (Min. 1,500 IP)

Player	W	L	IP	H	BB	BR/9
Addie Joss	160	97	2336	1895	370	8.73
Ed Walsh	195	126	2964	2346	617	9.00
Christy Mathewson	373	188	4783	4216	846	9.52
Three Finger Brown	239	129	3172	2708	673	9.59
Walter Johnson	416	279	5924	4925	1405	9.62
Babe Adams	194	140	2995	2841	430	9.83
Juan Marichal	243	142	3509	3153	709	9.91
Rube Waddell	191	145	2961	2460	803	9.92
Deacon Phillippe	185	110	2607	2518	363	9.95
Sandy Koufax	165	87	2324	1754	817	9.96
Chief Bender	210	128	3028	2645	712	9.98
Eddie Plank	327	192	4513	3956	1072	10.03
Tom Seaver	311	205	4782	3971	1390	10.09
Grover Alexander	373	208	5189	4868	953	10.10
Hoyt Wilhelm	143	122	2254	1757	778	10.12
Cy Young	511	313	7356	7092	1217	10.17
Hooks Wiltse	141	90	2112	1892	498	10.18
Don Sutton	310	239	5003	4402	1272	10.21
Catfish Hunter	224	166	3448	2958	954	10.21
Sam Leever	194	100	2661	2449	587	10.27
Ferguson Jenkins	284	226	4500	4142	997	10.28
Ed Reulbach	185	104	2633	2117	892	10.29
Andy Messersmith	130	99	2230	1719	831	10.29
Barney Pelty	91	117	1918	1663	532	10.30
Jeff Tesreau	118	72	1679	1350	572	10.30
Gary Nolan	110	70	1675	1505	413	10.31
Don Drysdale	209	166	3432	3084	855	10.33

Fewest Base Runners per Nine Innings, Career (Min. 1,500 IP) *(cont'd)*

Player	W	L	IP	H	BB	BR/9
Old Hoss Radbourn	308	191	4535	4335	875	10.34
Ernie Bonham	103	72	1551	1501	287	10.38
Eddie Cicotte	210	148	3224	2897	827	10.40
Rollie Fingers	114	118	1701	1474	492	10.40
Dick Rudolph	121	108	2049	1971	402	10.42
Orval Overall	106	71	1532	1230	551	10.46
Denny McLain	131	91	1886	1646	548	10.47
Frank Smith	138	111	2273	1975	676	10.49
Carl Hubbell	253	154	3589	3463	724	10.50
John Candelaria	141	89	2017	1876	477	10.50
Robin Roberts	286	245	4689	4582	902	10.53
Slim Sallee	172	143	2819	2726	572	10.53
Mario Soto	95	83	1612	1273	617	10.55
Bert Blyleven	229	197	3987	3605	1072	10.56
Ron Guidry	163	80	2219	2030	580	10.59
Jim Bunning	224	184	3760	3433	1000	10.61
Jack Taylor	150	139	2617	2502	582	10.61
Gaylord Perry	314	265	5351	4938	1379	10.62
Jim Palmer	268	152	3948	3349	1311	10.62
Fernando Valenzuela	99	68	1554	1295	540	10.63
Joe McGinnity	247	145	3459	3276	812	10.64
Jesse Tannehill	195	119	2770	2800	478	10.65
Luis Tiant	229	172	3486	3075	1104	10.67
Ralph Terry	107	99	1849	1748	446	10.68
Bob Gibson	251	174	3885	3279	1336	10.69
Fred Toney	137	102	2206	2037	583	10.69
Harry Brecheen	132	92	1908	1731	536	10.69
Fritz Peterson	133	131	2218	2217	426	10.72
Joe Horlen	116	117	2001	1829	554	10.72
Jim Scott	107	113	1872	1624	609	10.74
Eddie Fisher	85	70	1538	1398	438	10.74
Warren Spahn	363	245	5244	4830	1434	10.75
Dave Stieb	95	80	1654	1434	544	10.76
Mike Cuellar	185	130	2808	2538	822	10.77
Ken Johnson	91	106	1737	1670	413	10.79
Hippo Vaughn	176	137	2730	2461	817	10.81
Don Newcombe	149	90	2155	2102	490	10.83
Howie Camnitz	133	106	2085	1852	656	10.83
Carl Mays	208	126	3020	2912	734	10.87
John Clarkson	326	177	4536	4295	1191	10.88
Dennis Eckersley	151	128	2495	2401	624	10.91
Sonny Siebert	140	114	2153	1919	692	10.91
Dean Chance	128	115	2148	1864	739	10.91
Don Wilson	104	92	1748	1479	640	10.91
Dizzy Dean	150	83	1966	1927	458	10.92
Don Mossi	101	80	1548	1493	385	10.92
Dave McNally	184	119	2729	2488	826	10.93
Ron Reed	146	140	2476	2374	633	10.93
Bob Welch	100	77	1569	1427	479	10.93
Whitey Ford	236	106	3170	2766	1086	10.94
Mort Cooper	128	75	1841	1666	571	10.94

Fewest Base Runners per Nine Innings, Career (Min. 1,500 IP) *(cont'd)*

Player	W	L	IP	H	BB	BR/9
Frank Tanana	159	153	2757	2596	772	10.95
Larry Dierker	139	123	2334	2130	711	10.96
Mel Stottlemyre	164	139	2662	2435	809	10.97

Most Complete Games, Season, AL

Player	Team	Year	CG
Jack Chesbro	NY	1904	48
George Mullin	DET	1904	42
Ed Walsh	CHI	1908	42
Cy Young	BOS	1902	41
	BOS	1904	40
Joe McGinnity	BAL	1901	39
Bill Dinneen	BOS	1902	39
Eddie Plank	PHI	1903	39
Rube Waddell	PHI	1904	39
Cy Young	BOS	1901	38
Jack Powell	NY	1904	38
Walter Johnson	WAS	1910	38
Bill Dinneen	BOS	1904	37
Casey Patten	WAS	1904	37
Eddie Plank	PHI	1904	37
Ed Walsh	CHI	1907	37
Frank Smith	CHI	1909	37
Al Orth	WAS	1902	36
Jack Powell	STL	1902	36
Al Orth	NY	1906	36
Walter Johnson	WAS	1911	36
	WAS	1916	36
Bob Feller	CLE	1946	36
Chick Fraser	PHI	1901	35
Roscoe Miller	DET	1901	35
Bill Bernhard	CLE	1904	35
Harry Howell	STL	1905	35
George Mullin	DET	1905	35
Eddie Plank	PHI	1905	35
George Mullin	DET	1906	35
	DET	1907	35
Jack Coombs	PHI	1910	35
Joe Wood	BOS	1912	35
Walter Johnson	WAS	1915	35
Babe Ruth	BOS	1917	35

Ed Walsh (*left*) compiled a 1.82 lifetime ERA over 14 seasons—an all-time record. Don Sutton (*above*) joined the 300-win club in 1986 despite having won 20 games in a season just once, in 1976.

Most Complete Games, Season, NL since 1900

Player	Team	Year	CG	Player	Team	Year	CG
Vic Willis	BOS	1902	45	Irv Young	BOS	1906	37
Joe McGinnity	NY	1903	44	Wild Bill Donovan	BKN	1901	36
Noodles Hahn	CIN	1901	41	Christy Mathewson	NY	1901	36
Irv Young	BOS	1905	41	Togie Pittinger	BOS	1902	36
Jack Taylor	STL	1904	39	Vic Willis	BOS	1905	36
Vic Willis	BOS	1904	39	Grover Alexander	PHI	1915	36
Oscar Jones	BKN	1904	38	Togie Pittinger	BOS	1903	35
Joe McGinnity	NY	1904	38	Christy Mathewson	NY	1904	35
Grover Alexander	PHI	1916	38	Kid Nichols	STL	1904	35
Dummy Taylor	NY	1901	37	Grover Alexander	PHI	1917	35
Christy Mathewson	NY	1903	37				

Most Innings Pitched, Season, AL

Player	Team	Year	IP	Player	Team	Year	IP
Ed Walsh	CHI	1908	464	Bill Dinneen	BOS	1902	371
Jack Chesbro	NY	1904	455	Walter Johnson	WAS	1916	371
Ed Walsh	CHI	1907	422	Bob Feller	CLE	1946	371
	CHI	1912	393	Ed Walsh	CHI	1910	370
Jack Powell	NY	1904	390		CHI	1911	369
Cy Young	BOS	1902	385	Walter Johnson	WAS	1912	368
Rube Waddell	PHI	1904	383	Eddie Plank	PHI	1904	365
Joe McGinnity	BAL	1901	382	Frank Smith	CHI	1909	365
George Mullin	DET	1904	382	Wilbur Wood	CHI	1973	359
Cy Young	BOS	1904	380	Casey Patten	WAS	1904	358
Wilbur Wood	CHI	1972	377	George Uhle	CLE	1923	358
Mickey Lolich	DET	1971	376	George Mullin	DET	1907	357
Walter Johnson	WAS	1910	373	Jack Coombs	PHI	1910	353
	WAS	1914	372	Red Faber	CHI	1922	353
Cy Young	BOS	1901	371	Dizzy Trout	DET	1944	352

Most Innings Pitched, Season, NL sicne 1900

Player	Team	Year	IP	Player	Team	Year	IP
Joe McGinnity	NY	1903	434	Grover Alexander	PHI	1911	367
Vic Willis	BOS	1902	410	Christy Mathewson	NY	1903	366
Joe McGinnity	NY	1904	408	Grover Alexander	CHI	1920	363
Christy Mathewson	NY	1908	391	George McQuillan	PHI	1908	360
Togie Pittinger	BOS	1902	389	Irv Young	BOS	1906	358
Grover Alexander	PHI	1916	389	Grover Alexander	PHI	1914	355
	PHI	1917	388	Dummy Taylor	NY	1901	353
Irv Young	BOS	1905	378	Togie Pittinger	BOS	1903	352
Oscar Jones	BKN	1904	377	Jack Taylor	STL	1904	352
Grover Alexander	PHI	1915	376	Stoney McGlynn	STL	1907	352
Noodles Hahn	CIN	1901	375	Wild Bill Donovan	BKN	1902	351
Christy Mathewson	NY	1904	368	Vic Willis	BOS	1904	350

Most Grand Slams Allowed, Career

Player	Total
Ned Garver	9
Jim Kaat	9
Milt Pappas	9
Jerry Reuss	9
Jim Brewer	8
Roy Face	8
Bob Feller	8
Johnny Klippstein	8
Lindy McDaniel	8
Tug McGraw	8
Early Wynn	8
Larry French	7
Jim Hearn	7
Gaylord Perry	7
Ray Sadecki	7
Jack Sanford	7
Mike Torrez	7
Lon Warneke	7

Most Extra-Inning Home Runs Allowed, Career

Player	Total
Roy Face	21
Hoyt Wilhelm	14
Lindy McDaniel	13
Dick Radatz	12
Johnny Sain	12
Gaylord Perry	11
Willie Hernandez	10
Johnny Klippstein	9
Don McMahon	9
Turk Lown	8

Milt Pappas (*right*) pitched for 11 years before experiencing his first losing season in 1968. *Far right*: Despite a 194–163 lifetime record, Jerry Reuss is 0–7, 5.45 ERA in League Championship Series play.

Most Wins after Age 40

Player	Birth Date	W	L	Player	Birth Date	W	L
Phil Niekro	Apr 1, 1939	114	90	Red Faber	Sep 8, 1888	38	57
Jack Quinn	Jul 5, 1884	89	72	Dazzy Vance	Mar 4, 1891	33	31
Cy Young	Mar 29, 1867	76	60	Connie Marrero	Apr 25, 1911	32	20
Warren Spahn	Apr 23, 1921	75	62	Jerry Koosman	Dec 23, 1942	31	26
Hoyt Wilhelm	Jul 26, 1923	52	41	Babe Adams	May 18, 1882	30	25
Gaylord Perry	Sep 15, 1938	50	59	Don Sutton	Apr 2, 1945	30	21
Grover Alexander	Feb 26, 1887	46	30				

Won 20 and Hit .300 in Same Year, AL

Player	Team	Year	W	L	AB	H	HR	RBI	BA
Clark Griffith	CHI	1901	24	7	89	27	2	14	.303
Cy Young	BOS	1903	28	9	137	44	1	14	.321
Ed Killian	DET	1907	25	13	122	39	0	11	.320
Jack Coombs	PHI	1911	28	12	141	45	2	23	.319
Babe Ruth	BOS	1917	24	13	123	40	2	12	.325
Carl Mays	NY	1921	27	9	143	49	2	22	.343
Joe Bush	NY	1922	26	7	95	31	0	12	.311
George Uhle	CLE	1923	26	16	144	52	0	22	.361
Joe Shaute	CLE	1924	20	17	107	34	1	10	.318
Walter Johnson	WAS	1925	20	7	97	42	2	20	.433
Ted Lyons	CHI	1930	22	15	122	36	1	15	.311
Wes Ferrell	CLE	1931	22	12	116	37	9	30	.319
Schoolboy Rowe	DET	1934	24	8	109	33	2	22	.303
Wes Ferrell	BOS	1935	25	14	150	52	7	32	.347
Red Ruffing	NY	1939	21	7	114	35	1	20	.307
Ned Garver	STL	1951	20	12	95	29	1	9	.305
Catfish Hunter	OAK	1971	21	11	103	36	1	12	.350

Won 20 and Hit .300. in Same Year, NL

Player	Team	Year	W	L	AB	H	HR	RBI	BA
Jesse Tannehill	PIT	1900	20	6	110	37	0	17	.336
Brickyard Kennedy	BKN	1900	20	13	123	37	0	15	.301
Claude Hendrix	PIT	1912	24	9	121	39	1	15	.322
Burleigh Grimes	BKN	1920	23	11	111	34	0	16	.306
Wilbur Cooper	PIT	1924	20	14	104	36	0	15	.346
Pete Donohue	CIN	1926	20	14	106	33	0	14	.311
Burleigh Grimes	PIT	1928	25	14	131	42	0	16	.321
Curt Davis	STL	1939	22	16	105	40	1	17	.381
Bucky Walters	CIN	1939	27	11	120	39	1	16	.325
Johnny Sain	BOS	1947	21	12	107	37	0	18	.346
Don Newcombe	BKN	1955	20	5	117	42	7	23	.359
Warren Spahn	MIL	1958	22	11	108	36	2	15	.333
Don Drysdale	LA	1965	23	12	130	39	7	19	.300
Bob Gibson	STL	1970	23	7	109	33	2	19	.303

Top: Possessor of a .623 lifetime winning percentage and a .271 batting average, Don Newcombe never managed a win or a hit in three World Series. Wes Ferrell (*above*) batted .280, slugged .446, and won 60 percent of his games over 15 seasons.

Most Home Runs, Pitcher, Career

Player	HR
Wes Ferrell	38
Bob Lemon	37
Red Ruffing	36
Warren Spahn	35
Earl Wilson	35
Don Drysdale	29
John Clarkson	24
Bob Gibson	24
Walter Johnson	24
Jack Stivetts	21
Milt Pappas	20
Dizzy Trout	20
Jack Harshman	19
Gary Peters	19
Schoolboy Rowe	18
Cy Young	18
Jim Tobin	17
Early Wynn	17
Jim Kaat	16
Johnny Antonelli	15
Don Cardwell	15
Dick Donovan	15
Lefty Grove	15
Jouett Meekin	15
Don Newcombe	15
Joe Nuxhall	15
Claude Passeau	15
Pedro Ramos	15
Babe Ruth	15
Hal Schumacher	15
Rick Wise	15

Three Home Runs in One Game, Pitcher

Player	Team	Date
Guy Hecker	LOU AA	Aug 15, 1886
Jim Tobin	BOS N	May 13, 1942

Two Home Runs in One Game, Pitcher, AL

Player	Team	Date
Ed Summers	DET	Sep 17, 1910
Ed Willett	DET	Jun 30, 1912
Jim Shaw	WAS	May 2, 1919
Garland Buckeye	CLE	Sep 10, 1925
Jess Doyle	DET	Sep 28, 1925
Red Ruffing	NY	Sep 18, 1930
Wes Ferrell	CLE	Aug 31, 1931
Chief Hogsett	DET	Aug 31, 1932

Two Home Runs in One Game, Pitcher, AL *(cont'd)*

Player	Team	Date	Player	Team	Date
Wes Ferrell	BOS	Jul 13, 1934	Billy Hoeft	DET	Jul 14, 1957
	BOS	Aug 22, 1934	Jack Harshman	BAL	Jul 16, 1958
	BOS	Jul 31, 1935		BAL	Sep 23, 1958
Mel Harder	CLE	Jul 31, 1935	Milt Pappas	BAL	Aug 27, 1961
Red Ruffing	NY	Jun 17, 1936	Dick Donovan	CLE	May 18, 1962
Wes Ferrell	BOS	Aug 12, 1936	Pedro Ramos	CLE	May 30, 1962
Eldon Auker	DET	Aug 14, 1937	Dick Donovan	CLE	Aug 31, 1962
Jack Wilson	BOS	Jun 16, 1940	Pedro Ramos	CLE	Jul 31, 1963
Spud Chandler	NY	Jul 26, 1940	Earl Wilson	BOS	Aug 16, 1965
Bob Lemon	CLE	Jul 24, 1949	Jim Rooker	KC	Jul 7, 1969
Babe Birrer	DET	Jul 19, 1955	Sonny Siebert	BOS	Sep 2, 1971
Dixie Howell	CHI	Jun 16, 1957			

Two Home Runs in One Game, Pitcher, NL

Player	Team	Date	Player	Team	Date
Monte Ward	NY	May 3, 1883	Don Newcombe	BKN	May 30, 1955
Fred Goldsmith	CHI	May 27, 1884	Jim Hearn	NY	Jun 9, 1955
John Clarkson	CHI	Oct 9, 1884	Don Newcombe	BKN	Sep 19, 1956
Harry Staley	BOS	Jun 1, 1893	Lew Burdette	MIL	Aug 13, 1957
Scott Stratton	CHI	Jul 27, 1894		MIL	Jul 10, 1958
Frank Foreman	CIN	Jul 4, 1895	Don Drysdale	LA	Aug 23, 1958
Jack Stivetts	BOS	Jun 12, 1896	Don Cardwell	CHI	Sep 2, 1960
Art Nehf	NY	Jul 29, 1924	Glen Hobbie	CHI	Jul 2, 1961
Tony Kaufmann	CHI	Jul 4, 1925	Tony Cloninger	ATL	Jun 16, 1966
Jack Knight	PHI	Jun 24, 1926		ATL	Jul 3, 1966
Phil Collins	PHI	Jul 22, 1930	Rick Wise	PHI	Jun 23, 1971
Hal Schumacher	NY	Apr 24, 1934		PHI	Aug 28, 1971
Bill Lee	CHI	May 7, 1941	Ferguson Jenkins	CHI	Sep 1, 1971
Bucky Walters	CIN	May 20, 1945	Larry Christenson	PHI	Sep 5, 1976
Dave Koslo	NY	Jul 7, 1949	Randy Lerch	PHI	Sep 30, 1978
Ben Wade	BKN	Jul 6, 1952	Walt Terrell	NY	Aug 6, 1983
Don Newcombe	BKN	Apr 14, 1955	Jim Gott	SF	May 12, 1985

Two Home Runs in One Game, Pitcher, Other Leagues

Player	Team	Date	Player	Team	Date
Bob Caruthers	STL AA	Aug 16, 1886	Jack Stivetts	STL AA	Aug 6, 1891
Jack Stivetts	STL AA	Jun 10, 1890			

Two Home Runs in One Game Twice in One Season, Pitcher

Player	Team	Date	Player	Team	Date
Wes Ferrell	BOS A	Jul 13, 1934	Dick Donovan	CLE A	May 18, 1962
	BOS A	Aug 22, 1934		CLE A	Aug 31, 1962
Don Newcombe	BKN N	Apr 14, 1955	Tony Cloninger	ATL N	Jun 16, 1966
	BKN N	May 30, 1955		ATL N	Jul 3, 1966
Jack Harshman	BAL A	Jul 16, 1958	Rick Wise	PHI N	Jun 23, 1971
	BAL A	Sep 23, 1958		PHI N	Aug 28, 1971

Schoolboy Rowe (*left*) led the N.L. with 15 pinch hits in 1943 while going 14–8 for the Phillies. Pitcher Tony Cloninger (*below*) is the only National Leaguer to hit two grand slams in one game.

Pinch-Hit Grand Slams, Pitcher

Player	Team	Date	Opp.	Opp. Pitcher
Mike O'Neill	STL N	Jun 3, 1902	BOS	Togie Pittinger
Schoolboy Rowe	PHI N	May 2, 1943	BOS	Al Javery
Zeb Eaton	DET A	Jul 15, 1945	NY	Hank Borowy
Early Wynn	WAS A	Sep 15, 1946	DET	Johnny Gorsica
Tommy Byrne	CHI A	May 16, 1953	NY	Ewell Blackwell

Grand Slams, Pitcher, AL

Player	Team	Date	Opp.	Opp. Pitcher
Cy Falkenberg	WAS	Jul 18, 1906	CHI	Frank Owen
Walter Johnson	WAS	Jun 21, 1914	DET	George Boehler
Jim Shaw	WAS	May 5, 1919	PHI	Jing Johnson
Babe Ruth	BOS	May 20, 1919	STL	Dave Davenport
George Uhle	CLE	Apr 28, 1921	DET	Dutch Leonard
Red Ruffing	NY	Aug 14, 1933	BOS	Bob Weiland

Grand Slams, Pitcher, AL *(cont'd)*

Player	Team	Date	Opp.	Opp. Pitcher
Lefty Grove	BOS	Jul 27, 1935	PHI	George Blaeholder
Wes Ferrell	BOS	Aug 12, 1936	PHI	Hod Lisenbee
Lynn Nelson	PHI	Jul 21, 1937	CLE	Ivy Andrews
Monty Stratton	CHI	Jun 10, 1938	BOS	Charlie Wagner
Schoolboy Rowe	DET	Jul 22, 1939	PHI	Nels Potter
Spud Chandler	NY	Jul 26, 1940	CHI	Pete Appleton
Zeb Eaton	DET	Jul 15, 1945	NY	Hank Borowy
Early Wynn	WAS	Sep 15, 1946	DET	Johnny Gorsica
Carl Scheib	PHI	May 8, 1948	CHI	Bob Gillespie
Dizzy Trout	DET	Jul 28, 1949	WAS	Al Gettel
	DET	Jun 23, 1950	NY	Tommy Byrne
Saul Rogovin	DET	Jul 23, 1950	NY	Ed Lopat
Ellis Kinder	BOS	Aug 6, 1950	CHI	Billy Pierce
Tommy Byrne	STL	Sep 18, 1951	WAS	Sid Hudson
Bob Porterfield	WAS	May 5, 1953	DET	Bill Wight
Tommy Byrne	CHI	May 16, 1953	NY	Ewell Blackwell
Don Larsen	NY	Apr 22, 1956	BOS	Frank Sullivan
Bob Grim	KC	Apr 15, 1959	CHI	Barry Latman
Camilo Pascual	WAS	Aug 14, 1960	NY	Bob Turley
Pedro Ramos	CLE	May 30, 1962	BAL	Chuck Estrada
Orlando Pena	KC	May 31, 1963	WAS	Don Rudolph
Camilo Pascual	MIN	Apr 27, 1965	CLE	Stan Williams
Mel Stottlemyre	NY	Jul 20, 1965	BOS	Bill Monbouquette
Earl Wilson	DET	Aug 13, 1966	BOS	Dan Osinski
John O'Donoghue	CLE	Jun 1, 1967	DET	Denny McLain
Gary Peters	CHI	May 5, 1968	NY	Al Downing
Dave McNally	BAL	Aug 26, 1968	OAK	Chuck Dobson
Fred Talbot	SEA	Jul 9, 1969	CAL	Eddie Fisher
Steve Dunning	CLE	May 11, 1971	OAK	Diego Segui

Grand Slams, Pitcher, NL

Player	Team	Date	Opp.	Opp. Pitcher
Mike O'Neill	STL	Jun 3, 1902	BOS	Togie Pittinger
Patsy Flaherty	BOS	May 24, 1907	NY	Hooks Wiltse
Deacon Phillippe	PIT	Jul 22, 1910	BKN	Fred Miller
George Ferguson	BOS	Sep 22, 1910	CIN	Jack Rowan
Lee Meadows	PHI	Apr 28, 1921	BOS	Jack Scott
Mule Watson	NY	Jun 8, 1924	PIT	Johnny Morrison
Jimmy Ring	PHI	May 12, 1925	PIT	Vic Aldridge
Phil Collins	PHI	Jun 23, 1929	BOS	Kent Greenfield
Bill Walker	NY	May 5, 1930	PIT	Larry French
Freddie Fitzsimmons	NY	May 10, 1931	CHI	Pat Malone
Roy Parmelee	NY	Jul 17, 1934	CHI	Lon Warneke
Clay Bryant	CHI	Aug 28, 1937	BOS	Frank Gabler
Curt Davis	STL	Apr 26, 1938	CIN	Al Hollingsworth
Al Hollingsworth	CIN	May 28, 1938	STL	Lon Warneke
Claude Passeau	CHI	May 19, 1941	BKN	Hugh Casey
Schoolboy Rowe	PHI	May 2, 1943	BOS	Al Javery
Ox Miller	CHI	Sep 7, 1947	PIT	Kirby Higbe

Grand Slams, Pitcher, NL *(cont'd)*

Player	Team	Date	Opp.	Opp. Pitcher
Monte Kennedy	NY	Jul 3, 1949	BKN	Morrie Martin
Erv Palica	BKN	Sep 24, 1950	PHI	Bubba Church
Lew Burdette	MIL	Jul 10, 1958	LA	Johnny Podres
Bob Purkey	CIN	Aug 1, 1959	CHI	John Buzhardt
Don Drysdale	LA	Aug 9, 1961	MIL	Don Nottebart
Art Mahaffey	PHI	Aug 2, 1962	NY	Craig Anderson
Carl Willey	NY	Jul 15, 1963	HOU	Ken Johnson
Bob Gibson	STL	Sep 29, 1965	SF	Gaylord Perry
Tony Cloninger	ATL	Jul 3, 1966	SF	Bob Priddy
	ATL	Jul 3, 1966	SF	Ray Sadecki
Jack Hamilton	NY	May 20, 1967	STL	Al Jackson
Al McBean	PIT	Jul 28, 1968	STL	Larry Jaster
Mike Corkins	SD	Sep 4, 1970	CIN	Jim Merritt
Rick Wise	PHI	Aug 28, 1971	SF	Don McMahon
Burt Hooton	CHI	Sep 16, 1972	NY	Tom Seaver
Bob Gibson	STL	Jul 26, 1973	NY	John Strohmayer
Rick Wise	STL	Aug 21, 1973	ATL	Roric Harrison
Jim Lonborg	PHI	Jun 29, 1974	MON	Chuck Taylor
Don Stanhouse	MON	Jul 6, 1977	CHI	Bill Bonham
Larry Christenson	PHI	Sep 27, 1977	CHI	Dennis Lamp
Bruce Kison	PIT	Aug 26, 1979	SD	Bob Shirley
Enrique Romo	PIT	Oct 1, 1980	NY	Roy Lee Jackson
Scott Sanderson	MON	Sep 11, 1982	CHI	Randy Martz
Joaquin Andujar	STL	May 15, 1984	ATL	Jeff Dedmon
Steve Carlton	PHI	May 16, 1984	LA	Fernando Valenzuela
Don Robinson	PIT	Sep 12, 1985	CHI	Warren Brusstar
Bob Forsch	STL	Aug 10, 1986	PIT	Mike Bielecki

Most Home Runs, Pitcher, Season

Player	Team	Year	HR
Wes Ferrell	CLE A	1931	9
Jack Stivetts	STL AA	1890	7
Wes Ferrell	BOS A	1935	7
Bob Lemon	CLE A	1949	7
Don Newcombe	BKN N	1955	7
Don Drysdale	LA N	1958	7
	LA N	1965	7
Earl Wilson	BOS A	1966	
	DET A	1966	7
	DET A	1968	7

Most Hits, Pitcher, Career

Player	H
Cy Young	618
Walter Johnson	542
Red Ruffing	520
George Mullin	397
George Uhle	393
Red Lucas	392
Al Orth	389
Burleigh Grimes	380
Grover Alexander	378
Early Wynn	365
Ted Lyons	364
Warren Spahn	363
Christy Mathewson	355
Steve Carlton	346
Brickyard Kennedy	333
Eddie Plank	331
Wes Ferrell	316
Jack Powell	308
Joe Bush	306

Pitchers Who Stole Home, AL

Player	Team	Date	Inn.	Opp.
Win Mercer	WAS	Aug 10, 1901	4	PHI
Frank Owen	CHI	Aug 2, 1904	3	WAS
	CHI	Jun 13, 1905	8	WAS
Wild Bill Donovan	DET	Sep 14, 1905	4	CLE
	DET	May 7, 1906	5	CLE
Frank Owen	CHI	Apr 27, 1908	9	STL
Ed Walsh	CHI	Jun 13, 1908	7	NY
	CHI	Jul 2, 1909	6	STL
Eddie Plank	PHI	Aug 30, 1909	2	CHI
Jack Warhop	NY	Aug 27, 1910	6	CHI
	NY	Jul 12, 1912	3	STL
Ray Fisher	NY	May 3, 1915	4	PHI
Red Faber	CHI	Jul 14, 1915	4	PHI
Reb Russell	CHI	Aug 7, 1916	3	BOS
Jim Bagby	CLE	May 20, 1917		
Babe Ruth	BOS	Aug 24, 1918	2	STL
Dickie Kerr	CHI	Jul 8, 1921	7	NY
Red Faber	CHI	Apr 23, 1923	4	STL
George Mogridge	WAS	Aug 15, 1923	12	CHI
Joe Haynes	CHI	Sep 17, 1944	8	STL
Fred Hutchinson	DET	Aug 29, 1947	3	STL
Harry Dorish	STL	Jun 2, 1950	5	WAS

Pitchers Who Stole Home, NL since 1900

Player	Team	Date	Inn.	Opp.
Jesse Tannehill	PIT	Sep 20, 1900		
Jock Menefee	CHI	Jul 15, 1902	5	BKN
Joe McGinnity	NY	Aug 8, 1903	3	BKN
Henry Schmidt	BKN	Aug 15, 1903		
Joe McGinnity	NY	Apr 29, 1904	7	BOS
Jake Weimer	CIN	Jul 28, 1907		
Lefty Leifield	PIT	Jul 27, 1911		
Christy Mathewson	NY	Sep 12, 1911	3	BOS
Red Ames	NY	May 22, 1912	5	BKN
Rube Benton	CIN	Jun 23, 1912		
Christy Mathewson	NY	Jun 28, 1912	4	BOS
Slim Sallee	STL	Jul 22, 1913	3	NY
Jack Quinn	BOS	Sep 15, 1913		
Sherry Smith	BKN	Apr 19, 1916	3	NY
Tom Seaton	CHI	Jun 23, 1916	5	CIN
Bob Steele	NY	Jul 26, 1918	7	STL
Hippo Vaughn	CHI	Aug 9, 1919	8	NY
Dutch Ruether	CIN	Sep 3, 1919	4	CHI
Jesse Barnes	NY	Jul 27, 1920	6	STL
Dutch Ruether	BKN	May 4, 1921	5	NY
Johnny Vander Meer	CIN	Sep 23, 1943	5	NY
Bucky Walters	CIN	Apr 20, 1946	6	PIT
Don Newcombe	BKN	May 26, 1955	9	PIT
Curt Simmons	STL	Sep 1, 1963	2	PHI

In his last nine seasons, Hippo Vaughn (*top*) wo games with a 2.33 ERA. Since being traded aw Houston in 1981, Joaquin Andujar (*above*) has 80 games, 14 of them shutouts, for St. Louis Oakland.

Easiest Pitcher to Strike Out, Season since 1900

Player	Team	Year	SO	AB	Pct.
Bill Stoneman	MON N	1969	55	73	.753
Dean Chance	CAL A	1965	56	75	.747
	CAL A	1966	54	76	.711
Gary Gentry	NY N	1969	52	74	.703
Jerry Koosman	NY N	1968	62	91	.681
Dean Chance	MIN A	1968	63	93	.677
Jim Nash	OAK A	1968	50	74	.676
Steve Barber	BAL A	1965	43	65	.662
Gary Gentry	NY N	1970	39	59	.661
Jerry Koosman	NY N	1970	46	70	.657
Bill Stoneman	MON N	1971	61	93	.656

Right: Bob Buhl's 0-for-62 was his worst year, but he also hit .032 (1-for-31) in 1954, .057 (4-for-70) in '59, and .060 (4-for-67) in '65. Before becoming a pitcher, Bucky Walters (*below*) spent four years as an infielder, including 1934 when he hit 24 doubles, seven triples, and eight home runs.

Most Times Struck Out, Pitcher, Career since 1900

Player	SO	AB
Lefty Grove	593	1369
Bob Feller	505	1282
Warren Spahn	487	1872
Red Faber	417	1269
Milt Pappas	406	1073
Bob Buhl	389	857
Sandy Koufax	386	776
Bob Friend	375	1137
Robin Roberts	372	1525
Mel Harder	369	1203
Don Drysdale	359	1169
Dean Chance	353	662
Sad Sam Jones	346	1243
Bill Doak	332	905
Early Wynn	330	1704
Bob Purkey	325	645
Jim Bunning	317	1275
Larry Jackson	310	1089
Danny MacFayden	309	910
Stan Coveleski	304	1058

Most At-Bats with No Hits, Pitcher, Season since 1900

Player	Team	Year	AB	Player	Team	Year	AB
Bob Buhl	MIL N	1962		Steve Stone	SF N	1971	34
	CHI N	1962	70	Ed Lynch	NY N	1982	33
Bill Wight	CHI A	1950	61	Ellis Kinder	BOS A	1952	32
Ron Herbel	SF N	1964	47	Luke Walker	PIT N	1969	32
Karl Drews	STL A	1949	46	Bob Miller	MIN A	1969	31
Ernie Koob	STL A	1916	41	Don Carman	PHI N	1986	31
Randy Tate	NY N	1975	41	Karl Adams	CHI N	1915	30
Ed Rakow	DET A	1964	39	Rick Wise	PHI N	1966	30
Harry Parker	NY N	1974	36				

Best-Hitting Pitchers, Season, AL

Player	Team	Year	G	AB	R	H	2B	3B	HR	RBI	BA
Walter Johnson	WAS	1925	36	97	12	42	6	1	2	20	.433
Red Ruffing	BOS	1930									
	NY	1930	58	110	17	40	8	2	4	22	.364
George Uhle	CLE	1923	58	144	23	52	10	3	0	22	.361
Gene Bearden	STL	1952	45	65	6	23	3	0	0	8	.354
Win Mercer	WAS	1901	24	68	13	24	4	1	0	10	.353
Catfish Hunter	OAK	1971	38	103	14	36	1	1	1	12	.350
Wes Ferrell	BOS	1935	75	150	25	52	7	1	7	32	.347
Elam Vangilder	STL	1922	45	93	16	32	10	2	2	11	.344
Carl Mays	NY	1921	51	143	18	49	5	1	2	22	.343
George Uhle	DET	1929	40	108	18	37	1	1	0	17	.343
Chad Kimsey	STL	1930	60	70	14	24	4	1	2	14	.343
George Mullin	DET	1902	35	111	19	38	4	3	0	11	.342
Joe Bush	NY	1924	60	124	13	42	9	3	1	14	.339
Red Ruffing	NY	1935	50	109	13	37	10	0	2	18	.339

Best-Hitting Pitchers, Season, NL since 1900

Player	Team	Year	G	AB	R	H	2B	3B	HR	RBI	BA
Jack Bentley	NY	1923	52	89	9	38	6	2	1	14	.427
Curt Davis	STL	1939	63	105	10	40	5	0	1	17	.381
Don Newcombe	LA	1958									
	CIN	1958	50	72	11	26	1	0	1	9	.361
	BKN	1955	57	117	18	42	9	1	7	18	.359
Erv Brame	PIT	1930	50	116	20	41	5	0	3	22	.353
Dutch Ruether	BKN	1921	49	97	12	34	5	2	2	13	.351
Wilbur Cooper	PIT	1924	38	104	11	36	5	2	0	15	.346
Dolf Luque	CIN	1926	34	78	8	27	5	0	0	8	.346
Johnny Sain	BOS	1947	40	107	13	37	7	0	0	18	.346
Joe Bowman	PIT	1939	70	96	9	33	8	1	0	18	.344
Bill Phillips	CIN	1902	38	114	11	39	1	3	0	11	.342
Doc Crandall	NY	1910	44	73	10	25	2	4	1	13	.342
Jack Scott	BOS	1921	51	88	14	30	5	1	1	12	.341
Jesse Tannehill	PIT	1900	29	94	16	32	7	0	0	15	.340

Best-Hitting Pitchers, Career

Player	AB	R	H	2B	3B	HR	RBI	BA
Babe Ruth	490	75	149	34	11	15	73	.304
George Uhle	1363	172	393	60	21	9	187	.288
Doc Crandall	573	77	163	23	15	8	91	.284
Red Lucas	1388	150	392	60	13	3	183	.282
Wes Ferrell	1128	169	316	55	12	38	202	.280
Al Orth	1400	166	389	54	28	11	165	.278
Ad Gumbert	832	134	230	30	17	13	109	.276
Jack Scott	678	67	186	31	4	5	73	.274
Don Newcombe	878	94	238	33	3	15	108	.271
Sloppy Thurston	648	65	175	38	10	5	79	.270
Red Ruffing	1932	207	520	97	13	36	273	.269
Carl Mays	1085	113	291	32	21	5	110	.268

Best-Hitting Pitchers, Career ***(cont'd)***

Player	AB	R	H	2B	3B	HR	RBI	BA
Nixey Callahan	683	100	181	24	12	1	79	.265
Johnny Marcum	533	56	141	18	1	5	70	.265
George Mullin	1504	162	397	70	23	3	135	.264
Jesse Tannehill	1091	147	288	44	21	5	111	.264
Schoolboy Rowe	909	116	239	36	9	18	153	.263
Fred Hutchinson	649	71	171	23	3	4	83	.263
Brickyard Kennedy	1275	150	333	50	21	1	148	.261
Dutch Ruether	947	81	245	30	11	7	109	.259
Joe Shaute	657	63	170	28	4	1	63	.259

Left: Red Ruffing's career included two 20-loss seasons with Boston before moving on to World Series glory with the Yankees. George Uhle (*above*) batted .308 and led the A.L. in pinch hits with 11 in 1924, to offset a 9–15 performance for the Indians.

Worst-Hitting Pitchers, Career (Min. 100 AB)

Player	AB	H	BA
Ron Herbel	206	6	.029
Ed Klepfer	125	6	.048
Andy McGaffigan	103	5	.049
Bill Butler	117	6	.051
Taylor Phillips	113	6	.053
Bill Trotter	109	6	.055
Don Johnson	155	9	.058
Luke Walker	188	11	.059
Buster Narum	118	7	.059
Ryne Duren	114	7	.061
Marv Breuer	157	10	.064
Rip Hagerman	123	8	.065
Dean Chance	662	44	.066
Joe Engel	104	7	.067
Jose DeLeon	130	9	.069
Bob Bowman	101	7	.069
Billy McCool	101	7	.069
Ernie Koob	128	9	.070
Mike Kilkenny	114	8	.070
Bill Greif	166	12	.072
Rick Camp	175	13	.074
Clem Labine	227	17	.075
Pete Burnside	132	10	.076
Dick Drago	274	21	.077
Dan Spillner	130	10	.077
Dick Woodson	117	9	.077
Bill Hands	472	37	.078
Wayne Simpson	153	12	.078
Steve Bedrosian	128	10	.078
Kent Tekulve	116	9	.078
Brent Strom	102	8	.078
Lee Stange	305	24	.079
Gary Lavelle	111	9	.081
Karl Drews	254	21	.083
Steve Bedrosian	133	11	.083
Wilbur Wood	322	27	.084
Ed Rakow	226	19	.084
Roger Craig	448	38	.085
Hank Aguirre	388	33	.085
Ike Delock	361	31	.086
Bill Stoneman	338	29	.086
Dave Wickersham	324	28	.086
Bob Kuzava	256	22	.086
Bob Savage	104	9	.087

Player	AB	H	BA
Dick Ellsworth	673	59	.088
Hoyt Wilhelm	432	38	.088
Dean Stone	170	15	.088
Bob Buhl	857	76	.089
George Brunet	418	37	.089
Pete Broberg	101	9	.089
Bruce Sutter	101	9	.089
Tom Gorman	155	14	.090
Johnny Broaca	254	23	.091
Jim Hannan	209	19	.091
Atlee Hammaker	176	16	.091
LaMarr Hoyt	110	10	.091
Kent Peterson	110	10	.091
Ron Kline	491	45	.092
Hal Woodeshick	174	16	.092
Howie Judson	150	14	.093
Bob Keefe	107	10	.093
Wally Bunker	331	31	.094
Tommie Sisk	235	22	.094
Art Decatur	159	15	.094
Gary Gentry	285	27	.095
Bob Hendley	243	23	.095
Charles Hudson	210	20	.095
Tom Kelley	116	11	.095
Rollie Sheldon	209	20	.096
Hi Bell	178	17	.096
Ron Perranoski	167	16	.096
Bob Johnson	157	15	.096
Jack Lamabe	156	15	.096
Dick Kelley	125	12	.096
Sandy Koufax	776	75	.097
John Montefusco	455	44	.097
George Smith	349	34	.097
Satchel Paige	124	12	.097
Al Benton	512	50	.098
Clay Kirby	478	47	.098
Cannonball Titcomb	224	22	.098
Dave Hillman	163	16	.098
Carl Willey	263	26	.099
Les Tietje	171	17	.099
Craig McMurtry	152	15	.099
Casey Cox	151	15	.099
Lee Tunnell	121	12	.099
Rick Matula	111	11	.099

Individual Fielding Records

Fewest Errors by Position, Season, AL (Min. 150 G, excl. Pitchers)

Player	Team	Year	Pos.	G	E	TC
Stuffy McInnis	BOS	1921	1B	152	1	1652
Jerry Adair	BAL	1964	2B	153	5	822
Bobby Grich	BAL	1973	2B	162	5	945
Don Money	MIL	1974	3B	157	5	472
Ed Brinkman	DET	1972	SS	156	7	735
Rocky Colavito	CLE	1965	OF	162	0	274
Brian Downing	CAL	1982	OF	158	0	330
Jim Sundberg	TEX	1979	C	150	4	833
Walter Johnson	WAS	1913	P	47	0	103

Fewest Errors by Position, Season, NL (Min. 150 G, excl. Pitchers)

Player	Team	Year	Pos.	G	E	TC
Steve Garvey	SD	1984	1B	159	0	1319
Joe Morgan	CIN	1977	2B	151	5	715
Ryne Sandberg	CHI	1986	2B	153	5	806
Ken Reitz	STL	1980	3B	150	8	387
Larry Bowa	PHI	1972	SS	150	9	715
Danny Litwhiler	PHI	1942	OF	151	0	317
Curt Flood	STL	1966	OF	159	0	396
Terry Puhl	HOU	1979	OF	152	0	359
Randy Hundley	CHI	1967	C	152	4	928
Randy Jones	SD	1976	P	40	0	112

Most Errors by Position, Season, AL

Player	Team	Year	Pos.	G	E
Jerry Freeman	WAS	1908	1B	154	41
Kid Gleason	DET	1901	2B	136	64
Sammy Strang	CHI	1902	3B	137	62
John Gochnaur	CLE	1903	SS	128	98
Roy Johnson	DET	1929	OF	146	31
Oscar Stanage	DET	1911	C	141	41
Jack Chesbro	NY	1904	P	55	15
Rube Waddell	PHI	1905	P	46	15
Ed Walsh	CHI	1912	P	62	15

Bobby Grich holds the record for lifetime fielding average at second base, .984, and won four Gold Glove awards.

Most Errors by Position, Season, NL since 1900

Player	Team	Year	Pos.	G	E
Jack Doyle	NY	1900	1B	130	41
George Grantham	CHI	1923	2B	150	55
Piano Legs Hickman	NY	1900	3B	118	91
Rudy Hulswitt	PHI	1903	SS	138	81
Cy Seymour	CIN	1903	OF	135	36
Red Dooin	PHI	1909	C	140	40
Doc Newton	CIN	1901	P	33	17

Most Consecutive Errorless Games by Position, AL

Player	Pos.	G	Began	Ended
Mike Hegan	1B	178	1970	1973
Jerry Adair	2B	89	1964	1965
Don Money	3B	88	1973	1974
Ed Brinkman	SS	72	1972	1972
Brian Downing	OF	244	1981	1983
Yogi Berra	C	148	1957	1958
Paul Lindblad	P	385	1966	1974

Most Consecutive Errorless Games by Position, NL

Player	Pos.	G	Began	Ended
Steve Garvey	1B	193	1983	1985
Joe Morgan	2B	91	1977	1978
Jim Davenport	3B	97	1966	1968
Buddy Kerr	SS	68	1946	1947
Curt Flood	OF	226	1965	1966
Johnny Edwards	C	138	1970	1971
Ron Reed	P	297	1978	1983

Above: Joe Morgan's back-to-back MVP seasons in 1975–76 led Sparky Anderson's Reds to consecutive World Championships. Since 1981 Brian Downing (*above right*) has committed only eight errors in 688 games in the outfield. Steve Garvey (*right*) has played 162 games at first in five separate seasons.

Double and Triple Plays

Unassisted Triple Plays

Player	Team	Date	Pos.	Opp.	Opp. Batter
Neal Ball	CLE	Jul 19, 1909	SS	BOS	Amby McConnell
Bill Wambsganss	CLE	Oct 10, 1920	2B	BKN	Clarence Mitchell
George Burns	BOS	Sep 14, 1923	1B	CLE	Frank Brower
Ernie Padgett	BOS	Oct 6, 1923	SS	PHI	Walter Holke
Glenn Wright	PIT	May 7, 1925	SS	STL	Jim Bottomley
Jimmy Cooney	CHI	May 30, 1927	SS	PIT	Paul Waner
Johnny Neun	DET	May 31, 1927	1B	CLE	Homer Summa
Ron Hansen	WAS	Jul 29, 1968	SS	CLE	Joe Azcue

Best Double-Play Combinations, Season

Player	Team	Year	DP
Bill Mazeroski	PIT N	1966	161
Gene Alley	PIT N	1966	128
Total			289
Gerry Priddy	DET A	1950	150
Johnny Lipon	DET A	1950	126
Total			276
Bill Mazeroski	PIT N	1962	138
Dick Groat	PIT N	1962	126
Total			264
Bobby Doerr	BOS A	1949	134
Vern Stephens	BOS A	1949	128
Total			262
Bill Mazeroski	PIT N	1961	144
Dick Groat	PIT N	1961	117
Total			261
Jerry Coleman	NY A	1950	137
Phil Rizzuto	NY A	1950	123
Total			260
Bobby Knoop	CAL A	1966	135
Jim Fregosi	CAL A	1966	125
Total			260
Hughie Critz	CIN N	1928	124
Hod Ford	CIN N	1928	128
Total			252
Johnny Temple	CIN N	1954	117
Roy McMillan	CIN N	1954	129
Total			246
Ray Mack	CLE A	1943	123
Lou Boudreau	CLE A	1943	122
Total			245
Bobby Doerr	BOS A	1950	130
Vern Stephens	BOS A	1950	115
Total			245
Bill Mazeroski	PIT N	1958	118
Dick Groat	PIT N	1958	127
Total			245

Player	Team	Year	DP
Dave Cash	PHI N	1974	141
Larry Bowa	PHI N	1974	104
Total			245
Jackie Robinson	BKN N	1951	137
Pee Wee Reese	BKN N	1951	106
Total			243
Nellie Fox	CHI A	1960	126
Luis Aparicio	CHI A	1960	117
Total			243
Bobby Richardson	NY A	1961	136
Tony Kubek	NY A	1961	107
Total			243
Glenn Hubbard	ATL N	1985	127
Rafael Ramirez	ATL N	1985	115
Total			243
Glenn Hubbard	ATL N	1982	111
Rafael Ramirez	ATL N	1982	130
Total			241
Damaso Garcia	TOR A	1980	112
Alfredo Griffin	TOR A	1980	126
Total			238
Red Schoendienst	STL N	1954	137
Alex Grammas	STL N	1954	100
Total			237
Dave Stapleton	BOS A	1980	90
Rick Burleson	BOS A	1980	147
Total			237
Bernie Allen	MIN A	1962	109
Zoilo Versalles	MIN A	1962	127
Total			236
Bill Mazeroski	PIT N	1967	131
Gene Alley	PIT N	1967	105
Total			236
Rob Wilfong	MIN A	1979	92
Roy Smalley	MIN A	1979	144
Total			236

Best Double-Play Combinations, Season ***(cont'd)***

Player	Team	Year	DP
Joe Gordon	NY A	1942	121
Phil Rizzuto	NY A	1942	114
Total			235
Willie Randolph	NY A	1979	128
Bucky Dent	NY A	1979	107
Total			235
Joe Gordon	NY A	1939	116
Frankie Crosetti	NY A	1939	118
Total			234
Lonny Frey	CIN N	1943	112
Eddie Miller	CIN N	1943	121
Total			233
Don Blasingame	STL N	1957	128
Alvin Dark	STL N	1957	105
Total			233
Bobby Doerr	BOS A	1948	119
Vern Stephens	BOS A	1948	113
Total			232
Bobby Grich	BAL A	1974	132
Mark Belanger	BAL A	1974	100
Total			232
Eddie Stanky	NY N	1951	117
Alvin Dark	NY N	1951	114
Total			231
Tommy Herr	STL N	1985	120
Ozzie Smith	STL N	1985	111
Total			231
Joe Gordon	CLE A	1947	110
Lou Boudreau	CLE A	1947	120
Total			230
Cass Michaels	CHI A	1949	135
Luke Appling	CHI A	1949	95
Total			230
Johnny Temple	CIN N	1955	119
Roy McMillan	CIN N	1955	111
Total			230
Bobby Grich	BAL A	1973	130
Mark Belanger	BAL A	1973	100
Total			230
Eddie Stanky	NY N	1950	128
Alvin Dark	NY N	1950	101
Total			229

Player	Team	Year	DP
Cookie Rojas	KC A	1974	114
Freddie Patek	KC A	1974	115
Total			229
Bobby Doerr	BOS A	1938	118
Joe Cronin	BOS A	1938	110
Total			228
Ryne Sandberg	CHI N	1983	126
Larry Bowa	CHI N	1983	102
Total			228
Charlie Gehringer	DET A	1933	111
Billy Rogell	DET A	1933	116
Total			227
Pep Young	PIT N	1938	120
Arky Vaughan	PIT N	1938	107
Total			227
Jackie Robinson	BKN N	1950	133
Pee Wee Reese	BKN N	1950	94
Total			227
Bobby Grich	BAL A	1975	122
Mark Belanger	BAL A	1975	105
Total			227
Jackie Hayes	CHI A	1937	115
Luke Appling	CHI A	1937	111
Total			226
Nellie Fox	CHI A	1958	141
Luis Aparicio	CHI A	1958	85
Total			226
Marv Breeding	BAL A	1960	116
Ron Hansen	BAL A	1960	110
Total			226
Bill Mazeroski	PIT N	1963	131
Dick Schofield	PIT N	1963	95
Total			226
Bucky Harris	WAS A	1923	120
Roger Peckinpaugh	WAS A	1923	105
Total			225
Ray Mack	CLE A	1940	109
Lou Boudreau	CLE A	1940	116
Total			225
Bobby Doerr	BOS A	1946	129
Johnny Pesky	BOS A	1946	96
Total			225

Perhaps the slickest glove man ever to play second, Bill Mazeroski's bottom-of-the-ninth homer off Ralph Terry in Game Seven of the 1960 World Series gave Pittsburgh the championship over the Yankees.

Most Double Plays, Second Baseman, Season, AL

Player	Team	Year	DP
Gerry Priddy	DET	1950	150
Nellie Fox	CHI	1957	141
Buddy Myer	WAS	1935	138
Jerry Coleman	NY	1950	137
Bobby Richardson	NY	1966	136
Cass Michaels	CHI	1949	135
Bobby Knoop	CAL	1966	135
Bobby Doerr	BOS	1949	134
	BOS	1942	132
Gerry Priddy	STL	1948	132
Bobby Grich	BAL	1974	132
Bobby Doerr	BOS	1950	130
Bobby Grich	BAL	1973	130

Most Double Plays, Second Baseman, Season, NL

Player	Team	Year	DP
Bill Mazeroski	PIT	1966	161
	PIT	1961	144
Dave Cash	PHI	1974	141
Bill Mazeroski	PIT	1962	138
Jackie Robinson	BKN	1951	137
Red Schoendienst	STL	1954	137
Jackie Robinson	BKN	1950	133
Bill Mazeroski	PIT	1963	131
	PIT	1967	131
Tommy Helms	CIN	1971	130

Most Double Plays, Shortstop, Season, AL

Player	Team	Year	DP
Rick Burleson	BOS	1980	147
Roy Smalley	MIN	1979	144
Lou Boudreau	CLE	1944	134
Spike Owen	SEA	1986	
	BOS	1986	133
Vern Stephens	BOS	1949	128
Zoilo Versalles	MIN	1962	127
Eddie Joost	PHI	1949	126
Johnny Lipon	DET	1950	126
Leo Cardenas	MIN	1969	126
Alfredo Griffin	TOR	1980	126
Jim Fregosi	CAL	1966	125
Alfredo Griffin	TOR	1979	124
Phil Rizzuto	NY	1950	123
Cal Ripken	BAL	1985	123
Lou Boudreau	CLE	1943	122
Cal Ripken	BAL	1984	122
Roy Smalley	MIN	1978	121
Frankie Crosetti	NY	1938	120
Lou Boudreau	CLE	1947	120

Most Double Plays, Shortstop, Season, NL

Player	Team	Year	DP
Bobby Wine	MON	1970	137
Rafael Ramirez	ATL	1982	130
Roy McMillan	CIN	1954	129
Hod Ford	CIN	1928	128
Gene Alley	PIT	1966	128
Dick Groat	PIT	1958	127
	PIT	1962	126
Eddie Miller	CIN	1943	123
	BOS	1940	122

Unassisted Double Plays, Outfielder

Player	Team	Date	Pos.	Opp.
Billy Sunday	PIT N	Sep 11, 1888	CF	WAS
Steve Brodie	BOS N	Jun 29, 1891	CF	NY
Tommy McCarthy	BOS N	Apr 30, 1894	LF	PHI
Fielder Jones	CHI A	Jul 1, 1904	CF	STL
Sam Mertes	NY N	Jul 24, 1905	LF	CIN
George Stone	STL A	Aug 23, 1905	LF	NY
Socks Seybold	PHI A	Aug 15, 1907	RF	CLE
	PHI A	Sep 10, 1907	RF	BOS
Tris Speaker	BOS A	Jun 1, 1909	CF	PHI
	BOS A	Apr 23, 1910	CF	PHI
	BOS A	Apr 21, 1914	CF	PHI
	BOS A	Aug 8, 1914	CF	DET
Elmer Smith	CLE A	Jul 15, 1915	RF	BOS
Bill Hinchman	PIT N	Apr 28, 1916	RF	CIN
Benny Kauff	NY N	Jul 19, 1916	CF	CHI
Tris Speaker	CLE A	Apr 18, 1918	CF	DET
	CLE A	Apr 29, 1918	CF	CHI
Elmer Smith	CLE A	Sep 6, 1920	RF	STL
	NY A	Jul 18, 1923	RF	DET
Sam Rice	WAS A	Jul 21, 1923	RF	CLE
Ty Cobb	DET A	Jul 15, 1924	CF	PHI
Elmer Smith	CIN N	Jul 13, 1925	RF	BOS
Jack Smith	STL N	Aug 5, 1925	RF	BOS
Ty Tyson	NY N	Aug 2, 1926	CF	STL
Ty Cobb	PHI A	Apr 26, 1927	RF	BOS
Adam Comorosky	PIT N	May 31, 1931	LF	CHI
	PIT N	Jun 13, 1931	LF	NY
Al Simmons	CHI A	Apr 20, 1933	LF	STL
Danny Taylor	BKN N	Jun 20, 1933	CF	STL
Dom DiMaggio	BOS A	Aug 2, 1942	CF	DET
George Case	WAS A	Jun 8, 1944	CF	PHI
Leon Culberson	BOS A	May 25, 1945	CF	STL
Curt Flood	STL N	Jun 19, 1967	CF	HOU
Jose Cardenal	CLE A	Jun 8, 1968	CF	DET
	CLE A	Jul 16, 1968	CF	CAL
Bobby Bonds	SF N	May 31, 1972	RF	NY
Billy North	OAK A	Jul 28, 1974	CF	CHI

Most Games Caught, Season

Player	Team	Year	Total
Randy Hundley	CHI N	1968	160
Frankie Hayes	PHI A	1944	155
Ray Mueller	CIN N	1944	155
Jim Sundberg	TEX A	1975	155
Johnny Bench	CIN N	1968	154
Ted Simmons	STL N	1975	154
Carlton Fisk	BOS A	1978	154
Ted Simmons	STL N	1973	153
Gary Carter	MON N	1982	153

Player	Team	Year	Total
Jim Hegan	CLE A	1949	152
Randy Hundley	CHI N	1967	152
Gary Carter	MON N	1978	152
Ray Schalk	CHI A	1920	151
Frankie Hayes	PHI A		
	CLE A	1945	151
Johnny Edwards	HOU N	1969	151
Randy Hundley	CHI N	1969	151
Manny Sanguillen	PIT N	1974	151

Most Games Caught, Season *(cont'd)*

Player	Team	Year	Total	Player	Team	Year	Total
Carlton Fisk	BOS A	1977	151	Buck Rodgers	LA A	1962	150
Jim Sundberg	TEX A	1980	151	Jim Sundberg	TEX A	1979	150
George Gibson	PIT N	1909	150	Jody Davis	CHI N	1983	150
Mike Tresh	CHI A	1945	150				

Most Games Caught, Career

Player	G Cau	Yrs.	BA	Player	G Cau	Yrs.	BA
Al Lopez	1918	19	.261	Frank Snyder	1249	16	.265
Bob Boone	1808	15	.251	Chief Zimmer	1239	19	.269
Rick Ferrell	1806	18	.281	Ivy Wingo	1231	17	.260
Gabby Hartnett	1790	20	.297	Steve Yeager	1230	15	.228
Ted Simmons	1747	19	.286	Hank Severeid	1225	15	.289
Johnny Bench	1744	17	.267	Walker Cooper	1223	18	.285
Jim Sundberg	1741	13	.250	Andy Seminick	1213	15	.243
Ray Schalk	1726	18	.253	Tom Haller	1199	12	.257
Bill Dickey	1712	17	.313	George Gibson	1196	14	.236
Yogi Berra	1696	19	.285	Malachi Kittredge	1196	16	.219
Carlton Fisk	1642	17	.271	Red Dooin	1194	15	.240
Jim Hegan	1629	17	.228	Butch Wynegar	1193	11	.256
Deacon McGuire	1611	26	.278	Roy Campanella	1183	10	.276
Bill Freehan	1581	15	.262	Mickey Owen	1175	13	.255
Sherm Lollar	1571	18	.264	Johnny Kling	1168	13	.271
Luke Sewell	1561	20	.259	Smoky Burgess	1139	18	.295
Ernie Lombardi	1542	17	.306	Elston Howard	1138	14	.274
Steve O'Neill	1528	17	.263	Billy Sullivan	1121	16	.212
Gary Carter	1522	13	.271	Manny Sanguillen	1114	13	.296
Darrell Porter	1499	16	.247	Cy Perkins	1111	17	.259
Rollie Hemsley	1495	19	.262	Birdie Tebbetts	1108	14	.270
Del Crandall	1479	16	.254	Alan Ashby	1104	14	.242
Johnny Roseboro	1476	14	.249	Phil Masi	1101	14	.264
Mickey Cochrane	1451	13	.320	Earl Battey	1087	13	.270
Wally Schang	1439	19	.284	Oscar Stanage	1074	14	.234
Muddy Ruel	1413	19	.275	Jack Clements	1073	17	.286
Johnny Edwards	1392	14	.242	Ed Bailey	1064	14	.256
Tim McCarver	1387	21	.271	Lance Parrish	1039	10	.263
Gus Mancuso	1360	14	.265	Milt May	1034	15	.263
Jimmie Wilson	1359	18	.284	Jack Warner	1032	14	.249
Bob O'Farrell	1338	21	.273	Sammy White	1027	11	.262
Jerry Grote	1325	15	.251	Randy Hundley	1026	14	.236
Rick Dempsey	1321	18	.238	Mike Tresh	1019	12	.249
Wilbert Robinson	1316	17	.273	Buck Martinez	1009	17	.225
Frankie Hayes	1309	14	.259	Bill Killefer	1006	13	.238
Spud Davis	1291	16	.308	Clay Dalrymple	1003	12	.233
Thurman Munson	1278	11	.288	Duke Farrell	1003	18	.275
Del Rice	1249	17	.237				

Most No-Hitters Caught, Career

Player	Team	Date	Opp.	No-Hit Pitcher
Ray Schalk	CHI A	May 14, 1914	WAS	Jim Scott
	CHI A	May 31, 1914	CLE	Joe Benz
	CHI A	Apr 14, 1917	STL	Eddie Cicotte
	CHI A	Apr 30, 1922	DET	Charlie Robertson
Lou Criger	BOS A	May 5, 1904	PHI	Cy Young
	BOS A	Jun 30, 1908	NY	Cy Young
	NY A	Aug 30, 1910	CLE	Tom Hughes
Bill Carrigan	BOS A	Jul 29, 1911	STL	Joe Wood
	BOS A	Jun 21, 1916	NY	Rube Foster
	BOS A	Aug 30, 1916	STL	Dutch Leonard
Val Picinich	PHI A	Aug 26, 1916	CLE	Joe Bush
	WAS A	Jul 1, 1920	BOS	Walter Johnson
	BOS A	Sep 7, 1923	PHI	Howard Ehmke
Luke Sewell	CLE A	Apr 29, 1931	STL	Wes Ferrell
	CHI A	Aug 31, 1935	STL	Vern Kennedy
	CHI A	Jun 1, 1937	STL	Bill Dietrich
Jim Hegan	CLE A	Jul 10, 1947	PHI	Don Black
	CLE A	Jun 30, 1948	DET	Bob Lemon
	CLE A	Jul 1, 1951	DET	Bob Feller
Yogi Berra	NY A	Jul 12, 1951	CLE	Allie Reynolds
	NY A	Sep 28, 1951	BOS	Allie Reynolds
	NY A	Oct 8, 1956	BKN	Don Larsen
Roy Campanella	BKN N	Jun 19, 1952	CHI	Carl Erskine
	BKN N	May 12, 1956	NY	Carl Erskine
	BKN N	Sep 25, 1956	PHI	Sal Maglie
Del Crandall	MIL N	Jun 12, 1954	PHI	Jim Wilson
	MIL N	Aug 18, 1960	PHI	Lew Burdette
	MIL N	Sep 16, 1960	PHI	Warren Spahn
Jeff Torborg	LA N	Sep 9, 1965	CHI	Sandy Koufax
	LA N	Jul 20, 1970	PHI	Bill Singer
	CAL A	May 15, 1973	KC	Nolan Ryan
Alan Ashby	HOU N	Apr 4, 1979	ATL	Ken Forsch
	HOU N	Sep 26, 1981	LA	Nolan Ryan
	HOU N	Sep 25, 1986	SF	Mike Scott
Herm McFarland	CHI A	Sep 20, 1902	DET	Nixey Callahan
	CHI A	Sep 6, 1905	DET	Frank Smith
Bill Bergen	BKN N	Aug 1, 1906	PIT	Harry McIntyre
	BKN N	Sep 5, 1908	BOS	Nap Rucker
Nig Clarke	CLE A	Oct 2, 1908	CHI	Addie Joss
	CLE A	Apr 20, 1910	CHI	Addie Joss
Art Wilson	NY N	Sep 6, 1912	PHI	Jeff Tesreau
	CHI N	May 2, 1917	CIN	Hippo Vaughn
Hank Gowdy	BOS N	Sep 9, 1914	PHI	George Davis
	BOS N	Jun 16, 1916	PIT	Tom Hughes
Rollie Hemsley	STL A	Sep 18, 1934	BOS	Bobo Newsom
	CLE A	Apr 16, 1940	CHI	Bob Feller
Ernie Lombardi	CIN N	Jun 11, 1938	BOS	Johnny Vander Meer
	CIN N	Jun 15, 1938	BKN	Johnny Vander Meer
Walker Cooper	STL N	Aug 30, 1941	CIN	Lon Warneke
	BOS N	Aug 11, 1950	BKN	Vern Bickford
Buddy Rosar	PHI A	Sep 9, 1945	STL	Dick Fowler

Most No-Hitters Caught, Career *(cont'd)*

Player	Team	Date	Opp.	No-Hit Pitcher
Buddy Rosar	PHI A	Sep 3, 1947	WAS	Bill McCahan
Smoky Burgess	CIN N	May 26, 1956	MIL	Johnny Klippstein
			MIL	Hersh Freeman
			MIL	Joe Black
	PIT N	May 26, 1959	MIL	Harvey Haddix
Gus Triandos	BAL A	Sep 20, 1958	NY	Hoyt Wilhelm
	PHI N	Jun 21, 1964	NY	Jim Bunning
Bob Tillman	BOS A	Jun 26, 1962	LA	Earl Wilson
	BOS A	Sep 16, 1965	CLE	Dave Morehead
Jim Pagliaroni	BOS A	Aug 1, 1962	CHI	Bill Monbouquette
	OAK A	May 8, 1968	MIN	Catfish Hunter
Johnny Roseboro	LA N	Jun 30, 1962	NY	Sandy Koufax
	LA N	May 31, 1963	SF	Sandy Koufax
John Bateman	HOU N	May 17, 1963	PHI	Don Nottebart
	MON N	Apr 17, 1969	PHI	Bill Stoneman
Joe Azcue	CLE A	Jun 10, 1966	WAS	Sonny Siebert
	CAL A	Jul 3, 1970	OAK	Clyde Wright
Johnny Edwards	CIN N	Aug 19, 1965	CHI	Jim Maloney
	STL N	Sep 18, 1968	SF	Ray Washburn
Ted Simmons	STL N	Aug 14, 1971	PIT	Bob Gibson
	STL N	Apr 16, 1978	PHI	Bob Forsch
Tim McCarver	PHI N	Jun 23, 1971	CIN	Rick Wise
	MON N	Oct 2, 1972	NY	Bill Stoneman
Randy Hundley	CHI N	Apr 16, 1972	PHI	Burt Hooton
	CHI N	Sep 2, 1972	SD	Milt Pappas
Fran Healy	KC A	Apr 27, 1973	DET	Steve Busby
	KC A	Jun 19, 1974	MIL	Steve Busby
Darrell Porter	KC A	May 14, 1977	TEX	Jim Colborn
	STL N	Sep 26, 1983	MON	Bob Forsch

Ray Schalk (*far left*) was one of the few clean regulars on the 1919 Black Sox. Bob Boone (*left*) has established the first realistic shot at Al Lopez's record for career games caught.

Most Putouts, Outfielder, Game

Player	Team	Date	Pos.	PO	Inns.
Fred Treacey	NY N	Jul 10, 1876	LF	12	16
Harry Bay	CLE A	Jul 19, 1904	CF	12	12
Earl Clark	BOS N	May 10, 1929	CF	12	
Carden Gillenwater	BOS N	Sep 11, 1946	CF	12	17
Tom McBride	WAS A	Jul 2, 1948	LF	12	
Lloyd Merriman	CIN N	Sep 7, 1951	CF	12	18
Lyman Bostock	MIN A	May 25, 1977	CF	12	
Ruppert Jones	SEA A	May 16, 1978	CF	12	16
Rick Manning	MIL A	Jun 11, 1983	CF	12	15
Garry Maddox	PHI N	Jun 10, 1984	CF	12	12
Gary Pettis	CAL A	Jun 4, 1985	CF	12	15
Oddibe McDowell	TEX A	Jul 20, 1985	CF	12	15
Fred Treacey	NY N	Jul 8, 1876	LF	11	15
Dick Harley	STL N	Jun 30, 1898	LF	11	
Topsy Hartsel	CHI N	Sep 10, 1901	LF	11	
George Burns	NY N	Jul 17, 1914	LF	11	21
Roy Massey	BOS N	Jul 31, 1918	CF	11	21
Ty Cobb	DET A	Aug 4, 1918	CF	11	18
Burt Shotton	WAS A	Aug 4, 1918	LF	11	18
Hy Myers	BKN N	Apr 30, 1919	CF	11	20
Happy Felsch	CHI A	Jun 23, 1919	CF	11	
Max Carey	PIT N	Jul 25, 1921	CF	11	
Johnny Mostil	CHI A	May 22, 1928	CF	11	
Harry Rice	NY A	Jun 12, 1930	CF	11	
Johnny Hopp	STL N	May 3, 1944	CF	11	
Paul Lehner	PHI A	Jun 25, 1950	LF	11	
Irv Noren	WAS A	Sep 22, 1951	CF	11	
Willie Horton	DET A	Jul 18, 1969	LF	11	
Mickey Stanley	DET A	Jul 13, 1973	CF	11	
Dave Henderson	SEA A	Apr 27, 1982	CF	11	11
Tony Armas	OAK A	Jun 12, 1982	RF	11	

Most Assists, Outfielder, Game

Player	Team	Date	Pos.	A	Inns.
Harry Schafer	BOS N	Sep 26, 1877	RF	4	
Bill Crowley	BUF N	May 24, 1880	CF	4	
	BUF N	Aug 27, 1880	CF	4	
Dusty Miller	CIN N	May 30, 1895	LF	4	11
Ducky Holmes	CHI A	Aug 21, 1903	LF	4	
Fred Clarke	PIT N	Aug 23, 1910	LF	4	
Lee Magee	NY A	Jun 28, 1916	CF	4	
Happy Felsch	CHI A	Aug 14, 1919	CF	4	
Bob Meusel	NY A	Sep 5, 1921	CF	4	
Sam Langford	CLE A	May 1, 1928	CF	4	
Wally Berger	BOS N	Apr 27, 1931	CF	4	

Most Putouts in Nine Innings, First Baseman

Player	Team	Date	PO	Player	Team	Date	PO
Tom Jones	STL A	May 11, 1906	22	Hal Chase	NY A	Aug 5, 1905	21
Hal Chase	NY A	Sep 21, 1906	22	Jiggs Donahue	CHI A	May 31, 1908	21
Ernie Banks	CHI N	May 9, 1963	22	Jake Daubert	BKN N	May 6, 1910	21
Cap Anson	CHI N	Aug 19, 1880	21	Hal Chase	NY A	Jun 23, 1911	21
Harry Stovey	WOR N	Sep 24, 1880	21	Vic Saier	CHI N	Sep 7, 1913	21
Ed Swartwood	PIT AA	Jun 25, 1883	21	Stuffy McInnis	BOS A	Jul 19, 1918	21
Charlie Householder	BKN AA	Jun 9, 1884	21	Harvey Cotter	CHI N	Jul 14, 1924	21
Billy O'Brien	WAS N	Sep 22, 1888	21	Bill Sweeney	BOS A	Jun 24, 1931	21
John Anderson	BKN N	Aug 26, 1896	21	Bill Terry	NY N	Apr 17, 1932	21
Jake Beckley	CIN N	Sep 27, 1898	21	Elbie Fletcher	PIT N	Jun 6, 1941	21

Most Assists, First Baseman, Game

Player	Team	Date	A	Inns.
Ferris Fain	PHI A	Jun 9, 1949	8	12
Bob Skinner	PIT N	Jul 22, 1954	8	14
Bob Robertson	PIT N	Jun 21, 1971	8	
Kitty Bransfield	PIT N	May 3, 1904	7	
George Stovall	STL A	Aug 7, 1912	7	
Fred Luderus	PHI N	Aug 22, 1918	7	

Most Putouts, Second Baseman, Game

Player	Team	Date	PO	Inns.
Jake Pitler	PIT N	Aug 22, 1917	15	22
Thorny Hawkes	TRO N	Jul 30, 1879	12	10
Lou Bierbauer	PHI AA	Jun 22, 1888	12	
Billy Gardner	BAL A	May 21, 1957	12	16
Bobby Knoop	CAL A	Aug 30, 1966	12	
Vern Fuller	CLE A	Apr 11, 1969	12	16

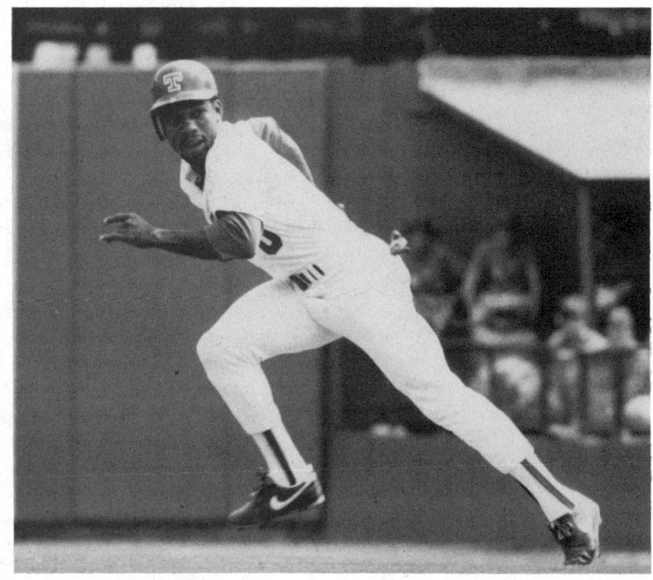

A member of the 1984 U.S. Olympic Baseball Team, Texas' Oddibe McDowell (*left*) has 36 home runs and 58 stolen bases in his first two seasons. Mr. Cub, Ernie Banks (*above*), slugged a record 293 homers at shortstop, and another 219 from other positions.

Most Assists, Second Baseman, Game

Player	Team	Date	A	Inns.
Lave Cross	PHI N	Aug 5, 1897	15	12
Morrie Rath	CIN N	Aug 26, 1919	13	15
Bobby Avila	CLE A	Jul 1, 1952	13	19
Willie Randolph	NY A	Aug 25, 1976	13	19
Fred Dunlap	CLE N	Jul 24, 1882	12	
Sam Crane	NY AA	Jun 1, 1883	12	
Monte Ward	BKN N	Jun 10, 1892	12	
Danny Richardson	WAS N	Jun 20, 1892	12	
Danny Murphy	PHI A	Oct 6, 1907	12	14
Joe Gedeon	STL A	Aug 19, 1918	12	14
Lee Magee	BKN N	Apr 30, 1919	12	20
Frankie Frisch	NY N	Aug 21, 1923	12	10
Billy Herman	CHI N	Jun 29, 1933	12	12
Hughie Critz	NY N	Jul 3, 1933	12	18
Don Heffner	STL A	May 22, 1938	12	13
Pep Young	PIT N	May 30, 1938	12	17
Don Gutteridge	STL A	Jul 4, 1944	12	14
Gerry Priddy	WAS A	Sep 6, 1946	12	11
Jim Gilliam	BKN N	Jul 21, 1956	12	
Red Schoendienst	MIL N	Aug 17, 1957	12	11
Vern Fuller	CLE A	Apr 11, 1969	12	16
Don Money	MIL A	Jun 24, 1977	12	
Ryne Sandberg	CHI N	Jun 12, 1983	12	
Glenn Hubbard	ATL N	Apr 14, 1985	12	
Juan Samuel	PHI N	Apr 20, 1985	12	
Tony Phillips	OAK A	Jul 6, 1986	12	
Harold Reynolds	SEA A	Aug 27, 1986	12	

Most Putouts, Third Baseman, Game

Player	Team	Date	PO
Willie Kuehne	PIT N	May 24, 1889	10
Pat Dillard	STL N	Jun 18, 1900	9
Art Devlin	NY N	May 23, 1908	8

Most Assists, Third Baseman, Game

Player	Team	Date	A	Inns.
Bobby Byrne	PIT N	Jun 18, 1910	12	11
Jerry Denny	PRO N	Aug 17, 1882	11	18
Deacon White	BUF N	May 16, 1884	11	
Jerry Denny	NY N	May 29, 1890	11	
Frank Baker	NY A	May 24, 1918	11	19
Damon Phillips	BOS N	Aug 29, 1944	11	
Ken McMullen	WAS A	Sep 26, 1966	11	
Mike Ferraro	NY A	Sep 14, 1968	11	
Doug DeCinces	CAL A	May 7, 1983	11	12

Don Money (*top*) played every infield position, as well as the outfield, and was voted to the All-Star team at second and third base. *Above*: In three full seasons, Phillie Juan Samuel has amassed 44 triples, 167 SB, and 451 strikeouts.

Most Putouts, Shortstop, Game

Player	Team	Date	PO	Inns.
Monte Cross	PHI N	Jul 7, 1899	14	11
Shorty Fuller	NY N	Aug 20, 1895	11	
Joe Cassidy	WAS A	Sep 30, 1904	11	
Russ Wrightstone	PHI N	Sep 4, 1922	11	16
Hod Ford	CIN N	Sep 18, 1929	11	

Most Assists, Shortstop, Game

Player	Team	Date	A	Inns.
Rick Burleson	CAL A	Apr 13, 1982	15	20
Herman Long	BOS N	May 6, 1892	14	14
Tommy Corcoran	CIN N	Aug 7, 1903	14	
Heinie Wagner	BOS A	Aug 7, 1907	14	14
Rogers Hornsby	STL N	May 26, 1917	14	15
Rabbit Maranville	PIT N	Jul 26, 1923	14	12
Bud Harrelson	NY N	May 24, 1973	14	19
Arthur Irwin	WOR N	Aug 31, 1880	13	14
Danny Richardson	WAS N	Jun 30, 1892	13	
Otto Krueger	STL N	Aug 17, 1902	13	18
Dave Bancroft	PHI N	Jul 13, 1918	13	21
Ivy Olson	BKN N	Aug 11, 1920	13	
Bobby Reeves	WAS A	Aug 7, 1927	13	
Bill Almon	SD N	May 4, 1977	13	
Germany Smith	BKN AA	Jun 29, 1889	12	
Bill Shindle	PHI P	Sep 26, 1890	12	
Bobby Wallace	STL N	May 4, 1901	12	
Kid Elberfeld	DET A	Sep 2, 1901	12	
Freddy Parent	BOS A	Jul 9, 1902	12	17
Bill Dahlen	NY N	Aug 16, 1906	12	
Art Fletcher	NY N	May 21, 1916	12	
Hod Ford	BOS N	Jun 16, 1921	12	
Eddie Miller	BOS N	Jun 27, 1939	12	23
Lou Boudreau	CLE A	Sep 14, 1939	12	

Above: Brooks Robinson, the human vacuum cleaner, won a record 16 consecutive Gold Gloves from 1960–75. *Right*: Luke Appling's .310 lifetime batting average and dazzling play at shortstop never received a postseason showcase *Below*: Phil Rizzuto's 10 stolen bases in nine World Series ranks third on the all-time list.

Rookie Records

Two Hundred or More Hits, Rookie, AL

Player	Team	Year	H
Tony Oliva	MIN	1964	217
Dale Alexander	DET	1929	215
Harvey Kuenn	DET	1953	209
Hal Trosky	CLE	1934	206
Joe DiMaggio	NY	1936	206
Johnny Pesky	BOS	1942	205
Earle Combs	NY	1925	203
Roy Johnson	DET	1929	201
Dick Wakefield	DET	1943	200

Two Hundred or More Hits, Rookie, NL

Player	Team	Year	H
Lloyd Waner	PIT	1927	223
Jimmy Williams	PIT	1899	217
Frank McCormick	CIN	1938	209
Johnny Frederick	BKN	1929	206
Billy Herman	CHI	1932	206
Vada Pinson	CIN	1959	205
Dick Allen	PHI	1964	201

Thirty or More Home Runs, Rookie, AL

Player	Team	Year	HR
Al Rosen	CLE	1950	37
Hal Trosky	CLE	1934	35
Rudy York	DET	1937	35
Ron Kittle	CHI	1983	35
Walt Dropo	BOS	1950	34
Jimmie Hall	MIN	1963	33
Jose Canseco	OAK	1986	33
Tony Oliva	MIN	1964	32
Ted Williams	BOS	1939	31
Bob Allison	WAS	1959	30
Pete Incaviglia	TEX	1986	30

Thirty or More Home Runs, Rookie, NL

Player	Team	Year	HR
Wally Berger	BOS	1930	38
Frank Robinson	CIN	1956	38
Earl Williams	ATL	1971	33
Jim Ray Hart	SF	1964	31
Willie Montanez	PHI	1971	30

Above: Frank Robinson topped his rookie mark of 38 home runs just twice on his way to 586 career blasts. Cleveland star Al Rosen (*right*) hit 192 homers and drove in 712 runs in his seven full seasons.

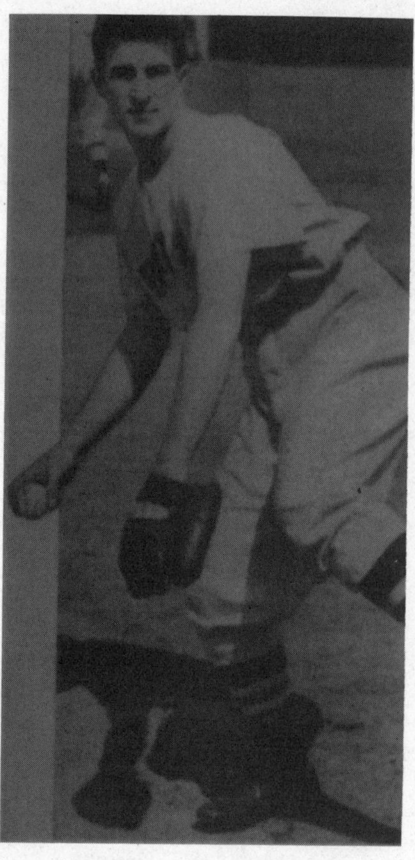

Lloyd Waner (*above*) batted .348 and scored 388 runs in his first three years for Pittsburgh. Johnny Pesky (*right*) collected 200+ hits in each of his first three seasons with the Red Sox.

.300 Average in Rookie Year Only, AL

Player	Team	Year	BA
Claude Rossman	CLE	1906	.308
Simon Nicholls	PHI	1907	.302
Bucky Harris	WAS	1920	.300
Tex Vache	BOS	1925	.313
Joe Boley	PHI	1927	.311
Hank Steinbacher	CHI	1938	.331
Charlie Keller	NY	1939	.334
Ralph Hodgin	CHI	1943	.314
Sam Mele	BOS	1947	.302
Walt Dropo	BOS	1950	.322
Jim Finigan	PHI	1954	.302
Manny Jimenez	KC	1962	.301
Willie Smith	LA	1964	.301

.300 Average in Rookie Year Only, NL

Player	Team	Year	BA
Fred Snodgrass	NY	1910	.321
Johnny Gooch	PIT	1922	.329
Bert Griffith	BKN	1922	.308
Dick Cox	BKN	1925	.329
Buzz Arlett	PHI	1931	.313
Les Mallon	PHI	1931	.309
Tuck Stainback	CHI	1934	.306
Les Scarsella	CIN	1936	.313
Johnny Rizzo	PIT	1938	.301
Bama Rowell	BOS	1940	.305

Most Hits in First Game

Player	Team	Date	H	2B	3B	HR
Fred Clarke	LOU N	Jun 30, 1894	5	1	0	0
Cecil Travis	WAS A	May 16, 1933	5	0	0	0
Casey Stengel	BKN N	Jul 17, 1912	4	0	0	0
Art Shires	CHI A	Aug 20, 1928	4	0	1	0
Russ Van Atta	NY A	Apr 25, 1933	4	0	1	0
Spook Jacobs	PHI A	Apr 13, 1954	4	0	0	0
Willie McCovey	SF N	Jul 30, 1959	4	0	2	0
Mack Jones	MIL N	Jul 13, 1961	4	1	0	0
Ted Cox	BOS A	Sep 17, 1977	4	0	0	0

Most Doubles, Rookie, AL

Player	Team	Year	2B
Fred Lynn	BOS	1975	47
Roy Johnson	DET	1929	45
Hal Trosky	CLE	1934	45
Bob Johnson	PHI	1933	44
Joe DiMaggio	NY	1936	44
Ted Williams	BOS	1939	44
Dale Alexander	DET	1929	43
Earl Averill	CLE	1929	43
Tony Oliva	MIN	1964	43
Carl Lind	CLE	1928	42
Bob Meusel	NY	1920	40

Most Doubles, Rookie, NL

Player	Team	Year	2B
Johnny Frederick	BKN	1929	52
Vada Pinson	CIN	1959	47
Billy Herman	CHI	1932	42
Warren Cromartie	MON	1977	41
Johnny Bench	CIN	1968	40
Kiddo Davis	PHI	1932	39
Alvin Dark	BOS	1948	39
Ray Grimes	CHI	1921	38
Gene Moore	BOS	1936	38
Orlando Cepeda	SF	1958	38
Dick Allen	PHI	1964	38

Most Triples, Rookie, AL

Player	Team	Year	3B
Joe Cassidy	WAS	1904	19
Charlie Gehringer	DET	1926	17
Russ Scarritt	BOS	1929	17
Hobe Ferris	BOS	1901	15
Del Pratt	STL	1912	15
Red Barnes	WAS	1928	15
Dale Alexander	DET	1929	15
Joe DiMaggio	NY	1936	15
Socks Seybold	PHI	1901	14
Tony Lazzeri	NY	1926	14
Doug Taitt	BOS	1928	14
Roy Johnson	DET	1929	14
Joe Vosmik	CLE	1931	14
Barney McCosky	DET	1939	14
Minnie Minoso	CLE	1951	
	CHI	1951	14
Jake Wood	DET	1961	14

Most Triples, Rookie, NL

Player	Team	Year	3B
Jimmy Williams	PIT	1899	27
Tommy Long	STL	1915	25
Paul Waner	PIT	1926	22
Juan Samuel	PHI	1984	19
Harry Lumley	BKN	1904	18
Glenn Wright	PIT	1924	18
Ival Goodman	CIN	1935	18
George Treadway	BAL	1893	17
Kip Selbach	WAS	1894	17
Jim Gilliam	BKN	1953	17

One Hundred or More RBIs, Rookie, AL

Player	Team	Year	RBI
Ted Williams	BOS	1939	145
Walt Dropo	BOS	1950	144
Hal Trosky	CLE	1934	142
Dale Alexander	DET	1929	137
Joe DiMaggio	NY	1936	125
Joe Vosmik	CLE	1931	117
Jose Canseco	OAK	1986	117
Al Rosen	CLE	1950	116
Alvin Davis	SEA	1984	116
Tony Lazzeri	NY	1926	114
Smead Jolley	CHI	1930	114
Ken Keltner	CLE	1938	113
Ping Bodie	CHI	1911	112
Zeke Bonura	CHI	1934	110
Luke Easter	CLE	1950	107
Fred Lynn	BOS	1975	105
Rudy York	DET	1937	103
Al Simmons	PHI	1924	102
Jim Rice	BOS	1975	102
Ron Kittle	CHI	1983	100
Wally Joyner	CAL	1986	100

One Hundred or More RBIs, Rookie, NL

Player	Team	Year	RBI
Wally Berger	BOS	1930	119
Jimmy Williams	PIT	1899	116
Ray Jablonski	STL	1953	112
Johnny Rizzo	PIT	1938	111
Gus Suhr	PIT	1930	107
Del Bissonette	BKN	1928	106
Bill Brubaker	PIT	1936	102
Jim Greengrass	CIN	1953	102
Babe Young	NY	1940	101

Left: Fred Lynn's three-run homer in the first inning of Game Six of the 1975 World Series began one of the greatest games in baseball history. Casey Stengel (*above*) batted .284 in 14 years before retiring to the dugout.

Highest Batting Average, Rookie, AL (Min. 300 AB)

Player	Team	Year	BA
Wade Boggs	BOS	1982	.349
Dale Alexander	DET	1929	.343
Patsy Dougherty	BOS	1902	.342
Earle Combs	NY	1925	.342
Al Bumbry	BAL	1973	.337
Socks Seybold	PHI	1901	.334
Heinie Manush	DET	1923	.334
Charlie Keller	NY	1939	.334
Mickey Cochrane	PHI	1925	.331
Earl Averill	CLE	1929	.331
Hank Steinbacher	CHI	1938	.331
Johnny Pesky	BOS	1942	.331
Fred Lynn	BOS	1975	.331

Highest Batting Average, Rookie, NL (Min. 300 AB)

Player	Team	Year	BA
George Watkins	STL	1930	.373
Jimmy Williams	PIT	1899	.355
Lloyd Waner	PIT	1927	.355
Chick Stahl	BOS	1897	.354
Kiki Cuyler	PIT	1924	.354
Fielder Jones	BKN	1896	.353
Ginger Beaumont	PIT	1899	.352
Dan Gladden	SF	1984	.351
Cuckoo Christensen	CIN	1926	.350
Paul Waner	PIT	1926	.336

Rookie No-Hitters, AL

Player	Team	Date	Score	Opp.
Earl Moore	CLE	May 9, 1901	2-4	CHI
Charlie Robertson	CHI	Apr 30, 1922	2-0	DET
Bobo Newsom	STL	Sep 18, 1934	1-2	BOS
Vern Kennedy	CHI	Aug 31, 1935	5-0	CLE
Bill McCahan	PHI	Sep 3, 1947	3-0	WAS
Bobo Holloman	STL	May 6, 1953	6-0	PHI
Bo Belinsky	LA	May 5, 1962	2-0	BAL
Vida Blue	OAK	Sep 21, 1970	6-0	MIN
Steve Busby	KC	Apr 27, 1973	3-0	DET
Jim Bibby	TEX	Jul 30, 1973	8-0	OAK
Mike Warren	OAK	Sep 29, 1983	3-0	CHI

Rookie No-Hitters, NL

Player	Team	Date	Score	Opp.
Lee Richmond	WOR	Jun 12, 1880	1-0	CLE
Larry Corcoran	CHI	Aug 19, 1880	6-0	BOS
Bumpus Jones	CIN	Oct 15, 1892	7-1	PIT
Jim Hughes	BAL	Apr 22, 1898	8-0	BOS
Deacon Phillippe	LOU	May 25, 1899	7-0	NY
Christy Mathewson	NY	Jul 15, 1901	5-0	STL
Nick Maddox	PIT	Sep 20, 1907	2-1	BKN
Jeff Tesreau	NY	Sep 6, 1912	3-0	PHI
Paul Dean	STL	Sep 21, 1934	3-0	BKN
Don Wilson	HOU	Jun 18, 1967	2-0	ATL
Burt Hooton	CHI	Apr 16, 1972	4-0	NY

Wade Boggs has a .352 batting average for his first five years in the majors.

Rookie No-Hitters, Other Leagues

Player	Team	Date	Score	Opp.
Tony Mullane	LOU AA	Sep 11, 1882	2-0	CIN
Guy Hecker	LOU AA	Sep 19, 1882	3-1	PIT
Al Atkinson	PHI AA	May 24, 1884	10-1	PIT
Ed Morris	COL AA	May 29, 1884	5-0	PIT
Sam Kimber	BKN AA	Oct 4, 1884	0-0	TOL
Matt Kilroy	BAL AA	Oct 6, 1886	6-0	PIT
Ted Breitenstein	STL AA	Oct 4, 1891	8-0	LOU

Twenty or More Wins, Rookie, AL

Player	Team	Year	W	L
Russ Ford	NY	1910	26	6
Ed Summers	DET	1908	24	12
Vean Gregg	CLE	1911	23	7
Roscoe Miller	DET	1901	23	13
Monte Weaver	WAS	1932	22	10
Wes Ferrell	CLE	1929	21	10
Boo Ferriss	BOS	1945	21	10
Reb Russell	CHI	1913	21	17
Scott Perry	PHI	1918	21	19
Bob Grim	NY	1954	20	6
Gene Bearden	CLE	1948	20	7
Hugh Bedient	BOS	1912	20	9
Alex Kellner	PHI	1949	20	12
Roy Patterson	CHI	1901	20	16

Twenty or More Wins, Rookie, NL since 1900

Player	Team	Year	W	L
Grover Alexander	PHI	1911	28	13
Larry Cheney	CHI	1912	26	10
Jeff Pfeffer	BKN	1914	23	12
George McQuillan	PHI	1908	23	17
Larry Jansen	NY	1947	21	5
Johnny Beazley	STL	1942	21	6
Henry Schmidt	BKN	1903	21	13
Bill Voiselle	NY	1944	21	16
King Cole	CHI	1910	20	4
Jake Weimer	CHI	1903	20	8
Jack Pfiester	CHI	1906	20	8
Cliff Melton	NY	1937	20	9
Harvey Haddix	STL	1953	20	9
Tom Browning	CIN	1985	20	9
Lou Fette	BOS	1937	20	10
Jim Turner	BOS	1937	20	11
Christy Mathewson	NY	1901	20	17
Irv Young	BOS	1905	20	21

Burt Hooton (*top*) won 96 games in his first seven seasons in L.A., helping the Dodgers into three World Series. *Above*: Tom Browning's 35–22 record with 316 strikeouts in two years has today's Cincinnati fans recalling the days of the Big Red Machine.

ERA Under 2.00, Rookie, AL (Min. 130 IP)

Player	Team	Year	ERA
Harry Krause	PHI	1909	1.39
Bob Lee	LA	1964	1.51
Ed Summers	DET	1908	1.64
Russ Ford	NY	1910	1.65
Frank Lange	CHI	1910	1.65
Otto Hess	CLE	1904	1.67
Bill Burns	WAS	1908	1.69
Mark Eichhorn	TOR	1986	1.72
Rube Bressler	PHI	1914	1.77
Vean Gregg	CLE	1911	1.81
Hippo Vaughn	NY	1910	1.83
Ernie Shore	BOS	1914	1.89
Reb Russell	CHI	1913	1.91
Scott Perry	PHI	1918	1.98
Doug Corbett	MIN	1980	1.99

ERA Under 2.00, Rookie, NL since 1900 (Min. 130 IP)

Player	Team	Year	ERA
Babe Adams	PIT	1909	1.11
Ed Reulbach	CHI	1905	1.42
George McQuillan	PHI	1908	1.53
Steve Rogers	MON	1973	1.54
Jack Pfiester	CHI	1906	1.56
King Cole	CHI	1910	1.80
Jeff Tesreau	NY	1912	1.96
Carl Lundgren	CHI	1902	1.97
Jeff Pfeffer	BKN	1914	1.97

Three Hundred or More Innings Pitched, Rookie, AL

Player	Team	Year	IP
Roscoe Miller	DET	1901	332
Scott Perry	PHI	1918	332
Reb Russell	CHI	1913	316
Elmer Myers	PHI	1916	315
Roy Patterson	CHI	1901	312
Bill Reidy	MIL	1901	301
Ed Summers	DET	1908	301
Russ Ford	NY	1910	300

Three Hundred or More Innings Pitched, Rookie, NL since 1900

Player	Team	Year	IP
Irv Young	BOS	1905	378
Grover Alexander	PHI	1911	367
George McQuillan	PHI	1908	360
Christy Mathewson	NY	1901	336
Oscar Jones	BKN	1903	324
Ed Scott	CIN	1900	323
Orval Overall	CIN	1905	318
Al Mattern	BOS	1909	316
Jeff Pfeffer	BKN	1914	315
Bill Voiselle	NY	1944	313
Jack Harper	STL	1901	309
Harry McIntyre	BKN	1905	309
Long Tom Hughes	CHI	1901	308
Vive Lindaman	BOS	1906	307
Larry Cheney	CHI	1912	303
Jesse Haines	STL	1920	302
Henry Schmidt	BKN	1903	301

Most Strikeouts, Rookie, AL

Player	Team	Year	SO
Herb Score	CLE	1955	245
Russ Ford	NY	1910	209
Bob Johnson	KC	1970	206
Mark Langston	SEA	1984	204
Gary Peters	CHI	1963	189
Elmer Myers	PHI	1916	182
Ken McBride	LA	1961	180
Frank Tanana	CAL	1974	180
Tom Phoebus	BAL	1967	179
Ron Guidry	NY	1977	176

Most Strikeouts, Rookie, NL since 1900

Player	Team	Year	SO
Dwight Gooden	NY	1984	276
Grover Alexander	PHI	1911	227
Long Tom Hughes	CHI	1901	225
Christy Mathewson	NY	1901	221
John Montefusco	SF	1975	215
Don Sutton	LA	1966	209
Gary Nolan	CIN	1967	206
Tom Griffin	HOU	1969	200
Sam Jones	CHI	1955	198
Dizzy Dean	STL	1932	191

Most Complete Games, Rookie, AL

Player	Team	Year	CG
Roscoe Miller	DET	1901	35
Elmer Myers	PHI	1916	31
Roy Patterson	CHI	1901	30
Ed Siever	DET	1901	30
Fred Glade	STL	1904	30
Scott Perry	PHI	1918	30
Chief Bender	PHI	1903	29
Russ Ford	NY	1910	29
Earl Moore	CLE	1901	28
Eddie Plank	PHI	1901	28
Bill Reidy	MIL	1901	28
Addie Joss	CLE	1902	28

Most Complete Games, Rookie, NL since 1900

Player	Team	Year	CG
Irv Young	BOS	1905	41
Christy Mathewson	NY	1901	36
Ed Scott	CIN	1900	32
Long Tom Hughes	CHI	1901	32
Orval Overall	CIN	1905	32
Vive Lindaman	BOS	1906	32
George McQuillan	PHI	1908	32
Oscar Jones	BKN	1903	31
Grover Alexander	PHI	1911	31
Henry Schmidt	BKN	1903	29
Harry McIntyre	BKN	1905	29

Most Shutouts, Rookie, AL

Player	Team	Year	ShO
Russ Ford	NY	1910	8
Reb Russell	CHI	1913	8
Harry Krause	PHI	1908	7
Fred Glade	STL	1904	6
Gene Bearden	CLE	1948	6
Addie Joss	CLE	1902	5
Ed Summers	DET	1908	5
Hippo Vaughn	NY	1910	5
Vean Gregg	CLE	1911	5
Boo Ferriss	BOS	1945	5
Mike Garcia	CLE	1949	5
Ron Guidry	NY	1977	5
Mike Boddicker	BAL	1983	5

Most Shutouts, Rookie, NL since 1900

Player	Team	Year	ShO
Fernando Valenzuela	LA	1981	8
Irv Young	BOS	1905	7
George McQuillan	PHI	1908	7
Grover Alexander	PHI	1911	7
Jerry Koosman	NY	1968	7
Ewell Blackwell	CIN	1946	6
Harvey Haddix	STL	1953	6
Christy Mathewson	NY	1901	5
Henry Schmidt	BKN	1903	5
Ed Reulbach	CHI	1905	5
Dazzy Vance	BKN	1922	5
Paul Dean	STL	1934	5
Lou Fette	BOS	1937	5
Jim Turner	BOS	1937	5
Don Newcombe	BKN	1949	5
Ray Culp	PHI	1963	5
Larry Jaster	STL	1966	5
Gary Nolan	CIN	1967	5

Right: Dick Williams's stewardship led Oakland to consecutive World Championships. *Below*: Sparky Anderson's teams boast a 33–17 postseason record, and include World Series victors in 1975–76 (Reds) and 1984 (Tigers).

Pennant-Winning Rookie Managers, AL

Manager	Team	Year	W	L	Pct.
Clark Griffith	CHI	1901	83	55	.610
Hughie Jennings	DET	1907	92	58	.613
Kid Gleason	CHI	1919	88	52	.629
Bucky Harris	WAS	1924	92	62	.597
Joe Cronin	WAS	1933	99	53	.651
Mickey Cochrane	DET	1934	101	53	.656
Ralph Houk	NY	1961	109	53	.678
Yogi Berra	NY	1964	99	63	.611
Dick Williams	BOS	1967	92	70	.568
Jimmy Frey	KC	1980	97	65	.599

Pennant-Winning Rookie Managers, NL

Manager	Team	Year	W	L	Pct.
Frank Chance	CHI	1906	116	36	.763
Pat Moran	PHI	1915	90	62	.592
Gabby Street	STL	1930	92	62	.597
Charlie Grimm	CHI	1932	90	44	.584
Bill Terry	NY	1933	91	61	.599
Gabby Hartnett	CHI	1938	89	63	.586
Eddie Dyer	STL	1946	98	58	.628
Sparky Anderson	CIN	1970	102	60	.630
Tommy Lasorda	LA	1977	98	64	.605

Team Records

Most Wins, Season, AL

Team	Year	W	L	Pct.	Place
CLE	1954	111	43	.721	1
NY	1927	110	44	.714	1
NY	1961	109	53	.673	1
BAL	1969	109	53	.673	1
BAL	1970	108	54	.667	1
PHI	1931	107	45	.704	1
NY	1932	107	47	.695	1
NY	1939	106	45	.702	1
BOS	1912	105	47	.691	1

Most Wins, Season, NL

Team	Year	W	L	Pct.	Place
CHI	1906	116	36	.763	1
PIT	1909	110	42	.724	1
CIN	1975	108	54	.667	1
NY	1986	108	54	.667	1
CHI	1907	107	45	.704	1
NY	1904	106	47	.693	1
STL	1942	106	48	.688	1
NY	1905	105	48	.686	1
STL	1943	105	49	.682	1
STL	1944	105	49	.682	1
BKN	1953	105	49	.682	1

The Chicago Cubs, led by Frank Chance (*left*), averaged an incredible 102 wins per season from 1906–12. *Below*: Diminutive Miller Huggins (5′ 6½″, 140 lbs.) was the first great Yankee skipper, leading New York to six pennants.

Connie Mack, the dean of managers, led the Philadelphia Athletics from 1901–50, winning 3776 games, nine pennants, and five World Series.

Most Losses, Season, AL

Team	Year	W	L	Pct.	Place
PHI	1916	36	117	.235	8
WAS	1904	38	113	.251	8
BOS	1932	43	111	.279	8
STL	1939	43	111	.279	8
WAS	1909	42	110	.276	8
PHI	1915	47	109	.283	8
TOR	1979	53	109	.327	7
STL	1937	46	108	.299	8
OAK	1979	54	108	.333	7
STL	1910	47	107	.305	8
STL	1911	45	107	.296	8
BOS	1926	46	107	.301	8
TOR	1977	54	107	.335	7
PHI	1920	48	106	.312	8
WAS	1963	56	106	.346	10
CHI	1970	56	106	.346	6
BOS	1906	49	105	.318	8
BOS	1925	47	105	.309	8
PHI	1943	49	105	.318	8
PHI	1946	49	105	.318	8
KC	1964	57	105	.352	10

Most Losses, Season, NL

Team	Year	W	L	Pct.	Place
NY	1962	40	120	.250	10
BOS	1935	38	115	.248	8
PIT	1952	42	112	.273	8
NY	1965	50	112	.309	10
PHI	1941	43	111	.279	8
NY	1963	51	111	.315	10
MON	1969	52	110	.321	6
SD	1969	52	110	.321	6
PHI	1928	43	109	.283	8
PHI	1942	42	109	.278	8
NY	1964	53	109	.327	10
BOS	1909	45	108	.294	8
PHI	1945	46	108	.299	8
BOS	1911	44	107	.291	8
PHI	1961	47	107	.305	8
MON	1976	55	107	.340	6
PHI	1939	45	106	.298	8
STL	1908	49	105	.318	8
PHI	1938	45	105	.300	8

Most Consecutive Wins, AL

Team	Year	W	Home	Away	Team	Year	W	Home	Away
CHI	1906	19	11	8	KC	1977	16	9	7
NY	1947	19	6	13	NY	1906	15	12	3
NY	1953	18	3	15	PHI	1913	15	13	2
WAS	1912	17	1	16	BOS	1946	15	11	4
PHI	1931	17	5	12	NY	1960	15	9	6
NY	1926	16	12	4					

Most Consecutive Wins, NL

Team	Year	W	Home	Away	Team	Year	W	Home	Away
NY	1916	26	26	0	PHI	1887	16	5	11
CHI	1880	21	11	10	PHI	1890	16	14	2
CHI	1935	21	18	3	PHI	1892	16	11	5
PRO	1884	20	16	4	PIT	1909	16	12	4
CHI	1885	18	14	4	NY	1912	16	11	5
BOS	1891	18	16	2	NY	1951	16	13	3
BAL	1894	18	13	5	DET	1886	15	12	3
NY	1904	18	13	5	PIT	1903	15	11	4
BOS	1897	17	16	1	BKN	1924	15	3	12
NY	1907	17	14	3	CHI	1936	15	11	4
NY	1916	17	0	17	NY	1936	15	7	8

Most Consecutive Losses, AL

Team	Year	L	Home	Away	Team	Year	L	Home	Away
BOS	1906	20	19	1	WAS	1959	18	3	15
PHI	1916	20	1	19	BOS	1926	17	14	3
PHI	1943	20	3	17	BOS	1907	16	9	7
DET	1975	19	9	10	BOS	1927	15	10	5
PHI	1920	18	0	18	PHI	1937	15	10	5
WAS	1948	18	8	10	TEX	1972	15	5	10

Most Consecutive Losses, NL

Team	Year	L	Home	Away	Team	Year	L	Home	Away
CLE	1899	24	3	21	TRO	1882	16	5	11
PIT	1890	23	1	22	DET	1884	16	5	11
PHI	1961	23	6	17	CLE	1899	16	0	16
LOU	1894	20	0	20	BOS	1907	16	5	11
MON	1969	20	12	8	BOS	1911	16	8	8
BOS	1906	19	3	16	BKN	1944	16	0	16
CIN	1914	19	6	13	BOS	1909	15	0	15
CIN	1876	18	9	9	STL	1909	15	11	4
LOU	1894	18	0	18	BOS	1927	15	0	15
WAS	1894	17	7	10	BOS	1935	15	0	15
NY	1962	17	7	10	NY	1963	15	8	7
ATL	1977	17	8	9	NY	1982	15	6	9

Above: Casey Stengel's Yankees celebrated 10 pennants and seven World Championships between 1949–60. *Right*: At the start of the twentieth century the Chicago Cubs were the best team in baseball, boasting four future Hall of Famers in their lineup: Three Finger Brown, Joe Tinker, Johnny Evers, and Frank Chance.

Forfeited Games

Team	Date	Loser	Site	Inns.	Score
DET A	May 2, 1901	CHI	CHI	9	7-5
NY N	May 13, 1901	BKN	NY	9	7-7
DET A	May 31, 1901	BAL	DET	9	5-5
NY N	Jun 9, 1901	CIN	CIN	9	25-13
CLE A	Jul 23, 1901	WAS	CLE	9	4-4
DET A	Aug 21, 1901	BAL	BAL	4	7-4
PIT N	Jun 16, 1902	BOS	BOS	4	4-0
BOS A	Jun 28, 1902	BAL	BAL	8	9-4
STL A	Jul 17, 1902	BAL	BAL	0	
DET A	Aug 8, 1903	CLE	CLE	11	6-5
STL N	Oct 4, 1904	NY	NY	4	2-1
PIT N	Aug 5, 1905	NY	PIT	9	5-5
WAS A	Aug 22, 1905	DET	DET	11	2-1
PIT N	Jun 9, 1906	PHI	PHI	8	7-1
NY A	Jul 2, 1906	PHI	PHI	9	5-1
CHI N	Aug 7, 1906	NY	NY	0	
NY A	Sep 3, 1906	PHI	NY	9	3-3
PHI N	Apr 11, 1907	NY	NY	8	3-0
STL N	Oct 5, 1907	CHI	STL	4	0-2
NY N	Oct 4, 1909	PHI	NY	4	1-1
STL N	Jul 6, 1913	CHI	CHI	3	4-0
PHI A	Jun 26, 1914	WAS	PHI	4	2-0
BKN N	Jul 18, 1916	CHI	CHI	10	4-4
CHI A	Sep 9, 1917	CLE	CHI	10	3-3
CLE A	Jul 20, 1918	PHI	PHI	9	9-1
CHI A	Aug 20, 1920	PHI	PHI	9	5-2
NY A	Jun 13, 1924	DET	DET	9	10-6
CLE A	Apr 26, 1925	CHI	CHI	9	7-2
STL N	Jun 6, 1937	PHI	PHI	4	8-2
BOS A	Aug 15, 1941	WAS	WAS	8	3-6
BOS N	Sep 26, 1942	NY	NY	8	2-5
NY N	Aug 21, 1949	PHI	PHI	9	4-2
PHI N	Jul 18, 1954	STL	STL	4	8-1
NY A	Sep 30, 1971	WAS	WAS	9	5-7
TEX A	Jun 4, 1974	CLE	CLE	9	5-5
TOR A	Sep 15, 1977	BAL	TOR	5	4-0
DET A	Jul 12, 1979	CHI	CHI	0	

Most Lopsided Wins since 1900

Team	Date	Loser	Score	Diff.
BOS A	Jun 8, 1950	STL	29-4	25
CLE A	Jul 7, 1923	BOS	27-3	24
CIN N	Jun 4, 1911	BOS	26-3	23
NY A	May 24, 1936	PHI	25-2	23
CLE A	Aug 12, 1948	STL	26-3	23
CHI A	Apr 23, 1955	KC	29-6	23
CIN N	May 13, 1902	PHI	24-2	22
PHI A	May 18, 1912	DET	24-2	22
STL N	Jul 6, 1929	PHI	28-6	22
CHI N	Jul 3, 1945	BOS	24-2	22
PIT N	Sep 16, 1975	CHI	22-0	22
CAL A	Aug 25, 1979	TOR	24-2	22
DET A	Sep 15, 1901	CLE	21-0	21
NY N	Sep 10, 1924	BOS	22-1	21
NY A	Jun 28, 1939	PHI	23-2	21
NY A	Aug 13, 1939	PHI	21-0	21
CIN N	Jun 8, 1940	BKN	23-2	21
NY A	Aug 12, 1953	WAS	22-1	21
CLE A	Aug 7, 1923	WAS	22-2	20
NY A	Sep 28, 1923	BOS	24-4	20
STL N	Sep 16, 1926	PHI	23-3	20
NY A	Jul 4, 1927	WAS	21-1	20
NY A	May 2, 1939	DET	22-2	20
BOS A	Sep 27, 1940	WAS	24-4	20
BOS A	Jun 18, 1953	DET	23-3	20
CIN N	Jun 1, 1957	CHI	22-2	20

Longest Games, AL

Team	Date	Opp.	Inns.	Score
CHI	May 8, 1984	MIL	25	7-6
PHI	Sep 1, 1906	BOS	24	4-1
DET	Jul 21, 1945	PHI	24	1-1
NY	Jun 24, 1962	DET	22	9-7
WAS	Jun 12, 1967	CHI	22	6-5
MIL	May 12, 1972	MIN	22	4-3
DET	May 24, 1929	CHI	21	6-5
OAK	Jun 4, 1971	WAS	21	5-3
CHI	May 26, 1973	CLE	21	6-3
PHI	Jul 4, 1905	BOS	20	4-2
WAS	Aug 9, 1967	MIN	20	9-7
NY	Aug 29, 1967	BOS	20	4-3
BOS	Jul 27, 1969	SEA	20	5-3
OAK	Jul 9, 1971	CAL	20	1-0
WAS	Sep 14, 1971	CLE	20	8-6
SEA	Sep 3, 1981	BOS	20	8-7
CAL	Apr 13, 1982	SEA	20	4-3

Brooklyn's Leon Cadore (*top*) and Boston's Joe Oeschger (*above*) dueled to a 26-inning, 1–1 tie in baseball's longest game. Cadore finished the season 15–14, but lost Game Four of the World Series to the eventual-champion Indians. Oeschger also won 15 games that year, and 20 the next, but never pitched in the World Series.

Longest Games, NL

Team	Date	Opp.	Inns.	Score
BKN	May 1, 1920	BOS	26	1-1
STL	Sep 11, 1974	NY	25	4-3
HOU	Apr 15, 1968	NY	24	1-0
BKN	Jun 27, 1939	BOS	23	2-2
SF	May 31, 1964	NY	23	8-6
BKN	Aug 22, 1917	PIT	22	6-5
CHI	May 17, 1927	BOS	22	4-3
NY	Jul 17, 1914	PIT	21	3-1
CHI	Jul 17, 1918	PHI	21	2-1
PIT	Aug 1, 1918	BOS	21	2-0
SF	Sep 1, 1967	CIN	21	1-0
HOU	Sep 24, 1971	SD	21	2-1
SD	May 21, 1977	MON	21	11-8
LA	Aug 17, 1982	CHI	21	2-1
CHI	Jun 30, 1892	CIN	20	7-7
CHI	Aug 24, 1905	PHI	20	2-1
BKN	Apr 30, 1919	PHI	20	9-9
STL	Aug 28, 1930	CHI	20	8-7
BKN	Jul 5, 1940	BOS	20	6-2
PHI	May 4, 1973	ATL	20	5-4
PIT	Jul 6, 1980	CHI	20	5-4
HOU	Aug 15, 1980	SD	20	3-1

Career Spent With One Team (15 or more years)

Player	Team	Yrs.	Pos.
Brooks Robinson	BAL A	23	3B
Carl Yastrzemski	BOS A	23	OF-1B
Cap Anson	CHI N	22	1B
Al Kaline	DET A	22	OF
Stan Musial	STL N	22	OF-1B
Mel Ott	NY N	22	OF
Fred Clarke	LOU N		
	PIT N	21	OF
Walter Johnson	WAS A	21	P
Ted Lyons	CHI A	21	P
Willie Stargell	PIT N	21	OF-1B
Honus Wagner	LOU N		
	PIT N	21	SS
Luke Appling	CHI A	20	SS
Red Faber	CHI A	20	P
Mel Harder	CLE A	20	P
Ernie Banks	CHI N	19	SS-1B
Charlie Gehringer	DET A	19	2B
Jim Palmer	BAL A	19	P
Ted Williams	BOS A	19	OF
Ossie Bluege	WAS A	18	3B
Roberto Clemente	PIT N	18	OF
Bob Feller	CLE A	18	P
Ed Kranepool	NY N	18	1B-OF
Mickey Mantle	NY A	18	OF-IB
Bill Russell	LA N	18	SS
Johnny Bench	CIN N	17	C
Dave Concepcion	CIN N	17	SS
Frankie Crosetti	NY A	17	SS
Bill Dickey	NY A	17	C
Lou Gehrig	NY A	17	1B
Bob Gibson	STL N	17	P
Bill Mazeroski	PIT N	17	2B
Pie Traynor	PIT N	17	3B
Tommy Bridges	DET A	16	P
Whitey Ford	NY A	16	P
Stan Hack	CHI N	16	3B
Carl Hubbell	NY N	16	P
Vern Law	PIT N	16	P
Clyde Milan	WAS A	16	OF
Pee Wee Reese	BKN N		
	LA N	16	SS
Hooks Dauss	DET A	15	P
Dwight Evans	BOS A	15	OF
Bill Freehan	DET A	15	C
Carl Furillo	BKN N		
	LA N	15	OF
John Hiller	DET A	15	P
Travis Jackson	NY N	15	SS-3B
Bob Lemon	CLE A	15	P
Tony Oliva	MIN A	15	OF
Mike Schmidt	PHI N	15	3B
Paul Splittorff	KC A	15	P
Mickey Stanley	DET A	15	OF
Roy White	NY A	15	OF

Retired Numbers, AL

Player	Team	No.
Earl Weaver	BAL	4
Brooks Robinson	BAL	5
Frank Robinson	BAL	20
Jim Palmer	BAL	22
Joe Cronin	BOS	4
Ted Williams	BOS	9
Gene Autry	CAL	26
Rod Carew	CAL	29
Nellie Fox	CHI	2
Luke Appling	CHI	4
Minnie Minoso	CHI	9
Luis Aparicio	CHI	11
Earl Averill	CLE	3
Lou Boudreau	CLE	5
Bob Feller	CLE	19
Charlie Gehringer	DET	2
Hank Greenberg	DET	5
Al Kaline	DET	6
Hank Aaron	MIL	44
Harmon Killebrew	MIN	3
Billy Martin	NY	1
Babe Ruth	NY	3
Lou Gehrig	NY	4
Joe DiMaggio	NY	5
Mickey Mantle	NY	7
Yogi Berra	NY	8
Bill Dickey	NY	8
Roger Maris	NY	9
Phil Rizzuto	NY	10
Thurman Munson	NY	15
Whitey Ford	NY	16
Elston Howard	NY	32
Casey Stengel	NY	37

Brooks Robinson (*below*) came to bat in an Orioles uniform over 10,000 times, helping Baltimore to four A.L. pennants. In 23 years in Boston Carl Yastrzemski (*right*) hit 452 home runs and drove in 1844 runs.

Pie Traynor (*above*) had 11 seasons with 10 or more triples, and a .320 career average. Duke Snider (*right*) hit 40 homers for the Dodgers five years in a row (1953–57).

Retired Numbers, NL

Player	Team	No.
Warren Spahn	ATL	21
Phil Niekro	ATL	35
Eddie Mathews	ATL	41
Hank Aaron	ATL	44
Ernie Banks	CHI	14
Fred Hutchinson	CIN	1
Johnny Bench	CIN	5
Jim Umbricht	HOU	32
Don Wilson	HOU	40
Pee Wee Reese	LA	1
Duke Snider	LA	4
Jim Gilliam	LA	19
Walter Alston	LA	24
Sandy Koufax	LA	32
Roy Campanella	LA	39
Jackie Robinson	LA	42
Don Drysdale	LA	53
Gil Hodges	NY	14
Casey Stengel	NY	37
Richie Ashburn	PHI	1
Robin Roberts	PHI	36
Billy Meyer	PIT	1
Willie Stargell	PIT	8
Pie Traynor	PIT	20
Roberto Clemente	PIT	21
Honus Wagner	PIT	33
Danny Murtaugh	PIT	40
Bill Terry	SF	3
Mel Ott	SF	4
Carl Hubbell	SF	11
Willie Mays	SF	24
Juan Marichal	SF	27
Willie McCovey	SF	44
Stan Musial	STL	6
Ken Boyer	STL	14
Dizzy Dean	STL	17
Lou Brock	STL	20
Bob Gibson	STL	45
August A. Busch, Jr.	STL	85

Most Wins, Manager, Career

Manager	Yrs.	W	L	Pct.	Manager	Yrs.	W	L	Pct.
Connie Mack	53	3776	4025	.484	Wilbert Robinson	19	1397	1395	.500
John McGraw	33	2840	1984	.589	Ned Hanlon	19	1315	1165	.530
Bucky Harris	29	2159	2219	.493	Frank Selee	16	1299	872	.598
Joe McCarthy	24	2126	1335	.614	Cap Anson	20	1297	957	.575
Walter Alston	23	2040	1613	.556	Charlie Grimm	19	1287	1069	.546
Leo Durocher	24	2010	1710	.540	Chuck Tanner	17	1271	1262	.502
Casey Stengel	25	1926	1867	.508	Billy Rigney	18	1239	1321	.484
Bill McKechnie	25	1898	1724	.524	Joe Cronin	15	1236	1055	.540
Gene Mauch	25	1826	1950	.484	Billy Martin	15	1209	976	.553
Ralph Houk	20	1619	1534	.514	Lou Boudreau	16	1162	1224	.487
Fred Clarke	19	1602	1179	.576	Frankie Frisch	16	1137	1078	.513
Sparky Anderson	17	1513	1122	.574	Hughie Jennings	14	1131	972	.538
Clark Griffith	20	1491	1367	.522	Danny Murtaugh	15	1115	950	.540
Earl Weaver	17	1479	1060	.583	Billy Southworth	13	1064	729	.593
Dick Williams	19	1470	1334	.524	Harry Wright	18	1042	848	.551
Al Lopez	17	1422	1026	.581	Steve O'Neill	14	1039	819	.559
Miller Huggins	17	1413	1134	.555	Chuck Dressen	16	1037	993	.511
Jimmy Dykes	21	1407	1538	.478	Red Schoendienst	13	1028	944	.521

Ralph Houk, "The Major," led the Yankees to the World Series in each of his first three seasons in the dugout, and never came close again in his 20-year career.

Pennant-Winning Managers in AL and NL

Manager	Team	Year	W	L
Joe McCarthy	CHI N	1929	98	54
	NY A	1932	107	47
	NY A	1936	102	51
	NY A	1937	102	52
	NY A	1938	99	53
	NY A	1939	106	45
	NY A	1941	101	53
	NY A	1942	103	51
	NY A	1943	98	56
Sparky Anderson	CIN N	1970	102	60
	CIN N	1972	95	59
	CIN N	1975	108	54
	CIN N	1976	102	60
	DET A	1984	104	58
Dick Williams	BOS A	1967	92	70
	OAK A	1972	93	62
	OAK A	1973	94	68
	SD N	1984	92	70
Alvin Dark	SF N	1962	103	62
	OAK A	1974	90	72
Yogi Berra	NY A	1964	99	63
	NY N	1973	82	79

Most League Pennants Won, Manager

Manager	Total
John McGraw	10
Casey Stengel	10
Connie Mack	9
Joe McCarthy	9
Walter Alston	7
Miller Huggins	6
Sparky Anderson	5
Cap Anson	5
Ned Hanlon	5
Frank Selee	5

Brother Batteries, AL

Player	Team	Pos.	First	Last
Tommy Thompson	NY	P	1912	1912
Homer Thompson	NY	C		
Milt Gaston	BOS	P	1929	1929
Alex Gaston	BOS	C		
Wes Ferrell	BOS	P	1934	1937
Rick Ferrell	BOS	C		
Wes Ferrell	WAS	P	1937	1937
Rick Ferrell	WAS	C		
Bobby Shantz	PHI	P	1954	1954
Billy Shantz	PHI	C		
Bobby Shantz	KC	P	1955	1955
Billy Shantz	KC	C		
Bobby Shantz	NY	P	1960	1960
Billy Shantz	NY	C		

Brother Batteries, NL

Player	Team	Pos.	First	Last
Will White	BOS	P	1877	1877
Deacon White	BOS	C		
Will White	CIN	P	1878	1879
Deacon White	CIN	C		
Pete Wood	BUF	P	1885	1885
Fred Wood	BUF	C		
John Ewing	NY	P	1891	1891
Buck Ewing	NY	C		
Mike O'Neill	STL	P	1902	1903
Jack O'Neill	STL	C		
Lefty Tyler	BOS	P	1914	1914
Fred Tyler	BOS	C		
Mort Cooper	STL	P	1940	1945
Walker Cooper	STL	C		
Mort Cooper	NY	P	1947	1947
Walker Cooper	NY	C		
Elmer Riddle	CIN	P	1941	1941
Johnny Riddle	CIN	C		
Elmer Riddle	CIN	P	1944	1945
Johnny Riddle	CIN	C		
Elmer Riddle	PIT	P	1948	1948
Johnny Riddle	PIT	C		
Jim Bailey	CIN	P	1959	1959
Ed Bailey	CIN	C		
Larry Sherry	LA	P	1959	1962
Norm Sherry	LA	C		

Brother Batteries, Other Leagues

Player	Team	Pos.	First	Last
Ed Dugan	RIC AA	P	1884	1884
Bill Dugan	RIC AA	C		
Dick Conway	BAL AA	P	1886	1886
Bill Conway	BAL AA	C		
John Ewing	NY P	P	1890	1890
Buck Ewing	NY P	C		

Pitching Brothers, Same Team, AL

Player	Team	First	Last	W	L
Vean Gregg	CLE	1913	1913	20	13
Dave Gregg	CLE			0	0
Ted Blankenship	CHI	1922	1923	17	24
Homer Blankenship	CHI			1	1
Alex Kellner	PHI	1952	1953	23	26
Walt Kellner	PHI			0	0
Gaylord Perry	CLE	1974	1975	27	22
Jim Perry	CLE			18	18
Phil Niekro	NY	1985	1985	16	12
Joe Niekro	NY			2	1

Pitching Brothers, Same Team, NL

Player	Team	First	Last	W	L
Larry Corcoran	CHI	1884	1884	35	23
Mike Corcoran	CHI			0	1
John Clarkson	BOS	1892	1892	8	6
Dad Clarkson	BOS			1	0
Frank Foreman	CIN	1896	1896	15	6
Brownie Foreman	CIN			0	4
Christy Mathewson	NY	1906	1907	46	25
Henry Mathewson	NY			0	1
Howie Camnitz	PIT	1909	1909	25	6
Harry Camnitz	PIT			0	0
Grover Lowdermilk	STL	1911	1911	0	1
Lou Lowdermilk	STL			3	4
Jesse Barnes	NY	1919	1923	76	42
Virgil Barnes	NY			3	4
Johnny Morrison	PIT	1921	1921	9	7
Phil Morrison	PIT			0	0
Dizzy Dean	STL	1934	1937	95	42
Paul Dean	STL			43	28
Eddie O'Brien	PIT	1956	1958	1	0
Johnny O'Brien	PIT			1	3
Lindy McDaniel	STL	1957	1958	18	16
Von McDaniel	STL			7	5
Dennis Bennett	PHI	1964	1964	12	14
Dave Bennett	PHI			0	0
Phil Niekro	ATL	1973	1974	33	23
Joe Niekro	ATL			5	6
Rick Reuschel	CHI	1975	1976	25	29
Paul Reuschel	CHI			5	5
Mickey Mahler	ATL	1979	1979	5	11
Rick Mahler	ATL			0	0

Three or More Brothers in Baseball

Player	First	Last
Dick Allen	1963	1977
Hank Allen	1965	1973
Ron Allen	1972	1972
Felipe Alou	1958	1974
Matty Alou	1960	1974
Jesus Alou	1963	1979
Cloyd Boyer	1949	1955
Ken Boyer	1955	1969
Clete Boyer	1955	1971
John Clarkson	1882	1894
Dad Clarkson	1891	1896
Walter Clarkson	1904	1908
Amos Cross	1885	1887
Lave Cross	1887	1907
Frank Cross	1901	1901
Jose Cruz	1970	
Hector Cruz	1973	1982
Tommy Cruz	1973	1977
Ed Delahanty	1888	1903
Tom Delahanty	1894	1897
Jim Delahanty	1901	1915
Frank Delahanty	1905	1915
Joe Delahanty	1907	1909
Joe DiMaggio	1936	1951
Vince DiMaggio	1937	1946
Dom DiMaggio	1940	1953

Player	First	Last
Mike Edwards	1977	1980
Dave Edwards	1978	1982
Marshall Edwards	1981	1983
Hugh High	1913	1918
Charlie High	1919	1920
Andy High	1922	1934
Mike Mansell	1879	1884
Tom Mansell	1879	1884
John Mansell	1882	1882
Mike O'Neill	1901	1907
Jack O'Neill	1902	1906
Steve O'Neill	1911	1928
Jim O'Neill	1920	1923
Eddie Sadowski	1960	1966
Ted Sadowski	1960	1962
Bob Sadowski	1963	1966
Joe Sewell	1920	1933
Luke Sewell	1921	1942
Tommy Sewell	1927	1927
Len Sowders	1886	1886
John Sowders	1887	1890
Bill Sowders	1888	1890
George Wright	1876	1882
Sam Wright	1876	1881
Harry Wright	1876	1877

Most Wins by Brothers

Player	Yrs.	W	L
Gaylord Perry	22	314	265
Jim Perry	17	215	174
Total	39	529	439
Phil Niekro	23	311	261
Joe Niekro	20	213	190
Total	43	524	451
John Clarkson	12	326	177
Dad Clarkson	6	39	39
Walter Clarkson	5	18	16
Total	23	383	232
Christy Mathewson	17	373	188
Henry Mathewson	2	0	1
Total	19	373	189
Pud Galvin	14	361	309
Lou Galvin	1	0	2
Total	15	361	311
Old Hoss Radbourn	11	308	191
George Radbourn	1	1	2
Total	12	309	193

Player	Yrs.	W	L
Stan Coveleski	14	215	142
Harry Coveleski	9	81	55
Total	23	296	197
Gus Weyhing	14	264	234
John Weyhing	2	3	4
Total	16	267	238
Bob Forsch	13	143	116
Ken Forsch	16	114	113
Total	29	257	229
Will White	10	229	166
Deacon White	2	0	0
Total	12	229	166
Jesse Barnes	13	153	149
Virgil Barnes	9	61	59
Total	22	214	208
Dizzy Dean	12	150	83
Paul Dean	9	50	34
Total	21	200	117

In their six years together on the Cardinals mound, Dizzy and Paul Dean (*left*) went 154–77 and recorded all four St. Louis wins in the 1934 World Series. Big Poison (Paul) and Little Poison (Lloyd)—The Waners (*below left*)—hit .330 with 300 triples in 14 seasons with Pittsburgh. *Below*: Less prolific than his brother, Jim Perry won "only" 215 games in 17 seasons.

Best-Hitting Brothers

Player	Yrs.	G	H	2B	3B	HR	RBI	BA
Paul Waner	20	2549	3152	603	190	112	1309	.333
Lloyd Waner	18	1992	2459	281	118	28	598	.316
Total	38	4541	5611	884	308	140	1907	.325
Ed Delahanty	16	1835	2597	522	185	100	1464	.346
Jim Delahanty	13	1186	1159	191	60	18	489	.283
Frank Delahanty	6	287	223	22	82	5	94	.222
Joe Delahanty	3	269	222	30	15	4	100	.238
Tom Delahanty	3	19	16	5	0	0	6	.239
Total	41	3596	4217	770	282	127	2153	.311
Bob Meusel	11	1407	1693	368	95	156	1067	.309
Irish Meusel	11	1294	1521	250	92	107	820	.310
Total	22	2701	3214	618	187	263	1887	.309
Jim O'Rourke	19	1774	2304	414	132	51	830	.310
John O'Rourke	3	230	279	58	24	11	98	.285
Total	22	2004	2583	472	156	62	928	.309
Dixie Walker	18	1905	2064	376	96	105	1023	.306
Harry Walker	11	807	786	126	37	10	214	.296
Total	19	2712	2850	502	133	115	1237	.303
Hank Aaron	23	3298	3771	624	98	755	2297	.305
Tommie Aaron	7	437	216	42	6	13	94	.229
Total	30	3735	3987	666	104	768	2391	.300
Joe DiMaggio	13	1737	2219	389	131	361	1507	.325
Dom DiMaggio	11	1399	1680	308	57	87	618	.298
Vince DiMaggio	10	1110	959	209	24	125	584	.249
Total	34	4245	4853	906	212	573	2739	.298
Bob Johnson	13	1863	2051	396	95	288	1283	.296
Roy Johnson	10	1153	1292	275	83	58	556	.296
Total	23	3016	3343	671	178	346	1839	.296
Joe Sewell	14	1902	2226	436	68	49	1051	.312
Luke Sewell	20	1630	1393	273	56	20	696	.259
Tommy Sewell	1	1	0	0	0	0	0	.000
Total	35	3533	3619	709	124	69	1747	.292
Lave Cross	21	2275	2644	411	135	47	1344	.292
Amos Cross	3	117	118	16	7	1		.268
Frank Cross	1	1	3	0	0	0	0	.600
Total	25	2393	2765	427	142	48	1344	.291
Gee Walker	15	1783	1991	399	76	124	997	.294
Hub Walker	5	297	205	43	6	5	60	.263
Total	20	2080	2196	442	82	129	1057	.291
Dick Allen	15	1749	1848	320	79	351	1119	.292
Hank Allen	7	389	212	27	9	6	128	.241
Ron Allen	1	7	1	0	0	1	1	.091
Total	23	2145	2061	347	88	358	1248	.285
Felipe Alou	17	2082	2101	359	49	206	852	.286
Matty Alou	15	1667	1777	236	50	31	427	.307
Jesus Alou	15	1380	1216	170	27	32	377	.280
Total	47	5129	5094	765	126	269	1656	.280
Lee May	18	2071	2031	340	31	354	1244	.267
Carlos May	10	1165	1127	172	23	90	536	.274
Total	28	3236	3158	512	54	444	1780	.269
Ken Boyer	15	2034	2143	318	68	282	1141	.287

Best-Hitting Brothers *(cont'd)*

Player	Yrs.	G	H	2B	3B	HR	RBI	BA
Clete Boyer	16	1725	1396	200	33	162	654	.242
Cloyd Boyer	5	113	20	5	1	0	8	.167
Total	36	3872	3559	523	102	444	1803	.266
Tony Conigliaro	8	876	849	139	23	166	516	.264
Billy Conigliaro	5	347	289	56	10	40	128	.256
Total	13	1223	1138	195	33	206	644	.262
Steve O'Neill	17	1586	1259	248	34	13	537	.263
Jack O'Neill	5	303	185	24	5	1	74	.196
Mike O'Neill	5	137	97	14	9	2	41	.255
Jim O'Neill	2	109	94	18	7	1	43	.287
Total	29	2135	1635	304	55	17	695	.254

Fathers and Sons in Baseball

Player	First	Last
Bobby Adams	1946	1959
Mike Adams	1972	1978
Angel Aragon	1914	1917
Jack Aragon	1941	1941
Earl Averill	1929	1941
Earl Averill	1956	1963
Jim Bagby	1912	1923
Jim Bagby	1938	1947
Clyde Barnhart	1920	1928
Vic Barnhart	1944	1946
Charlie Beamon	1956	1958
Charlie Beamon	1978	1981
Gus Bell	1950	1964
Buddy Bell	1972	
Yogi Berra	1946	1965
Dale Berra	1978	
Charlie Berry	1884	1884
Charlie Berry	1925	1938
Joe Berry	1902	1902
Joe Berry	1921	1922
Bobby Bonds	1968	1981
Barry Bonds	1986	
Ray Boone	1948	1960
Bob Boone	1972	
Fred Brickell	1926	1933
Fritzie Brickell	1958	1961
Earle Brucker	1937	1943
Earle Brucker	1948	1948
Dolf Camilli	1933	1945
Doug Camilli	1960	1969
Al Campanis	1943	1943
Jim Campanis	1966	1973
Joe Coleman	1942	1955
Joe Coleman	1965	1979
Eddie Collins	1906	1930
Eddie Collins	1939	1942
Ed Connolly	1929	1932
Ed Connolly	1964	1967
Jimmy Cooney	1890	1892
Jimmy Cooney	1917	1928
Johnny Cooney	1921	1944
Red Corriden	1910	1915
John Corriden	1946	1946
Bill Crouch	1910	1910
Bill Crouch	1939	1945
Herm Doscher	1879	1882
Jack Doscher	1903	1908
Jim Eschen	1915	1915
Larry Eschen	1942	1942
Tito Francona	1956	1970
Terry Francona	1981	
Len Gabrielson	1939	1939
Len Gabrielson	1960	1970
Charlie Ganzel	1884	1897
Babe Ganzel	1927	1928
Larry Gilbert	1914	1915
Charlie Gilbert	1940	1947
Tookie Gilbert	1950	1953
Peaches Graham	1902	1912
Jack Graham	1946	1949
Freddie Green	1959	1964
Gary Green	1986	
Ray Grimes	1920	1926
Oscar Grimes	1938	1946
Ross Grimsley	1951	1951
Ross Grimsley	1971	1982
Sam Hairston	1951	1951
Jerry Hairston	1973	1977
John Hairston	1969	1969
Jim Hegan	1941	1960

Fathers and Sons in Baseball *(cont'd)*

Player	First	Last
Mike Hegan	1964	1977
Ken Heintzelman	1937	1952
Tom Heintzelman	1973	1978
Wally Hood	1920	1922
Wally Hood	1949	1949
Julian Javier	1960	1972
Stan Javier	1984	
Adam Johnson	1914	1918
Adam Johnson	1941	1941
Ernie Johnson	1912	1925
Don Johnson	1943	1948
Bob Kennedy	1939	1957
Terry Kennedy	1978	
Marty Keough	1956	1966
Matt Keough	1977	
Lew Krausse	1931	1932
Lew Krausse	1961	1974
Bill Kunkel	1961	1963
Jeff Kunkel	1984	
Joe Landrum	1950	1952
Bill Landrum	1986	
Max Lanier	1938	1953
Hal Lanier	1964	1973
Vern Law	1950	1967
Vance Law	1980	
Thornton Lee	1933	1948
Don Lee	1957	1966
Dutch Lerchen	1910	1910
George Lerchen	1932	1933
Glenn Liebhardt	1906	1909
Glenn Liebhardt	1930	1938
Freddie Lindstrom	1924	1934
Charlie Lindstrom	1958	1958
Jack Lively	1911	1911
Bud Lively	1947	1949
Connie Mack	1886	1896
Earle Mack	1910	1914
Harl Maggert	1907	1912
Harl Maggert	1938	1938
Charlie Malay	1905	1905
Joe Malay	1933	1935
Barney Martin	1953	1953
Jerry Martin	1974	1984
Wally Mattick	1912	1918
Bobby Mattick	1938	1942
Pinky May	1939	1943
Milt May	1970	1984
Frank Meinke	1884	1885
Bob Meinke	1910	1910
Willie Mills	1901	1901
Art Mills	1927	1928
Gene Moore	1909	1912
Gene Moore	1931	1945
Guy Morton	1914	1924
Guy Morton	1954	1954
Walter Mueller	1922	1926
Don Mueller	1948	1959
Bill Narleski	1929	1930
Ray Narleski	1954	1959
Chet Nichols	1926	1932
Chet Nichols	1951	1964
Ron Northey	1942	1957
Scott Northey	1969	1969
Frank Okrie	1920	1920
Len Okrie	1948	1952
Jim O'Rourke	1876	1904
Queenie O'Rourke	1908	1908
Patsy O'Rourke	1908	1908
Joe O'Rourke	1929	1929
Tiny Osborne	1922	1925
Bobo Osborne	1957	1963
Steve Partenheimer	1913	1913
Stan Partenheimer	1944	1945
Herman Pillette	1917	1924
Duane Pillette	1949	1956
Mel Queen	1942	1952
Mel Queen	1964	1972
Walt Ripley	1935	1935
Allen Ripley	1978	1982
Ebba St. Claire	1951	1954
Randy St. Claire	1984	
Ralph Savidge	1908	1909
Don Savidge	1929	1929
Dick Schofield	1953	1971
Dick Schofield	1983	
Joe Schultz	1912	1925
Joe Schultz	1939	1948
Earl Sheely	1921	1931
Bud Sheely	1951	1953
Dick Siebert	1932	1945
Paul Siebert	1974	1978
George Sisler	1915	1930
Dick Sisler	1946	1953
Dave Sisler	1956	1962
Bob Skinner	1954	1966
Joel Skinner	1983	
Roy Smalley	1948	1958
Roy Smalley	1975	
Joe Stephenson	1945	1947
Jerry Stephenson	1963	1970
Ron Stillwell	1961	1962
Kurt Stillwell	1986	

Fathers and Sons in Baseball *(cont'd)*

Player	First	Last
Billy Sullivan	1899	1916
Billy Sullivan	1931	1947
Haywood Sullivan	1955	1963
Marc Sullivan	1982	
George Susce	1929	1944
George Susce	1955	1959
Jose Tartabull	1962	1970
Danny Tartabull	1984	
Ricardo Torres	1920	1922
Gil Torres	1940	1946
Mike Tresh	1939	1949
Tom Tresh	1961	1969
Hal Trosky	1933	1946
Hal Trosky	1958	1958
Dizzy Trout	1939	1957
Steve Trout	1978	
Al Unser	1942	1945
Del Unser	1968	1982
Ozzie Virgil	1956	1969
Ozzie Virgil	1980	
Howard Wakefield	1905	1907
Dick Wakefield	1941	1952
Dixie Walker	1909	1912
Dixie Walker	1931	1949
Harry Walker	1940	1955
Ed Walsh	1904	1917
Ed Walsh	1928	1932
Jo-Jo White	1932	1944
Mike White	1963	1965
Maury Wills	1959	1972
Bump Wills	1977	1982
Bobby Wine	1960	1972
Robbie Wine	1986	
Joe Wood	1908	1922
Joe Wood	1944	1944
Del Young	1909	1915
Del Young	1937	1940

Two Grand Slams in One Inning, Team

Player	Team	Date	Inn.	Opp.	Opp. Pitcher
Tom Burns	CHI N	Aug 16, 1890	5	PIT	Bill Phillips
Malachi Kittredge	CHI N	Aug 16, 1890	5	PIT	Bill Phillips
Bob Allison	MIN A	Jul 18, 1962	1	CLE	Jim Perry
Harmon Killebrew	MIN A	Jul 18, 1962	1	CLE	Jim Perry
Denis Menke	HOU N	Jul 30, 1969	9	NY	Cal Koonce
Jimmy Wynn	HOU N	Jul 30, 1969	9	NY	Ron Taylor
Cecil Cooper	MIL A	Apr 11, 1980	2	BOS	Mike Torrez
Don Money	MIL A	Apr 11, 1980	2	BOS	Chuck Rainey
Larry Sheets	BAL A	Aug 6, 1986	4	TEX	Bobby Witt
Jim Dwyer	BAL A	Aug 6, 1986	4	TEX	Jeff Russell

Two Pinch-Hit Home Runs in One Inning, Team, AL

Player	Team	Date	Inn.	Opp.
Bob Cerv	NY	Jul 23, 1955	9	KC
Elston Howard	NY	Jul 23, 1955	9	KC
Vic Roznovsky	BAL	Aug 26, 1966	9	BOS
Boog Powell	BAL	Aug 26, 1966	9	BOS
Bob Stinson	SEA	Apr 27, 1979	8	NY
Dan Meyer	SEA	Apr 27, 1979	8	NY
Dave Engle	MIN	May 16, 1983	9	OAK
Mickey Hatcher	MIN	May 16, 1983	9	OAK
Wayne Gross	BAL	Aug 12, 1985	9	CLE
Larry Sheets	BAL	Aug 12, 1985	9	CLE
Oddibe McDowell	TEX	Sep 1, 1986	9	BOS
Darrell Porter	TEX	Sep 1, 1986	9	BOS

Two Pinch-Hit Home Runs in One Inning, Team, NL

Player	Team	Date	Inn.	Opp.
Bobby Hofman	NY	Jun 20, 1954	6	STL
Dusty Rhodes	NY	Jun 20, 1954	6	STL
Hank Sauer	SF	Jun 4, 1958	10	MIL
Bob Schmidt	SF	Jun 4, 1958	10	MIL
Frank Howard	LA	Aug 8, 1963	5	CHI
Bill Skowron	LA	Aug 8, 1963	5	CHI
Willie Crawford	LA	Jul 23, 1975	9	STL
Lee Lacy	LA	Jul 23, 1975	9	STL

Back-to-Back Pinch-Hit Home Runs, Team

Player	Team	Date	Inn.	Opp.	Opp. Pitcher
Hank Sauer	SF N	Jun 4, 1958	10	MIL	Ernie Johnson
Bob Schmidt	SF N	Jun 4, 1958	10	MIL	Ernie Johnson
Frank Howard	LA N	Aug 8, 1963	5	CHI	Bob Buhl
Bill Skowron	LA N	Aug 8, 1963	5	CHI	Don Elston
Vic Roznovsky	BAL A	Aug 26, 1966	9	BOS	Lee Stange
Boog Powell	BAL A	Aug 26, 1966	9	BOS	Lee Stange
Willie Crawford	LA N	Jul 23, 1975	9	MON	Claude Raymond
Lee Lacy	LA N	Jul 23, 1975	9	MON	Claude Raymond
Wayne Gross	BAL A	Aug 12, 1985	9	CLE	Jerry Reed
Larry Sheets	BAL A	Aug 12, 1985	9	CLE	Jerry Reed
Oddibe McDowell	TEX A	Sep 1, 1986	9	BOS	Steve Crawford
Darrell Porter	TEX A	Sep 1, 1986	9	BOS	Steve Crawford

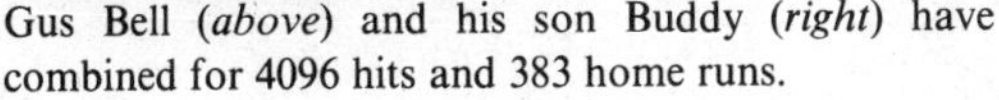

Gus Bell (*above*) and his son Buddy (*right*) have combined for 4096 hits and 383 home runs.

Home Runs by First Two Batters in Game, AL

Player	Team	Date	Opp.	Opp. Pitcher
Boze Berger	CHI	Sep 2, 1937	BOS	Johnny Marcum
Mike Kreevich	CHI	Sep 2, 1937	BOS	Johnny Marcum
Barney McCosky	DET	Jun 22, 1939	PHI	Lynn Nelson
Earl Averill	DET	Jun 22, 1939	PHI	Lynn Nelson
Hank Bauer	NY	Apr 27, 1955	CHI	Virgil Trucks
Andy Carey	NY	Apr 27, 1955	CHI	Virgil Trucks
Bill Tuttle	KC	Sep 18, 1958	BOS	Ted Bowsfield
Roger Maris	KC	Sep 18, 1958	BOS	Ted Bowsfield
Lenny Green	MIN	May 10, 1962	CLE	Jim Perry
Vic Power	MIN	May 10, 1962	CLE	Jim Perry
Luis Aparicio	BOS	May 1, 1971	MIN	Jim Perry
Reggie Smith	BOS	May 1, 1971	MIN	Jim Perry
Graig Nettles	CLE	Jun 19, 1971	DET	Dean Chance
Vada Pinson	CLE	Jun 19, 1971	DET	Dean Chance
Rick Miller	BOS	Jun 20, 1973	MIL	Bill Parsons
Reggie Smith	BOS	Jun 20, 1973	MIL	Bill Parsons
Don Money	MIL	Jul 29, 1975	BOS	Diego Segui
Darrell Porter	MIL	Jul 29, 1975	BOS	Diego Segui
Rick Burleson	BOS	Jun 17, 1977	NY	Catfish Hunter
Fred Lynn	BOS	Jun 17, 1977	NY	Catfish Hunter
Rickey Henderson	OAK	Sep 9, 1983	TOR	Jim Clancy
Mike Davis	OAK	Sep 9, 1983	TOR	Jim Clancy
Darryl Motley	KC	May 3, 1984	MIL	Don Sutton
Pat Sheridan	KC	May 3, 1984	MIL	Don Sutton
Dwight Evans	BOS	Sep 5, 1985	CLE	Neal Heaton
Wade Boggs	BOS	Sep 5, 1985	CLE	Neal Heaton
Kirby Puckett	MIN	Jul 18, 1986	BAL	Scott McGregor
Gary Gaetti	MIN	Jul 18, 1986	BAL	Scott McGregor
Lou Whitaker	DET	Aug 5, 1986	CLE	Jose Roman
Alan Trammell	DET	Aug 5, 1986	CLE	Jose Roman

Home Runs by First Two Batters in Game, NL

Player	Team	Date	Opp.	Opp. Pitcher
Roy Johnson	BOS	Aug 6, 1937	CHI	Tex Carleton
Rabbit Warstler	BOS	Aug 6, 1937	CHI	Tex Carleton
Pete Coscarart	PIT	Jul 6, 1945	BOS	Don Hendrickson
Jim Russell	PIT	Jul 6, 1945	BOS	Don Hendrickson
Grady Hatton	CIN	Apr 19, 1952	PIT	Mel Queen
Bobby Adams	CIN	Apr 19, 1952	PIT	Mel Queen
Whitey Lockman	SF	Jul 6, 1958	STL	Jim Brosnan
Willie Kirkland	SF	Jul 6, 1958	STL	Jim Brosnan
Curt Flood	STL	Aug 17, 1958	LA	Sandy Koufax
Gene Freese	STL	Aug 17, 1958	LA	Sandy Koufax
Chuck Hiller	SF	May 27, 1964	STL	Bob Gibson
Duke Snider	SF	May 27, 1964	STL	Bob Gibson
Pete Rose	CIN	Apr 7, 1969	LA	Don Drysdale
Bobby Tolan	CIN	Apr 7, 1969	LA	Don Drysdale
Pete Rose	CIN	Aug 17, 1969	PIT	Steve Blass
Bobby Tolan	CIN	Aug 17, 1969	PIT	Steve Blass

Home Runs by First Two Batters in Game, NL *(cont'd)*

Player	Team	Date	Opp.	Opp. Pitcher
Pete Rose	CIN	Jun 28, 1970	HOU	Don Wilson
Bobby Tolan	CIN	Jun 28, 1970	HOU	Don Wilson
Omar Moreno	PIT	Jul 5, 1982	HOU	Joe Niekro
Johnny Ray	PIT	Jul 5, 1982	HOU	Joe Niekro
Juan Samuel	PHI	Jul 29, 1984	MON	Bill Gullickson
Von Hayes	PHI	Jul 29, 1984	MON	Bill Gullickson
Gary Redus	PHI	Jul 7, 1986	ATL	David Palmer
Juan Samuel	PHI	Jul 7, 1986	ATL	David Palmer

Home Runs by First Two Batters in Game, Other Leagues

Player	Team	Date	Opp.	Opp. Pitcher
Tom Brown	BOS AA	Jun 25, 1891	BAL	Sadie McMahon
Bill Joyce	BOS AA	Jun 25, 1891	BAL	Sadie McMahon
Jim McTamany	PHI AA	Aug 21, 1891	BOS	Darby O'Brien
Henry Larkin	PHI AA	Aug 21, 1891	BOS	Darby O'Brien

White Sox outfielder Mike Kreevich (*above*) led the A.L. with 16 triples on his way to a second consecutive .300 season in 1937. Reggie Smith (*right*) ranks sixth on the all-time World Series home run percentage list with six homers in 73 AB.

Four Consecutive Home Runs, Team

Player	Team	Date	Inn.	Player	Team	Date	Inn.
Eddie Mathews	MIL N	Jun 8, 1961	7	Tony Oliva	MIN A	May 2, 1964	11
Hank Aaron	MIL N	Jun 8, 1961		Bob Allison	MIN A	May 2, 1964	
Joe Adcock	MIL N	Jun 8, 1961		Jimmie Hall	MIN A	May 2, 1964	
Frank Thomas	MIL N	Jun 8, 1961		Harmon Killebrew	MIN A	May 2, 1964	
Woodie Held	CLE A	Jul 31, 1963	6				
Pedro Ramos	CLE A	Jul 31, 1963					
Tito Francona	CLE A	Jul 31, 1963					
Larry Brown	CLE A	Jul 31, 1963					

Three Consecutive Home Runs, Team, AL

Player	Team	Date	Inn.	Player	Team	Date	Inn.
Nap Lajoie	CLE	Jun 30, 1902	6	Vern Stephens	BOS	Jun 6, 1948	
Piano Legs Hickman	CLE	Jun 30, 1902		Larry Doby	CLE	Jul 28, 1950	3
Bill Bradley	CLE	Jun 30, 1902		Al Rosen	CLE	Jul 28, 1950	
Tilly Walker	PHI	May 2, 1922	4	Luke Easter	CLE	Jul 28, 1950	
Cy Perkins	PHI	May 2, 1922		Harry Simpson	CLE	Sep 2, 1951	1
Bing Miller	PHI	May 2, 1922		Al Rosen	CLE	Sep 2, 1951	
Bob Meusel	NY	Sep 10, 1925	4	Luke Easter	CLE	Sep 2, 1951	
Babe Ruth	NY	Sep 10, 1925		Clint Courtney	STL	Jul 16, 1953	5
Lou Gehrig	NY	Sep 10, 1925		Dick Kryhoski	STL	Jul 16, 1953	
Babe Ruth	NY	May 4, 1929	7	Jim Dyck	STL	Jul 16, 1953	
Lou Gehrig	NY	May 4, 1929		Harvey Kuenn	DET	Jul 7, 1956	7
Bob Meusel	NY	May 4, 1929		Earl Torgeson	DET	Jul 7, 1956	
Al Simmons	PHI	Jun 18, 1930	5	Charlie Maxwell	DET	Jul 7, 1956	
Jimmie Foxx	PHI	Jun 18, 1930		Don Buddin	BOS	Sep 7, 1959	2
Bing Miller	PHI	Jun 18, 1930		Jerry Casale	BOS	Sep 7, 1959	
Bob Johnson	PHI	Jul 17, 1934	4	Pumpsie Green	BOS	Sep 7, 1959	
Jimmie Foxx	PHI	Jul 17, 1934		Jim Gentile	BAL	Apr 30, 1961	7
Pinky Higgins	PHI	Jul 17, 1934		Gus Triandos	BAL	Apr 30, 1961	
Ben Chapman	CLE	Jun 25, 1939	7	Ron Hansen	BAL	Apr 30, 1961	
Hal Trosky	CLE	Jun 25, 1939		Norm Cash	DET	May 23, 1961	9
Jeff Heath	CLE	Jun 25, 1939		Steve Boros	DET	May 23, 1961	
Ted Williams	BOS	Sep 24, 1940	6	Dick Brown	DET	May 23, 1961	
Jimmie Foxx	BOS	Sep 24, 1940		Gene Green	WAS	Jun 27, 1961	1
Joe Cronin	BOS	Sep 24, 1940		Willie Tasby	WAS	Jun 27, 1961	
Joe DiMaggio	NY	May 23, 1946	5	Dale Long	WAS	Jun 27, 1961	
Nick Etten	NY	May 23, 1946		Jerry Kindall	CLE	Jun 17, 1962	2
Joe Gordon	NY	May 23, 1946		Bubba Phillips	CLE	Jun 17, 1962	
Roy Cullenbine	DET	Apr 23, 1947	8	Jim Mahoney	CLE	Jun 17, 1962	
Dick Wakefield	DET	Apr 23, 1947		Gino Cimoli	KC	Aug 19, 1962	7
Hoot Evers	DET	Apr 23, 1947		Wayne Causey	KC	Aug 19, 1962	
Charlie Keller	NY	May 13, 1947	6	Billy Bryan	KC	Aug 19, 1962	
Joe DiMaggio	NY	May 13, 1947		Lee Thomas	LA	Aug 28, 1962	4
Johnny Lindell	NY	May 13, 1947		Leon Wagner	LA	Aug 28, 1962	
Stan Spence	BOS	Apr 19, 1948	2	Buck Rodgers	LA	Aug 28, 1962	
Vern Stephens	BOS	Apr 19, 1948		Brooks Robinson	BAL	Sep 10, 1965	8
Bobby Doerr	BOS	Apr 19, 1948		Curt Blefary	BAL	Sep 10, 1965	
Ted Williams	BOS	Jun 6, 1948	6	Jerry Adair	BAL	Sep 10, 1965	
Stan Spence	BOS	Jun 6, 1948		Tony Oliva	MIN	Jun 9, 1966	7

Three Consecutive Home Runs, Team, AL ***(cont'd)***

Player	Team	Date	Inn.	Player	Team	Date	Inn.
Don Mincher	MIN	Jun 9, 1966		Tony Armas	OAK	Jun 3, 1980	
Harmon Killebrew	MIN	Jun 9, 1966		Cecil Cooper	MIL	May 28, 1982	6
Bobby Richardson	NY	Jun 29, 1966	3	Don Money	MIL	May 28, 1982	
Mickey Mantle	NY	Jun 29, 1966		Gorman Thomas	MIL	May 28, 1982	
Joe Pepitone	NY	Jun 29, 1966		Robin Yount	MIL	Jun 5, 1982	7
Frank Howard	WAS	Jul 2, 1966	6	Cecil Cooper	MIL	Jun 5, 1982	
Don Lock	WAS	Jul 2, 1966		Ben Oglivie	MIL	Jun 5, 1982	
Ken McMullen	WAS	Jul 2, 1966		Ron Washington	MIN	Jun 7, 1982	8
Ted Kubiak	OAK	Jun 22, 1969	3	Tom Brunansky	MIN	Jun 7, 1982	
Reggie Jackson	OAK	Jun 22, 1969		Kent Hrbek	MIN	Jun 7, 1982	
Sal Bando	OAK	Jun 22, 1969		Cecil Cooper	MIL	Sep 12, 1982	3
Bobby Murcer	NY	Aug 10, 1969	6	Ted Simmons	MIL	Sep 12, 1982	
Thurman Munson	NY	Aug 10, 1969		Ben Oglivie	MIL	Sep 12, 1982	
Gene Michael	NY	Aug 10, 1969		Steve Henderson	SEA	Aug 2, 1983	3
Frank Robinson	BAL	Sep 4, 1969	9	Dave Henderson	SEA	Aug 2, 1983	
Boog Powell	BAL	Sep 4, 1969		Domingo Ramos	SEA	Aug 2, 1983	
Brooks Robinson	BAL	Sep 4, 1969		Carlton Fisk	CHI	Sep 9, 1983	1
Duke Sims	CLE	Aug 22, 1970	6	Tom Paciorek	CHI	Sep 9, 1983	
Graig Nettles	CLE	Aug 22, 1970		Greg Luzinski	CHI	Sep 9, 1983	
Eddie Leon	CLE	Aug 22, 1970		Reggie Jackson	CAL	Apr 14, 1984	4
Jim Northrup	DET	Apr 17, 1971	7	Brian Downing	CAL	Apr 14, 1984	
Norm Cash	DET	Apr 17, 1971		Bobby Grich	CAL	Apr 14, 1984	
Willie Horton	DET	Apr 17, 1971		Willie Upshaw	TOR	Apr 26, 1984	6
Aurelio Rodriguez	DET	Jun 27, 1972	1	George Bell	TOR	Apr 26, 1984	
Al Kaline	DET	Jun 27, 1972		Jesse Barfield	TOR	Apr 26, 1984	
Willie Horton	DET	Jun 27, 1972		Don Mattingly	NY	May 29, 1984	6
George Mitterwald	MIN	Jul 15, 1973	8	Don Baylor	NY	May 29, 1984	
Joe Lis	MIN	Jul 15, 1973		Dave Winfield	NY	May 29, 1984	
Jim Holt	MIN	Jul 15, 1973		Oscar Gamble	NY	Jun 3, 1984	4
Al Kaline	DET	Jul 29, 1974	1	Steve Kemp	NY	Jun 3, 1984	
Bill Freehan	DET	Jul 29, 1974		Toby Harrah	NY	Jun 3, 1984	
Mickey Stanley	DET	Jul 29, 1974		Andre Thornton	CLE	Jun 29, 1984	5
Bobby Bonds	CAL	May 11, 1977	2	Mel Hall	CLE	Jun 29, 1984	
Don Baylor	CAL	May 11, 1977		Jerry Willard	CLE	Jun 29, 1984	
Ron Jackson	CAL	May 11, 1977		Darryl Motley	KC	Aug 19, 1984	7
Fred Lynn	BOS	Jul 4, 1977	8	Frank White	KC	Aug 19, 1984	
Jim Rice	BOS	Jul 4, 1977		Steve Balboni	KC	Aug 19, 1984	
Carl Yastrzemski	BOS	Jul 4, 1977		Rudy Law	CHI	Aug 24, 1985	9
George Scott	BOS	Aug 13, 1977	6	Ron Kittle	CHI	Aug 24, 1985	
Butch Hobson	BOS	Aug 13, 1977		Harold Baines	CHI	Aug 24, 1985	
Dwight Evans	BOS	Aug 13, 1977		Cal Ripken	BAL	Sep 16, 1985	8
Eddie Murray	BAL	May 8, 1979	6	Eddie Murray	BAL	Sep 16, 1985	
Lee May	BAL	May 8, 1979		Fred Lynn	BAL	Sep 16, 1985	
Gary Roenicke	BAL	May 8, 1979		Kirk Gibson	DET	Jul 8, 1986	4
Tony Perez	BOS	May 31, 1980	6	Lance Parrish	DET	Jul 8, 1986	
Carlton Fisk	BOS	May 31, 1980		Darrell Evans	DET	Jul 8, 1986	
Butch Hobson	BOS	May 31, 1980		George Brett	KC	Sep 28, 1986	4
Dave Revering	OAK	Jun 3, 1980	9	Frank White	KC	Sep 28, 1986	
Mitchell Page	OAK	Jun 3, 1980		Jamie Quirk	KC	Sep 28, 1986	

Since joining the Brewers in 1977, Cecil Cooper has collected 908 RBIs, two Gold Glove awards, and has topped .300 seven times.

Three Consecutive Home Runs, Team, NL

Player	Team	Date	Inn.
Frank Shugart	STL	May 10, 1894	7
Doggie Miller	STL	May 10, 1894	
Heinie Peitz	STL	May 10, 1894	
Bill Terry	NY	Aug 13, 1932	4
Mel Ott	NY	Aug 13, 1932	
Freddie Lindstrom	NY	Aug 13, 1932	
Paul Waner	PIT	Jun 10, 1935	8
Arky Vaughan	PIT	Jun 10, 1935	
Pep Young	PIT	Jun 10, 1935	
Tony Cuccinello	BOS	Jul 9, 1938	3
Max West	BOS	Jul 9, 1938	
Elbie Fletcher	BOS	Jul 9, 1938	
Burgess Whitehead	NY	Jun 6, 1939	4
Manny Salvo	NY	Jun 6, 1939	
Joe Moore	NY	Jun 6, 1939	
Alex Kampouris	NY	Aug 13, 1939	4
Bill Lohrman	NY	Aug 13, 1939	
Joe Moore	NY	Aug 13, 1939	
Phil Cavarretta	CHI	Aug 11, 1941	5
Stan Hack	CHI	Aug 11, 1941	
Bill Nicholson	CHI	Aug 11, 1941	
Walker Cooper	STL	Jun 11, 1944	8
Whitey Kurowski	STL	Jun 11, 1944	
Danny Litwhiler	STL	Jun 11, 1944	
Grady Hatton	CIN	Aug 11, 1946	8
Max West	CIN	Aug 11, 1946	
Ray Mueller	CIN	Aug 11, 1946	
Johnny Mize	NY	Jun 20, 1948	8
Willard Marshall	NY	Jun 20, 1948	
Sid Gordon	NY	Jun 20, 1948	
Whitey Lockman	NY	Jun 4, 1949	6
Sid Gordon	NY	Jun 4, 1949	
Willard Marshall	NY	Jun 4, 1949	
Roy Campanella	BKN	Apr 19, 1952	7
Andy Pafko	BKN	Apr 19, 1952	
Duke Snider	BKN	Apr 19, 1952	
Ralph Kiner	PIT	Sep 27, 1952	7
Joe Garagiola	PIT	Sep 27, 1952	
Gus Bell	PIT	Sep 27, 1952	
Wes Westrum	NY	Sep 4, 1953	4
Al Corwin	NY	Sep 4, 1953	
Whitey Lockman	NY	Sep 4, 1953	
Bobby Hofman	NY	Jun 20, 1954	6
Wes Westrum	NY	Jun 20, 1954	
Dusty Rhodes	NY	Jun 20, 1954	
Gus Bell	CIN	Aug 15, 1954	9
Ted Kluszewski	CIN	Aug 15, 1954	
Jim Greengrass	CIN	Aug 15, 1954	

Three Consecutive Home Runs, Team, NL *(cont'd)*

Player	Team	Date	Inn.
Randy Jackson	CHI	Apr 16, 1955	2
Ernie Banks	CHI	Apr 16, 1955	
Dee Fondy	CHI	Apr 16, 1955	
Jerry Lynch	PIT	Jul 6, 1955	6
Frank Thomas	PIT	Jul 6, 1955	
Dale Long	PIT	Jul 6, 1955	
Eddie Mathews	MIL	May 30, 1956	1
Hank Aaron	MIL	May 30, 1956	
Bobby Thomson	MIL	May 30, 1956	
Gus Bell	CIN	May 31, 1956	9
Ted Kluszewski	CIN	May 31, 1956	
Frank Robinson	CIN	May 31, 1956	
Duke Snider	BKN	Jun 29, 1956	9
Randy Jackson	BKN	Jun 29, 1956	
Gil Hodges	BKN	Jun 29, 1956	
Hank Thompson	NY	Jul 8, 1956	4
Daryl Spencer	NY	Jul 8, 1956	
Wes Westrum	NY	Jul 8, 1956	
Frank Thomas	PIT	Apr 21, 1957	3
Paul Smith	PIT	Apr 21, 1957	
Dick Groat	PIT	Apr 21, 1957	
Hank Aaron	MIL	Jun 26, 1957	5
Eddie Mathews	MIL	Jun 26, 1957	
Wes Covington	MIL	Jun 26, 1957	
Bob Skinner	PIT	May 7, 1958	5
Ted Kluszewski	PIT	May 7, 1958	
Frank Thomas	PIT	May 7, 1958	
Hank Aaron	MIL	May 31, 1958	1
Eddie Mathews	MIL	May 31, 1958	
Wes Covington	MIL	May 31, 1958	
Hank Aaron	MIL	Jun 18, 1961	3
Joe Adcock	MIL	Jun 18, 1961	
Frank Thomas	MIL	Jun 18, 1961	
	NY	Apr 28, 1962	6
Charlie Neal	NY	Apr 28, 1962	
Gil Hodges	NY	Apr 28, 1962	
Willie Mays	SF	Aug 27, 1963	3
Orlando Cepeda	SF	Aug 27, 1963	
Felipe Alou	SF	Aug 27, 1963	
Ken Boyer	STL	Jul 18, 1964	8
Bill White	STL	Jul 18, 1964	
Tim McCarver	STL	Jul 18, 1964	
Dave Marshall	SF	Aug 5, 1969	5
Ron Hunt	SF	Aug 5, 1969	
Bobby Bonds	SF	Aug 5, 1969	
Dave Marshall	NY	May 18, 1970	8
Joe Foy	NY	May 18, 1970	
Jerry Grote	NY	May 18, 1970	
Bob Robertson	PIT	Aug 1, 1970	7
Willie Stargell	PIT	Aug 1, 1970	
Jose Pagan	PIT	Aug 1, 1970	
Nate Colbert	SD	Jul 16, 1974	9
Willie McCovey	SD	Jul 16, 1974	
Dave Winfield	SD	Jul 16, 1974	
George Theodore	NY	Jul 20, 1974	5
Rusty Staub	NY	Jul 20, 1974	
Cleon Jones	NY	Jul 20, 1974	
Larry Biittner	CHI	May 17, 1977	5
Bobby Murcer	CHI	May 17, 1977	
Jerry Morales	CHI	May 17, 1977	
Greg Luzinski	PHI	Sep 30, 1977	2
Richie Hebner	PHI	Sep 30, 1977	
Garry Maddox	PHI	Sep 30, 1977	
Gary Matthews	ATL	Aug 14, 1978	3
Jeff Burroughs	ATL	Aug 14, 1978	
Bob Horner	ATL	Aug 14, 1978	
Tony Perez	MON	Jun 17, 1979	4
Gary Carter	MON	Jun 17, 1979	
Ellis Valentine	MON	Jun 17, 1979	
Jerry Turner	SD	Jul 11, 1979	1
Dave Winfield	SD	Jul 11, 1979	
Gene Tenace	SD	Jul 11, 1979	
Ken Griffey	CIN	May 27, 1980	3
George Foster	CIN	May 27, 1980	
Dan Driessen	CIN	May 27, 1980	
Reggie Smith	SF	Jul 11, 1982	2
Milt May	SF	Jul 11, 1982	
Champ Summers	SF	Jul 11, 1982	
Enos Cabell	HOU	Jun 24, 1984	5
Phil Garner	HOU	Jun 24, 1984	
Jose Cruz	HOU	Jun 24, 1984	
Juan Samuel	PHI	Aug 17, 1985	7
Glenn Wilson	PHI	Aug 17, 1985	
Mike Schmidt	PHI	Aug 17, 1985	
Gary Carter	NY	Jul 27, 1986	3
Darryl Strawberry	NY	Jul 27, 1986	
Kevin Mitchell	NY	Jul 27, 1986	

Three Consecutive Home Runs, Team, Other Leagues

Player	Team	Date	Inn.
George Gore	NY P	May 31, 1890	8
Buck Ewing	NY P	May 31, 1890	
Roger Connor	NY P	May 31, 1890	

Most Home Runs in One Inning, Team, AL

Player	Team	Date	Inn.	Player	Team	Date	Inn.
Rich Rollins	MIN	Jun 9, 1966	7	Andy Etchebarren	BAL	May 17, 1967	7
Zoilo Versalles	MIN	Jun 9, 1966		Sam Bowens	BAL	May 17, 1967	
Tony Oliva	MIN	Jun 9, 1966		Boog Powell	BAL	May 17, 1967	
Don Mincher	MIN	Jun 9, 1966		Davey Johnson	BAL	May 17, 1967	
Harmon Killebrew	MIN	Jun 9, 1966		Al Kaline	DET	Jul 29, 1974	1
Ted Williams	BOS	Sep 24, 1940	6	Bill Freehan	DET	Jul 29, 1974	
Jimmie Foxx	BOS	Sep 24, 1940		Mickey Stanley	DET	Jul 29, 1974	
Joe Cronin	BOS	Sep 24, 1940		Ed Brinkman	DET	Jul 29, 1974	
Jim Tabor	BOS	Sep 24, 1940		Rick Burleson	BOS	Jun 17, 1977	1
Dizzy Trout	DET	Jun 23, 1950	4	Fred Lynn	BOS	Jun 17, 1977	
Gerry Priddy	DET	Jun 23, 1950		Carlton Fisk	BOS	Jun 17, 1977	
Vic Wertz	DET	Jun 23, 1950		George Scott	BOS	Jun 17, 1977	
Hoot Evers	DET	Jun 23, 1950		Fred Lynn	BOS	Jul 4, 1977	8
Gene Mauch	BOS	May 22, 1957	7	Jim Rice	BOS	Jul 4, 1977	
Ted Williams	BOS	May 22, 1957		Carl Yastrzemski	BOS	Jul 4, 1977	
Dick Gernert	BOS	May 22, 1957		George Scott	BOS	Jul 4, 1977	
Frank Malzone	BOS	May 22, 1957		Dave Stapleton	BOS	May 31, 1980	4
Norm Zauchin	BOS	Aug 26, 1957	7	Tony Perez	BOS	May 31, 1980	
Ted Lepcio	BOS	Aug 26, 1957		Carlton Fisk	BOS	May 31, 1980	
Jimmy Piersall	BOS	Aug 26, 1957		Butch Hobson	BOS	May 31, 1980	
Frank Malzone	BOS	Aug 26, 1957		Dave Engle	MIN	May 16, 1983	9
Woodie Held	CLE	Jul 31, 1963	6	Bobby Mitchell	MIN	May 16, 1983	
Pedro Ramos	CLE	Jul 31, 1963		Gary Gaetti	MIN	May 16, 1983	
Tito Francona	CLE	Jul 31, 1963		Mickey Hatcher	MIN	May 16, 1983	
Larry Brown	CLE	Jul 31, 1963		Chet Lemon	DET	Sep 10, 1986	4
Tony Oliva	MIN	May 2, 1964	11	Mike Heath	DET	Sep 10, 1986	
Bob Allison	MIN	May 2, 1964		Kirk Gibson	DET	Sep 10, 1986	
Jimmie Hall	MIN	May 2, 1964		Darnell Coles	DET	Sep 10, 1986	
Harmon Killebrew	MIN	May 2, 1964					

Most Home Runs in One Inning, Team, NL

Player	Team	Date	Inn.	Player	Team	Date	Inn.
Harry Danning	NY	Jun 6, 1939	4	Lou Bierbauer	PIT	Jun 6, 1894	
Frank Demaree	NY	Jun 6, 1939		Jake Stenzel	PIT	Jun 6, 1894	
Burgess Whitehead	NY	Jun 6, 1939		Cliff Heathcote	CHI	May 12, 1930	7
Manny Salvo	NY	Jun 6, 1939		Hack Wilson	CHI	May 12, 1930	
Joe Moore	NY	Jun 6, 1939		Charlie Grimm	CHI	May 12, 1930	
Del Ennis	PHI	Jun 2, 1949	8	Clyde Beck	CHI	May 12, 1930	
Andy Seminick	PHI	Jun 2, 1949		Zeke Bonura	NY	Aug 13, 1939	4
Willie Jones	PHI	Jun 2, 1949		Alex Kampouris	NY	Aug 13, 1939	
Schoolboy Rowe	PHI	Jun 2, 1949		Bill Lohrman	NY	Aug 13, 1939	
Andy Seminick	PHI	Jun 2, 1949		Joe Moore	NY	Aug 13, 1939	
Orlando Cepeda	SF	Aug 23, 1961	9	Erv Dusak	STL	Jun 6, 1948	6
Felipe Alou	SF	Aug 23, 1961		Red Schoendienst	STL	Jun 6, 1948	
Jim Davenport	SF	Aug 23, 1961		Enos Slaughter	STL	Jun 6, 1948	
Willie Mays	SF	Aug 23, 1961		Nippy Jones	STL	Jun 6, 1948	
John Orsino	SF	Aug 23, 1961		Davey Williams	NY	May 28, 1954	8
Jake Stenzel	PIT	Jun 6, 1894	3	Alvin Dark	NY	May 28, 1954	
Denny Lyons	PIT	Jun 6, 1894		Monte Irvin	NY	May 28, 1954	

Most Home Runs in One Inning, Team, NL ***(cont'd)***

Player	Team	Date	Inn.
Billy Gardner	NY	May 28, 1954	
Willie Mays	NY	Jul 8, 1956	4
Hank Thompson	NY	Jul 8, 1956	
Daryl Spencer	NY	Jul 8, 1956	
Wes Westrum	NY	Jul 8, 1956	
Eddie Mathews	MIL	Jul 8, 1961	7
Hank Aaron	MIL	Jul 8, 1961	
Joe Adcock	MIL	Jul 8, 1961	
Frank Thomas	MIL	Jul 8, 1961	
Joe Torre	MIL	Jun 8, 1965	10
Eddie Mathews	MIL	Jun 8, 1965	
Hank Aaron	MIL	Jun 8, 1965	
Gene Oliver	MIL	Jun 8, 1965	
Ivan Murrell	SD	Jul 10, 1970	9
Ed Spiezio	SD	Jul 10, 1970	
Dave Campbell	SD	Jul 10, 1970	
Clarence Gaston	SD	Jul 10, 1970	
Mike Lum	ATL	Jun 21, 1971	8
Hal King	ATL	Jun 21, 1971	
Hank Aaron	ATL	Jun 21, 1971	
Darrell Evans	ATL	Jun 21, 1971	
Andre Dawson	MON	Jul 30, 1978	3
Larry Parrish	MON	Jul 30, 1978	
Dave Cash	MON	Jul 30, 1978	
Andre Dawson	MON	Jul 30, 1978	
Juan Samuel	PHI	Aug 17, 1985	7
Glenn Wilson	PHI	Aug 17, 1985	
Mike Schmidt	PHI	Aug 17, 1985	
Darren Daulton	PHI	Aug 17, 1985	
Andre Dawson	MON	Apr 29, 1986	4
Hubie Brooks	MON	Apr 29, 1986	
Tim Wallach	MON	Apr 29, 1986	
Mike Fitzgerald	MON	Apr 29, 1986	

Teammates Davy Johnson (*left*) and Darrell Evans (*above*) combined in 1973 for 84 home runs, 203 RBIs, and a .551 slugging percentage, to complement the efforts of a teammate named Aaron.

Most Home Runs by Team, Game, AL

Player	Team	Date	HR	Score	Opp.
Babe Dahlgren	NY	Jun 28, 1939	2	23-2	PHI
Joe DiMaggio	NY	Jun 28, 1939	2		
Bill Dickey	NY	Jun 28, 1939	1		
Joe Gordon	NY	Jun 28, 1939	1		
Tommy Henrich	NY	Jun 28, 1939	1		
George Selkirk	NY	Jun 28, 1939	1		
Total			8		
Harmon Killebrew	MIN	Aug 29, 1963	2	14-2	WAS
Vic Power	MIN	Aug 29, 1963	2		
Bernie Allen	MIN	Aug 29, 1963	1		
Bob Allison	MIN	Aug 29, 1963	1		
Jimmie Hall	MIN	Aug 29, 1963	1		
Rich Rollins	MIN	Aug 29, 1963	1		
Total			8		
Fred Lynn	BOS	Jul 4, 1977	2	9-6	TOR
George Scott	BOS	Jul 4, 1977	2		
Carl Yastrzemski	BOS	Jul 4, 1977	1		
Jim Rice	BOS	Jul 4, 1977	1		
Butch Hobson	BOS	Jul 4, 1977	1		
Bernie Carbo	BOS	Jul 4, 1977	1		
Total			8		
Jimmy Dykes	PHI	Jun 3, 1921	2	15-9	DET
Frank Welch	PHI	Jun 3, 1921	2		
Tilly Walker	PHI	Jun 3, 1921	1		
Cy Perkins	PHI	Jun 3, 1921	1		
Joe Dugan	PHI	Jun 3, 1921	1		
Total			7		
Lou Gehrig	NY	Jun 3, 1932	4	20-13	PHI
Tony Lazzeri	NY	Jun 3, 1932	1		
Earle Combs	NY	Jun 3, 1932	1		
Babe Ruth	NY	Jun 3, 1932	1		
Total			7		
Clyde Vollmer	WAS	May 3, 1949	2	14-12	CHI
Mark Christman	WAS	May 3, 1949	1		
Gil Coan	WAS	May 3, 1949	1		
Eddie Robinson	WAS	May 3, 1949	1		
Al Evans	WAS	May 3, 1949	1		
Bud Stewart	WAS	May 3, 1949	1		
Total			7		
Bobby Doerr	BOS	Jun 8, 1950	3	29-4	STL
Ted Williams	BOS	Jun 8, 1950	2		
Walt Dropo	BOS	Jun 8, 1950	2		
Total			7		
Sherm Lollar	CHI	Apr 23, 1955	2	29-6	KC
Bob Nieman	CHI	Apr 23, 1955	2		
Walt Dropo	CHI	Apr 23, 1955	1		
Jack Harshman	CHI	Apr 23, 1955	1		
Minnie Minoso	CHI	Apr 23, 1955	1		
Total			7		
Mickey Mantle	NY	May 30, 1961	2	12-3	BOS
Roger Maris	NY	May 30, 1961	2		

Most Home Runs by Team, Game, AL *(cont'd)*

Player	Team	Date	HR	Score	Opp.
Bill Skowron	NY	May 30, 1961	2		
Yogi Berra	NY	May 30, 1961	1		
Total			7		
Rocky Colavito	CLE	Jul 17, 1966	2	15-2	DET
Chuck Hinton	CLE	Jul 17, 1966	2		
Max Alvis	CLE	Jul 17, 1966	1		
Buddy Booker	CLE	Jul 17, 1966	1		
Leon Wagner	CLE	Jul 17, 1966	1		
Total			7		
Paul Blair	BAL	May 17, 1967	1	12-8	BOS
Sam Bowens	BAL	May 17, 1967	1		
Boog Powell	BAL	May 17, 1967	1		
Andy Etchebarren	BAL	May 17, 1967	1		
Davey Johnson	BAL	May 17, 1967	1		
Brooks Robinson	BAL	May 17, 1967	1		
Frank Robinson	BAL	May 17, 1967	1		
Total			7		
Ben Oglivie	MIL	Apr 29, 1980	2	14-1	CLE
Sal Bando	MIL	Apr 29, 1980	2		
Sixto Lezcano	MIL	Apr 29, 1980	1		
Paul Molitor	MIL	Apr 29, 1980	1		
Larry Hisle	MIL	Apr 29, 1980	1		
Total			7		
Gorman Thomas	SEA	May 11, 1985	3	14-6	OAK
Al Cowens	SEA	May 11, 1985	1		
Jim Presley	SEA	May 11, 1985	1		
Phil Bradley	SEA	May 11, 1985	1		
Dave Henderson	SEA	May 11, 1985	1		
Total			7		
Eddie Murray	BAL	Aug 26, 1985	3	17-3	CAL
John Shelby	BAL	Aug 26, 1985	1		
Floyd Rayford	BAL	Aug 26, 1985	1		
Gary Roenicke	BAL	Aug 26, 1985	1		
Rick Dempsey	BAL	Aug 26, 1985	1		
Total			7		
Darrell Porter	TEX	Sep 13, 1986	2	14-1	MIN
Ruben Sierra	TEX	Sep 13, 1986	2		
Pete O'Brien	TEX	Sep 13, 1986	1		
Pete Incaviglia	TEX	Sep 13, 1986	1		
Steve Buechele	TEX	Sep 13, 1986	1		
Total			7		

Most Home Runs by Team, Game, NL

Player	Team	Date	HR	Score	Opp.
Jim Pendleton	MIL	Aug 30, 1953	3	19-4	PIT
Eddie Mathews	MIL	Aug 30, 1953	2		
Del Crandall	MIL	Aug 30, 1953	1		
Jack Dittmer	MIL	Aug 30, 1953	1		
Johnny Logan	MIL	Aug 30, 1953	1		
Total			8		
Bob Thurman	CIN	Aug 18, 1956	3	13-4	MIL
Ted Kluszewski	CIN	Aug 18, 1956	2		
Frank Robinson	CIN	Aug 18, 1956	2		
Wally Post	CIN	Aug 18, 1956	1		
Total			8		
Willie Mays	SF	Apr 30, 1961	4	14-4	MIL
Jose Pagan	SF	Apr 30, 1961	2		
Felipe Alou	SF	Apr 30, 1961	1		
Orlando Cepeda	SF	Apr 30, 1961	1		
Total			8		
Larry Parrish	MON	Jul 30, 1978	3	19-0	ATL
Andre Dawson	MON	Jul 30, 1978	2		
Tony Perez	MON	Jul 30, 1978	1		
Dave Cash	MON	Jul 30, 1978	1		
Chris Speier	MON	Jul 30, 1978	1		
Total			8		
Jack Rowe	DET	Jun 12, 1886	2	14-7	STL
Sam Thompson	DET	Jun 12, 1886	2		
Charlie Bennett	DET	Jun 12, 1886	1		
Dan Brouthers	DET	Jun 12, 1886	1		
Sam Crane	DET	Jun 12, 1886	1		
Total			7		
Roger Connor	NY	May 9, 1888	3	18-4	IND
George Gore	NY	May 9, 1888	1		
Tim Keefe	NY	May 9, 1888	1		
Danny Richardson	NY	May 9, 1888	1		
Mike Tiernan	NY	May 9, 1888	1		
Total			7		
Lou Bierbauer	PIT	Jun 6, 1894	2	27-11	BOS
Jake Stenzel	PIT	Jun 6, 1894	2		
Denny Lyons	PIT	Jun 6, 1894	1		
Connie Mack	PIT	Jun 6, 1894	1		
Frank Scheibeck	PIT	Jun 6, 1894	1		
Total			7		
Joe Moore	NY	Jun 6, 1939	2	17-3	CIN
Harry Danning	NY	Jun 6, 1939	1		
Mel Ott	NY	Jun 6, 1939	1		
Frank Demaree	NY	Jun 6, 1939	1		
Manny Salvo	NY	Jun 6, 1939	1		
Burgess Whitehead	NY	Jun 6, 1939	1		
Total			7		
Frank Demaree	NY	Aug 13, 1939	2	11-2	PHI
Joe Moore	NY	Aug 13, 1939	1		
Bob Seeds	NY	Aug 13, 1939	1		
Zeke Bonura	NY	Aug 13, 1939	1		

Most Home Runs by Team, Game, NL *(cont'd)*

Player	Team	Date	HR	Score	Opp.
Alex Kampouris	NY	Aug 13, 1939	1		
Bill Lohrman	NY	Aug 13, 1939	1		
Total			7		
Eddie Lake	STL	May 7, 1940	2	18-2	BKN
Johnny Mize	STL	May 7, 1940	2		
Stu Martin	STL	May 7, 1940	1		
Joe Medwick	STL	May 7, 1940	1		
Don Padgett	STL	May 7, 1940	1		
Total			7		
Ralph Kiner	PIT	Aug 16, 1947	3	12-7	STL
Hank Greenberg	PIT	Aug 16, 1947	2		
Billy Cox	PIT	Aug 16, 1947	2		
Total			7		
Wes Westrum	NY	Jun 24, 1950	3	12-2	CIN
Alvin Dark	NY	Jun 24, 1950	1		
Monte Irvin	NY	Jun 24, 1950	1		
Whitey Lockman	NY	Jun 24, 1950	1		
Hank Thompson	NY	Jun 24, 1950	1		
Total			7		
Joe Adcock	MIL	Jul 31, 1954	4	15-7	BKN
Eddie Mathews	MIL	Jul 31, 1954	2		
Andy Pafko	MIL	Jul 31, 1954	1		
Total			7		
Willie Mays	NY	Jul 8, 1956	2	16-1	PIT
Daryl Spencer	NY	Jul 8, 1956	2		
Wes Westrum	NY	Jul 8, 1956	2		
Hank Thompson	NY	Jul 8, 1956	1		
Total			7		
Frank Robinson	CIN	Jun 1, 1957	2	22-2	CHI
Ed Bailey	CIN	Jun 1, 1957	1		
Gus Bell	CIN	Jun 1, 1957	1		
Don Hoak	CIN	Jun 1, 1957	1		
Hal Jeffcoat	CIN	Jun 1, 1957	1		
Wally Post	CIN	Jun 1, 1957	1		
Total			7		
Adolfo Phillips	CHI	Jun 11, 1967	3	18-10	NY
Randy Hundley	CHI	Jun 11, 1967	2		
Ernie Banks	CHI	Jun 11, 1967	1		
Ron Santo	CHI	Jun 11, 1967	1		
Total			7		
Clete Boyer	ATL	Aug 3, 1967	2	10-3	CHI
Joe Torre	ATL	Aug 3, 1967	2		
Hank Aaron	ATL	Aug 3, 1967	1		
Tito Francona	ATL	Aug 3, 1967	1		
Denis Menke	ATL	Aug 3, 1967	1		
Total			7		
Bernie Carbo	CIN	Apr 21, 1970	2	13-8	STL
Johnny Bench	CIN	Apr 21, 1970	1		
Dave Concepcion	CIN	Apr 21, 1970	1		
Tony Perez	CIN	Apr 21, 1970	1		
Pete Rose	CIN	Apr 21, 1970	1		

Most Home Runs by Team, Game, NL *(cont'd)*

Player	Team	Date	HR	Score	Opp.
Bobby Tolan	CIN	Apr 21, 1970	1		
Total			7		
Jim Hickman	CHI	Aug 19, 1970	2	12-2	SD
Glenn Beckert	CHI	Aug 19, 1970	1		
Johnny Callison	CHI	Aug 19, 1970	1		
Ferguson Jenkins	CHI	Aug 19, 1970	1		
Joe Pepitone	CHI	Aug 19, 1970	1		
Billy Williams	CHI	Aug 19, 1970	1		
Total			7		
Henry Cruz	LA	May 5, 1976	2	14-12	CHI
Bill Buckner	LA	May 5, 1976	1		
Ron Cey	LA	May 5, 1976	1		
Bill Russell	LA	May 5, 1976	1		
Ed Goodson	LA	May 5, 1976	1		
Steve Yeager	LA	May 5, 1976	1		
Total			7		
Larry Biittner	CHI	May 17, 1977	2	28-6	SD
Steve Ontiveros	CHI	May 17, 1977	1		
Gene Clines	CHI	May 17, 1977	1		
Bobby Murcer	CHI	May 17, 1977	1		
Jerry Morales	CHI	May 17, 1977	1		
Dave Rosello	CHI	May 17, 1977	1		
Total			7		
Dusty Baker	LA	May 25, 1979	1	17-6	CIN
Rick Sutcliffe	LA	May 25, 1979	1		
Steve Garvey	LA	May 25, 1979	1		
Gary Thomasson	LA	May 25, 1979	1		
Joe Ferguson	LA	May 25, 1979	1		
Derrel Thomas	LA	May 25, 1979	1		
Davey Lopes	LA	May 25, 1979	1		
Total			7		

Most 40-Home Run Hitters, AL

Player	Team	Year	HR
Babe Ruth	NY	1927	60
Lou Gehrig	NY	1927	47
Babe Ruth	NY	1930	49
Lou Gehrig	NY	1930	41
Babe Ruth	NY	1931	46
Lou Gehrig	NY	1931	46
Roger Maris	NY	1961	61
Mickey Mantle	NY	1961	54
Rocky Colavito	DET	1961	45
Norm Cash	DET	1961	41
Rico Petrocelli	BOS	1969	40
Carl Yastrzemski	BOS	1969	40

Most 40-Home Run Hitters, NL

Player	Team	Year	HR
Davey Johnson	ATL	1973	43
Darrell Evans	ATL	1973	41
Hank Aaron	ATL	1973	40
Duke Snider	BKN	1953	42
Roy Campanella	BKN	1953	41
Gil Hodges	BKN	1954	42
Duke Snider	BKN	1954	40
Ted Kluszewski	CIN	1955	47
Wally Post	CIN	1955	40
Orlando Cepeda	SF	1961	46
Willie Mays	SF	1961	40
Johnny Bench	CIN	1970	45
Tony Perez	CIN	1970	40

The greatest power hitters in history: Together Gehrig and Ruth hit 30+ homers 23 times, drove in 100+ runs 26 times, slugged over .700 13 times, and combined for 25 World Series base-clearers while establishing the Yankees dynasty in the 1920s and '30s.

Most 30-Home Run Hitters, AL

Player	Team	Year	HR
Charlie Keller	NY	1941	33
Tommy Henrich	NY	1941	31
Joe DiMaggio	NY	1941	30
Harmon Killebrew	WAS	1959	42
Jim Lemon	WAS	1959	33
Bob Allison	WAS	1959	30
Harmon Killebrew	MIN	1963	45
Bob Allison	MIN	1963	35
Jimmie Hall	MIN	1963	33
Harmon Killebrew	MIN	1964	49
Bob Allison	MIN	1964	32
Tony Oliva	MIN	1964	32
Jim Rice	BOS	1977	39
George Scott	BOS	1977	33
Butch Hobson	BOS	1977	30
Gorman Thomas	MIL	1982	39
Ben Oglivie	MIL	1982	32
Cecil Cooper	MIL	1982	32

Most 30-Home Run Hitters, NL

Player	Team	Year	HR
Steve Garvey	LA	1977	33
Reggie Smith	LA	1977	32
Dusty Baker	LA	1977	30
Ron Cey	LA	1977	30
Chuck Klein	PHI	1929	43
Lefty O'Doul	PHI	1929	32
Don Hurst	PHI	1929	31
Johnny Mize	NY	1947	51
Willard Marshall	NY	1947	36
Walker Cooper	NY	1947	35
Gil Hodges	BKN	1950	32
Duke Snider	BKN	1950	31
Roy Campanella	BKN	1950	31
Duke Snider	BKN	1953	42
Roy Campanella	BKN	1953	41
Gil Hodges	BKN	1953	31
Frank Robinson	CIN	1956	38
Wally Post	CIN	1956	36
Ted Kluszewski	CIN	1956	35
Joe Adcock	MIL	1961	35
Hank Aaron	MIL	1961	34
Eddie Mathews	MIL	1961	32

Player	Team	Year	HR
Willie McCovey	SF	1963	44
Willie Mays	SF	1963	38
Orlando Cepeda	SF	1963	34
Willie Mays	SF	1964	47
Orlando Cepeda	SF	1964	31
Jim Ray Hart	SF	1964	31
Eddie Mathews	MIL	1965	32
Hank Aaron	MIL	1965	32
Mack Jones	MIL	1965	31
Hank Aaron	ATL	1966	44
Joe Torre	ATL	1966	36
Felipe Alou	ATL	1966	31
Willie Mays	SF	1966	37
Willie McCovey	SF	1966	36
Jim Ray Hart	SF	1966	33
Johnny Bench	CIN	1970	45
Tony Perez	CIN	1970	40
Lee May	CIN	1970	34
Davey Johnson	ATL	1973	43
Darrell Evans	ATL	1973	41
Hank Aaron	ATL	1973	40

Most 20-Home Run Hitters, AL

Player	Team	Year	HR
Roger Maris	NY	1961	61
Mickey Mantle	NY	1961	54
Bill Skowron	NY	1961	28
Yogi Berra	NY	1961	22
Elston Howard	NY	1961	21
Johnny Blanchard	NY	1961	21
Harmon Killebrew	MIN	1964	49
Bob Allison	MIN	1964	32
Tony Oliva	MIN	1964	32
Jimmie Hall	MIN	1964	25
Don Mincher	MIN	1964	23
Zoilo Versalles	MIN	1964	20
Darrell Evans	DET	1986	29
Kirk Gibson	DET	1986	28

Player	Team	Year	HR
Lance Parrish	DET	1986	22
Alan Trammell	DET	1986	21
Darnell Coles	DET	1986	20
Lou Whitaker	DET	1986	20
Jim Rice	BOS	1977	39
George Scott	BOS	1977	33
Butch Hobson	BOS	1977	30
Carl Yastrzemski	BOS	1977	28
Carlton Fisk	BOS	1977	26
Gary Gaetti	MIN	1986	34
Kirby Puckett	MIN	1986	31
Kent Hrbek	MIN	1986	29
Tom Brunansky	MIN	1986	23
Roy Smalley	MIN	1986	20

Most 20-Home Run Hitters, NL

Player	Team	Year	HR
Hank Aaron	MIL	1965	32
Eddie Mathews	MIL	1965	32
Mack Jones	MIL	1965	31
Joe Torre	MIL	1965	27
Felipe Alou	MIL	1965	23
Gene Oliver	MIL	1965	21

Player	Team	Year	HR
Frank Robinson	CIN	1956	38
Wally Post	CIN	1956	36
Ted Kluszewski	CIN	1956	35
Gus Bell	CIN	1956	29
Ed Bailey	CIN	1956	28

In nine years with the Yanks, Moose Skowron hit .294 with 165 home runs, but never had more homers or RBIs than Mickey Mantle or Roger Maris.

Home Run Trios, Season, AL

Player	Team	Year	HR
Roger Maris	NY	1961	61
Mickey Mantle	NY	1961	54
Bill Skowron	NY	1961	28
Total			143
Babe Ruth	NY	1927	60
Lou Gehrig	NY	1927	47
Tony Lazzeri	NY	1927	18
Total			125
Jimmie Foxx	PHI	1932	58
Al Simmons	PHI	1932	35
Mickey Cochrane	PHI	1932	23
Total			116
Harmon Killebrew	MIN	1963	45
Bob Allison	MIN	1963	35
Tony Oliva	MIN	1963	33
Total			113
Harmon Killebrew	MIN	1964	49
Bob Allison	MIN	1964	32
Tony Oliva	MIN	1964	32
Total			113
Joe DiMaggio	NY	1937	46
Lou Gehrig	NY	1937	37
Bill Dickey	NY	1937	29
Total			112
Hank Greenberg	DET	1938	58
Rudy York	DET	1938	33
Charlie Gehringer	DET	1938	20
Total			111

Home Run Trios, Season, NL

Player	Team	Year	HR
Davey Johnson	ATL	1973	43
Darrell Evans	ATL	1973	41
Hank Aaron	ATL	1973	40
Total			124
Johnny Mize	NY	1947	51
Willard Marshall	NY	1947	36
Walker Cooper	NY	1947	35
Total			122
Johnny Bench	CIN	1970	45
Tony Perez	CIN	1970	40
Lee May	CIN	1970	34
Total			119
Willie McCovey	SF	1963	44
Willie Mays	SF	1963	38
Orlando Cepeda	SF	1963	34
Total			116
Duke Snider	BKN	1953	42
Roy Campanella	BKN	1953	41
Gil Hodges	BKN	1953	31
Total			114
Ted Kluszewski	CIN	1955	47
Wally Post	CIN	1955	40
Gus Bell	CIN	1955	27
Total			114
Willie Mays	SF	1965	52
Willie McCovey	SF	1965	39
Jim Ray Hart	SF	1965	23
Total			114
Hank Aaron	ATL	1966	44
Joe Torre	ATL	1966	36
Felipe Alou	ATL	1966	31
Total			111
Eddie Mathews	MIL	1959	46
Hank Aaron	MIL	1959	39
Joe Adcock	MIL	1959	25
Total			110

Home Run Duos, Season, AL (25 each)

Player	Team	Year	HR
Roger Maris	NY	1961	61
Mickey Mantle	NY	1961	54
Total			115
Babe Ruth	NY	1927	60
Lou Gehrig	NY	1927	47
Total			107
Jimmie Foxx	PHI	1932	58
Al Simmons	PHI	1932	35
Total			93
Babe Ruth	NY	1931	46
Lou Gehrig	NY	1931	46
Total			92
Hank Greenberg	DET	1938	58
Rudy York	DET	1938	33
Total			91
Babe Ruth	NY	1930	49
Lou Gehrig	NY	1930	41
Total			90
Rocky Colavito	DET	1961	45
Norm Cash	DET	1961	41
Total			86
Joe DiMaggio	NY	1937	46
Lou Gehrig	NY	1937	37
Total			83

Player	Team	Year	HR
Frank Robinson	BAL	1966	49
Boog Powell	BAL	1966	34
Total			83
Ted Williams	BOS	1949	43
Vern Stephens	BOS	1949	39
Total			82
Mickey Mantle	NY	1956	52
Yogi Berra	NY	1956	30
Total			82
Babe Ruth	NY	1928	54
Lou Gehrig	NY	1928	27
Total			81
Babe Ruth	NY	1929	46
Lou Gehrig	NY	1929	35
Total			81
Harmon Killebrew	MIN	1964	49
Tony Oliva	MIN	1964	32
Total			81
Harmon Killebrew	MIN	1963	45
Bob Allison	MIN	1963	35
Total			80
Carl Yastrzemski	BOS	1969	40
Rico Petrocelli	BOS	1969	40
Total			80

Home Run Duos, Season, NL (25 each)

Player	Team	Year	HR
Hack Wilson	CHI	1930	56
Gabby Hartnett	CHI	1930	37
Total			93
Willie Mays	SF	1965	52
Willie McCovey	SF	1965	39
Total			91
Johnny Mize	NY	1947	51
Willard Marshall	NY	1947	36
Total			87
Ted Kluszewski	CIN	1955	47
Wally Post	CIN	1955	40
Total			87
Eddie Mathews	MIL	1959	46
Hank Aaron	MIL	1959	39
Total			85
George Foster	CIN	1977	52
Johnny Bench	CIN	1977	31
Total			83
Gil Hodges	BKN	1954	42
Duke Snider	BKN	1954	40
Total			82

Mickey Mantle (*right*) had to settle for 54 home runs in 1961 while his teammate Roger Maris (*left*) broke Babe Ruth's record with 61. The two bombers never combined for more than 63 home runs in one season again.

Home Run Duos, Career, AL

Player	Team	First	Last	HR
Babe Ruth	NY	1925	1934	424
Lou Gehrig	NY	1925	1934	348
Total				772
Harmon Killebrew	WAS	1958	1970	476
Bob Allison	MIN	1958	1970	256
Total				732
Mickey Mantle	NY	1951	1963	419
Yogi Berra	NY	1951	1963	283
Total				702
Norm Cash	DET	1960	1974	373
Al Kaline	DET	1960	1974	274
Total				647
Jim Rice	BOS	1974		351
Dwight Evans	BOS	1974		280
Total				631
Ted Williams	BOS	1939	1951	323
Bobby Doerr	BOS	1939	1951	216
Total				539
Boog Powell	BAL	1961	1974	303
Brooks Robinson	BAL	1961	1974	234
Total				537
Carl Yastrzemski	BOS	1963	1976	308
Rico Petrocelli	BOS	1963	1976	210
Total				518
Hank Greenberg	DET	1934	1945	250
Rudy York	DET	1934	1945	239
Total				489
Reggie Jackson	KC	1967	1975	254
Sal Bando	OAK	1967	1975	165
Total				419

Home Run Duos, Career, NL

Player	Team	First	Last	HR
Hank Aaron	MIL	1954	1966	442
Eddie Mathews	ATL	1954	1966	421
Total				863
Willie Mays	SF	1959	1971	430
Willie McCovey	SF	1959	1971	370
Total				800
Duke Snider	BKN	1947	1961	384
Gil Hodges	LA	1947	1961	361
Total				745
Billy Williams	CHI	1960	1973	376
Ron Santo	CHI	1960	1973	337
Total				713
Johnny Bench	CIN	1971	1981	277
George Foster	CIN	1971	1981	244
Total				521
Mike Schmidt	PHI	1972	1980	283
Greg Luzinski	PHI	1972	1980	220
Total				503
Dale Murphy	ATL	1978		264
Bob Horner	ATL	1978		215
Total				479
Willie Stargell	PIT	1962	1972	277
Roberto Clemente	PIT	1962	1972	175
Total				452
Ron Cey	LA	1971	1982	228
Steve Garvey	LA	1971	1982	210
Total				438
Mel Ott	NY	1926	1936	275
Bill Terry	NY	1926	1936	138
Total				413
Frank Robinson	CIN	1958	1965	257
Vada Pinson	CIN	1958	1965	147
Total				404
Ken Boyer	STL	1955	1963	218
Stan Musial	STL	1955	1963	183
Total				401

Most Home Runs by Team, Season, AL

Team	Year	HR
NY	1961	240
MIN	1963	225
MIN	1964	221
MIL	1982	216
BAL	1985	214
BOS	1977	213
DET	1962	209
DET	1985	205
BOS	1970	203
MIL	1980	203

Most Home Runs by Team, Season, NL

Team	Year	HR
NY	1947	221
CIN	1956	221
BKN	1953	208
ATL	1966	207
ATL	1973	206
SF	1962	204
BKN	1955	201

Most 100-RBI Hitters, AL

Player	Team	Year	RBI
Lou Gehrig	NY	1936	152
Joe DiMaggio	NY	1936	125
Tony Lazzeri	NY	1936	109
George Selkirk	NY	1936	107
Bill Dickey	NY	1936	107
Ken Williams	STL	1922	155
Marty McManus	STL	1922	109
George Sisler	STL	1922	105
Baby Doll Jacobson	STL	1922	102
Lou Gehrig	NY	1927	175
Babe Ruth	NY	1927	164
Bob Meusel	NY	1927	103
Tony Lazzeri	NY	1927	102
Lou Gehrig	NY	1931	184
Babe Ruth	NY	1931	163
Ben Chapman	NY	1931	122
Lyn Lary	NY	1931	107
Lou Gehrig	NY	1932	151
Babe Ruth	NY	1932	137
Tony Lazzeri	NY	1932	113
Ben Chapman	NY	1932	107
Hank Greenberg	DET	1934	139
Charlie Gehringer	DET	1934	127
Goose Goslin	DET	1934	100
Billy Rogell	DET	1934	100
Goose Goslin	DET	1936	125
Charlie Gehringer	DET	1936	116
Al Simmons	DET	1936	112
Marv Owen	DET	1936	105
Joe DiMaggio	NY	1939	126
Joe Gordon	NY	1939	111
Bill Dickey	NY	1939	105
George Selkirk	NY	1939	101
Jimmie Foxx	BOS	1940	119
Ted Williams	BOS	1940	113
Joe Cronin	BOS	1940	111
Bobby Doerr	BOS	1940	105
Jim Rice	BOS	1977	114
Butch Hobson	BOS	1977	112
Carlton Fisk	BOS	1977	102
Carl Yastrzemski	BOS	1977	102
Cecil Cooper	MIL	1982	121
Robin Yount	MIL	1982	112
Gorman Thomas	MIL	1982	110
Ben Oglivie	MIL	1982	102

Most 100-RBI Hitters, NL

Player	Team	Year	RBI
Glenn Wright	PIT	1925	121
Clyde Barnhart	PIT	1925	114
Pie Traynor	PIT	1925	106
Kiki Cuyler	PIT	1925	102
Hack Wilson	CHI	1929	159
Rogers Hornsby	CHI	1929	149
Riggs Stephenson	CHI	1929	110
Kiki Cuyler	CHI	1929	102
Chuck Klein	PHI	1929	145
Don Hurst	PHI	1929	125
Lefty O'Doul	PHI	1929	122
Pinky Whitney	PHI	1929	115

Most Runs in One Inning, Team, AL

Team	Date	R	Inn.	Opp.
BOS	Jun 18, 1953	17	7	DET
NY	Jul 6, 1920	14	5	WAS
BOS	Jul 4, 1948	14	7	PHI
CLE	Sep 21, 1950	14	1	PHI
CLE	Jul 7, 1923	13	6	BOS
PHI	Jun 15, 1925	13	8	CLE
DET	Jun 17, 1925	13	6	NY
CHI	Sep 26, 1943	13	4	WAS
NY	Jun 21, 1945	13	5	BOS
KC	Apr 21, 1956	13	2	CHI
CLE	Apr 10, 1977	13	8	BOS
CAL	Sep 14, 1978	13	9	TEX
PHI	Jul 8, 1902	12	6	BOS
CLE	Apr 14, 1925	12	8	STL
WAS	Jul 10, 1926	12	8	STL
PHI	May 22, 1929	12	5	BOS
NY	May 27, 1933	12	8	CHI
BOS	May 6, 1934	12	4	DET
BOS	Jul 25, 1936	12	5	DET
PHI	Aug 29, 1937	12	1	CHI
CLE	Jul 2, 1943	12	4	NY
BOS	Aug 4, 1945	12	4	WAS
NY	Sep 11, 1949	12	3	WAS
PHI	Sep 23, 1950	12	6	WAS
CHI	Jun 10, 1952	12	4	PHI
BOS	May 4, 1962	12	5	CHI

Most Runs in One Inning, Team, AL *(cont'd)*

Team	Date	R	Inn.	Opp.
BOS	Aug 10, 1965	12	5	BAL
CAL	Apr 30, 1966	12	8	BOS
TEX	Jul 3, 1983	12	15	OAK
BOS	Aug 21, 1986	12	6	CLE

Below: Rogers Hornsby (*on the right*), whose .358 lifetime batting average is second only to Ty Cobb, and Hack Wilson, who had the league high in homers four times and strikeouts five times, batted .339 together for three years with the Cubs. Brewers outfielder Ben Oglivie (*right*) has had three three-homer games since 1979. *Below right*: Another teammate of Hornsby and Wilson, Riggs Stephenson, posted a .336 career mark over 14 seasons.

Most Runs in One Inning, Team, NL

Team	Date	R	Inn.	Opp.
CHI	Sep 6, 1883	18	7	DET
BOS	Jun 18, 1894	16	1	BAL
HAR	May 13, 1876	15	4	NY
BKN	May 21, 1952	15	1	CIN
CLE	Aug 7, 1889	14	3	WAS
CIN	Jun 18, 1893	14	1	LOU
BAL	Apr 24, 1894	14	9	BOS
CHI	Aug 25, 1922	14	4	PHI
PRO	Jun 22, 1882	13	3	DET
NY	Sep 8, 1883	13	3	PHI
NY	Jul 19, 1890	13	2	CLE
CHI	Aug 16, 1890	13	5	PIT
BOS	Jul 25, 1900	13	1	STL
NY	May 13, 1910	13	1	STL
BKN	Aug 8, 1954	13	8	CIN
SF	May 7, 1966	13	3	STL
ATL	Sep 20, 1972	13	2	HOU
PRO	May 15, 1878	12	8	BOS
NY	Jun 7, 1887	12	3	PHI
CHI	May 8, 1890	12	6	CIN
PIT	Apr 22, 1892	12	1	STL
PIT	Jun 6, 1894	12	3	BOS
CHI	Jul 17, 1895	12	4	PHI
CIN	Jun 16, 1897	12	2	BKN
BKN	Sep 21, 1897	12	1	BOS
PHI	Oct 2, 1897	12	2	NY
PHI	Jul 21, 1923	12	6	CHI
CHI	May 28, 1925	12	7	CIN
NY	Sep 3, 1926	12	5	BOS
STL	Sep 16, 1926	12	3	PHI
NY	Jun 1, 1930	12	3	BOS
CHI	Aug 21, 1935	12	6	PHI
CHI	May 5, 1938	12	8	PHI
CIN	May 4, 1942	12	4	NY
BKN	May 24, 1953	12	8	PHI
BKN	Aug 30, 1953	12	7	STL
SF	Aug 23, 1961	12	9	CIN
HOU	May 31, 1975	12	8	PHI
CIN	Apr 25, 1977	12	5	SD
MON	Sep 24, 1985	12	5	CHI

Billy North used his speed to patrol Oakland's championship outfield and to lead the A.L. in stolen bases in 1974 and '76.

Most Runs in One Inning, Team, Other Leagues

Team	Date	R	Inn.	Opp.
PHI P	Jun 26, 1890	14	6	BUF
WAS AA	Jun 17, 1891	14	1	BAL
STL AA	May 12, 1887	12	5	BAL
STL AA	Jun 19, 1887	12	4	CIN
STL AA	Aug 25, 1889	12	3	BAL
NY P	May 31, 1890	12	8	PIT

Most Runs by Team, Game, AL

Team	Date	R	Opp.
BOS	Jun 8, 1950	29	STL
CHI	Apr 23, 1955	29	KC
CLE	Jul 7, 1923	27	BOS
CLE	Aug 12, 1948	26	STL
CLE	May 11, 1930	25	PHI
NY	May 24, 1936	25	PHI
PHI	May 18, 1912	24	DET
NY	Sep 28, 1923	24	BOS
CLE	Jul 29, 1928	24	NY
PHI	May 1, 1929	24	BOS
BOS	Sep 27, 1940	24	WAS
TOR	Jun 26, 1978	24	BAL
CAL	Aug 25, 1979	24	TOR
BOS	Aug 21, 1986	24	CLE

Most Runs by Team, Game, NL since 1900

Team	Date	R	Opp.
STL	Jul 6, 1929	28	PHI
CIN	Jun 4, 1911	26	BOS
CHI	Aug 25, 1922	26	PHI
NY	Apr 30, 1944	26	BKN
PHI	Apr 11, 1985	26	NY
NY	Jun 9, 1901	25	CIN
BKN	Sep 23, 1901	25	CIN
CIN	May 13, 1902	24	PHI
PIT	Jun 22, 1925	24	STL
NY	Sep 2, 1925	24	PHI
CHI	Jul 3, 1945	24	BOS

Most Runs by Team, Game, NL before 1900

Team	Date	R	Opp.
CHI	Jun 29, 1897	36	LOU
CHI	Jul 24, 1882	35	CLE
CHI	Jul 3, 1883	31	BUF
CHI	Jul 22, 1876	30	LOU
BOS	Jun 9, 1883	30	DET
CIN	Jun 18, 1893	30	LOU
BOS	Jun 20, 1883	29	PHI
NY	Jun 15, 1887	29	PHI
PHI	Aug 17, 1894	29	LOU
HAR	May 13, 1876	28	NY
PRO	Aug 21, 1883	28	PHI
BOS	Aug 27, 1887	28	PIT
CHI	Aug 25, 1891	28	BKN
BOS	Aug 21, 1894	28	CIN
BOS	Sep 3, 1896	28	STL

Most Runs by Team, Game, Other Leagues

Team	Date	R	Opp.
PHI P	Jun 26, 1890	30	BUF
STL AA	Apr 30, 1887	28	CLE
PHI AA	Apr 23, 1888	28	CLE
BKN P	Jul 12, 1890	28	BUF
CIN AA	Sep 11, 1883	27	PIT
LOU AA	Aug 12, 1886	27	BKN
LOU AA	May 26, 1887	27	BKN
BAL AA	Jun 30, 1887	27	NY

Most Stolen Bases by Team, Season, AL

Team	Year	SB
OAK	1976	341
NY	1910	288
WAS	1913	287
CHI	1901	280
DET	1909	280
DET	1911	276
WAS	1912	274
NY	1911	270
DET	1912	270
CHI	1902	265
PHI	1912	258
NY	1914	251

Most Stolen Bases by Team, Season, NL

Team	Year	SB
BAL	1899	364
NY	1911	347
NY	1912	319
STL	1985	314
CIN	1910	310
NY	1913	296
NY	1905	291
CIN	1911	289
NY	1906	288
NY	1904	283
CHI	1906	283
NY	1910	282
CIN	1909	280

Team	Year	SB
BKN	1900	274
BKN	1903	273
BKN	1899	271
CHI	1908	270
CHI	1905	267
NY	1903	264
PIT	1907	264
CHI	1905	263
STL	1986	262
PIT	1977	260
CHI	1903	259
BAL	1898	250
NY	1908	250

Stolen Base Duos, Season, AL

Player	Team	Year	SB
Rickey Henderson	OAK	1982	130
Davey Lopes	OAK	1982	28
Total			158
Rickey Henderson	OAK	1983	108
Mike Davis	OAK	1983	32
Total			140
Clyde Milan	WAS	1913	75
Danny Moeller	WAS	1913	62
Total			137
Ty Cobb	DET	1915	96
Donie Bush	DET	1915	35
Total			131
Ty Cobb	DET	1909	76
Donie Bush	DET	1909	53
Total			129
Billy North	OAK	1976	75
Bert Campaneris	OAK	1976	54
Total			129
Rickey Henderson	OAK	1980	100
Dwayne Murphy	OAK	1980	26
Total			126
Ty Cobb	DET	1911	83
Donie Bush	DET	1911	42
Total			125
Clyde Milan	WAS	1912	88
Danny Moeller	WAS	1912	30
Total			118
Ty Cobb	DET	1910	65
Donie Bush	DET	1910	49
Total			114
Willie Wilson	KC	1979	83
Amos Otis	KC	1979	30
Total			113

Player	Team	Year	SB
Fritz Maisel	NY	1914	74
Roger Peckinpaugh	NY	1914	38
Total			112
Dave Collins	TOR	1984	60
Damaso Garcia	TOR	1984	46
Total			106
Rickey Henderson	NY	1985	80
Bobby Meacham	NY	1985	25
Total			105
Mickey Rivers	CAL	1975	70
Jerry Remy	CAL	1975	34
Total			104
Eddie Collins	PHI	1912	63
Frank Baker	PHI	1912	40
Total			103
Ray Chapman	CLE	1917	52
Braggo Roth	CLE	1917	51
Total			103
Eddie Collins	PHI	1910	81
Frank Baker	PHI	1910	21
Total			102
Ty Cobb	DET	1912	61
Sam Crawford	DET	1912	41
Total			102
Rickey Henderson	NY	1986	87
Willie Randolph	NY	1986	15
Total			102
Amos Otis	KC	1971	52
Freddie Patek	KC	1971	49
Total			101
Rudy Law	CHI	1983	77
Julio Cruz	CHI	1983	24
Total			101

Stolen Base Duos, Season, NL

Player	Team	Year	SB
Vince Coleman	STL	1985	110
Willie McGee	STL	1985	56
Total			166
Ron LeFlore	MON	1980	97
Rodney Scott	MON	1980	63
Total			160
Lou Brock	STL	1974	118
Bake McBride	STL	1974	30
Total			148
Vince Coleman	STL	1986	107
Ozzie Smith	STL	1986	31
Total			138
Maury Wills	LA	1962	104

Player	Team	Year	SB
Willie Davis	LA	1962	32
Total			136
Omar Moreno	PIT	1980	96
Phil Garner	PIT	1980	32
Total			128
Frank Taveras	PIT	1977	70
Omar Moreno	PIT	1977	53
Total			123
Bob Bescher	CIN	1910	70
Dode Paskert	CIN	1910	51
Total			121
Juan Samuel	PHI	1984	72
Von Hayes	PHI	1984	48

Stolen Base Duos, Season, NL *(cont'd)*

Player	Team	Year	SB
Total			120
Maury Wills	LA	1965	94
Willie Davis	LA	1965	25
Total			119
Gene Richards	SD	1980	61
Ozzie Smith	SD	1980	57
Total			118
Bob Bescher	CIN	1911	80
Dick Egan	CIN	1911	37
Total			117
Omar Moreno	PIT	1978	71
Frank Taveras	PIT	1978	46
Total			117
Tim Raines	MON	1982	78
Andre Dawson	MON	1982	39
Total			117
Tim Raines	MON	1983	90
Andre Dawson	MON	1983	25
Total			115
Jimmy Sheckard	BKN	1903	67
Sammy Strang	BKN	1903	46
Total			113
Josh Devore	NY	1911	61
Fred Snodgrass	NY	1911	51
Total			112
Art Devlin	NY	1905	59
Sam Mertes	NY	1905	52
Total			111
Frank Chance	CHI	1906	57
Johnny Evers	CHI	1906	49
Total			106
Tim Raines	MON	1986	70
Mitch Webster	MON	1986	36
Total			106
Cesar Cedeno	HOU	1977	61
Jose Cruz	HOU	1977	44
Total			105

Player	Team	Year	SB
Honus Wagner	PIT	1907	61
Tommy Leach	PIT	1907	43
Total			104
Alan Wiggins	SD	1984	70
Tony Gwynn	SD	1984	33
Total			103
Bob Bescher	CIN	1912	67
Armando Marsans	CIN	1912	35
Total			102
Dave Collins	CIN	1980	79
Ken Griffey	CIN	1980	23
Total			102
Tim Raines	MON	1984	75
Miguel Dilone	MON	1984	27
Total			102
Tim Raines	MON	1981	71
Rodney Scott	MON	1981	30
Total			101
Ryne Sandberg	CHI	1985	54
Davey Lopes	CHI	1985	47
Total			101
Frank Chance	CHI	1903	67
Jimmy Slagle	CHI	1903	33
Total			100
Red Murray	NY	1910	57
Josh Devore	NY	1910	43
Total			100
Joe Morgan	CIN	1972	58
Bobby Tolan	CIN	1972	42
Total			100
Joe Morgan	CIN	1975	67
Dave Concepcion	CIN	1975	33
Total			100
Omar Moreno	PIT	1982	60
Lee Lacy	PIT	1982	40
Total			100

Most .300 Hitters, Season, AL (300 AB each)

Player	Team	Year	AB	BA
Al Simmons	PHI	1927	406	.392
Ty Cobb	PHI	1927	490	.357
Mickey Cochrane	PHI	1927	432	.338
Jimmy Dykes	PHI	1927	417	.324
Sammy Hale	PHI	1927	501	.313
Joe Boley	PHI	1927	370	.311
Walter French	PHI	1927	326	.304

Vince Coleman (*above*) is the only player to top 100 steals in a season in both the majors and the minors. Willie McGee (*right*), Coleman's partner in crime, has 52 triples in five years with the Cardinals. Joltin' Joe DiMaggio (*below right*) drove in 1537 runs in 13 years and never struck out more than 40 times in a season.

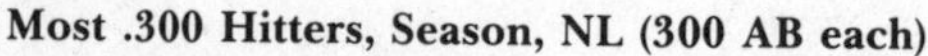

Most .300 Hitters, Season, NL (300 AB each)

Player	Team	Year	AB	BA
George Watkins	STL	1930	391	.373
Frankie Frisch	STL	1930	540	.346
Chick Hafey	STL	1930	446	.336
Jimmie Wilson	STL	1930	362	.318
Sparky Adams	STL	1930	570	.314
Jim Bottomley	STL	1930	487	.304
Charley Gelbert	STL	1930	513	.303
Taylor Douthit	STL	1930	664	.303
Kiki Cuyler	PIT	1925	617	.357
Max Carey	PIT	1925	542	.343
George Grantham	PIT	1925	359	.326
Clyde Barnhart	PIT	1925	539	.325
Pie Traynor	PIT	1925	591	.320
Earl Smith	PIT	1925	329	.313
Glenn Wright	PIT	1925	614	.308
Freddie Lindstrom	NY	1928	646	.358
Shanty Hogan	NY	1928	411	.333
Bill Terry	NY	1928	568	.326
Mel Ott	NY	1928	435	.322
Lefty O'Doul	NY	1928	354	.319
Andy Reese	NY	1928	406	.308
Jimmy Welsh	NY	1928	476	.307

.300-Hitting Outfields, AL

Player	Team	Year	BA
Patsy Dougherty	BOS	1902	.342
Chick Stahl	BOS	1902	.323
Buck Freeman	BOS	1902	.309
Tris Speaker	BOS	1911	.327
Harry Hooper	BOS	1911	.311
Duffy Lewis	BOS	1911	.307
Ty Cobb	DET	1919	.384
Bobby Veach	DET	1919	.355
Ira Flagstead	DET	1919	.331
Tris Speaker	CLE	1920	.388
Charlie Jamieson	CLE	1920	.319
Elmer Smith	CLE	1920	.316
Baby Doll Jacobson	STL	1920	.355
Jack Tobin	STL	1920	.341
Ken Williams	STL	1920	.307
Baby Doll Jacobson	STL	1921	.352
Jack Tobin	STL	1921	.352
Ken Williams	STL	1921	.349
Harry Heilmann	DET	1921	.394
Ty Cobb	DET	1921	.389
Bobby Veach	DET	1921	.338
Ken Williams	STL	1922	.332
Jack Tobin	STL	1922	.331
Baby Doll Jacobson	STL	1922	.317
Ty Cobb	DET	1922	.401
Harry Heilmann	DET	1922	.356
Bobby Veach	DET	1922	.327
Babe Ruth	NY	1923	.393
Whitey Witt	NY	1923	.314
Bob Meusel	NY	1923	.313
Harry Heilmann	DET	1923	.403
Ty Cobb	DET	1923	.340
Heinie Manush	DET	1923	.334
Tris Speaker	CLE	1923	.380
Charlie Jamieson	CLE	1923	.345
Homer Summa	CLE	1923	.328
Sam Rice	WAS	1923	.316
Nemo Leibold	WAS	1923	.305
Goose Goslin	WAS	1923	.300
Ken Williams	STL	1923	.357
Jack Tobin	STL	1923	.317
Baby Doll Jacobson	STL	1923	.309
Bing Miller	PHI	1924	.342
Bill Lamar	PHI	1924	.330
Al Simmons	PHI	1924	.308
Bibb Falk	CHI	1924	.352
Harry Hooper	CHI	1924	.328
Johnny Mostil	CHI	1924	.325
Al Simmons	PHI	1925	.384
Bill Lamar	PHI	1925	.356
Bing Miller	PHI	1925	.319
Harry Rice	STL	1925	.359
Baby Doll Jacobson	STL	1925	.341
Ken Williams	STL	1925	.331
Harry Heilmann	DET	1925	.393
Ty Cobb	DET	1925	.378
Al Wingo	DET	1925	.370
Goose Goslin	WAS	1926	.354
Sam Rice	WAS	1926	.337
Earl McNeely	WAS	1926	.303
Bibb Falk	CHI	1926	.345
Johnny Mostil	CHI	1926	.328
Bill Barrett	CHI	1926	.307
Heinie Manush	DET	1926	.378
Harry Heilmann	DET	1926	.367
Bob Fothergill	DET	1926	.367
Babe Ruth	NY	1927	.356
Earle Combs	NY	1927	.356
Bob Meusel	NY	1927	.337
Al Simmons	PHI	1927	.392
Ty Cobb	PHI	1927	.357
Walter French	PHI	1927	.304
Al Simmons	PHI	1928	.351
Bing Miller	PHI	1928	.329
Ty Cobb	PHI	1928	.323
Goose Goslin	WAS	1928	.379
Sam Rice	WAS	1928	.328
Red Barnes	WAS	1928	.302
Harry Heilmann	DET	1928	.328
Bob Fothergill	DET	1928	.317
Harry Rice	DET	1928	.302
Al Simmons	PHI	1929	.365
Bing Miller	PHI	1929	.335
Mule Haas	PHI	1929	.313
Harry Heilmann	DET	1929	.344
Roy Johnson	DET	1929	.314
Harry Rice	DET	1929	.304
Heinie Manush	WAS	1930	.362
Sam Rice	WAS	1930	.349
Sammy West	WAS	1930	.328
Dick Porter	CLE	1930	.350
Earl Averill	CLE	1930	.339
Charlie Jamieson	CLE	1930	.301
Babe Ruth	NY	1931	.373
Earle Combs	NY	1931	.318
Ben Chapman	NY	1931	.315
Sammy West	WAS	1931	.333
Sam Rice	WAS	1931	.310
Heinie Manush	WAS	1931	.307
Earl Averill	CLE	1931	.333
Joe Vosmik	CLE	1931	.320
Dick Porter	CLE	1931	.312

.300-Hitting Outfields, AL *(cont'd)*

Player	Team	Year	BA
Doc Cramer	PHI	1932	.336
Al Simmons	PHI	1932	.322
Mule Haas	PHI	1932	.305
Earl Averill	CLE	1932	.314
Joe Vosmik	CLE	1932	.312
Dick Porter	CLE	1932	.308
Gee Walker	DET	1936	.353
Al Simmons	DET	1936	.327
Goose Goslin	DET	1936	.315
Joe DiMaggio	NY	1936	.323
George Selkirk	NY	1936	.308
Jake Powell	NY	1936	.306
Beau Bell	STL	1937	.340
Sammy West	STL	1937	.328
Joe Vosmik	STL	1937	.325
Rip Radcliff	CHI	1937	.325
Dixie Walker	CHI	1937	.302
Mike Kreevich	CHI	1937	.302
George Case	WAS	1938	.305
Sammy West	WAS	1938	.302
Al Simmons	WAS	1938	.302
Ben Chapman	BOS	1938	.340
Joe Vosmik	BOS	1938	.324
Doc Cramer	BOS	1938	.301
Joe DiMaggio	NY	1939	.381
Charlie Keller	NY	1939	.334
George Selkirk	NY	1939	.306
Ted Williams	BOS	1940	.343
Doc Cramer	BOS	1940	.303
Dom DiMaggio	BOS	1940	.301
Dom DiMaggio	BOS	1950	.328
Al Zarilla	BOS	1950	.325
Ted Williams	BOS	1950	.317
Hoot Evers	DET	1950	.323
Vic Wertz	DET	1950	.308
Johnny Groth	DET	1950	.306

.300-Hitting Outfields, NL

Player	Team	Year	BA
Willie Keeler	BKN	1900	.368
Joe Kelley	BKN	1900	.319
Fielder Jones	BKN	1900	.309
Jesse Burkett	STL	1900	.363
Patsy Donovan	STL	1900	.316
Emmet Heidrick	STL	1900	.301
Ed Delahanty	PHI	1901	.354
Elmer Flick	PHI	1901	.336
Roy Thomas	PHI	1901	.309
Jesse Burkett	STL	1901	.382
Emmet Heidrick	STL	1901	.339
Patsy Donovan	STL	1901	.303
Ginger Beaumont	PIT	1901	.332
Fred Clarke	PIT	1901	.324
Lefty Davis	PIT	1901	.313
Patsy Donovan	STL	1902	.315
Homer Smoot	STL	1902	.311
George Barclay	STL	1902	.300
Jack Dalton	BKN	1914	.319
Zack Wheat	BKN	1914	.319
Casey Stengel	BKN	1914	.316
Edd Roush	CIN	1921	.352
Pat Duncan	CIN	1921	.308
Rube Bressler	CIN	1921	.307
Walt Cruise	BOS	1921	.346
Billy Southworth	BOS	1921	.308
Ray Powell	BOS	1921	.306
Turner Barber	CHI	1921	.314
George Maisel	CHI	1921	.310
Max Flack	CHI	1921	.301
Zack Wheat	BKN	1922	.335
Hy Myers	BKN	1922	.317
Tommy Griffith	BKN	1922	.316
Curt Walker	PHI	1922	.337
Cliff Lee	PHI	1922	.322
Cy Williams	PHI	1922	.308
Kiki Cuyler	PIT	1925	.357
Max Carey	PIT	1925	.343
Clyde Barnhart	PIT	1925	.325
Zack Wheat	BKN	1925	.359
Dick Cox	BKN	1925	.329
Eddie Brown	BKN	1925	.306
Billy Southworth	STL	1926	.317
Taylor Douthit	STL	1926	.308
Ray Blades	STL	1926	.305
Cuckoo Christensen	CIN	1926	.350
Edd Roush	CIN	1926	.323
Curt Walker	CIN	1926	.306
Cy Williams	PHI	1926	.345
Freddy Leach	PHI	1926	.329
Johnny Mokan	PHI	1926	.303
Paul Waner	PIT	1927	.380
Lloyd Waner	PIT	1927	.355
Clyde Barnhart	PIT	1927	.319
Riggs Stephenson	CHI	1927	.344
Hack Wilson	CHI	1927	.318

.300-Hitting Outfields, NL ***(cont'd)***

Player	Team	Year	BA
Earl Webb	CHI	1927	.301
Mel Ott	NY	1928	.322
Lefty O'Doul	NY	1928	.319
Jimmy Welsh	NY	1928	.307
Lloyd Waner	PIT	1928	.353
Paul Waner	PIT	1928	.336
Adam Comorosky	PIT	1928	.321
Riggs Stephenson	CHI	1929	.362
Kiki Cuyler	CHI	1929	.360
Hack Wilson	CHI	1929	.345
Chick Hafey	STL	1929	.338
Taylor Douthit	STL	1929	.336
Ernie Orsatti	STL	1929	.332
Lefty O'Doul	PHI	1929	.398
Chuck Klein	PHI	1929	.356
Denny Sothern	PHI	1929	.306
Babe Herman	BKN	1929	.381
Johnny Frederick	BKN	1929	.328
Rube Bressler	BKN	1929	.318
George Watkins	STL	1930	.373
Chick Hafey	STL	1930	.336
Taylor Douthit	STL	1930	.303
Riggs Stephenson	CHI	1930	.367
Hack Wilson	CHI	1930	.356
Kiki Cuyler	CHI	1930	.355
Chuck Klein	PHI	1932	.348
Kiddo Davis	PHI	1932	.309
Hal Lee	PHI	1932	.303
Chuck Klein	PHI	1933	.368
Wes Schulmerich	PHI	1933	.334
Chick Fullis	PHI	1933	.309
Kiki Cuyler	CHI	1934	.338
Babe Herman	CHI	1934	.304
Chuck Klein	CHI	1934	.301
Woody Jensen	PIT	1935	.324
Paul Waner	PIT	1935	.321
Lloyd Waner	PIT	1935	.309
Ernie Koy	STL	1940	.310
Enos Slaughter	STL	1940	.306
Terry Moore	STL	1940	.304
Pete Reiser	BKN	1941	.343
Joe Medwick	BKN	1941	.318
Dixie Walker	BKN	1941	.311
Goody Rosen	BKN	1945	.325
Luis Olmo	BKN	1945	.313
Dixie Walker	BKN	1945	.300
Tommy Holmes	BOS	1948	.325
Jeff Heath	BOS	1948	.319
Mike McCormick	BOS	1948	.303
Bobby Thomson	NY	1949	.309
Willard Marshall	NY	1949	.307
Whitey Lockman	NY	1949	.301
Carl Furillo	BKN	1953	.344
Duke Snider	BKN	1953	.336
Jackie Robinson	BKN	1953	.329
Felipe Alou	SF	1962	.316
Willie Mays	SF	1962	.304
Harvey Kuenn	SF	1962	.304
Rico Carty	MIL	1964	.330
Hank Aaron	MIL	1964	.328
Lee Maye	MIL	1964	.304
Matty Alou	PIT	1966	.342
Roberto Clemente	PIT	1966	.317
Willie Stargell	PIT	1966	.315
Pete Rose	CIN	1969	.348
Alex Johnson	CIN	1969	.315
Bobby Tolan	CIN	1969	.305
Roberto Clemente	PIT	1969	.345
Matty Alou	PIT	1969	.331
Willie Stargell	PIT	1969	.307
Pete Rose	CIN	1970	.316
Bobby Tolan	CIN	1970	.316
Bernie Carbo	CIN	1970	.310
Vic Davalillo	PIT	1972	.318
Roberto Clemente	PIT	1972	.312
Al Oliver	PIT	1972	.312
Bake McBride	STL	1974	.309
Reggie Smith	STL	1974	.309
Lou Brock	STL	1974	.306
Al Oliver	PIT	1974	.321
Richie Zisk	PIT	1974	.313
Willie Stargell	PIT	1974	.301
Ken Griffey	CIN	1976	.336
Cesar Geronimo	CIN	1976	.307
George Foster	CIN	1976	.306
Garry Maddox	PHI	1976	.330
Jay Johnstone	PHI	1976	.318
Greg Luzinski	PHI	1976	.304
Dan Gladden	SF	1984	.351
Chili Davis	SF	1984	.315
Jeffrey Leonard	SF	1984	.302

Teammates Who Finished 1-2 in Batting, AL

Player	Team	Year	AB	H	BA
Ty Cobb	DET	1907	605	212	.350
Sam Crawford	DET	1907	582	188	.323
Ty Cobb	DET	1908	581	188	.324
Sam Crawford	DET	1908	591	184	.311
Ty Cobb	DET	1919	497	191	.384
Bobby Veach	DET	1919	538	191	.355
Harry Heilmann	DET	1921	603	237	.394
Ty Cobb	DET	1921	507	197	.389
Ted Williams	BOS	1942	522	186	.356
Johnny Pesky	BOS	1942	620	205	.331
Ted Williams	BOS	1958	411	135	.328
Pete Runnels	BOS	1958	568	183	.322
Harvey Kuenn	DET	1959	561	198	.353
Al Kaline	DET	1959	511	167	.327
Norm Cash	DET	1961	535	193	.361
Al Kaline	DET	1961	586	190	.324
George Brett	KC	1976	645	215	.333
Hal McRae	KC	1976	527	175	.332
Rod Carew	MIN	1977	616	239	.388
Lyman Bostock	MIN	1977	592	199	.336
Don Mattingly	NY	1984	603	207	.343
Dave Winfield	NY	1984	567	193	.340

Teammates Who Finished 1-2 in Batting, NL

Player	Team	Year	AB	H	BA
George Gore	CHI	1880	322	116	.360
Cap Anson	CHI	1880	356	120	.337
King Kelly	CHI	1886	451	175	.388
Cap Anson	CHI	1886	504	187	.371
Cap Anson	CHI	1888	515	177	.344
Jimmy Ryan	CHI	1888	549	182	.332
Billy Hamilton	PHI	1893	355	135	.380
Sam Thompson	PHI	1893	600	222	.370
Honus Wagner	PIT	1903	512	182	.355
Fred Clarke	PIT	1903	427	150	.351
Rogers Hornsby	STL	1923	424	163	.384
Jim Bottomley	STL	1923	523	194	.371
Rogers Hornsby	STL	1925	504	203	.403
Jim Bottomley	STL	1925	619	227	.367
Bubbles Hargrave	CIN	1926	326	115	.353
Cuckoo Christensen	CIN	1926	329	115	.350
Chuck Klein	PHI	1933	606	223	.368
Spud Davis	PHI	1933	495	173	.349
Joe Medwick	STL	1937	633	237	.374
Johnny Mize	STL	1937	560	204	.364
Willie Mays	NY	1954	565	195	.345
Don Mueller	NY	1954	619	212	.342

Teammates Who Finished 1-2 in Batting, Other Leagues

Player	Team	Year	AB	H	BA
Fred Dunlap	STL U	1884	449	185	.412
Orator Shaffer	STL U	1884	467	168	.360
Guy Hecker	LOU AA	1886	345	118	.342
Pete Browning	LOU AA	1886	467	159	.340
Dan Brouthers	BOS AA	1891	486	170	.350
Hugh Duffy	BOS AA	1891	536	180	.336

Most 200-Hit Batters, AL

Player	Team	Year	AB	H	BA
Gee Walker	DET	1937	635	213	.335
Charlie Gehringer	DET	1937	564	209	.371
Pete Fox	DET	1937	628	208	.331
Hank Greenberg	DET	1937	594	200	.337
Eddie Collins	CHI	1920	601	222	.369
Joe Jackson	CHI	1920	570	218	.382
Buck Weaver	CHI	1920	630	210	.333
George Sisler	STL	1920	631	257	.407
Baby Doll Jacobson	STL	1920	609	216	.355
Jack Tobin	STL	1920	593	202	.341
Jack Tobin	STL	1921	671	236	.352
George Sisler	STL	1921	582	216	.371
Baby Doll Jacobson	STL	1921	599	211	.352
Dale Alexander	DET	1929	626	215	.343
Charlie Gehringer	DET	1929	634	215	.339
Roy Johnson	DET	1929	640	201	.314
Robin Yount	MIL	1982	635	210	.331
Cecil Cooper	MIL	1982	654	205	.315
Paul Molitor	MIL	1982	666	201	.302

Most 200-Hit Batters, NL

Player	Team	Year	AB	H	BA
Lefty O'Doul	PHI	1929	638	254	.398
Chuck Klein	PHI	1929	616	219	.356
Fresco Thompson	PHI	1929	623	202	.324
Pinky Whitney	PHI	1929	612	200	.327
Kiki Cuyler	CHI	1930	642	228	.355
Woody English	CHI	1930	638	214	.335
Hack Wilson	CHI	1930	585	208	.356
Chuck Klein	PHI	1930	648	250	.386
Pinky Whitney	PHI	1930	606	207	.342
Lefty O'Doul	PHI	1930	528	202	.383
Bill Terry	NY	1935	596	203	.341
Hank Leiber	NY	1935	613	203	.331
Joe Moore	NY	1935	681	201	.295
Dick Groat	STL	1963	631	201	.319
Curt Flood	STL	1963	662	200	.302
Bill White	STL	1963	658	200	.304

Far left: Chuck Klein's consecutive MVP seasons in 1931–32 totaled 69 HRs, 258 RBIs, and a .342 average. Bill Terry (*left*) collected six 200-hit seasons on his way to a lifetime .341 mark. *Below left*: Sam Crawford's record of 312 triples seems untouchable—no active player has half that many. Don Mattingly (*below*) has averaged 219 hits and 30 home runs over the last three seasons.

Most Hits by Team, Game, AL

Team	Date	H	Inns.	Opp.
CLE	Jul 10, 1932	33	18	PHI
NY	Sep 28, 1923	30		BOS
PHI	May 1, 1929	29		BOS
CLE	Aug 12, 1948	29		STL
CHI	Apr 23, 1955	29		KC
OAK	Jul 1, 1979	29	15	TEX
DET	Sep 29, 1928	28		NY
BOS	Jun 8, 1950	28		STL
NY	Aug 12, 1953	28		WAS

Most Hits by Team, Game, NL since 1900

Team	Date	H	Inns.	Opp.
NY	Jun 9, 1901	31		CIN
NY	Sep 2, 1925	30		PHI
BKN	Aug 22, 1917	28	22	PIT
NY	Jul 10, 1922	28		PIT
NY	Jun 15, 1929	28		PIT
STL	Jul 6, 1929	28		PHI
BKN	Jun 23, 1930	28		PIT
NY	Jul 11, 1931	28		PHI
CHI	Jul 3, 1945	28		BOS
MON	Jun 30, 1978	28		ATL
NY	Jul 4, 1985	28	19	ATL

Most Hits by Team, Game, NL before 1900

Team	Date	H	Opp.
PHI	Aug 17, 1894	36	LOU
CHI	Jul 3, 1882	32	DET
CHI	Jul 3, 1883	32	BUF
WAS	Jun 7, 1892	32	CIN
CIN	Jun 18, 1893	32	LOU
CHI	Jun 29, 1897	32	LOU
CHI	Jul 22, 1876	31	LOU
CHI	Sep 6, 1883	31	DET
NY	Jun 11, 1887	31	WAS
CHI	Jun 18, 1887	31	DET
HAR	May 13, 1876	30	NY
STL	Jun 1, 1895	30	NY
BOS	Sep 3, 1896	30	STL

Most Lopsided Shutouts, AL

Team	Date	Score	Opp.
DET	Sep 15, 1901	21-0	CLE
NY	Aug 13, 1939	21-0	PHI
BOS	Apr 30, 1950	19-0	PHI
CLE	May 18, 1955	19-0	BOS
DET	Apr 29, 1935	18-0	STL
NY	Jul 10, 1936	18-0	CLE
BOS	Jul 11, 1954	18-0	PHI
NY	Apr 24, 1909	17-0	WAS
NY	Jul 6, 1920	17-0	WAS
CHI	Sep 19, 1925	17-0	WAS
NY	Sep 17, 1931	17-0	STL
LA	Aug 23, 1963	17-0	WAS
BAL	Jul 27, 1969	17-0	CHI
CAL	Apr 23, 1980	17-0	MIN

Most Lopsided Shutouts, NL

Team	Date	Score	Opp.
PRO	Aug 21, 1883	28-0	PHI
NY	May 27, 1885	24-0	BUF
PHI	Jun 28, 1887	24-0	IND
PIT	Sep 16, 1975	22-0	CHI
CHI	May 28, 1886	20-0	WAS
PIT	Jul 15, 1893	19-0	WAS
PIT	Jul 8, 1896	19-0	WAS
CHI	Jun 7, 1906	19-0	NY
PIT	Aug 3, 1961	19-0	STL
CHI	May 13, 1969	19-0	SD
LA	Jun 28, 1969	19-0	SD
MON	Jul 30, 1978	19-0	ATL
CHI	Jul 20, 1876	18-0	LOU
BUF	Aug 4, 1884	18-0	DET

Team	Date	Score	Opp.
BOS	Oct 3, 1885	18-0	BUF
PHI	Jul 11, 1910	18-0	PIT
PHI	Jul 14, 1934	18-0	CIN
STL	Jun 10, 1944	18-0	CIN
CIN	Aug 8, 1965	18-0	LA
STL	Jun 1, 1876	17-0	PHI
CHI	Aug 11, 1881	17-0	DET
CHI	Sep 16, 1884	17-0	BOS
BAL	May 7, 1894	17-0	WAS
BOS	Sep 17, 1897	17-0	NY
PHI	Sep 4, 1899	17-0	WAS
STL	Aug 24, 1924	17-0	BKN
PHI	May 20, 1951	17-0	PIT

Most Lopsided Shutouts, Other Leagues

Team	Date	Score	Opp.
CIN AA	Jul 6, 1883	23-0	BAL
STL AA	May 7, 1889	21-0	COL
CIN AA	Aug 10, 1889	20-0	BAL
STL AA	Aug 15, 1886	19-0	BKN
PIT AA	Aug 3, 1886	18-0	BKN
BOS P	Aug 29, 1890	18-0	PIT
NY AA	Jul 4, 1884	17-0	STL
PIT AA	Jul 9, 1885	17-0	NY
BKN AA	Oct 3, 1889	17-0	PHI

Longest Shutouts, AL

Team	Date	Inns.	Score	Opp.	Team	Date	Inns.	Score	Opp.
OAK	Jul 9, 1971	20	1-0	CAL	CHI	Apr 20, 1912	15	0-0	STL
DET	Jul 16, 1909	18	0-0	WAS	STL	Apr 20, 1912	15	0-0	CHI
WAS	Jul 16, 1909	18	0-0	DET	WAS	Jul 3, 1913	15	1-0	BOS
WAS	May 15, 1918	18	1-0	CHI	NY	May 30, 1917	15	2-0	PHI
WAS	Jun 8, 1947	18	1-0	CHI	WAS	Jul 25, 1918	15	1-0	STL
CHI	Sep 13, 1967	17	1-0	CLE	NY	Jul 4, 1925	15	1-0	PHI
BAL	Sep 27, 1974	17	1-0	MIL	WAS	Apr 13, 1926	15	1-0	PHI
CHI	Aug 4, 1910	16	0-0	PHI	CLE	Aug 24, 1935	15	2-0	PHI
PHI	Aug 4, 1910	16	0-0	CHI	CLE	Jun 4, 1948	15	5-0	WAS
STL	Jun 5, 1942	16	1-0	PHI	CLE	May 14, 1961	15	1-0	BAL
BAL	Sep 11, 1959	16	1-0	CHI	LA	Apr 13, 1963	15	1-0	CHI
CAL	Sep 22, 1975	16	3-0	CHI	CHI	Jun 4, 1965	15	2-0	NY
WAS	Aug 14, 1903	15	1-0	STL	NY	Aug 27, 1976	15	5-0	CAL
BOS	May 11, 1904	15	1-0	DET	KC	May 23, 1981	15	1-0	MIN

Longest Shutouts, NL

Team	Date	Inns.	Score	Opp.	Team	Date	Inns.	Score	Opp.
HOU	Apr 15, 1968	24	1-0	NY	MON	Sep 21, 1981	17	1-0	PHI
PIT	Aug 1, 1918	21	2-0	BOS	BKN	Jul 7, 1915	16	0-0	BOS
SF	Sep 1, 1967	21	1-0	CIN	BOS	Jul 7, 1915	16	0-0	BKN
BKN	Sep 11, 1946	19	0-0	CIN	SF	Jul 2, 1963	16	1-0	MIL
CIN	Sep 11, 1946	19	0-0	BKN	PIT	Sep 30, 1964	16	1-0	CIN
PRO	Aug 17, 1882	18	1-0	DET	HOU	Apr 21, 1976	16	1-0	LA
NY	Jul 2, 1933	18	1-0	STL	CIN	Sep 11, 1906	15	0-0	PIT
NY	Oct 2, 1965	18	0-0	PHI	PIT	Sep 11, 1906	15	0-0	CIN
PHI	Oct 2, 1965	18	0-0	NY	CIN	Jun 11, 1915	15	1-0	BKN
PIT	Jun 7, 1972	18	1-0	SD	CIN	Jun 16, 1933	15	1-0	NY
CHI	Sep 21, 1901	17	1-0	BOS	PHI	Jun 22, 1944	15	1-0	BOS
PIT	Aug 22, 1908	17	1-0	BKN	PHI	Aug 7, 1951	15	1-0	BOS
NY	Jul 16, 1920	17	7-0	PIT	NY	Jun 4, 1969	15	1-0	LA
SF	Aug 19, 1968	17	1-0	NY	LA	Apr 14, 1970	15	1-0	NY
HOU	Aug 23, 1980	17	1-0	CHI	SF	Jul 21, 1980	15	2-0	CHI

Teams with Four 20-Game Winners

Player	Team	Year	W
Red Faber	CHI A	1920	23
Lefty Williams	CHI A	1920	22
Eddie Cicotte	CHI A	1920	21
Dickie Kerr	CHI A	1920	21
Dave McNally	BAL A	1971	21
Pat Dobson	BAL A	1971	20
Mike Cuellar	BAL A	1971	20
Jim Palmer	BAL A	1971	20

Teams with Three 20-Game Winners, AL

Player	Team	Year	W
Cy Young	BOS	1903	28
Bill Dinneen	BOS	1903	21
Long Tom Hughes	BOS	1903	20
Cy Young	BOS	1904	26
Bill Dinneen	BOS	1904	23
Jesse Tannehill	BOS	1904	21
Rube Waddell	PHI	1905	26
Eddie Plank	PHI	1905	25
Andy Coakley	PHI	1905	20
Bob Rhoads	CLE	1906	22
Addie Joss	CLE	1906	21
Otto Hess	CLE	1906	20
Wild Bill Donovan	DET	1907	25
Ed Killian	DET	1907	25
George Mullin	DET	1907	20
Doc White	CHI	1907	27
Ed Walsh	CHI	1907	24
Frank Smith	CHI	1907	23
Joe Wood	BOS	1912	34
Hugh Bedient	BOS	1912	20
Buck O'Brien	BOS	1912	20

Player	Team	Year	W
Jim Bagby	CLE	1920	31
Stan Coveleski	CLE	1920	24
Ray Caldwell	CLE	1920	20
Lefty Grove	PHI	1931	31
George Earnshaw	PHI	1931	21
Rube Walberg	PHI	1931	20
Bob Feller	CLE	1951	22
Mike Garcia	CLE	1951	20
Early Wynn	CLE	1951	20
Early Wynn	CLE	1952	23
Mike Garcia	CLE	1952	22
Bob Lemon	CLE	1952	22
Bob Lemon	CLE	1956	20
Herb Score	CLE	1956	20
Early Wynn	CLE	1956	20
Mike Cuellar	BAL	1970	24
Dave McNally	BAL	1970	24
Jim Palmer	BAL	1970	20
Ken Holtzman	OAK	1973	21
Catfish Hunter	OAK	1973	21
Vida Blue	OAK	1973	20

Teams with Three 20-Game Winners, NL since 1900

Player	Team	Year	W
Jack Chesbro	PIT	1902	28
Deacon Phillippe	PIT	1902	20
Jesse Tannehill	PIT	1902	20
Joe McGinnity	NY	1904	35
Christy Mathewson	NY	1904	33
Dummy Taylor	NY	1904	21
Christy Mathewson	NY	1905	31
Red Ames	NY	1905	22
Joe McGinnity	NY	1905	21

Player	Team	Year	W
Christy Mathewson	NY	1913	25
Rube Marquard	NY	1913	23
Jeff Tesreau	NY	1913	22
Fred Toney	NY	1920	21
Art Nehf	NY	1920	21
Jesse Barnes	NY	1920	20
Dolf Luque	CIN	1923	27
Pete Donohue	CIN	1923	21
Eppa Rixey	CIN	1923	20

Strikeout Duos, Season, AL

Player	Team	Year	SO
Nolan Ryan	CAL	1973	383
Bill Singer	CAL	1973	241
Total			624
Nolan Ryan	CAL	1976	327
Frank Tanana	CAL	1976	261
Total			588
Rube Waddell	PHI	1904	349
Eddie Plank	PHI	1904	201
Total			550
Sam McDowell	CLE	1968	283
Luis Tiant	CLE	1968	264
Total			547

Player	Team	Year	SO
Nolan Ryan	CAL	1974	367
Frank Tanana	CAL	1974	180
Total			547
Nolan Ryan	CAL	1977	341
Frank Tanana	CAL	1977	205
Total			546
Mickey Lolich	DET	1971	308
Joe Coleman	DET	1971	236
Total			544
Sam McDowell	CLE	1965	325
Sonny Siebert	CLE	1965	191
Total			516

Strikeout Duos, Season, NL

Player	Team	Year	SO
Sandy Koufax	LA	1965	382
Don Drysdale	LA	1965	210
Total			592
Sandy Koufax	LA	1963	306
Don Drysdale	LA	1963	251
Total			557
Sandy Koufax	LA	1966	317
Don Sutton	LA	1966	209

Player	Team	Year	SO
Total			526
Jim Bunning	PHI	1965	268
Chris Short	PHI	1965	237
Total			505
Mike Scott	HOU	1986	306
Nolan Ryan	HOU	1986	194
Total			500

Best Lefty-Righty Duos

Player	Team	LH/RH	First	Last	W	L
Warren Spahn	BOS N	LH	1951	1963	264	158
Lew Burdette	MIL N	RH	1951	1963	179	120
Total					443	278
Hooks Wiltse	NY N	LH	1904	1914	138	85
Christy Mathewson	NY N	RH	1904	1914	297	120
Total					435	205
Eddie Plank	PHI A	LH	1903	1914	225	118
Chief Bender	PHI A	RH	1903	1914	191	103
Total					416	221
Lefty Gomez	NY A	LH	1930	1942	189	101
Red Ruffing	NY A	RH	1930	1942	219	120
Total					408	221
Hal Newhouser	DET A	LH	1939	1952	200	147
Dizzy Trout	DET A	RH	1939	1952	161	153
Total					361	300
Carl Hubbell	NY N	LH	1931	1942	204	121
Hal Schumacher	NY N	RH	1931	1942	154	116
Total					358	237
Curt Simmons	PHI N	LH	1948	1960	114	110
Robin Roberts	PHI N	RH	1948	1960	233	189
Total					347	299
Sandy Koufax	BKN N	LH	1956	1966	163	85

Best Lefty-Righty Duos ***(cont'd)***

Player	Team	LH/RH	First	Last	W	L
Don Drysdale	LA N	RH	1956	1966	177	134
Total					340	219
Wilbur Cooper	PIT N	LH	1912	1924	202	159
Babe Adams	PIT N	RH	1912	1924	134	105
Total					336	264
Doc White	CHI A	LH	1904	1913	143	108
Ed Walsh	CHI A	RH	1904	1913	190	121
Total					333	229
Jerry Koosman	NY N	LH	1967	1977	137	122
Tom Seaver	NY N	RH	1967	1977	189	110
Total					326	232
Bill Sherdel	STL N	LH	1920	1930	142	110
Jesse Haines	STL N	RH	1920	1930	166	127
Total					308	237
Dave McNally	BAL A	LH	1965	1974	164	94
Jim Palmer	BAL A	RH	1965	1974	129	69
Total					293	163
Eppa Rixey	CIN N	LH	1921	1929	155	120
Dolf Luque	CIN N	RH	1921	1929	125	137
Total					280	257
Jim Kaat	MIN A	LH	1963	1972	151	109
Jim Perry	MIN A	RH	1963	1972	128	90
Total					279	199
Johnny Vander Meer	CIN N	LH	1938	1948	108	101
Bucky Walters	CIN N	RH	1938	1948	160	107
Total					268	208
Mike Flanagan	BAL A	LH	1975	1984	125	87
Jim Palmer	BAL A	RH	1975	1984	139	83
Total					264	170
Paul Splittorff	KC A	LH	1974	1983	125	107
Dennis Leonard	KC A	RH	1974	1983	136	93
Total					261	200
Tommy Bridges	DET A	LH	1933	1942	155	100
Schoolboy Rowe	DET A	RH	1933	1942	105	62
Total					260	162
Herb Pennock	NY A	LH	1923	1930	135	75
Waite Hoyt	NY A	RH	1923	1930	119	73
Total					254	148
Lefty Grove	PHI A	LH	1928	1933	152	41
George Earnshaw	PHI A	RH	1928	1933	98	58
Total					250	99

Jim Palmer (*above left*) led a stellar Baltimore pitching staff with eight 20-win seasons and a .638 winning percentage. Teammate Mike Cuellar (*above*) went 24–8 with 21 complete games for the O's during the 1970 championship season. Eddie Cicotte (*left*) won 28 and 29 games, respectively, in 1917 and 1919, leading the White Sox to two pennants before being barred from the game by Judge Landis for his role in throwing the Series.

Player Index

Hank Aaron
Most Grand Slams, Career 3
Most Grand Slams, Season, NL 4
Most Home Runs, Season, NL 7, 8
Most Home Runs, Career 9
Best Home Run Ratio, Career 10
Most Home Runs by Position, Career, NL 10
Two Home Runs in One Game Most Often 12
Three Home Runs in One Game, NL 18
Most Extra-Inning Home Runs, Career 23
Thirty Home Runs with 30 Stolen Bases, Season, NL 24
Brothers with Most Home Runs, Career 25
Home Runs by Brothers in One Game 26
Most Total Bases, Season, NL 30
Most Times Walked, Game, NL 32
Two Legs of Triple Crown, NL 48
The 3,000-Hit Club 54
The 3,000th Hit 54
Most Runs, Career 60
Most RBIs, Career 61
Most Runs Produced, Career 62
Longest Hitting Streaks, NL 71
Fewest Games Missed (10-Year Period) 72
Retired Numbers, AL 182
Retired Numbers, NL 183
Best-Hitting Brothers 189
Four Consecutive Home Runs, Team 196
Three Consecutive Home Runs, Team, NL 199
Most Home Runs in One Inning, Team, NL 201
Most Home Runs by Team, Game, NL 205
Most 40-Home Run Hitters, NL 206
Most 30-Home Run Hitters, NL 208
Most 20-Home Run Hitters, NL 208
Home Run Trios, Season, NL 209
Home Run Duos, Season, NL (25 each) 210
Home Run Duos, Career, NL 211
.300-Hitting Outfields, NL 221

Tommie Aaron
Brothers with Most Home Runs, Career 25
Home Runs by Brothers in One Game 26
Best-Hitting Brothers 189

Don Aase
Most Saves, Season, AL 122
Most Wins Plus Saves, Season 123

Ted Abernathy
Most Saves, Career 121
Most Saves, Season, NL 122

Ed Acosta
Shutout in First Start in Majors, NL 84

Jerry Adair
Easiest to Double Up, Career (Min. 1000 G) 41
Fewest Errors by Position, Season, AL (Min. 150 G, excl. Pitchers) 147
Most Consecutive Errorless Games by Position, AL 148
Three Consecutive Home Runs, Team, AL 196

Babe Adams
Most Shutouts, Career 79
Shutout with Most Hits Allowed, NL 86
Best Control Pitchers, Career 126
Most Innings Pitched, Game, NL 128
Fewest Base Runners per Nine Innings, Career (Min. 1,500 IP) 129
Most Wins after Age 40 134
ERA Under 2.00, Rookie, NL since 1900 (Min. 130 IP) 169
Best Lefty-Righty Duos 229

Bobby Adams
Most Consecutive Pinch Hits 70
Fathers and Sons in Baseball 190
Home Runs by First Two Batters in Game, NL 194

Karl Adams
Most At-Bats with No Hits, Pitcher, Season since 1900 141

Mike Adams
Fathers and Sons in Baseball 190

Sparky Adams
Most .300 Hitters, Season, NL (300 AB each) 218

Joe Adcock
Most Grand Slams, Career 3
Most Pinch-Hit Home Runs, Career 5
Best Home Run Ratio, Career 10
Four Home Runs in One Game, NL 20
Most Home Runs in Final Season 24
Most Extra-Base Hits, Game, NL 26
Most Total Bases, Game, NL 30
Easiest to Double Up, Career (Min. 1000 G) 41
Grounded into Most Double Plays, Game, NL 43
Four Consecutive Home Runs, Team 196
Three Consecutive Home Runs, Team, NL 199
Most Home Runs in One Inning, Team, NL 201
Most Home Runs by Team, Game, NL 205
Most 30-Home Run Hitters, NL 208
Home Run Trios, Season, NL 209

Tommie Agee
Grounded into Most Double Plays, Game, NL 43
Easiest to Strike Out, Career (Min. 1,000 G) 44
Cycle Hitters, NL 50

Hank Aguirre
Worst-Hitting Pitchers, Career (Min. 100 AB) 144

Willie Aikens
Grand Slam In Two Consecutive Games, AL 3

Eddie Ainsmith
The Worst Hitters (Min. 2,500 AB) 52
Stole 2nd, 3rd, and Home in One Game, AL 66

Jack Aker
Most Saves, Career 121
Most Saves, Season, AL 122

Most Wins Plus Saves, Season 123

Dale Alexander

Longest Hitting Streaks, AL 70
Two Hundred or More Hits, Rookie, AL 163
Most Doubles, Rookie, AL 165
Most Triples, Rookie, AL 165
One Hundred or More RBIs, Rookie, AL 166
Highest Batting Average, Rookie, AL (Min. 300 AB) 167
Most 200-Hit Batters, AL 223

Grover Alexander

Most Shutouts, Career 79
Most Shutout Losses, Career 80
Most Shutouts, Season, NL 81
Most Complete 1-0 Wins, Career 94
Thirty-Game Winners, NL since 1900 101
Most 20-Win Seasons 101
Most Wins, Career 102
The 300-Win Club 103
Most Wins by Age, Season, NL since 1900 104
Most Strikeouts, Season, NL since 1900 106, 107
Two Complete Game Wins in One Day, NL since 1900 124
Best Control Pitchers, Career 126
Lowest ERA, Season, NL 127
Triple-Crown Pitchers, NL (most wins, lowest ERA, most strikeouts) 129
Fewest Base Runners per Nine Innings, Career (Min. 1,500 IP) 129
Most Complete Games, Season, NL since 1900 132
Most Innings Pitched, Season, NL sicne 1900 132
Most Wins after Age 40 134
Most Hits, Pitcher, Career 139
Twenty or More Wins, Rookie, NL since 1900 168
Three Hundred or More Innings Pitched, Rookie, NL since 1900 169
Most Strikeouts, Rookie, NL since 1900 169
Most Complete Games, Rookie, NL since 1900 170
Most Shutouts, Rookie, NL since 1900 170

Bernie Allen

Best Double-Play Combinations, Season 149
Most Home Runs by Team, Game, AL 202

Dick Allen

Most Home Runs, Season, NL 8
Best Home Run Ratio, Career 10
Two Home Runs in One Game Most Often 12
Three Home Runs in One Game, NL 18
Brothers with Most Home Runs, Career 25
Most Times Walked, Game, NL 32
Most Times Struck Out, Game, NL 34
Easiest to Strike Out, Career (Min. 1,000 G) 44
Two Legs of Triple Crown, AL 46
Two Hundred or More Hits, Rookie, NL 163
Most Doubles, Rookie, NL 165
Three or More Brothers in Baseball 187
Best-Hitting Brothers 189

Frank Allen

No-Hitters, Other Leagues 91

Hank Allen

Brothers with Most Home Runs, Career 25
Three or More Brothers in Baseball 187
Best-Hitting Brothers 189

Johnny Allen

Most Consecutive Wins, AL 115

Ron Allen

Brothers with Most Home Runs, Career 25
Three or More Brothers in Baseball 187
Best-Hitting Brothers 189

Gene Alley

Best Double-Play Combinations, Season 149
Most Double Plays, Shortstop, Season, NL 151

Bob Allison

Most Grand Slams, Season, AL 4
Best Home Run Ratio, Career 10
Three Home Runs in One Game, AL 14
Most Times Struck Out, Game, AL 33
Easiest to Strike Out, Career (Min. 1,000 G) 44
Thirty or More Home Runs, Rookie, AL 163
Two Grand Slams in One Inning, Team 192
Four Consecutive Home Runs, Team 196
Most Home Runs in One Inning, Team, AL 200
Most Home Runs by Team, Game, AL 202
Most 30-Home Run Hitters, AL 207
Most 20-Home Run Hitters, AL 208
Home Run Trios, Season, AL 209
Home Run Duos, Season, AL (25 each) 210
Home Run Duos, Career, AL 211

Mel Almada

Longest Hitting Streaks, AL 70

Bill Almon

Most Assists, Shortstop, Game 159

Luis Aloma

Undefeated Seasons (5 or more wins) 101

Sandy Alomar

Hardest to Double Up, Career (Min. 1,000 G) 42
Most Consecutive Games Played 71

Felipe Alou

Leadoff Home Runs in Two Consecutive Games, NL 21
Most Leadoff Home Runs, Career 22
Brothers with Most Home Runs, Career 25
Home Runs by Brothers in One Game 26
Most Consecutive Hits, NL 74
Three or More Brothers in Baseball 187
Best-Hitting Brothers 189
Three Consecutive Home Runs, Team, NL 199
Most Home Runs in One Inning, Team, NL 200
Most Home Runs by Team, Game, NL 204
Most 30-Home Run Hitters, NL 208
Most 20-Home Run Hitters, NL 208
Home Run Trios, Season, NL 209
.300-Hitting Outfields, NL 221

Neal Ball
Unassisted Triple Plays 149

Dave Bancroft
Most Hits, Game, NL 36
Cycle Hitters, NL 50
Most Assists, Shortstop, Game 159

Chris Bando
Brothers with Most Home Runs, Career 25

Sal Bando
Most Home Runs by Position, Career, AL 10
Brothers with Most Home Runs, Career 25
Most Times Walked, Game, AL 32
Three Consecutive Home Runs, Team, AL 197
Most Home Runs by Team, Game, AL 203
Home Run Duos, Career, AL 211

Dan Bankhead
Home Run in First Appearance in Majors, NL 11

Ernie Banks
Most Grand Slams, Career 3
Most Grand Slams, Season, NL 4
Most Home Runs, Season, NL 7, 8
Most Home Runs, Career 9
Best Home Run Ratio, Career 10
Most Home Runs by Position, Career, NL 10
Most Home Runs by Position, Season, NL 11
Two Home Runs in One Game Most Often 12
Three Home Runs in One Game, NL 18
Most Triples, Game, NL 29
Two Legs of Triple Crown, NL 48
Most RBIs, Career 61
Most Consecutive Games Played 71
Most Putouts in Nine Innings, First Baseman 157
Career Spent With One Team (15 or more years) 181
Retired Numbers, NL 183
Three Consecutive Home Runs, Team, NL 199
Most Home Runs by Team, Game, NL 205

Floyd Bannister
Most Strikeouts, Season, AL 105
Most Strikeouts per Nine Innings, Career (Min. 1,500 IP) 114

Jimmy Bannon
Grand Slam In Two Consecutive Games, NL 3

Steve Barber
Easiest Pitcher to Strike Out, Season since 1900 141

Turner Barber
.300-Hitting Outfields, NL 220

George Barclay
.300-Hitting Outfields, NL 220

Jesse Barfield
Most Home Runs, Season, AL 7
Three Consecutive Home Runs, Team, AL 197

Len Barker
No-Hitters, AL (9 innings or more) 88
Perfect Games (9 innings or more) 94

Sam Barkley
Cycle Hitters, Other Leagues 51

Jesse Barnes
No-Hitters, NL (9 innings or more) 89
Best Control Pitchers, Career 126
Pitchers Who Stole Home, NL since 1900 140
Pitching Brothers, Same Team, NL 186
Most Wins by Brothers 187
Teams with Three 20-Game Winners, NL since 1900 227

Red Barnes
Most Triples, Rookie, AL 165
.300-Hitting Outfields, AL 219

Ross Barnes
Most Hits, Game, NL 35

Virgil Barnes
Pitching Brothers, Same Team, NL 186
Most Wins by Brothers 187

Rex Barney
No-Hitters, NL (9 innings or more) 89

Clyde Barnhart
Longest Hitting Streaks, NL 71
Fathers and Sons in Baseball 190
Most 100-RBI Hitters, NL 212
Most .300 Hitters, Season, NL (300 AB each) 218
.300-Hitting Outfields, NL 220

Vic Barnhart
Fathers and Sons in Baseball 190

Cuno Barragan
Home Run in First Appearance in Majors, NL 11

Bill Barrett
.300-Hitting Outfields, AL 219

Dick Bartell
Most Doubles, Game, NL 27

John Bateman
Struck Out Twice in One Inning, NL 33
The Worst Hitters (Min. 2,500 AB) 52
Most No-Hitters Caught, Career 155

Frank Bates
Worst Won-Lost Record, Season (12 or more losses) 95
Most Consecutive Losses, NL 116

Johnny Bates
Home Run in First Appearance in Majors, NL 11
Cycle Hitters, NL 50

Ray Bates
Most RBIs in One Inning, AL 63

Earl Battey
Easiest to Double Up, Career (Min. 1000 G) 41
Most Games Caught, Career 153

Hank Bauer
Leadoff Home Runs in Two Consecutive Games, AL 21
Most Leadoff Home Runs, Career 22
Most Consecutive Hits, AL 73
Home Runs by First Two Batters in Game, AL 194

Harry Bay
Longest Hitting Streaks, AL 70
Most Putouts, Outfielder, Game 156

Don Baylor
Most Grand Slams, Career 3
Three Home Runs in One Game, AL 15
Most Consecutive Hits, AL 73
Home Runs in Most Consecutive At-Bats, AL 76
Three Consecutive Home Runs, Team, AL 197

Charlie Beamon
Shutout in First Start in Majors, AL 83
Fathers and Sons in Baseball 190

Charlie Beamon
Fathers and Sons in Baseball 190

Gene Bearden
Best-Hitting Pitchers, Season, AL 142
Twenty or More Wins, Rookie, AL 168
Most Shutouts, Rookie, AL 170

Ginger Beaumont
Most Triples, Game, NL 28
Most Hits, Game, NL 36
Most Runs, Game, NL 60
Highest Batting Average, Rookie, NL (Min. 300 AB) 167
.300-Hitting Outfields, NL 220

Johnny Beazley
Twenty or More Wins, Rookie, NL since 1900 168

Clyde Beck
Most Home Runs in One Inning, Team, NL 200

Glenn Beckert
Longest Hitting Streaks, NL 71
Most Home Runs by Team, Game, NL 206

Jake Beckley
Three Home Runs in One Game, NL 17
Most Triples, Game, NL 28
Most Runs Produced, Career 62
Most Putouts in Nine Innings, First Baseman 157

Julio Becquer
Most Pinch Hits, Season, AL 68

Hugh Bedient
Twenty or More Wins, Rookie, AL 168
Teams with Three 20-Game Winners, AL 227

Steve Bedrosian
Worst-Hitting Pitchers, Career (Min. 100 AB) 144

Fred Beene
Undefeated Seasons (5 or more wins) 101

Mark Belanger
The Worst Hitters (Min. 2,500 AB) 52
Best Double-Play Combinations, Season 150

Bo Belinsky
No-Hitters, AL (9 innings or more) 88
Rookie No-Hitters, AL 167

Beau Bell
.300-Hitting Outfields, AL 220

Buddy Bell
Fathers and Sons in Baseball 190

George Bell
Three Consecutive Home Runs, Team, AL 197

Gus Bell
Three Home Runs in One Game, NL 18
Cycle Hitters, NL 50
Fathers and Sons in Baseball 190
Three Consecutive Home Runs, Team, NL 198, 199
Most Home Runs by Team, Game, NL 205
Most 20-Home Run Hitters, NL 208
Home Run Trios, Season, NL 209

Hi Bell
Two Complete Game Wins in One Day, NL since 1900 124
Worst-Hitting Pitchers, Career (Min. 100 AB) 144

Jay Bell
Home Run in First Appearance in Majors, AL 11

Kevin Bell
Most Times Struck Out, Game, AL 33

Les Bell
Three Home Runs in One Game, NL 17
Most Triples, Game, NL 29
Most Total Bases, Game, NL 30
Most Times Struck Out, Game, NL 34

Johnny Bench
Most Grand Slams, Career 3
Most Home Runs, Season, NL 7, 8
Best Home Run Ratio, Career 10
Most Home Runs by Position, Career, NL 10
Three Home Runs in One Game, NL 19
Most Times Walked, Game, NL 32
Two Legs of Triple Crown, NL 48
Most Games Caught, Season 152
Most Games Caught, Career 153
Most Doubles, Rookie, NL 165
Career Spent With One Team (15 or more years) 181
Retired Numbers, NL 183
Most Home Runs by Team, Game, NL 205
Most 40-Home Run Hitters, NL 206
Most 30-Home Run Hitters, NL 208
Home Run Trios, Season, NL 209
Home Run Duos, Season, NL (25 each) 210
Home Run Duos, Career, NL 211

Chief Bender
Most Shutouts, Career 79
No-Hitters, AL (9 innings or more) 87
Best Won-Lost Record, Season, AL (20 or more wins) 96
Most Wins, Career 102
Most Consecutive Wins, AL 115
Fewest Base Runners per Nine Innings, Career (Min. 1,500 IP) 129
Most Complete Games, Rookie, AL 170
Best Lefty-Righty Duos 228

Ray Benge
Shutout in First Start in Majors, AL 83

Juan Beniquez
Three Home Runs in One Game, AL 15

Charlie Bennett
Most Home Runs by Team, Game, NL 204

Dave Bennett
Pitching Brothers, Same Team, NL 186

Dennis Bennett
Pitching Brothers, Same Team, NL 186

Jack Bentley
Shutout in First Start in Majors, AL 83
Best-Hitting Pitchers, Season, NL since 1900 142

Al Benton
Worst-Hitting Pitchers, Career (Min. 100 AB) 144

Rube Benton
Shutout with Most Hits Allowed, NL 86
Pitchers Who Stole Home, NL since 1900 140

Joe Benz
No-Hitters, AL (9 innings or more) 87

Bill Bergen
The Worst Hitters (Min. 2,500 AB) 52
Most No-Hitters Caught, Career 154

Boze Berger
Home Runs by First Two Batters in Game, AL 194

Wally Berger
Two Legs of Triple Crown, NL 47
Most Assists, Outfielder, Game 156
Thirty or More Home Runs, Rookie, NL 163
One Hundred or More RBIs, Rookie, NL 166

Tony Bernazard
Switch-Hit Home Runs in One Game, AL 23

Bill Bernhard
Most Complete Games, Season, AL 131

Carlos Bernier
Most Triples, Game, NL 29

Dale Berra
Fathers and Sons in Baseball 190

Yogi Berra
Most Pinch-Hit Grand Slams, Career 6
Most Home Runs by Position, Career, AL 10
Most Consecutive Errorless Games by Position, AL 148
Most Games Caught, Career 153
Most No-Hitters Caught, Career 154
Pennant-Winning Rookie Managers, AL 171
Retired Numbers, AL 182
Pennant-Winning Managers in AL and NL 184
Fathers and Sons in Baseball 190
Most Home Runs by Team, Game, AL 203
Most 20-Home Run Hitters, AL 208
Home Run Duos, Season, AL (25 each) 210
Home Run Duos, Career, AL 211

Charlie Berry
Fathers and Sons in Baseball 190

Charlie Berry
Fathers and Sons in Baseball 190

Joe Berry
Fathers and Sons in Baseball 190

Joe Berry
Fathers and Sons in Baseball 190

Bob Bescher
Most Stolen Bases, Season, NL 65
Most Stolen Bases, Career 66
Stolen Base Duos, Season, NL 216, 217

Kurt Bevacqua
Most Pinch Hits, Season, NL 69
Most Pinch Hits, Career 69

Jim Bibby
No-Hitters, AL (9 innings or more) 88
Rookie No-Hitters, AL 167

Vern Bickford
No-Hitters, NL (9 innings or more) 89

Lou Bierbauer
Most Putouts, Second Baseman, Game 157
Most Home Runs in One Inning, Team, NL 200
Most Home Runs by Team, Game, NL 204

Carson Bigbee
Most Hits, Game, NL 36

Larry Biittner
Most Pinch Hits, Career 69
Three Consecutive Home Runs, Team, NL 199
Most Home Runs by Team, Game, NL 206

Steve Bilko
Most Times Struck Out, Game, NL 34

Babe Birrer
Two Home Runs in One Game, Pitcher, AL 136

Charlie Bishop
Most Consecutive Losses, AL 115

Max Bishop
Most Times Walked, Game, AL 31
More Walks than Hits, Season, AL 55

Del Bissonette
One Hundred or More RBIs, Rookie, NL 166

Don Black
No-Hitters, AL (9 innings or more) 87

Ewell Blackwell
No-Hitters, NL (9 innings or more) 89
Most Consecutive Wins, NL 115
Most Shutouts, Rookie, NL since 1900 170

Ray Blades
.300-Hitting Outfields, NL 220

Paul Blair
Three Home Runs in One Game, AL 15
Most Home Runs by Team, Game, AL 203

Johnny Blanchard
Home Runs in Most Consecutive At-Bats, AL 76
Most 20-Home Run Hitters, AL 208

Fred Blanding
Shutout in First Start in Majors, AL 83

Homer Blankenship
Pitching Brothers, Same Team, AL 186

Ted Blankenship
Pitching Brothers, Same Team, AL 186

Don Blasingame
Hardest to Double Up, Career (Min. 1,000 G) 42
No-Hit Spoilers - The Only Hit Most Often 56
Best Double-Play Combinations, Season 150

Curt Blefary
Three Home Runs in One Game, AL 14
Three Consecutive Home Runs, Team, AL 196

Lu Blue
Most Combined Hits and Walks, Season, AL 40

Vida Blue
Most Shutouts, Career 80
No-Hitters, AL (9 innings or more) 88
Most Wins, Career 102
Most Strikeouts, Season, AL 105
Most Strikeouts in Extra-Inning Game, AL 112
Most Games with 10 or More Strikeouts, Career 114
Rookie No-Hitters, AL 167
Teams with Three 20-Game Winners, AL 227

Ossie Bluege
Most Times Struck Out, Game, AL 33
Career Spent With One Team (15 or more years) 181

Bert Blyleven
Most Shutouts, Career 79
No-Hitters, AL (9 innings or more) 88
Most Complete 1-0 Wins, Career 94
Most Wins, Career 102
Most Strikeouts, Season, AL 105, 106
Most Strikeouts, Career 108
Most Games with 10 or More Strikeouts, Career 114
Most Strikeouts per Nine Innings, Career (Min. 1,500 IP) 114
Fewest Base Runners per Nine Innings, Career (Min. 1,500 IP) 130

John Boccabella
Two Home Runs in One Inning, NL 12
Most RBIs in One Inning, NL 63

Mike Boddicker
Most Shutouts, Rookie, AL 170

Ping Bodie
One Hundred or More RBIs, Rookie, AL 166

Wade Boggs
Most Combined Hits and Walks, Season, AL 39, 40
Longest Hitting Streaks, AL 70
Highest Batting Average, Rookie, AL (Min. 300 AB) 167
Home Runs by First Two Batters in Game, AL 194

Joe Boley
.300 Average in Rookie Year Only, AL 164

Most .300 Hitters, Season, AL (300 AB each) 217

Jim Bolger
Most Pinch Hits, Season, NL 69

Bobby Bolin
Most Strikeouts per Nine Innings, Career (Min. 1,500 IP) 114

Tommy Bond
Most Shutouts, Career 80
Most Shutouts, Season, NL 81
Most Shutout Losses, Season, NL 81
Triple-Crown Pitchers, NL (most wins, lowest ERA, most strikeouts) 129

Barry Bonds
Fathers and Sons in Baseball 190

Bobby Bonds
Grand Slam in First Major League Game 4
Leadoff Home Runs in Two Consecutive Games, NL 21
Most Leadoff Home Runs, Career 22
Thirty Home Runs with 30 Stolen Bases, Season, AL 24
Thirty Home Runs with 30 Stolen Bases, Season, NL 24
Easiest to Strike Out, Career (Min. 1,000 G) 44
Most Stolen Bases, Career 66
Unassisted Double Plays, Outfielder 152
Fathers and Sons in Baseball 190
Three Consecutive Home Runs, Team, AL 197
Three Consecutive Home Runs, Team, NL 199

Bill Bonham
Four Strikeouts in One Inning, NL 109

Ernie Bonham
Best Won-Lost Record, Season, AL (20 or more wins) 96
Best Control Pitchers, Career 126
Fewest Base Runners per Nine Innings, Career (Min. 1,500 IP) 130

Frank Bonner
Most Doubles, Game, NL 27

Zeke Bonura
Grounded into Most Double Plays, Game, AL 43
Grounded into Most Double Plays, Game, NL 43
One Hundred or More RBIs, Rookie, AL 166
Most Home Runs in One Inning, Team, NL 200
Most Home Runs by Team, Game, NL 204

Buddy Booker
Most Home Runs by Team, Game, AL 203

Bob Boone
Most Games Caught, Career 153
Fathers and Sons in Baseball 190

Ray Boone
Most Grand Slams, Season, AL 4
Fathers and Sons in Baseball 190

Pedro Borbon
Most Relief Wins, Season, NL 119

Frenchy Bordagaray
Most Pinch Hits, Season, NL 68

Steve Boros
Three Home Runs in One Game, AL 14
Three Consecutive Home Runs, Team, AL 196

Thad Bosley
Most Pinch Hits, Season, NL 68

Dick Bosman
No-Hitters, AL (9 innings or more) 88

Lyman Bostock
Cycle Hitters, AL 49
Batting Champion by Widest Margin, AL 56
Most Putouts, Outfielder, Game 156
Teammates Who Finished 1-2 in Batting, AL 222

Dave Boswell
Most Strikeouts, Season, AL 106

Ken Boswell
Most Pinch Hits, Season, NL 68

Jim Bottomley
Most Grand Slams, Season, NL 4
Most Triples, Game, NL 29
Twenty Doubles, 20 Triples, and 20 Home Runs, Season, NL 29
Most Hits, Game, NL 36
Two Legs of Triple Crown, NL 47
Cycle Hitters, NL 50
Most RBIs, Game, NL 64
Most .300 Hitters, Season, NL (300 AB each) 218
Teammates Who Finished 1-2 in Batting, NL 222

Lou Boudreau
Most Extra-Base Hits, Game, AL 26
Most Doubles, Game, AL 27
Best Double-Play Combinations, Season 149, 150
Most Double Plays, Shortstop, Season, AL 151
Most Assists, Shortstop, Game 159
Retired Numbers, AL 182
Most Wins, Manager, Career 184

Larry Bowa
Fewest Errors by Position, Season, NL (Min. 150 G, excl. Pitchers) 147
Best Double-Play Combinations, Season 149, 150

Sam Bowens
Most Home Runs in One Inning, Team, AL 200
Most Home Runs by Team, Game, AL 203

Bob Bowman
Worst-Hitting Pitchers, Career (Min. 100 AB) 144

Joe Bowman
Best-Hitting Pitchers, Season, NL since 1900 142

Bob Boyd
Most Pinch Hits, Season, AL 68

Clete Boyer
Brothers with Most Home Runs, Career 25
Three or More Brothers in Baseball 187
Best-Hitting Brothers 190
Most Home Runs by Team, Game, NL 205

Cloyd Boyer
Three or More Brothers in Baseball 187
Best-Hitting Brothers 190

Ken Boyer
Brothers with Most Home Runs, Career 25
Cycle Hitters, NL 50
Longest Hitting Streaks, NL 71
Retired Numbers, NL 183
Three or More Brothers in Baseball 187
Best-Hitting Brothers 189
Three Consecutive Home Runs, Team, NL 199
Home Run Duos, Career, NL 211

Buzz Boyle
Longest Hitting Streaks, NL 71

Jack Boyle
Most Hits, Game, NL 36

Bill Bradley
Most Triples, Game, AL 28
Cycle Hitters, AL 49
Longest Hitting Streaks, AL 70
Three Consecutive Home Runs, Team, AL 196

George Bradley
Most Shutouts, Season, NL 81
No-Hitters, NL (9 innings or more) 88

Phil Bradley
Most Home Runs by Team, Game, AL 203

Tom Bradley
Most Strikeouts, Season, AL 105

King Brady
Shutout in First Start in Majors, AL 83

Dave Brain
Most Triples, Game, NL 29

Erv Brame
Best-Hitting Pitchers, Season, NL since 1900 142

Kitty Bransfield
Most Assists, First Baseman, Game 157

Steve Braun
Most Pinch Hits, Season, NL 69
Most Pinch Hits, Career 69

Harry Brecheen
Fewest Base Runners per Nine Innings, Career (Min. 1,500 IP) 130

Marv Breeding
Best Double-Play Combinations, Season 150

Ted Breitenstein
No-Hitters, NL (9 innings or more) 89
No-Hitters, Other Leagues 91
Rookie No-Hitters, Other Leagues 168

Lynn Brenton
Struck Out Twice in One Inning, NL 33

Roger Bresnahan
Shutout in First Start in Majors, NL 84

Rube Bressler
Longest Hitting Streaks, NL 71
ERA Under 2.00, Rookie, AL (Min. 130 IP) 169
.300-Hitting Outfields, NL 220, 221

George Brett
Three Home Runs in One Game, AL 15
Twenty Doubles, 20 Triples, and 20 Home Runs, Season, AL 29
Cycle Hitters, AL 49
More RBIs than Games Played, Season, AL 65
Longest Hitting Streaks, AL 70
Three Consecutive Home Runs, Team, AL 197
Teammates Who Finished 1-2 in Batting, AL 222

Marv Breuer
Worst-Hitting Pitchers, Career (Min. 100 AB) 144

Jim Brewer
Most Saves, Career 121
Most Grand Slams Allowed, Career 133

Fred Brickell
Fathers and Sons in Baseball 190

Fritzie Brickell
Fathers and Sons in Baseball 190

Tommy Bridges
Most Walks in One Game, AL 113
Career Spent With One Team (15 or more years) 181
Best Lefty-Righty Duos 229

John Briggs
Most Hits, Game, AL 35

Ed Brinkman

The Worst Hitters (Min. 2,500 AB) 52
Fewest Errors by Position, Season, AL (Min. 150 G, excl. Pitchers) 147
Most Consecutive Errorless Games by Position, AL 148
Most Home Runs in One Inning, Team, AL 200

Johnny Broaca

Most Times Struck Out, Game, AL 33
Worst-Hitting Pitchers, Career (Min. 100 AB) 144

Pete Broberg

Worst-Hitting Pitchers, Career (Min. 100 AB) 144

Lou Brock

Most Leadoff Home Runs, Career 22
Twenty Home Runs with 50 Stolen Bases, Season 24
.300 Batting Average in Final Season (Min. 100 G) 39
Hardest to Double Up, Career (Min. 1,000 G) 42
Cycle Hitters, NL 50
The 3,000-Hit Club 54
The 3,000th Hit 54
No-Hit Spoilers - The Only Hit Most Often 58
Batted .300 after Age 40 59
Most Stolen Bases, Season, NL 65
Most Stolen Bases, Career 66
Longest Hitting Streaks, NL 71
Retired Numbers, NL 183
Stolen Base Duos, Season, NL 216
.300-Hitting Outfields, NL 221

Steve Brodie

Most Hits, Game, NL 36
Most Consecutive Games Played 71
Unassisted Double Plays, Outfielder 152

Jack Brohamer

Cycle Hitters, AL 49

Hubie Brooks

Most Home Runs in One Inning, Team, NL 201

Dan Brouthers

Three Home Runs in One Game, NL 17
Most Total Bases, Game, NL 30
Most Hits, Game, NL 36
Two Legs of Triple Crown, NL 47
Highest Batting Average, Career 53
Most Runs Produced, Season, NL 62
Most Home Runs by Team, Game, NL 204
Teammates Who Finished 1-2 in Batting, Other Leagues 223

Frank Brower

Most Hits, Game, AL 35

Boardwalk Brown

Most Walks in One Game, AL 113

Buster Brown

Most Consecutive Losses, NL 116

Clint Brown

Most Relief Wins, Season, AL 118

Dick Brown

Three Consecutive Home Runs, Team, AL 196

Eddie Brown

Most Consecutive Games Played 71
.300-Hitting Outfields, NL 220

Elmer Brown

Shutout in First Start in Majors, AL 83

Gates Brown

Most Pinch-Hit Home Runs, Career 5
Pinch-Hit Home Run in First At-Bat in Majors, AL 6
Home Run in First Appearance in Majors, AL 11
Most Pinch Hits, Season, AL 68
Most Pinch Hits, Career 69

Larry Brown

The Worst Hitters (Min. 2,500 AB) 52
Four Consecutive Home Runs, Team 196
Most Home Runs in One Inning, Team, AL 200

Mace Brown

Most Relief Wins, Season, NL 119

Three Finger Brown

Most Shutouts, Career 79
Most Shutouts, Season, NL 81
Shutout with Most Hits Allowed, NL 86
Most Complete 1-0 Wins, Career 94
Most 1-0 Losses, Career 95
Best Won-Lost Record, Season, NL (20 or more wins) 97
Most Wins, Career 102
Most Wins by Age, Season, NL since 1900 104
Best Control Pitchers, Career 126
Lowest ERA, Season, NL 127
Fewest Base Runners per Nine Innings, Career (Min. 1,500 IP) 129

Tom Brown

Most Leadoff Home Runs, Career 22
Most Triples, Game, Other Leagues 29
Home Runs by First Two Batters in Game, Other Leagues 195

Tommy Brown

Three Home Runs in One Game, NL 17

Pete Browning

Cycle Hitters, Other Leagues 51
The .400 Hitters, Other Leagues 53
Highest Batting Average, Career 53
Teammates Who Finished 1-2 in Batting, Other Leagues 223

Tom Browning
Twenty or More Wins, Rookie, NL since 1900 168

Bill Brubaker
Grounded into Most Double Plays, Game, NL 43
One Hundred or More RBIs, Rookie, NL 166

Bob Bruce
Most Shutout Losses, Season, NL 81
Perfect Innings, NL (3 strikeouts on 9 pitches) 110

Earle Brucker
Fathers and Sons in Baseball 190

Earle Brucker
Fathers and Sons in Baseball 190

Tom Brunansky
Three Consecutive Home Runs, Team, AL 197
Most 20-Home Run Hitters, AL 208

George Brunet
Worst-Hitting Pitchers, Career (Min. 100 AB) 144

Bill Bruton
Most Leadoff Home Runs, Career 22
Most Doubles, Game, AL 27
Hardest to Double Up, Career (Min. 1,000 G) 42

Billy Bryan
Three Consecutive Home Runs, Team, AL 196

Clay Bryant
Grand Slams, Pitcher, NL 138

Garland Buckeye
Two Home Runs in One Game, Pitcher, AL 135

Bill Buckner
Most Home Runs by Team, Game, NL 206

Don Buddin
Three Consecutive Home Runs, Team, AL 196

Steve Buechele
Most Home Runs by Team, Game, AL 203

Charlie Buffinton
Most 20-Win Seasons 101
Most Wins, Career 102
Most Strikeouts, Season before 1900 107
Most Strikeouts in Nine-Inning Game, NL 111
Most Consecutive Wins, NL 115
Most Consecutive Strikeouts, NL 116

Don Buford
Most Leadoff Home Runs, Career 22
Switch-Hit Home Runs in One Game, AL 23
Most Times Struck Out, Game, AL 33
Hardest to Double Up, Career (Min. 1,000 G) 42

Bob Buhl
Most Times Struck Out, Pitcher, Career since 1900 141
Most At-Bats with No Hits, Pitcher, Season since 1900 141
Worst-Hitting Pitchers, Career (Min. 100 AB) 144

Al Bumbry
Leadoff Home Runs in Two Consecutive Games, AL 21
Most Leadoff Home Runs, Career 22
Most Triples, Game, AL 28
No-Hit Spoilers - The Only Hit Most Often 57
Highest Batting Average, Rookie, AL (Min. 300 AB) 167

Wally Bunker
Most Wins by Age, Season, AL 103
Worst-Hitting Pitchers, Career (Min. 100 AB) 144

Jim Bunning
Most Shutouts, Career 80
Most Shutout Losses, Career 80
No-Hitters, AL (9 innings or more) 88
No-Hitters, NL (9 innings or more) 90
Most No-Hitters, Career 93
Perfect Games (9 innings or more) 94
Most 1-0 Losses, Career 95
Most Wins, Career 102
Most Strikeouts, Season, AL 106
Most Strikeouts, Season, NL since 1900 106, 107
Most Strikeouts, Career 108
Perfect Innings, AL (3 strikeouts on 9 pitches) 110
Most Games with 10 or More Strikeouts, Career 114
Most Strikeouts per Nine Innings, Career (Min. 1,500 IP) 114
Fewest Base Runners per Nine Innings, Career (Min. 1,500 IP) 130
Most Times Struck Out, Pitcher, Career since 1900 141
Strikeout Duos, Season, NL 228

Lew Burdette
No-Hitters, NL (9 innings or more) 90
Most Wins, Career 102
Best Control Pitchers, Career 126
Two Home Runs in One Game, Pitcher, NL 136
Grand Slams, Pitcher, NL 139
Best Lefty-Righty Duos 228

Smoky Burgess
Most Pinch-Hit Home Runs, Career 5
Three Home Runs in One Game, NL 18
Most RBIs, Game, NL 64
Most Pinch Hits, Season, AL 68
Most Pinch Hits, Career 69
Most Games Caught, Career 153
Most No-Hitters Caught, Career 155

Tom Burgmeier
Undefeated Seasons (5 or more wins) 101
Most Relief Wins, Career 117
Most Relief Losses, Career 120
Most Saves, Career 121

Bobby Burke
No-Hitters, AL (9 innings or more) 87
Most Walks in One Game, AL 113

Jesse Burkett
Leadoff Home Runs in Two Consecutive Games, NL 21
Most Combined Hits and Walks, Season, NL 41
The .400 Hitters, NL 52
Highest Batting Average, Career 53
Most Seasons with 200 Hits 54
Most Runs, Season, NL 59
Most Runs, Career 60
Most Runs Produced, Career 62
Most Walks in One Game, NL 113
.300-Hitting Outfields, NL 220

Rick Burleson
Best Double-Play Combinations, Season 149
Most Double Plays, Shortstop, Season, AL 151
Most Assists, Shortstop, Game 159
Home Runs by First Two Batters in Game, AL 194
Most Home Runs in One Inning, Team, AL 200

Johnny Burnett
Most Hits, Game, AL 35

Wally Burnette
Shutout in First Start in Majors, AL 83

Bill Burns
ERA Under 2.00, Rookie, AL (Min. 130 IP) 169

Dick Burns
No-Hitters, Other Leagues 91

George Burns
Most Hits, Game, AL 35
Unassisted Triple Plays 149

George Burns
Cycle Hitters, NL 50
Most Steals of Home, Career 67
Fewest Games Missed (10-Year Period) 72
Most Putouts, Outfielder, Game 156

Oyster Burns
Most Triples, Game, Other Leagues 29
Cycle Hitters, NL 50

Tom Burns
Two Grand Slams in One Inning, Team 192

Pete Burnside
Worst-Hitting Pitchers, Career (Min. 100 AB) 144

Jeff Burroughs
Most Grand Slams, Career 3
Most Grand Slams, Season, AL 4
Most Home Runs, Season, NL 8
Three Home Runs in One Game, AL 15
Easiest to Strike Out, Career (Min. 1,000 G) 44
Three Consecutive Home Runs, Team, NL 199

Ellis Burton
Switch-Hit Home Runs in One Game, NL 23

Jim Busby
Grand Slam In Two Consecutive Games, AL 3

Steve Busby
No-Hitters, AL (9 innings or more) 88
Most No-Hitters, Career 93
Rookie No-Hitters, AL 167

Donie Bush
Most Times Struck Out, Game, AL 33
Most Stolen Bases, Career 66
Stolen Base Duos, Season, AL 216

Guy Bush
Most Innings Pitched, Game, NL 128

Joe Bush
Most Shutouts, Career 80
No-Hitters, AL (9 innings or more) 87
Most Complete 1-0 Wins, Career 94
Highest Percentage of Team's Wins, AL 99
Won 20 and Hit .300 in Same Year, AL 134
Most Hits, Pitcher, Career 139
Best-Hitting Pitchers, Season, AL 142

Max Butcher
Most Consecutive Losses, NL 116

Bill Butler
Worst-Hitting Pitchers, Career (Min. 100 AB) 144

Bobby Byrne
Most Assists, Third Baseman, Game 158

Tommy Byrne
Most Walks in One Game, AL 113
Pinch-Hit Grand Slams, Pitcher 137
Grand Slams, Pitcher, AL 138

Marty Bystrom
Shutout in First Start in Majors, NL 85
Undefeated Seasons (5 or more wins) 101

Enos Cabell
Three Consecutive Home Runs, Team, NL 199

Leon Cadore
Shutout with Most Hits Allowed, NL 86
Most Innings Pitched, Game, NL 128

Earl Caldwell
Shutout in First Start in Majors, NL 84

Ray Caldwell
No-Hitters, AL (9 innings or more) 87

Teams with Three 20-Game Winners, AL 227

Nixey Callahan

Shutout with Most Hits Allowed, NL 86
No-Hitters, AL (9 innings or more) 87
Best-Hitting Pitchers, Career 143

Johnny Callison

Three Home Runs in One Game, NL 18
Cycle Hitters, NL 50
Most Home Runs by Team, Game, NL 206

Paul Calvert

Most Consecutive Losses, AL 115

Dolf Camilli

Two Legs of Triple Crown, NL 47
Fathers and Sons in Baseball 190

Doug Camilli

Fathers and Sons in Baseball 190

Harry Camnitz

Pitching Brothers, Same Team, NL 186

Howie Camnitz

Best Won-Lost Record, Season, NL (20 or more wins) 97
Fewest Base Runners per Nine Innings, Career (Min. 1,500 IP) 130
Pitching Brothers, Same Team, NL 186

Rick Camp

Worst-Hitting Pitchers, Career (Min. 100 AB) 144

Roy Campanella

Most Home Runs, Season, NL 8
Best Home Run Ratio, Career 10
Most Home Runs by Position, Career, NL 10
Most Home Runs by Position, Season, NL 11
Three Home Runs in One Game, NL 17
Easiest to Double Up, Career (Min. 1000 G) 41
Most Games Caught, Career 153
Most No-Hitters Caught, Career 154
Retired Numbers, NL 183
Three Consecutive Home Runs, Team, NL 198
Most 40-Home Run Hitters, NL 206
Most 30-Home Run Hitters, NL 208
Home Run Trios, Season, NL 209

Bert Campaneris

Home Run in First Appearance in Majors, AL 11
Home Run on First Pitch in Majors, AL 11
Most Leadoff Home Runs, Career 22
Most Triples, Game, AL 28
Hardest to Double Up, Career (Min. 1,000 G) 42
Most Stolen Bases, Career 66
Most Stolen Bases, Game, AL 66
Stolen Base Duos, Season, AL 216

Al Campanis

Fathers and Sons in Baseball 190

Jim Campanis

Fathers and Sons in Baseball 190

Bill Campbell

Most Relief Wins, Career 117
Most Relief Wins, Season, AL 118
Most Relief Losses, Career 120
Most Saves, Career 121
Most Saves, Season, AL 122
Most Wins Plus Saves, Season 122

Bruce Campbell

Most Hits, Game, AL 35
Longest Hitting Streaks, AL 70

Dave Campbell

Most Home Runs in One Inning, Team, NL 201

Vin Campbell

.300 Batting Average in Final Season (Min. 100 G) 39

John Candelaria

No-Hitters, NL (9 innings or more) 90
Best Won-Lost Record, Season, NL (20 or more wins) 97
Fewest Base Runners per Nine Innings, Career (Min. 1,500 IP) 130

Jose Canseco

Thirty or More Home Runs, Rookie, AL 163
One Hundred or More RBIs, Rookie, AL 166

Ben Cantwell

Most Consecutive Losses, NL 116

Bernie Carbo

Most Home Runs by Team, Game, AL 202
Most Home Runs by Team, Game, NL 205
.300-Hitting Outfields, NL 221

Jose Cardenal

Most Hits, Game, NL 37
Unassisted Double Plays, Outfielder 152

Leo Cardenas

Most Home Runs by Position, Career, NL 10
Most Home Runs in a Doubleheader, NL 20
Most Double Plays, Shortstop, Season, AL 151

Don Cardwell

No-Hitters, NL (9 innings or more) 90
Most Home Runs, Pitcher, Career 135
Two Home Runs in One Game, Pitcher, NL 136

Rod Carew

Most Grand Slams, Season, AL 4
Most Combined Hits and Walks, Season, AL 40
Cycle Hitters, AL 49
The 3,000-Hit Club 54
The 3,000th Hit 54

Best Home Run Ratio, Career 10
Most Home Runs by Position, Career, AL 10
Most Combined Hits and Walks, Season, AL 40
Three Consecutive Home Runs, Team, AL 196, 197
Most 40-Home Run Hitters, AL 206
Home Run Duos, Season, AL (25 each) 210
Home Run Duos, Career, AL 211
Teammates Who Finished 1-2 in Batting, AL 222

Joe Cassidy

Most Putouts, Shortstop, Game 159
Most Triples, Rookie, AL 165

Danny Cater

Easiest to Double Up, Career (Min. 1000 G) 41

Bill Caudill

Most Saves, Career 121
Most Saves, Season, AL 122
Most Wins Plus Saves, Season 122

Red Causey

Most Walks in One Game, NL 113

Wayne Causey

Three Consecutive Home Runs, Team, AL 196

Phil Cavarretta

No-Hit Spoilers - The Only Hit Most Often 58
Three Consecutive Home Runs, Team, NL 198

Cesar Cedeno

Twenty Home Runs with 50 Stolen Bases, Season 24
Cycle Hitters, NL 50
Most Stolen Bases, Career 66
Stolen Base Duos, Season, NL 217

Orlando Cepeda

Most Home Runs, Season, NL 7
Most Home Runs by Position, Career, NL 10
Three Home Runs in One Game, NL 19
Most Doubles, Game, AL 27
Two Legs of Triple Crown, NL 48
Most Doubles, Rookie, NL 165
Three Consecutive Home Runs, Team, NL 199
Most Home Runs in One Inning, Team, NL 200
Most Home Runs by Team, Game, NL 204
Most 40-Home Run Hitters, NL 206
Most 30-Home Run Hitters, NL 208
Home Run Trios, Season, NL 209

Bob Cerv

Most Pinch-Hit Home Runs, Career 5
Three Home Runs in One Game, AL 14
Two Pinch-Hit Home Runs in One Inning, Team, AL 192

Ron Cey

Most Consecutive Hits, NL 74
Most Home Runs by Team, Game, NL 206
Most 30-Home Run Hitters, NL 208
Home Run Duos, Career, NL 211

Cliff Chambers

No-Hitters, NL (9 innings or more) 90

Chris Chambliss

Most Pinch Hits, Season, NL 68

Dean Chance

Most Consecutive Times Struck Out, AL 74
Most Shutouts, Season, AL 80
No-Hitters, AL (9 innings or more) 88
Most Complete 1-0 Wins, Career 94
Most Strikeouts, Season, AL 105
Fewest Base Runners per Nine Innings, Career (Min. 1,500 IP) 130
Easiest Pitcher to Strike Out, Season since 1900 141
Most Times Struck Out, Pitcher, Career since 1900 141
Worst-Hitting Pitchers, Career (Min. 100 AB) 144

Frank Chance

Most Stolen Bases, Career 66
Pennant-Winning Rookie Managers, NL 171
Stolen Base Duos, Season, NL 217

Spud Chandler

Best Won-Lost Record, Season, AL (20 or more wins) 96
Two Home Runs in One Game, Pitcher, AL 136
Grand Slams, Pitcher, AL 138

Ben Chapman

Three Home Runs in One Game, AL 13
Most Triples, Game, AL 28
Most Times Walked, Game, AL 31
Most Steals of Home, Career 67
Three Consecutive Home Runs, Team, AL 196
Most 100-RBI Hitters, AL 212
.300-Hitting Outfields, AL 219, 220

Ray Chapman

.300 Batting Average in Final Season (Min. 100 G) 39
Stolen Base Duos, Season, AL 216

Sam Chapman

Three Home Runs in One Game, AL 14
Cycle Hitters, AL 49

Larry Chappell

Most Times Caught Stealing, Game, AL 68

Hal Chase

Most Triples, Game, AL 28
Longest Hitting Streaks, AL 70
Most Putouts in Nine Innings, First Baseman 157

Larry Cheney

Shutout with Most Hits Allowed, NL 86
Twenty or More Wins, Rookie, NL since 1900 168
Three Hundred or More Innings Pitched, Rookie, NL since 1900 169

Tom Cheney

Most Strikeouts in Extra-Inning Game, AL 112

Jack Chesbro

Most Shutouts, Career 80
Shutout with Most Hits Allowed, AL 86
Best Won-Lost Record, Season, NL (20 or more wins) 97
Highest Percentage of Team's Wins, AL 99
Thirty-Game Winners, AL 100
Most Wins by Age, Season, AL 103
Most Strikeouts, Season, AL 105
Most Consecutive Wins, AL 115
Most Complete Games, Season, AL 131
Most Innings Pitched, Season, AL 132
Most Errors by Position, Season, AL 147
Teams with Three 20-Game Winners, NL since 1900 227

Cuckoo Christensen

Highest Batting Average, Rookie, NL (Min. 300 AB) 167
.300-Hitting Outfields, NL 220
Teammates Who Finished 1-2 in Batting, NL 222

Larry Christenson

Two Home Runs in One Game, Pitcher, NL 136
Grand Slams, Pitcher, NL 139

Mark Christman

Most Home Runs by Team, Game, AL 202

Eddie Cicotte

Most Shutouts, Career 80
No-Hitters, AL (9 innings or more) 87
Most 1-0 Losses, Career 95
Best Won-Lost Record, Season, AL (20 or more wins) 96
Most Wins, Career 102
Most Wins by Age, Season, AL 103
Fewest Base Runners per Nine Innings, Career (Min. 1,500 IP) 130
Teams with Four 20-Game Winners 227

Gino Cimoli

Three Consecutive Home Runs, Team, AL 196

Bob Clark

Shutout in First Start in Majors, AL 83

Earl Clark

Most Putouts, Outfielder, Game 156

Jack Clark

Longest Hitting Streaks, NL 71

Watty Clark

Best Control Pitchers, Career 126

Will Clark

Home Run in First Appearance in Majors, AL 11

Fred Clarke

Most Games with Five or More Hits, Career 37
Cycle Hitters, NL 50
The .400 Hitters, NL 52
Most Runs Produced, Career 62
Longest Hitting Streaks, NL 71
Most Assists, Outfielder, Game 156
Most Hits in First Game 165
Career Spent With One Team (15 or more years) 181
Most Wins, Manager, Career 184
.300-Hitting Outfields, NL 220
Teammates Who Finished 1-2 in Batting, NL 222

Nig Clarke

Most No-Hitters Caught, Career 154

Dad Clarkson

Pitching Brothers, Same Team, NL 186
Three or More Brothers in Baseball 187
Most Wins by Brothers 187

John Clarkson

Most Shutouts, Career 80
Most Shutouts, Season, NL 81
No-Hitters, NL (9 innings or more) 89
Most 20-Win Seasons 101
Most Wins, Career 102
The 300-Win Club 103
Most Strikeouts, Season before 1900 107, 108
Most Strikeouts in Nine-Inning Game, NL 111
Most Consecutive Strikeouts, NL 116
Two Complete Game Wins in One Day, NL before 1900 125
Triple-Crown Pitchers, NL (most wins, lowest ERA, most strikeouts) 129
Fewest Base Runners per Nine Innings, Career (Min. 1,500 IP) 130
Most Home Runs, Pitcher, Career 135
Two Home Runs in One Game, Pitcher, NL 136
Pitching Brothers, Same Team, NL 186
Three or More Brothers in Baseball 187
Most Wins by Brothers 187

Walter Clarkson

Three or More Brothers in Baseball 187
Most Wins by Brothers 187

Mark Clear

Most Relief Wins, Season, AL 118
Most Relief Losses, Season, AL 120

Roger Clemens

Best Won-Lost Record, Season, AL (20 or more wins) 96
Most Strikeouts, Season, AL 105
Most Strikeouts in Nine-Inning Game, AL 110
Most Consecutive Wins, AL 115
Most Consecutive Strikeouts, AL 116

Roberto Clemente

Three Home Runs in One Game, NL 18
Most Triples, Game, NL 29

Most Games with Five or More Hits, Career 37
.300 Batting Average in Final Season (Min. 100 G) 39
Grounded into Most Double Plays, Game, NL 43
The 3,000-Hit Club 54
The 3,000th Hit 54
Career Spent With One Team (15 or more years) 181
Retired Numbers, NL 183
Home Run Duos, Career, NL 211
.300-Hitting Outfields, NL 221

Jack Clements

Most Games Caught, Career 153

Donn Clendenon

Easiest to Strike Out, Career (Min. 1,000 G) 44

Harlond Clift

No-Hit Spoilers - The Only Hit Most Often 58

Monk Cline

Most Runs, Game, Other Leagues 60

Gene Clines

Most Home Runs by Team, Game, NL 206

Lu Clinton

Cycle Hitters, AL 49

Tony Cloninger

Two Grand Slams in One Game 3
Most RBIs, Game, NL 64
Most Strikeouts, Season, NL since 1900 107
Two Home Runs in One Game, Pitcher, NL 136
Two Home Runs in One Game Twice in One Season, Pitcher 136
Grand Slams, Pitcher, NL 139

Otis Clymer

Cycle Hitters, AL 49

Gil Coan

Most Home Runs by Team, Game, AL 202

Ty Cobb

Three Home Runs in One Game, AL 13
Most Total Bases, Game, AL 30
Most Hits, Game, AL 35
Most Games with Five or More Hits, Career 37
Most Combined Hits and Walks, Season, AL 40
Triple Crown Winners, AL 45
Players Who Just Missed Triple Crowns, AL 45
Two Legs of Triple Crown, AL 46
The .400 Hitters, AL 52
Highest Batting Average, Career 53
The 3,000-Hit Club 54
The 3,000th Hit 54
Most Seasons with 200 Hits 54
Batted .300 after Age 40 59
Most Runs, Career 60
Most RBIs, Career 61
Most Runs Produced, Season, AL 61
Most Runs Produced, Career 62
Most RBIs in One Inning, AL 63
Most Stolen Bases, Season, AL 65
Most Stolen Bases, Career 66
Stole 2nd, 3rd, and Home in One Game, AL 66
Most Steals of Home, Career 67
Longest Hitting Streaks, AL 70
Most Consecutive Hits, AL 73
Unassisted Double Plays, Outfielder 152
Most Putouts, Outfielder, Game 156
Stolen Base Duos, Season, AL 216
Most .300 Hitters, Season, AL (300 AB each) 217
.300-Hitting Outfields, AL 219
Teammates Who Finished 1-2 in Batting, AL 222

Mickey Cochrane

Three Home Runs in One Game, AL 13
Cycle Hitters, AL 49
Most Games Caught, Career 153
Highest Batting Average, Rookie, AL (Min. 300 AB) 167
Pennant-Winning Rookie Managers, AL 171
Home Run Trios, Season, AL 209
Most .300 Hitters, Season, AL (300 AB each) 217

Rocky Colavito

Most Home Runs, Season, AL 7
Best Home Run Ratio, Career 10
Two Home Runs in One Game Most Often 12
Three Home Runs in One Game, AL 14
Four Home Runs in One Game, AL 20
Most Home Runs in a Doubleheader, AL 20
Most Total Bases, Game, AL 30
Most Hits, Game, AL 35
Home Runs in Most Consecutive At-Bats, AL 76
Fewest Errors by Position, Season, AL (Min. 150 G, excl. Pitchers) 147
Most Home Runs by Team, Game, AL 203
Most 40-Home Run Hitters, AL 206
Home Run Duos, Season, AL (25 each) 210

Nate Colbert

Three Home Runs in One Game, NL 19
Most Home Runs in a Doubleheader, NL 20
Three Consecutive Home Runs, Team, NL 199

Jim Colborn

No-Hitters, AL (9 innings or more) 88

King Cole

Shutout in First Start in Majors, NL 84
Best Won-Lost Record, Season, NL (20 or more wins) 97
Twenty or More Wins, Rookie, NL since 1900 168
ERA Under 2.00, Rookie, NL since 1900 (Min. 130 IP) 169

Ed Coleman

Three Home Runs in One Game, AL 13
Most Pinch Hits, Season, AL 68

Jerry Coleman

Best Double-Play Combinations, Season 149
Most Double Plays, Second Baseman, Season, AL 151

Joe Coleman
Most Strikeouts, Season, AL 105, 106
Fathers and Sons in Baseball 190
Strikeout Duos, Season, AL 228

Joe Coleman
Fathers and Sons in Baseball 190

John Coleman
Most Consecutive Losses, NL 116

Vince Coleman
Most Stolen Bases, Season, NL 65
Stolen Base Duos, Season, NL 216

Darnell Coles
Most Home Runs in One Inning, Team, AL 200
Most 20-Home Run Hitters, AL 208

Bill Collins
Cycle Hitters, NL 50

Dave Collins
Hardest to Double Up, Career (Min. 1,000 G) 42
Most Stolen Bases, Season, NL 65
Stolen Base Duos, Season, AL 216
Stolen Base Duos, Season, NL 217

Eddie Collins
Fathers and Sons in Baseball 190

Phil Collins
Two Home Runs in One Game, Pitcher, NL 136
Grand Slams, Pitcher, NL 138

Ray Collins
Two Complete Game Wins in One Day, AL 124

Shano Collins
Most Steals of Home, Career 67

Jackie Collum
Shutout in First Start in Majors, NL 84

Earle Combs
Most Leadoff Home Runs, Career 22
Most Triples, Game, AL 28
Longest Hitting Streaks, AL 70
Two Hundred or More Hits, Rookie, AL 163
Highest Batting Average, Rookie, AL (Min. 300 AB) 167
Most Home Runs by Team, Game, AL 202
.300-Hitting Outfields, AL 219

Adam Comorosky
Grounded into Most Double Plays, Game, NL 43
Unassisted Double Plays, Outfielder 152
.300-Hitting Outfields, NL 221

Dave Concepcion
Career Spent With One Team (15 or more years) 181
Most Home Runs by Team, Game, NL 205
Stolen Base Duos, Season, NL 217

Billy Conigliaro
Home Runs by Brothers in One Game 26
Best-Hitting Brothers 190

Tony Conigliaro
Home Runs by Brothers in One Game 26
Most Times Struck Out, Game, AL 33
Best-Hitting Brothers 190

Bill Connelly
Undefeated Seasons (5 or more wins) 101

Ed Connolly
Fathers and Sons in Baseball 190

Ed Connolly
Fathers and Sons in Baseball 190

Roger Connor
Three Home Runs in One Game, NL 17
Most Hits, Game, NL 36
Cycle Hitters, Other Leagues 51
Most Runs Produced, Career 62
Fewest Games Missed (10-Year Period) 72
Most Consecutive Hits, NL 74
Three Consecutive Home Runs, Team, Other Leagues 199
Most Home Runs by Team, Game, NL 204

Merv Connors
Three Home Runs in One Game, AL 13

Sandy Consuegra
Shutout in First Start in Majors, AL 83
Undefeated Seasons (5 or more wins) 101

Bill Conway
Brother Batteries, Other Leagues 185

Dick Conway
Brother Batteries, Other Leagues 185

Duff Cooley
Most Hits, Game, NL 36
Cycle Hitters, NL 50

Jack Coombs
Most Shutouts, Career 80
Most Shutouts, Season, AL 80
Shutout in First Start in Majors, AL 83
Thirty-Game Winners, AL 100
Most Strikeouts, Season, AL 105
Most Strikeouts in Extra-Inning Game, AL 112
Lowest ERA, Season, AL 127
Most Innings Pitched, Game, AL 127
Most Complete Games, Season, AL 131
Most Innings Pitched, Season, AL 132
Won 20 and Hit .300 in Same Year, AL 134

Jimmy Cooney
Unassisted Triple Plays 149
Fathers and Sons in Baseball 190

Jimmy Cooney
Fathers and Sons in Baseball 190

Johnny Cooney
Hardest to Strike Out, Career (Min. 1,000 G) 44
Batted .300 after Age 40 59
Fathers and Sons in Baseball 190

Cecil Cooper
Three Home Runs in One Game, AL 15
Most Times Struck Out, Game, AL 33
Two Grand Slams in One Inning, Team 192
Three Consecutive Home Runs, Team, AL 197
Most 30-Home Run Hitters, AL 207
Most 100-RBI Hitters, AL 212
Most 200-Hit Batters, AL 223

Mort Cooper
Most Shutouts, Season, NL 81
Fewest Base Runners per Nine Innings, Career (Min. 1,500 IP) 130
Brother Batteries, NL 185

Walker Cooper
Three Home Runs in One Game, NL 17
Most Total Bases, Game, NL 30
Most Hits, Game, NL 36
Easiest to Double Up, Career (Min. 1000 G) 41
Most RBIs, Game, NL 64
Most Games Caught, Career 153
Most No-Hitters Caught, Career 154
Brother Batteries, NL 185
Three Consecutive Home Runs, Team, NL 198
Most 30-Home Run Hitters, NL 208
Home Run Trios, Season, NL 209

Wilbur Cooper
Most Shutouts, Career 80
Shutout in First Start in Majors, NL 84
Most 1-0 Losses, Career 95
Most Wins, Career 102
Won 20 and Hit .300. in Same Year, NL 134
Best-Hitting Pitchers, Season, NL since 1900 142
Best Lefty-Righty Duos 229

Henry Coppola
Shutout in First Start in Majors, AL 83

Doug Corbett
ERA Under 2.00, Rookie, AL (Min. 130 IP) 169

Larry Corcoran
No-Hitters, NL (9 innings or more) 88
Most No-Hitters, Career 93
Most Consecutive Wins, NL 115
Rookie No-Hitters, NL 167
Pitching Brothers, Same Team, NL 186

Mike Corcoran
Pitching Brothers, Same Team, NL 186

Tommy Corcoran
Most Assists, Shortstop, Game 159

Fred Corey
Worst Won-Lost Record, Season (12 or more losses) 95

Mike Corkins
Grand Slams, Pitcher, NL 139

John Corriden
Fathers and Sons in Baseball 190

Red Corriden
Fathers and Sons in Baseball 190

Al Corwin
Three Consecutive Home Runs, Team, NL 198

Pete Coscarart
Home Runs by First Two Batters in Game, NL 194

Jim Cosman
Shutout in First Start in Majors, NL 84

Harvey Cotter
Most Putouts in Nine Innings, First Baseman 157

Bill Coughlin
Stole 2nd, 3rd, and Home in One Game, AL 66

Clint Courtney
Three Consecutive Home Runs, Team, AL 196

Harry Coveleski
Most Wins by Brothers 187

Stan Coveleski
Most Shutouts, Career 80
Shutout in First Start in Majors, AL 83
Most Complete 1-0 Wins, Career 94
Best Won-Lost Record, Season, AL (20 or more wins) 96
Most Wins, Career 102
Most Consecutive Wins, AL 115
Most Innings Pitched, Game, AL 127
Most Times Struck Out, Pitcher, Career since 1900 141
Most Wins by Brothers 187
Teams with Three 20-Game Winners, AL 227

Wes Covington
Three Consecutive Home Runs, Team, NL 199

Billy Cowan
Most Times Struck Out, Game, AL 33

Al Cowens
Most Home Runs by Team, Game, AL 203

Joe Cowley
No-Hitters, AL (9 innings or more) 88
Most Consecutive Strikeouts, AL 116

Billy Cox
Most Home Runs by Team, Game, NL 205

Casey Cox
Worst-Hitting Pitchers, Career (Min. 100 AB) 144

Dick Cox
.300 Average in Rookie Year Only, NL 164
.300-Hitting Outfields, NL 220

Ted Cox
Most Hits in First Game 165

Harry Craft
Cycle Hitters, NL 50

Roger Craig
Most Shutout Losses, Season, NL 81
Most Consecutive Losses, NL 116
Worst-Hitting Pitchers, Career (Min. 100 AB) 144

Doc Cramer
Most Hits, Game, AL 35
Cycle Hitters, AL 49
.300-Hitting Outfields, AL 220

Del Crandall
Most Grand Slams, Season, NL 4
Most Games Caught, Career 153
Most No-Hitters Caught, Career 154
Most Home Runs by Team, Game, NL 204

Doc Crandall
Best-Hitting Pitchers, Season, NL since 1900 142
Best-Hitting Pitchers, Career 142

Cannonball Crane
Four Strikeouts in One Inning, NL 109
Most Walks in One Game, NL 113
Two Complete Game Wins in One Day, Other Leagues 126

Sam Crane
Most Assists, Second Baseman, Game 158
Most Home Runs by Team, Game, NL 204

Gavvy Cravath
Most Doubles, Game, NL 27
Players Who Just Missed Triple Crowns, NL 45
Two Legs of Triple Crown, NL 47

Sam Crawford
Two Legs of Triple Crown, AL 46
Most Runs Produced, Career 62
Fewest Games Missed (10-Year Period) 72
Stolen Base Duos, Season, AL 216
Teammates Who Finished 1-2 in Batting, AL 222

Willie Crawford
Two Pinch-Hit Home Runs in One Inning, Team, NL 193
Back-to-Back Pinch-Hit Home Runs, Team 193

Lou Criger
The Worst Hitters (Min. 2,500 AB) 52
Most No-Hitters Caught, Career 154

Bill Cristall
Shutout in First Start in Majors, AL 83

Hughie Critz
Most Times Walked, Game, NL 32
Best Double-Play Combinations, Season 149
Most Assists, Second Baseman, Game 158

Warren Cromartie
Most Doubles, Rookie, NL 165

Joe Cronin
Most Home Runs by Position, Career, AL 10
Cycle Hitters, AL 49
Most Pinch Hits, Season, AL 68
RBI in Most Consecutive Games, AL 72
Best Double-Play Combinations, Season 150
Pennant-Winning Rookie Managers, AL 171
Retired Numbers, AL 182
Most Wins, Manager, Career 184
Three Consecutive Home Runs, Team, AL 196
Most Home Runs in One Inning, Team, AL 200
Most 100-RBI Hitters, AL 212

John Crooks
Leadoff Home Runs in Two Consecutive Games, NL 21

Frankie Crosetti
Most Leadoff Home Runs, Career 22
Struck Out Twice in One Inning, AL 32
Best Double-Play Combinations, Season 150
Most Double Plays, Shortstop, Season, AL 151
Career Spent With One Team (15 or more years) 181

Amos Cross
Three or More Brothers in Baseball 187
Best-Hitting Brothers 189

Frank Cross
Three or More Brothers in Baseball 187
Best-Hitting Brothers 189

Lave Cross
Cycle Hitters, NL 50
Most Runs Produced, Career 62
Most Assists, Second Baseman, Game 158
Three or More Brothers in Baseball 187

Best-Hitting Brothers 189

Monte Cross
The Worst Hitters (Min. 2,500 AB) 52
Most Putouts, Shortstop, Game 159

Bill Crouch
Fathers and Sons in Baseball 190

Bill Crouch
Fathers and Sons in Baseball 190

General Crowder
Best Won-Lost Record, Season, AL (20 or more wins) 96
Most Consecutive Wins, AL 115

George Crowe
Most Pinch-Hit Home Runs, Career 5
Most Pinch Hits, Season, NL 69
Most Pinch Hits, Career 69

Cap Crowell
Most Walks in One Game, AL 113

Bill Crowley
Most Assists, Outfielder, Game 156

Terry Crowley
Most Pinch-Hit Grand Slams, Career 6
Most Pinch Hits, Career 69

Walt Cruise
Grounded into Most Double Plays, Game, NL 43
.300-Hitting Outfields, NL 220

Hector Cruz
Three or More Brothers in Baseball 187

Henry Cruz
Most Home Runs by Team, Game, NL 206

Jose Cruz
Three or More Brothers in Baseball 187
Three Consecutive Home Runs, Team, NL 199
Stolen Base Duos, Season, NL 217

Julio Cruz
Stolen Base Duos, Season, AL 216

Tommy Cruz
Three or More Brothers in Baseball 187

Mike Cubbage
Cycle Hitters, AL 49
Most RBIs in One Inning, AL 63

Al Cuccinello
Home Runs by Brothers in One Game 26

Tony Cuccinello
Home Runs by Brothers in One Game 26
Most Hits, Game, NL 36
.300 Batting Average in Final Season (Min. 100 G) 39
Most Consecutive Games Played 71
Three Consecutive Home Runs, Team, NL 198

Mike Cuellar
Most Shutouts, Career 80
Most Strikeouts, Season, NL since 1900 107
Four Strikeouts in One Inning, AL 108
Fewest Base Runners per Nine Innings, Career (Min. 1,500 IP) 130
Teams with Four 20-Game Winners 227
Teams with Three 20-Game Winners, AL 227

Leon Culberson
Cycle Hitters, AL 49
Unassisted Double Plays, Outfielder 152

Roy Cullenbine
Most Home Runs in Final Season 24
More Walks than Hits, Season, AL 55
Three Consecutive Home Runs, Team, AL 196

Ray Culp
Most Consecutive Times Struck Out, AL 74
Most Strikeouts per Nine Innings, Career (Min. 1,500 IP) 114
Most Shutouts, Rookie, NL since 1900 170

George Culver
No-Hitters, NL (9 innings or more) 90

Candy Cummings
Two Complete Game Wins in One Day, NL before 1900 125

Bert Cunningham
Two Complete Game Wins in One Day, Other Leagues 126

Cliff Curtis
Shutout in First Start in Majors, NL 84
Most Consecutive Losses, NL 116

Guy Curtright
Longest Hitting Streaks, AL 70

Ed Cushman
No-Hitters, Other Leagues 91
Most Strikeouts in Nine-Inning Game, Other Leagues 112
Most Consecutive Strikeouts, Other Leagues 117

George Cutshaw
Most Hits, Game, NL 36

Kiki Cuyler
Most Hits, Game, NL 36

Most Combined Hits and Walks, Season, NL 41
Cycle Hitters, NL 50
Most Runs Produced, Season, NL 62
Most Consecutive Hits, NL 74
Highest Batting Average, Rookie, NL (Min. 300 AB) 167
Most 100-RBI Hitters, NL 212
Most .300 Hitters, Season, NL (300 AB each) 218
.300-Hitting Outfields, NL 220, 221
Most 200-Hit Batters, NL 223

Bill Dahlen
Most Triples, Game, NL 28
Most Runs Produced, Career 62
Longest Hitting Streaks, NL 71
Most Assists, Shortstop, Game 159

Babe Dahlgren
Most Home Runs by Team, Game, AL 202

One Arm Daily
No-Hitters, NL (9 innings or more) 88
Most Strikeouts, Season before 1900 107
Most Strikeouts in Nine-Inning Game, Other Leagues 112

Abner Dalrymple
Most Doubles, Game, NL 27
Cycle Hitters, Other Leagues 51

Clay Dalrymple
The Worst Hitters (Min. 2,500 AB) 52
Most Games Caught, Career 153

Jack Dalton
.300-Hitting Outfields, NL 220

Bill Damman
Shutout with Most Hits Allowed, NL 86

Bert Daniels
Cycle Hitters, AL 49

Harry Danning
Cycle Hitters, NL 50
Most Home Runs in One Inning, Team, NL 200
Most Home Runs by Team, Game, NL 204

Alvin Dark
Best Double-Play Combinations, Season 150
Most Doubles, Rookie, NL 165
Pennant-Winning Managers in AL and NL 184
Most Home Runs in One Inning, Team, NL 200
Most Home Runs by Team, Game, NL 205

Bobby Darwin
Most Times Struck Out, Game, AL 33

Jake Daubert
Most Putouts in Nine Innings, First Baseman 157

Rich Dauer
Easiest to Double Up, Career (Min. 1000 G) 41

Darren Daulton
Most Home Runs in One Inning, Team, NL 201

Hooks Dauss
Twenty Wins One Year, 20 Losses the Next, AL 98
Most Wins, Career 102
Career Spent With One Team (15 or more years) 181

Vic Davalillo
Hardest to Double Up, Career (Min. 1,000 G) 42
Most Pinch Hits, Season, NL 68
Most Pinch Hits, Career 69
.300-Hitting Outfields, NL 221

Dave Davenport
No-Hitters, Other Leagues 91
Two Complete Game Wins in One Day, AL 124

Jim Davenport
Most Consecutive Errorless Games by Position, NL 148
Most Home Runs in One Inning, Team, NL 200

Andre David
Home Run in First Appearance in Majors, AL 11

Alvin Davis
One Hundred or More RBIs, Rookie, AL 166

Bud Davis
Most Walks in One Game, AL 113

Chili Davis
Switch-Hit Home Runs in One Game, NL 23
.300-Hitting Outfields, NL 221

Curt Davis
Best Control Pitchers, Career 126
Won 20 and Hit .300. in Same Year, NL 134
Grand Slams, Pitcher, NL 138
Best-Hitting Pitchers, Season, NL since 1900 142

Dixie Davis
Most Innings Pitched, Game, AL 127

Eric Davis
Three Home Runs in One Game, NL 19
Twenty Home Runs with 50 Stolen Bases, Season 24
Most Stolen Bases, Season, NL 65

George Davis
No-Hitters, NL (9 innings or more) 89

George Davis
Most Triples, Game, NL 28
Most Hits, Game, NL 36
Most Runs Produced, Career 62

Longest Hitting Streaks, NL 71

Harry Davis

Two Legs of Triple Crown, AL 46
Cycle Hitters, AL 49

Jim Davis

Four Strikeouts in One Inning, NL 109

Jody Davis

Most Games Caught, Season 153

Jumbo Davis

Cycle Hitters, Other Leagues 51

Kiddo Davis

Most Doubles, Rookie, NL 165
.300-Hitting Outfields, NL 221

Lefty Davis

.300-Hitting Outfields, NL 220

Mark Davis

Most Relief Losses, Season, NL 120

Mike Davis

Home Runs by First Two Batters in Game, AL 194
Stolen Base Duos, Season, AL 216

Ron Davis

Most Consecutive Strikeouts, AL 116
Most Relief Wins, Season, AL 118
Most Relief Losses, Season, AL 120
Most Saves, Career 121
Most Saves, Season, AL 122

Spud Davis

Most Games Caught, Career 153
Teammates Who Finished 1-2 in Batting, NL 222

Tommy Davis

Two Legs of Triple Crown, NL 48
Most RBIs, Season, NL 60

Willie Davis

Most Hits, Game, NL 37
Longest Hitting Streaks, NL 71
Stolen Base Duos, Season, NL 216, 217

Andre Dawson

Two Home Runs in One Inning, NL 12
Three Home Runs in One Game, NL 19
Most RBIs in One Inning, NL 63
Most Home Runs in One Inning, Team, NL 201
Most Home Runs by Team, Game, NL 204
Stolen Base Duos, Season, NL 217

Dizzy Dean

Best Won-Lost Record, Season, NL (20 or more wins) 97
Thirty-Game Winners, NL since 1900 101
Most Strikeouts in Nine-Inning Game, NL 111
Fewest Base Runners per Nine Innings, Career (Min. 1,500 IP) 130
Most Strikeouts, Rookie, NL since 1900 169
Retired Numbers, NL 183
Pitching Brothers, Same Team, NL 186
Most Wins by Brothers 187

Dory Dean

Most Consecutive Losses, NL 116

Paul Dean

No-Hitters, NL (9 innings or more) 89
Rookie No-Hitters, NL 167
Most Shutouts, Rookie, NL since 1900 170
Pitching Brothers, Same Team, NL 186
Most Wins by Brothers 187

Hank DeBerry

Most Hits, Game, NL 36

Art Decatur

Worst-Hitting Pitchers, Career (Min. 100 AB) 144

Doug DeCinces

Three Home Runs in One Game, AL 15
Most Assists, Third Baseman, Game 158

George Decker

Longest Hitting Streaks, NL 71

Ivan DeJesus

Cycle Hitters, NL 50

Ed Delahanty

Four Home Runs in One Game, NL 20
Most Doubles, Game, NL 27
Most Total Bases, Game, NL 30
Most Hits, Game, NL 36
Most Hits, Game, Other Leagues 37
Most Games with Five or More Hits, Career 37
Batting Champion with Two Different Clubs 43
Two Legs of Triple Crown, NL 47
The .400 Hitters, NL 52
Highest Batting Average, Career 53
Most Runs Produced, Season, NL 62
Most Runs Produced, Career 62
Longest Hitting Streaks, NL 71
Most Consecutive Hits, NL 74
Three or More Brothers in Baseball 187
Best-Hitting Brothers 189
.300-Hitting Outfields, NL 220

Frank Delahanty

Three or More Brothers in Baseball 187
Best-Hitting Brothers 189

Jim Delahanty

Three or More Brothers in Baseball 187
Best-Hitting Brothers 189

Joe Delahanty
Three or More Brothers in Baseball 187
Best-Hitting Brothers 189

Tom Delahanty
Three or More Brothers in Baseball 187
Best-Hitting Brothers 189

Jose DeLeon
Worst-Hitting Pitchers, Career (Min. 100 AB) 144

Ike Delock
Worst-Hitting Pitchers, Career (Min. 100 AB) 144

Joe DeMaestri
Most Hits, Game, AL 35

Al Demaree
Shutout in First Start in Majors, NL 84
Two Complete Game Wins in One Day, NL since 1900 124

Frank Demaree
Most Hits, Game, NL 36
Most Home Runs in One Inning, Team, NL 200
Most Home Runs by Team, Game, NL 204

Don Demeter
Three Home Runs in One Game, NL 18

Rick Dempsey
Most Games Caught, Career 153
Most Home Runs by Team, Game, AL 203

Jerry Denny
Most Hits, Game, NL 36
Most Assists, Third Baseman, Game 158

Bucky Dent
Best Double-Play Combinations, Season 150

Paul Derringer
Most Shutout Losses, Career 80
Most Complete 1-0 Wins, Career 94
Most Wins, Career 102
Best Control Pitchers, Career 126

Russ Derry
Most Times Walked, Game, AL 32

Jim Deshaies
Most Consecutive Strikeouts, NL 116

Art Devlin
Most Putouts, Third Baseman, Game 158
Stolen Base Duos, Season, NL 217

Jim Devlin
Most Shutout Losses, Season, NL 81

Josh Devore
Stolen Base Duos, Season, NL 217

Buttercup Dickerson
Most Hits, Game, NL 35

Bill Dickey
Grand Slam In Two Consecutive Games, AL 3
Most Home Runs by Position, Career, AL 10
Three Home Runs in One Game, AL 14
Most Games Caught, Career 153
Career Spent With One Team (15 or more years) 181
Retired Numbers, AL 182
Most Home Runs by Team, Game, AL 202
Home Run Trios, Season, AL 209
Most 100-RBI Hitters, AL 212

Johnny Dickshot
.300 Batting Average in Final Season (Min. 100 G) 39

Murry Dickson
Twenty Wins One Year, 20 Losses the Next, NL since 1900 98

Larry Dierker
No-Hitters, NL (9 innings or more) 90
Most Strikeouts, Season, NL since 1900 106
Fewest Base Runners per Nine Innings, Career (Min. 1,500 IP) 131

Bill Dietrich
No-Hitters, AL (9 innings or more) 87

Pat Dillard
Most Putouts, Third Baseman, Game 158

Bob Dillinger
Longest Hitting Streaks, AL 70

Pop Dillon
Most Doubles, Game, AL 27

Miguel Dilone
Stolen Base Duos, Season, NL 217

Dom DiMaggio
Brothers with Most Home Runs, Career 25
Home Runs by Brothers in One Game 26
Longest Hitting Streaks, AL 70
Unassisted Double Plays, Outfielder 152
Three or More Brothers in Baseball 187
Best-Hitting Brothers 189
.300-Hitting Outfields, AL 220

Joe DiMaggio
Most Grand Slams, Career 3
Most Grand Slams, Season, AL 4
Most Home Runs, Season, AL 7
Best Home Run Ratio, Career 10

Harry Dorish
Pitchers Who Stole Home, AL 140

Herm Doscher
Fathers and Sons in Baseball 190

Jack Doscher
Fathers and Sons in Baseball 190

Patsy Dougherty
Most Triples, Game, AL 28
Cycle Hitters, AL 49
No-Hit Spoilers - The Only Hit Most Often 56, 57
Highest Batting Average, Rookie, AL (Min. 300 AB) 167
.300-Hitting Outfields, AL 219

Taylor Douthit
Most Consecutive Hits, NL 74
Most .300 Hitters, Season, NL (300 AB each) 218
.300-Hitting Outfields, NL 220, 221

Tommy Dowd
Cycle Hitters, NL 50

Pete Dowling
Most Times Struck Out, Game, NL 34

Al Downing
Most Strikeouts, Season, AL 105
Perfect Innings, AL (3 strikeouts on 9 pitches) 110
Most Strikeouts per Nine Innings, Career (Min. 1,500 IP) 114
Most Consecutive Strikeouts, NL 116

Brian Downing
Most Leadoff Home Runs, Career 22
Fewest Errors by Position, Season, AL (Min. 150 G, excl. Pitchers) 147
Most Consecutive Errorless Games by Position, AL 148
Three Consecutive Home Runs, Team, AL 197

Dave Downs
Shutout in First Start in Majors, NL 84

Jack Doyle
Most Hits, Game, NL 36
Most Errors by Position, Season, NL since 1900 147

Jess Doyle
Two Home Runs in One Game, Pitcher, AL 135

Larry Doyle
Most Steals of Home, Career 67

Slow Joe Doyle
Shutout in First Start in Majors, AL 83
Shutout in First Two Major League Games, AL 85

Moe Drabowsky
Undefeated Seasons (5 or more wins) 101

Dick Drago
Most Consecutive Times Struck Out, AL 74
Worst-Hitting Pitchers, Career (Min. 100 AB) 144

Chuck Dressen
Most Wins, Manager, Career 184

Karl Drews
Most At-Bats with No Hits, Pitcher, Season since 1900 141
Worst-Hitting Pitchers, Career (Min. 100 AB) 144

Dan Driessen
Three Consecutive Home Runs, Team, NL 199

Walt Dropo
Easiest to Double Up, Career (Min. 1000 G) 41
More RBIs than Games Played, Season, AL 64
Most Consecutive Hits, AL 73
Thirty or More Home Runs, Rookie, AL 163
.300 Average in Rookie Year Only, AL 164
One Hundred or More RBIs, Rookie, AL 166
Most Home Runs by Team, Game, AL 202

Don Drysdale
Most Home Runs by Position, Career, NL 10
Most Home Runs by Position, Season, NL 11
Most Shutouts, Career 79
Most Shutout Losses, Career 80
Most Wins, Career 102
Most Strikeouts, Season, NL since 1900 106, 107
Four Strikeouts in One Inning, NL 109
Most Games with 10 or More Strikeouts, Career 114
Most Strikeouts per Nine Innings, Career (Min. 1,500 IP) 114
Fewest Base Runners per Nine Innings, Career (Min. 1,500 IP) 129
Won 20 and Hit .300. in Same Year, NL 134
Most Home Runs, Pitcher, Career 135
Two Home Runs in One Game, Pitcher, NL 136
Grand Slams, Pitcher, NL 139
Most Home Runs, Pitcher, Season 139
Most Times Struck Out, Pitcher, Career since 1900 141
Retired Numbers, NL 183
Strikeout Duos, Season, NL 228
Best Lefty-Righty Duos 229

Clise Dudley
Home Run in First Appearance in Majors, NL 11
Home Run on First Pitch in Majors, NL 11

Hugh Duffy
Most Triples, Game, NL 28
Most Combined Hits and Walks, Season, NL 41
Triple Crown Winners, NL 45
The .400 Hitters, NL 52
Most Runs, Season, NL 59
Most Runs Produced, Season, NL 62
Most Runs Produced, Career 62

Dick Egan
Stolen Base Duos, Season, NL 217

Howard Ehmke
No-Hitters, AL (9 innings or more) 87
Twenty Wins with Last-Place Team, AL 99

Mark Eichhorn
Most Relief Wins, Season, AL 118
ERA Under 2.00, Rookie, AL (Min. 130 IP) 169

Kid Elberfeld
Most Times Walked, Game, AL 31
Most Assists, Shortstop, Game 159

Hod Eller
No-Hitters, NL (9 innings or more) 89
Perfect Innings, NL (3 strikeouts on 9 pitches) 110

Bob Elliott
Three Home Runs in One Game, NL 17
Cycle Hitters, NL 50
Batting Champion by Widest Margin, NL 56
No-Hit Spoilers - The Only Hit Most Often 58

Dock Ellis
No-Hitters, NL (9 innings or more) 90
Most Consecutive Wins, NL 115

Dick Ellsworth
Worst-Hitting Pitchers, Career (Min. 100 AB) 144

Joe Engel
Worst-Hitting Pitchers, Career (Min. 100 AB) 144

Dave Engle
Two Pinch-Hit Home Runs in One Inning, Team, AL 192
Most Home Runs in One Inning, Team, AL 200

Woody English
Most Combined Hits and Walks, Season, NL 40
Most 200-Hit Batters, NL 223

Del Ennis
Three Home Runs in One Game, NL 18
No-Hit Spoilers - The Only Hit Most Often 58
Most Home Runs in One Inning, Team, NL 200

Mike Epstein
Three Home Runs in One Game, AL 14
Home Runs in Most Consecutive At-Bats, AL 76

Frank Ernaga
Home Run in First Appearance in Majors, NL 11

Carl Erskine
No-Hitters, NL (9 innings or more) 90
Most No-Hitters, Career 93

Jim Eschen
Fathers and Sons in Baseball 190

Larry Eschen
Fathers and Sons in Baseball 190

Andy Etchebarren
The Worst Hitters (Min. 2,500 AB) 52
Most Home Runs in One Inning, Team, AL 200
Most Home Runs by Team, Game, AL 203

Nick Etten
Three Consecutive Home Runs, Team, AL 196

Al Evans
Most Home Runs by Team, Game, AL 202

Darrell Evans
Most Home Runs, Season, AL 7
Most Home Runs, Season, NL 8
Three Home Runs in One Game, NL 19
Three Consecutive Home Runs, Team, AL 197
Most Home Runs in One Inning, Team, NL 201
Most 40-Home Run Hitters, NL 206
Most 30-Home Run Hitters, NL 208
Most 20-Home Run Hitters, AL 208
Home Run Trios, Season, NL 209

Dwight Evans
Cycle Hitters, AL 49
Career Spent With One Team (15 or more years) 181
Home Runs by First Two Batters in Game, AL 194
Three Consecutive Home Runs, Team, AL 197
Home Run Duos, Career, AL 211

Steve Evans
.300 Batting Average in Final Season (Min. 100 G) 39

Hoot Evers
Cycle Hitters, AL 49
Three Consecutive Home Runs, Team, AL 196
Most Home Runs in One Inning, Team, AL 200
.300-Hitting Outfields, AL 220

Johnny Evers
Most Steals of Home, Career 67
Stolen Base Duos, Season, NL 217

Buck Ewing
Most Triples, Game, NL 28
Brother Batteries, NL 185
Brother Batteries, Other Leagues 185
Three Consecutive Home Runs, Team, Other Leagues 199

John Ewing
Brother Batteries, NL 185
Brother Batteries, Other Leagues 185

Red Faber

Stole 2nd, 3rd, and Home in One Game, AL 66
Highest Percentage of Team's Wins, AL 99
Most Wins, Career 102
Most Innings Pitched, Season, AL 132
Most Wins after Age 40 134
Pitchers Who Stole Home, AL 140
Most Times Struck Out, Pitcher, Career since 1900 141
Career Spent With One Team (15 or more years) 181
Teams with Four 20-Game Winners 227

Roy Face

Most Consecutive Wins, NL 115
Most Relief Wins, Career 117
Most Relief Wins, Season, NL 119
Most Relief Losses, Career 120
Most Relief Losses, Season, NL 120
Most Saves, Career 121
Most Grand Slams Allowed, Career 133
Most Extra-Inning Home Runs Allowed, Career 133

Ferris Fain

Most Assists, First Baseman, Game 157

Bibb Falk

.300-Hitting Outfields, AL 219

Cy Falkenberg

Grand Slams, Pitcher, AL 137

Ed Farmer

Most Saves, Season, AL 122

Sid Farrar

Most Triples, Game, Other Leagues 29

Dick Farrell

Most Strikeouts, Season, NL since 1900 107
Most Relief Losses, Career 120

Duke Farrell

Most Games Caught, Career 153

Bob Feller

Most Shutouts, Career 79
Most Shutouts, Season, AL 80
No-Hitters, AL (9 innings or more) 87
Most No-Hitters, Career 93
Most Wins, Career 102
Most Wins by Age, Season, AL 103
Most Strikeouts, Season, AL 105
Most Strikeouts, Career 108
Most Strikeouts in Nine-Inning Game, AL 110
Most Games with 10 or More Strikeouts, Career 114
Most Complete Games, Season, AL 131
Most Innings Pitched, Season, AL 132
Most Grand Slams Allowed, Career 133
Most Times Struck Out, Pitcher, Career since 1900 141
Career Spent With One Team (15 or more years) 181
Retired Numbers, AL 182
Teams with Three 20-Game Winners, AL 227

Happy Felsch

.300 Batting Average in Final Season (Min. 100 G) 39
Most Putouts, Outfielder, Game 156
Most Assists, Outfielder, Game 156

Terry Felton

Worst Won-Lost Record, Season (12 or more losses) 95
Most Consecutive Losses, AL 115

Charlie Ferguson

No-Hitters, NL (9 innings or more) 89
Two Complete Game Wins in One Day, NL before 1900 125

George Ferguson

Grand Slams, Pitcher, NL 138

Joe Ferguson

Most Times Walked, Game, NL 32
Most Home Runs by Team, Game, NL 206

Sid Fernandez

Most Strikeouts, Season, NL since 1900 107

Mike Ferraro

Most Assists, Third Baseman, Game 158

Rick Ferrell

Home Runs by Brothers in One Game 26
Most Games Caught, Career 153
Brother Batteries, AL 185

Wes Ferrell

Most Home Runs by Position, Career, AL 10
Most Home Runs by Position, Season, AL 11
Home Runs by Brothers in One Game 26
No-Hitters, AL (9 innings or more) 87
Most Consecutive Wins, AL 115
Won 20 and Hit .300 in Same Year, AL 134
Most Home Runs, Pitcher, Career 135
Two Home Runs in One Game, Pitcher, AL 135, 136
Two Home Runs in One Game Twice in One Season, Pitcher 136
Grand Slams, Pitcher, AL 138
Most Home Runs, Pitcher, Season 139
Most Hits, Pitcher, Career 139
Best-Hitting Pitchers, Season, AL 142
Best-Hitting Pitchers, Career 142
Twenty or More Wins, Rookie, AL 168
Brother Batteries, AL 185

Hobe Ferris

Longest Hitting Streaks, AL 70
Most Triples, Rookie, AL 165

Boo Ferriss

Shutout in First Start in Majors, AL 83

Shutout in First Two Major League Games, AL 85
Best Won-Lost Record, Season, AL (20 or more wins) 96
Twenty or More Wins, Rookie, AL 168
Most Shutouts, Rookie, AL 170

Lou Fette

Twenty or More Wins, Rookie, NL since 1900 168
Most Shutouts, Rookie, NL since 1900 170

Jesus Figueroa

Most Pinch Hits, Season, NL 69

Tom Filer

Undefeated Seasons (5 or more wins) 101

Dana Fillingim

Most Innings Pitched, Game, NL 128

Rollie Fingers

Most Strikeouts per Nine Innings, Career (Min. 1,500 IP) 114
Most Relief Wins, Career 117
Most Relief Wins, Season, AL 118
Most Relief Wins, Season, NL 119
Most Relief Losses, Career 120
Most Relief Losses, Season, AL 120
Most Relief Losses, Season, NL 120
Most Saves, Career 121
Most Saves, Season, NL 122
Most Wins Plus Saves, Season 123
Fewest Base Runners per Nine Innings, Career (Min. 1,500 IP) 130

Jim Finigan

.300 Average in Rookie Year Only, AL 164

Eddie Fisher

Most Relief Wins, Season, AL 118
Fewest Base Runners per Nine Innings, Career (Min. 1,500 IP) 130

Jack Fisher

Most Walks in One Game, AL 113

Ray Fisher

Pitchers Who Stole Home, AL 140

Carlton Fisk

Most Home Runs by Position, Career, AL 10
Most Home Runs by Position, Season, AL 11
Cycle Hitters, AL 49
Most Games Caught, Season 152, 153
Most Games Caught, Career 153
Three Consecutive Home Runs, Team, AL 197
Most Home Runs in One Inning, Team, AL 200
Most 20-Home Run Hitters, AL 208
Most 100-RBI Hitters, AL 212

Mike Fitzgerald

Home Run in First Appearance in Majors, NL 11
Most Home Runs in One Inning, Team, NL 201

Freddie Fitzsimmons

Most Wins, Career 102
Grand Slams, Pitcher, NL 138

Max Flack

.300-Hitting Outfields, NL 220

Ira Flagstead

Most Times Walked, Game, AL 31
.300-Hitting Outfields, AL 219

Patsy Flaherty

Most Shutout Losses, Season, AL 81
Grand Slams, Pitcher, NL 138

Mike Flanagan

Best Lefty-Righty Duos 229

Art Fletcher

Most Assists, Shortstop, Game 159

Elbie Fletcher

Most Putouts in Nine Innings, First Baseman 157
Three Consecutive Home Runs, Team, NL 198

Elmer Flick

Most Triples, Game, AL 28
Most Triples, Game, NL 28
Most Times Walked, Game, NL 32
.300-Hitting Outfields, NL 220

Curt Flood

Struck Out Twice in One Inning, NL 33
Most Consecutive Hits, NL 74
Fewest Errors by Position, Season, NL (Min. 150 G, excl. Pitchers) 147
Most Consecutive Errorless Games by Position, NL 148
Unassisted Double Plays, Outfielder 152
Home Runs by First Two Batters in Game, NL 194
Most 200-Hit Batters, NL 223

Ben Flowers

Shutout in First Start in Majors, AL 83

Doug Flynn

Most Triples, Game, NL 29

Jocko Flynn

Best Won-Lost Record, Season, NL (20 or more wins) 97
Most Consecutive Wins, NL 115

Curry Foley

Cycle Hitters, NL 50

Tim Foli

Most Times Walked, Game, NL 32
Cycle Hitters, NL 51

Dee Fondy

Three Consecutive Home Runs, Team, NL 199

Davy Force

Most Hits, Game, NL 35

Dan Ford

Three Home Runs in One Game, AL 15
Cycle Hitters, AL 49
Most Consecutive Hits, AL 73

Hod Ford

Best Double-Play Combinations, Season 149
Most Double Plays, Shortstop, Season, NL 151
Most Putouts, Shortstop, Game 159
Most Assists, Shortstop, Game 159

Russ Ford

Best Won-Lost Record, Season, AL (20 or more wins) 96
Twenty Wins One Year, 20 Losses the Next, AL 98
Most Strikeouts, Season, AL 105
Twenty or More Wins, Rookie, AL 168
ERA Under 2.00, Rookie, AL (Min. 130 IP) 169
Three Hundred or More Innings Pitched, Rookie, AL 169
Most Strikeouts, Rookie, AL 169
Most Complete Games, Rookie, AL 170
Most Shutouts, Rookie, AL 170

Whitey Ford

Most Shutouts, Career 79
Best Won-Lost Record, Season, AL (20 or more wins) 96
Most Wins, Career 102
Most Strikeouts, Season, AL 105
Most Consecutive Wins, AL 115
Fewest Base Runners per Nine Innings, Career (Min. 1,500 IP) 130
Career Spent With One Team (15 or more years) 181
Retired Numbers, AL 182

Brownie Foreman

Pitching Brothers, Same Team, NL 186

Frank Foreman

Two Home Runs in One Game, Pitcher, NL 136
Pitching Brothers, Same Team, NL 186

Mike Fornieles

Shutout in First Start in Majors, AL 83

Bob Forsch

No-Hitters, NL (9 innings or more) 90
Most No-Hitters, Career 94
Grand Slams, Pitcher, NL 139
Most Wins by Brothers 187

Ken Forsch

No-Hitters, NL (9 innings or more) 90
Most Wins by Brothers 187

Terry Forster

Most Saves, Career 121

George Foster

Most Grand Slams, Career 3
Most Home Runs, Season, NL 7, 8
Three Home Runs in One Game, NL 19
Easiest to Strike Out, Career (Min. 1,000 G) 44
Two Legs of Triple Crown, NL 48
Most RBIs, Season, NL 60
Three Consecutive Home Runs, Team, NL 199
Home Run Duos, Season, NL (25 each) 210
Home Run Duos, Career, NL 211
.300-Hitting Outfields, NL 221

Rube Foster

No-Hitters, AL (9 innings or more) 87

Bob Fothergill

Cycle Hitters, AL 49
Most Pinch Hits, Season, AL 68
Most Pinch Hits, Career 69
.300-Hitting Outfields, AL 219

Jack Fournier

Three Home Runs in One Game, NL 17
Most Hits, Game, NL 36
Most Consecutive Hits, NL 74

Dick Fowler

No-Hitters, AL (9 innings or more) 87

Nellie Fox

Hardest to Strike Out, Career (Min. 1,000 G) 44
Most Consecutive Games Played 71
Fewest Games Missed (10-Year Period) 72
Best Double-Play Combinations, Season 149, 150
Most Double Plays, Second Baseman, Season, AL 151
Retired Numbers, AL 182

Pete Fox

Longest Hitting Streaks, AL 70
Most 200-Hit Batters, AL 223

Jimmie Foxx

Most Grand Slams, Career 3
Grand Slam In Two Consecutive Games, AL 3
Most Grand Slams, Season, AL 4
Most Home Runs, Season, AL 7
Most Home Runs, Career 9
Best Home Run Ratio, Career 10
Most Home Runs by Position, Career, AL 10
Two Home Runs in One Game Most Often 12
Three Home Runs in One Game, AL 13
Most Home Runs in a Doubleheader, AL 20
Most Extra-Inning Home Runs, Career 23
Most Extra-Base Hits in a Doubleheader, AL 27
Most Total Bases, Game, AL 30
Most Total Bases, Season, AL 30
Most Times Walked, Game, AL 31
Most Hits, Game, AL 35
Most Combined Hits and Walks, Season, AL 39, 40

Lowest ERA, Season, NL 127
Fewest Base Runners per Nine Innings, Career (Min. 1,500 IP) 130
Won 20 and Hit .300. in Same Year, NL 134
Most Home Runs, Pitcher, Career 135
Grand Slams, Pitcher, NL 139
Career Spent With One Team (15 or more years) 181
Retired Numbers, NL 183

George Gibson

Most Games Caught, Season 153
Most Games Caught, Career 153

Kirk Gibson

Three Consecutive Home Runs, Team, AL 197
Most Home Runs in One Inning, Team, AL 200
Most 20-Home Run Hitters, AL 208

Sam Gibson

Most Walks in One Game, AL 113

Charlie Gilbert

Fathers and Sons in Baseball 190

Larry Gilbert

Fathers and Sons in Baseball 190

Tookie Gilbert

Fathers and Sons in Baseball 190

Wally Gilbert

Most Hits, Game, NL 36

George Gill

Shutout in First Start in Majors, AL 83
Worst Won-Lost Record, Season (12 or more losses) 95

Carden Gillenwater

Most Putouts, Outfielder, Game 156

Jim Gilliam

Most Assists, Second Baseman, Game 158
Most Triples, Rookie, NL 165
Retired Numbers, NL 183

Frank Gilmore

Most Strikeouts in Nine-Inning Game, NL 111
Most Consecutive Losses, NL 116

Dave Giusti

Most Saves, Career 121
Most Saves, Season, NL 122

Dan Gladden

Leadoff Home Runs in Two Consecutive Games, NL 21
Highest Batting Average, Rookie, NL (Min. 300 AB) 167
.300-Hitting Outfields, NL 221

Fred Gladding

Undefeated Seasons (5 or more wins) 101
Most Saves, Career 121

Fred Glade

Most Shutout Losses, Season, AL 81
Most Complete Games, Rookie, AL 170
Most Shutouts, Rookie, AL 170

Jack Glasscock

Most Hits, Game, NL 36
Cycle Hitters, NL 51

Kid Gleason

Longest Hitting Streaks, AL 70
Most Errors by Position, Season, AL 147
Pennant-Winning Rookie Managers, AL 171

Bill Glynn

Three Home Runs in One Game, AL 14

John Gochnaur

Most Errors by Position, Season, AL 147

Fred Goldsmith

Best Won-Lost Record, Season, NL (20 or more wins) 97
Two Home Runs in One Game, Pitcher, NL 136

Lefty Gomez

Struck Out Twice in One Inning, AL 32
Best Won-Lost Record, Season, AL (20 or more wins) 96
Triple-Crown Pitchers, AL (most wins, lowest ERA, most strikeouts) 128
Best Lefty-Righty Duos 228

Johnny Gooch

Most Hits, Game, NL 36
.300 Average in Rookie Year Only, NL 164

Wilbur Good

Stole 2nd, 3rd, and Home in One Game, NL 66

Dwight Gooden

Best Won-Lost Record, Season, NL (20 or more wins) 97
Most Wins by Age, Season, NL since 1900 104
Most Strikeouts, Season, NL since 1900 106, 107
Most Strikeouts in Nine-Inning Game, NL 111
Most Games with 10 or More Strikeouts, Career 114
Most Consecutive Wins, NL 115
Triple-Crown Pitchers, NL (most wins, lowest ERA, most strikeouts) 129
Most Strikeouts, Rookie, NL since 1900 169

Ival Goodman

Most Triples, Rookie, NL 165

Ed Goodson

Most Home Runs by Team, Game, NL 206

Joe Gordon

Most Home Runs by Position, Career, AL 10
Most Home Runs by Position, Season, AL 11
Most Home Runs in Final Season 24
Cycle Hitters, AL 49
Longest Hitting Streaks, AL 70
Best Double-Play Combinations, Season 150
Three Consecutive Home Runs, Team, AL 196
Most Home Runs by Team, Game, AL 202
Most 100-RBI Hitters, AL 212

Sid Gordon

Most Grand Slams, Season, NL 4
Two Home Runs in One Inning, NL 12
Easiest to Double Up, Career (Min. 1000 G) 41
Most Consecutive Hits, NL 74
Three Consecutive Home Runs, Team, NL 198

George Gore

Most Extra-Base Hits, Game, NL 26
Most Hits, Game, NL 35
Three Consecutive Home Runs, Team, Other Leagues 199
Most Home Runs by Team, Game, NL 204
Teammates Who Finished 1-2 in Batting, NL 222

Tom Gorman

Worst-Hitting Pitchers, Career (Min. 100 AB) 144

Goose Goslin

Three Home Runs in One Game, AL 13
Grounded into Most Double Plays, Game, AL 43
Cycle Hitters, AL 49
Most RBIs, Career 61
Most Runs Produced, Career 62
Longest Hitting Streaks, AL 70
Most 100-RBI Hitters, AL 212
.300-Hitting Outfields, AL 219, 220

Goose Gossage

Most Relief Wins, Career 117
Most Relief Wins, Season, AL 118
Most Relief Wins, Season, NL 119
Most Relief Losses, Career 120
Most Relief Losses, Season, AL 120
Most Saves, Career 121
Most Saves, Season, AL 122

Jim Gott

Two Home Runs in One Game, Pitcher, NL 136

Hank Gowdy

Most No-Hitters Caught, Career 154

Jack Graham

Fathers and Sons in Baseball 190

Peaches Graham

Fathers and Sons in Baseball 190

Alex Grammas

Best Double-Play Combinations, Season 149

Wayne Granger

Most Saves, Career 121
Most Saves, Season, NL 122
Most Wins Plus Saves, Season 123

Mudcat Grant

Shutout with Most Hits Allowed, AL 86

George Grantham

Most Errors by Position, Season, NL since 1900 147
Most .300 Hitters, Season, NL (300 AB each) 218

Freddie Green

Fathers and Sons in Baseball 190

Gary Green

Fathers and Sons in Baseball 190

Gene Green

Three Consecutive Home Runs, Team, AL 196

Lenny Green

Home Runs by First Two Batters in Game, AL 194

Pumpsie Green

Three Consecutive Home Runs, Team, AL 196

Hank Greenberg

Most Grand Slams, Career 3
Most Home Runs, Season, AL 7
Best Home Run Ratio, Career 10
Most Home Runs by Position, Season, AL 11
Two Home Runs in One Game Most Often 12
Most Home Runs in Final Season 24
Most Combined Hits and Walks, Season, AL 40
Two Legs of Triple Crown, AL 46
More Walks than Hits, Season, NL 55
Most RBIs, Season, AL 60
Most Runs Produced, Season, AL 61
More RBIs than Games Played, Season, AL 64, 65
Home Runs in Most Consecutive At-Bats, AL 76
Retired Numbers, AL 182
Most Home Runs by Team, Game, NL 205
Home Run Trios, Season, AL 209
Home Run Duos, Season, AL (25 each) 210
Home Run Duos, Career, AL 211
Most 100-RBI Hitters, AL 212
Most 200-Hit Batters, AL 223

Jim Greengrass

Most Doubles, Game, NL 27
One Hundred or More RBIs, Rookie, NL 166
Three Consecutive Home Runs, Team, NL 198

Dave Gregg

Pitching Brothers, Same Team, AL 186

Vean Gregg

Twenty or More Wins, Rookie, AL 168
ERA Under 2.00, Rookie, AL (Min. 130 IP) 169
Most Shutouts, Rookie, AL 170

Pitching Brothers, Same Team, AL 186

Bill Greif

Worst-Hitting Pitchers, Career (Min. 100 AB) 144

Bobby Grich

Three Home Runs in One Game, AL 15
Fewest Errors by Position, Season, AL (Min. 150 G, excl. Pitchers) 147
Best Double-Play Combinations, Season 150
Most Double Plays, Second Baseman, Season, AL 151
Three Consecutive Home Runs, Team, AL 197

Ken Griffey

Three Home Runs in One Game, NL 19
No-Hit Spoilers - The Only Hit Most Often 59
Three Consecutive Home Runs, Team, NL 199
Stolen Base Duos, Season, NL 217
.300-Hitting Outfields, NL 221

Alfredo Griffin

Hardest to Double Up, Career (Min. 1,000 G) 42
Best Double-Play Combinations, Season 149
Most Double Plays, Shortstop, Season, AL 151

Tom Griffin

Most Strikeouts, Season, NL since 1900 107
Most Strikeouts, Rookie, NL since 1900 169

Bert Griffith

.300 Average in Rookie Year Only, NL 164

Clark Griffith

Most 20-Win Seasons 101
Won 20 and Hit .300 in Same Year, AL 134
Pennant-Winning Rookie Managers, AL 171
Most Wins, Manager, Career 184

Tommy Griffith

.300-Hitting Outfields, NL 220

Bob Grim

Grand Slams, Pitcher, AL 138
Twenty or More Wins, Rookie, AL 168

Burleigh Grimes

Grounded into Most Double Plays, Game, NL 43
Most Shutouts, Career 80
Most Shutout Losses, Career 80
Most Wins, Career 102
Most Wins by Age, Season, NL since 1900 104
Most Consecutive Wins, NL 115
Most Consecutive Losses, NL 116
Most Innings Pitched, Game, NL 128
Won 20 and Hit .300. in Same Year, NL 134
Most Hits, Pitcher, Career 139

Oscar Grimes

Fathers and Sons in Baseball 190

Ray Grimes

Batting Champion by Widest Margin, NL 56
RBI in Most Consecutive Games, NL 72
Most Doubles, Rookie, NL 165
Fathers and Sons in Baseball 190

Charlie Grimm

Longest Hitting Streaks, NL 71
Pennant-Winning Rookie Managers, NL 171
Most Wins, Manager, Career 184
Most Home Runs in One Inning, Team, NL 200

Ross Grimsley

Fathers and Sons in Baseball 190

Ross Grimsley

Fathers and Sons in Baseball 190

Dan Griner

Shutout with Most Hits Allowed, NL 86

Dick Groat

Most Hits, Game, NL 36
Best Double-Play Combinations, Season 149
Most Double Plays, Shortstop, Season, NL 151
Three Consecutive Home Runs, Team, NL 199
Most 200-Hit Batters, NL 223

Heinie Groh

Most Times Walked, Game, NL 32
Cycle Hitters, NL 51

Bob Groom

Struck Out Twice in One Inning, AL 32
No-Hitters, AL (9 innings or more) 87
Most Consecutive Losses, AL 115

Greg Gross

Most Pinch Hits, Season, NL 68
Most Pinch Hits, Career 69

Wayne Gross

The Worst Hitters (Min. 2,500 AB) 52
Two Pinch-Hit Home Runs in One Inning, Team, AL 192
Back-to-Back Pinch-Hit Home Runs, Team 193

Jerry Grote

Most Consecutive Hits, NL 74
Most Games Caught, Career 153
Three Consecutive Home Runs, Team, NL 199

Johnny Groth

Most Consecutive Hits, AL 73
.300-Hitting Outfields, AL 220

Lefty Grove

Most Times Struck Out, Game, AL 33
Most Shutouts, Career 80
Best Won-Lost Record, Season, AL (20 or more wins) 96

Odell Hale
Cycle Hitters, AL 49

Sammy Hale
Grounded into Most Double Plays, Game, AL 43
Most Pinch Hits, Season, AL 68
Most .300 Hitters, Season, AL (300 AB each) 217

Ed Halicki
No-Hitters, NL (9 innings or more) 90

Dick Hall
Most Relief Wins, Career 117

George Hall
Most Triples, Game, NL 28

Jimmie Hall
Thirty or More Home Runs, Rookie, AL 163
Four Consecutive Home Runs, Team 196
Most Home Runs in One Inning, Team, AL 200
Most Home Runs by Team, Game, AL 202
Most 30-Home Run Hitters, AL 207
Most 20-Home Run Hitters, AL 208

Mel Hall
Three Consecutive Home Runs, Team, AL 197

Tom Haller
Most Games Caught, Career 153

Billy Hamilton
Most Triples, Game, NL 28
Most Triples, Game, Other Leagues 29
Most Combined Hits and Walks, Season, NL 40, 41
Highest Batting Average, Career 53
Most Runs, Season, NL 59
Most Runs, Career 60
Most Runs Produced, Season, NL 62
Longest Hitting Streaks, NL 71
Teammates Who Finished 1-2 in Batting, NL 222

Earl Hamilton
No-Hitters, AL (9 innings or more) 87
Undefeated Seasons (5 or more wins) 101

Jack Hamilton
Grand Slams, Pitcher, NL 139

Atlee Hammaker
Worst-Hitting Pitchers, Career (Min. 100 AB) 144

Bill Hands
Worst-Hitting Pitchers, Career (Min. 100 AB) 144

Ned Hanlon
Most Wins, Manager, Career 184
Most League Pennants Won, Manager 185

Jim Hannan
Worst-Hitting Pitchers, Career (Min. 100 AB) 144

Ron Hansen
The Worst Hitters (Min. 2,500 AB) 52
Unassisted Triple Plays 149
Best Double-Play Combinations, Season 150
Three Consecutive Home Runs, Team, AL 196

Mel Harder
Most Wins, Career 102
Two Home Runs in One Game, Pitcher, AL 136
Most Times Struck Out, Pitcher, Career since 1900 141
Career Spent With One Team (15 or more years) 181

Alex Hardy
Shutout in First Start in Majors, NL 84

Steve Hargan
Worst Won-Lost Record, Season (12 or more losses) 95

Bubbles Hargrave
Teammates Who Finished 1-2 in Batting, NL 222

Dick Harley
Most Hits, Game, NL 36
Most Putouts, Outfielder, Game 156

George Harper
Three Home Runs in One Game, NL 17

Jack Harper
Three Hundred or More Innings Pitched, Rookie, NL since 1900 169

Tommy Harper
Most Leadoff Home Runs, Career 22
Thirty Home Runs with 30 Stolen Bases, Season, AL 24
Most Stolen Bases, Season, AL 65
Most Stolen Bases, Career 66

Toby Harrah
Three Consecutive Home Runs, Team, AL 197

Bud Harrelson
Hardest to Double Up, Career (Min. 1,000 G) 42
Most Assists, Shortstop, Game 159

Ken Harrelson
Three Home Runs in One Game, AL 14

Bucky Harris
Best Double-Play Combinations, Season 150
.300 Average in Rookie Year Only, AL 164
Pennant-Winning Rookie Managers, AL 171
Most Wins, Manager, Career 184

Joe Harris
Most Shutout Losses, Season, AL 81
Most Consecutive Losses, AL 115

Most Innings Pitched, Game, AL 127

Lum Harris
Most Consecutive Losses, AL 115

Jack Harshman
Most Strikeouts in Nine-Inning Game, AL 110
Most Home Runs, Pitcher, Career 135
Two Home Runs in One Game, Pitcher, AL 136
Two Home Runs in One Game Twice in One Season, Pitcher 136
Most Home Runs by Team, Game, AL 202

Jim Ray Hart
Cycle Hitters, NL 51
Most RBIs in One Inning, NL 63
Thirty or More Home Runs, Rookie, NL 163
Most 30-Home Run Hitters, NL 208
Home Run Trios, Season, NL 209

Gabby Hartnett
Most Home Runs by Position, Career, NL 10
Longest Hitting Streaks, NL 71
Most Games Caught, Career 153
Pennant-Winning Rookie Managers, NL 171
Home Run Duos, Season, NL (25 each) 210

Topsy Hartsel
Most Putouts, Outfielder, Game 156

Ervin Harvey
Most Hits, Game, AL 35

Bill Hassamaer
Most Triples, Game, NL 28
Cycle Hitters, NL 51

Buddy Hassett
Most Consecutive Hits, NL 74

Mickey Hatcher
Two Pinch-Hit Home Runs in One Inning, Team, AL 192
Most Home Runs in One Inning, Team, AL 200

Grady Hatton
Home Runs by First Two Batters in Game, NL 194
Three Consecutive Home Runs, Team, NL 198

Joe Hauser
Three Home Runs in One Game, AL 13

Bill Hawke
No-Hitters, NL (9 innings or more) 89

Thorny Hawkes
Most Putouts, Second Baseman, Game 157

Chicken Hawks
.300 Batting Average in Final Season (Min. 100 G) 39

Frankie Hayes
Most Doubles, Game, AL 27
Most Games Caught, Season 152
Most Games Caught, Career 153

Jackie Hayes
Best Double-Play Combinations, Season 150

Von Hayes
Two Home Runs in One Inning, NL 12
Most RBIs in One Inning, NL 63
Home Runs by First Two Batters in Game, NL 195
Stolen Base Duos, Season, NL 216

Joe Haynes
Pitchers Who Stole Home, AL 140

Ed Head
No-Hitters, NL (9 innings or more) 89

Fran Healy
Most No-Hitters Caught, Career 155

Jim Hearn
Most Grand Slams Allowed, Career 133
Two Home Runs in One Game, Pitcher, NL 136

Jeff Heath
Twenty Doubles, 20 Triples, and 20 Home Runs, Season, AL 29
Three Consecutive Home Runs, Team, AL 196
.300-Hitting Outfields, NL 221

Mike Heath
Most Home Runs in One Inning, Team, AL 200

Cliff Heathcote
Cycle Hitters, NL 51
Most Home Runs in One Inning, Team, NL 200

Dave Heaverlo
Most Relief Losses, Season, AL 120

Wally Hebert
Worst Won-Lost Record, Season (12 or more losses) 95

Richie Hebner
Most Consecutive Times Struck Out, NL 74
Three Consecutive Home Runs, Team, NL 199

Guy Hecker
Most Hits, Game, Other Leagues 37
Most Runs, Game, Other Leagues 60
No-Hitters, Other Leagues 91
Most Strikeouts, Season before 1900 107
Most Strikeouts in Nine-Inning Game, Other Leagues 112
Two Complete Game Wins in One Day, Other Leagues 125
Three Home Runs in One Game, Pitcher 135

Rookie No-Hitters, Other Leagues 168
Teammates Who Finished 1-2 in Batting, Other Leagues 223

Don Heffner
Most Assists, Second Baseman, Game 158

Jim Hegan
The Worst Hitters (Min. 2,500 AB) 52
Most Games Caught, Season 152
Most Games Caught, Career 153
Most No-Hitters Caught, Career 154
Fathers and Sons in Baseball 190

Mike Hegan
Cycle Hitters, AL 49
Most Consecutive Errorless Games by Position, AL 148
Fathers and Sons in Baseball 191

Emmet Heidrick
.300-Hitting Outfields, NL 220

Harry Heilmann
The .400 Hitters, AL 52
Highest Batting Average, Career 53
Most Runs Produced, Career 62
Most Consecutive Hits, AL 73
.300-Hitting Outfields, AL 219
Teammates Who Finished 1-2 in Batting, AL 222

Ken Heintzelman
Fathers and Sons in Baseball 191

Tom Heintzelman
Fathers and Sons in Baseball 191

Woodie Held
Easiest to Strike Out, Career (Min. 1,000 G) 44
Four Consecutive Home Runs, Team 196
Most Home Runs in One Inning, Team, AL 200

Tommy Helms
Most Double Plays, Second Baseman, Season, NL 151

Charlie Hemphill
Most Times Walked, Game, AL 31

Rollie Hemsley
Most Games Caught, Career 153
Most No-Hitters Caught, Career 154

Solly Hemus
Most Times Walked, Game, NL 32

Dave Henderson
Most Putouts, Outfielder, Game 156
Three Consecutive Home Runs, Team, AL 197
Most Home Runs by Team, Game, AL 203

Hardie Henderson
Most Strikeouts, Season before 1900 107

Ken Henderson
Switch-Hit Home Runs in One Game, AL 23

Rickey Henderson
Most Leadoff Home Runs, Career 22
Twenty Home Runs with 50 Stolen Bases, Season 24
Most Times Walked, Game, AL 32
Most Stolen Bases, Season, AL 65
Most Stolen Bases, Career 66
Most Times Caught Stealing, Game, AL 68
Home Runs by First Two Batters in Game, AL 194
Stolen Base Duos, Season, AL 216

Steve Henderson
Three Consecutive Home Runs, Team, AL 197

Bob Hendley
Worst-Hitting Pitchers, Career (Min. 100 AB) 144

George Hendrick
Three Home Runs in One Game, AL 15

Harvey Hendrick
Stole 2nd, 3rd, and Home in One Game, NL 66
Longest Hitting Streaks, NL 71

Ellie Hendricks
Most Times Walked, Game, NL 32

Claude Hendrix
No-Hitters, Other Leagues 91
Won 20 and Hit .300. in Same Year, NL 134

Weldon Henley
No-Hitters, AL (9 innings or more) 87

Butch Henline
Three Home Runs in One Game, NL 17

Tommy Henrich
Most Grand Slams, Season, AL 4
Most Home Runs by Team, Game, AL 202
Most 30-Home Run Hitters, AL 207

Dutch Henry
Most Consecutive Losses, AL 115

John Henry
Shutout in First Start in Majors, NL 84

Ron Herbel
Most At-Bats with No Hits, Pitcher, Season since 1900 141
Worst-Hitting Pitchers, Career (Min. 100 AB) 144

Babe Herman
Three Home Runs in One Game, NL 17

Most Total Bases, Season, NL 30
Most Combined Hits and Walks, Season, NL 41
Grounded into Most Double Plays, Game, NL 43
Cycle Hitters, NL 51
Most Consecutive Hits, NL 74
.300-Hitting Outfields, NL 221

Billy Herman

Grounded into Most Double Plays, Game, NL 43
Most Assists, Second Baseman, Game 158
Two Hundred or More Hits, Rookie, NL 163
Most Doubles, Rookie, NL 165

Gene Hermanski

Three Home Runs in One Game, NL 17
Most Times Walked, Game, NL 32

Keith Hernandez

Most Grand Slams, Season, NL 4
Cycle Hitters, NL 51

Ramon Hernandez

Undefeated Seasons (5 or more wins) 101

Willie Hernandez

Most Saves, Career 121
Most Saves, Season, AL 122
Most Wins Plus Saves, Season 123
Most Extra-Inning Home Runs Allowed, Career 133

Larry Herndon

Three Home Runs in One Game, AL 15
Home Runs in Most Consecutive At-Bats, AL 76

Tommy Herr

Best Double-Play Combinations, Season 150

Troy Herriage

Worst Won-Lost Record, Season (12 or more losses) 95

Buck Herzog

Stole 2nd, 3rd, and Home in One Game, NL 66
Most Steals of Home, Career 67

Otto Hess

Most Innings Pitched, Game, NL 128
ERA Under 2.00, Rookie, AL (Min. 130 IP) 169
Teams with Three 20-Game Winners, AL 227

Joe Heving

Most Relief Wins, Season, AL 118

John Hibbard

Shutout in First Start in Majors, NL 84

Jim Hickman

Three Home Runs in One Game, NL 18
Easiest to Strike Out, Career (Min. 1,000 G) 44
Cycle Hitters, NL 51
Most Home Runs by Team, Game, NL 206

Piano Legs Hickman

Longest Hitting Streaks, NL 71
Undefeated Seasons (5 or more wins) 101
Most Walks in One Game, NL 113
Most Errors by Position, Season, NL since 1900 147
Three Consecutive Home Runs, Team, AL 196

Pinky Higgins

Three Home Runs in One Game, AL 13, 14
Cycle Hitters, AL 49
Most Consecutive Hits, AL 73
Three Consecutive Home Runs, Team, AL 196

Andy High

Hardest to Strike Out, Career (Min. 1,000 G) 44
Three or More Brothers in Baseball 187

Charlie High

Three or More Brothers in Baseball 187

Hugh High

Three or More Brothers in Baseball 187

Ted Higuera

Most Strikeouts, Season, AL 105

Carmen Hill

Shutout in First Start in Majors, NL 84

Chuck Hiller

Home Runs by First Two Batters in Game, NL 194

John Hiller

Most Consecutive Strikeouts, AL 116
Most Relief Wins, Career 117
Most Relief Wins, Season, AL 118
Most Relief Losses, Career 120
Most Relief Losses, Season, AL 120
Most Saves, Career 121
Most Saves, Season, AL 122
Most Wins Plus Saves, Season 122
Career Spent With One Team (15 or more years) 181

Dave Hillman

Worst-Hitting Pitchers, Career (Min. 100 AB) 144

Bill Hinchman

Unassisted Double Plays, Outfielder 152

Paul Hines

Most Hits, Game, NL 35
Triple Crown Winners, NL 45
Fewest Games Missed (10-Year Period) 72

Chuck Hinton

Most Home Runs by Team, Game, AL 203

Larry Hisle

Most Times Struck Out, Game, NL 34

Easiest to Strike Out, Career (Min. 1,000 G) 44
Cycle Hitters, AL 49
Most Home Runs by Team, Game, AL 203

Myril Hoag

Most Hits, Game, AL 35

Don Hoak

Most Times Struck Out, Game, NL 34
Most Home Runs by Team, Game, NL 205

Glen Hobbie

Two Home Runs in One Game, Pitcher, NL 136

Butch Hobson

Three Consecutive Home Runs, Team, AL 197
Most Home Runs in One Inning, Team, AL 200
Most Home Runs by Team, Game, AL 202
Most 30-Home Run Hitters, AL 207
Most 20-Home Run Hitters, AL 208
Most 100-RBI Hitters, AL 212

George Hockette

Shutout in First Start in Majors, AL 83

Johnny Hodapp

Two Hits in One Inning Twice in One Game 37
.300 Batting Average in Final Season (Min. 100 G) 39

Gomer Hodge

Most Pinch Hits, Season, AL 68

Gil Hodges

Most Grand Slams, Career 3
Most Home Runs, Season, NL 8
Best Home Run Ratio, Career 10
Most Home Runs by Position, Career, NL 10
Two Home Runs in One Game Most Often 12
Four Home Runs in One Game, NL 20
Most Total Bases, Game, NL 30
Cycle Hitters, NL 51
Most RBIs, Game, NL 64
Retired Numbers, NL 183
Three Consecutive Home Runs, Team, NL 199
Most 40-Home Run Hitters, NL 206
Most 30-Home Run Hitters, NL 208
Home Run Trios, Season, NL 209
Home Run Duos, Season, NL (25 each) 210
Home Run Duos, Career, NL 211

Ralph Hodgin

.300 Average in Rookie Year Only, AL 164

Billy Hoeft

Two Home Runs in One Game, Pitcher, AL 136

Bill Hoffer

Best Won-Lost Record, Season, NL (20 or more wins) 97

Bobby Hofman

Two Pinch-Hit Home Runs in One Inning, Team, NL 193
Three Consecutive Home Runs, Team, NL 198

Shanty Hogan

Most .300 Hitters, Season, NL (300 AB each) 218

Chief Hogsett

Two Home Runs in One Game, Pitcher, AL 135

Al Hollingsworth

Grand Slams, Pitcher, NL 138

Charlie Hollocher

Most Triples, Game, NL 29

Bobo Holloman

Shutout in First Start in Majors, AL 83
No-Hitters, AL (9 innings or more) 88
Rookie No-Hitters, AL 167

Ducky Holmes

Most Assists, Outfielder, Game 156

Tommy Holmes

Hardest to Strike Out, Career (Min. 1,000 G) 44
No-Hit Spoilers - The Only Hit Most Often 58
Longest Hitting Streaks, NL 71
.300-Hitting Outfields, NL 221

Jim Holt

Three Consecutive Home Runs, Team, AL 197

Ken Holtzman

No-Hitters, NL (9 innings or more) 90
Most No-Hitters, Career 93
Undefeated Seasons (5 or more wins) 101
Most Strikeouts, Season, NL since 1900 107
Teams with Three 20-Game Winners, AL 227

Wally Hood

Fathers and Sons in Baseball 191

Wally Hood

Fathers and Sons in Baseball 191

Harry Hooper

Leadoff Home Runs in Two Consecutive Games, AL 21
Most Leadoff Home Runs, Career 22
No-Hit Spoilers - The Only Hit Most Often 57
Most Steals of Home, Career 67
.300-Hitting Outfields, AL 219

Burt Hooton

No-Hitters, NL (9 innings or more) 90
Grand Slams, Pitcher, NL 139
Rookie No-Hitters, NL 167

Johnny Hopp
Most Hits, Game, NL 36
Most Putouts, Outfielder, Game 156

Joe Horlen
No-Hitters, AL (9 innings or more) 88
Fewest Base Runners per Nine Innings, Career (Min. 1,500 IP) 130

Bob Horner
Best Home Run Ratio, Career 10
Four Home Runs in One Game, NL 20
Three Consecutive Home Runs, Team, NL 199
Home Run Duos, Career, NL 211

Rogers Hornsby
Most Grand Slams, Career 3
Most Home Runs, Season, NL 8
Most Home Runs by Position, Career, NL 10
Most Home Runs by Position, Season, NL 11
Three Home Runs in One Game, NL 17
Most Total Bases, Season, NL 30
Most Combined Hits and Walks, Season, NL 40
Batting Champion with Two Different Clubs 43
Triple Crown Winners, NL 45
Players Who Just Missed Triple Crowns, NL 45
Two Legs of Triple Crown, NL 47
The .400 Hitters, NL 52
Highest Batting Average, Career 53
Most Seasons with 200 Hits 54
Batting Champion by Widest Margin, NL 56
Most RBIs, Season, NL 60
Most RBIs, Career 61
Most Runs Produced, Season, NL 62
Most Runs Produced, Career 62
More RBIs than Games Played, Season, NL 65
Most Consecutive Pinch Hits 70
Longest Hitting Streaks, NL 71
Most Consecutive Hits, NL 74
Most Assists, Shortstop, Game 159
Most 100-RBI Hitters, NL 212
Teammates Who Finished 1-2 in Batting, NL 222

Tony Horton
Three Home Runs in One Game, AL 15
Most Home Runs in Final Season 24
Cycle Hitters, AL 49

Willie Horton
Most Grand Slams, Season, AL 4
Two Home Runs in One Game Most Often 12
Three Home Runs in One Game, AL 15
Most Putouts, Outfielder, Game 156
Three Consecutive Home Runs, Team, AL 197

Pete Hotaling
Most Hits, Game, Other Leagues 37

Sadie Houck
Most Triples, Game, Other Leagues 29

Charlie Hough
Most Relief Wins, Season, NL 119
Most Relief Losses, Season, NL 120

Ralph Houk
Pennant-Winning Rookie Managers, AL 171
Most Wins, Manager, Career 184

Charlie Householder
Most Putouts in Nine Innings, First Baseman 157

Elston Howard
Most Games Caught, Career 153
Retired Numbers, AL 182
Two Pinch-Hit Home Runs in One Inning, Team, AL 192
Most 20-Home Run Hitters, AL 208

Frank Howard
Most Home Runs, Season, AL 7
Best Home Run Ratio, Career 10
Most Times Struck Out, Game, AL 33
Easiest to Double Up, Career (Min. 1000 G) 41
Easiest to Strike Out, Career (Min. 1,000 G) 44
Two Legs of Triple Crown, AL 46
Two Pinch-Hit Home Runs in One Inning, Team, NL 193
Back-to-Back Pinch-Hit Home Runs, Team 193
Three Consecutive Home Runs, Team, AL 197

Dixie Howell
Two Home Runs in One Game, Pitcher, AL 136

Harry Howell
Most Shutout Losses, Season, AL 81
Shutout with Most Hits Allowed, AL 86
Most Complete Games, Season, AL 131

Ken Howell
Most Relief Losses, Season, NL 120

Roy Howell
Most RBIs, Game, AL 64

LaMarr Hoyt
Most Consecutive Wins, AL 115
Worst-Hitting Pitchers, Career (Min. 100 AB) 144

Waite Hoyt
Shutout with Most Hits Allowed, AL 86
Most Wins, Career 102
Best Lefty-Righty Duos 229

Al Hrabosky
Most Relief Wins, Season, NL 119

Kent Hrbek
Most Grand Slams, Season, AL 4
Three Consecutive Home Runs, Team, AL 197
Most 20-Home Run Hitters, AL 208

Glenn Hubbard
Best Double-Play Combinations, Season 149
Most Assists, Second Baseman, Game 158

Carl Hubbell
Most Shutouts, Career 80
Most Shutouts, Season, NL 81
No-Hitters, NL (9 innings or more) 89
Best Won-Lost Record, Season, NL (20 or more wins) 97
Most Wins, Career 102
Most Consecutive Wins, NL 115
Best Control Pitchers, Career 126
Most Innings Pitched, Game, NL 128
Fewest Base Runners per Nine Innings, Career (Min. 1,500 IP) 130
Career Spent With One Team (15 or more years) 181
Retired Numbers, NL 183
Best Lefty-Righty Duos 228

Charles Hudson
Worst-Hitting Pitchers, Career (Min. 100 AB) 144

Johnny Hudson
Grounded into Most Double Plays, Game, NL 43

Sid Hudson
Most Walks in One Game, AL 113

Miller Huggins
Most Triples, Game, NL 29
Most Times Caught Stealing, Game, NL 68
Most Wins, Manager, Career 184
Most League Pennants Won, Manager 185

Jim Hughes
Shutout in First Start in Majors, NL 84
Shutout in First Two Major League Games, NL 85
No-Hitters, NL (9 innings or more) 89
Best Won-Lost Record, Season, NL (20 or more wins) 97
Rookie No-Hitters, NL 167

Long Tom Hughes
Most Strikeouts, Season, NL since 1900 107
Three Hundred or More Innings Pitched, Rookie, NL since 1900 169
Most Strikeouts, Rookie, NL since 1900 169
Most Complete Games, Rookie, NL since 1900 170
Teams with Three 20-Game Winners, AL 227

Roy Hughes
Grounded into Most Double Plays, Game, NL 43

Tom Hughes
No-Hitters, AL (9 innings or more) 87
No-Hitters, NL (9 innings or more) 89
Most No-Hitters, Career 93

Jim Hughey
Most Consecutive Losses, NL 116

Rudy Hulswitt
Most Errors by Position, Season, NL since 1900 147

Randy Hundley
Cycle Hitters, NL 51
Fewest Errors by Position, Season, NL (Min. 150 G, excl. Pitchers) 147
Most Games Caught, Season 152
Most Games Caught, Career 153
Most No-Hitters Caught, Career 155
Most Home Runs by Team, Game, NL 205

Ron Hunt
Three Consecutive Home Runs, Team, NL 199

Catfish Hunter
Most Shutouts, Career 79
No-Hitters, AL (9 innings or more) 88
Perfect Games (9 innings or more) 94
Best Won-Lost Record, Season, AL (20 or more wins) 96
Most Wins, Career 102
Most Consecutive Wins, AL 115
Fewest Base Runners per Nine Innings, Career (Min. 1,500 IP) 129
Won 20 and Hit .300 in Same Year, AL 134
Best-Hitting Pitchers, Season, AL 142
Teams with Three 20-Game Winners, AL 227

Don Hurst
Most 30-Home Run Hitters, NL 208
Most 100-RBI Hitters, NL 212

Fred Hutchinson
Pitchers Who Stole Home, AL 140
Best-Hitting Pitchers, Career 143
Retired Numbers, NL 183

Bill Hutchison
Most Strikeouts, Season before 1900 108
Two Complete Game Wins in One Day, NL before 1900 125

Tom Hutton
Most Pinch Hits, Career 69

Pete Incaviglia
Thirty or More Home Runs, Rookie, AL 163
Most Home Runs by Team, Game, AL 203

Hal Irelan
Grounded into Most Double Plays, Game, NL 43

Monte Irvin
Grounded into Most Double Plays, Game, NL 43
Most Home Runs in One Inning, Team, NL 200
Most Home Runs by Team, Game, NL 205

Arthur Irwin
Most Assists, Shortstop, Game 159

Mike Ivie
Most Pinch-Hit Grand Slams, Career 6

Ray Jablonski
One Hundred or More RBIs, Rookie, NL 166

Grant Jackson
Undefeated Seasons (5 or more wins) 101

Joe Jackson
Most Triples, Game, AL 28
.300 Batting Average in Final Season (Min. 100 G) 39
The .400 Hitters, AL 52
Highest Batting Average, Career 53
Stole 2nd, 3rd, and Home in One Game, AL 66
Longest Hitting Streaks, AL 70
Most 200-Hit Batters, AL 223

Larry Jackson
Most Shutouts, Career 80
Most 1-0 Losses, Career 95
Twenty Wins One Year, 20 Losses the Next, NL since 1900 98
Most Times Struck Out, Pitcher, Career since 1900 141

Randy Jackson
Grounded into Most Double Plays, Game, NL 43
Three Consecutive Home Runs, Team, NL 199

Reggie Jackson
Most Grand Slams, Career 3
Most Grand Slams, Season, AL 4
Most Pinch-Hit Grand Slams, Career 6
Most Home Runs, Season, AL 7
Most Home Runs, Career 9
Best Home Run Ratio, Career 10
Two Home Runs in One Game Most Often 12
Three Home Runs in One Game, AL 14, 15
Most Times Struck Out, Game, AL 33
Easiest to Strike Out, Career (Min. 1,000 G) 44
Two Legs of Triple Crown, AL 46
Most Runs Produced, Career 62
Most RBIs, Game, AL 64
Three Consecutive Home Runs, Team, AL 197
Home Run Duos, Career, AL 211

Ron Jackson
Three Consecutive Home Runs, Team, AL 197

Travis Jackson
Career Spent With One Team (15 or more years) 181

Spook Jacobs
Most Hits in First Game 165

Baby Doll Jacobson
Most Triples, Game, AL 28
Cycle Hitters, AL 49
Most 100-RBI Hitters, AL 212
.300-Hitting Outfields, AL 219
Most 200-Hit Batters, AL 223

Bob James
Most Saves, Season, AL 122
Most Wins Plus Saves, Season 123

Charlie Jamieson
Most Combined Hits and Walks, Season, AL 40
.300-Hitting Outfields, AL 219

Larry Jansen
Best Won-Lost Record, Season, NL (20 or more wins) 97
Twenty or More Wins, Rookie, NL since 1900 168

Ray Jarvis
Most Times Struck Out, Game, AL 33

Larry Jaster
Most Shutouts, Rookie, NL since 1900 170

Julian Javier
Fathers and Sons in Baseball 191

Stan Javier
Fathers and Sons in Baseball 191

Hal Jeffcoat
Most Home Runs by Team, Game, NL 205

Ferguson Jenkins
Most Shutouts, Career 79
Most Shutout Losses, Career 80
Most Shutout Losses, Season, NL 81
Most Complete 1-0 Wins, Career 94
Most 1-0 Losses, Career 95
Most 20-Win Seasons 101
Most Wins, Career 102
Most Strikeouts, Season, AL 105
Most Strikeouts, Season, NL since 1900 106
Most Strikeouts, Career 108
Most Games with 10 or More Strikeouts, Career 114
Best Control Pitchers, Career 126
Fewest Base Runners per Nine Innings, Career (Min. 1,500 IP) 129
Two Home Runs in One Game, Pitcher, NL 136
Most Home Runs by Team, Game, NL 206

Hughie Jennings
Most Runs, Season, NL 59
Most Runs Produced, Season, NL 62
Pennant-Winning Rookie Managers, AL 171
Most Wins, Manager, Career 184

Jackie Jensen
Easiest to Double Up, Career (Min. 1000 G) 41
Most RBIs, Game, AL 64

Woody Jensen
.300-Hitting Outfields, NL 221

Manny Jimenez
Three Home Runs in One Game, AL 14

.300 Average in Rookie Year Only, AL 164

Tommy John

Most Shutouts, Career 79
Most Wins, Career 102

Adam Johnson

Shutout in First Start in Majors, AL 83
Fathers and Sons in Baseball 191

Adam Johnson

Fathers and Sons in Baseball 191

Alex Johnson

.300-Hitting Outfields, NL 221

Bob Johnson

Most Strikeouts, Season, AL 105
Worst-Hitting Pitchers, Career (Min. 100 AB) 144
Most Strikeouts, Rookie, AL 169

Bob Johnson

Most Grand Slams, Season, AL 4
Brothers with Most Home Runs, Career 25
Most Hits, Game, AL 35
Cycle Hitters, AL 49
No-Hit Spoilers - The Only Hit Most Often 58
Most RBIs in One Inning, AL 63
Longest Hitting Streaks, AL 70
Most Doubles, Rookie, AL 165
Best-Hitting Brothers 189
Three Consecutive Home Runs, Team, AL 196

Bob Johnson

Most Consecutive Pinch Hits 70

Cliff Johnson

Most Pinch-Hit Home Runs, Career 5
Two Home Runs in One Inning, AL 12
Three Home Runs in One Game, AL 15

Davey Johnson

Most Pinch-Hit Grand Slams, Career 6
Most Home Runs, Season, NL 8
Most Home Runs by Position, Season, NL 11
Most Home Runs in One Inning, Team, AL 200
Most Home Runs by Team, Game, AL 203
Most 40-Home Run Hitters, NL 206
Most 30-Home Run Hitters, NL 208
Home Run Trios, Season, NL 209

Deron Johnson

Three Home Runs in One Game, NL 19
Struck Out Twice in One Inning, AL 32
Most Times Struck Out, Game, NL 34
Easiest to Strike Out, Career (Min. 1,000 G) 44
Home Runs in Most Consecutive At-Bats, NL 76

Don Johnson

Worst-Hitting Pitchers, Career (Min. 100 AB) 144

Don Johnson

Fathers and Sons in Baseball 191

Ernie Johnson

Fathers and Sons in Baseball 191

Jerry Johnson

Most Relief Wins, Season, NL 119

Ken Johnson

No-Hitters, NL (9 innings or more) 90
Fewest Base Runners per Nine Innings, Career (Min. 1,500 IP) 130

Roy Johnson

Brothers with Most Home Runs, Career 25
Most Errors by Position, Season, AL 147
Two Hundred or More Hits, Rookie, AL 163
Most Doubles, Rookie, AL 165
Most Triples, Rookie, AL 165
Best-Hitting Brothers 189
Home Runs by First Two Batters in Game, NL 194
.300-Hitting Outfields, AL 219
Most 200-Hit Batters, AL 223

Si Johnson

Most Consecutive Losses, NL 116

Tom Johnson

Most Relief Wins, Season, AL 118

Walter Johnson

Most Shutouts, Career 79
Most Shutout Losses, Career 80
Most Shutouts, Season, AL 80
Most Shutout Losses, Season, AL 81
Shutout with Most Hits Allowed, AL 86
No-Hitters, AL (9 innings or more) 87
Most Complete 1-0 Wins, Career 94
Most 1-0 Losses, Career 95
Best Won-Lost Record, Season, AL (20 or more wins) 96
Twenty Wins One Year, 20 Losses the Next, AL 98
Highest Percentage of Team's Wins, AL 99
Twenty Wins and 20 Losses in Same Year, AL 99
Thirty-Game Winners, AL 100
Most 20-Win Seasons 101
Most Wins, Career 102
The 300-Win Club 103
Most Wins by Age, Season, AL 103
Most Strikeouts, Season, AL 105, 106
Most Strikeouts, Career 108
Four Strikeouts in One Inning, AL 108
Most Strikeouts in Extra-Inning Game, AL 112
Most Games with 10 or More Strikeouts, Career 114
Most Consecutive Wins, AL 115
Lowest ERA, Season, AL 127
Most Innings Pitched, Game, AL 127
Triple-Crown Pitchers, AL (most wins, lowest ERA, most strikeouts) 128
Fewest Base Runners per Nine Innings, Career (Min. 1,500 IP) 129
Most Complete Games, Season, AL 131

Most Innings Pitched, Season, AL 132
Won 20 and Hit .300 in Same Year, AL 134
Most Home Runs, Pitcher, Career 135
Grand Slams, Pitcher, AL 137
Most Hits, Pitcher, Career 139
Best-Hitting Pitchers, Season, AL 142
Fewest Errors by Position, Season, AL (Min. 150 G, excl. Pitchers) 147
Career Spent With One Team (15 or more years) 181

Doc Johnston
Most Consecutive Hits, AL 73

Jimmy Johnston
Cycle Hitters, NL 51
Stole 2nd, 3rd, and Home in One Game, NL 66
Most Steals of Home, Career 67
Most Consecutive Hits, NL 74

Jay Johnstone
Most Pinch Hits, Career 69
.300-Hitting Outfields, NL 221

Smead Jolley
One Hundred or More RBIs, Rookie, AL 166

Bumpus Jones
No-Hitters, NL (9 innings or more) 89
Rookie No-Hitters, NL 167

Charley Jones
Two Home Runs in One Inning, NL 12
Most Triples, Game, Other Leagues 29

Cleon Jones
Three Consecutive Home Runs, Team, NL 199

Dalton Jones
Most Pinch Hits, Career 69

Fielder Jones
Unassisted Double Plays, Outfielder 152
Highest Batting Average, Rookie, NL (Min. 300 AB) 167
.300-Hitting Outfields, NL 220

Jimmy Jones
Shutout in First Start in Majors, NL 85

Mack Jones
Most Hits in First Game 165
Most 30-Home Run Hitters, NL 208
Most 20-Home Run Hitters, NL 208

Nippy Jones
Most Home Runs in One Inning, Team, NL 200

Oscar Jones
Most Complete Games, Season, NL since 1900 132
Most Innings Pitched, Season, NL sicne 1900 132
Three Hundred or More Innings Pitched, Rookie, NL since 1900 169
Most Complete Games, Rookie, NL since 1900 170

Randy Jones
Fewest Errors by Position, Season, NL (Min. 150 G, excl. Pitchers) 147

Ruppert Jones
Most Putouts, Outfielder, Game 156

Sad Sam Jones
Most Shutouts, Career 80
No-Hitters, AL (9 innings or more) 87
Most Wins, Career 102
Most Times Struck Out, Pitcher, Career since 1900 141

Sam Jones
No-Hitters, NL (9 innings or more) 90
Most Strikeouts, Season, NL since 1900 107
Most Strikeouts per Nine Innings, Career (Min. 1,500 IP) 114
Most Strikeouts, Rookie, NL since 1900 169

Tom Jones
Most Putouts in Nine Innings, First Baseman 157

Willie Jones
Most Doubles, Game, NL 27
Most Home Runs in One Inning, Team, NL 200

Eddie Joost
Most Leadoff Home Runs, Career 22
More Walks than Hits, Season, AL 55
Most Double Plays, Shortstop, Season, AL 151

Niles Jordan
Shutout in First Start in Majors, NL 84

Addie Joss
Most Shutouts, Career 79
Shutout in First Start in Majors, AL 83
No-Hitters, AL (9 innings or more) 87
Most No-Hitters, Career 93
Perfect Games (9 innings or more) 94
Most Complete 1-0 Wins, Career 94
Best Control Pitchers, Career 126
Lowest ERA, Season, AL 127
Fewest Base Runners per Nine Innings, Career (Min. 1,500 IP) 129
Most Complete Games, Rookie, AL 170
Most Shutouts, Rookie, AL 170
Teams with Three 20-Game Winners, AL 227

Bill Joyce
Three Home Runs in One Game, NL 17
Most Triples, Game, NL 28
Cycle Hitters, NL 51
Home Runs by First Two Batters in Game, Other Leagues 195

Mike O'Neill
Pinch-Hit Grand Slams, Pitcher 137

.300-Hitting Outfields, NL 220

Tom Kelley

Worst-Hitting Pitchers, Career (Min. 100 AB) 144

Alex Kellner

Twenty Wins One Year, 20 Losses the Next, AL 98
Twenty or More Wins, Rookie, AL 168
Pitching Brothers, Same Team, AL 186

Walt Kellner

Pitching Brothers, Same Team, AL 186

George Kelly

Most Grand Slams, Season, NL 4
Three Home Runs in One Game, NL 17
Most Total Bases, Game, NL 30

King Kelly

Most Triples, Game, NL 28
Most Hits, Game, NL 36
Most Runs, Game, NL 60
Teammates Who Finished 1-2 in Batting, NL 222

Ken Keltner

Three Home Runs in One Game, AL 14
One Hundred or More RBIs, Rookie, AL 166

Steve Kemp

Three Consecutive Home Runs, Team, AL 197

Bill Kennedy

Most Walks in One Game, AL 113

Bob Kennedy

Fathers and Sons in Baseball 191

Brickyard Kennedy

Won 20 and Hit .300. in Same Year, NL 134
Most Hits, Pitcher, Career 139
Best-Hitting Pitchers, Career 143

John Kennedy

Pinch-Hit Home Run in First At-Bat in Majors, AL 6
Home Run in First Appearance in Majors, AL 11

Monte Kennedy

Grand Slams, Pitcher, NL 139

Terry Kennedy

Fathers and Sons in Baseball 191

Vern Kennedy

No-Hitters, AL (9 innings or more) 87
Rookie No-Hitters, AL 167

Joe Keough

Pinch-Hit Home Run in First At-Bat in Majors, AL 6
Home Run in First Appearance in Majors, AL 11

Marty Keough

Fathers and Sons in Baseball 191

Matt Keough

Most Consecutive Losses, AL 115
Fathers and Sons in Baseball 191

Jim Kern

Most Relief Wins, Season, AL 118
Most Relief Losses, Career 120
Most Relief Losses, Season, AL 120
Most Wins Plus Saves, Season 123

Buddy Kerr

Home Run in First Appearance in Majors, NL 11
Most Consecutive Errorless Games by Position, NL 148

Dickie Kerr

Pitchers Who Stole Home, AL 140
Teams with Four 20-Game Winners 227

Don Kessinger

Most Hits, Game, NL 37

Mike Kilkenny

Worst-Hitting Pitchers, Career (Min. 100 AB) 144

Harmon Killebrew

Most Grand Slams, Career 3
Most Home Runs, Season, AL 7
Most Home Runs, Career 9
Best Home Run Ratio, Career 10
Two Home Runs in One Game Most Often 12
Three Home Runs in One Game, AL 14
Most Home Runs in a Doubleheader, AL 20
Most Extra-Inning Home Runs, Career 23
Easiest to Strike Out, Career (Min. 1,000 G) 44
Two Legs of Triple Crown, AL 46
Most RBIs, Career 61
Retired Numbers, AL 182
Two Grand Slams in One Inning, Team 192
Four Consecutive Home Runs, Team 196
Three Consecutive Home Runs, Team, AL 197
Most Home Runs in One Inning, Team, AL 200
Most Home Runs by Team, Game, AL 202
Most 30-Home Run Hitters, AL 207
Most 20-Home Run Hitters, AL 208
Home Run Trios, Season, AL 209
Home Run Duos, Season, AL (25 each) 210
Home Run Duos, Career, AL 211

Bill Killefer

Most Games Caught, Career 153

Ed Killian

Won 20 and Hit .300 in Same Year, AL 134
Teams with Three 20-Game Winners, AL 227

Matt Kilroy

No-Hitters, Other Leagues 91
Most Strikeouts, Season before 1900 107

Ted Kluszewski

Most Home Runs, Season, NL 7, 8
Three Home Runs in One Game, NL 18
Most Home Runs in Final Season 24
Two Legs of Triple Crown, NL 48
Three Consecutive Home Runs, Team, NL 198, 199
Most Home Runs by Team, Game, NL 204
Most 40-Home Run Hitters, NL 206
Most 30-Home Run Hitters, NL 208
Most 20-Home Run Hitters, NL 208
Home Run Trios, Season, NL 209
Home Run Duos, Season, NL (25 each) 210

Jack Knight

Two Home Runs in One Game, Pitcher, NL 136

Joe Knight

.300 Batting Average in Final Season (Min. 100 G) 39

Lon Knight

Most Hits, Game, Other Leagues 37
Cycle Hitters, Other Leagues 51

Ray Knight

Most Grand Slams, Season, NL 4
Two Home Runs in One Inning, NL 12
Easiest to Double Up, Career (Min. 1000 G) 41
Most RBIs in One Inning, NL 63

Bobby Knoop

Easiest to Strike Out, Career (Min. 1,000 G) 44
Best Double-Play Combinations, Season 149
Most Double Plays, Second Baseman, Season, AL 151
Most Putouts, Second Baseman, Game 157

Darold Knowles

Most Relief Losses, Career 120
Most Relief Losses, Season, AL 120
Most Saves, Career 121

Don Kolloway

Stole 2nd, 3rd, and Home in One Game, AL 66

Ed Konetchy

No-Hit Spoilers - The Only Hit Most Often 57
Most Consecutive Hits, NL 74

Jim Konstanty

Most Relief Wins, Season, NL 119

Ernie Koob

No-Hitters, AL (9 innings or more) 87
Most At-Bats with No Hits, Pitcher, Season since 1900 141
Worst-Hitting Pitchers, Career (Min. 100 AB) 144

Jerry Koosman

Most Consecutive Times Struck Out, NL 74
Twenty Wins One Year, 20 Losses the Next, NL since 1900 98
Most Wins, Career 102
Most Strikeouts, Season, NL since 1900 107
Most Strikeouts, Career 108
Most Games with 10 or More Strikeouts, Career 114
Most Wins after Age 40 134
Easiest Pitcher to Strike Out, Season since 1900 141
Most Shutouts, Rookie, NL since 1900 170
Best Lefty-Righty Duos 229

Dave Koslo

Two Home Runs in One Game, Pitcher, NL 136

Sandy Koufax

Most Consecutive Times Struck Out, NL 74
Most Shutouts, Career 80
Most Shutouts, Season, NL 81
No-Hitters, NL (9 innings or more) 90
Most No-Hitters, Career 93
Perfect Games (9 innings or more) 94
Most Complete 1-0 Wins, Career 94
Best Won-Lost Record, Season, NL (20 or more wins) 97
Most Strikeouts, Season, NL since 1900 106, 107
Perfect Innings, NL (3 strikeouts on 9 pitches) 110
Most Strikeouts in Nine-Inning Game, NL 111
Most Strikeouts in Extra-Inning Game, NL 112
Most Games with 10 or More Strikeouts, Career 114
Most Strikeouts per Nine Innings, Career (Min. 1,500 IP) 114
Triple-Crown Pitchers, NL (most wins, lowest ERA, most strikeouts) 129
Fewest Base Runners per Nine Innings, Career (Min. 1,500 IP) 129
Most Times Struck Out, Pitcher, Career since 1900 141
Worst-Hitting Pitchers, Career (Min. 100 AB) 144
Retired Numbers, NL 183
Strikeout Duos, Season, NL 228
Best Lefty-Righty Duos 228

Ernie Koy

Home Run in First Appearance in Majors, NL 11
.300-Hitting Outfields, NL 221

Jack Kralick

No-Hitters, AL (9 innings or more) 88

Ed Kranepool

Most Pinch Hits, Season, NL 69
Most Pinch Hits, Career 69
Career Spent With One Team (15 or more years) 181

Harry Krause

Lowest ERA, Season, AL 127
ERA Under 2.00, Rookie, AL (Min. 130 IP) 169
Most Shutouts, Rookie, AL 170

Lew Krausse

Fathers and Sons in Baseball 191

Lew Krausse

Shutout in First Start in Majors, AL 83

Dennis Lamp
Undefeated Seasons (5 or more wins) 101

Jim Landis
Most Times Struck Out, Game, AL 33

Ken Landreaux
Most Triples, Game, AL 28
Longest Hitting Streaks, AL 70

Bill Landrum
Fathers and Sons in Baseball 191

Joe Landrum
Fathers and Sons in Baseball 191

Bill Lange
.300 Batting Average in Final Season (Min. 100 G) 39

Frank Lange
ERA Under 2.00, Rookie, AL (Min. 130 IP) 169

Sam Langford
Most Assists, Outfielder, Game 156

Mark Langston
Most Strikeouts, Season, AL 105, 106
Most Consecutive Strikeouts, AL 116
Most Strikeouts, Rookie, AL 169

Hal Lanier
Easiest to Double Up, Career (Min. 1000 G) 41
The Worst Hitters (Min. 2,500 AB) 52
Fathers and Sons in Baseball 191

Max Lanier
Undefeated Seasons (5 or more wins) 101
Fathers and Sons in Baseball 191

Carney Lansford
Three Home Runs in One Game, AL 15

Paul LaPalme
Shutout in First Start in Majors, NL 84

Henry Larkin
Most Doubles, Game, Other Leagues 27
Most Hits, Game, NL 36
Most Hits, Game, Other Leagues 37
Cycle Hitters, Other Leagues 51
Home Runs by First Two Batters in Game, Other Leagues 195

Dave LaRoche
Most Relief Losses, Career 120
Most Relief Losses, Season, AL 120
Most Saves, Career 121

Don Larsen
No-Hitters, AL (9 innings or more) 88
Perfect Games (9 innings or more) 94
Grand Slams, Pitcher, AL 138

Lyn Lary
Most 100-RBI Hitters, AL 212

Tommy Lasorda
Pennant-Winning Rookie Managers, NL 171

Arlie Latham
Most Hits, Game, Other Leagues 37

Charlie Lau
Most Doubles, Game, AL 27

Cookie Lavagetto
Most Hits, Game, NL 36

Gary Lavelle
Most Relief Wins, Career 117
Most Relief Losses, Career 120
Most Saves, Career 121
Worst-Hitting Pitchers, Career (Min. 100 AB) 144

Jimmy Lavender
No-Hitters, NL (9 innings or more) 89

Rudy Law
Most Stolen Bases, Season, AL 65
Three Consecutive Home Runs, Team, AL 197
Stolen Base Duos, Season, AL 216

Vance Law
Fathers and Sons in Baseball 191

Vern Law
Most Innings Pitched, Game, NL 128
Career Spent With One Team (15 or more years) 181
Fathers and Sons in Baseball 191

Brooks Lawrence
Most Consecutive Wins, NL 115

Les Layton
Pinch-Hit Home Run in First At-Bat in Majors, NL 6
Home Run in First Appearance in Majors, NL 11

Tony Lazzeri
Two Grand Slams in One Game 3
Three Home Runs in One Game, AL 13
Most Total Bases, Game, AL 30
Cycle Hitters, AL 49
Most RBIs, Game, AL 64
Most Triples, Rookie, AL 165
One Hundred or More RBIs, Rookie, AL 166
Most Home Runs by Team, Game, AL 202
Home Run Trios, Season, AL 209
Most 100-RBI Hitters, AL 212

Charlie Lea
No-Hitters, NL (9 innings or more) 90

Freddy Leach
.300-Hitting Outfields, NL 220

Tommy Leach
Stolen Base Duos, Season, NL 217

Bill Lee
Shutout in First Start in Majors, NL 84
Shutout with Most Hits Allowed, NL 86
Two Home Runs in One Game, Pitcher, NL 136

Bob Lee
ERA Under 2.00, Rookie, AL (Min. 130 IP) 169

Cliff Lee
.300-Hitting Outfields, NL 220

Don Lee
Fathers and Sons in Baseball 191

Hal Lee
Three Home Runs in One Game, NL 17
.300-Hitting Outfields, NL 221

Thornton Lee
Fathers and Sons in Baseball 191

Sam Leever
Most Shutouts, Career 80
Best Won-Lost Record, Season, NL (20 or more wins) 97
Best Control Pitchers, Career 126
Fewest Base Runners per Nine Innings, Career (Min. 1,500 IP) 129

Bill LeFebvre
Home Run in First Appearance in Majors, AL 11

Jim Lefebvre
Switch-Hit Home Runs in One Game, NL 23

Joe Lefebvre
Most Hits, Game, NL 37

Ron LeFlore
Most Stolen Bases, Season, AL 65
Most Stolen Bases, Season, NL 65
Most Stolen Bases, Career 66
Longest Hitting Streaks, AL 70
Stolen Base Duos, Season, NL 216

Paul Lehner
Most Putouts, Outfielder, Game 156

Hank Leiber
Two Home Runs in One Inning, NL 12
Three Home Runs in One Game, NL 17
Most 200-Hit Batters, NL 223

Nemo Leibold
.300-Hitting Outfields, AL 219

Charlie Leibrandt
Shutout in First Start in Majors, NL 85

Lefty Leifield
Shutout in First Start in Majors, NL 84
Pitchers Who Stole Home, NL since 1900 140

Denny Lemaster
Most Strikeouts per Nine Innings, Career (Min. 1,500 IP) 114

Johnnie LeMaster
Home Run in First Appearance in Majors, NL 11
The Worst Hitters (Min. 2,500 AB) 52

Bob Lemon
Most Shutouts, Season, AL 80
No-Hitters, AL (9 innings or more) 87
Most 20-Win Seasons 101
Most Wins, Career 102
Most Home Runs, Pitcher, Career 135
Two Home Runs in One Game, Pitcher, AL 136
Most Home Runs, Pitcher, Season 139
Career Spent With One Team (15 or more years) 181
Teams with Three 20-Game Winners, AL 227

Chet Lemon
Most Home Runs in One Inning, Team, AL 200

Jim Lemon
Two Home Runs in One Inning, AL 12
Three Home Runs in One Game, AL 14
Most RBIs in One Inning, AL 63
Most 30-Home Run Hitters, AL 207

Dave Lemonds
Most Consecutive Times Struck Out, AL 74

Don Lenhardt
Most Grand Slams, Season, AL 4

Ed Lennox
Cycle Hitters, Other Leagues 51

Eddie Leon
Three Consecutive Home Runs, Team, AL 197

Dennis Leonard
Most Strikeouts, Season, AL 105
Best Lefty-Righty Duos 229

Dutch Leonard
No-Hitters, AL (9 innings or more) 87
Most No-Hitters, Career 93
Lowest ERA, Season, AL 127

Jeffrey Leonard
Cycle Hitters, NL 51
.300-Hitting Outfields, NL 221

Ted Lepcio
Most Home Runs in One Inning, Team, AL 200

Don Leppert
Home Run in First Appearance in Majors, NL 11
Three Home Runs in One Game, AL 14

Randy Lerch
Two Home Runs in One Game, Pitcher, NL 136

Dutch Lerchen
Fathers and Sons in Baseball 191

George Lerchen
Fathers and Sons in Baseball 191

Sam Leslie
Cycle Hitters, NL 51
Most Pinch Hits, Season, NL 68

Walt Leverenz
Worst Won-Lost Record, Season (12 or more losses) 95

Dutch Levsen
Two Complete Game Wins in One Day, AL 124

Duffy Lewis
.300-Hitting Outfields, AL 219

Jack Lewis
Most Triples, Game, Other Leagues 29

Sixto Lezcano
Most Home Runs by Team, Game, AL 203

Glenn Liebhardt
Fathers and Sons in Baseball 191

Glenn Liebhardt
Fathers and Sons in Baseball 191

Carl Lind
Most Doubles, Rookie, AL 165

Vive Lindaman
Most Shutout Losses, Season, NL 81
Shutout in First Start in Majors, NL 84
Three Hundred or More Innings Pitched, Rookie, NL since 1900 169
Most Complete Games, Rookie, NL since 1900 170

Paul Lindblad
Most Consecutive Errorless Games by Position, AL 148

Johnny Lindell
Most Doubles, Game, AL 27
Three Consecutive Home Runs, Team, AL 196

Charlie Lindstrom
Fathers and Sons in Baseball 191

Freddie Lindstrom
Cycle Hitters, NL 51
Longest Hitting Streaks, NL 71
Fathers and Sons in Baseball 191
Three Consecutive Home Runs, Team, NL 198
Most .300 Hitters, Season, NL (300 AB each) 218

Frank Linzy
Most Relief Wins, Season, NL 119
Most Relief Losses, Career 120
Most Relief Losses, Season, NL 120
Most Saves, Career 121

Johnny Lipon
Best Double-Play Combinations, Season 149
Most Double Plays, Shortstop, Season, AL 151

Joe Lis
Three Consecutive Home Runs, Team, AL 197

Danny Litwhiler
Fewest Errors by Position, Season, NL (Min. 150 G, excl. Pitchers) 147
Three Consecutive Home Runs, Team, NL 198

Bud Lively
Fathers and Sons in Baseball 191

Jack Lively
Fathers and Sons in Baseball 191

Winston Llenas
Most Pinch Hits, Season, AL 68

Hans Lobert
Stole 2nd, 3rd, and Home in One Game, NL 66

Don Lock
Three Consecutive Home Runs, Team, AL 197

Whitey Lockman
Home Run in First Appearance in Majors, NL 11
Leadoff Home Runs in Two Consecutive Games, NL 21
Hardest to Double Up, Career (Min. 1,000 G) 42
Home Runs by First Two Batters in Game, NL 194
Three Consecutive Home Runs, Team, NL 198
Most Home Runs by Team, Game, NL 205
.300-Hitting Outfields, NL 221

Skip Lockwood
Most Relief Losses, Season, NL 120

Johnny Logan
Most Home Runs by Team, Game, NL 204

Bill Lohrman
Three Consecutive Home Runs, Team, NL 198
Most Home Runs in One Inning, Team, NL 200
Most Home Runs by Team, Game, NL 205

Mickey Lolich
Most Shutouts, Career 79
Most Shutout Losses, Career 80
Most Wins, Career 102
Most Strikeouts, Season, AL 105, 106
Most Strikeouts, Career 108
Most Strikeouts in Nine-Inning Game, AL 111
Most Games with 10 or More Strikeouts, Career 114
Most Strikeouts per Nine Innings, Career (Min. 1,500 IP) 114
Most Innings Pitched, Season, AL 132
Strikeout Duos, Season, AL 228

Sherm Lollar
Two Hits in One Inning Twice in One Game 37
Easiest to Double Up, Career (Min. 1000 G) 41
Most Games Caught, Career 153
Most Home Runs by Team, Game, AL 202

Ernie Lombardi
Most Doubles, Game, NL 27
Most Hits, Game, NL 36
Easiest to Double Up, Career (Min. 1000 G) 41
Batting Champion with Two Different Clubs 43
Most Games Caught, Career 153
Most No-Hitters Caught, Career 154

Jim Lonborg
Most Strikeouts, Season, AL 105
Grand Slams, Pitcher, NL 139

Dale Long
Three Consecutive Home Runs, Team, AL 196
Three Consecutive Home Runs, Team, NL 199

Herman Long
Cycle Hitters, NL 51
Most Assists, Shortstop, Game 159

Tommy Long
Most Times Caught Stealing, Game, NL 68
Most Triples, Rookie, NL 165

Ed Lopat
Shutout with Most Hits Allowed, AL 86

Davey Lopes
Three Home Runs in One Game, NL 19
Most Leadoff Home Runs, Career 22
Most Total Bases, Game, NL 30
Most Stolen Bases, Season, NL 65
Most Stolen Bases, Career 66
Most Stolen Bases, Game, NL 66
Most Home Runs by Team, Game, NL 206
Stolen Base Duos, Season, AL 216
Stolen Base Duos, Season, NL 217

Al Lopez
Most Games Caught, Career 153
Most Wins, Manager, Career 184

Aurelio Lopez
Most Relief Wins, Season, AL 118

Hector Lopez
Three Home Runs in One Game, AL 14

Don Loun
Shutout in First Start in Majors, AL 83

Tom Lovett
No-Hitters, NL (9 innings or more) 89

Grover Lowdermilk
Pitching Brothers, Same Team, NL 186

Lou Lowdermilk
Pitching Brothers, Same Team, NL 186

Bobby Lowe
Two Home Runs in One Inning, NL 12
Four Home Runs in One Game, NL 20
Most Total Bases, Game, NL 30
Most Hits, Game, NL 36
Most Runs, Season, NL 59
Most Runs, Game, NL 60
Most Runs Produced, Season, NL 62
Home Runs in Most Consecutive At-Bats, NL 76

Turk Lown
Most Extra-Inning Home Runs Allowed, Career 133

Peanuts Lowrey
Most Pinch Hits, Season, NL 68
Most Consecutive Pinch Hits 70

Pat Luby
Most Consecutive Wins, NL 115

Johnny Lucadello
Switch-Hit Home Runs in One Game, AL 23

Red Lucas
Most Pinch Hits, Career 69
Best Control Pitchers, Career 126
Most Hits, Pitcher, Career 139
Best-Hitting Pitchers, Career 142

Fred Luderus
Most Consecutive Games Played 71
Most Assists, First Baseman, Game 157

Mike Lum
Three Home Runs in One Game, NL 19
Most Pinch Hits, Season, NL 69

Most Pinch Hits, Career 69
Most Home Runs in One Inning, Team, NL 201

Harry Lumley

Most Triples, Rookie, NL 165

Carl Lundgren

Lowest ERA, Season, NL 127
ERA Under 2.00, Rookie, NL since 1900 (Min. 130 IP) 169

Dolf Luque

Best-Hitting Pitchers, Season, NL since 1900 142
Teams with Three 20-Game Winners, NL since 1900 227
Best Lefty-Righty Duos 229

Billy Lush

Most Triples, Game, AL 28

Johnny Lush

No-Hitters, NL (9 innings or more) 89

Greg Luzinski

Easiest to Strike Out, Career (Min. 1,000 G) 44
Three Consecutive Home Runs, Team, AL 197
Three Consecutive Home Runs, Team, NL 199
Home Run Duos, Career, NL 211
.300-Hitting Outfields, NL 221

Sparky Lyle

Most Relief Wins, Career 117
Most Relief Wins, Season, AL 118
Most Relief Losses, Career 120
Most Saves, Career 121
Most Saves, Season, AL 122
Most Wins Plus Saves, Season 122

Ed Lynch

Most At-Bats with No Hits, Pitcher, Season since 1900 141

Jack Lynch

Most Strikeouts in Nine-Inning Game, Other Leagues 112

Jerry Lynch

Most Pinch-Hit Home Runs, Career 5
Most Pinch Hits, Season, NL 68
Most Pinch Hits, Career 69
Three Consecutive Home Runs, Team, NL 199

Fred Lynn

Three Home Runs in One Game, AL 15
Most Total Bases, Game, AL 30
Cycle Hitters, AL 49
Most RBIs, Game, AL 64
Most Doubles, Rookie, AL 165
One Hundred or More RBIs, Rookie, AL 166
Highest Batting Average, Rookie, AL (Min. 300 AB) 167
Home Runs by First Two Batters in Game, AL 194
Three Consecutive Home Runs, Team, AL 197
Most Home Runs in One Inning, Team, AL 200
Most Home Runs by Team, Game, AL 202

Denny Lyons

Most Hits, Game, Other Leagues 37
Most Home Runs in One Inning, Team, NL 200
Most Home Runs by Team, Game, NL 204

Ted Lyons

No-Hitters, AL (9 innings or more) 87
Most Wins, Career 102
Most Innings Pitched, Game, AL 127
Won 20 and Hit .300 in Same Year, AL 134
Most Hits, Pitcher, Career 139
Career Spent With One Team (15 or more years) 181

Rick Lysander

Shutout with Most Hits Allowed, AL 86

Bill Macdonald

Shutout in First Start in Majors, NL 84

Danny MacFayden

Most Times Struck Out, Pitcher, Career since 1900 141

Dave Machemer

Home Run in First Appearance in Majors, AL 11

Connie Mack

Most Wins, Manager, Career 184
Most League Pennants Won, Manager 185
Fathers and Sons in Baseball 191
Most Home Runs by Team, Game, NL 204

Denny Mack

Most Hits, Game, Other Leagues 37

Earle Mack

Fathers and Sons in Baseball 191

Ray Mack

Best Double-Play Combinations, Season 149, 150

Max Macon

Most Consecutive Pinch Hits 70

Garry Maddox

Most Putouts, Outfielder, Game 156
Three Consecutive Home Runs, Team, NL 199
.300-Hitting Outfields, NL 221

Nick Maddox

Shutout in First Start in Majors, NL 84
No-Hitters, NL (9 innings or more) 89
Rookie No-Hitters, NL 167

Tony Madigan

Worst Won-Lost Record, Season (12 or more losses) 95

Bill Madlock
Most Hits, Game, NL 37
Batting Champion with Two Different Clubs 43

Lee Magee
Most Times Caught Stealing, Game, AL 68
Most Assists, Outfielder, Game 156
Most Assists, Second Baseman, Game 158

Sherry Magee
Two Legs of Triple Crown, NL 47
No-Hit Spoilers - The Only Hit Most Often 57
Most Stolen Bases, Career 66
Most Steals of Home, Career 67

Harl Maggert
Fathers and Sons in Baseball 191

Harl Maggert
Fathers and Sons in Baseball 191

Sal Maglie
No-Hitters, NL (9 innings or more) 90

Art Mahaffey
Most Strikeouts in Nine-Inning Game, NL 111
Grand Slams, Pitcher, NL 139

Mickey Mahler
Pitching Brothers, Same Team, NL 186

Rick Mahler
Pitching Brothers, Same Team, NL 186

Jim Mahoney
Three Consecutive Home Runs, Team, AL 196

Duster Mails
Shutout with Most Hits Allowed, AL 86
Undefeated Seasons (5 or more wins) 101

Alex Main
No-Hitters, Other Leagues 91

Fritz Maisel
Most Stolen Bases, Season, AL 65
Stole 2nd, 3rd, and Home in One Game, AL 66
Most Steals of Home, Career 67
Most Times Caught Stealing, Game, AL 68
Stolen Base Duos, Season, AL 216

George Maisel
.300-Hitting Outfields, NL 220

Hank Majeski
Most Extra-Base Hits in a Doubleheader, AL 27

Charlie Malay
Fathers and Sons in Baseball 191

Joe Malay
Fathers and Sons in Baseball 191

Candy Maldonado
Most Pinch Hits, Season, NL 69

Les Mallon
.300 Average in Rookie Year Only, NL 164

Jim Maloney
No-Hitters, NL (9 innings or more) 90
Most No-Hitters, Career 93
Most Strikeouts, Season, NL since 1900 106, 107
Most Strikeouts in Nine-Inning Game, NL 111
Most Strikeouts in Extra-Inning Game, NL 112
Most Games with 10 or More Strikeouts, Career 114
Most Strikeouts per Nine Innings, Career (Min. 1,500 IP) 114
Most Consecutive Strikeouts, NL 116

Frank Malzone
Most Home Runs in One Inning, Team, AL 200

Gus Mancuso
Most Games Caught, Career 153

Pepe Mangual
Most Times Struck Out, Game, NL 34

Jack Manning
Three Home Runs in One Game, NL 17

Rick Manning
Most Times Struck Out, Game, AL 33
Most Putouts, Outfielder, Game 156

John Mansell
Three or More Brothers in Baseball 187

Mike Mansell
Three or More Brothers in Baseball 187

Tom Mansell
Three or More Brothers in Baseball 187

Mickey Mantle
Most Home Runs, Season, AL 7
Most Home Runs, Career 9
Best Home Run Ratio, Career 10
Most Home Runs by Position, Career, AL 10
Two Home Runs in One Game Most Often 12
Three Home Runs in One Game, AL 14
Switch-Hit Home Runs in One Game, AL 23
Most Extra-Inning Home Runs, Career 23
Most Home Runs in Final Season 24
Struck Out Twice in One Inning, AL 32
Most Combined Hits and Walks, Season, AL 40
Easiest to Strike Out, Career (Min. 1,000 G) 44
Triple Crown Winners, AL 45
Cycle Hitters, AL 49
More Walks than Hits, Season, AL 55

Tom McBride
Most RBIs in One Inning, AL 63
Most Putouts, Outfielder, Game 156

Bill McCahan
Shutout in First Start in Majors, AL 83
No-Hitters, AL (9 innings or more) 87
Rookie No-Hitters, AL 167

Dutch McCall
Most Consecutive Losses, NL 116

Joe McCarthy
Most Wins, Manager, Career 184
Pennant-Winning Managers in AL and NL 184
Most League Pennants Won, Manager 185

Tommy McCarthy
Unassisted Double Plays, Outfielder 152

Tim McCarver
Most Pinch Hits, Career 69
Most Games Caught, Career 153
Most No-Hitters Caught, Career 155
Three Consecutive Home Runs, Team, NL 199

Kirk McCaskill
Most Strikeouts, Season, AL 106

Billy McCool
Worst-Hitting Pitchers, Career (Min. 100 AB) 144

Barry McCormick
Most Hits, Game, NL 36

Frank McCormick
Most Consecutive Games Played 71
Two Hundred or More Hits, Rookie, NL 163

Jim McCormick
Most Shutout Losses, Career 80
Most Shutout Losses, Season, NL 81
Most 20-Win Seasons 101
Most Wins, Career 102
Most Strikeouts, Season before 1900 107
Most Consecutive Wins, NL 115

Mike McCormick
Most Wins by Age, Season, NL since 1900 104

Mike McCormick
.300-Hitting Outfields, NL 221

Barney McCosky
Most Triples, Rookie, AL 165
Home Runs by First Two Batters in Game, AL 194

Willie McCovey
Most Grand Slams, Career 3
Most Grand Slams, Season, NL 4
Most Pinch-Hit Home Runs, Career 5
Most Pinch-Hit Grand Slams, Career 6
Most Home Runs, Season, NL 7, 8
Most Home Runs, Career 9
Best Home Run Ratio, Career 10
Most Home Runs by Position, Career, NL 10
Two Home Runs in One Inning, NL 12
Two Home Runs in One Game Most Often 12
Three Home Runs in One Game, NL 18
Two Legs of Triple Crown, NL 48
Most Hits in First Game 165
Retired Numbers, NL 183
Three Consecutive Home Runs, Team, NL 199
Most 30-Home Run Hitters, NL 208
Home Run Trios, Season, NL 209
Home Run Duos, Season, NL (25 each) 210
Home Run Duos, Career, NL 211

Tom McCraw
Three Home Runs in One Game, AL 14

Tom McCreery
Three Home Runs in One Game, NL 17

Clyde McCullough
Three Home Runs in One Game, NL 17

Harry McCurdy
Most Consecutive Hits, AL 73

Lindy McDaniel
Most Relief Wins, Career 117
Most Relief Wins, Season, AL 118
Most Relief Wins, Season, NL 119
Most Relief Losses, Career 120
Most Saves, Career 121
Most Grand Slams Allowed, Career 133
Most Extra-Inning Home Runs Allowed, Career 133
Pitching Brothers, Same Team, NL 186

Von McDaniel
Shutout in First Start in Majors, NL 84
Pitching Brothers, Same Team, NL 186

Gil McDougald
Most RBIs in One Inning, AL 63

Oddibe McDowell
Leadoff Home Runs in Two Consecutive Games, AL 21
Cycle Hitters, AL 49
Most Putouts, Outfielder, Game 156
Two Pinch-Hit Home Runs in One Inning, Team, AL 192
Back-to-Back Pinch-Hit Home Runs, Team 193

Roger McDowell
Most Relief Wins, Season, NL 119

Sam McDowell
Most Strikeouts, Season, AL 105
Most Strikeouts in Nine-Inning Game, AL 111
Most Games with 10 or More Strikeouts, Career 114
Most Strikeouts per Nine Innings, Career (Min. 1,500 IP) 114

Craig McMurtry
Worst-Hitting Pitchers, Career (Min. 100 AB) 144

Dave McNally
Shutout in First Start in Majors, AL 83
Best Won-Lost Record, Season, AL (20 or more wins) 96
Most Strikeouts, Season, AL 106
Most Consecutive Wins, AL 115
Fewest Base Runners per Nine Innings, Career (Min. 1,500 IP) 130
Grand Slams, Pitcher, AL 138
Teams with Four 20-Game Winners 227
Teams with Three 20-Game Winners, AL 227
Best Lefty-Righty Duos 229

Earl McNeely
.300-Hitting Outfields, AL 219

Bid McPhee
Most Triples, Game, NL 28
Cycle Hitters, Other Leagues 51

Mox McQuery
Cycle Hitters, NL 51

George McQuillan
Most Shutout Losses, Season, NL 81
Most Innings Pitched, Season, NL sicne 1900 132
Twenty or More Wins, Rookie, NL since 1900 168
ERA Under 2.00, Rookie, NL since 1900 (Min. 130 IP) 169
Three Hundred or More Innings Pitched, Rookie, NL since 1900 169
Most Complete Games, Rookie, NL since 1900 170
Most Shutouts, Rookie, NL since 1900 170

George McQuinn
Cycle Hitters, AL 49
Longest Hitting Streaks, AL 70

Hal McRae
Most Extra-Base Hits in a Doubleheader, AL 27
Teammates Who Finished 1-2 in Batting, AL 222

Jim McTamany
Most Hits, Game, Other Leagues 37
Home Runs by First Two Batters in Game, Other Leagues 195

Cal McVey
Most Hits, Game, NL 35

Larry McWilliams
Struck Out Twice in One Inning, NL 33

Bobby Meacham
Stolen Base Duos, Season, AL 216

Lee Meadows
Most 1-0 Losses, Career 95
Grand Slams, Pitcher, NL 138

Joe Medwick
Most Extra-Base Hits in a Doubleheader, NL 27
Most Doubles, Game, NL 27
Most Total Bases, Season, NL 30
Triple Crown Winners, NL 45
Cycle Hitters, NL 51
Most RBIs, Season, NL 60
Longest Hitting Streaks, NL 71
Most Consecutive Hits, NL 74
Most Home Runs by Team, Game, NL 205
.300-Hitting Outfields, NL 221
Teammates Who Finished 1-2 in Batting, NL 222

Jouett Meekin
Most Triples, Game, NL 28
Shutout with Most Hits Allowed, NL 86
Most Home Runs, Pitcher, Career 135

Bob Meinke
Fathers and Sons in Baseball 191

Frank Meinke
Fathers and Sons in Baseball 191

Roman Mejias
Three Home Runs in One Game, NL 18

Sam Mele
Most RBIs in One Inning, AL 63
.300 Average in Rookie Year Only, AL 164

Oscar Melillo
Cycle Hitters, AL 49
Most Consecutive Hits, AL 73

Bill Melton
Three Home Runs in One Game, AL 14

Cliff Melton
Twenty or More Wins, Rookie, NL since 1900 168

Jock Menefee
Pitchers Who Stole Home, NL since 1900 140

Denis Menke
Leadoff Home Runs in Two Consecutive Games, NL 21
No-Hit Spoilers - The Only Hit Most Often 58
Two Grand Slams in One Inning, Team 192
Most Home Runs by Team, Game, NL 205

Win Mercer
Pitchers Who Stole Home, AL 140
Best-Hitting Pitchers, Season, AL 142

Fred Merkle
Most RBIs in One Inning, NL 63
Most Steals of Home, Career 67

Lloyd Merriman
Most Putouts, Outfielder, Game 156

Jim Merritt
Most Consecutive Strikeouts, AL 116

Sam Mertes
Leadoff Home Runs in Two Consecutive Games, NL 21
Most Times Walked, Game, NL 32
Cycle Hitters, NL 51
Unassisted Double Plays, Outfielder 152
Stolen Base Duos, Season, NL 217

Andy Messersmith
Most Strikeouts, Season, AL 105
Most Strikeouts, Season, NL since 1900 107
Most Strikeouts per Nine Innings, Career (Min. 1,500 IP) 114
Fewest Base Runners per Nine Innings, Career (Min. 1,500 IP) 129

Catfish Metkovich
Longest Hitting Streaks, AL 70

Roger Metzger
The Worst Hitters (Min. 2,500 AB) 52

Bob Meusel
Brothers with Most Home Runs, Career 25
Two Legs of Triple Crown, AL 46
Cycle Hitters, AL 49
Stole 2nd, 3rd, and Home in One Game, AL 66
Most Assists, Outfielder, Game 156
Most Doubles, Rookie, AL 165
Best-Hitting Brothers 189
Three Consecutive Home Runs, Team, AL 196
Most 100-RBI Hitters, AL 212
.300-Hitting Outfields, AL 219

Irish Meusel
Brothers with Most Home Runs, Career 25
Best-Hitting Brothers 189

Billy Meyer
Retired Numbers, NL 183

Dan Meyer
Two Pinch-Hit Home Runs in One Inning, Team, AL 192

Chief Meyers
Cycle Hitters, NL 51

Gene Michael
Three Consecutive Home Runs, Team, AL 197

Clyde Milan
Most Stolen Bases, Season, AL 65
Most Stolen Bases, Career 66
Most Stolen Bases, Game, AL 66
Most Consecutive Games Played 71
Career Spent With One Team (15 or more years) 181
Stolen Base Duos, Season, AL 216

Larry Milbourne
Switch-Hit Home Runs in One Game, AL 23

Felix Millan
Most Hits, Game, NL 37
Most RBIs in One Inning, NL 63

Bing Miller
Longest Hitting Streaks, AL 70
Three Consecutive Home Runs, Team, AL 196
.300-Hitting Outfields, AL 219

Bob Miller
Worst Won-Lost Record, Season (12 or more losses) 95
Most Consecutive Losses, NL 116
Most At-Bats with No Hits, Pitcher, Season since 1900 141

Doc Miller
Most Pinch Hits, Season, NL 68

Doggie Miller
Three Consecutive Home Runs, Team, NL 198

Dusty Miller
Most Assists, Outfielder, Game 156

Eddie Miller
Best Double-Play Combinations, Season 150
Most Double Plays, Shortstop, Season, NL 151
Most Assists, Shortstop, Game 159

Elmer Miller
Struck Out Twice in One Inning, AL 32

Hack Miller
Home Run in First Appearance in Majors, AL 11

John Miller
Home Run in First Appearance in Majors, AL 11

Ox Miller
Grand Slams, Pitcher, NL 138

Rick Miller
Most Doubles, Game, AL 27
Most Pinch Hits, Season, AL 68
Home Runs by First Two Batters in Game, AL 194

Roscoe Miller
Most Complete Games, Season, AL 131
Twenty or More Wins, Rookie, AL 168
Three Hundred or More Innings Pitched, Rookie, AL 169
Most Complete Games, Rookie, AL 170

Russ Miller
Worst Won-Lost Record, Season (12 or more losses) 95
Most Consecutive Losses, NL 116

Stu Miller
Shutout in First Start in Majors, NL 84
Most Relief Wins, Career 117
Most Relief Wins, Season, AL 118
Most Relief Wins, Season, NL 119
Most Relief Losses, Career 120
Most Saves, Career 121

Jocko Milligan
Most Doubles, Game, Other Leagues 27

Art Mills
Fathers and Sons in Baseball 191

Willie Mills
Fathers and Sons in Baseball 191

Eddie Milner
Leadoff Home Runs in Two Consecutive Games, NL 21
No-Hit Spoilers - The Only Hit Most Often 56

John Milner
Most Grand Slams, Career 3
Most Grand Slams, Season, NL 4
Most Pinch-Hit Grand Slams, Career 6

Don Mincher
Most Pinch-Hit Home Runs, Career 5
Three Consecutive Home Runs, Team, AL 197
Most Home Runs in One Inning, Team, AL 200
Most 20-Home Run Hitters, AL 208

Minnie Minoso
Most Triples, Rookie, AL 165
Retired Numbers, AL 182
Most Home Runs by Team, Game, AL 202

Greg Minton
Most Relief Losses, Season, NL 120
Most Saves, Career 121
Most Saves, Season, NL 122
Most Wins Plus Saves, Season 123

Bobby Mitchell
Most Home Runs in One Inning, Team, AL 200

Fred Mitchell
Most Walks in One Game, NL 113

Kevin Mitchell
Three Consecutive Home Runs, Team, NL 199

Mike Mitchell
Cycle Hitters, NL 51

George Mitterwald
Three Home Runs in One Game, NL 19
Three Consecutive Home Runs, Team, AL 197

Johnny Mize
Most Home Runs, Season, NL 7, 8
Best Home Run Ratio, Career 10
Most Home Runs by Position, Season, NL 11
Two Home Runs in One Game Most Often 12
Three Home Runs in One Game, AL 14
Three Home Runs in One Game, NL 17
Two Legs of Triple Crown, NL 47, 48
Cycle Hitters, NL 51
Most Pinch Hits, Season, AL 68
Most Consecutive Pinch Hits 70
Three Consecutive Home Runs, Team, NL 198
Most Home Runs by Team, Game, NL 205
Most 30-Home Run Hitters, NL 208
Home Run Trios, Season, NL 209
Home Run Duos, Season, NL (25 each) 210
Teammates Who Finished 1-2 in Batting, NL 222

Danny Moeller
Stole 2nd, 3rd, and Home in One Game, AL 66
Stolen Base Duos, Season, AL 216

Sam Moffett
Most Consecutive Losses, NL 116

Randy Moffitt
Most Relief Losses, Career 120

George Mogridge
No-Hitters, AL (9 innings or more) 87
Pitchers Who Stole Home, AL 140

Johnny Mokan
.300-Hitting Outfields, NL 220

Paul Molitor
Three Home Runs in One Game, AL 15
Most Leadoff Home Runs, Career 22
Most Home Runs by Team, Game, AL 203
Most 200-Hit Batters, AL 223

Bill Monbouquette
No-Hitters, AL (9 innings or more) 88
Most Strikeouts in Nine-Inning Game, AL 110

Rick Monday
Three Home Runs in One Game, NL 19
Most Leadoff Home Runs, Career 22
Most Times Struck Out, Game, AL 33
Hardest to Double Up, Career (Min. 1,000 G) 42
Easiest to Strike Out, Career (Min. 1,000 G) 44

Don Money
Most Leadoff Home Runs, Career 22
Fewest Errors by Position, Season, AL (Min. 150 G, excl. Pitchers) 147
Most Consecutive Errorless Games by Position, AL 148

Most Assists, Second Baseman, Game 158
Two Grand Slams in One Inning, Team 192
Home Runs by First Two Batters in Game, AL 194
Three Consecutive Home Runs, Team, AL 197

Sid Monge

Most Relief Wins, Season, AL 118

Willie Montanez

Thirty or More Home Runs, Rookie, NL 163

Rene Monteagudo

.300 Batting Average in Final Season (Min. 100 G) 39
Most Pinch Hits, Season, NL 69

John Montefusco

No-Hitters, NL (9 innings or more) 90
Most Strikeouts, Season, NL since 1900 107
Worst-Hitting Pitchers, Career (Min. 100 AB) 144
Most Strikeouts, Rookie, NL since 1900 169

Wally Moon

Home Run in First Appearance in Majors, NL 11

Charlie Moore

Cycle Hitters, AL 49

Donnie Moore

Most Saves, Season, AL 122

Earl Moore

No-Hitters, AL (9 innings or more) 87
Rookie No-Hitters, AL 167
Most Complete Games, Rookie, AL 170

Gene Moore

Most Doubles, Rookie, NL 165
Fathers and Sons in Baseball 191

Gene Moore

Fathers and Sons in Baseball 191

Henry Moore

.300 Batting Average in Final Season (Min. 100 G) 39

Joe Moore

Hardest to Double Up, Career (Min. 1,000 G) 42
Three Consecutive Home Runs, Team, NL 198
Most Home Runs in One Inning, Team, NL 200
Most Home Runs by Team, Game, NL 204
Most 200-Hit Batters, NL 223

Johnny Moore

Three Home Runs in One Game, NL 17

Roy Moore

Worst Won-Lost Record, Season (12 or more losses) 95
Most Consecutive Losses, AL 115

Terry Moore

Most Hits, Game, NL 36
Most Consecutive Hits, NL 74
.300-Hitting Outfields, NL 221

Bob Moose

No-Hitters, NL (9 innings or more) 90

Jerry Morales

Three Consecutive Home Runs, Team, NL 199
Most Home Runs by Team, Game, NL 206

Jose Morales

Grounded into Most Double Plays, Game, AL 43
Most Pinch Hits, Season, NL 68
Most Pinch Hits, Career 69

Pat Moran

Most Triples, Game, NL 29
Pennant-Winning Rookie Managers, NL 171

Dave Morehead

Shutout in First Start in Majors, AL 83
No-Hitters, AL (9 innings or more) 88

Omar Moreno

Hardest to Double Up, Career (Min. 1,000 G) 42
Most Stolen Bases, Season, NL 65
Most Stolen Bases, Career 66
Most Consecutive Games Played 71
Home Runs by First Two Batters in Game, NL 195
Stolen Base Duos, Season, NL 216, 217

Cy Morgan

Most Times Struck Out, Game, AL 33

Eddie Morgan

Pinch-Hit Home Run in First At-Bat in Majors, NL 6
Home Run in First Appearance in Majors, NL 11
Home Run on First Pitch in Majors, NL 11

Joe Morgan

Most Home Runs by Position, Career, NL 10
Most Leadoff Home Runs, Career 22
Twenty Home Runs with 50 Stolen Bases, Season 24
Most Times Walked, Game, NL 32
Most Hits, Game, NL 36
Hardest to Double Up, Career (Min. 1,000 G) 42
Most Runs Produced, Career 62
Most Stolen Bases, Career 66
Fewest Errors by Position, Season, NL (Min. 150 G, excl. Pitchers) 147
Most Consecutive Errorless Games by Position, NL 148
Stolen Base Duos, Season, NL 217

George Moriarty

Most Steals of Home, Career 67

John Morrill

Fewest Games Missed (10-Year Period) 72

Ed Morris

No-Hitters, Other Leagues 91
Most Strikeouts, Season before 1900 108
Rookie No-Hitters, Other Leagues 168

Jack Morris

No-Hitters, AL (9 innings or more) 88
Most Strikeouts, Season, AL 105

Johnny Morrison

Pitching Brothers, Same Team, NL 186

Phil Morrison

Pitching Brothers, Same Team, NL 186

Guy Morton

Worst Won-Lost Record, Season (12 or more losses) 95
Four Strikeouts in One Inning, AL 108
Most Consecutive Losses, AL 115
Fathers and Sons in Baseball 191

Guy Morton

Fathers and Sons in Baseball 191

Walt Moryn

Three Home Runs in One Game, NL 18

Wally Moses

Most Leadoff Home Runs, Career 22
Hardest to Double Up, Career (Min. 1,000 G) 42

Don Mossi

Fewest Base Runners per Nine Innings, Career (Min. 1,500 IP) 130

Johnny Mostil

Most Putouts, Outfielder, Game 156
.300-Hitting Outfields, AL 219

Manny Mota

Most Pinch Hits, Career 69

Darryl Motley

Home Runs by First Two Batters in Game, AL 194
Three Consecutive Home Runs, Team, AL 197

Frank Mountain

No-Hitters, Other Leagues 91

Don Mueller

Three Home Runs in One Game, NL 18
Cycle Hitters, NL 51
Fathers and Sons in Baseball 191
Teammates Who Finished 1-2 in Batting, NL 222

Emmett Mueller

Home Run in First Appearance in Majors, NL 11

Les Mueller

Most Innings Pitched, Game, AL 127

Ray Mueller

Most Games Caught, Season 152
Three Consecutive Home Runs, Team, NL 198

Walter Mueller

Fathers and Sons in Baseball 191

Hugh Mulcahy

Most Consecutive Losses, NL 116

Tony Mullane

No-Hitters, Other Leagues 91
Most 20-Win Seasons 101
Most Wins, Career 102
Most Strikeouts, Season before 1900 108
Two Complete Game Wins in One Day, Other Leagues 125
Most Innings Pitched, Game, NL 128
Rookie No-Hitters, Other Leagues 168

George Mullin

Most Shutouts, Career 80
No-Hitters, AL (9 innings or more) 87
Twenty Wins One Year, 20 Losses the Next, AL 98
Twenty Wins and 20 Losses in Same Year, AL 99
Most Wins, Career 102
Most Wins by Age, Season, AL 103
Two Complete Game Wins in One Day, AL 124
Most Complete Games, Season, AL 131
Most Innings Pitched, Season, AL 132
Most Hits, Pitcher, Career 139
Best-Hitting Pitchers, Season, AL 142
Best-Hitting Pitchers, Career 143
Teams with Three 20-Game Winners, AL 227

Pat Mullin

Three Home Runs in One Game, AL 14

Van Mungo

Struck Out Twice in One Inning, NL 33
Shutout in First Start in Majors, NL 84
Most Strikeouts, Season, NL since 1900 106
Most Consecutive Strikeouts, NL 116

Thurman Munson

Most Games Caught, Career 153
Retired Numbers, AL 182
Three Consecutive Home Runs, Team, AL 197

Bobby Murcer

Three Home Runs in One Game, AL 15
Most Home Runs in a Doubleheader, AL 20
Cycle Hitters, AL 49
Home Runs in Most Consecutive At-Bats, AL 76
Three Consecutive Home Runs, Team, AL 197
Three Consecutive Home Runs, Team, NL 199
Most Home Runs by Team, Game, NL 206

Dale Murphy
Best Home Run Ratio, Career 10
Three Home Runs in One Game, NL 19
Thirty Home Runs with 30 Stolen Bases, Season, NL 24
Most Times Walked, Game, NL 32
Easiest to Strike Out, Career (Min. 1,000 G) 44
Most Consecutive Games Played 71
Home Run Duos, Career, NL 211

Danny Murphy
Most Hits, Game, AL 35
Cycle Hitters, AL 49
Most Assists, Second Baseman, Game 158

Dwayne Murphy
Easiest to Strike Out, Career (Min. 1,000 G) 44
Stolen Base Duos, Season, AL 216

Eddie Murphy
Most Times Caught Stealing, Game, AL 68

Johnny Murphy
Most Relief Wins, Career 117
Most Relief Wins, Season, AL 118
Most Saves, Career 121

Rob Murphy
Undefeated Seasons (5 or more wins) 101

Tom Murphy
Most Shutout Losses, Season, AL 81

Dale Murray
Most Relief Wins, Season, NL 119
Most Relief Losses, Career 120

Eddie Murray
Most Grand Slams, Career 3
Most Grand Slams, Season, AL 4
Three Home Runs in One Game, AL 15
Switch-Hit Home Runs in One Game, AL 23
Brothers with Most Home Runs, Career 25
Two Legs of Triple Crown, AL 46
Most RBIs, Game, AL 64
Three Consecutive Home Runs, Team, AL 197
Most Home Runs by Team, Game, AL 203

Red Murray
Stolen Base Duos, Season, NL 217

Rich Murray
Brothers with Most Home Runs, Career 25

Ivan Murrell
Most Home Runs in One Inning, Team, NL 201

Danny Murtaugh
Retired Numbers, NL 183
Most Wins, Manager, Career 184

Tony Muser
Most Times Walked, Game, AL 32

Stan Musial
Most Home Runs, Career 9
Two Home Runs in One Game Most Often 12
Three Home Runs in One Game, NL 18
Most Home Runs in a Doubleheader, NL 20
Most Extra-Inning Home Runs, Career 23
Most Total Bases, Season, NL 30
Most Games with Five or More Hits, Career 37
Most Combined Hits and Walks, Season, NL 40, 41
Players Who Just Missed Triple Crowns, NL 45
Two Legs of Triple Crown, NL 48
Cycle Hitters, NL 51
The 3,000-Hit Club 54
The 3,000th Hit 54
Most Seasons with 200 Hits 54
Batting Champion by Widest Margin, NL 56
Batted .300 after Age 40 59
Most Runs, Career 60
Most RBIs, Career 61
Most Runs Produced, Career 62
Longest Hitting Streaks, NL 71
Most Consecutive Games Played 71
Fewest Games Missed (10-Year Period) 72
Home Runs in Most Consecutive At-Bats, NL 76
Career Spent With One Team (15 or more years) 181
Retired Numbers, NL 183
Home Run Duos, Career, NL 211

George Myatt
Most Hits, Game, AL 35

Buddy Myer
Most Combined Hits and Walks, Season, AL 40
Most Consecutive Hits, AL 73
Most Double Plays, Second Baseman, Season, AL 151

Elmer Myers
Shutout in First Start in Majors, AL 83
Three Hundred or More Innings Pitched, Rookie, AL 169
Most Strikeouts, Rookie, AL 169
Most Complete Games, Rookie, AL 170

Hy Myers
Most Times Caught Stealing, Game, NL 68
Most Putouts, Outfielder, Game 156
.300-Hitting Outfields, NL 220

Jack Nabors
Worst Won-Lost Record, Season (12 or more losses) 95
Most Consecutive Losses, AL 115

Doc Nance
Most Hits, Game, AL 35

Bill Narleski
Fathers and Sons in Baseball 191

Ray Narleski
Fathers and Sons in Baseball 191

Buster Narum
Home Run in First Appearance in Majors, AL 11
Worst-Hitting Pitchers, Career (Min. 100 AB) 144

Jim Nash
Easiest Pitcher to Strike Out, Season since 1900 141

Charlie Neal
Three Consecutive Home Runs, Team, NL 199

Greasy Neale
Stole 2nd, 3rd, and Home in One Game, NL 66

Art Nehf
Most Innings Pitched, Game, NL 128
Two Home Runs in One Game, Pitcher, NL 136
Teams with Three 20-Game Winners, NL since 1900 227

Dave Nelson
Stole 2nd, 3rd, and Home in One Game, AL 66

Lynn Nelson
Grand Slams, Pitcher, AL 138

Graig Nettles
Most Home Runs by Position, Career, AL 10
Most Home Runs in a Doubleheader, AL 20
Brothers with Most Home Runs, Career 25
Home Runs by Brothers in One Game 26
Home Runs by First Two Batters in Game, AL 194
Three Consecutive Home Runs, Team, AL 197

Jim Nettles
Brothers with Most Home Runs, Career 25
Home Runs by Brothers in One Game 26

Tex Neuer
Shutout in First Start in Majors, AL 83

Johnny Neun
Most Stolen Bases, Game, AL 66
Unassisted Triple Plays 149

Don Newcombe
Most Home Runs by Position, Season, NL 11
Shutout in First Start in Majors, NL 84
Best Won-Lost Record, Season, NL (20 or more wins) 97
Fewest Base Runners per Nine Innings, Career (Min. 1,500 IP) 130
Won 20 and Hit .300. in Same Year, NL 134
Most Home Runs, Pitcher, Career 135
Two Home Runs in One Game, Pitcher, NL 136
Two Home Runs in One Game Twice in One Season, Pitcher 136
Most Home Runs, Pitcher, Season 139
Pitchers Who Stole Home, NL since 1900 140
Best-Hitting Pitchers, Season, NL since 1900 142
Best-Hitting Pitchers, Career 142
Most Shutouts, Rookie, NL since 1900 170

Hal Newhouser
Most Wins, Career 102
Most Wins by Age, Season, AL 103
Most Strikeouts, Season, AL 105
Triple-Crown Pitchers, AL (most wins, lowest ERA, most strikeouts) 128
Best Lefty-Righty Duos 228

Bobo Newsom
Most Shutout Losses, Career 80
No-Hitters, AL (9 innings or more) 87
Best Won-Lost Record, Season, AL (20 or more wins) 96
Most Wins, Career 102
Most Strikeouts, Season, AL 105
Most Walks in One Game, AL 113
Most Consecutive Wins, AL 115
Most Consecutive Losses, AL 115
Rookie No-Hitters, AL 167

Doc Newton
Most Errors by Position, Season, NL since 1900 147

Simon Nicholls
.300 Average in Rookie Year Only, AL 164

Chet Nichols
Fathers and Sons in Baseball 191

Chet Nichols
Fathers and Sons in Baseball 191

Kid Nichols
Most Shutouts, Career 79
Most Complete 1-0 Wins, Career 94
Most 20-Win Seasons 101
Most Wins, Career 102
The 300-Win Club 103
Most Complete Games, Season, NL since 1900 132

Tricky Nichols
Worst Won-Lost Record, Season (12 or more losses) 95

Bill Nicholson
Three Home Runs in One Game, NL 17
Most Home Runs in a Doubleheader, NL 20
Hardest to Double Up, Career (Min. 1,000 G) 42
Two Legs of Triple Crown, NL 48
Home Runs in Most Consecutive At-Bats, NL 76
Three Consecutive Home Runs, Team, NL 198

George Nicol
Most Walks in One Game, NL 113

Steve Nicosia
Most Consecutive Times Struck Out, AL 74

Joe Niekro
Most Wins, Career 102
Pitching Brothers, Same Team, AL 186
Pitching Brothers, Same Team, NL 186
Most Wins by Brothers 187

Phil Niekro
Most Shutouts, Career 79
Most Shutout Losses, Career 80
No-Hitters, NL (9 innings or more) 90
Twenty Wins and 20 Losses, Season, NL since 1900 99
Most Wins, Career 102
The 300-Win Club 103
Most Wins by Age, Season, AL 104
Most Wins by Age, Season, NL since 1900 104
Most Strikeouts, Season, NL since 1900 106, 107
Most Strikeouts, Career 108
Four Strikeouts in One Inning, NL 109
Most Wins after Age 40 134
Retired Numbers, NL 183
Pitching Brothers, Same Team, AL 186
Pitching Brothers, Same Team, NL 186
Most Wins by Brothers 187

Bob Nieman
Home Run in First Appearance in Majors, AL 11
Most Home Runs by Team, Game, AL 202

Gary Nolan
Most Strikeouts, Season, NL since 1900 107
Fewest Base Runners per Nine Innings, Career (Min. 1,500 IP) 129
Most Strikeouts, Rookie, NL since 1900 169
Most Shutouts, Rookie, NL since 1900 170

Irv Noren
Most Putouts, Outfielder, Game 156

Jim Norris
Most Times Walked, Game, AL 32

Mike Norris
Shutout in First Start in Majors, AL 83

Billy North
Most Times Walked, Game, AL 32
Most Stolen Bases, Season, AL 65
Unassisted Double Plays, Outfielder 152
Stolen Base Duos, Season, AL 216

Ron Northey
Most Pinch-Hit Grand Slams, Career 6
Fathers and Sons in Baseball 191

Scott Northey
Fathers and Sons in Baseball 191

Jim Northrup
Two Grand Slams in One Game 3
Most Grand Slams, Season, AL 4
Most Hits, Game, AL 35
No-Hit Spoilers - The Only Hit Most Often 58
Three Consecutive Home Runs, Team, AL 197

Don Nottebart
No-Hitters, NL (9 innings or more) 90

Joe Nuxhall
Undefeated Seasons (5 or more wins) 101
Four Strikeouts in One Inning, NL 109
Most Home Runs, Pitcher, Career 135

Billy O'Brien
Most Putouts in Nine Innings, First Baseman 157

Buck O'Brien
Shutout in First Start in Majors, AL 83
Teams with Three 20-Game Winners, AL 227

Darby O'Brien
Most Hits, Game, Other Leagues 37

Eddie O'Brien
Pitching Brothers, Same Team, NL 186

Johnny O'Brien
Pitching Brothers, Same Team, NL 186

Pete O'Brien
Most Home Runs by Team, Game, AL 203

Danny O'Connell
Most Triples, Game, NL 29
Longest Hitting Streaks, NL 71

Billy O'Dell
Struck Out Twice in One Inning, NL 33
Shutout with Most Hits Allowed, NL 86

John O'Donoghue
Grand Slams, Pitcher, AL 138

Lefty O'Doul
Most Games with Five or More Hits, Career 37
Most Combined Hits and Walks, Season, NL 40
Batting Champion with Two Different Clubs 43
Most Consecutive Hits, NL 74
Most 30-Home Run Hitters, NL 208
Most 100-RBI Hitters, NL 212
Most .300 Hitters, Season, NL (300 AB each) 218
.300-Hitting Outfields, NL 221
Most 200-Hit Batters, NL 223

Joe Oeschger
Struck Out Twice in One Inning, NL 33
Twenty Wins One Year, 20 Losses the Next, NL since 1900 98
Perfect Innings, NL (3 strikeouts on 9 pitches) 110
Most Consecutive Losses, NL 116
Most Innings Pitched, Game, NL 128

Bob O'Farrell

Most Games Caught, Career 153

Rowland Office

Most Consecutive Pinch Hits 70
Longest Hitting Streaks, NL 71

Ben Oglivie

Most Home Runs, Season, AL 7
Three Home Runs in One Game, AL 15
Three Consecutive Home Runs, Team, AL 197
Most Home Runs by Team, Game, AL 203
Most 30-Home Run Hitters, AL 207
Most 100-RBI Hitters, AL 212

Bill O'Hara

Stole 2nd, 3rd, and Home in One Game, NL 66

Frank Okrie

Fathers and Sons in Baseball 191

Len Okrie

Fathers and Sons in Baseball 191

Charley O'Leary

The Worst Hitters (Min. 2,500 AB) 52

Tony Oliva

Three Home Runs in One Game, AL 15
Most Consecutive Hits, AL 73
Two Hundred or More Hits, Rookie, AL 163
Thirty or More Home Runs, Rookie, AL 163
Most Doubles, Rookie, AL 165
Career Spent With One Team (15 or more years) 181
Four Consecutive Home Runs, Team 196
Three Consecutive Home Runs, Team, AL 196
Most Home Runs in One Inning, Team, AL 200
Most 30-Home Run Hitters, AL 207
Most 20-Home Run Hitters, AL 208
Home Run Trios, Season, AL 209
Home Run Duos, Season, AL (25 each) 210

Al Oliver

Three Home Runs in One Game, AL 15
Most Home Runs in a Doubleheader, AL 20
Most Extra-Base Hits in a Doubleheader, AL 27
Two Legs of Triple Crown, NL 48
.300-Hitting Outfields, NL 221

Bob Oliver

Most Hits, Game, AL 35

Gene Oliver

Three Home Runs in One Game, NL 18
Most Home Runs in One Inning, Team, NL 201
Most 20-Home Run Hitters, NL 208

Luis Olmo

.300-Hitting Outfields, NL 221

Ivy Olson

Most Assists, Shortstop, Game 159

Jack O'Neill

Brother Batteries, NL 185
Three or More Brothers in Baseball 187
Best-Hitting Brothers 190

Jim O'Neill

Three or More Brothers in Baseball 187
Best-Hitting Brothers 190

Steve O'Neill

Most Games Caught, Career 153
Most Wins, Manager, Career 184
Three or More Brothers in Baseball 187
Best-Hitting Brothers 190

Tip O'Neill

Cycle Hitters, Other Leagues 51
The .400 Hitters, Other Leagues 53

Steve Ontiveros

Most Home Runs by Team, Game, NL 206

Jesse Orosco

Most Relief Wins, Season, NL 119
Most Saves, Season, NL 122
Most Wins Plus Saves, Season 123

Jim O'Rourke

Cycle Hitters, NL 51
Fewest Games Missed (10-Year Period) 72
Best-Hitting Brothers 189
Fathers and Sons in Baseball 191

Joe O'Rourke

Fathers and Sons in Baseball 191

John O'Rourke

Most Doubles, Game, NL 27
Best-Hitting Brothers 189

Patsy O'Rourke

Fathers and Sons in Baseball 191

Queenie O'Rourke

Fathers and Sons in Baseball 191

Dave Orr

Most Hits, Game, Other Leagues 37
.300 Batting Average in Final Season (Min. 100 G) 39
Cycle Hitters, Other Leagues 51

Ernie Orsatti

.300-Hitting Outfields, NL 221

John Orsino

Most Home Runs in One Inning, Team, NL 200

Most Wins, Career 102
Fewest Base Runners per Nine Innings, Career (Min. 1,500 IP) 130
Career Spent With One Team (15 or more years) 181
Retired Numbers, AL 182
Teams with Four 20-Game Winners 227
Teams with Three 20-Game Winners, AL 227
Best Lefty-Righty Duos 229

Larry Pape

Shutout in First Start in Majors, AL 83

Milt Pappas

Most Shutouts, Career 79
No-Hitters, NL (9 innings or more) 90
Most Wins, Career 102
Most Grand Slams Allowed, Career 133
Most Home Runs, Pitcher, Career 135
Two Home Runs in One Game, Pitcher, AL 136
Most Times Struck Out, Pitcher, Career since 1900 141

Freddy Parent

No-Hit Spoilers - The Only Hit Most Often 57
Most Assists, Shortstop, Game 159

Ace Parker

Pinch-Hit Home Run in First At-Bat in Majors, AL 6
Home Run in First Appearance in Majors, AL 11

Dave Parker

Most Pinch-Hit Grand Slams, Career 6

Harry Parker

Most At-Bats with No Hits, Pitcher, Season since 1900 141

Wes Parker

Switch-Hit Home Runs in One Game, NL 23
Cycle Hitters, NL 51

Roy Parmelee

Grand Slams, Pitcher, NL 138

Mel Parnell

No-Hitters, AL (9 innings or more) 88

Lance Parrish

Most Games Caught, Career 153
Three Consecutive Home Runs, Team, AL 197
Most 20-Home Run Hitters, AL 208

Larry Parrish

Most Grand Slams, Season, AL 4
Three Home Runs in One Game, AL 15
Three Home Runs in One Game, NL 19
Most Home Runs in One Inning, Team, NL 201
Most Home Runs by Team, Game, NL 204

Mike Parrott

Worst Won-Lost Record, Season (12 or more losses) 95
Most Consecutive Losses, AL 115

Tom Parrott

Cycle Hitters, NL 51

Stan Partenheimer

Fathers and Sons in Baseball 191

Steve Partenheimer

Fathers and Sons in Baseball 191

Camilo Pascual

Most Shutouts, Career 80
Most Strikeouts, Season, AL 105, 106
Most Games with 10 or More Strikeouts, Career 114
Most Strikeouts per Nine Innings, Career (Min. 1,500 IP) 114
Grand Slams, Pitcher, AL 138

Dode Paskert

Stole 2nd, 3rd, and Home in One Game, NL 66
Stolen Base Duos, Season, NL 216

Claude Passeau

Most Home Runs, Pitcher, Career 135
Grand Slams, Pitcher, NL 138

Jim Pastorius

Most Shutout Losses, Season, NL 81
Most Consecutive Losses, NL 116

Joe Pate

Undefeated Seasons (5 or more wins) 101

Freddie Patek

Three Home Runs in One Game, AL 15
Cycle Hitters, AL 49
Best Double-Play Combinations, Season 150
Stolen Base Duos, Season, AL 216

Casey Patten

Most Shutout Losses, Season, AL 81
Most Complete Games, Season, AL 131
Most Innings Pitched, Season, AL 132

Roy Patterson

Twenty or More Wins, Rookie, AL 168
Three Hundred or More Innings Pitched, Rookie, AL 169
Most Complete Games, Rookie, AL 170

Marty Pattin

Shutout with Most Hits Allowed, AL 86

Mike Paxton

Four Strikeouts in One Inning, AL 108

Monte Pearson

No-Hitters, AL (9 innings or more) 87

Roger Peckinpaugh

Most Times Walked, Game, AL 31
Longest Hitting Streaks, AL 70
Best Double-Play Combinations, Season 150
Stolen Base Duos, Season, AL 216

Heinie Peitz

Three Consecutive Home Runs, Team, NL 198

Eddie Pellagrini

Home Run in First Appearance in Majors, AL 11

Barney Pelty

Fewest Base Runners per Nine Innings, Career (Min. 1,500 IP) 129

Orlando Pena

Grand Slams, Pitcher, AL 138

Jim Pendleton

Three Home Runs in One Game, NL 18
Most Home Runs by Team, Game, NL 204

Herb Pennock

Most Shutouts, Career 80
Shutout with Most Hits Allowed, AL 86
Most Wins, Career 102
Best Lefty-Righty Duos 229

Joe Pepitone

Two Home Runs in One Inning, AL 12
Three Consecutive Home Runs, Team, AL 197
Most Home Runs by Team, Game, NL 206

Pascual Perez

Worst Won-Lost Record, Season (12 or more losses) 95

Tony Perez

Most Home Runs, Season, NL 8
No-Hit Spoilers - The Only Hit Most Often 58
Most RBIs, Career 61
Most Runs Produced, Career 62
Three Consecutive Home Runs, Team, AL 197
Three Consecutive Home Runs, Team, NL 199
Most Home Runs in One Inning, Team, AL 200
Most Home Runs by Team, Game, NL 204, 205
Most 40-Home Run Hitters, NL 206
Most 30-Home Run Hitters, NL 208
Home Run Trios, Season, NL 209

Cy Perkins

Most Games Caught, Career 153
Three Consecutive Home Runs, Team, AL 196
Most Home Runs by Team, Game, AL 202

Ron Perranoski

Most Relief Wins, Career 117
Most Relief Wins, Season, NL 119
Most Relief Losses, Career 120
Most Saves, Career 121
Most Saves, Season, AL 122
Most Wins Plus Saves, Season 123
Worst-Hitting Pitchers, Career (Min. 100 AB) 144

Pol Perritt

Shutout with Most Hits Allowed, NL 86
Two Complete Game Wins in One Day, NL since 1900 124

Gaylord Perry

Most Shutouts, Career 79
Most Shutout Losses, Career 80
Shutout with Most Hits Allowed, AL 86
No-Hitters, NL (9 innings or more) 90
Most Complete 1-0 Wins, Career 94
Most Wins, Career 102
The 300-Win Club 103
Most Strikeouts, Season, AL 105
Most Strikeouts, Season, NL since 1900 106, 107
Most Strikeouts, Career 108
Most Games with 10 or More Strikeouts, Career 114
Most Consecutive Wins, AL 115
Fewest Base Runners per Nine Innings, Career (Min. 1,500 IP) 130
Most Grand Slams Allowed, Career 133
Most Extra-Inning Home Runs Allowed, Career 133
Most Wins after Age 40 134
Pitching Brothers, Same Team, AL 186
Most Wins by Brothers 187

Jim Perry

Most Wins, Career 102
Pitching Brothers, Same Team, AL 186
Most Wins by Brothers 187
Best Lefty-Righty Duos 229

Scott Perry

Most Times Struck Out, Game, AL 33
Twenty Wins with Last-Place Team, AL 99
Highest Percentage of Team's Wins, AL 99
Twenty or More Wins, Rookie, AL 168
ERA Under 2.00, Rookie, AL (Min. 130 IP) 169
Three Hundred or More Innings Pitched, Rookie, AL 169
Most Complete Games, Rookie, AL 170

Johnny Pesky

Most Runs, Game, AL 60
Longest Hitting Streaks, AL 70
Most Consecutive Hits, AL 73
Best Double-Play Combinations, Season 150
Two Hundred or More Hits, Rookie, AL 163
Highest Batting Average, Rookie, AL (Min. 300 AB) 167
Teammates Who Finished 1-2 in Batting, AL 222

Gary Peters

Most Strikeouts, Season, AL 105, 106
Most Home Runs, Pitcher, Career 135
Grand Slams, Pitcher, AL 138
Most Strikeouts, Rookie, AL 169

Fritz Peterson

Most Shutout Losses, Career 80
Best Control Pitchers, Career 126

Fewest Base Runners per Nine Innings, Career (Min. 1,500 IP) 130

Kent Peterson

Worst-Hitting Pitchers, Career (Min. 100 AB) 144

Rico Petrocelli

Most Grand Slams, Season, AL 4
Most Home Runs, Season, AL 7
Most Home Runs by Position, Career, AL 10
Most Home Runs by Position, Season, AL 11
Most 40-Home Run Hitters, AL 206
Home Run Duos, Season, AL (25 each) 210
Home Run Duos, Career, AL 211

Gary Pettis

Most Putouts, Outfielder, Game 156

Big Jeff Pfeffer

No-Hitters, NL (9 innings or more) 89

Fred Pfeffer

No-Hit Spoilers - The Only Hit Most Often 57

Jeff Pfeffer

Most Innings Pitched, Game, NL 128
Twenty or More Wins, Rookie, NL since 1900 168
ERA Under 2.00, Rookie, NL since 1900 (Min. 130 IP) 169
Three Hundred or More Innings Pitched, Rookie, NL since 1900 169

Jack Pfiester

Most Strikeouts in Extra-Inning Game, NL 112
Lowest ERA, Season, NL 127
Twenty or More Wins, Rookie, NL since 1900 168
ERA Under 2.00, Rookie, NL since 1900 (Min. 130 IP) 169

Dave Philley

Most Pinch Hits, Season, AL 68
Most Pinch Hits, Season, NL 69
Most Pinch Hits, Career 69
Most Consecutive Pinch Hits 70
Most Consecutive Hits, NL 74

Deacon Phillippe

No-Hitters, NL (9 innings or more) 89
Most Consecutive Wins, NL 115
Best Control Pitchers, Career 126
Most Innings Pitched, Game, NL 128
Fewest Base Runners per Nine Innings, Career (Min. 1,500 IP) 129
Grand Slams, Pitcher, NL 138
Rookie No-Hitters, NL 167
Teams with Three 20-Game Winners, NL since 1900 227

Adolfo Phillips

Three Home Runs in One Game, NL 18
Most Home Runs in a Doubleheader, NL 20
Most Times Struck Out, Game, NL 34
Most Consecutive Times Struck Out, NL 74
Most Home Runs by Team, Game, NL 205

Bill Phillips

Best-Hitting Pitchers, Season, NL since 1900 142

Bubba Phillips

Three Consecutive Home Runs, Team, AL 196

Damon Phillips

Most Assists, Third Baseman, Game 158

Mike Phillips

Cycle Hitters, NL 51

Taylor Phillips

Worst-Hitting Pitchers, Career (Min. 100 AB) 144

Tony Phillips

Cycle Hitters, AL 49
Most Assists, Second Baseman, Game 158

Tom Phoebus

Shutout in First Start in Majors, AL 83
Shutout in First Two Major League Games, AL 85
No-Hitters, AL (9 innings or more) 88
Most Strikeouts, Rookie, AL 169

Bill Phyle

Shutout in First Start in Majors, NL 84

Wiley Piatt

Most Walks in One Game, NL 113

Val Picinich

Most No-Hitters Caught, Career 154

Billy Pierce

Most Shutouts, Career 80
Most Wins, Career 102

Jimmy Piersall

Most Hits, Game, AL 35
Most Home Runs in One Inning, Team, AL 200

Duane Pillette

Fathers and Sons in Baseball 191

Herman Pillette

Fathers and Sons in Baseball 191

George Pinckney

Most Hits, Game, Other Leagues 37
Most Consecutive Games Played 71

Lou Piniella

Easiest to Double Up, Career (Min. 1000 G) 41

Vada Pinson

Longest Hitting Streaks, NL 71
Most Consecutive Games Played 71

Two Hundred or More Hits, Rookie, NL 163
Most Doubles, Rookie, NL 165
Home Runs by First Two Batters in Game, AL 194
Home Run Duos, Career, NL 211

Jake Pitler

Most Putouts, Second Baseman, Game 157

Togie Pittinger

Twenty Wins One Year, 20 Losses the Next, NL since 1900 98
Most Complete Games, Season, NL since 1900 132
Most Innings Pitched, Season, NL sicne 1900 132

Juan Pizarro

Most Strikeouts per Nine Innings, Career (Min. 1,500 IP) 114

Eddie Plank

Most Shutouts, Career 79
Most Complete 1-0 Wins, Career 94
Most 1-0 Losses, Career 95
Best Won-Lost Record, Season, AL (20 or more wins) 96
Most 20-Win Seasons 101
Most Wins, Career 102
The 300-Win Club 103
Most Strikeouts, Season, AL 105, 106
Most Innings Pitched, Game, AL 127
Fewest Base Runners per Nine Innings, Career (Min. 1,500 IP) 129
Most Complete Games, Season, AL 131
Most Innings Pitched, Season, AL 132
Most Hits, Pitcher, Career 139
Pitchers Who Stole Home, AL 140
Most Complete Games, Rookie, AL 170
Teams with Three 20-Game Winners, AL 227
Strikeout Duos, Season, AL 228
Best Lefty-Righty Duos 228

Bud Podbielan

Most Walks in One Game, NL 113

Johnny Podres

Most Consecutive Strikeouts, NL 116

Darrell Porter

Most Games Caught, Career 153
Most No-Hitters Caught, Career 155
Two Pinch-Hit Home Runs in One Inning, Team, AL 192
Back-to-Back Pinch-Hit Home Runs, Team 193
Home Runs by First Two Batters in Game, AL 194
Most Home Runs by Team, Game, AL 203

Dick Porter

.300-Hitting Outfields, AL 219, 220

Henry Porter

No-Hitters, Other Leagues 91
Most Strikeouts in Nine-Inning Game, Other Leagues 112

Bob Porterfield

Grand Slams, Pitcher, AL 138

Wally Post

Most Pinch-Hit Home Runs, Career 5
Most Home Runs, Season, NL 8
Best Home Run Ratio, Career 10
Most Home Runs in a Doubleheader, NL 20
Easiest to Strike Out, Career (Min. 1,000 G) 44
Most Home Runs by Team, Game, NL 204, 205
Most 40-Home Run Hitters, NL 206
Most 30-Home Run Hitters, NL 208
Most 20-Home Run Hitters, NL 208
Home Run Trios, Season, NL 209
Home Run Duos, Season, NL (25 each) 210

Nels Potter

Most Relief Losses, Season, NL 120

Boog Powell

Best Home Run Ratio, Career 10
Three Home Runs in One Game, AL 14
Struck Out Twice in One Inning, AL 32
Two Pinch-Hit Home Runs in One Inning, Team, AL 192
Back-to-Back Pinch-Hit Home Runs, Team 193
Three Consecutive Home Runs, Team, AL 197
Most Home Runs in One Inning, Team, AL 200
Most Home Runs by Team, Game, AL 203
Home Run Duos, Season, AL (25 each) 210
Home Run Duos, Career, AL 211

Grover Powell

Shutout in First Start in Majors, NL 84

Jack Powell

Most Shutouts, Career 79
Most Shutout Losses, Career 80
Most 1-0 Losses, Career 95
Most Wins, Career 102
Most Strikeouts, Season, AL 106
Most Complete Games, Season, AL 131
Most Innings Pitched, Season, AL 132
Most Hits, Pitcher, Career 139

Jake Powell

.300-Hitting Outfields, AL 220

Ray Powell

Most Triples, Game, NL 29
.300-Hitting Outfields, NL 220

Vic Power

Home Runs by First Two Batters in Game, AL 194
Most Home Runs by Team, Game, AL 202

Del Pratt

.300 Batting Average in Final Season (Min. 100 G) 39
Most Triples, Rookie, AL 165

Jim Presley
Three Home Runs in One Game, AL 15
Grounded into Most Double Plays, Game, AL 43
Most Home Runs by Team, Game, AL 203

Tot Pressnell
Shutout in First Start in Majors, NL 84

Gerry Priddy
Best Double-Play Combinations, Season 149
Most Double Plays, Second Baseman, Season, AL 151
Most Assists, Second Baseman, Game 158
Most Home Runs in One Inning, Team, AL 200

Kirby Puckett
Leadoff Home Runs in Two Consecutive Games, AL 21
Cycle Hitters, AL 49
Home Runs by First Two Batters in Game, AL 194
Most 20-Home Run Hitters, AL 208

Terry Puhl
Most Leadoff Home Runs, Career 22
Hardest to Double Up, Career (Min. 1,000 G) 42
Fewest Errors by Position, Season, NL (Min. 150 G, excl. Pitchers) 147

Blondie Purcell
Most Consecutive Losses, NL 116

Bob Purkey
Shutout with Most Hits Allowed, NL 86
Best Won-Lost Record, Season, NL (20 or more wins) 97
Grand Slams, Pitcher, NL 139
Most Times Struck Out, Pitcher, Career since 1900 141

Billy Purtell
Struck Out Twice in One Inning, AL 32

Mel Queen
Fathers and Sons in Baseball 191

Mel Queen
Fathers and Sons in Baseball 191

Jack Quinn
Most Wins, Career 102
Most Wins by Age, Season, AL 104
Most Wins by Age, Season, NL since 1900 104
Best Control Pitchers, Career 126
Most Wins after Age 40 134
Pitchers Who Stole Home, NL since 1900 140

Jamie Quirk
Three Consecutive Home Runs, Team, AL 197

Dan Quisenberry
Most Relief Wins, Season, AL 118
Most Saves, Career 121
Most Saves, Season, AL 122
Most Wins Plus Saves, Season 122

Dick Radatz
Most Relief Wins, Season, AL 118
Most Relief Losses, Season, AL 120
Most Saves, Career 121
Most Wins Plus Saves, Season 122, 123
Most Extra-Inning Home Runs Allowed, Career 133

George Radbourn
Most Wins by Brothers 187

Old Hoss Radbourn
Most Shutouts, Career 80
Most Shutouts, Season, NL 81
No-Hitters, NL (9 innings or more) 88
Best Won-Lost Record, Season, NL (20 or more wins) 97
Most 20-Win Seasons 101
Most Wins, Career 102
The 300-Win Club 103
Most Strikeouts, Season before 1900 107, 108
Most Consecutive Wins, NL 115
Two Complete Game Wins in One Day, NL before 1900 125
Triple-Crown Pitchers, NL (most wins, lowest ERA, most strikeouts) 129
Fewest Base Runners per Nine Innings, Career (Min. 1,500 IP) 130
Most Wins by Brothers 187

Rip Radcliff
Most Hits, Game, AL 35
.300-Hitting Outfields, AL 220

Doug Rader
Easiest to Strike Out, Career (Min. 1,000 G) 44

Ken Raffensberger
Most 1-0 Losses, Career 95
Best Control Pitchers, Career 126

Pat Ragan
Perfect Innings, NL (3 strikeouts on 9 pitches) 110

Tim Raines
Most Stolen Bases, Season, NL 65
Stolen Base Duos, Season, NL 217

Ed Rakow
Most At-Bats with No Hits, Pitcher, Season since 1900 141
Worst-Hitting Pitchers, Career (Min. 100 AB) 144

Rafael Ramirez
Best Double-Play Combinations, Season 149
Most Double Plays, Shortstop, Season, NL 151

Domingo Ramos
Three Consecutive Home Runs, Team, AL 197

Pedro Ramos
Most Home Runs, Pitcher, Career 135
Two Home Runs in One Game, Pitcher, AL 136
Grand Slams, Pitcher, AL 138
Four Consecutive Home Runs, Team 196
Most Home Runs in One Inning, Team, AL 200

Toad Ramsey
Most Strikeouts, Season before 1900 107
Most Strikeouts in Nine-Inning Game, Other Leagues 112
Most Games with 10 or More Strikeouts, Career 114

Willie Randolph
Best Double-Play Combinations, Season 150
Most Assists, Second Baseman, Game 158
Stolen Base Duos, Season, AL 216

Merritt Ranew
Most Pinch Hits, Season, NL 69

Eric Rasmussen
Shutout in First Start in Majors, NL 85

Morrie Rath
Most Assists, Second Baseman, Game 158

Carl Ray
Most Walks in One Game, AL 113

Johnny Ray
Home Runs by First Two Batters in Game, NL 195

Floyd Rayford
Most Home Runs by Team, Game, AL 203

Bugs Raymond
Most Shutout Losses, Season, NL 81

Claude Raymond
Most Relief Losses, Career 120

Jeff Reardon
Most Saves, Career 121
Most Saves, Season, NL 122
Most Wins Plus Saves, Season 123

Gary Redus
Leadoff Home Runs in Two Consecutive Games, NL 21
Home Runs by First Two Batters in Game, NL 195

Ron Reed
Most Saves, Career 121
Fewest Base Runners per Nine Innings, Career (Min. 1,500 IP) 130
Most Consecutive Errorless Games by Position, NL 148

Andy Reese
Most .300 Hitters, Season, NL (300 AB each) 218

Pee Wee Reese
Most Home Runs by Position, Career, NL 10
Best Double-Play Combinations, Season 149, 150
Career Spent With One Team (15 or more years) 181
Retired Numbers, NL 183

Rich Reese
Most Pinch-Hit Grand Slams, Career 6

Bobby Reeves
Most Assists, Shortstop, Game 159

Bill Regan
Two Home Runs in One Inning, AL 12

Phil Regan
Most Consecutive Wins, NL 115
Most Relief Wins, Season, NL 119

Rick Reichardt
Two Home Runs in One Inning, AL 12
Most Times Struck Out, Game, AL 33

Bill Reidy
Three Hundred or More Innings Pitched, Rookie, AL 169
Most Complete Games, Rookie, AL 170

Long John Reilly
Most Triples, Game, NL 28
Most Hits, Game, Other Leagues 37
Cycle Hitters, NL 51
Cycle Hitters, Other Leagues 51
Most Runs, Game, Other Leagues 60

Pete Reiser
.300-Hitting Outfields, NL 221

Ken Reitz
Fewest Errors by Position, Season, NL (Min. 150 G, excl. Pitchers) 147

Jerry Remy
Most Hits, Game, AL 35
Stolen Base Duos, Season, AL 216

Rick Renick
Home Run in First Appearance in Majors, AL 11

Steve Renko
Most Consecutive Strikeouts, NL 116

Merv Rettenmund
Most Pinch Hits, Season, NL 68

Ed Reulbach
Most Shutouts, Career 80
Most Consecutive Wins, NL 115
Two Complete Game Wins in One Day, NL since 1900 124

Lowest ERA, Season, NL 127
Most Innings Pitched, Game, NL 128
Fewest Base Runners per Nine Innings, Career (Min. 1,500 IP) 129
ERA Under 2.00, Rookie, NL since 1900 (Min. 130 IP) 169
Most Shutouts, Rookie, NL since 1900 170

Paul Reuschel

Pitching Brothers, Same Team, NL 186

Rick Reuschel

Pitching Brothers, Same Team, NL 186

Jerry Reuss

Most Shutouts, Career 80
No-Hitters, NL (9 innings or more) 90
Most Grand Slams Allowed, Career 133

Dave Revering

Three Consecutive Home Runs, Team, AL 197

Allie Reynolds

Most Shutouts, Career 80
No-Hitters, AL (9 innings or more) 87
Most No-Hitters, Career 93

Carl Reynolds

Three Home Runs in One Game, AL 13

Craig Reynolds

Most Triples, Game, NL 29
Hardest to Double Up, Career (Min. 1,000 G) 42

Harold Reynolds

Most Assists, Second Baseman, Game 158

Ken Reynolds

Most Consecutive Losses, NL 116

Bob Rhoads

No-Hitters, AL (9 innings or more) 87
Teams with Three 20-Game Winners, AL 227

Dusty Rhodes

Three Home Runs in One Game, NL 18
Most Extra-Base Hits in a Doubleheader, NL 27
Two Pinch-Hit Home Runs in One Inning, Team, NL 193
Three Consecutive Home Runs, Team, NL 198

Del Rice

Most Games Caught, Career 153

Harry Rice

Most Putouts, Outfielder, Game 156
.300-Hitting Outfields, AL 219

Jim Rice

Most Home Runs, Season, AL 7
Two Home Runs in One Game Most Often 12
Three Home Runs in One Game, AL 15
Most Total Bases, Season, AL 30
Easiest to Double Up, Career (Min. 1000 G) 41
Two Legs of Triple Crown, AL 46
One Hundred or More RBIs, Rookie, AL 166
Three Consecutive Home Runs, Team, AL 197
Most Home Runs in One Inning, Team, AL 200
Most Home Runs by Team, Game, AL 202
Most 30-Home Run Hitters, AL 207
Most 20-Home Run Hitters, AL 208
Home Run Duos, Career, AL 211
Most 100-RBI Hitters, AL 212

Sam Rice

Hardest to Strike Out, Career (Min. 1,000 G) 44
Most Seasons with 200 Hits 54
Batted .300 after Age 40 59
Most Runs Produced, Career 62
Most Steals of Home, Career 67
Longest Hitting Streaks, AL 70
Most Consecutive Hits, AL 73
Unassisted Double Plays, Outfielder 152
.300-Hitting Outfields, AL 219

J. R. Richard

Most Strikeouts, Season, NL since 1900 106, 107
Most Games with 10 or More Strikeouts, Career 114
Most Strikeouts per Nine Innings, Career (Min. 1,500 IP) 114

Gene Richards

Most Hits, Game, NL 37
Stolen Base Duos, Season, NL 217

Bobby Richardson

Best Double-Play Combinations, Season 149
Most Double Plays, Second Baseman, Season, AL 151
Three Consecutive Home Runs, Team, AL 197

Danny Richardson

Most Hits, Game, NL 36
Most Assists, Second Baseman, Game 158
Most Assists, Shortstop, Game 159
Most Home Runs by Team, Game, NL 204

Hardy Richardson

Most Triples, Game, NL 28

Lance Richbourg

Most Triples, Game, NL 29

Pete Richert

Four Strikeouts in One Inning, NL 109
Most Consecutive Strikeouts, AL 116

Lee Richmond

No-Hitters, NL (9 innings or more) 88
Perfect Games (9 innings or more) 94
Twenty Wins with Last-Place Team, NL 99
Rookie No-Hitters, NL 167

Elmer Riddle
Brother Batteries, NL 185

Johnny Riddle
Brother Batteries, NL 185

Dave Righetti
No-Hitters, AL (9 innings or more) 88
Most Saves, Career 121
Most Saves, Season, AL 122
Most Wins Plus Saves, Season 122, 123

Billy Rigney
Most Wins, Manager, Career 184

Jose Rijo
Most Strikeouts in Nine-Inning Game, AL 111

Jimmy Ring
Grand Slams, Pitcher, NL 138

Cal Ripken
Cycle Hitters, AL 49
Most Consecutive Games Played 71
Most Double Plays, Shortstop, Season, AL 151
Three Consecutive Home Runs, Team, AL 197

Allen Ripley
Fathers and Sons in Baseball 191

Walt Ripley
Fathers and Sons in Baseball 191

Mickey Rivers
Most Leadoff Home Runs, Career 22
.300 Batting Average in Final Season (Min. 100 G) 39
Hardest to Double Up, Career (Min. 1,000 G) 42
Most Stolen Bases, Season, AL 65
Stolen Base Duos, Season, AL 216

Eppa Rixey
Most Shutouts, Career 80
Twenty Wins One Year, 20 Losses the Next, NL since 1900 98
Most Wins, Career 102
Teams with Three 20-Game Winners, NL since 1900 227
Best Lefty-Righty Duos 229

Johnny Rizzo
Most RBIs, Game, NL 64
.300 Average in Rookie Year Only, NL 164
One Hundred or More RBIs, Rookie, NL 166

Phil Rizzuto
Best Double-Play Combinations, Season 149, 150
Most Double Plays, Shortstop, Season, AL 151
Retired Numbers, AL 182

Robin Roberts
Most Shutouts, Career 79
Most Shutout Losses, Career 80
Shutout with Most Hits Allowed, AL 86
Best Won-Lost Record, Season, NL (20 or more wins) 97
Most Wins, Career 102
Most Wins by Age, Season, NL since 1900 104
Best Control Pitchers, Career 126
Fewest Base Runners per Nine Innings, Career (Min. 1,500 IP) 130
Most Times Struck Out, Pitcher, Career since 1900 141
Retired Numbers, NL 183
Best Lefty-Righty Duos 228

Bob Robertson
Most Assists, First Baseman, Game 157
Three Consecutive Home Runs, Team, NL 199

Charlie Robertson
No-Hitters, AL (9 innings or more) 87
Perfect Games (9 innings or more) 94
Rookie No-Hitters, AL 167

Dave Robertson
Cycle Hitters, NL 51

Sherry Robertson
Leadoff Home Runs in Two Consecutive Games, AL 21

Bill Robinson
Three Home Runs in One Game, NL 19

Brooks Robinson
Grand Slam In Two Consecutive Games, AL 3
Most Home Runs by Position, Career, AL 10
Cycle Hitters, AL 49
Fewest Games Missed (10-Year Period) 72
Career Spent With One Team (15 or more years) 181
Retired Numbers, AL 182
Three Consecutive Home Runs, Team, AL 196, 197
Most Home Runs by Team, Game, AL 203
Home Run Duos, Career, AL 211

Don Robinson
Grand Slams, Pitcher, NL 139

Eddie Robinson
Grounded into Most Double Plays, Game, AL 43
Most Home Runs by Team, Game, AL 202

Floyd Robinson
Most Hits, Game, AL 35

Frank Robinson
Two Grand Slams in One Game 3
Most Home Runs, Season, AL 7
Most Home Runs, Career 9
Best Home Run Ratio, Career 10

Two Home Runs in One Game Most Often 12
Three Home Runs in One Game, NL 18
Most Extra-Inning Home Runs, Career 23
Triple Crown Winners, AL 45
Cycle Hitters, NL 51
Most Runs, Career 60
Most RBIs, Career 61
Most Runs Produced, Career 62
Thirty or More Home Runs, Rookie, NL 163
Retired Numbers, AL 182
Three Consecutive Home Runs, Team, AL 197
Three Consecutive Home Runs, Team, NL 199
Most Home Runs by Team, Game, AL 203
Most Home Runs by Team, Game, NL 204, 205
Most 30-Home Run Hitters, NL 208
Most 20-Home Run Hitters, NL 208
Home Run Duos, Season, AL (25 each) 210
Home Run Duos, Career, NL 211

Jackie Robinson

Struck Out Twice in One Inning, NL 33
Cycle Hitters, NL 51
Stole 2nd, 3rd, and Home in One Game, NL 66
Most Steals of Home, Career 67
Best Double-Play Combinations, Season 149, 150
Most Double Plays, Second Baseman, Season, NL 151
Retired Numbers, NL 183
.300-Hitting Outfields, NL 221

Wilbert Robinson

Most Hits, Game, NL 35
Most RBIs, Game, NL 64
Most Games Caught, Career 153
Most Wins, Manager, Career 184

Andre Rodgers

Most Consecutive Pinch Hits 70

Buck Rodgers

Most Games Caught, Season 153
Three Consecutive Home Runs, Team, AL 196

Aurelio Rodriguez

Three Consecutive Home Runs, Team, AL 197

Ed Rodriguez

Undefeated Seasons (5 or more wins) 101

Preacher Roe

Best Won-Lost Record, Season, NL (20 or more wins) 97

Ed Roebuck

Struck Out Twice in One Inning, NL 33

Gary Roenicke

Three Consecutive Home Runs, Team, AL 197
Most Home Runs by Team, Game, AL 203

Billy Rogell

Most Times Walked, Game, AL 32
Best Double-Play Combinations, Season 150

Most 100-RBI Hitters, AL 212

Steve Rogers

Most Shutouts, Career 80
Most Strikeouts, Season, NL since 1900 107
ERA Under 2.00, Rookie, NL since 1900 (Min. 130 IP) 169

Mike Rogodzinski

Most Pinch Hits, Season, NL 69

Saul Rogovin

Grand Slams, Pitcher, AL 138

Billy Rohr

Shutout in First Start in Majors, AL 83

Cookie Rojas

Best Double-Play Combinations, Season 150

Rich Rollins

Most Home Runs in One Inning, Team, AL 200
Most Home Runs by Team, Game, AL 202

Bill Roman

Pinch-Hit Home Run in First At-Bat in Majors, AL 6
Home Run in First Appearance in Majors, AL 11

Eddie Rommel

Highest Percentage of Team's Wins, AL 99

Enrique Romo

Grand Slams, Pitcher, NL 139

Jim Rooker

Two Home Runs in One Game, Pitcher, AL 136

Charlie Root

Most Wins, Career 102

Buddy Rosar

Cycle Hitters, AL 49
Most No-Hitters Caught, Career 154, 155

Don Rose

Home Run in First Appearance in Majors, AL 11
Home Run on First Pitch in Majors, AL 11

Pete Rose

Three Home Runs in One Game, NL 19
Leadoff Home Runs in Two Consecutive Games, NL 21
Most Leadoff Home Runs, Career 22
Switch-Hit Home Runs in One Game, NL 23
Most Games with Five or More Hits, Career 37
Most Combined Hits and Walks, Season, NL 41
The 3,000-Hit Club 54
The 3,000th Hit 54
Most Seasons with 200 Hits 54
Batted .300 after Age 40 59
Most Runs, Career 60

Amos Rusie

No-Hitters, NL (9 innings or more) 89
Most 20-Win Seasons 101
Most Wins, Career 102
Most Strikeouts, Season before 1900 107, 108
Two Complete Game Wins in One Day, NL before 1900 125
Triple-Crown Pitchers, NL (most wins, lowest ERA, most strikeouts) 129

Bill Russell

Most Times Struck Out, Game, NL 34
Career Spent With One Team (15 or more years) 181
Most Home Runs by Team, Game, NL 206

Jim Russell

Switch-Hit Home Runs in One Game, NL 23
Home Runs by First Two Batters in Game, NL 194

Lefty Russell

Shutout in First Start in Majors, AL 83

Reb Russell

Shutout with Most Hits Allowed, AL 86
Pitchers Who Stole Home, AL 140
Twenty or More Wins, Rookie, AL 168
ERA Under 2.00, Rookie, AL (Min. 130 IP) 169
Three Hundred or More Innings Pitched, Rookie, AL 169
Most Shutouts, Rookie, AL 170

Dick Rusteck

Shutout in First Start in Majors, NL 84

Babe Ruth

Most Grand Slams, Career 3
Grand Slam In Two Consecutive Games, AL 3
Most Grand Slams, Season, AL 4
Most Home Runs, Season, AL 7
Most Home Runs, Career 9
Best Home Run Ratio, Career 10
Most Home Runs by Position, Career, AL 10
Two Home Runs in One Game Most Often 12
Three Home Runs in One Game, AL 13
Three Home Runs in One Game, NL 17
Most Extra-Inning Home Runs, Career 23
Most Consecutive Games with Extra-Base Hit 27
Most Total Bases, Season, AL 30
Struck Out Twice in One Inning, AL 32
Most Combined Hits and Walks, Season, AL 39, 40
Players Who Just Missed Triple Crowns, AL 45
Two Legs of Triple Crown, AL 46
Highest Batting Average, Career 53
Most Runs, Season, AL 59
Most Runs, Career 60
Most RBIs, Season, AL 60
Most RBIs, Career 61
Most Runs Produced, Season, AL 61
Most Runs Produced, Career 62
More RBIs than Games Played, Season, AL 64
Most Steals of Home, Career 67
Longest Hitting Streaks, AL 70
RBI in Most Consecutive Games, AL 72
Most Complete Games, Season, AL 131
Won 20 and Hit .300 in Same Year, AL 134
Most Home Runs, Pitcher, Career 135
Grand Slams, Pitcher, AL 137
Pitchers Who Stole Home, AL 140
Best-Hitting Pitchers, Career 142
Retired Numbers, AL 182
Three Consecutive Home Runs, Team, AL 196
Most Home Runs by Team, Game, AL 202
Most 40-Home Run Hitters, AL 206
Home Run Trios, Season, AL 209
Home Run Duos, Season, AL (25 each) 210
Home Run Duos, Career, AL 211
Most 100-RBI Hitters, AL 212
.300-Hitting Outfields, AL 219

Connie Ryan

Most Hits, Game, NL 36

Jimmy Ryan

Most Leadoff Home Runs, Career 22
Most Times Walked, Game, NL 32
Cycle Hitters, NL 51
Most Runs, Game, NL 60
Most Runs Produced, Career 62
Teammates Who Finished 1-2 in Batting, NL 222

Nolan Ryan

Most Shutouts, Career 79
Most Shutout Losses, Career 80
Most Shutout Losses, Season, AL 81
No-Hitters, AL (9 innings or more) 88
No-Hitters, NL (9 innings or more) 90
Most No-Hitters, Career 93
Most Complete 1-0 Wins, Career 94
Twenty Wins with Last-Place Team, AL 99
Most Wins, Career 102
Most Strikeouts, Season, AL 105
Most Strikeouts, Season, NL since 1900 106, 107
Most Strikeouts, Career 108
Perfect Innings, AL (3 strikeouts on 9 pitches) 110
Perfect Innings, NL (3 strikeouts on 9 pitches) 110
Most Strikeouts in Nine-Inning Game, AL 110, 111
Most Strikeouts in Nine-Inning Game, NL 111
Most Strikeouts in Extra-Inning Game, AL 112
Most Games with 10 or More Strikeouts, Career 114
Most Strikeouts per Nine Innings, Career (Min. 1,500 IP) 114
Most Consecutive Strikeouts, AL 116
Strikeout Duos, Season, AL 228
Strikeout Duos, Season, NL 228

Ray Sadecki

Most Shutout Losses, Season, NL 81
Most Strikeouts, Season, NL since 1900 107
Most Grand Slams Allowed, Career 133

Bob Sadowski

Most Times Struck Out, Game, NL 34

Bob Sadowski

Three or More Brothers in Baseball 187

Eddie Sadowski
Three or More Brothers in Baseball 187

Ted Sadowski
Three or More Brothers in Baseball 187

Vic Saier
Most Steals of Home, Career 67
Most Putouts in Nine Innings, First Baseman 157

Johnny Sain
Most Extra-Inning Home Runs Allowed, Career 133
Won 20 and Hit .300. in Same Year, NL 134
Best-Hitting Pitchers, Season, NL since 1900 142

Ebba St. Claire
Fathers and Sons in Baseball 191

Randy St. Claire
Fathers and Sons in Baseball 191

Bill Salkeld
Cycle Hitters, NL 51

Slim Sallee
Best Control Pitchers, Career 126
Fewest Base Runners per Nine Innings, Career (Min. 1,500 IP) 130
Pitchers Who Stole Home, NL since 1900 140

Manny Salvo
Three Consecutive Home Runs, Team, NL 198
Most Home Runs in One Inning, Team, NL 200
Most Home Runs by Team, Game, NL 204

Juan Samuel
Most Stolen Bases, Season, NL 65
Most Assists, Second Baseman, Game 158
Most Triples, Rookie, NL 165
Home Runs by First Two Batters in Game, NL 195
Three Consecutive Home Runs, Team, NL 199
Most Home Runs in One Inning, Team, NL 201
Stolen Base Duos, Season, NL 216

Raul Sanchez
Shutout in First Start in Majors, AL 83

Ryne Sandberg
Twenty Home Runs with 50 Stolen Bases, Season 24
Fewest Errors by Position, Season, NL (Min. 150 G, excl. Pitchers) 147
Best Double-Play Combinations, Season 150
Most Assists, Second Baseman, Game 158
Stolen Base Duos, Season, NL 217

Ben Sanders
No-Hitters, NL (9 innings or more) 89

Ken Sanders
Most Relief Losses, Season, AL 120
Most Saves, Season, AL 122

Reggie Sanders
Home Run in First Appearance in Majors, AL 11

Scott Sanderson
Grand Slams, Pitcher, NL 139

Fred Sanford
Shutout in First Start in Majors, AL 83

Jack Sanford
Most Consecutive Wins, NL 115
Most Grand Slams Allowed, Career 133

Manny Sanguillen
Most Games Caught, Season 152
Most Games Caught, Career 153

Ed Sanicki
Home Run in First Appearance in Majors, NL 11

Ron Santo
Most Home Runs by Position, Career, NL 10
Longest Hitting Streaks, NL 71
Fewest Games Missed (10-Year Period) 72
Most Home Runs by Team, Game, NL 205
Home Run Duos, Career, NL 211

Ed Sauer
Brothers with Most Home Runs, Career 25

Hank Sauer
Most Home Runs, Season, NL 8
Best Home Run Ratio, Career 10
Two Home Runs in One Game Most Often 12
Three Home Runs in One Game, NL 17, 18
Brothers with Most Home Runs, Career 25
Two Legs of Triple Crown, NL 48
Two Pinch-Hit Home Runs in One Inning, Team, NL 193
Back-to-Back Pinch-Hit Home Runs, Team 193

Bob Savage
Worst-Hitting Pitchers, Career (Min. 100 AB) 144

Don Savidge
Fathers and Sons in Baseball 191

Ralph Savidge
Fathers and Sons in Baseball 191

Steve Sax
Longest Hitting Streaks, NL 71

Doc Scanlan
Two Complete Game Wins in One Day, NL since 1900 124

Russ Scarritt
Most Triples, Rookie, AL 165

Les Scarsella
.300 Average in Rookie Year Only, NL 164

Harry Schafer
Most Assists, Outfielder, Game 156

Ray Schalk
Cycle Hitters, AL 49
Most Games Caught, Season 152
Most Games Caught, Career 153
Most No-Hitters Caught, Career 154

Wally Schang
Most Games Caught, Career 153

Carl Scheib
Worst Won-Lost Record, Season (12 or more losses) 95
Grand Slams, Pitcher, AL 138

Frank Scheibeck
Most Hits, Game, Other Leagues 37
Most Home Runs by Team, Game, NL 204

John Scheible
Shutout in First Start in Majors, NL 84

Richie Scheinblum
Most Consecutive Pinch Hits 70

Bob Schmidt
Two Pinch-Hit Home Runs in One Inning, Team, NL 193
Back-to-Back Pinch-Hit Home Runs, Team 193

Henry Schmidt
Pitchers Who Stole Home, NL since 1900 140
Twenty or More Wins, Rookie, NL since 1900 168
Three Hundred or More Innings Pitched, Rookie, NL since 1900 169
Most Complete Games, Rookie, NL since 1900 170
Most Shutouts, Rookie, NL since 1900 170

Mike Schmidt
Most Home Runs, Season, NL 7, 8
Most Home Runs, Career 9
Best Home Run Ratio, Career 10
Most Home Runs by Position, Career, NL 10
Most Home Runs by Position, Season, NL 11
Two Home Runs in One Game Most Often 12
Three Home Runs in One Game, NL 19
Four Home Runs in One Game, NL 20
Most Total Bases, Game, NL 30
Easiest to Strike Out, Career (Min. 1,000 G) 44
Two Legs of Triple Crown, NL 48
Home Runs in Most Consecutive At-Bats, NL 76
Career Spent With One Team (15 or more years) 181
Three Consecutive Home Runs, Team, NL 199
Most Home Runs in One Inning, Team, NL 201
Home Run Duos, Career, NL 211

Crazy Schmit
Most Walks in One Game, NL 113

Pete Schneider
Shutout in First Start in Majors, NL 84
Most Walks in One Game, NL 113
Most Consecutive Losses, NL 116

Red Schoendienst
Switch-Hit Home Runs in One Game, NL 23
Most Extra-Base Hits in a Doubleheader, NL 27
Most Pinch Hits, Season, NL 68
Longest Hitting Streaks, NL 71
Best Double-Play Combinations, Season 149
Most Double Plays, Second Baseman, Season, NL 151
Most Assists, Second Baseman, Game 158
Most Wins, Manager, Career 184
Most Home Runs in One Inning, Team, NL 200

Dick Schofield
The Worst Hitters (Min. 2,500 AB) 52
Best Double-Play Combinations, Season 150
Fathers and Sons in Baseball 191

Dick Schofield
Fathers and Sons in Baseball 191

Wes Schulmerich
.300-Hitting Outfields, NL 221

Wildfire Schulte
Most Grand Slams, Season, NL 4
Twenty Doubles, 20 Triples, and 20 Home Runs, Season, NL 29
Two Legs of Triple Crown, NL 47
Most Steals of Home, Career 67

Joe Schultz
Most Consecutive Pinch Hits 70
Fathers and Sons in Baseball 191

Joe Schultz
Fathers and Sons in Baseball 191

Hal Schumacher
Shutout with Most Hits Allowed, NL 86
Most Home Runs, Pitcher, Career 135
Two Home Runs in One Game, Pitcher, NL 136
Best Lefty-Righty Duos 228

Herb Score
Most Strikeouts, Season, AL 105
Most Strikeouts in Nine-Inning Game, AL 110
Most Strikeouts, Rookie, AL 169
Teams with Three 20-Game Winners, AL 227

Donnie Scott
Switch-Hit Home Runs in One Game, AL 23

Ed Scott

Three Hundred or More Innings Pitched, Rookie, NL since 1900 169
Most Complete Games, Rookie, NL since 1900 170

Everett Scott

Most Consecutive Games Played 71

George Scott

Most Times Struck Out, Game, AL 33
Easiest to Double Up, Career (Min. 1000 G) 41
Two Legs of Triple Crown, AL 46
Batting Champion by Widest Margin, AL 56
Three Consecutive Home Runs, Team, AL 197
Most Home Runs in One Inning, Team, AL 200
Most Home Runs by Team, Game, AL 202
Most 30-Home Run Hitters, AL 207
Most 20-Home Run Hitters, AL 208

Jack Scott

Best-Hitting Pitchers, Season, NL since 1900 142
Best-Hitting Pitchers, Career 142

Jim Scott

Shutout in First Start in Majors, AL 83
No-Hitters, AL (9 innings or more) 87
Twenty Wins and 20 Losses in Same Year, AL 99
Fewest Base Runners per Nine Innings, Career (Min. 1,500 IP) 130

Mike Scott

No-Hitters, NL (9 innings or more) 90
Most Strikeouts, Season, NL since 1900 106
Four Strikeouts in One Inning, NL 109
Strikeout Duos, Season, NL 228

Rodney Scott

Most Times Walked, Game, NL 32
Most Times Caught Stealing, Game, NL 68
Stolen Base Duos, Season, NL 216, 217

Tom Seaton

Pitchers Who Stole Home, NL since 1900 140

Tom Seaver

Most Shutouts, Career 79
Most Shutout Losses, Career 80
No-Hitters, NL (9 innings or more) 90
Most Wins, Career 102
The 300-Win Club 103
Most Strikeouts, Season, NL since 1900 106, 107
Most Strikeouts, Career 108
Most Strikeouts in Nine-Inning Game, NL 111
Most Strikeouts in Extra-Inning Game, NL 112
Most Games with 10 or More Strikeouts, Career 114
Most Strikeouts per Nine Innings, Career (Min. 1,500 IP) 114
Most Consecutive Strikeouts, NL 116
Fewest Base Runners per Nine Innings, Career (Min. 1,500 IP) 129
Best Lefty-Righty Duos 229

Bob Seeds

Most Home Runs by Team, Game, NL 204

Pat Seerey

Three Home Runs in One Game, AL 14
Four Home Runs in One Game, AL 20
Most Total Bases, Game, AL 30

Kip Selbach

Most Times Walked, Game, NL 32
Most Hits, Game, NL 36
Most Triples, Rookie, NL 165

Frank Selee

Most Wins, Manager, Career 184
Most League Pennants Won, Manager 185

George Selkirk

Most Home Runs by Team, Game, AL 202
Most 100-RBI Hitters, AL 212
.300-Hitting Outfields, AL 220

Andy Seminick

Two Home Runs in One Inning, NL 12
Three Home Runs in One Game, NL 17
Most Times Walked, Game, NL 32
Most Games Caught, Career 153
Most Home Runs in One Inning, Team, NL 200

Hank Severeid

Most Games Caught, Career 153

Ed Seward

No-Hitters, Other Leagues 91

Joe Sewell

Hardest to Strike Out, Career (Min. 1,000 G) 44
Most Consecutive Games Played 71
Three or More Brothers in Baseball 187
Best-Hitting Brothers 189

Luke Sewell

Most Games Caught, Career 153
Most No-Hitters Caught, Career 154
Three or More Brothers in Baseball 187
Best-Hitting Brothers 189

Tommy Sewell

Three or More Brothers in Baseball 187
Best-Hitting Brothers 189

Socks Seybold

Longest Hitting Streaks, AL 70
Unassisted Double Plays, Outfielder 152
Most Triples, Rookie, AL 165
Highest Batting Average, Rookie, AL (Min. 300 AB) 167

Cy Seymour

Two Legs of Triple Crown, NL 47
Most Walks in One Game, NL 113

Paul Siebert
Fathers and Sons in Baseball 191

Sonny Siebert
No-Hitters, AL (9 innings or more) 88
Fewest Base Runners per Nine Innings, Career (Min. 1,500 IP) 130
Two Home Runs in One Game, Pitcher, AL 136
Strikeout Duos, Season, AL 228

Ruben Sierra
Switch-Hit Home Runs in One Game, AL 23
Most Home Runs by Team, Game, AL 203

Ed Siever
Most Complete Games, Rookie, AL 170

Roy Sievers
Most Grand Slams, Career 3
Most Home Runs, Season, AL 7
Two Legs of Triple Crown, AL 46

Al Simmons
Most Grand Slams, Career 3
Three Home Runs in One Game, AL 13
Highest Batting Average, Career 53
Most Seasons with 200 Hits 54
Most RBIs, Season, AL 60
Most RBIs, Career 61
Most Runs Produced, Season, AL 61
Most Runs Produced, Career 62
Most RBIs in One Inning, AL 63
More RBIs than Games Played, Season, AL 64, 65
Longest Hitting Streaks, AL 70
RBI in Most Consecutive Games, AL 72
Unassisted Double Plays, Outfielder 152
One Hundred or More RBIs, Rookie, AL 166
Three Consecutive Home Runs, Team, AL 196
Home Run Trios, Season, AL 209
Home Run Duos, Season, AL (25 each) 210
Most 100-RBI Hitters, AL 212
Most .300 Hitters, Season, AL (300 AB each) 217
.300-Hitting Outfields, AL 219, 220

Curt Simmons
Most Shutouts, Career 80
Most Walks in One Game, NL 113
Pitchers Who Stole Home, NL since 1900 140
Best Lefty-Righty Duos 228

Nelson Simmons
Switch-Hit Home Runs in One Game, AL 23

Ted Simmons
Most Pinch-Hit Grand Slams, Career 6
Switch-Hit Home Runs in One Game, AL 23
Switch-Hit Home Runs in One Game, NL 23
Most Games Caught, Season 152
Most Games Caught, Career 153
Most No-Hitters Caught, Career 155
Three Consecutive Home Runs, Team, AL 197

Harry Simpson
Three Consecutive Home Runs, Team, AL 196

Wayne Simpson
Shutout in First Start in Majors, NL 84
Worst-Hitting Pitchers, Career (Min. 100 AB) 144

Duke Sims
Three Consecutive Home Runs, Team, AL 197

Bill Singer
No-Hitters, NL (9 innings or more) 90
Most Strikeouts, Season, AL 105
Most Strikeouts, Season, NL since 1900 106
Most Games with 10 or More Strikeouts, Career 114
Strikeout Duos, Season, AL 228

Ken Singleton
Easiest to Double Up, Career (Min. 1000 G) 41
Most Consecutive Hits, AL 73

Tommie Sisk
Most Consecutive Times Struck Out, NL 74
Worst-Hitting Pitchers, Career (Min. 100 AB) 144

Dave Sisler
Fathers and Sons in Baseball 191

Dick Sisler
Most Consecutive Hits, NL 74
Fathers and Sons in Baseball 191

George Sisler
Most Hits, Game, AL 35
.300 Batting Average in Final Season (Min. 100 G) 39
Most Combined Hits and Walks, Season, AL 40
Cycle Hitters, AL 49
The .400 Hitters, AL 52
Highest Batting Average, Career 53
Most Seasons with 200 Hits 54
Most Steals of Home, Career 67
Longest Hitting Streaks, AL 70
Most Consecutive Hits, AL 73
Fathers and Sons in Baseball 191
Most 100-RBI Hitters, AL 212
Most 200-Hit Batters, AL 223

Ted Sizemore
Most Times Walked, Game, NL 32

Bob Skinner
Most Assists, First Baseman, Game 157
Fathers and Sons in Baseball 191
Three Consecutive Home Runs, Team, NL 199

Joel Skinner
Fathers and Sons in Baseball 191

Bill Skowron
Most Pinch-Hit Grand Slams, Career 6

Most Times Struck Out, Game, AL 33
Easiest to Double Up, Career (Min. 1000 G) 41
Two Pinch-Hit Home Runs in One Inning, Team, NL 193
Back-to-Back Pinch-Hit Home Runs, Team 193
Most Home Runs by Team, Game, AL 203
Most 20-Home Run Hitters, AL 208
Home Run Trios, Season, AL 209

Gordon Slade
Home Run in First Appearance in Majors, NL 11

Jimmy Slagle
Stolen Base Duos, Season, NL 217

Enos Slaughter
No-Hit Spoilers - The Only Hit Most Often 58
Most Pinch Hits, Season, AL 68
Most Pinch Hits, Career 69
Most Home Runs in One Inning, Team, NL 200
.300-Hitting Outfields, NL 221

Roy Smalley
Cycle Hitters, NL 51
Fathers and Sons in Baseball 191

Roy Smalley
Switch-Hit Home Runs in One Game, AL 23
Most Times Walked, Game, AL 32
Most Times Struck Out, Game, AL 33
Best Double-Play Combinations, Season 149
Most Double Plays, Shortstop, Season, AL 151
Fathers and Sons in Baseball 191
Most 20-Home Run Hitters, AL 208

Al Smith
Most Leadoff Home Runs, Career 22

Bob Smith
Most Walks in One Game, NL 113
Most Innings Pitched, Game, NL 128

Charley Smith
Most Consecutive Pinch Hits 70

Dave Smith
Most Saves, Career 121
Most Saves, Season, NL 122

Earl Smith
Most .300 Hitters, Season, NL (300 AB each) 218

Elmer Smith
Longest Hitting Streaks, NL 71

Elmer Smith
Unassisted Double Plays, Outfielder 152
.300-Hitting Outfields, AL 219

Frank Smith
No-Hitters, AL (9 innings or more) 87
Most No-Hitters, Career 93
Fewest Base Runners per Nine Innings, Career (Min. 1,500 IP) 130
Most Complete Games, Season, AL 131
Most Innings Pitched, Season, AL 132
Teams with Three 20-Game Winners, AL 227

Fred Smith
Most Triples, Game, Other Leagues 29

George Smith
Shutout with Most Hits Allowed, NL 86
Worst-Hitting Pitchers, Career (Min. 100 AB) 144

Germany Smith
Most Assists, Shortstop, Game 159

Hal Smith
Shutout in First Start in Majors, NL 84

Jack Smith
Most Times Caught Stealing, Game, NL 68
Unassisted Double Plays, Outfielder 152

Lee Smith
Most Saves, Career 121
Most Saves, Season, NL 122
Most Wins Plus Saves, Season 123

Lonnie Smith
Most Stolen Bases, Game, NL 66

Ozzie Smith
Best Double-Play Combinations, Season 150
Stolen Base Duos, Season, NL 216, 217

Paul Smith
Three Consecutive Home Runs, Team, NL 199

Pop Smith
Most Times Walked, Game, NL 32

Reggie Smith
Three Home Runs in One Game, NL 19
Switch-Hit Home Runs in One Game, AL 23
Switch-Hit Home Runs in One Game, NL 23
Home Runs by First Two Batters in Game, AL 194
Three Consecutive Home Runs, Team, NL 199
Most 30-Home Run Hitters, NL 208
.300-Hitting Outfields, NL 221

Sherry Smith
Best Control Pitchers, Career 126
Most Innings Pitched, Game, NL 128
Pitchers Who Stole Home, NL since 1900 140

Willie Smith
.300 Average in Rookie Year Only, AL 164

Homer Smoot
.300-Hitting Outfields, NL 220

Duke Snider
Most Home Runs, Season, NL 8
Most Home Runs, Career 9
Best Home Run Ratio, Career 10
Two Home Runs in One Game Most Often 12
Three Home Runs in One Game, NL 17, 18
Struck Out Twice in One Inning, NL 33
Longest Hitting Streaks, NL 71
Retired Numbers, NL 183
Home Runs by First Two Batters in Game, NL 194
Three Consecutive Home Runs, Team, NL 198, 199
Most 40-Home Run Hitters, NL 206
Most 30-Home Run Hitters, NL 208
Home Run Trios, Season, NL 209
Home Run Duos, Season, NL (25 each) 210
Home Run Duos, Career, NL 211
.300-Hitting Outfields, NL 221

Fred Snodgrass
No-Hit Spoilers - The Only Hit Most Often 57, 58
.300 Average in Rookie Year Only, NL 164
Stolen Base Duos, Season, NL 217

Frank Snyder
Most Games Caught, Career 153

Tony Solaita
Three Home Runs in One Game, AL 15

Moose Solters
Three Home Runs in One Game, AL 13
Cycle Hitters, AL 49

Jose Sosa
Home Run in First Appearance in Majors, NL 11

Denny Sothern
Most Doubles, Game, NL 27
.300-Hitting Outfields, NL 221

Mario Soto
Most Strikeouts, Season, NL since 1900 106, 107
Four Strikeouts in One Inning, NL 109
Most Games with 10 or More Strikeouts, Career 114
Most Strikeouts per Nine Innings, Career (Min. 1,500 IP) 114
Fewest Base Runners per Nine Innings, Career (Min. 1,500 IP) 130

Billy Southworth
No-Hit Spoilers - The Only Hit Most Often 57
Most Wins, Manager, Career 184
.300-Hitting Outfields, NL 220

Bill Sowders
Three or More Brothers in Baseball 187

John Sowders
Three or More Brothers in Baseball 187

Len Sowders
Three or More Brothers in Baseball 187

Bob Spade
Shutout in First Start in Majors, NL 84

Warren Spahn
Most Home Runs by Position, Career, NL 10
Most Shutouts, Career 79
No-Hitters, NL (9 innings or more) 90
Most No-Hitters, Career 93
Most Complete 1-0 Wins, Career 94
Most 20-Win Seasons 101
Most Wins, Career 102
The 300-Win Club 103
Most Wins by Age, Season, NL since 1900 104
Most Strikeouts, Career 108
Most Strikeouts in Extra-Inning Game, NL 112
Fewest Base Runners per Nine Innings, Career (Min. 1,500 IP) 130
Most Wins after Age 40 134
Won 20 and Hit .300. in Same Year, NL 134
Most Home Runs, Pitcher, Career 135
Most Hits, Pitcher, Career 139
Most Times Struck Out, Pitcher, Career since 1900 141
Retired Numbers, NL 183
Best Lefty-Righty Duos 228

Al Spalding
Shutout in First Start in Majors, NL 84
Shutout in First Two Major League Games, NL 85

Tully Sparks
Most Innings Pitched, Game, NL 128

Tris Speaker
Most Grand Slams, Season, AL 4
Most Times Walked, Game, AL 31
Most Combined Hits and Walks, Season, AL 40
Hardest to Strike Out, Career (Min. 1,000 G) 44
Cycle Hitters, AL 49
Highest Batting Average, Career 53
The 3,000-Hit Club 54
The 3,000th Hit 54
Most Runs, Career 60
Most Runs Produced, Career 62
Most Stolen Bases, Career 66
Most Steals of Home, Career 67
Most Times Caught Stealing, Game, AL 68
Longest Hitting Streaks, AL 70
Most Consecutive Hits, AL 73
Unassisted Double Plays, Outfielder 152
.300-Hitting Outfields, AL 219

Chris Speier
Cycle Hitters, NL 51
Most Home Runs by Team, Game, NL 204

Stan Spence
Most Hits, Game, AL 35
Three Consecutive Home Runs, Team, AL 196

Daryl Spencer
Three Consecutive Home Runs, Team, NL 199
Most Home Runs in One Inning, Team, NL 201

Most Home Runs by Team, Game, NL 205

Ed Spiezio
Most Home Runs in One Inning, Team, NL 201

Charlie Spikes
Most Pinch Hits, Season, NL 69

Dan Spillner
Worst-Hitting Pitchers, Career (Min. 100 AB) 144

Paul Splittorff
Career Spent With One Team (15 or more years) 181
Best Lefty-Righty Duos 229

Karl Spooner
Shutout in First Start in Majors, NL 84
Shutout in First Two Major League Games, NL 85

Eddie Stack
Shutout in First Start in Majors, NL 84

Bill Stafford
Undefeated Seasons (5 or more wins) 101

Chick Stahl
Most Hits, Game, NL 36
Highest Batting Average, Rookie, NL (Min. 300 AB) 167
.300-Hitting Outfields, AL 219

Jake Stahl
No-Hit Spoilers - The Only Hit Most Often 57

Tuck Stainback
.300 Average in Rookie Year Only, NL 164

Gerry Staley
Most Relief Wins, Season, AL 118

Harry Staley
Most RBIs, Game, NL 64
Two Home Runs in One Game, Pitcher, NL 136

Oscar Stanage
The Worst Hitters (Min. 2,500 AB) 52
Most Errors by Position, Season, AL 147
Most Games Caught, Career 153

Lee Stange
Four Strikeouts in One Inning, AL 108
Worst-Hitting Pitchers, Career (Min. 100 AB) 144

Don Stanhouse
Grand Slams, Pitcher, NL 139

Eddie Stanky
Most Combined Hits and Walks, Season, NL 41
More Walks than Hits, Season, NL 55

Best Double-Play Combinations, Season 150

Bob Stanley
Most Saves, Career 121
Most Saves, Season, AL 122
Most Wins Plus Saves, Season 123

Mickey Stanley
Most Putouts, Outfielder, Game 156
Career Spent With One Team (15 or more years) 181
Three Consecutive Home Runs, Team, AL 197
Most Home Runs in One Inning, Team, AL 200

Leroy Stanton
Three Home Runs in One Game, AL 15

Dave Stapleton
Best Double-Play Combinations, Season 149
Most Home Runs in One Inning, Team, AL 200

Willie Stargell
Most Grand Slams, Career 3
Most Home Runs, Season, NL 7, 8
Most Home Runs, Career 9
Best Home Run Ratio, Career 10
Two Home Runs in One Game Most Often 12
Three Home Runs in One Game, NL 18, 19
Most Extra-Inning Home Runs, Career 23
Most Extra-Base Hits, Game, NL 26
Most Total Bases, Game, NL 30
Easiest to Strike Out, Career (Min. 1,000 G) 44
Two Legs of Triple Crown, NL 48
Cycle Hitters, NL 51
Most Consecutive Hits, NL 74
Career Spent With One Team (15 or more years) 181
Retired Numbers, NL 183
Three Consecutive Home Runs, Team, NL 199
Home Run Duos, Career, NL 211
.300-Hitting Outfields, NL 221

Ray Starr
Shutout in First Start in Majors, NL 84

Rusty Staub
Most Home Runs in a Doubleheader, NL 20
Most Pinch Hits, Season, NL 68, 69
Most Pinch Hits, Career 69
Most Consecutive Pinch Hits 70
Most Consecutive Times Struck Out, AL 74
Three Consecutive Home Runs, Team, NL 199

John Stearns
No-Hit Spoilers - The Only Hit Most Often 58

Bob Steele
Pitchers Who Stole Home, NL since 1900 140

Dave Stegman
Most Times Struck Out, Game, AL 33

George Stovall

Most Assists, First Baseman, Game 157

Harry Stovey

Most Triples, Game, NL 28
Most Triples, Game, Other Leagues 29
Most Times Struck Out, Game, NL 34
Cycle Hitters, Other Leagues 51
The .400 Hitters, Other Leagues 53
Most Putouts in Nine Innings, First Baseman 157

Sammy Strang

Most Times Walked, Game, AL 31
Most Consecutive Hits, NL 74
Most Errors by Position, Season, AL 147
Stolen Base Duos, Season, NL 217

Monty Stratton

Grand Slams, Pitcher, AL 138

Scott Stratton

Shutout with Most Hits Allowed, NL 86
Two Home Runs in One Game, Pitcher, NL 136

Darryl Strawberry

Three Home Runs in One Game, NL 19
Three Consecutive Home Runs, Team, NL 199

Gabby Street

Pennant-Winning Rookie Managers, NL 171

George Strickland

The Worst Hitters (Min. 2,500 AB) 52

George Strief

Most Extra-Base Hits, Game, Other Leagues 26
Most Triples, Game, Other Leagues 29

Brent Strom

Worst-Hitting Pitchers, Career (Min. 100 AB) 144

Sailor Stroud

Shutout in First Start in Majors, AL 83

Dick Stuart

Most Grand Slams, Season, AL 4
Most Home Runs, Season, AL 7
Best Home Run Ratio, Career 10
Three Home Runs in One Game, NL 18
Easiest to Strike Out, Career (Min. 1,000 G) 44

Johnny Stuart

Two Complete Game Wins in One Day, NL since 1900 124

Gus Suhr

Most Times Walked, Game, NL 32
Most Consecutive Games Played 71
One Hundred or More RBIs, Rookie, NL 166

Billy Sullivan

The Worst Hitters (Min. 2,500 AB) 52
Most Games Caught, Career 153
Fathers and Sons in Baseball 192

Billy Sullivan

Fathers and Sons in Baseball 192

Eddie Collins

Highest Batting Average, Career 53
The 3,000-Hit Club 54
The 3,000th Hit 54
Most Runs, Career 60
Most Runs Produced, Career 62
Most Stolen Bases, Season, AL 65
Most Stolen Bases, Career 66
Most Stolen Bases, Game, AL 66
Stole 2nd, 3rd, and Home in One Game, AL 66
Most Steals of Home, Career 67
Fathers and Sons in Baseball 190
Stolen Base Duos, Season, AL 216
Most 200-Hit Batters, AL 223

Haywood Sullivan

Fathers and Sons in Baseball 192

Marc Sullivan

Fathers and Sons in Baseball 192

Marty Sullivan

Most Triples, Game, NL 28

Homer Summa

.300-Hitting Outfields, AL 219

Champ Summers

Most Pinch-Hit Home Runs, Career 5
Most Pinch-Hit Grand Slams, Career 6
Three Consecutive Home Runs, Team, NL 199

Ed Summers

Two Complete Game Wins in One Day, AL 124
Most Innings Pitched, Game, AL 127
Two Home Runs in One Game, Pitcher, AL 135
Twenty or More Wins, Rookie, AL 168
ERA Under 2.00, Rookie, AL (Min. 130 IP) 169
Three Hundred or More Innings Pitched, Rookie, AL 169
Most Shutouts, Rookie, AL 170

Billy Sunday

Unassisted Double Plays, Outfielder 152

Jim Sundberg

Fewest Errors by Position, Season, AL (Min. 150 G, excl. Pitchers) 147
Most Games Caught, Season 152, 153
Most Games Caught, Career 153

Max Surkont

Most Consecutive Strikeouts, NL 116

George Susce
Fathers and Sons in Baseball 192

George Susce
Fathers and Sons in Baseball 192

Rick Sutcliffe
Most Consecutive Wins, NL 115
Most Home Runs by Team, Game, NL 206

Bruce Sutter
Perfect Innings, NL (3 strikeouts on 9 pitches) 110
Most Relief Losses, Career 120
Most Saves, Career 121
Most Saves, Season, NL 122
Most Wins Plus Saves, Season 122
Worst-Hitting Pitchers, Career (Min. 100 AB) 144

Don Sutton
Most Shutouts, Career 79
Most Wins, Career 102
The 300-Win Club 103
Most Strikeouts, Season, NL since 1900 107
Most Strikeouts, Career 108
Most Games with 10 or More Strikeouts, Career 114
Fewest Base Runners per Nine Innings, Career (Min. 1,500 IP) 129
Most Wins after Age 40 134
Most Strikeouts, Rookie, NL since 1900 169
Strikeout Duos, Season, NL 228

Ezra Sutton
Most Triples, Game, NL 28
Most Runs, Game, NL 60

Ed Swartwood
Most Putouts in Nine Innings, First Baseman 157

Bill Sweeney
Most Strikeouts, Season before 1900 107

Bill Sweeney
Longest Hitting Streaks, NL 71

Bill Sweeney
Most Putouts in Nine Innings, First Baseman 157

Charlie Sweeney
Most Strikeouts, Season before 1900 107
Most Strikeouts in Nine-Inning Game, NL 111

Bill Swift
Best Control Pitchers, Career 126

Bob Swift
The Worst Hitters (Min. 2,500 AB) 52

Ron Swoboda
Most Times Struck Out, Game, NL 34

Jim Tabor
Two Grand Slams in One Game 3
Three Home Runs in One Game, AL 14
Most Home Runs in a Doubleheader, AL 20
Most RBIs, Game, AL 64
Most Home Runs in One Inning, Team, AL 200

Doug Taitt
Most Triples, Rookie, AL 165

Fred Talbot
Grand Slams, Pitcher, AL 138

Vito Tamulis
Shutout in First Start in Majors, AL 83

Frank Tanana
Most Strikeouts, Season, AL 105, 106
Most Strikeouts in Nine-Inning Game, AL 110
Most Games with 10 or More Strikeouts, Career 114
Fewest Base Runners per Nine Innings, Career (Min. 1,500 IP) 131
Most Strikeouts, Rookie, AL 169
Strikeout Duos, Season, AL 228

Jesse Tannehill
No-Hitters, AL (9 innings or more) 87
Best Control Pitchers, Career 126
Fewest Base Runners per Nine Innings, Career (Min. 1,500 IP) 130
Won 20 and Hit .300. in Same Year, NL 134
Pitchers Who Stole Home, NL since 1900 140
Best-Hitting Pitchers, Season, NL since 1900 142
Best-Hitting Pitchers, Career 143
Teams with Three 20-Game Winners, AL 227
Teams with Three 20-Game Winners, NL since 1900 227

Lee Tannehill
The Worst Hitters (Min. 2,500 AB) 52

Chuck Tanner
Pinch-Hit Home Run in First At-Bat in Majors, NL 6
Home Run in First Appearance in Majors, NL 11
Home Run on First Pitch in Majors, NL 11
Most Wins, Manager, Career 184

Ted Tappe
Pinch-Hit Home Run in First At-Bat in Majors, NL 6
Home Run in First Appearance in Majors, NL 11

Danny Tartabull
Fathers and Sons in Baseball 192

Jose Tartabull
Fathers and Sons in Baseball 192

Willie Tasby
Three Consecutive Home Runs, Team, AL 196

Randy Tate

Most At-Bats with No Hits, Pitcher, Season since 1900 141

Jackie Tavener

Most Triples, Game, AL 28
Stole 2nd, 3rd, and Home in One Game, AL 66

Frank Taveras

Most Times Struck Out, Game, NL 34
Most Stolen Bases, Season, NL 65
Stolen Base Duos, Season, NL 216, 217

Carl Taylor

Most Pinch Hits, Season, NL 69

Danny Taylor

Unassisted Double Plays, Outfielder 152

Dummy Taylor

Most Complete Games, Season, NL since 1900 132
Most Innings Pitched, Season, NL sicne 1900 132
Teams with Three 20-Game Winners, NL since 1900 227

Jack Taylor

Twenty Wins One Year, 20 Losses the Next, NL since 1900 98
Undefeated Seasons (5 or more wins) 101
Lowest ERA, Season, NL 127
Most Innings Pitched, Game, NL 128
Fewest Base Runners per Nine Innings, Career (Min. 1,500 IP) 130
Most Complete Games, Season, NL since 1900 132
Most Innings Pitched, Season, NL sicne 1900 132

Tony Taylor

Most Pinch Hits, Season, NL 69

Birdie Tebbetts

Most Games Caught, Career 153

Kent Tekulve

Most Relief Wins, Career 117
Most Relief Losses, Career 120
Most Relief Losses, Season, NL 120
Most Saves, Career 121
Most Saves, Season, NL 122
Most Wins Plus Saves, Season 123
Worst-Hitting Pitchers, Career (Min. 100 AB) 144

Johnny Temple

Best Double-Play Combinations, Season 149, 150

Gene Tenace

Most Grand Slams, Season, AL 4
Easiest to Strike Out, Career (Min. 1,000 G) 44
More Walks than Hits, Season, AL 55
More Walks than Hits, Season, NL 55
Three Consecutive Home Runs, Team, NL 199

Fred Tenney

Most Times Walked, Game, NL 32
Most Hits, Game, NL 36

Jerry Terrell

Grounded into Most Double Plays, Game, AL 43

Walt Terrell

Two Home Runs in One Game, Pitcher, NL 136

Adonis Terry

No-Hitters, Other Leagues 91
Most No-Hitters, Career 94

Bill Terry

Three Home Runs in One Game, NL 17
Most Combined Hits and Walks, Season, NL 41
Cycle Hitters, NL 51
The .400 Hitters, NL 52
Highest Batting Average, Career 53
Most Seasons with 200 Hits 54
Most Putouts in Nine Innings, First Baseman 157
Pennant-Winning Rookie Managers, NL 171
Retired Numbers, NL 183
Three Consecutive Home Runs, Team, NL 198
Home Run Duos, Career, NL 211
Most .300 Hitters, Season, NL (300 AB each) 218
Most 200-Hit Batters, NL 223

Ralph Terry

Fewest Base Runners per Nine Innings, Career (Min. 1,500 IP) 130

Wayne Terwilliger

Most Consecutive Hits, NL 74

Jeff Tesreau

No-Hitters, NL (9 innings or more) 89
Fewest Base Runners per Nine Innings, Career (Min. 1,500 IP) 129
Rookie No-Hitters, NL 167
ERA Under 2.00, Rookie, NL since 1900 (Min. 130 IP) 169
Teams with Three 20-Game Winners, NL since 1900 227

George Theodore

Three Consecutive Home Runs, Team, NL 199

Henry Thielman

Most Consecutive Losses, NL 116

Claude Thomas

Shutout in First Start in Majors, AL 83

Derrel Thomas

Most Home Runs by Team, Game, NL 206

Frank Thomas

Three Home Runs in One Game, NL 18
Four Consecutive Home Runs, Team 196

Three Consecutive Home Runs, Team, NL 199
Most Home Runs in One Inning, Team, NL 201

Gorman Thomas

Most Home Runs, Season, AL 7
Best Home Run Ratio, Career 10
Three Home Runs in One Game, AL 15
Most Times Struck Out, Game, AL 33
Easiest to Strike Out, Career (Min. 1,000 G) 44
The Worst Hitters (Min. 2,500 AB) 52
Most Consecutive Times Struck Out, AL 74
Three Consecutive Home Runs, Team, AL 197
Most Home Runs by Team, Game, AL 203
Most 30-Home Run Hitters, AL 207
Most 100-RBI Hitters, AL 212

Lee Thomas

Three Home Runs in One Game, AL 14
Three Consecutive Home Runs, Team, AL 196

Roy Thomas

.300-Hitting Outfields, NL 220

Roy Thomas

Undefeated Seasons (5 or more wins) 101

Gary Thomasson

Most Home Runs by Team, Game, NL 206

Fresco Thompson

Most 200-Hit Batters, NL 223

Hank Thompson

Three Home Runs in One Game, NL 18
Three Consecutive Home Runs, Team, NL 199
Most Home Runs in One Inning, Team, NL 201
Most Home Runs by Team, Game, NL 205

Homer Thompson

Brother Batteries, AL 185

Jason Thompson

Most Home Runs in a Doubleheader, NL 20

Robby Thompson

Most Times Caught Stealing, Game, NL 68

Sam Thompson

Most Triples, Game, NL 28
Most Hits, Game, NL 36
Two Legs of Triple Crown, NL 47
Cycle Hitters, NL 51
The .400 Hitters, NL 52
Most RBIs, Season, NL 60
Most Runs Produced, Season, NL 62
Most Home Runs by Team, Game, NL 204
Teammates Who Finished 1-2 in Batting, NL 222

Tommy Thompson

Brother Batteries, AL 185

Bobby Thomson

Most Home Runs in a Doubleheader, NL 20
Three Consecutive Home Runs, Team, NL 199
.300-Hitting Outfields, NL 221

Andre Thornton

Most Grand Slams, Season, AL 4
Most Times Walked, Game, AL 31
Cycle Hitters, AL 49
Three Consecutive Home Runs, Team, AL 197

Walter Thornton

No-Hitters, NL (9 innings or more) 89

Bob Thurman

Three Home Runs in One Game, NL 18
Most Home Runs by Team, Game, NL 204

Sloppy Thurston

Twenty Wins with Last-Place Team, AL 99
Perfect Innings, AL (3 strikeouts on 9 pitches) 110
Best-Hitting Pitchers, Career 142

Luis Tiant

Most Shutouts, Career 79
Shutout in First Start in Majors, AL 83
Twenty Wins One Year, 20 Losses the Next, AL 98
Most Wins, Career 102
Most Strikeouts, Season, AL 105
Most Strikeouts in Nine-Inning Game, AL 111
Most Strikeouts in Extra-Inning Game, AL 112
Most Games with 10 or More Strikeouts, Career 114
Fewest Base Runners per Nine Innings, Career (Min. 1,500 IP) 130
Strikeout Duos, Season, AL 228

Dick Tidrow

Most Relief Wins, Season, NL 119

Mike Tiernan

Cycle Hitters, NL 51
Most Runs, Game, NL 60
Most Home Runs by Team, Game, NL 204

Les Tietje

Worst-Hitting Pitchers, Career (Min. 100 AB) 144

Bob Tillman

Three Home Runs in One Game, NL 18
Most No-Hitters Caught, Career 155

Joe Tinker

Most Steals of Home, Career 67

Cannonball Titcomb

No-Hitters, Other Leagues 91
Worst-Hitting Pitchers, Career (Min. 100 AB) 144

Jack Tobin

.300 Batting Average in Final Season (Min. 100 G) 39

Elmer Valo

Cycle Hitters, AL 49
Most Pinch Hits, Career 69

Russ Van Atta

Shutout in First Start in Majors, AL 83
Most Hits in First Game 165

Dazzy Vance

No-Hitters, NL (9 innings or more) 89
Best Won-Lost Record, Season, NL (20 or more wins) 97
Most Strikeouts, Season, NL since 1900 106, 107
Perfect Innings, NL (3 strikeouts on 9 pitches) 110
Most Strikeouts in Extra-Inning Game, NL 112
Most Games with 10 or More Strikeouts, Career 114
Most Consecutive Wins, NL 115
Most Consecutive Strikeouts, NL 116
Triple-Crown Pitchers, NL (most wins, lowest ERA, most strikeouts) 129
Most Wins after Age 40 134
Most Shutouts, Rookie, NL since 1900 170

Johnny Vander Meer

No-Hitters, NL (9 innings or more) 89
Most No-Hitters, Career 93
Most Strikeouts, Season, NL since 1900 107
Most Walks in One Game, NL 113
Pitchers Who Stole Home, NL since 1900 140
Best Lefty-Righty Duos 229

Bill Van Dyke

Cycle Hitters, Other Leagues 51

Elam Vangilder

Best-Hitting Pitchers, Season, AL 142

George Van Haltren

Most Runs Produced, Career 62
Fewest Games Missed (10-Year Period) 72
Most Walks in One Game, NL 113

Arky Vaughan

Most Combined Hits and Walks, Season, NL 41
Hardest to Double Up, Career (Min. 1,000 G) 42
Cycle Hitters, NL 51
Best Double-Play Combinations, Season 150
Three Consecutive Home Runs, Team, NL 198

Hippo Vaughn

Most Shutouts, Career 80
Most Shutout Losses, Career 80
No-Hitters, NL (9 innings or more) 89
Most Complete 1-0 Wins, Career 94
Triple-Crown Pitchers, NL (most wins, lowest ERA, most strikeouts) 129
Fewest Base Runners per Nine Innings, Career (Min. 1,500 IP) 130
Pitchers Who Stole Home, NL since 1900 140
ERA Under 2.00, Rookie, AL (Min. 130 IP) 169
Most Shutouts, Rookie, AL 170

Bobby Veach

Most Hits, Game, AL 35
Cycle Hitters, AL 49
.300-Hitting Outfields, AL 219
Teammates Who Finished 1-2 in Batting, AL 222

Bob Veale

Undefeated Seasons (5 or more wins) 101
Most Strikeouts, Season, NL since 1900 106, 107
Most Strikeouts in Nine-Inning Game, NL 111
Most Strikeouts in Extra-Inning Game, NL 112
Most Strikeouts per Nine Innings, Career (Min. 1,500 IP) 114

Otto Velez

Three Home Runs in One Game, AL 15
Most Home Runs in a Doubleheader, AL 20

Mickey Vernon

Cycle Hitters, AL 49

Zoilo Versalles

No-Hit Spoilers - The Only Hit Most Often 57
Best Double-Play Combinations, Season 149
Most Double Plays, Shortstop, Season, AL 151
Most Home Runs in One Inning, Team, AL 200
Most 20-Home Run Hitters, AL 208

George Vico

Home Run in First Appearance in Majors, AL 11
Home Run on First Pitch in Majors, AL 11

Ozzie Virgil

Fathers and Sons in Baseball 192

Ozzie Virgil

Fathers and Sons in Baseball 192

Bill Voiselle

Twenty or More Wins, Rookie, NL since 1900 168
Three Hundred or More Innings Pitched, Rookie, NL since 1900 169

Clyde Vollmer

Home Run in First Appearance in Majors, NL 11
Home Run on First Pitch in Majors, NL 11
Three Home Runs in One Game, AL 14
Most Home Runs by Team, Game, AL 202

Joe Vosmik

Most Triples, Rookie, AL 165
One Hundred or More RBIs, Rookie, AL 166
.300-Hitting Outfields, AL 219, 220

Rube Waddell

Most Shutouts, Career 79
Most Strikeouts, Season, AL 105
Perfect Innings, AL (3 strikeouts on 9 pitches) 110
Most Strikeouts in Nine-Inning Game, AL 110
Most Strikeouts in Extra-Inning Game, AL 112
Most Games with 10 or More Strikeouts, Career 114
Most Strikeouts per Nine Innings, Career (Min. 1,500 IP) 114

Ray Washburn
No-Hitters, NL (9 innings or more) 90

Claudell Washington
Three Home Runs in One Game, AL 15
Three Home Runs in One Game, NL 19

Ron Washington
Three Consecutive Home Runs, Team, AL 197

U. L. Washington
Switch-Hit Home Runs in One Game, AL 23

George Watkins
Three Home Runs in One Game, NL 17
Highest Batting Average, Rookie, NL (Min. 300 AB) 167
Most .300 Hitters, Season, NL (300 AB each) 218
.300-Hitting Outfields, NL 221

Bob Watson
Cycle Hitters, AL 49
Cycle Hitters, NL 51

Milt Watson
Most Innings Pitched, Game, NL 128

Mule Watson
Two Complete Game Wins in One Day, NL since 1900 124
Grand Slams, Pitcher, NL 138

Buck Weaver
.300 Batting Average in Final Season (Min. 100 G) 39
No-Hit Spoilers - The Only Hit Most Often 57
Stole 2nd, 3rd, and Home in One Game, AL 66
Most 200-Hit Batters, AL 223

Earl Weaver
Retired Numbers, AL 182
Most Wins, Manager, Career 184

Farmer Weaver
Most Hits, Game, Other Leagues 37
Cycle Hitters, Other Leagues 51

Monte Weaver
Twenty or More Wins, Rookie, AL 168

Sam Weaver
Most Consecutive Losses, NL 116

Earl Webb
.300-Hitting Outfields, NL 221

Mitch Webster
Stolen Base Duos, Season, NL 217

Ramon Webster
Most Pinch Hits, Season, NL 69

Dick Weik
Most Walks in One Game, AL 113

Bob Weiland
Shutout in First Start in Majors, AL 83

Carl Weilman
Most Times Struck Out, Game, AL 33

Jake Weimer
Pitchers Who Stole Home, NL since 1900 140
Twenty or More Wins, Rookie, NL since 1900 168

Phil Weintraub
Most RBIs, Game, NL 64

Bob Welch
Fewest Base Runners per Nine Innings, Career (Min. 1,500 IP) 130

Frank Welch
Most Home Runs by Team, Game, AL 202

Mickey Welch
Most Shutouts, Career 80
Most 20-Win Seasons 101
Most Wins, Career 102
The 300-Win Club 103
Most Strikeouts, Season before 1900 107
Most Consecutive Wins, NL 115
Most Consecutive Strikeouts, NL 116
Two Complete Game Wins in One Day, NL before 1900 125

Jimmy Welsh
Most .300 Hitters, Season, NL (300 AB each) 218
.300-Hitting Outfields, NL 221

Bill Werber
Most Doubles, Game, AL 27
Most Doubles, Game, NL 27
Most Steals of Home, Career 67

Perry Werden
.300 Batting Average in Final Season (Min. 100 G) 39

Vic Wertz
Most Grand Slams, Career 3
Most Grand Slams, Season, AL 4
Most Pinch-Hit Grand Slams, Career 6
Most Doubles, Game, AL 27
Cycle Hitters, AL 49
Most Pinch Hits, Season, AL 68
Most Consecutive Pinch Hits 70
Most Home Runs in One Inning, Team, AL 200
.300-Hitting Outfields, AL 220

Dave Wickersham

Worst-Hitting Pitchers, Career (Min. 100 AB) 144

Alan Wiggins

Most Stolen Bases, Season, NL 65
Most Stolen Bases, Game, NL 66
Stolen Base Duos, Season, NL 217

Bill Wight

Most At-Bats with No Hits, Pitcher, Season since 1900 141

Del Wilber

Three Home Runs in One Game, NL 17

Rob Wilfong

Best Double-Play Combinations, Season 149

Hoyt Wilhelm

Home Run in First Appearance in Majors, NL 11
No-Hitters, AL (9 innings or more) 88
Most Wins by Age, Season, NL since 1900 104
Most Relief Wins, Career 117
Most Relief Wins, Season, AL 118
Most Relief Wins, Season, NL 119
Most Relief Losses, Career 120
Most Saves, Career 121
Fewest Base Runners per Nine Innings, Career (Min. 1,500 IP) 129
Most Extra-Inning Home Runs Allowed, Career 133
Most Wins after Age 40 134
Worst-Hitting Pitchers, Career (Min. 100 AB) 144

Ted Wilks

Undefeated Seasons (5 or more wins) 101

Bob Will

Most Pinch Hits, Season, NL 69

Jerry Willard

Three Consecutive Home Runs, Team, AL 197

Ed Willett

Two Home Runs in One Game, Pitcher, AL 135

Carl Willey

Shutout in First Start in Majors, NL 84
Grand Slams, Pitcher, NL 139
Worst-Hitting Pitchers, Career (Min. 100 AB) 144

Nick Willhite

Shutout in First Start in Majors, NL 84

Billy Williams

Most Home Runs, Season, NL 8
Most Home Runs, Career 9
Two Home Runs in One Game Most Often 12
Three Home Runs in One Game, NL 18
Most Doubles, Game, NL 27
Cycle Hitters, NL 51
No-Hit Spoilers - The Only Hit Most Often 57
Most RBIs in One Inning, NL 63
Most Consecutive Games Played 71
Fewest Games Missed (10-Year Period) 72
Most Consecutive Hits, NL 74
Most Home Runs by Team, Game, NL 206
Home Run Duos, Career, NL 211

Cy Williams

Most Grand Slams, Season, NL 4
Most Pinch-Hit Home Runs, Career 5
Most Home Runs, Season, NL 8
Three Home Runs in One Game, NL 17
Cycle Hitters, NL 51
.300-Hitting Outfields, NL 220

Davey Williams

Most Home Runs in One Inning, Team, NL 200

Dick Williams

Most Pinch Hits, Season, AL 68
Pennant-Winning Rookie Managers, AL 171
Most Wins, Manager, Career 184
Pennant-Winning Managers in AL and NL 184

Earl Williams

Thirty or More Home Runs, Rookie, NL 163

Gus Williams

Most Triples, Game, AL 28

Jimmy Williams

Most Hits, Game, AL 35
Longest Hitting Streaks, NL 71
Two Hundred or More Hits, Rookie, NL 163
Most Triples, Rookie, NL 165
One Hundred or More RBIs, Rookie, NL 166
Highest Batting Average, Rookie, NL (Min. 300 AB) 167

Ken Williams

Two Home Runs in One Inning, AL 12
Three Home Runs in One Game, AL 13
Thirty Home Runs with 30 Stolen Bases, Season, AL 24
Two Legs of Triple Crown, AL 46
More RBIs than Games Played, Season, AL 64, 65
Longest Hitting Streaks, AL 70
Most 100-RBI Hitters, AL 212
.300-Hitting Outfields, AL 219

Lefty Williams

Most Times Struck Out, Game, AL 33
Most Innings Pitched, Game, AL 127
Teams with Four 20-Game Winners 227

Stan Williams

Most Strikeouts, Season, NL since 1900 107
Most Strikeouts per Nine Innings, Career (Min. 1,500 IP) 114

Ted Williams

Most Grand Slams, Career 3
Most Grand Slams, Season, AL 4

Jack Wilson
Two Home Runs in One Game, Pitcher, AL 136

Jim Wilson
No-Hitters, NL (9 innings or more) 90

Jimmie Wilson
Most Games Caught, Career 153
Most .300 Hitters, Season, NL (300 AB each) 218

Owen Wilson
Most Triples, Game, NL 29
Cycle Hitters, NL 51

Pete Wilson
Shutout in First Start in Majors, AL 83

Willie Wilson
Switch-Hit Home Runs in One Game, AL 23
Hardest to Double Up, Career (Min. 1,000 G) 42
Most Stolen Bases, Season, AL 65
Most Stolen Bases, Career 66
Stolen Base Duos, Season, AL 216

Hooks Wiltse
No-Hitters, NL (9 innings or more) 89
Four Strikeouts in One Inning, NL 109
Most Consecutive Strikeouts, NL 116
Fewest Base Runners per Nine Innings, Career (Min. 1,500 IP) 129
Best Lefty-Righty Duos 228

Bobby Wine
The Worst Hitters (Min. 2,500 AB) 52
Most Double Plays, Shortstop, Season, NL 151
Fathers and Sons in Baseball 192

Robbie Wine
Fathers and Sons in Baseball 192

Dave Winfield
Most Consecutive Hits, NL 74
Three Consecutive Home Runs, Team, AL 197
Three Consecutive Home Runs, Team, NL 199
Teammates Who Finished 1-2 in Batting, AL 222

Al Wingo
.300-Hitting Outfields, AL 219

Ivy Wingo
Most Games Caught, Career 153

Rick Wise
No-Hitters, NL (9 innings or more) 90
Most Home Runs, Pitcher, Career 135
Two Home Runs in One Game, Pitcher, NL 136
Two Home Runs in One Game Twice in One Season, Pitcher 136
Grand Slams, Pitcher, NL 139
Most At-Bats with No Hits, Pitcher, Season since 1900 141

Sam Wise
Most Hits, Game, NL 35
.300 Batting Average in Final Season (Min. 100 G) 39

Mike Witt
No-Hitters, AL (9 innings or more) 88
Perfect Games (9 innings or more) 94
Most Strikeouts, Season, AL 105
Most Strikeouts in Nine-Inning Game, AL 111

Whitey Witt
Most Times Walked, Game, AL 31
.300-Hitting Outfields, AL 219

Harry Wolverton
Most Triples, Game, NL 28

Fred Wood
Brother Batteries, NL 185

George Wood
Cycle Hitters, NL 51

Jake Wood
Most Triples, Rookie, AL 165

Joe Wood
Most Shutouts, Season, AL 80
No-Hitters, AL (9 innings or more) 87
Best Won-Lost Record, Season, AL (20 or more wins) 96
Thirty-Game Winners, AL 100
Most Wins by Age, Season, AL 103
Most Strikeouts, Season, AL 105
Most Consecutive Wins, AL 115
Lowest ERA, Season, AL 127
Most Complete Games, Season, AL 131
Fathers and Sons in Baseball 192
Teams with Three 20-Game Winners, AL 227

Joe Wood
Fathers and Sons in Baseball 192

Pete Wood
Brother Batteries, NL 185

Wilbur Wood
Twenty Wins One Year, 20 Losses the Next, AL 98
Twenty Wins and 20 Losses in Same Year, AL 99
Most Strikeouts, Season, AL 105
Most Relief Wins, Season, AL 118
Most Relief Losses, Season, AL 120
Most Innings Pitched, Season, AL 132
Worst-Hitting Pitchers, Career (Min. 100 AB) 144

Hal Woodeshick
Most Relief Wins, Season, NL 119
Worst-Hitting Pitchers, Career (Min. 100 AB) 144

Al Woods
Pinch-Hit Home Run in First At-Bat in Majors, AL 6
Home Run in First Appearance in Majors, AL 11

Dick Woodson
Worst-Hitting Pitchers, Career (Min. 100 AB) 144

Todd Worrell
Most Saves, Season, NL 122
Most Wins Plus Saves, Season 122

Al Worthington
Shutout in First Start in Majors, NL 84
Shutout in First Two Major League Games, NL 85
Most Relief Losses, Career 120
Most Saves, Career 121

Clyde Wright
No-Hitters, AL (9 innings or more) 88

George Wright
Three or More Brothers in Baseball 187

Glenn Wright
Most Consecutive Hits, NL 74
Unassisted Triple Plays 149
Most Triples, Rookie, NL 165
Most 100-RBI Hitters, NL 212
Most .300 Hitters, Season, NL (300 AB each) 218

Harry Wright
Most Wins, Manager, Career 184
Three or More Brothers in Baseball 187

Sam Wright
Three or More Brothers in Baseball 187

Taffy Wright
RBI in Most Consecutive Games, AL 72

Russ Wrightstone
Most Putouts, Shortstop, Game 159

John Wyatt
Most Saves, Career 121

John Wyckoff
Most Walks in One Game, AL 113

Butch Wynegar
Most Games Caught, Career 153

Early Wynn
Most Shutouts, Career 79
Most Shutout Losses, Career 80
Most Wins, Career 102
The 300-Win Club 103
Most Wins by Age, Season, AL 103
Most Grand Slams Allowed, Career 133
Most Home Runs, Pitcher, Career 135
Pinch-Hit Grand Slams, Pitcher 137
Grand Slams, Pitcher, AL 138
Most Hits, Pitcher, Career 139
Most Times Struck Out, Pitcher, Career since 1900 141
Teams with Three 20-Game Winners, AL 227

Jimmy Wynn
Three Home Runs in One Game, NL 18, 19
Easiest to Strike Out, Career (Min. 1,000 G) 44
More Walks than Hits, Season, NL 55
No-Hit Spoilers - The Only Hit Most Often 58
Two Grand Slams in One Inning, Team 192

Carl Yastrzemski
Most Grand Slams, Season, AL 4
Most Home Runs, Season, AL 7
Most Home Runs, Career 9
Three Home Runs in One Game, AL 15
Most Times Walked, Game, AL 32
Most Combined Hits and Walks, Season, AL 40
Triple Crown Winners, AL 45
Cycle Hitters, AL 49
The 3,000-Hit Club 54
The 3,000th Hit 54
Most Runs, Career 60
Most RBIs, Career 61
Most Runs Produced, Career 62
Career Spent With One Team (15 or more years) 181
Three Consecutive Home Runs, Team, AL 197
Most Home Runs in One Inning, Team, AL 200
Most Home Runs by Team, Game, AL 202
Most 40-Home Run Hitters, AL 206
Most 20-Home Run Hitters, AL 208
Home Run Duos, Season, AL (25 each) 210
Home Run Duos, Career, AL 211
Most 100-RBI Hitters, AL 212

Steve Yeager
Easiest to Strike Out, Career (Min. 1,000 G) 44
The Worst Hitters (Min. 2,500 AB) 52
Most Games Caught, Career 153
Most Home Runs by Team, Game, NL 206

Rudy York
Two Grand Slams in One Game 3
Most Grand Slams, Career 3
Most Grand Slams, Season, AL 4
Three Home Runs in One Game, AL 14
Two Legs of Triple Crown, AL 46
Most RBIs, Game, AL 64
Thirty or More Home Runs, Rookie, AL 163
One Hundred or More RBIs, Rookie, AL 166
Home Run Trios, Season, AL 209
Home Run Duos, Season, AL (25 each) 210
Home Run Duos, Career, AL 211

Eddie Yost
Most Leadoff Home Runs, Career 22
Most Combined Hits and Walks, Season, AL 40
More Walks than Hits, Season, AL 55
Most Consecutive Games Played 71